ESSAYS IN KOREAN SOCIAL HISTORY

Shin Yong-ha

2003

Essays in Korean Social History
Copyright © 2003 by Shin, Yong-ha

Published by Jisik-sanup Publications Co. Ltd.
35-18 Tongui-dong, Jongno-gu
Seoul, Korea
Telephone: (+82 2)734-1978   Fax: (+82 2)720-7900
http://www.jisik.co.kr
e-mail: jsp@jisik.co.kr
        jisikco@chollian.net

초판 인쇄   2003. 1. 23
초판 발행   2003. 1. 27

지은이   신용하
펴낸이   김경희
펴낸곳   ㈜지식산업사
주소   서울시 종로구 통의동 35-18
전화   (02)734-1978(대)
팩스   (02)720-7900
홈페이지   http://www.jisik.co.kr
e-mail   jsp@jisik.co.kr, jisikco@chollian.net

등록번호   1-363
등록날짜   1969. 5. 8

책값   38,000원

© 신용하(Shin, Yong-ha), 2003
ISBN 89-423-1067-2 93910

이 책을 읽고 지은이에게 문의하고자 하는 이는 지식산업사 e-mail로 연락 바랍니다

PREFACE

Over the years I keenly felt the necessity of writing and publishing some books in English on Korean history and society, as I realized that the world at large has not yet properly and adequately understood the richness, importance and complexity of Korea's historical experience. This book is a collection of my papers in English on Korean social history, especially in the following three fields.

The first part of this book consists of 6 papers on the history of Korean rural community which was the core of Korean traditional society, focusing on land, labor and culture of peasants. Some discussions on land reform are also included.

The second part includes 7 papers on Korea's response to Western challenges in the nineteenth century. I studied some Korean efforts to modernize their own society and country along the lines of national independence and liberty.

The third part includes 7 papers on the Korean national independence movement during the period of Japanese occupation. I have researched some aspects of Korean struggle to regain and preserve freedom, independence and national identity against Japanese aggression and colonial policy.

I would like to thank Mr. Kim Kyung-hee, the president of the Jisik-sanup Publications Company, and his staff for their editorial suggestions and publication of this book.

I hope this book will help readers around the world in forming a better understanding of Korean society and history.

Shin Yong-ha

Seoul National University

September 2002

CONTENTS

PART I

Land, Labor and Culture

in Korean Rural Society

1. Social History of *Ture* Community and *Nongak* (*P'ungmul*) Music

1. Introduction

There was joint labor cooperative body in the traditional society of Korea, called *ture* (두레), organized by and innate to Korean farmers. *Ture* was the most important joint; labor team throughout the paddy-field farming regions in the Chosŏn dynasty. It was much transformed and disappeared in the period of the Japanese occupation of Korea, but was widely seen in the farming community south of the central region of Korea. Following the liberation of Korea from Japan in 1945, it was still a folk practice traces of which could be found in some farming regions. *Ture* was an organization in which "all" male members of the village carried out paddy-field work on "all" lots of the irrigated farms through a "joint labor" system, by means of "mutual help," in solidarity as a community. *Ture* had brought about *nongak* in the process, creating and developing an idiosyncratic peasant culture combining labor and *nongak* (farmers' music).

What has to be noted here in particular is that joint labor through *ture* was much more efficient than the labor carried out by each individual farmer was and it had an astonishing effect in changing the toil of labor to a "delightful physical exercise." By this alone, *ture* may be called a sagacious institution and culture created by Korean people and by Korean farmers in its history.

Ture was called variously from one region to another, *konggul, kungguri, cheri, chari, chori, dolge, dolgaegim, dongne nonmaegi, hyangdu p'umŏry* and many other names. *Ture* was denoted in Chinese characters, in general, as *sa* (社, society or association) and in the period of the Japanese occupation, it was also recorded by various names—*nongsa* (farming society), *nonggye* (farming covenant), *nonch'ŏng* (farming office), *kyech'ŏng* (convenant office), *kŏsa* (contributory association), *mokch'ŏng* (farm-tending office), *kongch'ŏng* (public office), *nonggi* (farmers' banner) or *nongak* (farmers music) and so forth.

Ture may be summed up in a few words as a "joint labor community (*Arbeitsgemeinschaft* in German) of adult males for the joint field work of the village which existed idiosyncratically in Korean society." While it was a community-like institution, it was basically concerned with "labor." Besides *ture*, there were *p'umashi* (or *p'umdŭri*, namely, "labor for exchange") or other forms of *kye* (covenant) as a means of joint labor in the farming community. While *p'umashi* or *kye* was a form of "Gesellschaft," organized at will for the pecuniary interest of individuals, not a "Gemeinschaft," *ture* was a community (Gemeinschaft) organized obligatorily putting the interest of the community before that of individuals. The content and the structure of *ture* was quite innate to Korea in the course of its social development, thus deserving to be called *ture-gemeinschaft.* This paper attempts to briefly survey the structure, functions and changing modes of *ture-gemeinschaft.*[1]

2. Genesis and Transformation of *Ture*

Some different views are put forward on the etymological origin of the word "*Ture*."

First, Kang Chŏng-t'aek holds that *ture* means "rotation"[2] and In Chŏng-shik, has a similar view. According to In Chŏng-shik, when four farmers, A, B, C and D, take part in *ture*, they till the paddy-fields of all four in turn from A's to B's, C's and D's in a joint labor team. He sees that the word *ture* came from the joint tilling of paddy-fields in rotation, and that the word expresses a pattern of toil but does not denote the structure of joint labor itself.[3]

Second, Yi Pyŏng-do holds that the work came, etymologically, from *tull* or *tullyŏ* which means a circumference or a circling of a round. According to him, this is the same case as in English where a circle, meaning a circumference, also means a party or a society, and in German where *Verein*, meaning unification or a unifier, also means an association and *Genosse*, meaning a comrade, also means a member of a guild, a party or an association. He maintains that the names for an association in Korean−*to* (徒, circle), *chŏp* (接, face to face group), *kye* (契, association) or *sa* (社, society)-are all a translation of *ture* into Chinese characters.[4]

Third, according to my own view, *ture* is a noun deriving from the ancient word of *turŭda* (to circle whole, to cover whole) and as can be seen in the meaning of a verb of *turŭda*, the word *turu* is an adverb denoting all or wholly. In other words, *ture* is a noun meaning the whole as in the adverbial meaning of *turu* and since the intrinsic characteristics of a community consists in its totality, the word *ture* is an ancient Korean word denoting the 'community' itself. And while *tulle* is a noun denoting the circumference and its neighboring space, *ture* is a word denoting the whole and totality of the circumference and its neighboring space. Therefore, *tulle* is a derivative word from *ture* but is a noun with a differentiating meaning. The verb *turŭda* (to circle whole, to cover whole) also means at the same time (1) to mark the circumference, (2) to include the whole and (3) to pass around. When the word *turŭda* changes into the adverb *turu*, the adverbial meaning also carries "everybody," "as a whole" or "in a group," or "evenly" or "without the absence of any." Such a word as *turŭda* or *turu* became a noun *ture* meaning "all," "whole," "evenly," "without the absence of any" as a genuine Korean word indicating the community itself.

The foregoing three definitions are mutually supplementary, not conflicting against one another since the word *ture* carries the meaning of (1) including all members of the community "evenly without the absence of any," (2) of marking the line of demarcation from the outside world, drawing the line of *tulle*, and (3) of doing labor "in rotation."

The origin of *ture* dates back quite far and mention of it appears in the bibliographical data of the period of the Three Hans and Three Kingdoms. The development of *ture* can be classified into three stages from its genesis down to 1945. The criteria, applied in terms of social history, are (1) the extent of social stratification within a village or a community and (2) the types of work necessitating the joint labor of *ture*.

The first stage of *ture* was when all adult members of the community took part obligatorily while there was almost no stratification in the social status of community members. The *ture* in this stage is assumed to have been applied to hunting, fishing, prevention of natural disasters, defense against foreign invasions and all other community affairs in addition to farm labor. This stage must have lasted from the time when *ture* had emerged until the village community began to disintegrate, and joint tilling in the village was being replaced by individual toil by a household unit in the period of the Three Kingdoms. The second stage of *ture* was when the nobility and landlords did not take park: only commoners and farmers participated in *ture* following the stratification of social status among community members into nobility and commoners. *Ture* in this stage was mainly applied to work which required a concentrated input of the labor force. This stage corresponds to the period from the unification of the Three Kingdoms to the last period of the Chosŏn dynasty. The third stage of *ture* was when it was transformed under the influence of Japanese colonial policy while the monetary economy was infiltrating into the agricultural sector. *Ture* in this stage will be discussed later in a separate chapter.

Mention of the *ture* of the first stage occurs in the Chinese record of the customs of the Three Hans. In the passages of *Tung-i-ch'uan* (Story of the Eastern Barbarians), *Weichih* (Account of Wei), *Sankuochih* (History of Three States), describing the folk customs of Chinhan, it was said that "They all call themselves *tu* ("*to*" in Korean, meaning group members),"[5] Yi Pyong-do interprets this "*tu*" as the Chinese translation of *ture* in its pronunciation and in its meaning.[6] This seems to be a very sharp insight. Again in the passage on Han in the *Houhanshu*, it is recorded that the people of the Three Kingdoms, following the ploughing in spring, held a rite to worship shpirits, drank and ate throughout the night, singing and dancing in groups, and that they also did the same in October after all the farming work was finished.[7] Similar records occur in *Tung-i-ch'uan, Weichih, Sankuochih*.[8] These can be seen as an observation of the ancient forms of *homi-ssishi* or *ture nori* which will be discussed later. The passage on Yuri *nisakŭm* (King Yuri) in *Samguk Sagi* (History of the Three Kingdoms) also records that the king divided six clans into two groups, let his two royal princesses command one team each, let them compete in weaving work in joint labor for a month, judged the victor on August 15, and made the defeated side prepare food to treat the victor and they all enjoyed singing, dancing and playing games.[9] This shows the origin of *kilssam ture* and suggests that in this period weaving work was carried out in joint labor.

By means of such fragmentary records, we can confirm that the joint labor community of *ture* existed in the period of the Three Hans and the Three Kingdoms. *Ture* in this stage was a joint labor community not only of commoners but of all people of every status and class and we can see that the joint labor was concerned not only with farming but with all types of work such as weaving work, military drills and so forth. But it is also easily assumed that *ture* of this nature was in gradual decline as the farming work and social life got based on individual households and the social need for joint labor was decreasing. In Korea, particularly, the incessant growth of small-scale farming by individual households was the very cause that drove *ture* of the first stage into extinction.

Ture of the second stage was much transformed in character from the first stage: while the nobility or landlords were not participating, commoners and working hands carried out the works of irrigated farming such as taking care of irrigation, rice seedling, transplanting, weeding and harvesting in joint labor. Irrigated farming was not suitable for each individual household to do but necessitated joint labor since (1) it needed irrigation and (2) it required a concentrated input of labor within a short span of time. Such social needs seem to have revived *ture* into a new form which experienced many changes in character.

In the farming history of Korea, the incessant growth of small-scale farming by each individual household was driving out *ture* of the first stage while the gradual development of irrigated farming was bringing about *ture* of the second stage. The changing patterns of these two types of *ture* were the very reason which caused the extinction of *ture* in non-irrigated farming regions and which gave rise to *ture* of the second stage in irrigated farming regions.

The start of irrigated farming in Korea dates back far to the period of Three Kingdoms. The passages on Pyŏnhan and Chinhan in *Sankuochih*, say "they cultivate five kinds of grains and paddy"[10] and it is a well-known fact that paddy seeds were unearthed from the shell heaps of the period of Kara in Kimhae, Kyŏngsangnam-do province. The passage on the 6th year of King Taru of Paekche in the *History of the Three Kingdoms* records that "In February, paddy farming was first introduced in the counties and regions in the south of the country."[11] Around 33 A.D., rice farming started in the regions, now Chŏlla-do province. The fact that rice farming at the time was partially done in irrigated farming can be seen in a passage on King Hŭlhae in the *History of the Three Kingdoms* — "In the 21st year (330 A.D.), the Pyŏkkolji pond was first built and the length of the dike was 1,800 *po* (a unit of length, a stride)."[12] In other words, as early as the period of Three Kingdoms, a largescale irrigation work was carried out for the Pyŏkkolje dike in Kimje, Chŏllabuk-do province, for the sake of irrigated farming. However, it was in the Chosŏn dynasty that irrigated farming was generally propagated and a research indicates that it was in the later part of the Chosŏn dynasty that rice-seedling transplantation became widely popular.[13]

It was also in the Chosŏn dynasty that *ture* of the second stage came into wide use and it was, especially, in the latter part of the dynasty that its use reached its apex. This can be easily ascertained by research on the latter part of the dynasty. In fact, *ture* was the most popular joint labor pattern adopted by farmers everywhere in the irrigated farming areas south of the central part of the peninsula. Particularly in the latter part of the Chosŏn dynasty, even though rulers left behind voluminous records, *ture* of the second stage hardly remains in record today simply because it was a "joint labor pattern popular among the lowest rungs of farmers." The exceptional cases in which *yangban* bureaucrats left behind any fragmentary mention of *ture* were only on such occasions as it was related to other events.

For instance, an event on November 17 by the lunar calendar in 1738 indirectly suggests that *ture* was in wide use at the time. In September, 1737, Wŏn Kyŏng-ha passed the civil service state examination and was appointed as a special royal envoy to the Honam (Chŏlla-do province) region and he was sent on an secret inspection tour to the region.[14] Arriving at Puan, he found the farmers' banner and musical instruments of *nongak*, suspected that they could be possible military equipment in case of rebellion and confiscated them from the farmers. Then, the former county magistrate of Puan, An Pok-chun, took them as his own after turning them into scrap iron. In 1738, Nam T'ae-ryang, the king's secret inspector, was sent to Chŏlla-do province, and reported the fact to the king impeaching the former magistrate. Thus, the king, Right Prime Minister, other high court officials and the secret inspector convened a conference at the office of Border Defense Council to decide the case.[15]

In this conference, the king and his ministers derisively called the farmer who participated in *ture*, *minbae* (hoodlum-like folk) and the king was not able to tell 'sa' (社, *ture*) from 'sa' (寺, Buddhist temple), thinking that the banners and *nongak* instruments had been confiscated from Buddhist temples, not from farmers' *ture*.[16] Hearing the explanation from his court officials, he asked why the farmers used *kkwaenggwari* (small gong) and *ching* (large metallic gong). *Sŭngjŏngwŏn Ilgi* (Diary of the Royal Secretariat) records that the Right Prime Minister Song In-myŏng replied — "Farmers of *minbae* cheer those working or harvesting on the farm with these musical instruments" and the *Yŏngjo Sillok* also records his reply — "When there are some farmers who are not active enough while everyone is working hard on the farm, these metallic gongs are sounded to cheer them up."[17] The king again asked whether the banner of the farmers for *ture* was similar to that used in war, and the special envoy to Honam replied that "banners and musical instruments of *nongak* are useless as military equipment and that it is difficult to ban the use of them since these (indicating *ture* and *nongak*) had been in folk practice for more than a hundred years."

From these fragmentary records, we can easily learn that the joint labor system of *ture* was quite popular throughout the Honam region, and *nongak* came from *ture*, and that *ture* and *nongak* were established folk practices for more than a hundred years. Here, the folk practices of more than "one hundred years" should be taken to mean a long established practice, not exactly indicating the length of duration. We can also learn that the ruling circles of the Chosŏn dynasty were never favorably disposed toward *ture* and *nongak*, and they were, rather, hostile to these folk practices. However, in the latter period of the *Chosŏn* dynasty, *ture* spread widely to Ch'ungch'ŏng, Chŏlla, Kyŏnggi, Kyŏngsang, Kangwŏn and Hwanghae provinces, emerging as the most important form of farmers' joint labor. Thus, some scholars of *shilhak* (practical learning) came to incorporate the notion of *ture* community in their ideas for social reformation. The land reform plan of Chŏng Yak-yong (Tasan) based on *yŏjŏn* (village cooperative farm) system, arguing for joint labor and a cooperative farming system of joint tilling, was based on the real practice and the use of *ture* of the time.[18]

A report which surveyed selectively the provinces of Kyŏnggi, Ch'ungch'ŏng and Kangwŏn in the closing period of the Chosŏn dynasty presented the following account.

> If there is anything which took us by surprise in the farming methods of Koreans, it must be the ploughing by the use of cattle and joint labor. Joint labor is the working arrangement most needed under the present conditions of Korea's farming and it is most frequently used in transplantation of rice seedlings and in weeding. We witness that music is played and singing is done to encourage the weeding work.
>
> They raise a banner on which is written "Farming is the basis of the world" or "Farming is an occupation inherited from Shên Nung (the legendary god of farming)," and go to work around the banner. Walking around the countryside in the weeding season in summer, one hears the sound of gongs and this is where farmers play *nongak* during the break raising the farmers' banner. Particularly when they feel tired after a day of hard toil, especially in the late afternoon, some farmers change their hands from weeding to musical instruments and start playing exciting strains of *nongak* for the workers. Then, the farmers feel refreshed, forgetting the fatigue and continue their weeding work more vigorously in a natural way.[19]

This report says that in the surveyed Kangwŏn-do province, *ture* was quite popular, particularly, at Ch'ŏnggan, Yangyang, Ich'ŏn and Anhyŏp, in Kyŏnggi-do province at Yŏnch'ŏn, Changdan, Kaesŏng, Yangch'ŏn, Suwŏn, Chinwi and Namyang, and in Ch'ungch'ŏng-do province at T'aean, Haemi, Hyŏlsŏng, Taehŭng, Ch'ŏngyang and Sŏch'ŏn.[20]

This report also presents a similar account with respect to Chŏlla-do province surveyed selectively in the closing period of Chosŏn dynasty.

During transplantation, weeding and harvesting, they frequently organize joint labor with neighbors or with village members.

Imp'a, Chŏllabuk-do province: Many village affairs are done jointly and farm work is customarily done through mutual help.

Chŏnju, Chŏllabuk-do province: Transplantation or weeding is done jointly by groups of 30 to 50 farmers. But, the harvest is customarily done individually.

Magok-myŏn, Kwangju-gun, Chŏllanam-do province: Transplantation, irrigation work and harvesting are done jointly by village members.

Naju, Chŏllanam-do province: Transplantation is done by villagers jointly. In case some farmers cannot do harvesting due to some reasons, neighbors assemble to help them out working jointly.

Chindo, Chŏllanam-do province: Transplantation and harvesting are often done jointly. In transplantation work, gongs are played to the singing of folk songs to encourage up to transplanting work.[21]

This report says that in Kyŏngsang-do province which was selectively surveyed, *ture* was popular.

Hwamok-ri, Ch'ilsan, Kimhae-gun, Kyŏngsangnam-do province: Transplanting and harvesting are often done jointly by neighbors.

Waekwan, Indong-gun, Kyŏngsangbuk-do province: In the busiest season for transplantation and harvesting, work is frequently done jointly in rotation through consultation among villagers.

Indong, Kyŏngsangbuk-do province: Transplantation of rice seedlings is done jointly.

Thus, there are many occasions when work is carried out jointly.[22]

Even through such fragmentary data, we can see easily that until the final period of the Chosŏn dynasty *ture* was popular and widespread in the irrigated farming regions in the southern part of Korea.

3. Organization of *Ture*

Materials on the organization of *ture* extant today are only those related to the latter period of Chosŏn and the Japanese occupation period and are only fragmentary at that. Even so, I would like to survey these fragmentary data in order to explore and reconstruct the ideal patterns of the traditional structures of *ture* that must have existed in the latter period of Chosŏn and in the initial period of the Japanese occupation days before they were greatly distorted by the monetary economy and by Japanese colonial policies.

Membership of *ture* covered all adult males of a settlement (a village of natural growth) ranging in age from 16 to 55 years old, with an average number of 20 to 30 people. However, there were many other *ture* consisting of 50 persons.[23] Members of *ture* were usually called *turekkun* or *turep'ae*. Females were originally excluded from *ture* and there seemed to have been three reasons for non-membership of women. First, the nature of work for *ture* was customarily for men. Second, *ture* was organized with a unit of even labor load for an adult male, but the labor of women was considered to be short of the unit of labor. Third, *ture* also functioned as a form of group entertainment and the participation of women was considered not to be adequate. And, those under age and old people were originally excluded from membership of *ture* because they were also considered to be short of an average labor unit. Thus, *ture* was made up of young and middle-aged males, and male youth members formed the core of the labor force. As a result, *ture* became a structure of joint labor of youth and middle-aged male members with an even labor load.

Ture was by necessity formed as a village unit (a natural maŭl settlement or a natural community). *Dong* or *ri* as an administrative unit was not a unit for *ture* formation. For instance, Kuryong-ri, Kumsŏng-myŏn, Chech'ŏn-gun, Ch'ungch'ŏngbuk-do province was an administrative unit consisting of three natural settlements called Kuryong-ri (minor), Chagam-dong and Hanch'ŏn-dong and each had its own *ture*.[24] In the latter period of Japanese occupation days, there were *dong ture* organized in each administrative unit[25] and there were two or three *ture* in the same settlement but they were all exceptional distorted forms of *ture*. *Ture* was originally organized one in each natural settlement (village).

Male adults of each settlement were obligated to join *ture* so long as they had a unit of labor load. In other words, its membership was obligatory and of a totalistic nature. In case an adult male with a normal unit of labor load refused to join it, settlement members either alienated him from ordinary contact, cut the daily relationship, imposed whipping punishment or expelled him from the village. In the original form of *ture*, regardless of the number of adult males, a family had, they were all obliged to join it. However, in the latter period of Chosŏn and in the initial period of Japanese occupation while the monetary economy was spreading to the countryside, there appeared a pattern of *ture* in which only one adult male from a family joined it in order to even the labor load for each family.

In the original pattern of *ture*, the family of a widow and the sick or the weak with no adult male, were exempted from its membership. However they benefited evenly from the common labor of *ture*.

On the other hand, those under age and labor hands immigrating from other villages (wanderers or beggars) were refused *ture* membership even if they wanted it.

When an under-age boy was recognized as an adult male, reaching the age of 16, he had to undergo a rite called *chumŏk tadŭmi* (fist polishing) before he joined *ture*.[26] Seen as a residue of the rite for coming of age, the custom took the form of providing a reception for *ture* members in the latter period of Chosŏn. The rite was called *chinsŏt'ŏk*, consisting of about two *tu* (a unit of liquid quantity, about 16 liters) of rice wine. If the under aged boy was admitted to *ture* following the rite, his labor was rated as a unit of an adult male in an exchange of labor or in the hired work as a labor hand in the village. *Chumŏk tadŭmi* was called by various names from one region to another; *chinsŏ* (進鋤), *shinimnye* (新入禮), *kongbae* (公配).[27] When wanderers or beggars from other villages joined *ture*, his employer provided a reception for other *ture* members to get formal recognition of his membership and this reception was called *paguri*. This may be seen as a rite of initiation to a communal labor organization.

In case *yangban*, landlords and plutocrats lived together in the same settlement, after the *yangban* and landlord system became general in the Chosŏn dynasty, they were seen as non-laboring class and did not join *ture*. Instead, they let their servants join it. *Ture* was an organization consisting only of commoners of the village. In fact, it was a working unit of independent farmers, tenant farmers, farm servants *mŏsŭm* and farm hands who all engaged in labor, in other words, in a working community of people.

As the membership of *ture* had to undergo a certain form of screening, withdrawal from *ture* membership had also to go through a certain screening. Withdrawal from *ture* was impossible unless there were certain reasons to be recognized by the community and withdrawal was also subject to group obligation.

Officers of *ture* were as follows, each being assigned his own function.

(1) Representative, in command of *ture*— This position was called from one

region to another by various names; *yŏngjwa* (領座), *chwasang* (座上), *haengsu* (行首), *yŏngsu* (領首), *pansu* (班首) or *chwajang* (座長). The role of *yŏngjwa* was to control the members, decide on labor plans and the order of labor rotation and instruct the disposition of revenues and other related affairs of *ture*. *Yŏngjwa* was usually elected from among independent farmers with rich experience, a reputation for virtue and good discretion in human affairs.

(2) Officers assisting the representative—This position was called *togam* (都監), *kongwŏn* (公員), *chipsa* (執事) or *soim* (少任). The role of *togam* was to assist *yŏngjwa* and relay his instructions to *ture* members and oversee the affairs of *ture*.

(3) Foreman at the working place—This position was called such'onggak (首總角) or ch'onggak taebang (總角大方). His role was to be in charge of the work in the fields. He was the bearer of the farmers' banner and he was usually elected from among the sagacious tenant farmers or farm servants *mŏsŭm*.

(4) Assistant foreman—He was called either chosa ch'onggak (調査總角), ch'ŏngsu (靑首) or *chinsugun*. His role was to assist the foreman and to encourage the work in the fields. The assistant foreman was usually selected from among witty farm servants *mŏsŭm* or unmarried youth.

(5) Accountant-secretary—This position was generally called *yusa* (有司). His role was to check the roster, do the accounting and carry out the secretarial work. He also took care of washing hoes and was in charge of *nongak*. The position was usually given to a man well versed in letters and in accounting.

(6) Herdsman—This position was usually called *pangmokkam* (放牧監). His role was to watch the cattle and protect the farm lest they feed on farm produce. The position was usually given to the boys who would soon join *ture* or to a few of the oldest members of *ture*.

These officers were an exemplary pattern and the case *ture* was very small, the number of officers was cut down.

In an actual case, the officers of the *ture* of Ulsan region, Kyŏngsangnam-do province, were as follows.[28]

(1) *Haengsu*—Leader of *ture*

(2) *Togam*—An assistant to *Haengsu*

(3) *Such'onggak*—Foreman and banner-bearer

(4) *Chosa ch'onggak*—An assistant to *Such'onggak* and overseer of *ture* work.

(5) *Yusa*—Accountant and secretary

(6) *Pangmokkam*—Herdsman

Another case in the *ture* of Chŏngsŏn and P'yŏngch'ang regions of

Kangwŏn-do province was as follows.[29]

(1) *Yŏngjwa* — The over-all leader

(2) *Togam* — Assistant to the leader and the overseer of *ture*

(3) *Ch'onggak taebang* — Foreman at the field

(4) *Ch'ŏngsu* — One who watches for idle members and metes out punishment

(5) *Yusa* — Accountant and secretary

(6) *Pangmokkam* — Herdsman (usually a boy)

Officers were usually elected at the plenary session of the members by means of verbal voting.

Within the organization of *ture*, democratic practices were thoroughly observed. All officers including *yŏngjwa* took part in joint labor like any other member, carrying out their assigned parts, and even *yŏngjwa* could not dictate or act of his own, running *ture* very democratically. Thus, it may be said that farmers' democracy was dominant. However, discipline was strict and members also strictly abode by the rules. Orders and instructions of *yŏngjwa* were well observed and members worked according to the rules.

Membership carried a "great prestige" generally in and around the farming community. Villagers addressed officers of *ture* as Yi *Yŏngjwa*, Kim *Tŏgam*, Pak *Yusa* and so forth by their official titles, expressing their sense of respect.[30] The term of *ture* officers was usually a year but replacement was quite rare unless there was a plausible reason.

Ture was a common labor system, not to be organized a new each year but was a long-term community institution always there year in year out. A yearly calendar for *ture* was divided into a "period of labor" and a "period of preparation." The labor period was generally from May when the transplanting of rice seedlings starts to July when weeding is done and the hoes are washed. The preparation period covered from the end of the busiest farming season until the time of rice-seedling transplantation next year. At the start of the labor period, all *ture* members gathered at a farming office for a plenary meeting to elect officers and start the *ture* work. When the labor period was over, every member went back as an individual farmer. *Ture*, however, was not disbanded and went into the preparation period. So *ture* began the preparation for labor next year under the command of *yŏngjwa*. Thus, *ture* was maintained through the cycles of labor and preparation periods.

When *ture* was at its apex, there was a public building in the center of the village used as the *ture* office called nongch'ŏng (農廳),[31] kongch'ŏng (公廳), tongsa (洞舍), or konghoedang (公會堂). This was a common meeting place for members, providing an indoor space for common work and a common space for rest. Unmarried members used to sleep and eat in this building. The farmers' banner and farming implements were also kept here. A sturdy hedge was put up around the office for the purpose of guarding it and members watched the office in rotation.

Ture by necessity had a farmers' banner and *nongak* (*p'ungmul*). The farmers' banner was also called *turegi* (*ture* banner). It was a big streamer with Chinese letters written on it, "Farming is the basis of the world." The banner was the symbol of *ture* like a military flag for the army, symbolizing the pride and the sense of union of farmers. Therefore, farmers regarded the banner with a sense of awe.[32] When the banner was hoisted, any *yangban* in whatever high position could not pass by it riding a horse. They had to dismount from the horse and pass in front of it after paying due respect to the banner. The violation of this practice was to be punished by *ture*.[33] Neglect or disregard for the farmers' banner was taken as neglect or disregard for farmers themselves, thus provoking farmers to indignation.

There were grades of prestige in farmers' *ture* flags from one village to another. According to (1) the length of the history of *ture*, (2) outcome of the tug-of-war matches, cock-fighting, stone-throwing and other games, (3) outcome of *ture* matches, and (4) merits and grades of performance at statute labor, there were grades of *ture*: *sŏnsaeng* (teachers) and *cheja* (pupils), and *hyŏng* (elder brother) and *au* (younger brother). Thus, the prestige of each farmers' *ture* flag was graded. When *ture* from one village entered the field of the match or the field of the statute labor hoisting a farmers' flag, other farmers' flags with a low grade of prestige should lower itself to pay respect to the farmers' flag of a higher grade of honor. Whenever two *ture* met crossing the same road, the farmers' flag of lower prestige should step aside to make way for the farmers' flag of higher prestige. Otherwise, there followed a fierce fight between the two since the lack of such respect was considered to be insulting.

Nongak (*p'ungmul*) was obligatory to *ture*, constituting an important element of *ture*. In principle, there was no *ture* without *nongak*. Thus, in some regions, *ture* itself was sometimes called *nongak*. *Nongak* heightened the working efficiency of joint labor, encouraging the members and contributing greatly to making *ture* into a joint labor unit. *Nongak* will be further examined in the forthcoming chapter.

Such was the original and typical pattern of *ture*. However, some observers in the days of Japanese colonial rule have also reported on some other kinds of *ture* which derived from the original patterns.

One of them was women's *ture* with a long history. They organized *ture* to weave hemp and cotton clothes working in shifts. A women's *ture* for hemp cloth was called "*turesam* (hemp)" and the one for cotton cloth *ture pe*. The women worked in group, delighting themselves in group activity and they divided the process of labor according to the talents of each members so as to increase productivity.[34] And it was also reported that in some regions there were *ture* for children and *ture* for old people who originally had no qualification to join the ordinary *ture*.[35] In the regions where there was *ai ture* (*ture* for children), the original *ture* was called *ŏrŭn* (adults) *ture* and *ai ture* was supervised by *ŏrŭn ture*. *Ai ture* mainly did the grass cutting work.[36] Or, some special jobs were carried out by organizing a *ture* suitable for the job. For instance, grass cutting work for the making of fertilizer was done by adults organizing a *ture* for the work and the grass cut by this *ture* was called *ture p'ul* (grass).[37] Of course, such *ture* did not use farmers' flags or *nongak*, there were no officers or formal organization and membership was not obligatory on all members of the village. Such *ture* may be called an out-growth from the original patterns of *ture*.

4. Joint Labor of *Ture*

The kinds of works assigned to *ture* varied from one region to another but they are largely divided into three kinds: first, all covering irrigation, rice-seedlings transplanting, weeding and harvesting,[38] second, work including irrigation, transplanting and weeding[39] and third, only the weeding work.[40] Among these three, the second type of *ture* was most widespread.[41]

Ture labor covered the entire farm lands of the settlement. *Ture* regarded all the farming lots of the settlement as a unit of farming of its own and here appears strongly the communal nature. However, all the farming lots of the settlement was classified, according to the grade of benefits from *ture*, into the farmland of the settlement by common possession, the farmland of those lacking labor capacity such as widows, the sick or the weak, farming lots of ordinary farmers and farming lots of landlords.

The settlement farmland of communal possession existed somewhat by the time the "land survey project" by the Japanese was conducted in the final days of the Chosŏn dynasty.[42] This land was obligatory for joint labor by villagers.

The farms of widows, the sick and the weak received the greatest benefit from *ture*. *Ture* provided labor for free for this land even though widows or the sick could not contribute working hands. Especially for the sick, a caring hand was extended in a generous way and joint labor was readily provided.

For farms of this nature, *ture* had the nature of communal help for those unfortunate farmers who could not provide their due share of labor.

Farming land for ordinary farmers was in fact the private farm of each farmer participating in *ture* and *ture* also had the function of "mutual help" toward farms of this nature.[43] Self-tilling farms and tenant farms were all included in this category, thus constituting the greatest share of land.

The farming land of landlords was where landlords used farm servants or farm hands for tilling. Even though landlords let farm hands take part in *ture* for joint labor, the land received a greater benefit from the joint labor of *ture* in proportion to its size. Therefore, landlords were, by practice, to pay a consideration to *ture*, as calculated by the accountant of *ture*, in proportion to the benefit he received from *ture*, either in kind or in cash.

Ture thus firmly guaranteed, for all the farming lots of various kinds in the settlement, not to miss the best timing for irrigated farming, since it would greatly influence the outcome of the harvest. At the arrival of transplanting season each year, *ture* members gathered at the *ture* office for a meeting to screen new members and to elect new officers. Once officers were elected, under the guidance of *yŏngjwa*, the work days of the year for joint labor were calculated in proportion to the total area of the farm and to the number of *ture* members. The order of joint labor was also decided. The order of joint labor was determined usually to the urgency of the work needed and by custom but it varied greatly in view of conditions and other circumstances of the settlement.[44] At this meeting, work days for cattle were also calculated. Cattle (mostly oxen and cows) were mobilized from the village and they were all put to work on shifts and the quantity of labor by cattle was not counted in the accounting. Once the preparation was over, *ture* members conducted *homi modum* (gathering of hoes) and held a *nongak* meeting on the eve for a preparatory occasion of *ture* work. In general, they gathered at the *ture* office to conduct *chinsŏ tŏk* — a simple reception to celebrate the opening of *ture* work. Until late into the night, they played *nongak* and danced to its music.

When *ture* members went to the working lots, they gathered at the *ture* office and marched to the place in formation or they went directly to the working place each from his home. The former method was taken when the working lots were far from the village and the latter method was sometimes taken when the working lots were located near the village. In both cases, the departure time was at daybreak. On the days of *ture* work, a *nongak* troupe played drums or *nongak* strains at the archery range located on small green of the village to herald the time for gathering. Then, *ture* members gathered either at the *ture* office or at the shooting range and marched to the working lots in formation. At the front of the formation, *such'onggak* hoisted the farmers' banner as the standard bearer. Then followed *yŏnggi* (signal banner) to guard the farmers' flag and *nongak* followed. *Nongak* was made into a unit under the command of *sangsoe* and played a marching strain called *kil kunak* (road military music) in a militant and strong rhythm until the *ture* formation reached the working lots, After that, *ture* members, with hoes on their shoulders, marched in single file to the music. The sight of *ture* members marching from the *ture* office to the working lots was a real spectacle.

Once members reached the working lots, *yŏngjwa* erected the farmers' flag and the signal banner and ordered the start of the work. The members then went right into work under the command of *yŏngjwa*.

In case the working lot was near the village, officers of *ture* went to the lot beforehand, erecting the banners, and sounded the signal of gathering. Then *ture* members, at the signal, gathered around the banners and started the work at the command of *yŏngjwa*.[45]

One of the major characteristics of *ture* joint labor was "working with singing." A talented *ture* member was chosen as *solsori* (lead singer) and he took the lead of singing. Then other *ture* members in unison responded to him. In order to stimulate the singing, a *ture* member, standing behind other *ture* members on the bank, beat the gongs to add to the excitement.[46] W. R. Carles, who visited Korea around 1884, was very much impressed seeing such a scene and recorded, "Koreans always enjoy working in group and most of them were singing while working."[47] When the leading singer got tired, *ture* members grouped into two and both teams sang songs in turn. They sang in unison all songs they knew such as the song of the good harvest, the song of farmers and the song of great peace of the world. When they ran out of songs they knew, the leading singer improvised new songs to lead the chorus. In this process, a number of new farming songs were created. In *ture* work, songs were sung all day long until they finished the work of the day. The working-and-singing method of *ture* contributed greatly to lessening the pain of labor by means of delightful feelings of the heart and to turning the hard labor into a "delightful work."

Ture work proceeded in good order and with good efficiency under the command of *such'onggak*. The speed of work was faster than when the work was done individually and the work proceeded like a battle charge. The rapid speed of work, discipline and common coordination were three characteristics of *ture* work. Thus, the outcome of joint labor by *ture* was always greater than the sum of each individual labor with higher efficiency and with higher productivity. Usually, some large *ture*, in order to stimulate working efficiency, provided a drummer who played a big drum on the embankment of the farm and a gong player who played behind *ture* members in the paddy-field. At dusk when *ture* members began feeling tired, some members took *nongak* instruments instead of hoes and played *nongak* among their colleagues in order to stimulate them. Then other members felt quite refreshed and they could wield their hoes more vigorously, increasing the working speed.[48]

One of the distinct features of *ture* joint labor was "joint meals" and "joint rest." Farmers called the joint meals with meat and rice wine a "wet *chori*" and joint meals without meat and wine a "dry *chori*." *Ture* was always a wet *chori* and the joint meal was one of the very important events of *ture*. A joint meal was, according to the words of farmers, "eating rice from the same cauldron," functioning to solidify the sense of unity and bond among farmers. Again, for poor farmers and other farm hands, the joint meals were good occasions of the year for them to enjoy hearty meals. *Ture* members strengthened their sense of communal unity and bond in the pleasure and joy through the joint meals. Joint meals were prepared by women of the village or by each farming household in rotation.[49]

Joint rest was integrated with the joint meal. No rest time was programmed separately but the time for joint meals was amply scheduled so that joint rest could be taken. Farmers called the joint meal accompanied by joint rest a *ch'am* (a lapse of time). In *ture*, joint rest was taken quite regularly in joint as was joint meal. For instance, one could not finish up his work ahead of others or even if one finished his meal ahead of others, he could not lay down or smoke while others were still taking their meal.[50] Joint meals of *ture* usually occurred five times a day.[51] The joint meals were breakfast, *kyŏttŭri* (snack), lunch, *kyŏttŭri* and dinner.

Joint labor of *ture* usually started at daybreak for about an hour and then stopped for breakfast. Then, the morning work followed for about 2-3 hours and then a rest while taking a *kyŏttŭri*. *Kyŏttŭri* usually consisted of rice wine called *makkŏlli* and some snacks. Work resumed then and at noon, the joint meal and joint rest for lunch followed. Joint meal and joint rest for lunch was particularly good. The joint meal of lunch had to be hot food with fish or meat and wine so that *ture* members could enjoy a hearty meal. After lunch, there followed the playing of *nongak* and the farmers sang the above-mentioned songs and danced in unison. Following the *nongak*, the farmers took a nap for about an hour in the shade of trees. Observing such a scene, foreigners left behind records saying they couldn't understand such a practice.[52] Such joint rest and joint recreation were important ingredients of *ture* to reduce the pain of work, to help them recover from fatigue quickly and to heighten the spirit for labor.

Following the joint rest after lunch, *ture* members were reinvigorated and proceeded with the same procedure of work as in the morning until the time for another snack and the joint meal and joint rest at dinner. The work of the day ended with the setting of the sun.

The working hours of *ture* for a day were about 12 hours but the actual hours for labor were about eight hours and the remaining four hours were spent at joint meals, joint rest and joint recreation. When coming back to the *ture* office following a day of work, they filed in a line with the farmers' banner at the front, playing *nongak* as in the morning.[53] Even though they must have been tired in the evening, they were none the less vigorous, singing songs and dancing on their way home.[54]

The wisdom and sagacity of the Korean people was thus incorporated in the system of *ture* joint labor which enabled them to heighten labor efficiency, to turn painful work into a pleasant form of work and enable them to work for production in pleasure accompanied with singing and dancing.

When the joint labor of *ture* finished the work on the final farm, they chose the best and the most diligent worker of *ture* of the year and called him a *ture changwŏn* (No. 1 ace).[55] When all the work of weeding on the final farm was finished, the head of the *ture changwŏn* was decorated with a laurel of flowers or of willow and his face was touched up with make-up. Then, he was put on the back of a cow on which was put a cotton costume. Playing *nongak* and singing a song called *ojansori* in unison, they marched to the front of the house of the *ture changwŏn* and around the village. *Ture changwŏn* was usually picked from among hard-working farm hands and the landlord employing him was supposed to provide a banquet in the name of the rite of *changwŏn* or the rite of *tŭngp'ung*.[56] On the night of the final day of *ture* work, its members pleased themselves singing and dancing at such a banquet late into the night. When the events for *ture changwŏn* and the rite of *changwŏn* were over, the work period for *ture* of the year was almost over for the time being and there followed the event of *homi-ssishi* in preparation for the next work.

5. *Homi-modum* and *Homi-ssishi*

Ture had special rites or events called *homi-modum* (lit. "collection of hoes") and *homi-ssishi* (lit. "washing of hoes").[57] *Homi-modum* was a rite for all *ture* members to bring their hoes to the *ture* office on the day after they elected *ture* officers and finished the preparation for the joint labor (in reality, the work of transplantation). This was to signify the re-banding of joint labor for the year and to confirm the unity of *ture* at the same time. Customarily *ture* members received their hoes at the *ture* office before they went out to the field and they returned them to the *ture* office after the work of the day. The rite of storing the farming implements together‒ *homi-modum*‒ lasted until the end of all *ture* joint labor which was marked by the rite of *homi-ssishi*. Only after *homi-ssishi* was over did *ture* members bring their hoes back home. *Homi-modum* was meant to symbolize that *ture* was not a mere band of farmers but was a solid "community of joint labor."

Homi-ssishi was a "festival" to celebrate the achievement of the joint labor of the year after the weeding work was finished. The name probably, came from an assumption‒"Since the joint labor of the year is all finished let us wash the dirt and soil off the hoes to prepare for the work next year." *Homi-ssishi* was called variously from one region to another‒ *nadari, konggul, konghoe, paekchung nori, ture nori, mŏsŭm nori* or *sulmegi*. *Homi-ssishi* usually took place on the day of *Paekchung* on July 15 by the lunar calendar. However if the work on the final field was incomplete due to inevitable circumstances, *homi-ssishi* was held on an auspicious day fixed by divination. There were some regions where they used to hold festivals of *nadari*[58] or *ssŏre-ssich'im* (lit. "washing of harrows") in addition to *homi-ssishi* after transplantation was finished.[59]

It was customary to hold *homi-ssishi* on a hill of the village or in a field near the village. *Homi-ssishi* consisted of (1) a village conference, (2) *nongak* (instrumental music of farmers) and entertainment and (3) a banquet. In days when there existed a village autocracy, the village conference was held on the day of *homi-ssishi* to discuss and decide on matters concerning village affairs and to enjoy themselves afterwards by *nongak* and games. However, when the village autocracy disappeared, there was no need for the village conference and farmers went directly into *nongak* and games.

Nongak for *homi-ssishi* was bigger in size than the main *nongak* during the *ture* joint labor. At *homi-ssishi*, the number of *sogojabi* (small drum players) and *pŏpkojabi* (temple-drum players) were increased so that all *ture* members could take part in the music. The program was designed with full variety (*chapsaek*)‒ *mudong* (dancing children on the top of the shoulder of men), *p'osu* (dancer dressed as a hunter), monks, lasses, *yangban* (aristocrats), *ch'angbu* (male clowns) all sang and danced in group, and drama, well-meant remarks and acrobatics were added to increase the excitement. The *nongak* musicians marched around with the farmers' flag at the front led by *snagsoe* (the first gong player), playing a mass game called *chinbŏp nori* containing a number of episodes and styles. It was obligatory for all *ture* members either to be a player of *nongak* or to take some role in a variety show. In some regions, *ssirŭm* (a kind of wrestling matches) or tug-of-war contests were held in addition to *nongak*.

The banquet at *homi-ssishi* was particularly gorgeous. Cows or hogs were butchered and part of the meat was distributed among villagers to cheer the offering of their labor and *ture* members and male workers were treated to alcohol and meat. On this day, even impoverished villages also held an abundant banquet. In principle, *ture* members and male workers only were supposed to take part in *homi-ssishi* but since women of the village were mobilized for the preparation of the banquet, women also took part in the event as helpers and onlookers. *Homi-ssishi* became a festival for the whole village, the "biggest festival" for farmers. *Ture* members and adult villagers dissipated their fatigue through *homi-ssishi* consolidating the consciousness of unity among them.

After *homi-ssishi*, the *yusa* (accountant) of *ture* made his accounting for the year. Before the money economy deeply permeated the agricultural community, no individual accounting was made even among *ture* members, let along the family of the sick and widows.[60] Labor costs were precisely calculated against acreage and payment was taken only from landlords and big farmers. However, when the money economy became the rule of the day, individual accounting was made precisely for *ture* members except only for the farms of the sick and widows. Landlords and big farmers were supposed to pay a certain amount of money in proportion to the size of their land holding and the accountant also collected money from *ture* members whose land holdings were bigger than the average in proportion to the input of labor.

However, the income for *ture* was not divided among members but was used to meet the common expenses of *ture*. Herein, *ture* still maintained its communal character even after the rise of the money economy. With the income, the expense of *homi-ssishi* was paid in the first place and the rest was used to cover the purchase or the repair of *nongak* instruments. When there still remained some balance, the money was put into village savings such as *kye* (mutual financing association) so as to be spent for the common purpose of the village.[61] However, after the Japanese came to occupy the land by force, there arose big changes in the way of disposing of the income and in the way of distributing the money among members.

6. *Ture* and *Nongak* (*P'ungmul*)

Nongak was an important element in the *ture* community. A point to be stressed here is the fact that *nongak* derived originally from *ture*. The writer holds the view that *nongak* developed from a group labor music, a by-product of the *ture* joint labor and it became an indispensable part of the *ture* community, further developing into various forms.[62] *Nongak* was called variously from one region to another — *p'ungmul, p'ungjang, kŏlgung, maegut, maegwi, kunmul* or *sangdu*. Since the writer is a stranger to music, a sociological note will be made briefly concerning the relation between *ture* and *nongak*.

Korean farmers came to invent *nongak* and combined it with *ture* basically in order to make the *ture* joint labor pleasant and to heighten labor efficiency. Since *ture* was for joint labor, *nongak* could develop as a form of group labor music. Effects exerted by *nongak* on the *ture* joint labor may be summarized as follows:

First, *nongak* contributed greatly to the promotion of labor efficiency since it provided rhythm to the labor. Second, it combined music with the labor creating the "pleasure" of labor and managed to turn painful labor into a "pleasant exercise." Third, it combined labor and rest organically and helped farmers greatly to recover from labor fatigue fast. Fourth, it provided heightened morale to farmers by providing militant, heart-beating music and rhythm. Fifth, it managed to instill a sense of pride and confidence into farmers by providing pleasure and the sense of worthiness. Last, it provided entertainment and a sense of unity among *ture* members and contributed greatly in re-generating the common labor of farmer.

On the other hand, the fact that *nongak* derived from the *ture* joint labor and became an important element of *ture* came to assign a special attribute to it which can be easily discerned from other forms of music. Its characteristics of rhythm and tune are ① dynamic, ② exciting, ③ militant, ④ grandiose, ⑤ passionate, ⑥ optimistic, ⑦ productive and ⑧ sturdy and robust. Such characteristics cannot be understood if one does not note the fact that it was a product of the *ture* joint labor.

Instruments and props used in *nongak* basically were ① *nonggi* (farmers' banner), ② *yŏnggi* (command flag), ③ *kkwaenggwari* (small gong), ④ *ching* (big gong), ⑤ *changgo* (sandglass-shaped drum), ⑥ *k'ŭnbuk* (big drum), ⑦ *chagŭnbuk* (small drum), ⑧ *pŏpko* (temple drum), ⑨ *nallari* (shawm) and ⑩ *chapsaek* (variety of props). However, the number and the roles of instruments and props varied from one to another and accordingly, there was a wide difference in size. Based on the *nongak* of the three southern provinces in the closing days of the Chosŏn dynasty, a model pattern of *nongak* may be reconstructed as follows:

1) *nonggi⁻* a symbolical emblem of *ture*. Since it was described earlier, no more details will be made here. In general, it was a banner on which the Chinese characters meaning "Farming is the great basis of the world" were written, narrow horizontally and wide vertically in shape. On the top of the flag, a globe made from collected tail feathers of a pheasant, called *kkwŏngjangmok*, was put and on both sides below the tassel, two wooden poles with dragon head figures decorated in color were attached. Since the flag was the symbol of *ture*, it was made from cloth of the best quality.[63]

2) *yŏnggi⁻* a flag of the escort for *nonggi*, used as a signal flag for the *nongak* band and for *chin pŏp nori* play, a little shorter vertically than horizontally in an almost rectangular shape. In the middle of the flag, the Chinese character *yŏng* (令) meaning command was written and the rim was decorated with laces. At the end of the flagpole, either a single-pronged spear or a three-pronged spear made from brass or iron was attached. This flag usually used two colors of red and blue.

3) *sangsoe⁻* the first player of *kkwaenggwari*, the virtual leader of *nongak*. *Sangsoe* used the masculine *kkwaenggwari* with the most sonorous and strong sound, wearing *sangmo* (decorated headwear).

4) *pusoe⁻* the second *kkwaenggwari* player, assisting *sangsoe* and using the feminine *kkwaenggwari* with a soft sound, also wearing *sangmo*.

5) *samsoe⁻* the third *kkwaenggwari* player, using the same *kkwaenggwari* as *pusoe*, wearing *sangmo*.

6) *sujing⁻* the first *ching* player, wearing not *sangmo* but *kokkal* (paper cowl).

7) *pujing⁻* the second *ching* player, assisting *suching*, wearing a paper cowl.

8) *sangjanggo⁻* the first *changgo* player, wearing a paper cowl.

9) *pujanggo⁻* the second *changgo* player, wearing a paper cowl.

10) *k'ŭnbuk-chabi⁻* the first player of a big drum, wearing a paper cowl. Depending on the size of *nongak*, two big drums were often used.

11) *sangsogo⁻* the first player of a small drum, wearing not a paper cowl but *sangmo*. Beating the drum, he played a *sogo* dance, raising his knees high as if leaping into the air whirling around.

12) *pusogo⁻* the second *sogo* player, wearing *sangmo*.

13) *samsogo*‑ the third *sogo* player, wearing *sangmo*. Depending on the size of *nongak*, *sogo* players could number up to eight at most.

14) *sangbŏpko*‑ the first *pŏpko* player, *Pŏpko* was a drum a little smaller than *sogo*. The player wore *sangmo*. In some *nongak*, there was no distinction made between *sogo* and *pŏpko*, using both as the same. Beating *pŏpko*, players danced *pŏpko* dance.

15) *pubŏpko*‑ the second *pŏpko* player, wearing *sangmo*. Others same as *sangbŏpko*.

16) *sambŏpko*‑ the third *pŏpko* player, wearing *sangmo*. The number of *pŏpko* players could be extended up to eight. The first *pŏpko* player sometimes wore *sangmo* with a long streamer about 18 meters long and twirled the streamer.

17) *nallari-jabi*‑ the shawm player wearing a paper cowl.

Such were the basic constituents of *nongak* used for the *ture* joint labor. However, for the rest time or for the occasions of *homi-ssishi* or *ture* play, *chapsaek* was added to heighten the excitement, enriching the content of the play. The cast of *chapsaek* varied from one region to another, but its principal constituents used in the three southern provinces were as follows:

18) *mudong* (dancing children on the top of shoulder of men)‑ boys who danced on the shoulders of the adults. They wore yellow blouses, red skirts and purple overalls, dressed as women. Holding a towel in hand and wearing a cowl, they danced a female dance. *Mudong* usually played 2 or 3 story formation of a human wall up to a 5 story human wall formation. The number of *mudong* was counted the same as the number of *sogo* and *pŏpko* players (usually six, up to the maximum number of eight).[64]

19) *p'osu*‑ a dancer dressed as a hunter. Wearing a hunting cap of animal fur with a wooden gun and a net bag for pheasant on his shoulder, he played a dance but sometimes played a gag and well-meant remarks in addition.

20) *chung* (monk)‑ a dancer dressed as a monk. Putting on a white overall with a surplice, wearing a paper cowl, carrying a sack on the back, he held a rosary in his hand. Besides an adult monk, a child monk (*sami*) was also used.

21) *kakssi* (lass)‑ a male dancer dressed as a girl. He put on colorful coat and skirt in order to heighten the air of merriment, putting a white cloth on his head, and danced a female dance. Two or three *kakssi* were usually used.

22) *yangban* (aristocrat)‑ A dancer disguised as *yangban*. Putting on a robe, wearing a horny horse-hair coronet on his head, with a beard and holding a fan or a bamboo pipe in hand, he danced. In *nongak*, *yangban* were treated as

belittled strangers.

23) *ch'angbu* (male clowns)—He was a male clown dressed as a shaman and played as a dancer and singer. Putting a bamboo hat (*p'aeraengi*) on his head, he danced a shaman dance while singing.

24) *t'al kwangdae* (masked clown)—A masked dancer. Usually, a hag *kwangdae* or an oldster (male) *kwangdae* was used. Both of them danced facing each other and exchanged witty words in a gag play to excite the spectators.

Those who played the *nongak* instruments of "original" *nongak* were called *chaebi* or *chabi*. Their costume had a certain style. The original form of *nongak* costume seems to have derived from the military costume but in practice, they just put on ordinary clothes with a belt on it for the sake of convenience. Belts used three colors of red, blue and yellow. Belts of red and blue colors were called *karŭmtti* and were put on askew from both sides of the shoulder down and the yellow belt was called *hŏritti* (waist belt) which was bound around the waist tucking both red and blue belts inside. Only *sangsoe* put on an extra yellow belt on both sides of the shoulder to indicate that he was the leader.

Sangmo for *nongak* was a variation of a military cap with a flower decoration on it. On the top of *sangmo*, a revolving device (*toldae*) was put with a wooden stick (*ch'ori*) attached to it so as to put a long streamer to it. In pinciple, ① *kkwaenggwari* players ② *sogo* players and ③ *pŏpko* players wore *sangmo* and the rest wore paper cowls. Among *sangmo* wearers, *kkwaenggwari* players whirled their *sangmo* with a streamer made of tail feathers of birds attached to *ch'ori* and *sogo* and *pŏpko* players twirled their *sangmo* with a streamer, about 4.5 meters long and made of white paper. The paper streamer was called *pujŏnji*. Therefore, those who displayed the feat of twirling the long streamers were *sogo* and *pŏpko* players. The last *pŏpko* player was selected from among the most adroit streamer players and his role was to twirl the long streamer about 18 meters long. Cowls worn by players of *ching*, big drum, sandglass-shaped drum and shawm were decorated with paper flowers on top and on the sides.

The structure of a *nongak* band described so far was modeled after an ideal form, and bands of bigger size than this have been organized depending on the size of the *ture* joint labor. Since its size was big, the maintenance and management of *nongak* called for a big amount of money and its maintenance was difficult if there was no support from the *ture* income. It was customary for *nongak* to play without the addition of *chapsaek* when *ture* members moved from one labor site to another or when they came back from work. On such occasions, *nongak* played the militant and stimulating marching themes called *kilgunak* (marching military music) like at a military parade. During labor in the fields, strains were simplified. While a big drum player played the big drum on the embankment, a *kkwaenggwari* player tuned into the play and *ture* members worked in tune to the rhythm produced by these players. *Nongak* was not played during an ordinary course of labor but when *ture* members came to feel tired, *nongak* was played regularly.[65] During the rest hour, *nongak* was played in full, usually with the addition of *chapsaek* such as *mudong*.

Ture nongak reached its climax at *homi-ssishi* or at *ture* play. On such occasions, *chapsaek* was added in abundance to the full playing of *nongak*—constituting a combined ethnic music play consisting of five elements. The five elements were ① playing of percussion instruments led by the *kkwaenggwari* of *sangsoe* at the front, ② leading song and singing in unison in tune to the rhythm, ③ various dances by *nongak* players and by *chapsaek* players, ④ gag play and drama play led by *chapsaek* players and ⑤ twirling of streamers of *sangmo* and some acrobatic feats. Thus, *nongak* developed as an outdoor group music and group dance integrating all these forms of entertainment. On such occasions, *sangsoe* led the rhythm and the march. Rhythms or beats favored by farmers in *nongak* were *kilgunak*, *manjangdan*, *tŏngdŏkkungi*, *tadŭraegi*, *kutkŏri*, *chungmori*, *chajinmori*, *hwimori*, *changp'ungjang*, and *ch'umjangdan* and so on.[66] *Changdan* (lit. "long-short" meaning rhythm or beat) of *nongak* strains was designated in number according to the number of gong beats in a bar. The bigger the number, the faster the tempo. *Sangsoe* of *ture nongak* in the closing days of the Chosŏn dynasty was said to have been able to beat, usually, 12 times in the duration of a bar.

Dancing was also dynamic and vigorous. Among various dances, not only *sogo* and *pŏpko* dance in which dancers, raising one knee high, whirled around kicking the other leg against the ground, but also *nongak* dance in which dancers, shaking their torsos violently from left to right and vice versa in tune to a quick tempo, strode around the ground in a brisk movement to be suddenly interrupted by a motionless position was a dance all *ture* members and farmers liked best to play. Since *nongak* for *homi-ssishi* and *ture* plays consisted of around 30 players, the form in which players marched in a file leaping around was also stylized as a form of art, thus creating a sort of mass game called *chinbŏp nori*. Of *chinbŏp nori* (mass game) loved by *ture* farmers, there were *p'alchindobŏp, mŏngsŏkmari, sat'ongbaegi, tangsanbŏllim, kasae-mallim, kallimbŏpko* and *kosari-kkŏkki* etc.[67]

Sangmo, twirled around by commoner-farmers of the lowest rank attired in red, blue and yellow while dancing a militant and vigorous dance in tune to or playing the instruments of *nongak*, well symbolized that farmers in the days of Chosŏn feudal society were robust, dynamic and optimistic in their life even amid exploitation by the aristocrats and landlords. And even in the dark days under Japanese colonial rule, sonorous tunes of *nongak*, militantly leaping dances and resounding and optimistic choruses of Korean farmers also well symbolized the unbending will to life and the optimistic way of life of the Korean people even under the pressure of the Japanese imperialists. The criticism of *ture nongak* by Japanese observers —"Farming by Korean farmers is most of all the turmoil coming from festivity"[68]— seems to have derived more or less from a sense of jealousy.

Though *nongak* derived from *ture* and was an important element of *ture* joint labor, *nongak*, once having attained its own right of being, provided art and recreation for the entire farming community not only on the occasions of *ture* joint labor and *homi-ssishi*, but for all occasions of festivity and holidays. For instance, on such farmers' occasions as New Year's Day, Full Moon Day, *Tano* (May Festival), *Paekchung* or Korean Thanksgiving Day (all by lunar calender), *nongak* bands of *ture* played and again on such occasions as village rites. The *nongak* for *madangbabki* (lit. "ground stamping") played on the First Full Moon Day was really splendid. Such *nongak* can be seen as a secondary service form for villagers by *ture nongak*.

Since the social position of commoners (ordinary folk and farm servants) was improved in pace with the growth of commercial capital and the rise of commoners' culture in the closing days of the Chosŏn period, *nongak* which sprang from *ture* and became an important element of *ture* came to be detached from *ture* itself while improving itself as an independent art of the people. The specialization of *nongak* from *ture* may have undergone the following three stages from a sociological viewpoint.

First stage was a "house-call *nongak*." When the *nongak* band of *ture* needed money either to buy new instruments or to repair them or for their own expenses for an outing, they called at the houses of villagers, especially of rich farmers, in the leisurely time of farming, to play for them and receive donations for their entertainment. However, even though the house-call *nongak* started from *ture nongak*, it was not entirely a free service of entertainment or art and it was still within the bounds of village affairs since the income from *nongak* playing was secondary concern. Nevertheless, this was the start of the growth of *nongak* as a specialized form of entertainment activity.

The second stage was "*kŏllipp'ae nongak*" (kollipp'ae lit. means "begging-rice troupe"). Village farmers organized *nongak* from the start for the purpose of earning income. They called at houses not only of their villagers but of other villagers or they played in the market place to collect rice or money. *Kŏllipp'ae* used a number of *chapsaek* and it was characteristic that they played more *kut* (shamanistic rite) *nongak*. Thus, they were sometimes called "*kut* players' *nongak*." They played *kut nongak* such as *tangsan kut, saem kut, kosa kut, madang kut, p'an kut, t'ŏju kut,* or *chowang kut.* Individual plays such as *sangsoe, changgo, pŏpko, sangmo* with 18-metre-long streamers, and *mudong nori* were developed and added to *nongak*, making their play look more like an entertaining performance. This *nongak* was a form distinctively specialized from *ture.*

The third stage was "*namsadangp'ae* (troupe of strolling actors) *nongak*." Specialists in *nongak* organized their own independent band, going from one market place to another, from one town to another, supporting themselves from income derived from such performances.[69] *Namsadangp'ae nongak* added tight-rope dancing, acrobatics, saucer-spinning, clown play, mask-dance and other programs in addition to the regular programs of *nongak* in order to make it more amusing. Their performance was refined and was quite professional. *Nongak* played by a troupe of strolling actors was big in size, colorful and professional, more suitable as a staged performance for public entertainment. This *nongak* was a performing form completely specialized from *ture* origin.

The three kinds of *nongak* so far described indicate the process in which *nongak* was specialized from *ture*, reflecting the patterns of *nongak* which co-existed with the original *nongak* since the latter days of Chosŏn period. One thing to be noted here is the fact that *nongak* originally derived from *ture* and that (1) house-call *nongak*, (2) *kŏllipp'ae nongak* and (3) *namsadangp'ae nongak* all developed from *ture nongak.*

7. Social Functions of *Ture*

Ture played some important roles and functions in farming society.

1) Training Ground for Cooperative Life

Ture played the function of providing training for cooperative work based on joint labor in the struggle against nature and, at the same time, of providing villagers with training for systematic cooperative actions in the overall social life of an agricultural society. Such training contributed greatly to enabling farmers to effectively overcome the strenuous struggle against nature and the difficulty of their poor social life as farmers, so that they might manage to lead a social life based on the communal relations among them.

2) Function of Turning Labor into Pleasure

Ture played the role of turning painful labor into a kind of pleasure. Toiling with simple farming instruments was arduous and painful work but *ture* played the role of turning such painful labor into pleasurable work. Since it is a noble thing for man in society to do work with a joyful mind, role of *ture* must be evaluated highly.

3) Heightening of Labor Efficiency

The joint labor of *ture* served to raise the labor efficiency and to raise the productivity of labor. The achievement of *ture* labor was always greater than the sum of each individual labor. For instance, in case of Chŏktŏkri, Kŭmsŏng-myŏn, Chech'ŏn-gun, Ch'ungch'ŏngbuk-do province. "What would take three days for each farming household to finish, *ture* could finish in two days."[70] In other words, joint labor of *ture* could accomplish 50 per cent more than what could be done by the aggregate of individual labor. This bespeaks how effective *ture* was in an economic sense. *Ture* also contributed greatly to raising the total harvest of the village and to elevating the land productivity of the whole land holding of the village by enabling the villagers not to lose time in the input of labor so that the input of labor could be finished in the most opportune time.

4) Role of Mutual Help

Ture played an important role of mutual help by providing free service for the families of widows and the sick in the village. The role of mutual help by providing free service for the families of widows and the sick in the village. The role of mutual help functioned as forming social security for widows and the sick of the village and for all the villagers at the same time in case of any emergency among them. Such a function of *ture* played a big role in maintaining the communal character of the village even long after the farming community was disbanded in the tide of modernization.

5) Role of Mutual Entertainment

Ture provided entertainment for the villagers. *Nongak* and accompanying plays of *ture* in particular, played a big role in providing the often monotonous life in the countryside with joyful entertainment. Especially, the entertainment provided by *ture* was not only productive and wholesome but was directly connected to the re-generation of labor by farmers, to the improvement of the life of farmers and to the raising of productivity.

6) Role of Enlivening Life

Ture played an important role in enlivening the life of farmers which tended to be tedious and dull naturally and socially. Since the farming community had to stand against powerful nature, armed only with simple farming implements, and exploitation and suppression by the rulers had been piled up in the course of history life was apt to become tedious and dull. *Ture* played a big role in encouraging farmers and fostering the pride as farmers engaging in the "great basis of the world" thus contributing greatly to activating the social life of farmers.

7) Role as Common Norm

Ture played an important role in providing the village and farming society with common norms and rules as a means of autonomy. Common rules of *ture*, in particular, provided a sense of discipline to "young and adult males," core members of the farming community, helping the whole village maintain order.

8) Role of Social Integration

Ture played an important role of social integration so that members of the village would unite without being disrupted among them. *Ture* produced social solidarity and unity among village members by means of common labor, common mutual help, common entertainment and common rules, and functioned as a catalyst in integrating the village as a cooperative community of life.

9) Role of Fostering Community Spirit

Ture played an important role in fostering community spirit among villagers. In the course of the social transition in which the organizing principles of the village as a farming community were being lost as the elements of "Gesellschaft" were infiltrating into the farming community, *ture* played a big role in fostering the "we" consciousness and community spirit among villagers by means of periodic events of common labor, common donation, common entertainment and common receptions.

10) Role of Creating a Farmers' Culture

Ture became the womb of a farmers' culture. *Ture* gave birth to *nongak*, creating a number of farmers' plays, music and dance, enriching the content of folklore. Since farmers were a dominant part of population until before the coming of the modern age, this meant that *ture* also created a part of idiosyncratic ethnic culture. Farmers' culture and culture created out of *ture* were characterized by a rich content of productive and wholesome patterns directly related to labor and life.

Since *ture* played such important roles in sociological terms, farmers came to regard *ture* as valuable and something in which to take pride.

8. Changing Patterns of *Ture* from 1910 to 1945

From 1910 through 1945, money economy further infiltrated into farming communities and *ture* came to be drastically changed by the influence of the Japanese colonial policies. The change in *ture* during the Japanese days can be characterized by ① decline and disappearance of *ture*, ② the changed nature of the surviving *ture* and ③ decline and disappearance of *nongak*.

During the Japanese occupation, the communities of *ture* drastically declined and a number of *ture* disappeared. The observation reports in the closing period of the Japanese occupation remarked that *ture*, which was quite fashionable until the last days of the Chosŏn dynasty, disappeared 20 or 10 years or a few years before and the report referred to villages where there no longer existed *ture*.[71] The cause and reason for the decline and disappearance of *ture* during the Japanese occupation could be cited as follows:

First, since money economy further infiltrated into the farming sector, intensifying its influence, individualistic "pursuit of interest" became widespread and more popular. The infiltration of money economy into the farming sector withered the communal character of the village and the exclusive nature of village life was much discolored. As village members came to pursue their own personal interests ahead of any, the traditional mutual-help and cooperative system of the village came into a sharp decline.

Second, one cannot help referring to the disappearance of village communal land due to the land survey projects by the Japanese imperialists.[72] Though most land was held by personal title and there was very small land held commonly by villages at the end of the Chosŏn period, small strips of land of common holding were one of the material foundations sustaining the existence of *ture*. The land survey projects by the Japanese imperialists dissolved almost all of the remaining land of common holding and invalidated the right of village members to reclaim unclaimed wide open spaces of land, thus denying the economic right of *ture* for joint labor. This means that one of the economic basis for the survival of *ture* was forced to disappear.

Third, the Japanese colonial policies functioned to obliterate the "autonomy" of villages. Even by the end of the Chosŏn period, there still existed a strong remnant of autonomy among villagers. However, fearful and wary of the independent, autonomous and nationalistic character of the villages, the Japanese forced to destroy the autonomy of villages by incorporating the villages into the Japanese administrative jurisdiction (*myŏn* offices and the stationing of resident police in the village) so as to govern the farming communities in an authoritarian and fascistic way. Accordingly, the *ture* community of a voluntary nature came to decline and disappear in the course of time.

Fourth, during the Japanese occupation, cash-earning farm hands came to advance into farming communities. The intensified Japanese colonial policies including the land survey projects accelerated the diversification of the status of farmers, expediting the decline of owner-farmers down to impoverished tenant farmers and bringing about, at the same time, a number of cash-earning farm hands deprived of the possession of any land.[73] Cash-earning farm hands perpetually came to be employed by big farmers or by rich farmers at a low wage and even in the peak days demanding the most labor power, work contracts for daily wage were made possible, drastically decreasing the social need of *ture*.

Fifth, women advanced into the agricultural labor scene. As has been mentioned in the report on farming communities in Namwŏn-gun, Chŏllabuk-do province in the closing period of Japanese colonial rule, women took part in rice seedling transplantation and to a lesser extent, they also took park in weeding.[74] The advance of women into agriculture helped decrease the rising demand for male labor, and accordingly, lessened the social need of joint labor by *ture*.

Sixth, the decline of owner-farmers during the Japanese occupation greatly weakened the social strata of the farming community which could maintain the joint labor community of *ture*. Owner-farmers were the backbone of the farming community as the protector of farmers' culture.[75] The decline of such farmers eroded the social basis not only for *nongak* but the joint labor community of *ture* itself.

Seventh, brewing of farmers' rice-wine, *makkŏlli*, was prohibited by the Japanese imperialists who also held a hostile attitude to *nongak*. In order to ship more rice to Japan from Korea, the Japanese prohibited the private brewing of *makkŏlli* which was indispensable to the maintenance of farming labor by Korean farmers and to *ture*. They also regarded *nongak*, strangely enough, as a "wasteful" folk practice. Such a policy helped the decline and disappearance of *ture*, destroying some integral elements of *ture* – the common form of entertainment and the common banquet.

Eighth, the change in the structure of farming enterprise in association with the colonial policy by the Japanese and the introduction of weeding machines into farming also accelerated the decline of *ture*. The agricultural policy of imperialist Japan made compulsory the farming of cotton and tobacco in addition to sericulture in order to supply more raw material for the industry in Japan. Thus, the diversified and distorted forms of structure for farming enterprise and the rise of sericultural farmers also indirectly helped the decline of *ture*. Weeding machines were primitive, not so effective in labor efficiency and were only beginning to appear in the closing period of Japanese rule. They played a very small influence in the decline of *ture*. But the nature of weeding machines could expedite the disappearane of *ture* in weeding work.

Ninth, the Japanese authorities took suppressive measures against *ture* with an alternative choice for another form of "common labor team." Following the outbreak of the Second World War, the Japanese organized "common labor teams" by units of "patriotic teams" in which men and women above 14-15 years took part and disbanded the traditional form of *ture*.[76] This policy greatly decreased the number of *ture* in the closing period of colonial rule.

Despite the suppressive measures of the Japanese, *ture* was quite widespread by dint of its positive social function in the beginning period of Japanese colonial rule and was able to sustain its life as a dominant form of the supply of labor force for farming even in the closing period of Japanese rule. For instance, in the case of Hongsŏng-gun, Ch'ungch'ŏngnam-do province, 197 *ture* were existing as of 1915 (See Table 1). The number was smaller than that of the farming settlements (natural villages) but was bigger by 58 than the number of the administrative units of *ri*. At this time, it was reported that most weeding work in summer in this area was done through *ture* joint labor.[77] It was also reported that in this period, in Chŏlla-do and Ch'ungch'ŏng-do provinces generally, the work of rice seedling transplantation and weeding was quite heavily dependent on *ture*.[78]

By the end of Japanese occupation, *ture* remained in the southern regions of Korea as one of the dominant labor patterns of society. *Ture* of such nature can be classified into the following three types: ① a traditional type of *ture* which preserved communal characteristics despite the pressure from the Japanese imperialists and the influence from the money economy, ② a transformed type of *ture* which was transformed by the pressure of the Japanese imperialists and the money economy, ③ a new derivative type of *ture* which came to bear a new pattern due to various influence of the time.

Ture type 1 needs no explanation since it preserved the traditional nature of *ture* as it was. *Ture* type 2 can be characterized by ① recession of a communal nature of *ture*, ② prevalence of paying for labor and ③ a new introduction of contract labor system.

The transformed *ture* under Japanese suppression began to change from that of a communal nature to that of receiving cash payment for the labor for widows and the sick.[79] The labor wage was relatively small as a wage for labor of such nature but it reflected the change in quality in terms of labor free for the common benefit prevalent during Chosŏn dynasty days. At the same time, the compulsory membership of *ture* and the communal obligation for the *ture* members were also greatly weakened while "voluntary choice" of members became more dominant. In the transformed *ture*, the counting of wages became very compulsive. Wage counting was made even for labor done for land possessed by *ture* members. The whole acreage under cultivation and each holding of land by members were counted against the labor days required for *ture* work and the wage to be paid by each landowner and to be received by each *ture* member was counted. Even among *ture* members, in case one's land holding was bigger than the average wage to be paid for *ture* members, the balance was exactly counted out and paid back to *ture* and vice versa.[80] Thus, in case any farmer provided two or three members to *ture* and his land holding was relatively small, he received the wage balance in proportion to the excess labor service rendered.[81] Landlords and rich farmers were also naturally required to pay more money to *ture* in proportion to the balance between their land holdings.

One of the most striking characteristics of *ture* transformed under the Japanese pressure was that the income of *ture* was not used for *ture* for common purposes but was paid out as wages for *ture* members as the first thing to do. Then, the rest of the income, if any at all, was used for the occasions of *homi-ssishi* and for the maintenance of *nongak*. This was a big change in contrast to the former practice in which the income was first used for *ture* as a whole and no wage was paid out to *ture* members on an individual basis. Thus, in the transformed *ture*, the occasion of *homi-ssishi* became reduced in size and the maintenance of *nongak* or the purchase of *nongak* instruments became difficult.

In the transformed *ture* under the Japanese occupation, landlords or rich farmers first stipulated the wage for their land possession and made a labor contract with *ture*. In such cases, meals for *ture* members were provided by landlords. Since the labor efficiency by *ture* was higher than the sum of individual labor when the work was done separately, even in the transformed *ture*, the wage for *ture* members was not below the level of the wage for individual labor done separately and the sum to be paid out by landlords was not greater than the landlord would pay each member of the labor force he employed.

(Table 1) Number of *Ture* and *Nongak* in Hongsŏng-gun, Ch'ungch'ŏngnam-do Province (1915)

Name of *Myŏn*	Number of *Ri*	Number of *Ture*			Number of *Nongak*
		With *Nongak*	Without *Nongak*	Sum	
Hongyang	10	7	–	7	49
Hongbuk	14	21	–	21	84
Kŭmma	13	12	–	12	72
Hongdong	18	21	16	37	105
Changgok	16	27	–	27	166
Kwangch'ŏn	10	20	9	29	100
Ŭnha	11	3	2	5	15
Yongch'ŏn	11	10	–	10	50
Sŏbu	10	15	–	15	70
Kodo	14	16	6	22	111
Kuhang	12	12	–	12	60
Total	139	164	33	197	882

Source: The number of ture and nongak referred to the paper by Toyota Chuichi and that of ri to the statistics in the directory prepared by Etsuji Yuishichi.

In the case of Hongsŏng-gun, Ch'ungch'ŏngnam-do province, a landlord was supposed to pay 17 *chŏn* (a monetary unit; one hundredth of *won*) for a unit of land (about 1,000 m²) in case he resorted to the common labor of *ture* but in case he employed labor hands individually, he was supposed to spend 23 *chŏn*. In other words, the wage for *ture* was cheaper by 26 per cent than for individual labor contract. As Table 2 and Table 3 show, even inclusive of meals and banquet for *ture*, the cost of *ture* for a unit of land was 32 *chŏn* while the cost for the employment of each labor hand by contract was 35.5 *chŏn*, thus the cost of *ture* was cheaper by 9.1 per cent. For instance, a landlord with 30 units of land could save 120 *chŏn* on weeding for one round if he resorted to *ture*. Furthermore, if the landlord resorted to *ture* labor hours could be reduced greatly.[82] Because of these advantages; landlords living in the southern regions of Korea resorted to the transformed *ture* for rice seedling transplantation and weeding considering *ture* as a sort of system for labor contract. The transformed *ture* came to be called by such names as *modum ch'arye* or others from one region to another.[83]

Representative of the changed derivative form of *ture* under the social pressure of the time of Japanese occupation was a system of *kojidae*.[84] As the decline of farmers under Japanese rule was expedited with the rise of impoverished farmers and cash labor hands in farming, petty farmers and farming laborers organized a labor unit patterning after *ture*, and they could obtain contracts with landlords or with rich farmers beforehand and could be paid wages in advance during the time of scarcity of food (December—March) so as to tide over the crisis supporting their families with pre-paid wages. In the busy time of farming, they performed their contract duty and were paid the rest of the wage and such a labor system was called *kojidae*. Though patterned after traditional *ture*, it did not have a communal nature at all—it was a voluntary organization for extremely impoverished farmers and cash labor hands. It was a special labor union as a remedy for impoverished farmers and cash labor hands who had no choice but starvation otherwise under the extreme exploitation by the Japanese. Therefore, *kojidae* was an entirely different labor system from *ture* and it should be studied independently from *ture*.

Another change in *ture* to be noted was the decline and disappearance of *nongak*. The transformed *ture* was unable to buy *nongak* instruments or to repair them and *nongak* was declining as days went by. Since the Japanese saw *nongak* as nationalistic and "wasteful," the decline of *nongak* was the more expedited. As a result, there were a number of *ture* during the days of Japanese occupation that did not have *nongak*.

(Table 2) Wages and Cost of Weeding Work by *Ture* (1915)

Item	Acreage and Labor Hands	Unit Cost for a Unit of Land	Cost for 30 Units of Land	Remarks
Wages	30 Units of Land	0.170 *yen*	5.100 *yen*	60 *ture* members could finish the work in half a day
Meals and Drink	60 men	0.075 *yen*	4.500 *yen*	Drink once in the morning, lunch once, 7.3 *chŏn* per head
Total			9.600 *yen*	32 *chŏn* per unit of land

For instance, in the case of Hongsŏng-gun, Ch'ungch'ŏngnam-do province, by 1915, out of the total 197 *ture*, only 164 *ture*, 83.2 per cent, had *nongak* and the *ture* without *nongak* were 33, constituting 16.8 per cent of the total. The size of a *nongak* band was also greatly reduced and *nongak* were reduced to the extreme, with 8 or 5 members.[85] The Japanese started the compulsory rice appropriation from farmers upon the outbreak of the Second World War and took away the metal music instruments from farmers in the name of offering war materials to the country. Thus, with no instruments left, *nongak* rapidly disappeared from the scene.

Ture was greatly transformed, declined and disappeared from the scene as has been observed. Nevertheless, the *ture* community which could survive the Japanese suppression played a great role in maintaining the national tradition through mutual help even under the exploitative policy of the Japanese imperialists and despite the Japanese policy to extinguish Korean ethnicity.

(Table 3) Wages and Cost for Weeding Work by Individual Labor Hands (1915)

Item	Acreage and Labor Hands	Unit Cost for a Unit of Land	Cost for 30 Units of Land	Remarks
Wages	30 Units of Land	0.230 *yen*	6.900 *yen*	30 hands work on a unit of land for a day per head
Meals and Drink	30 men	0.100 *yen*	3000 *yen*	Drink twice for a.m. and p.m., lunch for once
Cost for the Family Members of 30 men (Meals and Drink)	15 persons	0.050 *yen*	0.750 *yen*	Lunch cost for auxiliary 15 persons
Total			10.650 *yen*	35.5 *chŏn* for weeding for a unit of land

9. Conclusion

As has been examined so far, *ture* and *nongak* were part of a sagacious social institution and culture which the Korean people devised and nurtured over the long span of history. Since man has come to create culture through labor struggling against nature, labor has become a toil too painful for man to bear. Man has endeavored to turn this painful labor into a joyful exercise of physical power but not to much avail.

Ture has succeeded in creating a common labor system, raising labor efficiency by being connected with *nongak*, and turning painful labor to joyful.

Korean farmers developed a mutual cooperative way of life through the community of *ture*, cementing the unity of the group members. Korean farmers also developed folk art and ethnic art such as beautiful and militant music and dance combined with the productive life of farming, working and enjoying together in group.

It is true that the conventional approach to the history of Korea has been obsessed with the history of politics in the central arena of the nation and with the history of rulers. However, this approach may end up in throwing light only on a small aspect of history. The "social history" as a new discipline of history has to also explore the history of the lives of the people at large which sustained the main stream of society so as to throw light into the depth of the "whole." Study of *ture* in times to come has to be able to supplement the conventional interpretation of history through the study of the lives of the people at the core of society.

Since Koreans underwent colonial rule by the Japanese while the nation was at a critical moment in the task of modernization, a number of beautiful and creative national traditions and cultural heritages were not handed down or preserved. However, it is fortunate that in recent times a new movement is taking place, though belatedly, to unearth the national cultural heritage and adapt it to the changing reality of the time.

In the task of unearthing our genuine cultural heritage buried in Korean cultural tradition, the subject of *ture* and *nongak* may have to be raised first of all before anything else. If joint common labor, the transfer of painful labor into joyful, and the practice of mutual help are things needed in any time, now is the time for us to examine *ture* and *nongak* to see whether they are really important cultural inheritances to be creatively handed down and developed further in times to come.

FOOTNOTES (Part I – 1)

1. Since I got interested in the history of farmers and farming villages, I set up a special file to collect data concerning the ture subject. But, data collected ever since were quite meager in comparison to other subject files. It was, though partly due to my own negligence, mainly due to the fact that rulers had almost no interest in the affairs and institutions of the people and no reliable data has been recorded. Despite a number of people have been interested in ture, no full-scale paper has been published on the subject since the liberation of Korea from Japan. Knowing there could be many defects due to paucity of data and material, I decided to publish this paper anyhow in its imperfect form and intend to supplement any defects by further study.

2. Kang Chŏng-t'aek, "Organization of Joint Labor and Its Historical Transformation in Korea," *Study of Agricultural Economy*, Vol. 17, No. 4, 1941.

3. In Chŏng-shik, *Comments on Korea's Farming Villages*, 1943, pp. 2-3.

4. Yi Pyŏng-do, "Study on Public Offices of the Ancient Times," *Collected Papers of Seoul National University*, Vol. 1, 1954.

5. See the "Account of the Eastern Barbarians" (Tung-i-ch'uan), *Sankuochih* (History of Three States).

6. Yi pyŏng-do, *op.cit.*

7. See the "Account of the Eastern Barbarians," *Houhanshu* (History of Latter Han).

8. *Sankuochih.*

9. Refer to the passages on King Yuri, *Samkuk Sagi* (History of Three Kingdoms), Vol. 1.

10. *Sankuochih.*

11. *Samkuk Sagi*, Vol. 23.

12. *Samkuk Sagi*, Vol. 2.

13. Kim Yong-sŏp, "Irrigated Rice Farming Technique in the Latter Period of Chosŏn," *Study of the Agricultural History of the Latter Period of Chosŏn*, 1971, Ilchogak, Seoul, pp. 2-103.

14. Refer to the passages of the day of Chŏnghae, September of the 13th year of King Yŏngjo, *Yŏngjo Sillok* (Chronicle of King Yŏngjo), Vol. 45.

15. Refer to the record of November 17, 14th year of King Yŏngjo, *Pibyŏnsadŭngnok* (Copied Record of the Office of Border Defense Council), Vol. 104.

16. Refer to the record of November 17, 14th year of King Yŏngjo, *Sŭngjŏngwŏn Ilgi* (Diary of the Royal Secretariat), Vol. 881.

17. Refer to the record of the day of Ŭlch'uk, November, 14th year of Yŏngjo, *Yŏngjo*

Sillok, Vol. 47.

18. Shin Yong-ha, "Land Reform Thought of Chŏng Yak-yong," *Kyujanggak*, Vol. 7, 1983.

19. *Report on Agricultural Products of Korea*, 1906, pp. 425-426.

20. *Ibid.*, pp. 426-428.

21. *Ibid.*, pp. 369-370.

22. *Ibid.*, p. 370.

23. *Ibid.*, pp. 370-371.

24. Eitaro Suzuki, "Study of Korean Village Settlements," *Study of East Asian Societies*, Vol. 1, 1943; *Study of Korea's Agricultural Society*, 1973, p. 23; "Travelogue on Korea's Agricultural Society," *ibid.*, p. 252.

25. Juichi Toyota, "Study of Ture and Nongak," *Chosen Magazine*, April 1916.

26. Kang Chŏng-t'aek, *op. cit*; In Chŏngshik, *op.cit.*, p. 4.

27. Kenichi Hisama, "Study of Farmers' Family Economy and Its Enterprise Scale," *Modern Aspects of Agriculture in Korea*, 1935, pp. 162-163.

28. Kang Chŏng-t'aek, *op.cit.*

29. Han Sang-bok, "Ture, Working and Playing Together," *Koreans*, November 1983.

30. Ture members called ture officers by such titles, possibly, in order to demonstrate against yangban class who called themselves among themselves such titles and this reflects the high sense of self-pride of ture members.

31. Since nongch'ŏng (farming office) was the headquarters and the meeting place of ture, there were regions where ture was called nongch'ŏng.

32. Yi Kak-chong, "Survey on Kye," *Chosen*, July 1923.

33. Chang Ki-ch'ang, "On Farmers' Association," *Chosen Magazine*, August 1917.

34. Kang Chŏng-t'aek, *op.cit.*

35. Eitaro Suzuki, "Travelogue on Korea's Agricultural Society," *op.cit.*, p. 200.

36. Eitaro Suzuki, "Notes on the Survey of Farming Regions in Honam Area," *Chosen*, No. 352, October 1944; *op.cit.*, p. 323.

37. Kang Chŏng-t'aek, *op.cit.*

38. *Report on Agricultural Products of Korea*, p. 369.

39. *Ibid.*, p. 425.

40. Matsuro Kato, *On Korea's Agriculture*, 1904, p. 168; Refer to the case of Suwon, *Report on Agricultural Products of Korea*, p. 426.

41. There were reports referring to the use of ture even in non-irrigated farming in Samnam (three southern provinces) but this was an exceptional case. In general, ture was used in irrigated farming.

　　Refer to the "Report on Common-tilled Farms," *Monthly Report of the Government-General of Chosŏn*, March 1913. p. 139. According to the report by April 1912, the common-tilled farms throughout the country reached 900 units with a total acreage of 1,621.6 chŏngbo (A chŏngbo is equivalent to 0.992 hectare). This indicates that there still remained a few common-tilled farms by the end of Chosŏn dynasty.

42.   In the traditional form of ture, rich farmers tended to get more benefit from ture than small farmers. Thus, they voluntarily provided the banquet, common meals and some other forms of donation to make up the balance of benefit they got from ture.

43.   Kang Chŏng-t'aek, *op.cit.* According to him, there were some distorted forms of ture in which the work on the farms of big farmers was done first and ture members were treated to meals and drink in return for the priority, during the Japanese days.

44.   Kang Chŏng-t'aek, *ibid.* According to him, the "assemble call" by bugles was played as a signal for the assemblage of ture members. This seemed to be miswritten in writing in Japanese. In Nongak, bugles were not used but shawms.

45.   Eitaro Suzuki, "Gleanings from the Travel in Korea's Agricultural Society," *Study of Ethnicity Research*, New Volume 1, No. 1, 1943; *op.cit.*, p. 122.

46.   W.R. Carles, *Life in Corea*, London, 1894, p. 180. "About 100 of them were at work... Coreans always seem to enjoy working in company, and many of the men were singing."

47.   *Report on Korea's Agricultural Products*, p. 426.

48.   In Chŏng-shik, *op.cit.*, pp. 11-12.

49.   Kang Chŏng-t'aek, op.cit.

50.   *Settlements of Korea*, Vol. 2, Government-General of Chosŏn, 1933, p. 175.

51.   E.S. Brunner, "Rural Korea: A Preliminary Survey of Economic, Social, and Religious Condition," *The Christian Mission in Relation to Rural Problems*, New York, 1928, p. 116. "In his stay in Japan, the author rarely saw an idle man. In Korea it is no unusual thing to see men smoking at their ease, even sleeping in mid afternoon out in the field." Thus, the author seems to criticize the napping practice of ture members as idleness and this must be a superficial observation by a foreigner who did not know the structure and practice of *ture*.

52.   Kenichi Hisama, "System of Labor Unit and Kojidae," *Modern Aspects of Agriculture in Korea*, p.220.

53.   *Report on Korea's Agricultural Products*, p. 426.

54.   The practice of changwŏn (passage of the state examination with the top honor) of ture seemed to be a practice of ture reflecting the high sense of self-pride of ture members as a counter contention to the culture and practice of yangban class.

55.   In case the landlord was not residing in the village or in case an ordinary farmer, not an farm servant, was elected in ture changwŏn, the banquet for changwŏn was provided by rich farmers and by ture members in turn.

56.   According to *Folk Entertainment in Korea*, Survey Material of the Government-General of Chosŏn, Vol. 47, 1941, the practice of homi-ssishi was a universal and prevalent custom seen anywhere in the provinces of Kyŏnggi, Ch'ungch'ŏng, Chŏlla, Kyŏngsang and Kangwŏn. The practice was also seen in Chŏngju of P'yŏnganbuk-do province (p.322), in Ch'ŏlsan (p.324), in Anbyŏn of Hamkyŏngbuk- do province (p.343).

The distribution of homi-ssishi practice seemed to indicate the distribution of ture system.

57. Kang Chŏng-t'aek, *op.cit.* According to it, in Ulsan area of Kyŏngsangnam-do province, a day was chosen for the banquet after the rice seedling transplantation and the first round of weeding work and this day was called nadari or banquet for washing hands.

58. Eitaro Suzuki, "Notes on the Survey of Farming Regions in Honam Area," *op.cit.*, p. 320. A small banquet called ssŏre-ssich'im was held after the rice seedling transplantation work in the Posŏng area of Chŏllanam-do province.

59. When landholding among ture members was relatively equal and even, no counting was needed among ture members since a rational counting of labor input was automatically made.

60. Chang Ki-ch'ang, *op.cit.*; Zenichi Itai, *Economic History of Korea*, 1928, p. 36.

61. According to *Folk Entertainment of Korea*, the distribution of Nongak generally corresponded with those of ture and homi-ssishi. Nongak was a universal practice throughout the provinces of Kyŏnggi, Ch'ungch'ŏng, Chŏlla, Kyŏngsang, Hwanghae and Kangwŏn and the practice of Nongak was also reported from Hamju of Hamkyŏngnam-do province (p.336) and Kilchu of Hamkyŏngbuk-do province (p.357).

62. *Report on Korea's Agricultural Products*, p. 427. Two farmers' flags were illustrated on this page, one from Suwŏn-gun, Kyŏnggi-do province, 6×2 ch'ŏk^2 (abt. 1.8×0.6m^2) in size, written on it Chinese characters meaning "Farming is the great basis of the world" and the other from Hyŏn'gok-dong of Suwŏn-gun, written on it Chinese character meaning "work inherited from the god of farming." However, the characters on the flag of the former were more generally used.

63. *Report on Korea's Agricultural Products*, pp. 427-428; "Photographs of Dancing Children," *Folk Entertainment of Korea*, appendix, p. 12.

64. *Report on Korea's Agricultural Products*, p. 426.

65. Office of Cultural Properties, *Comprehensive Report on Korea' Folk Practice*, 13 Vols., 1969-1982. Nongak was reported from various regions, and Yi Po-hyŏng is recording the strains of Nongak on musical notes. I was helped by this report in writing this paper.

66. See chapters on "Nongak, Fishing Festival for Good Harvest and Folk Songs," *Comprehensive Report on Korea's Folk Practice*, Vol. 13.

67. *Report on the Observation of Korea's Agricultural Society* (anonymous), 1930. Requoted from Kang Chŏng-t'aek, *op.cit.*

68. Singing actors of Nongak were classified as one of "seven despicable professions" of the time and such a social discrimination greatly hindered the development of Nongak as an art.

69. Eitaro Suzuki, "Travelogue on Korea's Agricultural Society," *op.cit.*, p. 253.

70. Kang Chŏng-t'aek, *op.cit.*; Eitaro Suzuki, "On Korea's Agricultural Settlements," *Monthly Report of the Government-General of Chosŏn*, Vol. 14, No. 9, 11 and 12,

1943; "Travelogue on Korea's Agricultural Society," *op.cit.*, p. 199.

71. Shin Yong-ha, *Study on Land Survey Project in Korea*, 1982, p. 102.

72. Farm labor hands began to appear in the agricultural society of Korea already in the closing periods of the Chosŏn dynasty, but under Japanese rule, they were established as a distinct social group, beginning to play a social role.

73. Yasu Ono, "Realistic Study of Korea's Farming Villages," *Collected Monographs of Taido School*, Vol. 4, 1938.

74. Pak Myŏng-gyu, "Reflections on the Nature of Land-Owning Farmers under the Japanese Imperialist Rule," in a mimeographed form, 1980.

75. Eitaro Suzuki, "Notes on the Survey of Farming Regions of Honam Area," *op.cit.*, pp. 316-317.

76. Juichi Toyoda, *op.cit.*

77. Chang Ki-ch'ang, *op.cit.*;Kang Chŏng-t'aek, *op.cit.*

78. Kang Chŏng-t'aek, *ibid.*

79. Eitaro Suzuki, "On Korea's Agricultural Settlements," *op.cit.*, pp. 34-35.

80. Eitaro Suzuki, "Travelogue on Korea's Agricultural Society," *ibid.*, p. 252.

81. According to Juichi Toyoda, *op.cit.*, there was some defect in the joint labor of ture but such defect could be made up for by not losing the opportune timing for farming by means of ture work.

82. Eitaro Suzuki, "Notes of the Survey of Farming Regions in Honam Area," *op.cit.*, pp. 317-319. *Modum Ch'arye* prevalent in Chŏllanam-do province was a transformed form of ture in which the farming lots of the big agricultural company of the area were first tilled by all the village laborers and they were paid the wages from the company.

83. Kenichi Hisama, "System of Labor Units and Kojidae," *op.cit.*, pp. 211-297.

84. Juichi Toyoda, *op.cit.*

2. *Kwajŏn* Land Reform and the Establishment of Private Landlordism in The Early Chosŏn Dynasty Korea, 1391-1470

1. Introduction

One of the most important things which a researcher of Asian social and economic history should keep in mind is to distinguish practice from theory with regard to social and economic facts and to isolate realities from ideals. There have frequently existed great discrepancies between theory and practice or ideal and reality in the socio-economic institutions and socio-economic policies in the histories of Asian countries.

In Korea from 1391 to 1466, an historic land reform called *Kwajŏn-pob* was carried out by the founder of the Chosŏn dynasty (1392-1910) and successive kings. When we review he studies of the *Kwajŏn* land reform and the land system of the early Chosŏn dynasty Korea, we find that two opposing approaches have developed in parallel.

One group of scholars has interpreted the *Kwajŏn* land reform as the establishment of a system of state ownership of land. This follows the theory of the planners of the *Kwajŏn* land reform who clearly explained that the ideal land reform was to re-establish the state ownership of land, taking the tenth century land reform of Kongjŏn-je or the 'public land system' as their model. Therefore, according to them, in its basic structure the land system of Chosŏn dynasty Korea is a system of state ownership of land.

The other group notes the development of private landlordism in sixteenth century Korea and interprets the *Kwajŏn* land reform as containing private land in the system from the very beginning. Although the *Kwajŏn* land reform established the state ownership of land, when private land grew on a national scale at the end of the fifteenth century, the *Kwajŏn* land reform vanished and private landlordism was established. According to them, the land system of the Chosŏn dynasty was basically one of private ownership of land, since the system of state ownership of land was very short-lived (less than one century and in an imperfect way at that) while the system of private ownership of land was practiced for a longer time, more than four centuries.

It seems to me that those two interpretations have been confusing the theory of the *Kwajŏn* land reform with its practice, and its relation to the establishment of private landlordism.

This paper will trace the practice or reality of the *Kwajŏn* land reform and the process of the establishment of private landlordism in the early Chosŏn dynasty focusing on the following questions.

(1) Did the *Kwajŏn* land reform establish state ownership of land following the model of the tenth century 'public land' system? What was the basic structure of the *Kwajŏn* land reform?

(2) Did the *Kwajŏn* land reform suppress the establishment and development of private landlordism? What was the actual relationship between the *Kwajŏn* land reform and private landlordism?

(3) Was the system of private ownership of land established after the disorganization of the *Kwajŏn* land reform through the growth of privately-held land? Was private landlordism established after the disappearance of the *Kwajŏn* land reform at the end of the fifteenth century?

The origin of private landlordism in Korea can be traced at least to as early as the ninth century when powerful local families emerged as the landed class occupying the peasants' land and trying to establish their own domains in local areas.[1]

This emergence of landlordism in the ninth century, however, was entirely arrested before it reached maturity by the land reform of the *Koryŏ* dynasty (918 A.D.-1392 A.D.) which was founded as a centralized kingdom. The founder of the *Koryŏ* dynasty, Wang Kŏn considered the owner-peasant system of ancient Korea and the Chun-t'ien or 'equal land' system of T'ang China[2] the ideal and modified them in his own way to establish a new system called Kongjŏn-je, the 'public land' system. He abolished the manors and landlordism which had been rapidly emerging in local areas and tried to establish an independent owner-peasant system under government supervision. In 998 King Mokjong developed a well-organized system of "public land."

Under the 'public land' system, the ownership of land was divided into two dimensions. The King or state had nominal ownership of all land based on the ancient oriental concept that 'under heaven every spot is the sovereign's ground,' and the commoner-peasant had actual ownership of cultivated land. This did not allow any interposition of landlord between them. Under this system, the peasants had the right to receive land from the government according to their family size and had an obligation to pay a land-tax called *Cho* (租), labor service called *Yong* (庸) and pay a tax in craft-products called *Jo* (調). The rate of the land-tax was 10 per cent of the gross yield.[3] (It temporarily increased to 25 per cent of the yield in 992, [4)] but 10 per cent was the official rate of land-tax throughout the *Koryŏ* dynasty.) The labor service and the tax in craft-products were not very heavy in the first half of the *Koryŏ* period.

Under the 'public land' system, all the arable land was divided into small family-sized holdings. The commoner-peasant could inherit land or leave the land at will, but buying and selling of land was not allowed in order to prevent the rise of landlordism. However, the peasants everywhere could have land holdings, since every peasant household had the right to be allotted the land by the government. Scholars of the traditional period felt that this was a system of state ownership of land.

The social status of peasants under the 'public land' system seems to have been in between that of the serf of the medieval manor of Western Europe and that of a free farmer.

As in any medieval society, *Koryŏ* aristocrats were not engaged in any economic production but occupied official posts as bureaucrats. Therefore, the King or the state had to provide measures to secure their livelihood. Thus the *Koryŏ* dynasty government gave the aristocratic officials the right to collect tax (or rent) called *Sujokwon* on certain acreages. This tax, along with their salaries, provided their income. This system was called *Chŏnsikwa*, "grade land and forest." [5)] Under this system the aristocratic bureaucrats were divided into 18 grades and were allotted the 'land and forest' according to their official rank. [6)] The scale of this allotment of the 'grade land and forest' in 998 is shown in the following Table 1.

(Table 1) The scale of the allotment of 'grade land and forest.'

Grades	Lands	Forests	Grades	Lands	Forests
1	100 kyŏl	70 kyŏl	11	50 kyŏl	25 kyŏl
2	95	65	12	45	22
3	90	60	13	40	20
4	85	55	14	35	15
5	80	50	15	30	10
6	75	45	16	27	none
7	70	40	17	23	none
8	65	35	18	20	none
9	60	33	outside of grade	17	none
10	55	30			

The right to collect tax (or rent) from 'grade land and forest' was valid only for the lifetime of the recipient, and it returned to the state immediately upon his death. Thus the system of the 'grade land and forest' economically guaranteed the aristocratic social status of officials for only one generation. It is important to note that the right to collect tax (or rent) on 'grade land and forest' in the 'public land' system of the *Koryŏ* dynasty was not hereditary.

The 'public land' system of the *Koryŏ* dynasty allotted *Kunin-jŏn* (軍人田) or 'soldiers land' for 'military households' (*Kunho*) as reward for their military service.[7] The scale for the allotment of 'soldiers land' was 25 *kyŏl*[8] for cavalry soldiers and 20 *kyŏl* for infantrymen and others. The total number of military households was 120,000.[9]

The 'public land' system of the *Koryŏ* dynasty also allotted *Konghaejŏnsi* (公廨田柴), the 'land and forest of government office,' to central government offices, local officer post stations and other government organizations in order to meet the expenditures of the administration at the place itself and to save transportation expenses. Besides the above lands, there were several other special categories of land in the 'public land' system which are not mentioned here.

However, the 'public land' system of the *Koryŏ* dynasty established some hereditary lands or hereditary rights to collect tax (or rent) for special purposes. This was to guarantee forever the economic security of high ranking aristocrats. Since official posts were not hereditary, the social status of aristocrats was economically unstable unless their descendents were successful in official careers or unless they had the privileged hereditary lands. The regulation of hereditary lands was somewhat complicated. However, its essential parts can be described as follows:

(1) The 'land and forest of merit-protection': The *Koryŏ* dynasty government allotted hereditary rights to collect tax (or rent) to merit subjects and officials of the 5th grade and above.[10] This was called *Kongumjŏnsi* (功陰田柴) or the 'land and forest of merit-protection.' However, the acreage of the allotment was rather small. The scale of the distribution of the 'land and forest of merit-protection'[11] of 1049 is shown in the following Table 2.

(Table 2) The scale of the allotment of 'land and forest of merit-protection'

Grades	Lands	Forests
1	25 *kyŏl*	15 *kyŏl*
2	22	12
3	20	10
4	17	8
5	15	5

(2) The 'royal family manor': The *Koryŏ* dynasty government also gave the special hereditary right to collect tax (or rent) to royal relations such as princes, princesses, and so forth in order to secure their economic lives and royal family status. This was called *Naejangjŏn* (內莊田) or the 'royal family manor.'[12] The scale of the allotment of the 'royal family manor' was not uniformly standardized, but its scale was larger than that of the 'land and forest of merit-protection' even though its number was smaller.

(3) The 'monastic land': Since Buddhism was the state religion of the *Koryŏ* dynasty and was believed in and respected by various sorts of people,[13] the *Koryŏ* dynasty government donated land to the Buddhist monasteries and allowed the Buddhist priests and nuns the privileged hereditary right to collect tax (or rent). This was called *Sasajŏn* (寺社田) or 'monastic land.' The scale of the donation of 'monastic land' was very large. For instance, one King donated 1,240 *kyŏl* (結) of 'military colony' land for one Buddhist monastery[14] in 1020. We also can find many records of small scale donations by Buddhist believers.

The 'public land' system of the *Koryŏ* dynasty presupposed a strong centralized government authority. The 'public land' system was well operated, and agricultural productivity increased considerably from the tenth to the twelfth centuries when the central government exercised strong control over the aristocrats and indeed over all the country. However, as the central government began to lose its controlling power after the military coup d'etat of 1196 and the Mongol invasion of 1231-1260, the 'public land' system began to be disrupted from the bottom.

The first symptom of the disintegration of the 'public land' system appeared in the 'land and forest of merit-protection.' Powerful aristocratic officials made the 'land and forest of merit-protection' their own and thus began an encroachment on royal control of land. In many cases high officials who had real power frequently asked the weak king to issue them land certificates (Sap'ae) for peasants' cultivated land, public land or virgin soil and occupied it as their private land.[15]

Royal family members carried out an encroachment on land based on their already privileged hereditary 'royal family manor,' competing with the powerful officials in extending the acreage of their private lands.[16] By the late fourteenth century, manors owned by royal family members numbered than 360 throughout the country.[17]

Buddhist monasteries also carried out extensive land encroachment and established their manors around the temples. Since 'monastic land' was exempt from land-tax, labor service and tax in craft-products, the concentration of land by monasteries accelerated.[18]

A fatal blow to the 'public land' system came when the 'grade land and forest,' which was land to be returned to the state after the death of an official, tended not to be returned but to be illegally inherited. In other words, the process of transformation of the 'grade land and forest' into private-owned land proceeded on a large scale. This meant the collapse of the principle of the 'public land' system of the *Koryŏ* dynasty in its essential part.[19]

The 'soldiers land' which was supposed to be non-hereditary also tended to be illegally inherited without any succession of the obligation of military service. That is, the process of the transformation of the 'soldiers land' into the private-owned land was advanced widely.[20]

Finally, the violent occupation of commoner-peasants' land by powerful aristocratic officials also took place. We can find many such cases in detail in the History of the *Koryŏ* kingdom.[21]

Thus, in fourteenth century Korea, there appeared a new phenomena which was different from that of the tenth and twelfth centuries in land system and agricultural organization. That is, large scale private manors were established in various places bound by high mountains and big rivers.[22] These manors were owned basically by four groups: ① the King and royal families, ② high ranking aristocratic officials, ③ Buddhist monasteries and ④ local powerful families.

The owners of the manors claimed their privileges and did not pay land-tax, labor service, or tax in craft-products to the state. Therefore, the government revenue was entirely dependent on the owner-peasant who had not been annexed by manors yet, and the burden on the peasants became heavier and heavier. This trend accelerated the fall of the owner-peasant and the development of manors in the fourteenth century. The major factors which hastened the process of the manorization of land in this period were as follows:

1) The powerful aristocrats acquired 'land-certificates' from the King giving them the right to collect tax (or rent) in certain areas and established their own manors there. This could be called the factor of political power.[23]

2) In some cases, the powerful aristocrats and wealthy families reclaimed waste and fallow lands and established their own manors.[24]

3) In some cases, the peasants entrusted their lands to the powerful aristocrats to seek security and to avoid the increasing burden of labor service, land-tax and tax in craft-products. This was called *T'ut'ak* or the 'entrust.'[25]

4) In some cases, peasants became debtors to the owner of the manor who also made usurious loans. They often handed over their lands in order to pay their debts and fell into the state of tenant-peasant of the manor.[26]

5) Dealing in land was also practiced to some extent in this period, and some times wealthy families bought the lands of poor peasants.[27]

6) And the donation of lands for the Buddhist monasteries also accelerated the establishment and the development of manors in this period. Donation of land was very common, ranging from the large scale donations of the King and powerful aristocrats to the donation of whole small holdings by devoted believer-peasants.[28]

The manors of the fourteenth century in Korea can be classified into three types by its form of operation.

1) The first one was the manor which formed a large scale estate in one place and was directly operated by the owner with a labor force of his own private slaves or former commoner-peasants.[29] In this case the former commoner-peasants or former house-slaves of aristocrats turned into a serf-something like the serfs of the early medieval European manor and in almost the same social and economic condition as they. This type of manor appeared mainly in the manors owned by royal families and some powerful high ranking aristocrats. In some cases, very powerful aristocrats lured the free commoner-peasants into serfdom by using as bait exemption from land-tax, labor service and tax in craft-products as well as political protection. Or sometimes the powerful aristocrats made the free commoner-peasants serfs by force. At the time, this was called *Apriang-wich'on* (壓良爲賤)[30] or the forcing free of a commoner into bondage.

2) The second type of manor which was formed was a large scale estate in one place not operated directly by the owner but rather leased out to tenants. In this case, the land of the manor was partitioned off into family-sized small holdings within the manor. Each tenant household cultivated his tenured holdings and paid rent to the owner of the manor. The tenant-cultivators were usually the same peasants who were former owner-peasants of the land. They simply lost their land ownership and were incorporated into the manor. The owner of the manor of this type was not concerned with the actual cultivation of land but simply sent his retainers to collect rent at the time of harvest.[31] This type appeared mainly in the manors which were located in places distant from the capital city where the owners of manors usually lived. The manors owned by Buddhist monasteries were also operated in this way. This type of manor was the prevailing one in this period. The social status of the tenant in this type was of two types; that is, the commoner-tenant and the serf-tenant (or the slave-tenant). The serf-tenant was bound to the land but the commoner-tenant was not. Generally speaking, the peasants were more free in this type than in the first type of manor.

3) The third type of manor was not a single large estate but was divided into small manors and was scattered over several districts.[32] This type of small scale manor was usually owned by powerful local families. Manors established through land reclamation also usually took this form. In this kind of manor, the tenants were mainly commoner-tenants, and accordingly they were not bound to the land and landlord but were considerably freer.

There still remained a considerable portion of independent free owner-peasants, though their state was very unstable, being threatened by annexation by powerful aristocrats. At the present stage of research, it is very hard to calculate any reliable statistics on the portion of manorized land and that of the remaining peasants' land in the fourteenth century.

We have only a few sources on the rate of rent in the manors. If a generalization is allowed with these given records, the rent-rate in the manor can be described as follows.

1) In the first type of manor which was operated directly by the owner with a labor force of his own serfs (or slaves) and former commoner-peasants, all surplus above the substance consumption of cultivators were collected as rent and this might be equivalent to at least 50 per cent of the gross yield.[33]

2) In the second type of manor, the rate of rent was either 33 per cent or 50 per cent of the yield. It is hard to say which rate was more prevalent. A low rate of rent resulted from on two factors. That is, the social status of the majority of tenants was free-commoners who had formerly paid 10 per cent of their yield to the state on one hand, and on the other the landlord could collect a great deal in total rents since the whole scale of the manor was very large.

3) In the third type of manor, which was small in scale and whose holdings were scattered over several districts, the rent-rate was either 33 per cent or 50 per cent of the yield. In this type, however, 50 per cent rent seems to have been more prevalent.[34] This may be the result of three factors. That is, (1) the landlords were mostly powerful local families who knew the rural situation of landless peasants very well, (2) the scale of the manor was relatively small and (3) the landlords were usually engaged in land reclamation. In the case of reclamation of private land, there was no rent for the first year, but from the second year onwards the rate of rent was 50 per cent of the yield.[35]

It should be remembered that the peasants who were annexed into a manor had to pay rent of 33 per cent or 50 per cent of the yeild to the landlords while the independent commoner-peasant paid 10 per cent of the yield to the state (or government).

The development of the manor in the fourteenth century shook the economic foundation of the *Koryŏ* dynasty.

1) Firstly, the revenue of the central government was greatly reduced because the owners of manors did not pay the land-tax, labor service or tax in craft-products.[36] This did not mean the revenue of royal families was reduced since their own manor were separated from government finances. The shortage of the revenue of the central government was so serious that the prime minister whose salary was supposed to have been 360 *sŏk* actually received only 20 *sŏk*.[37]

2) The revenue of local offices was also reduced significantly since a great deal of the local government-owned land had been invaded by powerful aristocrats and was incorporated into their manors.[38] In order to compensate for the deficit in the local office budgets, the local officials frequently imposed an illegally heavy tax on the peasants' lands.

3) The supply of military food was seriously reduced because the 'soldiers land' had become privately owned land and a certain part of it was annexed into manors. The soldiers were reduced to a state where they themselves had to supply their own provisions. This situation caused the collapse of the military system of the *Koryŏ* dynasty which was known as *Pubyŏng*, or the 'militia troops' system.[39] The owners of manors began to raise their own private troops to guard their manors instead of supplying military provisions for the national army. These trends seriously weakened the national defense capacity.

4) The frustrations and resistance of the peasants were also serious as frequent peasant revolts prove.[40]

The agrarian problem of the fourteenth century caused serious tension all over the country and directly brought about the political issue. Many scholar-officials and soldiers being supported by various groups of peasants requested a land reform. Thus in the fourteenth century, in the capital city of *Kaesŏng*, the two opposing political groups engaged in a power struggle which centered around the problem of land reform.

One was a group which tried to maintain and develop the manor system as an established economic institution. This group was mainly composed of royal families and high ranking aristocratic officials and was supported by the Buddhist monasteries which had great influence among various people.[41]

The other was a group which urged a land reform and reestablishment of the 'public land' system. This group was mainly composed of scholar-officials and was supported by soldiers and peasants.[42]

The first group had strong financial background based on the manorial system and occupied most of the important official posts and were strongly tied in with the influential Buddhist monasteries and its priests. The other group had rather weak financial background, but its members were more energetic and more learned scholar-officials who were well versed in practical business. This group was greatly influenced by Neo-Confucianism and already had a hostile feeling against Buddhism and Buddhist monasteries.

All the political conflicts in this period were related to the agrarian problem in one way or another.[43] At this time King *Kongmin* tried to reinforce centralized authority of the government and attempted to carry out a land reform for it, but his attempt was stopped by the opposition of the powerful aristocrats and the King himself was assassinated by them in 1374. After this incident, the possibility of a land reform by the *Koryŏ* dynasty court diminished and accordingly the possibility of a compromise of the different opinions between the two groups was also reduced.

Yi Sŏng-gye, the vice-commander-in-chief of the national army and a national hero after the successful annihilation of the Japanese pirates on the coast line, withdrew his soldiers from Wihwa Island on the Yalu River, disobeying the King's edict to conquer Manchuria. Returning to the capital city, he successfully carried out a coup d'etat in 1388. After seizing all real power for himself and his group, Yi Sŏng-gye set up the puppet king Kongyang, the last king of the *Koryŏ* dynasty, and prepared a land reform.

2. The First Land Reform (*Kwajŏn-pŏb*)

The first policy that Yi Sŏng-gye and his group carried out was the land reform which they had urged for a long time.

Their theory of land reform was that the whole kingdom was basically the 'Kings' land' or 'state-owned land.'[44] Therefore, if the land system fell into disorder, the king would have the right and duty to correct the system through the redistribution of land.[45]

According to the planners of the land reform, the lands of the *Koryŏ* dynasty could be divided into two categories, one is *Kongjŏn*, or 'public land,' and the other is *Sajŏn* (私田) or 'private land.' The *Sajŏn* or 'private land' included the 'grade land and forest,' the 'merit-protection land,' the 'royal family manors,' the 'soldiers land,' the 'monastic land' and a few others of the same kind; and the peasants' land, the 'land and forest of government office' and the rest were categorized as *Kongjŏn* or 'public land.' This classification was made by the standard of the collection of *cho* or tax (or rent): If the tax (or rent) of a land went to a 'private household,' it was 'private land'; and if the tax (or rent) went to the state, it was categorized as a 'public land.' According to them 'public land' was beneficial to the state because it increased the state revenue, but 'private land' was harmful because it reduced the revenue of the government.[46] The previous disorders of the land system were due to the expansion of 'private land.' The new land reform would have to halt the expansion of 'private land,' establish the state ownership of land, and collect tax (or rent) from all the classifications of land.[47]

According to them, scholar-officials should be specially treated since they were the backbone of the state, protecting and guarding the King and administering the state's affairs.[48] And the land tenure custom called *Ch'agyong* (借耕) should be abolished because the landowner (*Chŏnju*: 田主) took half of the yield without doing anything while the tenant-peasant (*Chŏnho*: 佃戶) could hardly maintain their subsistances.[49]

As a preparation for the land reform, in 1391 they first measured the arable land all over the country except two frontier areas.[50] The result of the measurements is shown in the following Table 3.

(Table 3) The result of the measurement of cultivated land in 1391

Province	Panted area	Fallow	Total
Kyŏnggi province	131,755 *kyŏl*	8,387 *kyŏl*	140,142 kyŏl
Six other provinces	491,342	166,643	657,985
Two frontier provinces	Unmeasured	unmeasured	unmeasured
Total	623,097	175,030	798,127

In order to carry out the reform, they declared the invalidity of the *Sap'ae* or the 'land-certificate' issued by former *Koryŏ* dynasty kings and burnt all the existing records and land registration documents in the central square of the capital city. It is recorded in the *Dynastic History of the Koryŏ Kingdom* that its flame had continued for several days.[51] This meant the declaration of the confiscation of the manors owned by aristocrats.

In 1391, they promulgated the historic act of the *Kwajŏn* land reform, the *Kwajŏn-pob* or the 'Act of the System of Grade Land.' The theory of the *Kwajŏn* land reform drafted by Neo-Confucian scholar-officials such as *Chong To-jon*[52] and Cho Chun[53] was to establish the system of state ownership of land and the owner-peasant system, taking the 'public land' system of the tenth century as a model. But, in reality, it turned out to be a unique *yangban*[54] style land reform which was different from that of th 'public land' system of the beginning of the *Koryŏ* dynasty. Now we are going to examine the reality or practice of the *Kwajŏn* land reform in detail.

Some of the major articles from the Act of the *Kwajŏn* land reform are as follows[55]:

(1) '*Kwajŏn* (科田)' or the 'grade land' shall be distributed to the *yangban* bureaucrats according to their grades after dividing them into 18 grades. The article will apply to all bureaucrats who protect and defend the king and who live in the capital city without consideration to their actual duty or to retirement. But the distribution of 'grade land' shall only apply to the lands of Kyŏnggi province.

(2) '*Kunjŏn* (軍田)' or 'military land' shall be distributed to *Halliang* or local *yangban*. The scale of the distribution of the 'military land' shall be 5 or 10 *kyŏl*, depending on their previously owned land.

(3) '*Kongsinjŏn* (功臣田)' or 'merit-subject land' shall be distributed to merit subjects who were nominated in 1390, and this land shall be hereditary.

(4) The 'military supply lands' which have diminished due to encroachment by powerful aristocrats shall be restored to their original state at the time of King Munjong (1047-1088). And the unmeasured lands of the two East and West frontier provinces, lands newly reclaimed and surplus land after the land measurement also shall supplement the 'military supply lands.'

(5) The royal house-owned lands such as *Nungch'imjŏn* (陵寢田) or the 'tomb-guard land,' *Ch'anggojŏn* (倉庫田) or the 'granary land' *Kungsajŏn* (宮司田) or the 'royal palace land' and so forth, shall be restored to their original state at the time of King Munjong after the survey and arrangement of land registration.

(6) If there is a shortage of local office-owned lands, the original state at the time of King Munjong shall be restored after the survey and arrangement of land registration.

(7) No one shall donate lands to Buddhist monasteries and temples. Violators shall be punished by law.

(8) The rate of rent for all kinds of land shall be 30 *tu*[56] of rice per *kyŏl* in paddy fields and 30 *tu* of miscellaneous grain per *kyŏl* in dry fields. The collection of rent above this rate shall be severely punished by law.

(9) The degree of loss of yield due to crop failure will be classified into 10 grades. If the yield is reduced by 10 per cent, the rent also shall be reduced by 10 per cent; if yield is reduced by 20 per cent, then the rent also shall be reduced by 20 per cent; and shall be reduced in this degree until the yield is reduced by 80 per cent, when all the rent shall be exempted.

(10) The field survey for the estimation of yield in the government-owned land shall be executed by local officials of cities and counties, and that of the yield in the 'grade land' and other private land will be performed by the landowner who shall collect rent according to the regulated rate in the

previous article.

(11) Owner of all kinds of land shall pay a land tax to the state. Its rate will be 2 *tu* of rice per *kyŏl* in paddy-fields and 2 *tu* of yellow beans per *kyŏl* in dry fields. The royal house hold lands and the 'merit-subject land' shall be exempted from the land tax.

(12) In times of emergency when a great army is mobilized and its military provisions are short, the government shall temporarily collect a certain amount of grain, according to what is needed, from all of public and private lands; and when the emergency is over, taxes shall return to the normal state.

In 1392, the year after the promulgation of the Act of the *Kwajŏn* land reform, Yi Sŏng-gye's group formally dethroned the puppet King Kongyang and inaugurated his own Chosŏn (Yi) dynasty. The founder of the Chosŏn dynasty executed the *Kwajŏn* land reform as one of the most important works for making a solid foundation for the new dynasty.[57] The successive kings also continued the land reform act. That is, the *Kwajŏn* land reform was carried out on a national scale during the period of King T'aejo (Yi Song-gye's throne name) but it was also practiced for generations as a basic policy of the Chosŏn dynasty. In 1394, they moved the capital city to Hanyang (present-day Seoul) to cut off the remaining influence of old aristocrats and to reinforce the execution of the *Kwajŏn* land reform.[58]

According to the *Kwajŏn* land reform, the Chosŏn dynasty government distributed *Kwajŏn* or 'grade land' to *yangban* bureaucrats in addition to their salaries. The scale of distribution of 'grade land'[59] is shown in the following Table 4.

(Table 4) The scale of the distribution of 'grade land'

Grades	Lands	Grades	Lands
1	150 *kyŏl*	10	65 *kyŏl*
2	130	11	57
3	125	12	50
4	115	13	43
5	105	14	35
6	97	15	25
7	89	16	20
8	81	17	15
9	73	18	10

The estimates of the recipients of the 'grade land' proved that the required acreage for this purpose was about 100,000 *kyŏl*. Since the cultivated land of Kyŏnggi province was far below what was needed for this purpose, Yi Sŏng-gye extended the boundaries of the province from 15 *hyŏn* (county) to 45 *hyŏn* which expanded the area to 130,000 *kyŏl* of cultivated land. It is noteworthy that this extended Kyŏnggi region became the first geographical and economic seat of the *yangban* class after the land redistribution of the *Kwajŏn* land reform.

The 'grade land' was distributed to all *yangban* bureaucrats without considering their actual official post or retirement. In this sense, 'grade land' can be interpreted as an allocation of income sources for their privileged social status in the form of rewards for their loyalty to the King and state. From 1392 to 1402, 84,100 *kyŏl* of the 'grade land' was actually distributed to *yangban* bureaucrats in the extended Kyŏnggi province.[60]

The 'grade land' of the *Chosŏn* dynasty *Kwajŏn* land reform looks similar to the 'grade land and forest' of the *Koryŏ* dynasty, but in reality it is quite different.

Firstly, in the 'grade land and forest' of the *Koryŏ* dynasty, the right to collect tax (or rent) was strictly limited to the lifetime of the aristocratic officials and should be returned to the state immediately after the death of the official. In the 'grade land' of the *Chosŏn* dynasty, however, it was inherited by the bereaved family members and was not returned to the government from the very beginning of the reform.

The wife of a deceased bureaucrat who had a child and did not remarry inherited all the 'grade land' of her husband. If she had no child, she inherited only half of her husband's 'grade land' under another title. This was called *Susinjon* or 'chastity land.'[61] And if a descendent of a deceased bureaucrat was very young, he inherited all the 'grade land' of his father under another title until he became twenty years of age and then received the formal 'grade land' according to his own rank. This was called *Hyulyangjŏn* or 'relief-support land.'[62] Even though the tiles of land were changed in theory, it was actually a transmission by heredity of the 'grade land,' since all the 'chastity land' and 'relief-support land' were the holdings of their deceased husband's or father's 'grade land.' Moreover, even in the case of the adoption of a son, the grade land could be inherited.[63] Generally speaking, the 'grade land' of the Chosŏn dynasty was transmitted by heredity from the very beginning. This fact was recognized by many officials of that time. The *Chronological History of Chosŏn Kingdom*, says that "the grade land is distributed as land held in perpetuity."[64] or "the grade land is inherited by descendents."[65] In 1414, there was an effort to restrict the inheritence of 'chastity land' and the 'relief-support land' but it proved a failure.

Secondly, in the 'grade land and forest' of the *Koryŏ* dynasty, the government office collected the rent and redistributed it to the recipients of 'land and forest.' In the 'grade land' of the Chosŏn dynasty, however, the recipients of land collected the rent themselves.[66]

This reflected the fact that the *Kwajŏn* land reform recognized the custom of rent collection by the landowner of the fourteenth century on the one hand, and recognized the character of the private land of 'grade land' on the other. The custom of rent collection by the recipient of 'grade land' led to the illegally excessive collection of rent by the landowner. Thus King Sejong tried to restrict excessive rent collection by means of collection and redistribution through government officials in 1420, but it was not realized.

Thirdly, the allotment of the 'grade land and forest' of the *Koryŏ* dynasty was done from land all over the country, but the 'grade land' of the Chosŏn dynasty was distributed with the land within the Kyŏnggi province. This measure was taken to check the encroachment of land and the development of manors by limiting the distribution of the 'grade land' within Kyŏnggi province which was near to the capital city and was easily checked by the government. They did not want to repeat the failures of the *Koryŏ* dynasty which allowed the allotment of 'grade land and forest' in distant areas and then has not able to check the encroachment of this land or the development of private manors. This principle partly collapsed[67] in 1414 but was reestablished[68] by King Sejong in 1431.

(Table 5) A example of scale of the distribution of the 'merit-subject land'

Classification	Number of Merit Subjects	Scale of Land Distribution	Total Distributed Land
1st class merit subject	10	158 *kyŏl*	1,500 *kyŏl*
2nd class merit subject	3	100	300
3rd class merit subject	21	80	1,680
4th class merit subject	23	60	1,380
Total	57	-	4,860

The *Kwajŏn* land reform distributed *Kongsinjŏn*, or 'merit-subject land,' to cetain officials who were nominated as merit subjects for their meritorious deeds for the King or state. The 'merit-subject land' was extra land added to the 'grade land.' Therefore, the merit subjects who were usually top-ranking officials, had three sources of income, 'merit-subject land,' 'grade land' and their salaries. 'Merit subject land' was to be hereditary as private land without limitations. The scale of the distribution of 'merit-subject land' varied. Generally speaking, the merit subjects were divided into three or four classes, and to each class there applied a different scale as is shown in the following example[69] of 'merit-subject land' distribution of 1401.

The character of the 'merit-subject land' can be interpreted as an extra guarantee of the privileged social status and economic security of top ranking *yangban* bureaucrats and their descendents even within the *yangban* class. The distribution of 'merit-subject land' together with the distribution of 'grade land' reinforced the hierarchical order among *yangban* bureaucrats.

Since 'merit-subject land' was very important in the allocation of wealth for the high ranking bureaucrats, there was keen competition and even severe struggle to get the title of merit subject. Thus, quite a large number of merit subjects were created whenever important events occurred concerning the fate of the King or the Dynasty. Accurate calculations of 'merit-subject land' distributed during the early Chosŏn dynasty period is a large subject yet to be researched. So far estimates have varied depending on the researchers. If we rely on some estimates,[70] the amount of 'merit-subject land' from the beginning of the *Kwajŏn* land reform to the end of fifteenth century is as follows in Table 6.

(Table 6) The distributed amounts of the merit-subject land in 15th Century

Year	Number of merit-subject	Acreage of merit-subject land	Accumulated total
1392	39	31,440	
1393	?	5,150	36,590
1398	18	6,650	43,240
1401	38	4,850	48,090
1453	37	6,050	54,140
1455	41	4,420	58,570
1467	41	4,860	63,430
1468	38	3,770	67,200
1471	75	1,410	68,610

There is a discrepancy between the accumulated total and the amount of 'merit-subject land' that actually existed. This was because some merit-subjects were later disgraced and their 'merit-subject lands' confiscated by the government. Further the actual distribution of 'merit-subject land' was done step-by-step through long periods. In 1402, the actual amount of 'merit-subject land' was 21,240 *kyŏl*,[71] and in 1471 it is estimated that it increased at least as much as 43,000 *kyŏl*.[72] The increase of 'merit-subject land' together with the increase of 'grade land' intensified the shortage of cultivated land in Kyŏnggi province and caused the proposal for the 'moved-distribution' of 'grade land' and 'merit-subject land' to the southern three provinces.

The 'merit-subject land' of the Chosŏn dynasty appears to be like the 'merit-protection land' of the *Koryŏ* dynasty, but its contents are a little different.

First, the 'merit-protection land' of the *Koryŏ* was allotted to all high ranking aristocratic officials of 5th grade and above, while the 'merit-subject lands' of the Chosŏn dynasty was distributed only to specific top ranking officials who were nominated as merit subjects.

This can be interpreted as reflecting the lack of a specific need to give hereditary land to all the high ranking officials. The 'grade land' was already hereditary in the Chosŏn dynasty on the one hand, and on the other hand, under the influence of Neo-Confucianism hierarchical differentiation of bureaucrats was a little more intensified in the Chosŏn dynasty.

Second, the allotment of 'merit-protection land' of the *Koryŏ* dynasty was small in scale to the extent that first class subjects received only 25 *kyŏl*. In the 'merit-subject land' of the Chosŏn dynasty, however, the scale of distribution of the 'merit-subject land' was rather large in that first class merit-subjects usually received from 150 to 220 *kyŏl* of cultivated land. Some top ranking officials were appointed as merit-subjects several times and sometimes received more than 1,000 *kyŏl*.[73]

Third, the 'merit-protection land' of the *Koryŏ* was allotted from land all over the country, while the 'merit-subject land' of the Chosŏn dynasty was distributed only from land in Kyŏnggi province with the exception of 'Wŏnjong merit-subject land' which was allotted in officials' home districts. This measure was taken to check the encroachment of land and the development of private manors in distant local areas by powerful merit subjects just as in the case of the 'grade land.' Later this principle was violated by the policy of the 'moved distribution' and 'merit-subject land' to the southern three provinces.

Chosŏn dynasty kings also bestowed *Pyŏlsajŏn* (別賜田) or 'special grant land' to bureaucrats who carried out small meritorious deeds for the king or the state.[74] This 'special grant land' was formally allowed to be hereditary.[75] Thus the structure of the 'special grant land' was almost the same as the 'merit-subject land.' The minor differences were as follows: ① the scale of the distribution of the 'special grant land' was very small; ② the 'special grant land' was bestowed only occasionally by the king depending on the case, and ③ thus the character of 'special grant land' was to encourage or command individual meritorious deeds.[76]

In theory the *Kwajŏn* land reform distributed *Kunjŏn* or 'military land' to local *yangban* families called *Halliang* who had the obligation to go to the capital city and guard the royal palace and state as cavalrymen. 'Military land' could be transmitted by heredity if the son took over his father's obligation. The scale of the distribution of 'military land' was 5 to 10 *kyŏl* per household depending on the recipient's previous land holdings.

In theory, the 'military land' was a reward for the service of local *yangban* for guarding the royal palace, and if they did not carry out this obligation, they should return the land to the government. In reality, since the guarding of the royal palace relied on a professional military guards system called *Owi-je* (五衛制), and local *Halliang* did not need to serve, 'military land' was transmitted by heredity even though local *yangban* did not carry out their obligation. Actually the distribution of 'military land' was held only once in 1392 and after that there were no more distributions of 'military land' and no returning of the 'military land' to the government. It is proper to say that the 'military land' of the *Kwajŏn* land reform was actually allowed to be hereditary just as the 'grade land' was from the beginning.[77]

The 'soldiers land' of the *Koryŏ* dynasty and the 'military land' of the *Kwajŏn* land reform are different from one another in character, since the 'soldiers land' was allotted to real soldiers or military households in relation to the militia troops system, while the 'military land' of the Chosŏn dynasty was distributed to local *yangban* in the name of military obligation.

The *Kwajŏn* land reform established the central government-owned land called *Wijŏn* (位田) or 'office land' and local office-owned land called *Wirokjŏn* (衛祿田) or 'official salary land,' *Kongsujŏn* (公須田), 'government supply land,' *Oeyŏkjŏn* (外役田) and 'local official land,' *Chapsaekwijon* (雜色位田) and 'miscellaneous office land,' *Tunjŏn*, and 'military colony' and a few others to supply revenue for the expenditures of the central and local government administration at its actual residence. And for the military, the *Kwajŏn* land reform established *Kunjawijŏn* (軍資位田) or 'military supply land' in Kyŏnggi province and in various local provinces.

At the present stage of research, it is very difficult to calculate exactly how much acreage of government-owned land the *Kwajŏn* land reform established. According to the original plan, the government aimed at establishing 50,000 *kyŏl* of government-owned land for official salaries and 100,000 *kyŏl* of 'military supply land' for military provisions.[78] It is not clear if this original goal was achieved or not, but it seems to have been achieved to a considerable extent. For instance, the total government revenue of 1392 was 400,000 *sŏk* and the accumulation of military provisions for the three years of 1399-1401 was 20,000 *sŏk*.[79] But, in 1413, the total government provisions, including the military provisions kept in storage in the government granaries, increased to

3,568,700 *sŏk*.[80] This indicates that the *Kwajŏn* land reform succeeded in increasing government revenue and military provisions.

The *Kwajŏn* land reform not only prohibited the donation of land to the Buddhist monasteries but also persecuted the Buddhists and confiscated much of the *Sasajŏn* or 'monastic land.' The major attacks on Buddhist 'monastic land' by the *Chosŏn* government in the early fifteenth century were as follows.

1) In the fourth month of 1402, the government authorized the land of only 70 monasteries and some local temples which had more than 100 monks, and confiscated all the rest of the 'monastic land.'[81]

2) In the fourth month of 1406, the government ordered a reduction in the size of monastic land from 20 to 200 *kyŏl* per monastery depending on the size of temples and authorized only 212 temples throughout the country, confiscating the rest of the monastic land.[82]

3) In the tenth month of 1409, the government confiscated half of the yield of the 'monastic land' and the remaining acreage was only 11,100 *kyŏl* for 'monastic land' after this.[83]

4) In the fourth month of 1424, the government again confiscated as much as 3,000 *kyŏl* of 'monastic land' and the total acreage of the 'monastic land' was then reduced from 11,100 *kyŏl* to 9,156 *kyŏl*.[84]

5) In the twelfth month of 1434, the government increased the rate of land tax on monastic land from 1 *tu* to 2 *tu* of rice per *kyŏl*.[85]

By attacks on the Buddhist 'monastic land,' the *Chosŏn* dynasty government reduced temples' land holding from the hundred thousand *kyŏl* held at the end of the *Koryŏ* dynasty to 8,156 *kyŏl* as early as 1424. The reduction of the 'monastic land' continued even in later periods.[86]

Since the *Kwajŏn* land reform set up the principle of the distribution of 'grade land,' 'merit subject land' and 'special grant land' only within Kyŏnggi province, even immediately after the land reform most of the cultivated land of Kyŏnggi province was used up as land grants to *yangban* bureaucrats. The state of the distributed land[87] in Kyŏnggi province in 1402 is shown in the following Table 7.

(Table 7) The land distributed by the reform in Kyŏnggi in 1402

Kinds of land	Distributed acreage
Grade land	84,100 *kyŏl*
Merit-subject land	21,240
Monastic land	4,680
Sother	39,280
Total	149,300

However, this 'Kyŏnggi principle' brought some problems to both sides, to the government as distributor and to the *yangban* bureaucrats as recipients.

From the standpoint of the government, the shortage of cultivated land in Kyŏnggi province became more and more serious because the number of *yangban* bureaucrats and merit subjects to whom the government had to distribute land according to the Act of the *Kwajŏn* land reform increased very rapidly and far beyond that forecast.

And from the standpoint of the *yangban* bureaucrats, they could not get rid of the supervision of the central government in order to expand their private lands. The *yangban* bureaucrats who were the recipients of the distribution of lands desired the 'moved distribution' of land in distant local provinces. Thus some *yangban* bureaucrats conducted a campaign for the 'moved distribution' of 'grade land' to the southern three provinces: That is, Ch'ungch'ŏng, Chŏlla and Kyŏngsang provinces. And they finally succeeded in getting it. The key events in the campaign were as follows:

1) In the sixth month of 1403, the Royal Advisory Council proposed 'moved distribution' of half of the 'grade land' and 'merit subject land' from Kyŏnggi to Kyŏngsang province, but it was rejected.[88]

2) In the fourth month of 1405, a Minister of Finance, being supported by all the ministers, proposed 'moved distribution' of one-third of the 'grade land' and 'merit subject land' to Kyŏngsang and Chŏlla provinces, but this was also rejected.[89]

3) In the eighth month of 1414, a Grand Inspector proposed that half of the 'grade land' and 'merit subject land' become 'moved distribution land' in the Southern three provinces on the pretext of the excessive collection of rent in the redistributed land of Kyŏnggi province. At this time, incidently, the third shipwreck occurred in transporting collected tax grain and King Taejong reconsidered the proposal and ordered the Ministry of Finance to make a draft of the moved distribution of the lands.[90]

4) In the fifth month of 1416, the Chosŏn dynasty government decided on the 'moved distribution' of half of the 'grade land' and 'merit subject land' to the southern three provinces. But they could not execute it, since an important elder subject strongly opposed the proposal. He insisted 'moved distribution' would cause a new discontent of local people and proposed a substitute measure for the revision of the regulation of rent collection in th Act of the *Kwajŏn* land reform.[91]

5) In the seventh month of 1417, (the seventeenth year of King Taejong's reign), King Taejong and his government revised the draft of the 'moved

distribution' to one-third of the 'grade land' and half of the 'merit subject land' instead and put it into effect.[92]

The 'moved distribution' of the lands to the southern three provinces soon caused the following problems: (1) excessive collection of rent in the 'moved' lands, (2) rapid development of the encroachment of land, and (3) reduction of food supply of the capital.

First of all, the 'moved distribution' of lands for *yangban* bureaucrats greatly contributed to the encroachment of land and the development of landlordism by the powerful high ranking *yangban* officials in local areas.[93] By this 'moved distribution' of lands, the *yangban* bureaucrats developed private landlordism on a nation-wide scale more rapidly and extended their geographic and economic control from Kyŏnggi province to other areas. Some scholar-officials still urged the revival of the 'Kyŏnggi principle' because of land encroachment and the rapid development of private landlordism in local areas.

In 1431 (the thirteenth year of his reign), King Sejong and some scholar-officials boldly decided to restore the 'Kyŏnggi principle' and forced it into effect.[94] Thus after about fifteen years, the 'Kyŏnggi principle' was revived, but during these years land encroachment and private landlordism spread deep roots into local areas. After all the 'moved distribution' of one-third of the 'grade land,' 'merit subject land' and 'special grant land' ended in accelerating the development of private landlordism without solving any problems, and the old problem of the shortage of cultivated land in Kyŏnggi province was raised again.

3. The Second Land Reform (*Chikjŏn-pŏb*)

At the beginning of the *Kwajŏn* land reform, the cultivated land in the extended Kyŏnggi province was well suited for the purpose of land redistribution. But after half a century as we have previously seen, the shortage of land in Kyŏnggi province became more and more serious because the distributed 'grade land,' 'merit-subject land' and 'special grant land' had actually become hereditary, and the number of new scholar-officials who had the right to receive 'grade land' had increased very rapidly far beyond the estimates of the planners. As a result, the *Chosŏn* government could not distribute the specified scale of 'grade land' to newly appointed officials. Some measures had to be taken to solve this problem.

In order to solve the problem of the shortage of available land, King Sejo, one of the most powerful and strong-minded kings of the Chosŏn dynasty, halted the distribution of the 'grade land' and established a new system of *Chikjŏn-pŏb* (職田法) or 'post land' in 1466 (the twelfth year of King Sejo's reign).[95]

Under the new system of 'post land,' the government distributed land to *yangban* bureaucrats only during the period that the official held the actual post, and the distributed land was then to be returned to the government immediately after the retirement of the bureaucrat from the post. By this measure the *Chosŏn* government could circulate a certain amount of land among new *yangban* bureaucrats.

The scale of the distribution of the 'post land' for *yangban* bureaucrats was also reduced for each grade[96] as is shown in the following Table 8.

(Table 8) The scale of distribution of 'post land'

Grades	Lands	Grades	Lands
Prince (a)	225 *kyŏl*	9	40 *kyŏl*
Prince (b)	180	10	35
1	110	11	30
2	105	12	25
3	95	13	20
4	85	14	20
5	65-60	15	15
6	55	16	15
7	50	17	10
8	45	18	10

The second land reform system came as a heavy blow to the family members of deceased bureaucrats, that is, the former recipients of 'chastity land' and 'relief-support land.' Therefore, some *yangban* bureaucrats strongly opposed the new reform, but the powerful King Sejo executed the system, rejecting the opposition. Grieved by it one Grand Inspector said, "the descendents of the retired aristocratic scholar-officials cannot have even one *kyŏl* of land under the system."[97]

Apart from the fact that the *Chosŏn* government did not have enough land in Kyŏnggi province to distribute to all *yangban* bureaucrats, the new measures that the government effected reduced the scale of distribution of 'post land' and did not provide any measures to secure the livelihood of retired bureaucrats and their families. This indicates that the authority of the Chosŏn dynasty royal house had become quite stable compared to its beginning. By this time, however, many *yangban* bureaucrats already had their own private land and did not need to rely on the special protection of the government.

In my opinion, the second land reform of the 'post land' is similar to the system of 'public land' of the *Koryŏ* dynasty in its structure and is close to the theory of state ownership of land in the traditional sense.

However, the system of the 'post land' caused a serious problem. In order to collect and accumulate personal wealth, the bureaucrats who were the recipients of the 'post land' squeezed the peasants as far as they could, since the right to collect rent in the 'post land' was only allowed during the time they held the official post and they did not know when they would be transferred or dismissed.[98]

The excessive collection of rent took the form of an additional tax called *Ch'ose* (草稅) or the 'hay-tax.' The recipient of the 'post land' collected hay from the peasants for their horses, though it was usually substituted for by rice or money. The rate of the 'hay-tax' was illegally as high as the original rent and both the rent and the 'hay-tax' imposed a heavy burden on the peasants.[99]

As the frustration of the peasants and the criticism from scholar-officials became heated, the *Chosŏn* government revised the system of 'post land' to *Chikjŏnseje* (職田稅制) or the system of the 'post allowance' in 1470 (the first year of King Sŏngjong's reign).[100] Therefore, the new system of 'post land' was practiced for only four years.

Under the system of the 'post allowance,' the peasant paid the tax and rent to the government granary instead of directly to the official-recipients of the land and then the government redistributed the collected rent to the bureaucrats according to the regulated scale. Actually, it was a system of the collection of tax by the government and the payment of allowances to bureaucrats by the government. In other words, it was a transformation from the land-distribution to an allowance-in-kind for the bureaucrats. Since the Chosŏn bureaucrats received salaries in rice and textile goods besides the 'grade land' or the 'post land,' the transformation of the 'post land' into the 'post allowance' system meant the establishment of an extra allowance, or bonus, added to the original salary.

The system of the 'post allowance' was short-lived, though we cannot find the exact dates of the formal abolition of this system.[101] There are some records showing that during the period of 1483-1484 the government temporarily stopped payment of the 'post allowance' because of crop failure of famine.[102] And finally we find a record of 1557 in the '*Chronological History of the Chosŏn Kingdom*' that the system of 'post allowance' had already been abolished.[103] From these records, we can assume that the system of 'post allowance' had actually been abolished several decades before 1557, which might be the end of the fifteenth century or the beginning of the sixteenth century.

The abolition of the system of the 'post allowance' with the bureaucrats' relying on their salaries did not mean hard times for the bureaucrats but rather meant they already possessed private-owned land on which they could rely for a high standard of living even without the 'post allowance.'

The transformation of the system of the 'post land' to the 'post allowance' and its abolition was the finale of the two land reforms of the Chosŏn dynasty. After this period, the government did not concern itself with land redistribution, and the land system of the Chosŏn dynasty was uniformly integrated into private-owned land with landlordism, which had developed side-by-side with the first *Kwajŏn* land reform from the beginning of the dynasty. And from this time on the possession and the encroachment of land by *yangban* bureaucrats was carried on by means of purchase and by reclamation which did not have any direct relation to official posts, even though in some cases the power of high official post indirectly influenced the accumulation of private property. I think it is quite proper to say that the privileged distribution of land for the *yangban* class through government authority ended in 1470 when the system of 'post land' was transformed into the system of the 'post allowance.'

4. The Establishment of Private Landlordism

As we have previously seen, in the land reforms of the early Chosŏn dynasty, the redistribution of land was confined to *yangban* bureaucrats, and the central and local government-owned lands were expanded to secure government revenue and military supply. In this sense, some scholars have indicated that the land reform of the early Chosŏn dynasty was to supply military provisions and to make a solid foundation for the new dynasty by procuring the loyalty of the scholar-officials by means of distributing land to them.[104] It is quite true that the dream of the tanant-peasants to become owner-peasants, just as in the 'public land' system, dissipated after the actual practice of the *Kwajŏn* land reform. However, I think there is also another aspect to which we have to turn our attention in order to understand the whole system of land reform during this period. That is the *Kwajŏn* land reform's legal endorsement of private landlordism on one hand, and also its providing some measures to protect tenants on the other.

The *Kwajŏn* land reform restricted and reduced the rate of rent to 30 *tu* (=2 *sŏk*) of rice per *kyŏl* in paddy-field and 30 *tu* (=2 *sŏk*) of miscellaneous grain per *kyŏl* in dry-field.[105] Since the productivity of one *kyŏl* at the time of the beginning of Chosŏn dynasty was about 20-30 *sŏk*,[106] this regulated rate of rent was equivalent to 10 per cent of the yield.

The rent-rate of 10 per cent of the yield was a considerably reduced rate compared to the rent-rate of 33-50 per cent of the yield in the fourteenth century manors. If this rent-rate of 10 per cent were practiced, the burdens on the tenants of the Chosŏn dynasty would be the same as that of the owner-peasant of the *Koryŏ* dynasty even though their economic status was different for one was a tenant and the other, an owner. Moreover, the *Kwajŏn* land reform imposed *cho* of the same 10 per cent of the yield on the owner-peasant. By this measure, in theory, the burden of the tenant-peasant and the owner-peasant became equalized even though the reform legally endorsed the land tenure system or private landlordism. Thus, the idea of the *Kwajŏn* land reform can be interpreted as having two important factors, that the founder of Chosŏn dynasty endorsed private landlordism for the landed official class to get their support for the solid foundation of the new dynasty on the one hand, and that the reduction of the rent rate from 33-50 per cent to 10 per cent of the yield for tenants was to pacify their frustration on the other. This reduction was to equalize the position of the tenants with that of their previous position of owner-peasant. However, since this regulated rent-rate was not well practiced in reality, its end result was to publically pave the road for the establishment and development of private landlordism in early fifteenth century Korea.

As a result of the legal endorsement of private landlordism in the *Kwajŏn* land reform, the land tax and the rent were separated from one another in the Chosŏn dynasty which was unlike the 'public land' system in which the land-tax and rent were combined together into one entity called *cho*. Thus according to the *Kwajŏn* land reform the land owner could collect 10 per cent of the yield from the tenant and had to pay the land-tax of 2 *tu* per *kyŏl* or 0.7 per cent of the yield to the government. The owner-peasants had to pay 10 per cent of *cho* to the state. Whether the 10 per cent *cho* levied on the owner-peasant after the *Kwajŏn* land reform is basically a land-tax or a rent is a problem yet to be discussed. In my opinion, it is essentially a land-tax since the private ownership of land in peasants' land and private landlordism in all kinds of lands had been legally established after the *Kwajŏn* land reform.

The *Kwajŏn* land reform also provided certain measures to protect the tenants in their relationship with landlords. The major regulations on their relationship in the Act of the *Kwajŏn* land reform are as follows.[107]

1) If a landowner deprives a tenant of cultivated land without any good reason, the landowner shall be punished. If the amount is over one *kyŏl*, the

violator's land itself shall be transmitted to other persons (or another person).

2) A tenant shall not sell or transfer his cultivated land to another person.

3) When a tenant dies without an heir or moved to another place or when a tenant's land is uncultivated due to excessive acreage held by the tenant, the government shall dispose of it after consulting with the landowner.

4) Every peasant can make fodder, graze and hunt in the commons and in waste lands in Kyŏnggi province. Anyone who interferes with this right shall be punished by law.

From the above regulations we can find that the *Kwajŏn* land reform of the Chosŏn dynasty protected the right of the peasants, the right to cultivate land for tenants, and the right to use commons and waste lands by all kinds of peasants, while it endorsed the land tenure system for landlords.

The above regulations were commonly practiced until the end of the Chosŏn dynasty, unlike the regulation on the rate of rent.

It is especially noteworthy that the *Chosŏn* government formally acknowledged the buying and selling of land in this period. In 1424, a Governor of Kyŏnggi province memorialized:

The person who sells his land usually does so because of his parent's funeral, debts, fines, poverty or the impossibility of maintaining the land. All dealing in land has been practiced owing to certain unavoidable circumstances. Therefore, it is regrettable that the government offices must confiscate the money of the price of land when the dealing is detected. And it is also unreasonable that only the dealing in land in the provinces has been prohibited while the dealing in building ground and vegetable land in the capital city has been allowed. I propose that our Majesty permit the buying and selling of land and punish according to the law only those who do not register it with the government office or do not carry out payment of taxes and to take the registration certificate.[108]

King Sejong and his ministers approved this proposal, an epoch making legal acknowledgement of the freedom to deal in land as early as 1424.

From 1424 onwards, the policy of dealing in land as well as its inheritance, transfer and mortgage was freely carried out, and the private-ownership of land was finally established and legally institutionalized. The obligation of a buyer of land was simply to report and register the private-ownership of land at the government office and to take the registration certificate of land ownership after paying a fee. In the *Kyongguk Taejon* (The Grand Code of the Chosŏn Kingdom), which is the comprehensive code of the Chosŏn dynasty compiled in 1474, are listed the regulations for the protection of the private-ownership of land and for the solution of disputes which might arises in land dealings.[109]

The establishment of free dealing in land and the institutionalization of private- ownership of land accelerated the development of private landlordism in early fifteenth century Korea.

By the legal institutionalization of the private-ownership of land in the early fifteenth century, trade in peasants' land, which was called 'public land' by the planners of the *Kwajŏn* land reform, was freely carried out.

Actually after the establishment of the private ownership of land, the previous concept of *Kongjŏn* (公田) or the 'public land' and *Sajŏn* (私田) or the 'private land' changed into another conception. That is, the meaning of 'public land' had been reduced to indicate *Kwanjŏn* (官田) or 'government-owned lands' and the previous 'peasants' land' and 'private lands' were lumped together in the term *Minjŏn* (民田) or 'people's private land.'[110] This new distinction was made in regard to the standard of possession of landownership. That is, if the ownership of land belonged to a private person it was called *Minjŏn*, or the 'people's private land,' and if the ownership of land belonged to public offices it was called *Kongjŏn*, 'public land,' or Kwanjŏn, the 'government-owned land.'

After the *Kwajŏn* land reform and the legal endorsement of private ownership of land, private landlordism was established and was further developed in the 'people's private land' by means of dealing in land. A land buyer was protected by law after the registration of his name and the location and acreage of his land with the government office.[111] Taking this institutional setting as an advantage, the *yangban* bureaucrats and the powerful local families established their estates by buying land while a number of peasants who sold their land fell into the state of tenancy.

Private landlordism was also established and developed in all kinds of land redistributed by the *Kwajŏn* land reform.

1) Firstly, private landlordism was established and developed rapidly in the 'merit-subject land' and the 'special grant land.' As we have already seen, the 'merit-subject land' was distributed as hereditary private land on a large scale even in local areas as well as in Kyŏnggi province from the beginning. Thus, in the course of time, the merit subjects turned into the biggest landlords in Kyŏnggi province and also in local areas. Some merit subjects became the very biggest landlords, owning more than 1,000 *kyŏl*.[112] They still pushed

forward the encroachment of land, and their holdings became larger and larger. The 'special grant land' traced the same course as the 'merit-subject land.'

2) Private landlordism was also established and developed in the 'grade land.' In theory, the 'grade land' itself was not hereditary, but in reality, inheritance was permitted under another name, 'chastity land' or 'relief-support land,' as we have seen. Therefore, 'grade land' turned into privately owned land and was operated in the same way the land tenure system was, just as with the 'merit-subject land.' Thus in the course of time, the high ranking *yangban* bureaucrats who were the recipients of the larger portions of 'grade land' turned out to be the bigger landlords and the low ranking *yangban* bureaucrats who were the recipients of smaller portions of 'grade land' became the small landlords. The recipients of 'grade land' also continued the land encroachment and developed private landlordism in the fifteenth century.[113]

3) Private landlordism was also established and developed in the 'military land' which was distributed to the local *yangban* called *Halliang*. In theory, the 'military land' could be hereditary only when descendents succeeded in fulfilling the father's military obligation, but in reality, the 'military land' was inherited by the descendents without any succession of obligations just as with the 'grade land.' Thus, basically *Halliang* turned out to be small landlords in local areas.[114] Some successful *Halliang* encroached upon land and became well established big landlords in local areas and, of course, some did not.[115]

4) Private landlordism was also established and developed in 'royal house lands' such as '*Nŭngch'imjŏn*,' the 'tomb-guard land,' *Ch'anggojŏn*, the 'granary land' and *Kungsajŏn*, the 'royal palace land.' In 1423, 'royal house land' was established under the name of *Naesujŏn* or 'palace supply land' and at a later period under the name of *Kungbangjon*, 'royal palace land.' Along with the development of private landlordism in the fifteenth century, the royal house applied the land-tenure system to their own land and became one of the biggest landlords of the time.[116]

Thus, in fifteenth century Korea, the correlation between the socio-economic class and the traditional social estate system was rather close.

1) The landlords were composed of *yangban* (兩班) bureaucrats, royal families and government offices. The high ranking *yangban* bureaucrats beginning with the merit subjects and royal family established themselves as the biggest landlords, and the low ranking *yangban* and local *yangban* became small landlords. Within the landlord class, officials rank and the size of the holdings of landlords was closely correlated at the beginning of Chosŏn dynasty.

2) The independent owner-peasants were composed of *yangin* (良人) or commoners. In the later Chosŏn period some poor local *yangban*'s descendents cultivated the land as independent owner-peasants, but in the fifteenth century these owner-peasants were commoners in terms of their social status.

3) The tenant-peasants were composed of the commoners and *ch'onmin* (賤民) or 'lower people' mainly *nobi* (奴婢) or 'serfs' or slaves. In the lands owned by royal families and government offices, the portion of the serf-tenants sometimes seemed to be larger than that of commoner-tenants, but in the land owned by private *yangban*, that of commoner-tenants was much larger than the serf-tenants. The serf-tenants could have their independent household but were bound to the land and landlord. However, the commoner-tenants were freeman and could leave the land whenever they wished and land tenure itself was practiced based on contracts in the case of the commoner-tenants.

The pattern of the operation of private landlordism in the early Chosŏn dynasty can be divided into two types. One is the manor-type operation, and the other is the non-manor type operation.

1) In the manor-type operation, landlords established a large scale estate in a certain area, and the estate was cultivated by tenants.[117] In the later *Koryŏ* dynasty period many manors were cultivated by serfs (or slaves) but in the process of the *Kwajŏn* land reform, many of this type of manors were confiscated and many serf-tenants (or slave-tenants) were emancipated.[118] Thus, in the fifteenth century Chosŏn period, the cultivators of the manor were composed of a large number of commoner-tenants and a small number of serf-tenants (or slave-tenants), and the land was usually enclosed into family-sized holdings within the manor. This type was equivalent to the second type of manor in the *Koryŏ* dynasty which we have already seen. However, these manors were different from those of medieval Europe or Japan or the late *Koryŏ* dynasty Korea in the sense that the landlords had no privilege of immunity and the social status of tenants was a little improved.

2) In the non-manor type operation, the land of one landlord was scattered over several districts, being divided into small holdings. The cultivators were mostly composed of commoner-tenants and a small number of serf-tenants (or slave-tenants). In the case of commoner-tenants, they were not bondsmen even though they were economically poor, and the lands were tenured based on contracts either in written or in oral form. In the case of serf-tenants (or slave-tenants), if they were cultivating their master's land, they were bound to the land and the landlord, but if they cultivated another landlord's land, they were not bound to the land or the landlord, and land-tenure was based on a contract,

and the tenure had to pay 2 *pil* or rolls of textile to their own master.

In the fifteenth century, non-manor type operations were more common than manor-type.[119] The reasons were that ① the *Kwajŏn* land reform divided many large scale estates into rather small ones in order to redistribute the land for the new scholar-officials, and ② the encroachment of land in the fifteenth century was carried out by means of buying land or reclamation and it was almost impossible to buy out all the holdings in one area unlike the fourteenth century *Koryŏ* dynasty in which land encroachment was mainly carried out through the occupation of one area by force.

The average scale of the land operation per peasant household enclosed in the manor is estimated at about 5 *kyŏl*, although its range was from 2.5 *kyŏl* to more than 50 *kyŏl*. We do not have statistics for the whole country in this period, but we can find valuable data of Kangwŏn province of 1436[120] *in the Chronological History of Chosŏn Kingdom* (*The Chronicle of King Sejong*) which can be re-established as in Table 9.

(Table 9) The size of farm operation per household of Kangjwŏn Province

Scale of operation	Number of households	Percentage of household	Acreage	Percentage of acreage	Average scale per household
50 *kyŏl* and above	10	0.1%	800 *kyŏl*	1.5%	80.0 *kyŏl*
20-49	71	0.6	2,499	4.0	34.5
10-19	1,641	14.3	23,795	38.0	14.5
6-9	2,043	17.5	15,322	25.0	7.5
1-5	7,773	67.4	19,432	31.0	2.5
Total	11,338	100.0	61,799	100.0	5.4

As we can see in the table, the number of large scale operations above 20 *kyŏl* was rather small, the medium scale operations of 10-19 *kyŏl* was 14.3 per cent of the total households, and the small scale family sized operation below 10 *kyŏl* prevailed by as much as 84.9 per cent of total households. And the average scale of operation per household was 5.4 *kyŏl* in this area. From this data we can assume that the average scale of the operation per household of the whole country was about 5 *kyŏl* in this period.

A big landlord usually employed bailiffs as his proxies in his manor or near to his leased lands. These bailiffs were called *Marŭm* (마름), *Kasin* (家臣), *Sŏje* (書題) or *Pandang* (半倘).[121] The major role of bailiffs was as follows:

① collection of the rent, ② storage and transportation of the rent, ③ supervision of the leased land or manor, and ④ payment of the land-tax for the landlords.

Bailiffs on the high ranking bureaucrat's manors usually came from the commoner class and were often exempted by the government from labor service. The power of bailiffs in rural villages was rather strong and they frequently oppressed the weak tenants.

In fifteenth century Korea, land-tenure was practiced in *Pyŏngjak* (竝作) method under which the rate or fraction of the rent was fixed by agreement between landlord and tenant. Thus, under this method, the amount of rent fluctuated depending on the year's harvest. The *Pyongjak* method was sometimes called the 'one-half method' since the rate of rent was usually one-half or 50 per cent of the yield.[122] Sometimes, a rent-rate of 33 per cent was applied, but generally speaking, it was 50 per cent of the yield and it usually accompanied another tax, the 'half-collection' or *Pyŏngjak-Pansu* (竝作半收).

The rent-rate of 50 per cent of the yield was illegally high, far beyond the legal rent rate of 10 per cent of the yield stipulated by the Act of the *Kwajŏn* land reform. The landlords who had been accustomed to the rent-rate of 50 per cent of the yield throughout the fourteenth century did not willingly observe the regulation of rent of the Act of the *Kwajŏn* land reform in the fifteenth century. The local government office did not have enough power to control the illegal collection of high rates of rent, since most of the landlords were merit subjects, *yangban* bureaucrats and local powerful families who were much more powerful and much higher ranking officials than the local government officials, so the landlords generally violated the Act of the *Kwajŏn* land reform and generally collected 50 per cent of the yield from the tenants.[123] The Chosŏn dynasty court vainly attempted to control the rate of rent according to the Act of the *Kwajŏn* land reform. Thus, as early as 1406, one vice prime minister memorialized the throne that high ranking officials and local powerful families were pushing forward land-encroachment and collecting illegal rent-rates of up to 50 per cent of the yield.[124]

Since the powerful *yangban* landlords did not observe the regulations on the rent-rate of 10 per cent of the yield of the Act of the *Kwajŏn* land reform and collected the customary rent-rate of 50 per cent of the yield, the 10 per cent *Cho* on the owner-tenant clearly appeared as a land tax. Thus, there actually existed great differences in the burdens of three groups after the *Kwajŏn* land reform. The landlord paid a land-tax of 2 *tu* (0.7 per cent of the yield) to the state. The owner-peasant paid a land-tax of 30 *tu* (10 per cent of the yield) to the state. The tenant-peasant paid rent of 100-150 *tu* (50 per cent of the yield) to the landlord.

Two different rates of land-tax applied to landlord and owner-peasant, and there was a great gap between the burdens of owner-peasant and tenant-peasant.

In 1444 (the twenty-sixth year of King Sejong's reign), King Sejong carried out a great tax reform to make an adjustment to the new situation of increased agricultural production and the development of private landlordism.[125] According to the new tax reform, the cultivated land of the whole country was classified into 6 classes according to the degree of its fertility. And the tax rate was fixed as 5 per cent of the yield was equivalent to 20 *tu* per *kyŏl* in a normal year since agricultural productivity had increased. And if there was any crop failure, the amount of land-tax was reduced on the following scale.

(Table 10) The sliding scale of Land-tax of the reform of 1444

Rate of crop loss	Scale of land-tax	Rate of crop loss	Scale of land-tax
normal year %	20 tu	50%	10 tu
10	18	60	8
20	16	70	6
30	14	80	4
40	12	90	none

By this tax reform, the land-tax on landlords increased from 2 *tu* to 20 *tu* and the land-tax on owner-peasants was reduced from 30 *tu* to 20 *tu* per *kyŏl* in normal year, and the different rate of land-tax for the two groups was unified as 5 per cent of the yield. This fact indicates that the 10 per cent Cho on owner-peasant was clearly identified as a land-tax, and that agricultural productivity had increased considerably since the *Kwajŏn* land reform was carried out.

However, in 1445, the year after the tax reform, the rate of the land-tax on the landlord went back to 2 *tu* again following the Act of the *Kwajŏn* land reform. Thus, the two different rates of land-tax on different groups were revived. From 1445 onwards, the burden on each socio-economic group became as follows.

1) The landlord paid a land-tax of 0.5 per cent of the yield (2 *tu*) to the state.

2) The owner-peasant paid a land-tax of 5 per cent of the yield (20 *tu*) to the state.

3) The tenant-peasant paid a rent of 50 per cent of the yield to the landlord.

The rent was mostly collected in kind.[126] The labor service as a rent was negligible in this period and money-rent was not usual.

We can find some record showing that the landlord sometimes collected money from the tenants to meet the expense of the transportation of rent,[127] but we have not yet found any direct records about the payment of rent in money in the fifteenth century. It is quite clear that rent in kind was most prevalent throughout the country in this period.

Since the Act of the *Kwajŏn* land reform formally endorsed the land tenure system with its rent-rate of 10 per cent of the yield, private landlordism was legally established immediately after the *Kwajŏn* land reform and further developed in the first half of the fifteenth century in the *Minjŏn* or 'people's private land' which included peasants' land, 'merit-subject land,' 'royal house land,' 'special grant land,' 'grade land,' 'military land,' 'monastic land,' and so forth. And during the fifteenth as well as later centuries private landlordism developed throughout the country with the rent-rate of 50 per cent of the yield.

From the middle of the fifteenth century on, even the lands owned by the central and local government offices were operated as part of the land-tenure system matching private landlordism in private-owned land and collecting rent of 50 per cent of the yield.[128] Thus the regulation of the rent-rate of the Act of the *Kwajŏn* land reform was ignored by the government itself in the later half of the fifteenth century and the development of private landlordism was far more rapid.

Thus, from fifteenth century on, it is proper to classify the lands and peasants into two groups: that is, tenured land and tenant-peasants on the one hand, and owner-land and owner-peasants on the other. The government did not survey the acreage, the number or the portion of tenured land and tenant-peasants regularly. But we can find a record that shows that the portion of tenant-peasants was about 30 per cent and that of owner-peasants was about 70 per cent of total peasant households as early as 1458.[129]

After its legal establishment in the *Kwajŏn* land reform, private landlordism developed for more than five long centuries as a basic socio-economic institution on Korean history until the 'Land Reform of 1950' finally abolished it.

5. Conclusion

In conclusion, we can say that the *Kwajŏn* land reform claimed state ownership of all land in the Kingdom, taking the 'public land' system of *Koryŏ* dynasty as the ideal model in theory, but it actually was a land reform which redistributed some private lands for *yangban* bureaucrats and which legally endorsed the private ownership of land and private landlordism in reality. The theory of the state ownership of land held by the planners of the *Kwajŏn* land reform simply provided the theoretical ground for the confiscation and redistribution of land in the new land reform and ended in imposing the land-tax on all kinds of land.

The *Kwajŏn* land reform did not include all the cultivated land of the country in its redistribution but did include the land of Kyŏnggi province and some part of the land in local areas. Actually, the *Kwajŏn* land reform did not establish state ownership of land in the country.

1) Since the peasants' land, which was not included in the reform, was legally endorsed as privately-owned land as early as 1424, it does not provide any basis for the classical theory of the state ownership of land but does offer evidence of the private ownership of land in early Chosŏn dynasty Korea.

2) Since the 'merit-subject land,' the 'special grant land' and the 'royal house lands' which were included in the reform were distributed as privately owned land in both theory and reality, these do not provide any foundation for the theory of the state ownership of land but do provide support for the theory of the private ownership of land in the early Chosŏn dynasty Korea.

3) The 'grade land' and the 'military land' which were included in the reform were not privately owned land in theory, but in reality they were passed on the descendents just like the 'merit-subject land.' Therefore, these lands do not offer any ground for the theory of the state ownership of land in early Chosŏn dynasty Korea.

4) The 'lands owned by government offices' which were extended by the *Kwajŏn* land reform do provide a foundation for the theory of the state ownership of land in the early Chosŏn dynasty. However, the proportion of this government owned land was rather small so that it was only about 10 per cent of the total cultivated land. Therefore, with this small portion, it is hardly possible to build a theory of state ownership of land in early Chosŏn dynasty.

5) In my opinion, the second land reform, the 'post land' system of 1466, was really an attempt to establish a kind of state ownership of land. However, the 'post land' system comprised only a small portion of the cultivated land in Kyŏnggi province and the system itself was very short-lived, being abolished in 1470. It was as an experiment that failed.

In short, the classical theory of the state ownership of land of the early Chosŏn dynasty has been too much influenced by the theories and ideals of the planners of the *Kwajŏn* land reform and has neglected reality. It is clear that the classical interpretation of the *Kwajŏn* land reform and the theory of state ownership of land of Chosŏn dynasty Korea does not accord with the actual historical and social facts.

The existing interpretation that the *Kwajŏn* land reform checked the development of the private ownership of land of the fourteenth century also does not accord with the facts. The *Kwajŏn* land reform did not check the private ownership of land though it did check the development of private manors.

The *Kwajŏn* land reform primarily confiscated and broke up the first type of manor of the *Koryŏ* dynasty, the large scale estate of the former hereditary powerful aristocrats which were operated directly by the owner with the labor of his own serfs or slaves, but the reform never denied the private ownership of land. On the contrary, the government legally endorsed the private ownership of land by approving and protecting free dealing in land as well as inheritance, transfer and mortgage in 1424, which was the period in which the *Kwajŏn* land reform was carried out. From 1424 on, the system of the registration of dealings in land and the registration of the private ownership of land and that of issuing certificates of land ownership was institutionalized.

Along with the development of private ownership of land, the general conception of land had also changed: that is, the *Kongjŏn* or the 'public land' which had indicated peasants' land in the *Koryŏ* dynasty changed into *Minjŏn* or 'people's private land,' and the conception of the 'public land' itself was reduced to indicate *Kwanjŏn* or the 'government-owned land' after the *Kwajŏn* land reform.

Since the *Kwajŏn* land reform abolished the immunity of manors and imposed the land-tax on all private-owned lands, there was no contradiction between the establishment of private ownership of land and state revenue unlike the case of the 'public land' system of the *Koryŏ* dynasty in which the privileged private lands claimed imunity and reduced the revenue of the state.

Generally speaking, we can conclude that the land system of the early Chosŏn dynasty, which was systemized by the *Kwajŏn* land reform, was a system of private ownership of land.

Some scholars, who have doubted the classical theory of the state ownership of land in Chosŏn dynasty, have emphasized the growth of the private land such as the 'merit-subject land' and the 'special grant land' which were contradictory to the principle of the *Kwajŏn* land reform and the tendency of the transformation of 'grade land' and 'military land' into private land in the course of time, even though the *Kwajŏn* land reform itself was the establishment of state ownership of land. They think that the land system of the Chosŏn dynasty must be the system of the private ownership of land because the system of the state ownership of land by the *Kwajŏn* land reform was short-lived, less than one century and that in an imperfect way, while for more than four centuries the system of the private ownership of land prevailed.

This theory does not accord with the facts very well either. This interpretation applied the same process of the disintegration of the 'public land' system of the *Koryŏ* dynasty to the system of the *Kwajŏn* land reform of a little earlier time, and is a misunderstanding which holds that the land reform of the 'public land' system of the *Koryŏ* dynasty and the *Kwajŏn* land reform of the Chosŏn dynasty had basically the same structure and the same reform. This new interpretation is still confusing theory with reality in the *Kwajŏn* land reform.

As we have previously seen, the *Kwajŏn* land reform legally endorsed private landlordism with the regulated rent-rate of 10 per cent of the yield. Therefore, private landlordism was established and developed not only after the disorganization of the *Kwajŏn* land reform in the late fifteenth century, but was legally established and developed from the very beginning of the *Kwajŏn* land reform of 1391 by the legal endorsement of private landlordism by the Act of the *Kwajŏn* land reform.

In reality, the *Kwajŏn* land reform paved the way for the development of private landlordism in the fifteenth century. This interpretation might sound a little bold, but it is quite in accord with the reality of the *Kwajŏn* land reform, when we do not consider simply the theory of the planners of the reform.

In my opinion, the *Kwajŏn* land reform of the Chosŏn dynasty actually accepted and internalized the established fact of the development of private landlordism in the fourteenth century in its system, while the land reform of the 'public land' system of the tenth century *Koryŏ* dynasty rejected and abolished the established fact of the emergence and development of private landlordism in the eighth and ninth century and established the 'public land' system both in theory and reality. In this sense, the character and structure of the *Kwajŏn* land reform of the Chosŏn dynasty is quite different from that of the 'public land' system of the *Koryŏ* dynasty.

The difference between the private landlordism before the *Kwajŏn* land reform and the private landlordism after the reform was that the former was not endorsed by law and had developed in the direction of the manor which had tax immunity, while the latter was legally endorsed and developed in the direction of the non-manor type absentee-landlordism.

In short, the basic structure of the *Kwajŏn* land reform can be summarized as follows.

1) The *Kwajŏn* land reform confiscated mainly the first type of manor of the end of the *Koryŏ* dynasty, that is the large scale estate which had tax immunity and was directly operated by the owner with the labor of his own serfs or slaves and some lands of old aristocrats; and it redistributed some of the confiscated land and the cultivated land of Kyŏnggi province to the new scholar-officials. The *Kwajŏn* land reform distributed 'grade land,' 'merit-subject land' and 'special grant land' for the central *yangban* scholar-officials,

and 'military land' for the local *yangban*. The redistribution of land was confined to *yangban* bureaucrats only. In this sense, we can say that the *Kwajŏn* land reform was a *yangban* land reform. By the *Kwajŏn* land reform, many of the old hereditary aristocrats fell and the new scholar-officials established themselves as the privileged landed class.

2) Land redistribution among *yangban* bureaucrats was done hierarchically according to their social status. The exemplary case of 'grade land' and 'merit-subject land' reinforced the hierarchical distribution of land. As a result, the distributed scale of the land supported the hierarchical order of status even within the *yangban* class. In this sense, we can say that even the method of the redistribution of land of the *Kwajŏn* land reform was typical *yangban* style.

Through the hierarchical redistribution of land by the *Kwajŏn* land reform, high-ranking *yangban* scholar-officials turned into bigger landlords, and low-ranking *yangban* officials and local *yangban* became small landlords after the *Kwajŏn* land reform.

3) The *Kwajŏn* land reform abolished the immunity of all manors and imposed the land-tax on all kinds of land in the kingdom and increased the state revenue. The reform also reestablished and extended the government owned land to meet the expenses of the central government and local offices and increased the acreage of the 'military supply land' to secure and increase military provisions. In this sense, we can say that the *Kwajŏn* land reform was a reform to reestablish the system of centralized government authority, checking the tendency of decentralization of the fourteenth century.

Because of the *yangban* characteristics of the *Kwajŏn* land reform, many scholars have disregarded its relation to the peasants. However, it is to be noted that the *Kwajŏn* land reform also tried to give some benefits to the peasants.

4) In confiscating and breaking up the first type of manor of the end of the *Koryŏ* dynasty, the *Kwajŏn* land reform emancipated many serf-tenants who were forcibly 'oppressed from free commoners into bondsmen or slaves,' and gave them the status of free-commoner. Accordingly, there was significant upward mobility of serf-tenants (or slave-tenants) to commoner-tenants in the period of the *Kwajŏn* land reform.

5) While the *Kwajŏn* land reform legally endorsed the land-tenure system or private landlordism in *Minjŏn* or 'people's private land,' it also called for reduction of the rent-rate to 10 per cent of the yield. As we have previously seen, this regulation was not observed by the powerful *yangban* landlords, and actually the customary rent-rate of 50 per cent of the yield was continued. However, it is to be remembered that the reform itself tried to reduce the

burden of the tenant-peasants.

6) And the *Kwajŏn* land reform also protected the permanent right of tenants to cultivate land. By the reform, tenants acquired the right to cultivate the tenured land permanently unless they did not pay the rent or they abandoned the tenured land. If a landlord violated this regulation he was to be punished by law, while the commoner-tenants and some of the serf-tenants (or slave-tenants) who cultivated land other than their master's could leave the land freely at any time after the harvest. This regulation was relatively well observed throughout Chosŏn dynasty.

Since the reduction of the rent-rate was not applied, the actual benefits of the reform for the tenants were significantly reduced. However, it is to be noted that the *Kwajŏn* land reform succeeded in protecting the permanent right to cultivate the tenured land for the tenants.

It is clear that the land reform of the early Chosŏn dynasty greatly contributed to the increase in agricultural productivity. At the present stage of research, however, it is very hard to measure the increased rate of agricultural productivity per unit of land because of the lack of materials on this subject. But we can find many statements that agricultural production had increased to a cónsiderable degree when the land-tax reform was carried out in 1444. Actually, the land-tax reform itself was an adjustment to increased agricultural production and to the development of private landlordism after the *Kwajŏn* land reform.

Of course, the increased agricultural production was partly the result of the agricultural development policy of the early Chosŏn dynasty government, but it also is clear that the emancipation of the serf-tenants and slaves and the establishment of enclosed independent farm operations through the *Kwajŏn* land reform greatly contributed to this change. The establishment of the private ownership of land and private landlordism accelerated the reclamation of land and resulted in an increase in the acreage of cultivated land. The trends of the horizontal expansion of the cultivated land in the early fifteenth century Chosŏn dynasty are shown in the following table 11.

(Table 11) The increased acreage of the cultivated land after the land reform

Year	Total cultivated land	Increased acreage
1391	798,127 [1] *kyŏl*	*kyŏl*
1413	1,071,977	273,850
1444	1,632,066	460,189

(1) A small acreage of the cultivated land in the North East and West frontier areas are not included. Taejong SIllok (The Chronicle of the King Taejong) Vol. 3, p. 8; KHCC ed., Chosŏn Wang jo Sillok, Vol. 1, p. 225.

Since the land survey of 1391 omitted the small acreage of the cultivated land of the North-East and West frontier areas, it would be not quite correct to compare this with those of the later years in which the land surveys covered the whole country. But from only 1413 to 1444, the acreage of the cultivated land of the whole country greatly increased from 1,071,977 *kyŏl*[130] to 1,632,066 *kyŏl*,[131] that is 52.3% in 32 years.

The increased acreage of the cultivated land after the *Kwajŏn* land reform also greatly contributed to the increase in agricultural production of the early Chosŏn dynasty. And it is to be noted that increased agricultural production economically supported the brilliant cultural achievements of the early Chosŏn dynasty.

FOOTNOTES (Part I - 2)

1. *Koryŏsa* (The History of the Koryŏ Kingdom), Vol. 78, p. 1 and p. 21, Yonsei University edition, Vol. 2, p. 705 and p. 714.
2. *Ibid.*, Vol. 78, p. 2; Y.U. edition, Vol. 2, p. 705.
3. *Ibid.*, Vol. 78, p. 47; Y.U. edition, Vol. 2, p. 728.
4. *Ibid.*, Vol. 78, p. 44; Y.U. edition, Vol. 2, p. 726.
5. *Ibid.*, Vol. 78, pp. 6-15; Y.U. edition, Vol. 2, pp. 707-712.
6. For a comprehensive description on this, see: Kang Chin'-ch' ŏl 'Hankuk Tojijedosa (sang)' (A history of Korean land system Part I) in *Hankuk Munwhasa Taegye* (An Outline of Korean Cultural History) Vol. 2, 1965, Seoul.
7. Some elaborate studies were done on this by Yi Ki-baik, Koryŏ Pyŏngjesa Yŏngu (Studies in the History of the Military System of the Koryŏ Kingdom) 1968, Seoul, and Kang Chin-ch'ŏl, Koryŏ Ch'ogi ui Kuninjon (The Soldiers land of the early Koryŏ period) in *Collection of Theses* of Sukmyong Woman's University, Vol. 3, 1963, Seoul.
8. *Op.cit.*, Vol. 118, pp. 20-21; Y.U. edition., Vol. 3 pp. 597-598.
9. *Ibid.*, Vol. 78, pp. 17-20; Y.U. edition, Vol. 2, pp. 713-714.
10. *Ibid.*, Vol. 78, p. 15; Y.U. edition, Vol. 2, p. 712.
11. *Ibid.*, Vol. 78, pp. 15-16; Y.U. edition, Vol. 2, p. 712.
12. *Ibid.*, Vol. 1, p. 11 and Vol. 8, p. 13; Y.U. edition, Vol. 1, p. 39 and p. 168.
13. *Ibid.*, Vol. 78, pp. 26-27; Y.U. edition, Vol. 2, pp. 717-718.
14. *Ibid.*, Vol. 4, p. 34; Y.U. edition, Vol. 1, p. 102.
15. *Ibid.*, Vol. 128, pp. 1-15, Vol. 78, p. 16 and pp. 29-30; Y.U. edition Vol. 3, pp. 774-780 and Vol. 2, p. 712 and p. 719.
16. *Koryŏsajŏlyo* (The Chronicle of the Koryŏ Kingdom), Vol. 20, p. 40; Kakushuin University edition, p. 534.
17. *Ibid.*, Vol. 78, p. 31; Y.U. edition, Vol. 2, p. 720: Also see Sudo, Yoshiyuki, 'Koraijo yori Lijo sho ni itaru Oshitsu Chaisei (The finance of the Royal House from the Koryŏ Kingdom to early Chosŏn dynasty)' in *Tohakakuho* (The Journal of Oriental Studies), Vol. 10, No. 1, 1939, Tokyo.
18. *Ibid.*, Vol. 84, p. 24; Y.U. edition, Vol. 2, p. 844.
19. *Ibid.*, Vol. 78, pp. 29-30; Y.U. edition, Vol. 2, p. 719.
20. *Ibid.*, Vol. 78, p. 22; Y.U. edition, Vol. 2, p. 715.
21. *Ibid.*, Vol. 28, p. 22, Vol. 30, p. 19 and Vol. 123, pp. 7-8; Y.U. edition, Vol. 1, p. 574

and p. 622 and Vol. 3, p. 674.

22. *Ibid.*, Vol. 78, p. 1, pp. 23-24, p. 29 and Vol. 79, p. 2; Y.U. edition, Vol. 2, p. 705, p. 719 and p. 732.

23. *Koryŏsa*, Vol. 78, p. 16 and p. 19; Y.U. edition, Vol. 2, p. 712 and p. 714.

24. In the thirteenth and fourteenth centuries, there existed a vast acreage of the fallow and the waste lands which were awaiting reclamation, and the government also enacted a 'reclamation-encouragement act' to increase agricultural production and allowed certain privileges such as the exemption of land-tax for the first several years. See *Koryŏsa*, Vol. 78, p. 46, Y.U. edition, Vol. 2, p. 727.

25. In the fourteenth century the Koryŏ dynasty, central and local government officials illegally imposed heavy burdens of labor service and tax in craft-products as well as land-tax and the independent owner-peasants were in such an unstable state that they did not know when they would be invaded and be annexed into manors by the powerful aristocrats. See *Koryŏsajolyo* (The Chronicle of Koryŏ Kingdom), Vol. 20, p. 42; K.U. edition, p. 538.

26. *Koryŏsa*, Vol. 129, pp. 41-43; Y.U. edition, Vol. 1, pp. 809-810.

27. See Yi Wu-Song, Koryŏ ui Yongopjon (The land held in perpetuity in Koryŏ Period) in *Yogsa hagbo* (Korean Historical Review) Vol. 28, 1965, Seoul. in his article. A new interpretation is presented on the private ownership of land and its dealing and inheritance under the 'public land' system.

28. *Koryŏsa*, Vol. 4, p. 34; Y.U. edition, Vol. 1, p. 102.

29. *Ibid.*, Vol. 126, pp. 10-11; Y.U. edition, Vol. 1, pp. 736-737.

30. *Ibid.*, Vol. 79, p. 3; Y.U. edition, Vol. 2, p. 733.

31. *Koryŏsa*, Vol. 130, p. 17; Y.U. edition, Vol. 1, p. 825.

32. *Taejo Sillok* (The Chronicle of King Taejo), Vol. 2, p. 6; Korean History Compilation Committee edition, Chosŏn Wangjo Sillok (The Chronological Historiography of Chosŏn Kingdom), Vol. 1, p. 6.

33. In this period, the highest rent-rate on the serfs who maintained their independent households was about 50 per cent of the yield. Therefore, it would be proper to assume that the rent-rate in the first type of manor was about or more than 50 per cent of the yield.

34. Chŏng Tojŏn: *Sambong-jip* (The Collection of Sambong's Works), Vol. 7, Korean History Compilation Committee edition, p. 214.

35. *Koryŏsa*, Vol. 78, p. 46; Y.U. edition, Vol. 2, p. 727.

36. *Koryŏsa*, Vol. 78, p. 5; Y.U. edition, Vol. 2, p. 707.

37. *Ibid.*, p. 22; Vol. 2, p. 715. 1 sŏk was about 1.5 bushels.

38. *Ibid.*, Vol. 128, p. 27; Y.U. edition, Vol. 3, p. 787.

39. *Ibid.*, Vol. 78, p. 32; Y.U. edition, Vol. 2, p. 720.

40. Hatada, Takashi, 'Korai Meiso Chinso Chidai ni okeru Nomin Ikki (The peasant revolt in the time of kings Myongjong and Sinjong of the Koryŏ period)' in *Rekishigaku*

Kenkyu (The Journal of Historical Science Society) Vol. 2, 1934, Tokyo.

41.   *Koryŏsa*, Vol. 118, pp. 3-4; Y.U. edition, Vol. 3, p. 589.

42.   The leading figures who claimed the land reform were Yi Sŏng-gye (李成桂), Chŏng To-jŏn (鄭道傳), Cho Chun (趙浚), Yi Haeng (李行), Hwang Sun-sang (黃順常), Cho In-ok (趙仁沃), Hŏ Ung (許應) and others.

43.   Lee Sang-baik, 'Koryŏ Malgi ui Chŏngjaeng kwa Chŏnjegaihyŏk Wundong kwaui Kwangye (The Relationship between the Political Struggle and the Land Reform Movement at the end of Koryŏ dynasty)' in *Yi-jo Kŏnguk ui Yŏngu* (Studies in the Founding of Chosŏn dynasty), 1949, Seoul.

44.   *Koryŏsa*, Vol. 78, p. 47; Y.U. edition, Vol. 2, p. 728.

45.   *Ibid.*, pp. 28-31; Vol. 2, pp. 718-720.

46.   *Ibid.*, p. 35; Vol. 2, p. 722.

47.   *Ibid.*, pp. 41-42; Vol. 2, p. 725.

48.   *Koryŏsa*, Vol. 78, p. 37; Y.U. edition, Vol. 2, p. 723.

49.   Chŏng To-jŏn, *Sambong-jip* (The collections of Sambong's Works), Vol. 7, Korean History Commmpliation Committee edition, p. 215.

50.   *Koryŏsa*, Vol. 78, p. 38; Y.U. edition, Vol. 2, p. 723.

51.   *Ibid.*, Vol. 78, p. 38; Y.U. edition, Vol. 2, p. 723.

52.   Chŏng To-jŏn's land reform draft is not well preserved but only a small part of it is compiled in *Sambong-jip* (The Collection of Sambong's Works), Vol. 7, Korean History Compilation Committee Edition, pp. 244-246.

53.   Cho Chun's land reform draft is recorded in *Koryŏsa*, Vol. 78, pp. 20-28 and pp. 34-42; Y.U. edition, Vol. 2, pp. 714-718 and pp. 721-725.

54.   Originally the term *yangban* indicated the civil and military servants for states in Koryŏ period, but from Chosŏn dynasty period on it had become label of the aristocratic scholar-officials.

55.   *Koryŏsa*, Vol. 78, pp. 38-43; Y.U. edition, Vol. 2, pp. 723-926.

56.   1 tu was about 3.3 quarts and 15 tu made 1 sŏk. Therefore 30 tu was equivalent to 2 sŏk.

57.   Lee Sang-baik, 'Koryŏ Malgi ui Chŏnjegaehyŏk Wundong kwa Yi Sŏng-gye waui Kwangye (The Relationship between the land Reform Movement and Yi Sŏnggye at the end of the Koryŏ dynasty) in *Yi-jo Kŏnguk ui Yŏngu* (Studies in the Founding of Chosŏn dynasty) 1949, Seoul.

58.   For a comprehensive description, Chŏn Kwan-wu, 'Hankuk Tojijedosa, Ha (A history of Korean land system, part. II) in *Hankuk Munwhasa Taegye* (An Outline of Korean Cultural History) Vol. 2, 1965, Seoul. And also see, Sudo, Yoshiyuki, 'Koraijo yori Lijo shogi ni itaru Tenseigaigaku (Land reform from the end of Koryŏ to the beginning of Chosŏn dynasty)' in *Toagak* (Orientica, Journal of Oriental studies) Vol. 3, 1940, Tokyo; Fukaya, Toshidetsu, 'Sensho no Tochiseito Ippan (An outline of the land system of the early Chosŏn dynasty)' in *Shigaku Za sshi* (Japanese Journal of

History), Vol. 50, No. 5-6, 1939, Tokyo.

59. *Koryŏsa*, Vol. 78, pp. 38-39; Y.U. edition, Vol. 2, pp. 723-724.

60. *Taejong Sillok* (The Chronicle of King Taejong), Vol. 3, p. 8, Korean History Compilation Committee Edition; *Chosŏn Wangjo Sillok* (The Chronological History of Chosŏn Kingdom), Vol. 1, p. 225.

61. *Koryŏsa*, Vol. 78, p. 40; Y.U. edition Vol. 2, p. 724.

62. *Ibid.*

63. *Sejong Sillok* (The Chronicle of King Sejong), Vol. 106, p. 10, Korean History Compilation Committee edition; Chosŏn Sillok, Vol. 4, p. 588.

64. *Ibid.*, Vol. 5, p. 17, KHCC edition, *ibid.*, Vol. 2, p. 337.

65. *Ibid.*, Vol. 49, p. 33, KHCC edition, *ibid.*, Vol. 3, p. 260.

66. *Koryŏsa*, Vol. 78, p. 43; Y.U. edition, Vol. 2, p. 726.

67. *Taejong Sillok* (The Chronicle of King Taejong), Vol. 34, p. 6; Korean History Compilation Committee edition, *Chosŏn Wangjo Sillok* (The Chronological Historiography of Chosŏn Kingdom), Vol. 2, p. 180.

68. *Sejong Sillok* (The Chronicle of King Sejong), Vol. 51, p. 11; KHCC edition, *Chosŏn Wangjo Sillok*, Vol. 3, p. 292.

69. *Taejong Sillok* (The Chronicle of King Taejong), Vol. 1, pp. 8-9; KHCC edition, Vol. 1, pp. 193-194.

70. The number of the merit subjects relies on the estimation of Ch'ŏn Kwan-Wu; Hankuk Tojijedosa (Ha) (A History of Korean Land system: Part II) in *Hankuk Munwhasa Taegye* (An Outline of Korean Cultural History) Vol. 2, Seoul, 1965, pp. 1447-1448; And the acreage of the merit-subject land relies on the estimation of Sohn Po-Kee; *Social History of the Early Chosŏn dynasty, 1392-1592*: With Emphasis on the Functional Aspects of Governmental Structure (Ph.D. Thesis) 1963. University of California, Berkeley. pp. 180-181.

71. *Taejong-Sillok* (The Chronicle of King Taejong), Vol. 3, p. 8; KHCC edition, *Chosŏn Wangjo Sillok*, Vol. 1, p. 225.

72. The most uncertain case of the 'merit-subject land' is 5,150 *kyŏl* of 1393 and the confiscated acreage later is estimate about 20,000 *kyŏl*. Therefore the actually existing acreage of the 'merit-subject land' must be more than 43,000 *kyŏl* in 1471.

73. *Taejong Sillok* (The Chronicle of King Taejong), Vol. 18, p. 44; KHCC edition, *Chosŏn Wangjo Sillok*, Vol. 1, p. 518.

74. *Sejong Sillok* (The Chronicle of King Sejong), Vol. 88, p. 32; KHCC edition, Vol. 4, p. 276.

75. *Kyŏngguk Taejŏn* (The Grand Code of Chosŏn Kingdom), Vol. 3; The Legislation Board edition, Vol. 1, p. 330.

76. *Sejong Sillok* (The Chronicle of King Sejong), Vol. 88; KHCC edition, Vol. 4, p. 276.

77. *Taejong Sillok* (The Chronicle of King Taejong), Vol. 7, p. 24; KHCC edition, *Chosŏn Wangjo Sillok*, Vol. 1, p. 299.

78. *Taejong Sillok* (The Chronicle of King Taejong), Vol. 5, p. 26; KHCC edition, *Chosŏn Wangjo Sillok*, Vol. 1, p. 276.

79. *Ibid.*, 1 sŏk (=15 tu) was about 1.5 bushels and one tu was about 3.3 quarts.

80. *Ibid.*, Vol. 26, p. 10; KHCC edition, *ibid.*, Vol. 1. p. 680.

81. *Ibid.*, Vol. 3, pp. 23-24; KHCC edition, *ibid.*, Vol. 1, pp. 232-233.

82. *Ibid.*, Vol. 11, p. 13; KHCC edition, Vol. 1, p. 352.

83. *Ibid.*, Vol. 18, p. 36; KHCC edition Vol. 1, p. 514.

84. *Sejong Sillok* (The Chronicle of King Sejong), Vol. 7, pp. 13-14 and Vol. 24, pp. 24-25; KHCC edition *Chosŏn Wangjo Sillok*, Vol. 2, pp. 367-368 and pp. 591-592.

85. *Ibid.*, Vol. 26, pp. 27-28; KHCC edition, Vol. 2, pp. 638-639.

86. Han Wu-Kun, 'Ryomal Sonch'o ui Pulgyo Chŏngch'aek (The policies on the Buddhism at the end of Koryŏ and in the early Chosŏn dynasty)' in *Seoul National University Journal*; Humanities and Social Sciences, Vol. 6, 1957, Seoul. Lee Sang-baik: 'Yu-Pul Yanggyo Kyodh'e ui Kiyon e Kwanhan il Yŏngu (A Study on the Motivation of the persecution of the Buddhism by the Confucianism) in *Hankuk Munwhasa Yŏngurongyo* (Some Studies in the Origins of Korean Social Customs) 1948, Seoul.

87. *Taejong Sillok* (The Chronicle of King Taejong), Vol. 3, p. 8; KHCC edition. Chosŏn Wangjo Sillok Vol. 1, p. 225.

88. *Ibid.*, *Taejong Sillok* (The Chronicle of King Taejong), Vol. 5, pp. 26-27; KHCC edition. *ibid.*, Vol. 1, p. 267.

89. *Ibid.*, Vol. 9 , p. 14; KHCC edition, Vol. 1, p. 324.

90. *Taejong Sillok*, Vol. 28, pp. 13-14; KHCC edition. Vol. 2, pp. 31-32.

91. *Ibid.*, Vol. 31, pp. 39-40; KHCC edition, Vol. 2, pp. 116-117.

92. *Ibid.*, Vol. 34, p. 6; KHCC edition Vol. 2, p. 180.

93. *Sejong Sillok* (The Chronicle of King Sejong), Vol. 51, p. 11; KHCC edition, *Chosŏn Wangjo Sillok*, Vol. 3 , p.292

94. *Sejong Sillok*, Vol. 51, p. 11; KHCC edition, Vol. 3, p. 292.

95. *Sejo Sillok* (The Chronicle of King Sejo), Vol. 39, p. 34; KHCC edition, *Chosŏn Wangjo Sillok*, Vol. 8, p. 37.

96. *Kyŏngguk Taejon* (The Grand Code of Chosŏn Kingdom), Vol. 2; Legislation Board edition Vol. 1, pp. 170-174.

97. *Sejo Sillok* (The Chronicle of King Sejo), Vol. 40, pp. 9-11; KHCC edition, *Chosŏn Wangjo Sillok*, Vol. 8, pp. 46-47.

98. *Yejong Sillok* (The Chronicle of King Yejong), Vol. 3, pp. 37-38; KHCC edition, *Chosŏn Wangjo Sillok*, Vol. 8, pp. 334-336.

99. *Ibid.*, Vol. 6, pp. 23-24; KHCC edition, Vol. 8, p. 394-395.

100. *Sŏngjong Sillok* (The Chronicle of King Sŏngjong), Vol. 4, p. 28; KHCC edition *Chosŏn Wangjo Sillok*, Vol. 8, p. 490.

101. *Taejon Hoet'ong* (The complete Collection of Grand Code), Vol. 2, p. 9.

102. *Sŏngjong Sillok* (The Chronicle of King Sŏngjong), Vol. 261, pp. 17-18; *Chungjong Sillok* (The Chronicle of King Chungjong), Vol. 7; KHCC edition, *Chosŏn Wangjo Sillok*, Vol. 12, pp. 136-137.

103. *Myŏngjong Sillok* (The Chronicle of King Myŏngjong), Vol. 20, p. 55; KHCC edition. *Chosŏn Wangjo Sillok*, Vol. 20, p. 344.

104. Lee Sang-baik, 'Yi Sŏng-gye ui Chŏnjegaehyok Wundong kwa ku siljŏk (The land reform movement of Yi Sŏng-gye's group and its result)' in *Yi-jo Kŏnguk ui Yŏngu* (Studies in the Founding of Chosŏn Dynasty), 1949, Seoul.

105. *Koryŏsa*, Vol. 78, p. 41; Y.U. edition, Vol. 2, p. 725.

106. *Chungbo Munhŏn Pigo* (The Revised Source Book of Historical Documents), Vol. 148, p. 14; Classics Compilation Committee edition, Vol. 2, p. 712.

107. *Koryŏsa*, Vol. 78, pp. 41-42; Y.U. edition, Vol. 2, p. 725.

108. *Sejong Sillok*, Vol. 23, p. 37; KHCC edition, Vol. 2, p. 589.

109. *Kyŏngguk Taejŏn* (The Grand Code of Chosŏn Kingdom), Vol. 2, Legislation Board edition Vol. 1, pp. 178-179 and p. 188.

110. *Sŏngjong Sillok*, Vol. 2, p. 19; KHCC edition Vol. 9, p. 606.

111. *Sŏngjong Sillok*, Vol. 20, p. 8; KHCC edition, Vol. 8, p. 672.

112. *Taejong Sillok*, Vol. 18, p. 44; KHCC edition, Vol. 1, p. 518.

113. *Taejong Sillok*, Vol. 12, pp. 35-36; KHCC edition, Vol. 1, pp. 379-380.

114. *Tanjong Sillok* (The Chronicle of King Tanjong), Vol. 9, p. 37; KHCC edition, *Chosŏn Wangjo Sillok*, Vol. 6, p. 654.

115. *Sejong Sillok*, Vol. 23, p. 30; KHCC edition, Vol. 2, p. 586.

116. *Kyŏngguk Taejŏn* (The Grand Code of Chosŏn Kingdom), Vol. 1, Legislation Board edition, pp. 76-77.

117. *Taejong Sillok* (The Chronicle of King Taejong), Vol. 19, p. 42; KHCC ed., *Chosŏn Wangjo Sillok*, Vol. 1, p. 544.

118. *Taejo Sillok* (The Chronicle of King Taejo), Vol. 1, p. 53; KHCC ed., *Chosŏn Wangjo Sillok*, Vol. 1, p. 27.

119. *Sejo Sillok* (The Chronicle of King Sejo), Vol. 9, pp. 26-27; KHCC ed., *Chosŏn Wangjo Sillok*, Vol. 7, p. 231.

120. *Sejong Sillok* (The Chronicle of King Sejong), Vol. 74, pp. 3-4; KHCC ed., *Chosŏn Wangjo Sillok*, Vol. 4, p. 22.

121. *Sŏngjong Sillok* (The Chronicle of King Songjong), Vol 44, p. 13; KHCC ed., *Chosŏn Wangjo Sillok*, Vol. 9, p. 122.

122. *Taejong Sillok* (The Chronicle of King Sejong), Vol. 12, pp. 35-36; KHCC ed., *Chosŏn Wangjo Sillok*, Vol. 1, pp. 379-380.

123. *Taejong Sillok* (The Chronicle of King Taejong), Vol. 28, pp. 13-14; KHCC ed., *Chosŏn Wangjo Sillok*, Vol. 2, pp. 31-32.

124. *Ibid.*, Vol. 12, p. 35; KHCC ed., Vol. 1, p. 379.

125. *Sejong Sillok* (The Chronicle of King Sejong), Vol. 106, pp. 21-23; KHCC ed.,

Chosŏn Wangjo Sillok, Vol. 4, pp. 595-596.
126. Chŏng To-jŏn, *Sambongjip* (The Collections of Sambong's works), Vol. 7, Korean History Compilation Committee ed., pp. 214-215.
127. *Ibid.*, Vol. 7; KHCC ed., p. 215 and pp. 211-212.
128. *Yejong Sillok* (The Chronicle of King Yejong), Vol. 6, pp. 9-10; KHCC ed., *Chosŏn Wangjo Sillok*, Vol. 8, pp. 387-388.
129. *Sejo Sillok* (The Chronicle of King Sejo), Vol. 11, p. 3; KHCC ed., *Chosŏn Wangjo Sillok*, Vol. 7, p. 249.
130. The Acreage of the cultivated land of Kyŏnggi-do is the measurement of 1402. See, *Taejong Sillok* (The *Chronicle* of King Taejong), Vol. 3, p. 8; KHCC ed., *Chosŏn Wangjo Sillok*, Vol. 1, p. 225: And those of the other provinces are the survey of up to 1413. See, *Chŭngbo Munhŏn Pigo* (The Revised Source Book of Historical Documents) Vol. 141, pp. 9-10; Classics Compilation Committee ed., Vol. 5, p. 626.
131. The total sum of the cultivated land of each province recorded in *Sejong Sillok* (The Chronicles of King Sejong), Vol. 148-155; KHCC ed., *Chosŏn Wangjo Sillok*, Vol. 5, pp. 613-701.

3. Landlordism in the Late Chosŏn Dynasty

1. Introduction

I have already made it clear that private landlordism of Chosŏn dynasty Korea was established and developed in the 15th century.[1] This paper is intended to review the development of landlordism in general tenant land between the turn of the century and 1910 and to outline the social state of tenant farming in that period.

By so doing we can identify the structural features of landlordism toward the end of the Chosŏn dynasty which preceded the system of landlord and tenant introduced following the Korean Land Survey Project by the Japanese colonial authorities. This is necessary to compare and analyze the differences between the former and the latter. On landlordism under the Japanese, I have published a separate paper.[2]

Besides the general landlordism-tenancy, there developed in the declining years of the Chosŏn dynasty a special form of tenancy based on what was called *Tojikwŏn* (賭地權). Since it is dealt with in another paper, this paper will confine itself to examining the ordinary tenant farming system prior to the rise of the special land tenure system.[3]

The writer has drawn freely on data provided by the Japanese as well as on materials and literature originating from the Chosŏn dynasty. In preparation for the eventual expropriation of land and farm produce from the Koreans, the Japanese undertook a series of field surveys on landlordism in the late Chosŏn dynasty around 1905 when the Japanese Residency-General was established.

The data and survey results made available through these Japanese efforts were meant to serve the cause of Japanese aggression and colonization of Korea. However, they shed much light on the situation of landlordism in the 19th century. Landlordism is an institution not subject to frequent changes. Consequently, the data explored by the Japanese in 1905-1909 will be of great help in identifying landlordism in the immediately preceding period.

The purpose of this paper is to draw and present a real picture of the landlordism that prevailed in the late Chosŏn dynasty on the basis of all available data.

2. Types of Landlordism

The landlordism of the late Chosŏn dynasty consisted of *"Pyŏngjakpŏb"* (竝作法) and *Tojakpŏb* (賭作法).[4] Another formula trichotomizes it into *Pyŏngjakpŏb*, *Chŏngtopŏb* (定賭法) and *Chipsupob* (執穗法).[5]

1) *Pyŏngjakpŏb*

The first division was known variously by the name of *T'ajakpŏb* (打作法), *Chŏlpanpŏb* (折半法) or *Panjakpŏb* (半作法). Under the system the tenant pays a previously fixed rate of rent from each year's crop. The rent was fixed at a certain ratio, thus the actual amount varied depending on the harvest of the year.

The generally prevailing ratio was 50 per cent of raw produce. Hence, farmers were wont to call it *Chŏlpanpŏb* or *Panjakpŏb*, both meaning farming on halves. This *Pyŏngjakpŏb* was most commonly practiced in the latter period of the Chosŏn dynasty.

It was this method with which philosophers of the *Silhak* (practical learning) school took issue as a typically irrational tenancy in the late 18th century and early 19th century.

Chŏng Yak-yong (pen name Tasan) criticized the tenancy based on *Pyŏngjakpŏb* that prevailed in the late 18th century and early 19th century on grounds that the landlord sitting idly by earns five-tenths of the produce whereas the tenant farmer is deprived of six-tenths of his crop—five-tenths in rent plus one-tenth in land tax.[6]

Chŏng gave this description of the private landlordism of the time: It is common practice for the landlord to take 50 per cent in rent and the favorite formula is *Pyŏngjakpŏb*, but its contents vary depending on localities.

In Kyŏnggi and Ch'ungch'ŏng provinces, rents are paid on the day when crops are harvested and threshed, while in Chŏlla province (southern province) the farmer stacks them in the field and later threshes them in the deep of winter to pay his rent. In Kyŏnggi and Ch'ungch'ŏng provinces the landlord is responsible for providing land tax and grain seeds, taking half of the produce, including straw. In Chŏlla province land tax and seeds must be provided by the tenant who gets all the straw, while the landlord obtains 50 per cent of the produce in rent.[7]

Chŏng clarified the local differences in tenancy in a written appeal to the king and deplored that th rich and influential owning land further expanded the system of landlord versus tenant. He points out that the owners of land are the king and the farmer who cultivates the land. But the rich and the influential have expropriated land for private ownership and emerged as the third owner, taking rent.

Farmers are charged private rent besides tax to the state. Land tax collected by the government accounts for only about one-twentieth of the total produce under legal provisions, but private rents amount to 50 per cent of the produce, and the latter is the main cause of impoverishing the people. In Kyŏnggi province the landlord pays land tax and provides seeds, while collecting 50 per cent rent, so the burden on tenants is less heavy.

In other provinces, however, the tenant pays land tax and should provide seeds, in addition to rent. Thus, the share for the tenant is reduced to far below 50 per cent of the crop. Chŏng deplored this exploitative practice and called for the reform of the tenant system.[8]

In his *Mokminsimsŏ* (Book on Shepherding the People), Chŏng writes as follows:

"Let us pause and think how can people bear it? One *kyŏl* (結) of land produces 800 to 400 *tu* (斗). Farmers do not own land but till the land of others. They work hard all day long but when the harvest comes in autumn, one half of the crop is taken away by the landlord. Out of 600 *tu* only 300 *tu* is available for food and wages to neighborhood workers. If seeds are taken, debts are paid and provisions for the remainder of the year are deducted from the sum, there will be only 100 *tu* left. Take tax from what little there remains, and farmers will have nothing left. Also, how can people make both ends meet?"[9]

In his *Kyungseyup'yo* (經世遺表) Chŏng Yak-yong gave the following illustration of the poor lot of tenant farmers who get no more than two-tenths of their produce on account of rents to landlords and various levies.

"For example, ten *tu* of seeds sown in rice paddies in the southern region will produce about 20 *sŏk* (石) of grain. Out of the crop 10 *sŏk* goes to the landlord in rent, 2 *sŏk* is kept as seed, 2 sŏk is contributed to the state food reserve, 2 *sŏk* goes in various leveis (too numerous to list here) and the tenant farmer will have 3 or 4 *sŏk* for his own consumption. The tithe under previous kings has now increased seven or eight times, making it difficult for the common people to survive."[10]

Pak Chi-wŏn (pen name, Yŏnam) elaborated on the situation in a rural county as follows:

> "At present less than one-tenth or two-tenths of farm households cultivate their own land. Six tenths of their produce is taken away−one-tenth in public levy and five-tenths in private rents."[11]

He then lamented that such harsh deprivation under the exacting landlordism forced people to vagrancy and starvation no matter how hard they worked.

The cases raised by these *Silhak* scholars were all those of the *Pyŏngjak* system of letting land by halves.

There were two methods in *Pyŏngjakpŏb*—*Yebunpŏb* (刈分法) and *Kŏkpunpŏb* (穀分法). The former divided the harvested crop before threshing and the latter divided the grains after threshing. The former prevailed mainly in the northern provinces and the latter was common in the south.

Yepunpŏb was designed by the landlords to prevent deliberate deflation of rent assessment caused by false reporting of the yield by the tenant. Under *Tojakpŏb* rent was paid in grains following threshing, but under *Pyŏngjakpŏb* bundled crops were collected immediately upon cutting them from the paddies. In some localities *Pyŏngjakpŏb* was also called *Yebunpŏb*.[12] Accordingly, *Yebunpŏb* was considered a kind of *Pyŏngjakpŏb*.

2) *Tojakpŏb*

Tojakpŏb was sometimes called *Tojopŏb* (賭租法) or *Tojipŏb* (賭地法). The arrangement calls for the payment of a fixed amount of rent every year regardless of the year's yield.[13] It adopted two different methods.[14]

The first known as *Chipsu* (執穗), *Tujijŏng* (頭支定) or *Chipjo* (執租), employed an assessor responsible for surveying the farm field prior to the year's harvest, in the presence of the tenant and determining the rent on the basis of his forecast of the harvest. Under the arrangement the ratio of rent was fixed but the actual amount of rent fluctuated depending on the crop returns of the year.[15]

The second, named *Chŏngtopŏb* (定賭法), *Chŏngtojo* (定賭租), *Yŏngjŏngtoji* (永定賭只), or *Yŏngse* (永稅), decides on the amount of rent in advance regardless of the year's crop returns. In determining the rent *Chŏngtopŏb* used three criteria:

(1) Average annual yield: A permanently fixed rent is levied each year under *Chŏngtopŏb*, or the average annual yield up to the previous year is made the

basis for deciding rent prior to the year's farming.[16] It was common for most landlords to refer to *Ch'usugi* (秋收記), a record of the harvests and rent payment up to the previous year, in fixing rent.[17]

(2) Price of land.[18]

(3) Area of farmland.[19]

Of the three (2) and (3) were exceptional and (1) was the most widespread. "A Survey on Tenant Farmers" classifies Tojakpob as follows:[20]

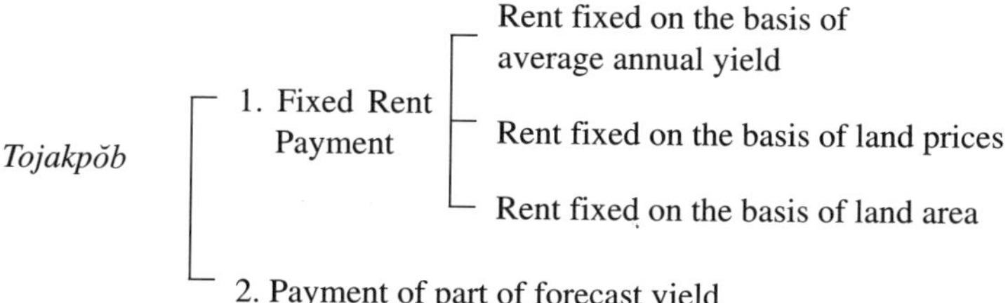

Of these methods fixed rent payment is *Chŏngtopŏb* and payment of part of the forecast yield may be regarded as *Chipsupŏb*.

Here we should pay attention to the confusion of the two methods of *Tojakpŏb*, distinct in content. As was the case with *Chipsupŏb*, assessing the year's rent on the basis of field survey prior to the harvest in accordance with a permanent ratio was different from levying a constant amount of rent year after year without regard for the crop returns of the particular year.

The former method approached in essence *Pyŏngjakpob* in that the annual rent changed each year even though it was decided on the basis of the forecast yield. The latter was rather akin to *Chŏngjopŏb* in light of the permanently constant amount of rent not affected by the year's yield.

The two essentially different kinds of tenant system were confused probably because the same rent ratio was applied to the same type of land owned by the same landlord. *Tojakpŏb* was adopted mostly in *Yŏktunt'o* (驛屯土) or *Kungbangjŏn* (宮房田) and partly in fertile rice paddies or dry fields of private ownership located far off. The ratio of rental was relatively low—one quarter or one-third of the produce.[21] Its difference from *Pyŏngjakpŏb* seems to have led to the combination of the two distinct systems of tenancy into one *Tojakpŏb*.

Tojakpŏb was not so widespread as *Pyŏngjakpŏb*, but it was common in Chŏlla province and Kyŏngsang province.[22] In other areas great landlords having land in distant places probably adopted it.[23] Therefore, trichotomy appears more relevant than dichotomy in classifying landlordism toward the end of the Chosŏn dynasty.

It may be assumed that *Pyŏngjakpŏb* and *Tojakpŏb* were distributed in the Kyŏngsang-do area at the following ratios:[24]

A. *Tojakpŏb* 32%
    1. Fixed rent is determined – 20%
        a. Annually fixed rent for many years – 14%
        b. Rent fixed in spring – 6%
    2. Assessing the rent on the basis of forecast yield in accordance with the already fixed tenancy ratio – 12%

B. *Pyŏngjakpŏb* – 68%

C. *Chŏngtopŏb* – Same as A 1 of *Tojopŏb*

If we include the distribution of *Chipsupŏb* (12%) of A 2 in *Pyŏngjakpŏb*, the distribution ratio of the latter would rise to 80 per cent, while *Chŏngtopŏb* would be 20 per cent. Under trichotomy the distribution ratio would be 68 per cent for Pyongjakpob, 20 per cent for *Chŏngtopŏb* and 12 per cent for *Chipsupŏb*.

The situation in Kyongsang province provides indicators by which we can assume the distribution ratios of various tenant systems throughout Korea.

3. Development of Parasitic Landlordism

Landlords in the late Chosŏn dynasty were parasitic landlords who did not involve themselves directly in agricultural operation. They were not interested in soil improvement, increased productivity or additional investment. Their main concern was how to enlarge tenant land and increase rent collection.[25] Tenants were responsible for farm production and operation with landlords living on the produce.

Such parasitic landlords included resident landlords living in the rural community and absentee-landlords living far away in Seoul or in provincial towns. According to "A Survey on Tenant Farmers" prepared by the Japanese authorities, most medium and large landlords resided in Seoul, while landlords in Chŏlla-do and other provinces had their homes in provincial cities and towns.[26]

The survey gives the following reasons for most landlords living in Seoul.[27]

1) Land was controlled jointly by officials.

2) Most local officials, including inspectors and county magistrates, were dispatched from Seoul and returned to the capital city upon the expiration of their tour of duty.

3) Inhabitants of Seoul, be they officials or private citizens, considered

investing their fortunes in rural land as the safest bet.

4) Oppressive administration and heavy taxation were carried to extremes in the countryside, and therefore, the rich migrated to Seoul to keep their property safe. Much land was sold to people from Seoul.

The report attributed the concentration of medium and large landlords in cities and towns other than Seoul to the following factors:[28]

1) Since rural communities were exposed to constant threat of bandits to lives and assets the propertied people were attracted to cities and towns.

2) The moneyed people found land purchase the safest method of investment.

3) Upon retirement those officials who owned land in their home towns and villages made it a rule to go back to local cities and towns to reside.

The growth of parasitic landlordism vastly prompted the stratification of the farmer class and reduction of small landowners to the status of tenant farmers in the late Chosŏn dynasty. Thus, an increasing number of farmers became tenants.

A census taken by the Finance Ministry in 1909 showed that owner-farmers accounted for 30 per cent and tenant farmers 70 per cent of the nation's rural population. Such areas as Kangwŏn and Hamgyŏng provinces had more owner-farmers.[29] The number of rural households in various categories in the late Chosŏn dynasty is compared with that of Japan and France of that period in the following table.

As can be seen in the foregoing table, the institution of parasitic landlordism was more prevalent in the late Chosŏn dynasty in Korea than in other countries, with the tenant farmer class snowballing.

(Table 1) Comparison with Japan and France

Country	Owner-farmer	Tenant	Owner-tenant	
Korea (N. Ch'ungch'ŏng Province)	12.1%	61.2%	26.7%	The province is considered typical
Japan	32.8%	27.7%	39.5%	Statistics of Agri. & Commerce Ministry
France	71.5%	10.0%	18.5%	As of 1890

4. Ratio and Forms of Rent

1) Ratio of Rent

Ratios of rent varied depending upon the type of landlord-tenant relationship. As the name indicates, *Pyŏngjakpŏb* called for farming on halves, that is 50 per cent.[30] There were cases where it was reduced to one-third or increased to two-thirds provided the landlord subsidized tax, seeds and working cost, but these cases were exceptional.

The favorite method of *Pyŏngjakpŏb* was 50 per cent of the produce in rent while the landlord paid land tax and the tenant supplied seeds.[31] The methods of financing the tax payment and purchase of seeds were variegated, and they affected the rent ratio in many ways. Some examples may be cited here:[32]

(1) The landlord pays land tax and the tenant provides seeds with the ratio of rent set at 50 per cent.

(2) Rent is fixed at 50 per cent and the landlord is responsible for paying land tax and providing seeds.

(3) The rent is 50 per cent and the tenant pays land tax and provides his own seeds.

(4) A sum amounting to land tax and cost of seeds is deducted from the produce and 50 per cent of the remainder is taken in rent.

(5) The landlord specifies the kind of crop to be grown and collects 50 per cent in rent, while paying land tax and providing seeds.

(6) The landlord takes 50 per cent in rent and also the straw, while paying land tax. The tenant provides seeds.

(7) The landlord provides seeds and takes 50 per cent in rent. The tenant gets the straw but pays land tax.

(8) The tenant pays land tax and seeds are provided jointly by the landlord and the tenant who gets the straw. Rent is 50 per cent.

(9) The landlord pays land tax and provides seeds and takes two-thirds of the produce in rent.

(10) The landlord pays land tax and purchases fertilizer for the tenant who provides seeds. Two-thirds of the produce is paid in rent.

Of the ten variations listed above (1) and (2) are the most widely practiced methods, followed by (3) and (4). The rest were rather exceptional.

Sambunpŏb (dividing into three) was often called and *Tojakpŏb* called for one-third in rent.[33] However in actuality, the rent ranged from one-quarter to four-tenths depending on the assessment of forecast yield.[34] Especially when an agent of the landlord was assigned to act as assessor, the outcome was likely to turn out in favor of the landlord: thus the ratio of rent often rose slightly above one-third. It is believed that rent was fixed somewhere between one-third and one-half.[35] As a matter of principle, however, the standard ratio of *Tojakpŏb* was one-third of the produce.

The ratio of *Tojakpŏb* was generally lower than that of *Pyŏngjakpŏb*. Therefore, the former carried with it various other burdens such as payment of land tax and provision of seeds by the tenant.[36] It was a general rule for the tenant to take all the straw.[37]

Chŏngtopŏb was generally considered a variation on *Tojopŏb* and tenants used to identify the two. But toward the end of the Chosŏn dynasty the former emerged as an independent method of collecting rent. A report of the Finance Ministry's taxation bureau says that it was widespread in P'yŏngan province and the ratio was 23-33 per cent depending on the fertility of land.[38]

It should be kept in mind here that the common ratio of 50 per cent in the late Chosŏn dynasty was the ceiling on land rent at that time. The ceiling was rarely ignored. The low agricultural productivity in that period seems to be largely responsible for the 50 per cent ceiling.[39] The exacting burden of rent that corresponded to all of the surplus product and occasionally ate into even the necessary product was aptly pointed out by Chŏng Yak-yong.

The ratio of rent was sometimes below one-third under *Tojakpŏb* in the late Chosŏn dynasty in some newly reclaimed areas. But the actual burden was heavier because forced labor, contributions and other taxes were added to it.

Since the rent on the tenant land of predominant private landlords was 50 per cent, any downward departure from the level had to be made up for by other forms of levy. There existed an internal movement to approach 50 per cent in parallel with another internal movement to bring down the rent to 33 per cent.

In such fertile area as Chŏlla province the tenants were sometimes subject to other forms of taxation besides the ground rent of 50 per cent,[40] but imposition of such additional burdens upon the tenant was not common. In case such burdens were imposed, the rent would be reduced to 33 per cent.

Under *Pyŏngjakpŏb* the amount of rent rose or fell automatically in accordance with the crop returns of the year. However, *Tojakpŏb* made it a rule to abide by the standing pact on rent, neither increasing nor decreasing the rent depending upon the annual yeild. When the tenant requested exemption or reduction of rent for reasons of bad crop, the landlord decided on it after a field survey.[41]

Besides rent, tenants in many areas were expected to offer free labor to help in the wedding and funeral services of the landlord. Near Sŏnch'ŏn in N. Pyŏngan Province it was customary for the landlord to engage the free labor of tenants three times a year — twice in August by the lunar calendar (once for house repair and once for gathering firewood) and once in February (roof replacement).[42]

There was another custom that the tenant supplied labor for soil improvement, irrigation and repair of farm implements and the landlord gave the money required for major improvement projects.[43]

2) Forms of Rent

Rent was mostly collected in kind with a few exceptional instances of cash payment under *Chŏngtopŏb*.[44] When the landlord was far removed from the tenant land and farm products were hard to deliver to him, or he specifically required cash payment, the rent in kind was converted into monetary value at the current price and it was paid in currency instead (Taegumnap: 代金納).[45] Under *Tojakpŏb* cash payment was more frequently made.[46] Such rent payment in cash was partly practiced on state-owned or royal lands, such as *Kungjangt'o* or *Yŏktunt'o*, and became gradually widespread.

In collecting rent in kind there were slight variations. Under *Pyŏngjakpŏb* all the crops raised on the tenant land were collected in kind, thus the contents of the rent were variegated. However, under *Tojakpŏb*, the rent was paid in the chief product of the region — for instance, rice for paddies and beans (or barley and milet) for dry fields. In some areas rice was uniformly requested as rent. In Hwanghae province. P'yŏngan province and Hamgyŏng province where milet was the main product, it was the standard grain to be paid in rent.[47]

Under *Pyŏngjakpŏb* rent was collected at the time of harvest. The tenant would notify the landlord of the date of gathering in or threshing crops and the landlord would send his agent over to witness the harvest. Under *Tojopŏb* the landlord collected rents mostly in November and December.[48]

It was customary under both *Pyŏngjakpŏb* and *Tojakpŏb* for tenants to bring their rents to the home of the landlord or a place the latter appointed. In case the home or the appointed place was far from where the tenant lived, the landlord was supposed to pay for the cost of transportation. The standard distance ranged from 10 *ri* (4 km) to 50 *ri*.[49]

5. Tenure and Contract of Tenancy

1) Length of the Tenure of Tenancy

The length of the tenure of tenancy was not usually predetermined but lasted indefinitely unless the tenant was derelict of rent payment.[50]

> "There is no such thing as the length of the tenure of tenancy. Those who apply themselves fully to farming will retain tenancy for ever, while those who are negligent will forfeit tenancy."[51]

The tenant was rarely asked to relinquish his tenant farming unless he failed to pay rents or utterly neglected farming. As long as the tenant was interested in keeping the farm, the landlord-tenant relationship continued for many years and decades or even generation after generation.[52]

Thus, there did not exist any fixed duration of tenancy, and once tenancy was granted, it would last almost indefinitely in the absence of serious dereliction on the part of the tenant. It was quite uncommon for the landlord to arbitrarily transfer tenancy.[53]

The Japanese who investigated the tenure-term of tenancy in Korea were divided into two groups. The first group contends that the term of tenancy lasted one year, and the tenancy contract was renewed if the tenant was found to be hard working and dutiful. The second group holds that the tenancy contract once entered into continued in effect indefinitely unless it was dissolved by either party. The second theory was confirmed to be more relevant.[54]

2) Tenancy Contract

The most common practice was to conclude a verbal contract between the tenant and the landlord or his agent, *Marŭm* or *Saŭm* (舍音).[55] In some places such a verbal contract was followed by a written note from either the landlord or the tenant.[56] *Tojakpŏb* frequently adopted the written form of contract.[57] One such contract paper issued by the landlord to the tenant was called *P'aeji* (牌旨) or *Ch'ach'ŏp* (差帖).

A paper in the reverse was called *Chijŏngp'yo* (支定標) or *Tojip'yo* (賭支標).

A tenancy contract could be dissolved by either the landlord or the tenant. Dissolution by the landlord was possible only when there were justifiable reasons in light of prevailing customs. But no dissolution could take place during the period between the vernal equinox and autumnal equinox,[58] or the period from the outset of cultivation to harvest.[59]

In case tenancy had lasted several years and an implied accord on its continuation the next year was considered to exist, the party wishing to dissolve the contract unilaterally (in the period between the harvest and sowing of seeds) was held responsible for making due compensation. If, for instance, the landlord was to terminate a tenancy contract, he was expected to provide the tenant with farmland as a substitute.

The tenant was also supposed to make up for any damage that might arise from dissolution of his instance.[60]

6. Tenant Management

A small landlord looked after his land by himself, but medium and large landlords or one who resided far off from his land had a *Saŭm* or *Marum* appointed to represent him.[61] Other names for *Saŭm* included *Taet'aegin* (大宅人) and *Nongmak chuin* (農幕主人). In P'yŏngan Province the most trusted tenant was chosen to act as the landlord's agent under the name of *Sujagin* (首作人).[62]

The powers and functions of *Saŭm* varied widely depending upon locality and the contents of the agreement between the landlord and his agent. The basic powers and functions of *Saŭm* may be listed as follows:

(1) Collection of rents[63]
(2) Selection of tenants
(3) Dissolution of tenancy
(4) Change of tenant
(5) Delivery of collected rents to the landlord
(6) Assessment of yield and rent[64]
(7) Storage of rents
(8) Marketing of rents
(9) Supervision of tenants
(10) Management of tenant land
(11) Payment of tax
(12) Rehabilitation of farms stricken by natural disasters
(13) Improvement and reclassification of land[65]
(14) Increase or reduction of rents
(15) Preservation of seeds under *Pyŏngjakpŏb*[66]

However, such important decisions as the improvement and reclassification of land or changes in rent assessment were subject to prior approval of the landlord.

The methods and amounts of paying for the service of *Saŭm* varied widely, but the typical one consisted of ① taking a fraction of the collected rents (usually one to five per cent) ② exemption or lightening of the rent levied on the farm tenanted by the agent, and ③ Lease of land free of rent.[67]

The amount of remuneration was highest in Kyŏnggi Province and its environs where the agent got nearly 10 per cent of the collected rents.[68] In Kyŏngsang provinces the agent was leased 3-10 *turak* (斗落, unit of land) free of rent or given about 2.5 per cent of the collected rents.[69] In N. Chŏlla Province 3-5 per cent was paid to the agent.[70] In S. Chu'ngch'ŏng Province one *turak* of land was offered free plus one *sŏk* (unit of grain) of the crop, for 20 *turak* to be looked after or 2. 5 per cent of the rent was given.[71] In P'yŏngan Province 15 *sŏk* was given for 100 *turak* tenant land under the care of the agent.[72]

People eligible for *Saŭm* would be 1) a trustworthy local small landlord, 2) a relative, 3) most trusted tenant.[73]

A big landlord appointed a *Tosaum* (都舍音) for an aggregate area of 1,000 *turak* to supervise subordinate *Saŭms*. *Tosaum* had the power to select or dismiss *Saŭms*.[74] A big landlord sometimes had one or more *T'ajakkwan* (打作官) in addition to *Saŭm*. The former stayed with the landlord or was hired temporarily in autumn to work together with *Saŭm* in surveying the yield and disposing of rents.[75]

7. Social Status of Tenants and Tenancy Rights

The social status of tenants under the landlordism of the 19th century was very different from that of the 15th century when the landlordism of the Chosŏn dynasty was firmly established. Under the landlordism of the 15th century, the landlord used to have his slaves as tenant farmers. Tenant rights were protected and guaranteed only for those *yangin* (良人, commoners) who were not slaves.

As landlordism expanded and developed in the 19th century, many a former *yangin* farmer became a tenant farmer, and as the class system declined the slave-turned tenant farmer was freed from any segregation as far as tenancy was concerned, except for two rolls of cloth paid as tribute to the landlord.

An increasing number of tenant farmers who had been private slaves came to lease and till the land belonging to landlords other than their own master. In this case, no servitude originating from their status was imposed upon them.

Especially, those former *yangin* who became tenants were not subject to constraints in terms of status, and they secured free status as tenant farmers. Aristocratic *yangban* (兩班) family background was no longer required of all landlords. Thus, there emerged many *yangin* landowners and *yangin* tenants.[76]

The landlordism of the 19th century came to be dominated by an economic relationship that replaced the formerly extra-economic relationship based on social estates. This may indicate that the landlordism of the period represented a time when the feudal system was disintegrating. The disintegration of feudalism was in progress in parallel with the spreading circulation of money and merchandise as well as the growth of commercial agriculture in the neighborhood of cities.

The opening of the country to foreign intercourse further accelerated the circulation of money and merchandise, introducing greater economic dimensions into landlordism. The Kabo Reform of 1894 touched off by *Tonghak* peasants' revolution put an end to the existing social estate system and private slavery. Abolition of slavery led to legal assurance of free status as tenants for former private slaves.

Legal abolition only would not do away with segregation against tenants by landlords overnight. But the reform of 1894 virtually completed the already ongoing process of disintegration of the social estate system and slavery, thus eliminating the last vestige of extra-economic restraints imposed upon tenants.

The marked improvement in the social status of tenant farmers, regardless of their former class background reduced the landlord-tenant relationship in the late 19th century to a merely economic one.[77]

Worthy of special note is the emergence and growth of the "customary right to tillage" of the tenant farmer on tenant land along with the enhancement of the social status of tenant farmers under the landlordism of the 19th century. It was in the 15th century that the customary right to tillage was first established simultaneously with the consolidation of private land ownership and development of private landlordism. Toward the end of the 19th century it seems to have entrenched itself as a very important right.

A survey report prepared by the Japanese colonial authorities commented on the customary right as follows:

"It has been pointed out that no length of the tenure is specified on tenancy in Korea. Be it *Tojakpŏb* or *T'ajakpŏb*, tenancy generally lasts several years or decades unless the tenant is derelict of rent payment or accused of misdeeds. Not rarely tenancy is passed on from generation to generation as long as the relations between the landlord and the tenant remain cordial.

Advance contract of tenancy term is unheard of.

In some localities the landlord finds it difficult to remove the tenant for reasons of long-standing intercourse dating back many generations. In case the landlord tries to coerce a tenant to leave, his fellow tenants band together to boycott the farm of the landlord by way of embarrassing him. The landlord has to yield to their pressure and recognize that his land is not always at his disposal."[78]

Similar examples are to be found in abundance in many surveys.[79] One survey reports that the tenant is entitled to indefinite tillage of tenant land as long as he pays rent.

"No definite duration is set for tenancy. The tenancy contract will last indefinitely as long as the tenant works hard and pays the agreed rent. The tenancy contract will be dissolved if the tenant is responsible for reduced crop or failure to pay the rent the contract requires. The length of the tenure of tenancy depends entirely upon the diligence and dutifulness of the tenant."[80]

"Most of the Korean farmers are tenants and they seldom request dissolution of a tenancy contract once entered into. The landlord makes it a rule not to replace tenants arbitrarily unless the tenant has committed some wrong. According to some landlords, frequent replacement of tenants without any blame on the latter's part will not be in the interest of landlords. Therefore, tenancy is not terminated unless there exist some serious reasons calling for such termination."[81]

This indicates the fact that the "right to tillage" or the tenant right was evolved and protected by custom.[82] The so-called customary right to tillage, however, was still a rather vulnerable right. Since it was not a right to counter a third party,[83] it could be transferred to others with the consent of the landlord only,[84] and without it the right was not alienable or releasable.[85]

When the ownership of land went over to another landlord, the tenant could not claim continued tenancy from the new owner.[86] The tenant's customary right to tillage was similar to that of credit[87] and not entitled to the protection under written law as a written right.[88] It was no more than a right of the tenant to continue to farm the tenant land indefinitely unless the tenant developed causes sufficient for deprivation of tenancy.

As the customary right of the tenant to tillage was still a vulnerable one, some wayward and highhanded landlords or their agents, *Saŭm*, took away the right[89] and gave it to another tenant on various pretexts.[90] Despite of such highhandedness, the existence of the customary right to tillage served to provide tenant farmers with a relatively stable socio-economic status to a certain extent. The customary right on the part of the tenant farmer was characteristic of the landlordism toward the close of the Chosŏn dynasty.

8. Living Conditions of Tenant Farmers

In the closing years of the Chosŏn dynasty tenant farmers were not exposed to severe discrimination on account of their social estate, but their economic life was marked by privation.

Impoverished and tilling a small patch of farmland, the tenant who had to pay 50 per cent of his harvest to the landlord could not stand on his own economically. Most of the tenants ran out of food before barley or rice was harvested. They used to gather and eat premature grains or live on edible herbs and grasses.[91]

To pull through the perennial spring famine tenant farmers were forced to borrow money from Kye (契: community mutual fund) and usurers at high interest, gradually running deep into debt.[92]

According to a sample survey conducted by the Agriculture, Commerce and Industry Ministry of the Empire of Korea (name of the late Chosŏn dynasty) on the economic state of farmers, the annual balance sheet of a rural household at the end of the Chosŏn dynasty was in the red. On an average throughout the nation, each family of 4.7 persons went 6.528 *wŏn* in the red a year. By province life was harder in Kyŏnggi, Ch'ungch'ŏng, Chŏlla, Kyŏng-sang and Hwanghae provinces. Such northern areas as P'yŏngan and Hamg-yŏng provinces were barely out of the red.[93]

They were out of the red not because of relative affluence but because of cheaper and crude foodstuff. The standard diet of poor tenant farmers in these areas consisted of: 1 per cent rice, 4 per cent barley, 19 per cent millet, 13 per cent barnyard millet, 33 per cent corn, 6 per cent Indian millet, 8 per cent red beans, 14 per cent beans and 2 per cent potatoes and miscellaneous crops.[94] Thus their dietary conditions were miserable, depending largely on subsidiary grains other than rice or barley.[95]

Most of the tenants who accepted usurious loans to make up for the deficit in household economy paid back their debts in crops or labor the following year. The debt snowballed, forcing them out of tenancy and breaking up their families to end up in vagrancy. To keep their families from dislocation, farmers used to harvest still-unripe crops to eat and take any edible plants for bare survival.[96] Such a distressing situation prevailed more or less throughout the country.[97]

The survey cited in the foregoing further shows that their cost of living ranged from a high of 45.78 *wŏn* per capita to a low of 6.65 *wŏn*— an average of 24.10 *wŏn*. As for food grains, people in the southern provinces consumed more rice and barley, while northerners relied more on such miscellaneous grains as millet. They ate the product of each season because they had no surplus from the previous season to be preserved.[98]

Clothes for tenant farmers were barely enough to shelter them from heat or cold, and one set of clothes was usually worn out over a few years. One hemp suit for summer cost 1 *wŏn* and one cotton dress for winter cost 2 *wŏn*.[99] The hard-pressed life of tenant farmers was the order of the day in all parts of the country.[100]

The same survey reports that tenant farmers had to bear the burden of paying, in addition to the expenses for farming, such public levies as land tax, house tax, tobacco and local spending tax.[101]

As has been described above, the tenant farmers of the late Chosŏn dynasty, though they commanded an improved social status, were impoverished and distressed because of heavy tenant rents, accumulated usurious debts and exacting taxes and levies.

9. Characteristics of Landlordism in the Late Chosŏn Dynasty

A question may be raised here as to the nature of landlordism of the late Chosŏn dynasty. Was it a feudalistic landlordism, or a modern capitalistic landlordism or a third type of landlordism? To answer this question the following three criteria should be examined:

1) How the surplus produce was expropriated;
2) Extra-economic coercion originating from social estate;
3) Various forms of rent payment in labor, kind or currency.[102]

Rents for farmland were paid out of the surplus product exclusive of the product required for the reproduction of labor by the tenant. The landlord acquired the surplus product in rent. In feudal times the landowner took all of the surplus product in confrontation with the tenant; the feudal landlord possessed tenants as serfs and took away the surplus yield not under legitimate machinery of economic law but by means of extra-economic coercion based on the social estate system.

However, under the modern capitalistic system only part of the surplus product is taken in rent that is paid as part of deduction from the "profit" to be acquired by the agricultural capitalist. Since profit is generated only through the medium of currency, ground rents also take the form of money.[103]

The high rate of rent paid to the landlord in the late Chosŏn dynasty approximated 50 per cent of the farm yield, and it corresponded to all of the surplus product, not part. It sometimes ate into the "required product" for the tenant to which the landowner was not entitled. The landlords in the late Chosŏn dynasty were parasitic landlords interested not in improving soil or increasing agricultural productivity but only in getting rents.[104]

Without the intervention of agricultural capitalists or profit, the landlord expropriated the sum total of the surplus product form the tenant. In that sense the rents under the landlordism of the late Chosŏn dynasty did not represent the ground rent or profit of modern capitalism but rather belonged to the category of precapitalistic rents. Coupled with the aspect of extra-economic coercion, its structure and nature would readily land itself to classification as feudalistic rents.[105]

In the second place, the collection of rents under the landlordism of the late Chosŏn dynasty depended more on economic coercion than on the dwindling extra-economic coercion. Tenant farmers coming from the *yangin* class were not subject to any social estate-oriented discrimination and even slaves who become tenant farmers could tenant land not owned by their landlord, without incurring any such discrimination.

Only those slaves who turned tenant farmers who worked on the land of their master were subject to extra-economic coercion stemming from class background, but its intensity was watered down in the 19th century until 1894 when it was ended with the liberation of slaves. Rent collection at that time represented a combination of economic coercion and some remnants of extra-economic coercion.[106]

As has been reviewed earlier, in most cases rents were paid in kind with some exceptional cases of cash payment. This means the rents under the landlordism of the late Chosŏn dynasty belonged to the category of pre-capitalistic rents.[107]

From this we can arrive at a tentative conclusion that the landlordism of the late Chosŏn dynasty was neither a purely feudalistic landlordism nor a modern capitalistic landlordism. It could be called a semi-feudalistic landlordism in that it was a transitional landlordism spanning feudal landlordism and modern landlordism. It was an outcome of the decline of the social estate system that accompanied the disintegration of feudalism.[108)]

The landlordism of the late Chosŏn dynasty may be characterized as a semi-feudal parasitic landlordism that followed the decline of social estate-oriented extra-economic coercion as a result of vanishing feudalistic rents.

10. Conclusion

The landlordism of the closing years of the Chosŏn dynasty was highlighted by its high rate of rent—33 per cent of the farm produce under *Tojakpŏb* and 50 per cent under *Pyŏngjakpŏb*.

Landlordism was widespread in the late 18th century and early 19th century. Chŏng Yak-yong estimated the distribution of landlords, owner-farmers and tenant farmers in the south western provinces as follows: landlords—5 per cent; landed farmers—25 per cent; and tenant farmers—70 per cent.[109)]

He observed that if the institution of landlord-tenant were abolished, the tenant farmers (70 per cent) would be delighted and the owner farmers (25 per cent) would also be happy over the relief of poor tenants, thus bringing the percentage of supporters of such land reform up to 95 per cent, while only 5 per cent, landlords, would be opposed to the abolition.[110)]

Expressing his regret over the hard-pressed living conditions of farmers in the southwestern provinces he witnessed, Chŏng called upon the king to undertake the reform supported by 95 per cent of the rural people, both tenant farmers and landed farmers.

Increasing deprivation of farmers as could be seen in the number of owner farmers turning into tenant farmers toward the end of the Chosŏn dynasty laid bare the growing evil of parasitic landlordism.[111)]

In the late Chosŏn dynasty the concept of state or royal ownership of land no longer prevailed and landlords and tenants laid claim to their independent rights. The government and the royal household only retained *Amun tunjŏn* (衙門屯田) and *Kungbangjŏn*.

The institution of private land ownership developed to bolster the growing private landlordism.

The tenant farmers for their part developed their right to tenant land. In some cases, they nurtured *"Tojikwŏn"* (賭地權) as an ownership deriving from real rights, while developing the customary right to tillage as a sort of claim.

Extra-economic coercion originating from social estate almost disappeared toward the end of the Chosŏn dynasty and there emerged a semi-feudal parasitic landlordism characteristic of the transition period.

Landlordism took away too much from farmers and vastly impeded the growth of agricultural productivity. And early reform was in order.

FOOTNOTES (Part I - 3)

1. Shin Yong-ha, "Kwajŏn Land Reform and the Establishment of Private Landlordism in Early Chosŏn Dynasty Korea, 1391-1470," *Seoul* National *University Economic Review*, Vol. 4, No. 1, 1970.

2. Shin Yong-ha, "Land Tenure System in Korea, 1910-1945," *Social Science Journal*, Korean National Commission for Unesco, Seoul, 1973.

3. Shin Yong-ha, "Relations between Tojikwŏn of Late Chosŏn Dynasty and Long-Lease Tenancy under Japanese Occupation," *Economic Review*, Vol. 6, No. 1, 1967.

4. *Report on Land and Agricultural Survey of Korea*, 1906, Volume on Kyŏnggi, Knagwŏn and Ch'ungch'ŏng Provinces, p. 502; *Report on Survey of Customs*, 1913, Chosŏn Government-General, p. 118.

5. *Ibid.*, Volume on Kyŏngsang and Chŏlla Provinces, p. 446. Society for Investigation of Real Estate Law, *Records on Investigation of Real Estate in Korea*, 1906, p. 43.

6. *Collected Works of Chŏng Tasan*, Chŏng-pŏpchip, *Kyŏngseyup'yo*; Chigwansuje and Chŏnje, 4.

7. *Ibid.*, *Mokminsimsŏ*, Vol. 5, p. 11.

8. *Ibid.*, *Simunjip*, Vol. 9, p. 60.

9. *Ibid.*, *Mokminsimsŏ*, Vol. 12, Chŏnjŏng.

10. *Ibid.*, *Kyŏngseyupyo*, "Chikwanhojo," No. 2.

11. "anminmyŏngjŏnui" (限民名田議), *Kwanŏngsoch'o* (課農小抄).

12. *Report on Land and Agricultural Survey of Korea*, Volume on P'yŏngan-do, p. 181; Volume on Hamgyŏng-do, p. 147.

13. *A Survey on Tenant Farmers*, Chosŏn Government-General, 1911, p. 3.

14. Ministry of Finance, *Reference Materials on Land Survey*, No. 2, 1909, pp. 73-74.

15. *Ibid.*, No. 3, 1909, pp. 95-97.

16. *Tenancy Customs of Korea*, Vol. 2, "Survey Materials on Korean Tenancy Customs," p. 105. Chŏngtopŏb calling for a permanently fixed amount of rent over many years was called also Yŏngtopŏb or Yŏng-chŏngtoji. It was a prototype of the fixed rent formula and later ramified into Chŏngjopŏb.

17. *Report on Land and Agricultural Survey of Korea*, Volume on Kyŏngsang and Chŏlla Provinces, pp. 446-447.

18. Materials on Survey of Traditional Tenancy Customs of Korea, p. 105.

19. *Ibid.*, p. 106.

20. *A Survey on Tenant Farmers*, p. 3.

21. *Report on Lnad and Agricultural Survey of Korea*, Volume on Kyŏnggi and Ch'ungch'ŏng Provinces, p. 502.

22. *A Survey on Tenant Farmers* p. 3-4, 5.

23. *Report on Land and Agricultural Survey of Korea*, Volume on Kyŏngsang and Chŏlla provinces pp. 446-447.

24. *Materials on Survey of Traditional Tenancy Customs of Korea*, p. 46.

25. *A Survey on Tenant Farmers*, pp. 2-44, 45.

26. *Ibid.*

27. *Ibid.*, p. 45-46.

28. *Ibid.*, pp. 2-46,47.

29. *Ibid.*, pp. 2-53,54.

30. Society for Investigation of Real Estate Law, *Rights to Land in Korea*, 1907, pp. 54-55.

31. *Report on Land and Agricultural Survey of Korea*, Volume on Kyŏnggi, Ch'ungch'ŏng and Kangwŏn Provinces, pp. 502-508; *ibid.*, Volume on P'yŏngan Province, p. 181.

32. *Materials on Survey of Traditional Tenancy Customs of Korea*, pp. 97-98 and pp. 106-107.

33. *Rights to Land in Korea, op.cit.*, p. 53.

34. *Reference Materials on Land Survey*, No. 2, pp. 82-83.

35. *Ibid.*, No. 3, pp. 95-97.

36. *Report on Land and Agricultural Survey of Korea*, Volume on Kyŏngsang-do and Chŏlla-do, pp. 447-458; Volume on Hamgyŏng-do, pp. 147-148; *Reference Materials on Land Survey*, No. 2, p. 106.

37. *Materials on Survey of Traditional Tenancy Customs of Korea*, pp. 46-47, p. 106.

38. *Reference Materials on Land Survey*, No. 3, p. 94.

39. Exemption of rents for the first three years and graded increase in rents in subsequent years for newly developed farmland was partly intended to encourage land reclamation and also reflective of the low productivity of such new paddies.

40. Chŏng, *op.cit.*, *Simunjip*, Mun Vol. I, No. 9, p. 60.

41. *Reference Materials on Land Survey*, No. 2, pp. 85-86.

42. *Op.cit.*, p. 88.

43. *Op.cit.*, No. 3, pp. 93-94.

44. *Materials on Survey of Traditional Tenancy Customs of Korea*, p. 49.

45. *Reference Materials on Land Survey*, No. 2, p. 84 and *Materials on Survey of Traditional Tenancy Customs of Korea*, p. 83.

46. *Op.cit.*, pp. 47-48.

47. *Reference Materials on Land Survey*, No. 2, pp. 84-85; *Materials on Survey of Traditional Tenancy Customs of Korea*, p. 83, p. 110.

48. *Reference Materials on Land Survey*, No. 2, pp. 86-87. The landlord used to collect rents mostly in October and November for the tenant was most likely to consume the

grain to be paid in rent in winter if it had been left uncollected. Then, rent collection had to be put off until the next harvest.

49. *Reference Materials on Land Survey*, No. 2, p. 86.

50. *Records on Investigation of Realestate in Korea*, 1906, p. 67.

51. *Materials on Survey of Traditional Tenancy Customs of Korea*, p. 50.

52. *Reference Materials on Land Survey*, No. 2, p. 77; *Materials on Survey of Traditional Tenancy Customs of Korea*, p. 109.

53. *Ibid.*, pp. 76-78 and pp. 109-110.

54. *Ibid.*, pp. 109-110.

55. *Reference Materials on Land Survey*, No. 2, pp. 71-73.

56. *Ibid.*, No. 3, p. 79.

57. *Ibid.*, No. 2, p. 71; *Materials on Survey of Traditional Tenancy Customs of Korea*, pp. 108-109, pp. 374-375.

58. *Reference Materials on Land Survey*, No. 3, p. 89.

59. *Materials on Survey of Traditional Tenancy Customs of Korea*, p.79; *Reference Materials on Land Survey*, No. 2, pp. 78-79.

60. *Reference Materials on Land Survey*, No. 3, p. 90. The report cites a few examples of some highhanded landlords arbitrarily imposing dissolution of tenancy contracts upon the tenants without due compensation.

61. *Materials on Traditional Tenancy Customs of Korea*, p. 86, p. 101.

62. *A Survey on Tenant Farmers*, pp. 3-51, 52.

63. For 1) to 5) see *Materials on Survey of Traditional Tenancy Customs of Korea*, p. 59 and *Survey Materials on Tenant Farmers*, pp. 3-52, 53.

64. For 6) to 12) see *Materials on Survey of Traditional Tenancy Customs of Korea*, pp. 114-115.

65. For 13) to 15) see *Materials on Survey of Traditional Tenancy Customs of Korea*, p. 60.

66. *Materials on Survey of Traditional Tenancy Customs of Korea*, p. 64.

67. *A Survey on Tenant Farmers*, p. 3 and p. 54. Also *Materials on Survey of Traditional Tenancy Customs of Korea*, pp. 115-116.

68. *Materials on Survey of Traditional Tenancy Customs of Korea*, p. 59.

69. *Ibid.*, p. 60.

70. *A Survey on Tenant Farmers*, p. 3 and p. 55; *Materials on Survey of Traditional Tenancy Customs of Korea*, pp. 62-63.

71. *Materials on Survey of Traditional Tenancy Customs of Korea*, pp. 64-65

72. *A Survey on Tenant Farmers*, p. 3 and p. 56; *Materials on Survey of Traditional Tenancy Customs of Korea*, p. 60.

73. *A Survey on Tenant Farmers*, p. 3-52; *Materials on Survey of Traditional Tenancy Customs of Korea*, pp. 100-101.

74. *Materials on Survey of Traditional Tenancy Customs of Korea*, p. 64.

75. *Report on Land Agricultural Survey of Korea*, Volume on Ch'ungch'ŏng and Kangwŏn Provinces, p. 501.

76. Shin Yong-ha, "A Study of Landlordism in Korea⁻ On Tenant Farming System under Japanese Occupation," *Economic Review*, Vol. 5, No. 3, 1966, p. 93.

77. *Report on Land and Agricultural Survey of Korea*, Volume on Kyŏnggi Ch'ungch'ŏng and Kangwŏn provinces, pp. 258-260 and p. 501.

78. *Materials on Survey of Traditional Tenancy Customs of Korea*, pp. 109-110.

79. *Reference Materials on Land Survey*, No. 2, p. 78.

80. *Materials on Survey of Traditional Tenancy Customs of Korea*, p. 56.

81. *Reference Materials on Land Survey*, No. 2, p. 79; *Materials on Survey of Traditional Tenancy Customs of Korea*, pp. 79-80 and p. 128.

82. *Society for Investigation of Real Estate Law, Rights to Land in Korea*, pp. 46-52. It reports that Korean tenants enjoyed a right to utilize land.

83. *Materials on Survey of Traditional Tenancy Customs of Korea*, pp. 38-39.

84. *Records on Investigation of Real Estate in Korea*, pp. 70-71.

85. *Materials on Survey of Traditional Tenancy Customs of Korea*, p. 39 and p. 114.

86. *Ibid.*, p. 39.

87. *Reports on Survey of Customs*, pp. 118-119.

88. *Materials on Survey of Traditional Tenancy Customs of Korea*, p. 27.

89. *Ibid.*, p. 127.

90. *Ibid.*, p. 66.

91. *A Survey on Tenant Farmers*, 1 in p. 4.

92. *Ibid.*, 1-2 in p. 4.

93. *Ibid.*, 2 in p. 4.

94. *Ibid.*, 15 in p. 4.

95. *Ibid.*, 14-15 in p. 4.

96. *Ibid.*, 3-4 in pp. 4.

97. *Ibid.*, 4-8 in pp. 4.

98. *Ibid.*, 9 in p. 4.

99. *Ibid.*, 10 in p. 4.

100. *Ibid.*, 10-16 in p. 4. Examples of the living conditions of tenant farmers in many parts of the country are given, but they were little different from each other.

101. *Ibid.*, 23-44 in p. 4.

102. The three criteria cited here need some elaboration. 1) The manner of expropriating surplus product represents a mode of production expressed most saliently in ground rent; 2) the extra-economic coercion represents the means and social relationship of collecting rents; 3) the forms of rents represent specific stages of development of rents prescribed by the above two criteria. It is believe that an examination of the historic nature of landlordism or the historic category of ground rents should be based on a unified analysis of these three criteria.

103. Ground rent under capitalism is predicated on the emergence of a capitalistic mode of production in agriculture. Rents are paid to the landlord out of that part of the profit gained from farming in excess of the average profit. Therefore, extra-economic coercion becomes unnecessary under a capitalistic system and is bound to decline. Payment of rents by means of exchange of commodities is conducted in accordance with socio-economic principles. Moreover, capital rents are part of profit and profit is generated through the medium of currency. Thus, ground rents will inevitably take the form of cash rents. Under the existing socio-economic conditions of the time, such an idealistic form does not occur frequently, but the same principle is applicable to all its variation.

104. *A Survey on Tenant Farmers*, 44-45 in p. 2.

105. The landlords of the late Chosŏn Dynasty could hardly fulfill the role of landed capitalist for most of them were parasitic landlords and the capitalistic mode of production was yet to be introduced. Toward the end of the Chosŏn Dynasty these parasitic landlords directly took all of the surplus product from tenant farmers.

106. We should take note of the fact that erosion of extra-economic coercion did not mean the immediate elimination of feudalistic ground rent or the instant emergence of modern capitalistic rents. Extra-economic coercion was a way of collecting feudal rent and an apparatus of social relationship, not only a constituent element of feudalistic rent. However, it was an important factor of feudalistic landlordism and its erosion certainly heralded the eventual disintegration of such feudalistic landlordism.

107. Cash payment of rents was prevalent in many countries during the period of decline of feudalistic landlordism. The rent payment in kind in the late Chosŏn Dynasty may well be regarded as a transitional form of tenancy that precedes capitalistic rents.

108. The semi-feudal landlordism mentioned here refers to the landlordism under which the legacies of extra-economic coercion originating from the social estate system eroded. Dynamically speaking, it means a landlordism in transition from the declining feudalistic landlordism to the modern capitalistic landlordism.

109. Chŏng, *op.cit.*, *Simunjip*, Mun I, Vol. 9, p. 61.

110. It is assumed that the 70 percent cited by Chŏng Yak-yong included not only pure tenant farmers but also those who were at once landed owner-tenants. Chŏng reckoned those partial tenants who paid rents to the landlord among the category of tenant farming, and this category accounted for 70 percent of the rural population in the southwestern provinces at that time. Chŏng termed them not tenant farmers but rent payers probably for this reason.

111. *A Survey on Tenant Farmers*, 1-6 in p. 5.

4. Tasan Chŏng Yak-yong's Land Reform Thought

1. Introduction

Chŏng Yak-yong (pen name Tasan, 1762-1836), was a great *Shilhak* (Practical Learning) scholar. He established unique ideas and systems in almost all branches of learning including politics, economics, social affairs, culture, national defense, and some aspects of the natural sciences, as well as presented methods of social reform.

Tasan's land reform thought formed one of the pivotal elements in his social reform thought. His land reform thought includes the *yŏjŏn* system (閭田制) he developed in *Chŏnlon* (田論)[1] which he wrote at the age of 38 and the *Chŏngjŏn* system (井田制) he developed in *Kyŏngse Yup'yo* (經世遺表; Design for Good Government),[2] which he wrote at the age of 56.

When he was still young, Tasan made public his radical land reform ideas. When he reached academic maturity later, however, he conceived and presented his new land reform thought on the basis of the *Chŏngjŏn* system.

Nevertheless, dissertations on his land reform thought centering on the *Chŏngjŏn* system have not yet been published actively at home and abroad.[3]

This paper aims at examining Tasan's *Chŏngjŏn* theory as one aspect of the social sciences.

2. Problem-Consciousness in Tasan's Theory

In Tasan's time there were many serious land problems including the expanding landlord system.[4] Some of the most serious of these land problems were as follows:

(1) Rapid land encroachment by privileged *yangban* landlords and other private landowners and degradation of peasants into tenants.

(2) Enforcement of the government office land system and its rapid expansion.

(3) Enforcement of the palace land system and increasing monopoly.

(4) Rapid spread of the phenomenon that peasants were drifting away from their farms and the rapid increase in the number of roaming people.

(5) Slowness in the growth of agricultural productivity and failure to coordinate farming and farm labor.

(6) Increase of the practice of concealing the acreage under crops, generalization of the habit of local petty officials of indulging in intermediary exploitation, and financial destitution facing the state treasury.

It is necessary first of all to point out that Tasan's land reform thought sprang from his consciousness of the following five problems.

First comes the problem of how to increase agricultural productivity. Discussing the *Chǒngjǒn* system in *Kyǒngse Yup'yo*, he clarified that "seeing along this line, it becomes clear that what is important in the principle of dividing the land is how to govern the land and not how to govern the property"[5]

"How to govern the land" means how to increase agricultural productivity and "how to govern the property" means how to achieve economic equality. He believed that to increase social wealth by elevating agricultural productivity would gradually bring about the welfare of all peasants. He clarified as follows:

> If the land is entrusted to competent persons and if they till the land diligently, crop production will increase, and, if crop production increases, it will enrich the people's living, and, if the people's living is enriched, all including invalids, sick persons, aged persons, infants, handicraftsmen, merchants, etc. will be pleased. Thus, the people's living is affected by crop production. We find here the will of all sages.[6]

Second, he was concerned with measures to protect the people from intermediary exploitation by local petty officials. He expressed one of the measures as an "even tax."

According to Tasan, the petty officials kept both an official register and a private register at the same time. They reduced the acreage under cultivation and expanded the uncultivated acreage in the official register while listing private farms owned by peasants and even abandoned farms in the private register as a means merciless exploitation on the peasants. They became fat through this intermediary exploitation.[7] He wrote:

> As I see it, it is recorded in the legal code that the tax from 1 *kyǒl* of land is generally 21 *tu* of rice (add 3 *tu* in case of Hwanghae do province) and 5 *chǒn* of money. Nevertheless, a peasant is asked to pay a tax no less than 40

tu of rice, 10 *tu* of millet, and 3 to 4 *nyang* (1 *nyang* = 10 *chŏn*) of money a year. Ten years ago a peasant could bear the tax burden because it did not exceed 100 *tu* from 1 *kyŏl*. Today, however, even a tax amounting to 100 *tu* is considered insufficient.[8]

In other words, the local petty officials collected from peasants a tax more than twice the amount they actually submitted to the government. Tasan tried to protect the people by rooting out this evil practice.

The third problem concerned measures to strengthen the foundation of the state finances by blocking intermediary embezzlement by petty officials in the local branches of government. The practice of concealing the acreage under cultivation existed on a wide scale at that time as a result of tricks played by petty officials and wealthy landlords. Consequently the state treasury plunged into a state of extreme destitution. The petty officials also embezzled a considerable amount of the tax. Tasan lamented:

> The state revenue does not exceed 120,000 *sŏk* in an ordinary year. The amount of tax brought to the capital does not exceed tens of thousands of sŏk in a lean year. How can the government meet its expenses with this amount?[9]

He went on lamenting that "whether the people become healthy or effete or whether the country rises or falls depends on the honesty of the petty officials.[10] He wrote:

> The lowest officials divide the revenue into three. One part is submitted to the government as a public tax while they embezzle the remaining two. Only after this evil practice is rooted out with an extraordinary measure or through reform, can the state function properly.[11]

Fourth, Tasan asserted that the wandering people be given land to settle and engage in production. He called this "jobs for all." He advised that idling and roaming men of the literati class who amounted to a considerable number throughout the country be given jobs so that they could engage in productive activities.

Fifth, Tasan tried to remove the harm the expanding government and palace lands did to the people's production.

Tasan believed that the *Chŏngjŏn* system was ideal for resolving all these five problems. However, his *Chŏngjŏn* theory did not intend a return to the

Chŏngjŏn system of the Zhou (周) dynasty in China which was presented as an ideal system under which all land problems could be solved by many *Shilhak* thinkers. In other words, Tasan tried to solve actual problems arising in his society by borrowing dignity from Zhou institutions.

3. Discussions on the Possibility of the *Chŏngjŏn* System

Tasan divided the *Chŏngjŏn* chapter in *Kyŏngse Yup'yo* into "Chŏngjŏn-non" and "Chŏngjŏnŭi." In the former, he pointed out misunderstandings by Confucian scholars while interpreting the *Chŏngjŏn* system (井田制) in bygone days and introduced his own understanding of the *Chŏngjŏn* system as a means of new land reform.

While regarding the *Chŏngjŏn* theories presented by Chinese Confucian scholars and Korean senior Confucian scholars of the Chosŏn dynasty as an ideal, he criticized the opinion that it was impossible to enforce the *Chŏngjŏn* system.[12]

He first discussed problems connected with terrain which was pointed out as the cause of impracticability of the system. Many, including Yi Ik, asserted its impracticability because there were many paddies and many mountainous farms in the Chosŏn kingdom making it impossible to divide the land in the form of 井 as against the kingdom of Zhou where most of the farms were dry fields and there were many plains. Recognizing the validity of this assertion, however, Tasan asserted that the essence of the *Chŏngjŏn* system does not exist in a specific form of the terrain making it possible to draw lines to divide the land into nine even blocks. The system is possible, he said, only when there are eight even acreage of blocks of land for the same number of peasants as their private farms and one public farm to be cultivated by them jointly. He went on to explain that they submit the yield from the public farm to the government as a tax and possess the yield from their respective private farms as their personal gains. He said:

> There were only dry fields in ancient times but today we have many paddies. They also say that as Korea is covered with mountainous terrain and has less humidity, it is truly impossible to develop paddies. There is one method, however. Even if our *Chŏngjŏn* system has no form, it would be all right if it has essence. If there are nine farms, each amounting to one kyŏl, and farmers are allowed to own eight out of the nine, with the remaining one designated as their public farm to be cultivated by them jointly, submitting the

yield from the public farm as a tax to the government while possessing the yield from their respective farms as their personal gains without setting aside a bit of the personal income for tax or public dues, this would constitute the *Chŏngjŏn* system.[13]

Another basis of the assertion that it would be impossible to put the *Chŏngjŏn* system into practice was that there was a large population but a small acreage of farms in the Chosŏn kingdom whereas there had been a scanty population but a large acreage of farms in the Zhou kingdom. Tasan pointed out as follows. Those who discussed the *Chŏngjŏn* system in his time first compared the total acreage of farms with the total population, reaching the conclusion that the acreage was insufficient for the large population. On the basis of this comparison, they said that even though it had been possible to enforce the *Chŏngjŏn* system in ancient times when there had been a large acreage of farms but a small population, it would be impossible to put it in force in the Chosŏn period when the population was growing day by day. Tasan wrote that this was a wrong conclusion.[14]

According to Tasan, agriculture, industry, and commerce had already been differentiated from each other, each pursuing its own different role. Those to whom farms were to be allotted would be only people who were engaged in agriculture. Overpopulation, therefore, did not pose any problem to Tasan. Concerning the social specialization of agriculture, industry, and commerce he wrote as follows:

> No matter how precious rice may be, all would become poor and finally die if all people returned to farms. If artisans do not make metal pieces, timber, chinaware, tiles, bricks, and other utensils, there would be only death. If workers do not produce timber in forests, if our domestic animals do not increase in pastures, and if our womenfolk do not weave cloth with hemp yarn, there would be only death. All of them cannot be considered as farmers and so they are not entitled to land. It is wrong to calculate the ratio between the population and the acreage.[15]

As we have seen, Tasan emphasized the need of specialization very much. He tried to solve the population problem by upholding the principle that "only those who are engaged in farming should be entitled to land and those who are not engaged in farming be excluded from land,"[16] while stressing the need of specialization of industry and commerce from agriculture. In other words,

Tasan saw no factor preventing the *Chŏngjŏn* system from being enforced.

4. Criticism Against the *Kyunjŏn* and *Hanjŏn* Theories.

On the basis of supporting the *Chŏngjŏn* theory, Tasan criticized the *Kyunjŏn* (均田制) and *Hanjŏn* theories (限田制).

He pointed out that although it had been enforced several times since ancient times, the *Kyunjŏn* system was abolished repeatedly, and although various means were devised for its proper enforcement, the results were failure.[17] He said that the basic cause of the failure was that farms were distributed evenly among the people, including those who were not engaged in farming.

> The *Kyunjŏn* system of Latter Wei (後魏) was not a principle left behind by the preceding kings and, furthermore, it was not their intention. Their intention was not to distribute farms among all people but to distribute jobs evenly among all people. Those who are given jobs as farmers will engage in farming, those who are given jobs as potters will make vessels, and those who are given jobs as merchants will engage in commerce... All can earn their livelihood in this manner. As those whose occupation was farming constituted the majority among the people, the deceased kings attached importance to farmers. What they really wanted was not to see that all people would return to farming or to see that all people would get farms. The principle the preceding kings advocated was that only farmers should be entitled to farms and those who were not engaged in farming be excluded from the land distribution. However, scholars of later ages who studied the Confucian classics, while ignoring the true intention of the principle advocated by the deceased kings, wanted only to see that all people, whether they were engaged in farming or not, would get farms evenly. What law is this, and when was this law enforced, and in what book is this law recorded? If even one among those who are not engaged in farming is given a farm, this would certainly run counter to out ancient law. What will happen if farms are distributed evenly among all people? If those who are not engaged in farming are allowed to get half of the yield while farmers are asked to submit six-tenths of the yield, this would certainly violate the principle of the deceased kings.[18]

In "*Chŏnlon*," Tasan clarified the impracticability of the *Kyunjŏn* system on account of ceaseless changes in the population and in the degree of land fertility. He said:

Are we to enforce the *Kyunjŏn* system in the near future? It is impossible to put the system in practice. The *Kyunjŏn* theory calls for even distribution of farms in consideration of the acreage of land and the population. The population increases or decreases every month and changes every year, so that we must distribute farms at Ratio A this year and redistribute them at Ratio B next year. The difference between the two ratios is so small and delicate that we cannot measure it with any accuracy. The degree of land fertility or sterility is also very delicate and it is impossible to make it even.[19]

Tasan also criticized the *Hanjŏn* theory proposed by Yi Ik and Pak Chi-wŏn because he did not see any effectiveness in it. Tasan foresaw the possibility that one could surpass the limit imposed on the acreage of land ownership as much as on wished by borrowing names. He said:

Shall we put the *Hanjŏn* system in force in the future? No. It is simply impossible to enforce the *Hanjŏn* system. The *Hanjŏn* system imposes a certain limit on the amount of land one is permitted to buy as well as on the amount of land one is permitted to sell. However, who knows when I, for instance, buy land beyond the limit, by borrowing names and when others decrease their land by borrowing my name? Therefore, the *Hanjŏn* system cannot be enforced.[20]

According to Tasan, the greatest defect of the *Kyunjŏn* and *Hanjŏn* theories was that they proposed distribution of land even among persons who were not engaged in farming. The result would be the same as teaching that it was all right for one to eat while idling away one's time. He criticized the theories bitterly as follows:

It is right to permit only those who are engaged in farming to own land while forbidding those who are not engaged in farming to own it. The *Kyunjŏn* and *Hanjŏn* theories, however, propose a measure to permit not only those who are engaged in farming but those who are not engaged in farming to own land in the future. Furthermore, they also propose land ownership to be granted to people who are not engaged in either handicraft or commerce. To permit even those who are not engaged in either handicraft or commerce to own land is tantamount to teaching that it is all right for all people in the world to eat while idling away their time. We can never consider this as a right principle.[21]

According to Tasan, both the *Kyunjŏn* and *Hanjŏn* theories could not be enforced and, therefore, land reform required a new measure. As the new measure he first conceived the *Yŏjŏn* system (閭田制) when he was young and then proposed the *Chŏngjŏn* system (井田制) when he grew mature.

5. Method of Land Distribution in the *Chŏngjŏn* Theory

1) Principle of Land Distribution

The method of land distribution in the *Chŏngjŏn* land reform proposed by Tasan was based on two principles.

The first principle called for land distribution only among those who were engaged in farming. He expressed this as the principle that "those who are engaged in farming can get land and those who are not engaged in farming cannot get it."[22] On the basis of this principle, he excluded literati, craftsmen, and merchants from land distribution. This was the creative aspect of Tasan's *Chŏngjŏn* theory.

Chŏngjŏn theories since ancient times presented methods of distributing land among all people in the national population. However, Tasan, paying attention to social specialization which had progressed remarkably during his time, namely, the considerable development of handicrafts and commerce, established the new principle of distributing land only among peasants by excluding craftsmen and merchants as well as literati who formed an unproductive segment of society. This was the result of his new interpretation of the *Chŏngjŏn* theories.

Second was the principle of land distribution on the basis of "family labor force." This has been interpreted as being based on the traditional "family" or as the principle of distributing land "according to ability."[23] However, the two interpretations cannot be considered correct. The family of that time was a comprehensive living unit as well as a unit of production and a unit of consumption. It was even a unit of distribution as well as a unit of education. Hence, to see a family as a unit of distribution makes Tasan's assertion obscure. "Ability" as the standard for distributing property in the modern sense as expressed in the phrase "according to ability" must mean "ability" where the degree of achievement differs from an investment of the same amount of labor. The ability Tasan advised to adopt as the standard for distributing land, however, was the "labor force" of a family or, in a strict sense, its "labor strength." Tasan himself compared this to the "ability standard" to be adopted when appointing government officials. However, this was a metaphor and the "ability standard" to be adopted when distributing land was considered as different from the "ability standard" to be adopted when appointing government officials. Tasan himself knew this well and distinguished "strength" from "ability," the former being the principle to be adopted when distributing land and the latter being the principle to be adopted when appointing government officials.

One thing to which we must pay special attention here is that Tasan distinguished "labor" from "labor force" and, consequently, "family labor" from "family labor force."

Tasan did not intent to distribute a greater amount of land or fertile land to any particular family on the basis of "family labor," but he intended to distribute a greater amount of land or fertile land to families whose labor force was greater on the basis of the "family labor force." In other words, although he adopted the "amount of labor" as the standard in land distribution, he intended to distribute a greater amount of land or more fertile land to families with labor force that was greater or stronger in both quantity and quality. With this measure he tried to distribute land in such a manner as to maximize the productivity of the total social labor force by mobilizing it rationally.

> Families that are strong can get better land, and families that are weak worse land in consideration of the amount and the strength of their labor. This certainly does not mean that we distribute land in consideration of the number of mouths to be fed. If the aim is to help peasants govern their property, it should be adopted as the principle to entitle one who has a small number of family members and who is weak to have better land so that he can alleviate his toil and one who has a large number of family members and who is strong to have better land so that he can display his diligence. However, the principle adopted here for land distribution runs counter to the above because the aim is to govern not the property but the land. When a wealthy landlord gives his land to tenants, he selects those who have more young men and oxen and gives fertile land to them. Those who are weak are given abandoned land. This is not different from the method of land distribution adopted by the

preceding kings.[24]

This is Tasan's explanation of the principle to be adopted for land distribution among peasants. In other words, he called on the government to give more land to families that were strong with a greater labor force in an effort to elevate agricultural productivity, like landlords who give more land with greater fertility to tenants who are able to improve the productivity of the land. Tasan made it clear that his *Chŏngjŏn* theory was aimed primarily at elevating agricultural productivity (governing the land) and not at achieving economic equality (governing the property).

If so, did Tasan ignore economic equality totally? No. His main concern was ultimately to achieve increased productivity together with economic equality. He merely believed that economic equality could be achieved not by the method of "governing the property" but by the method of "governing the land." It is very clear, however, that his primary aim was to elevate productivity rather than achieving economic equality.

One thing we must take note of here is how to interpret "in consideration of the amount" in the clause "in consideration of the amount and the strength."[25] It seems proper to interpret the "amount" as the "quantity" of labor force and the "strength" as its "quality."

The matter will differ greatly if we interpret the "amount" as the amount of "production means" (capital). If we follow this interpretation, it would mean that Tasan considered the family labor force not merely as manpower but as a sum of power and the various production means a peasant had (such as farming implements, draft animal, capital, etc.). In this case the standard for land distribution would be based on the "productivity of the family labor force," namely, on how much the family labor force would elevate its productivity by using its production tools and capital. In this case Tasan's *Chŏngjŏn* theory would become a land reform measure that would prove profitable only to wealthy peasants and his theory would be understood as a land reform measure that could provide support for enterprise in agriculture. Although it is apparent that Tasan considered draft cattle as a supplement to the family labor force, it is difficult to see that he included even production tools and capital in means that would elevate the productivity of the family labor force.

2) Method of Land Distribution

On the basis of this principle, Tasan divided the peasants among whom land was to be distributed into 'proto peasants' and 'residual peasants.'

His *Chŏngjŏn* theory, in principle, calls for division of land in the form of 井 with nine blocks of an equal size, the central block to be designated as a public farm for joint cultivation by eight proto peasants, submitting the yield from it as tax to the government, and the eight blocks surrounding the public farm to be designated as private farms for the same number of proto peasants, possessing the yield from their respective farms as their personal gains without setting aside a bit of the personal income for tax. The farmers to whom the private farms are to be given are called 'proto peasants.'

It was made the standard for the proto peasant that his family comprised eight members. However, we can assume that there would be great differences in the "family labor force" depending on the composition of family members. When we calculate the quantity of the labor force on the basis of counting each male adult as one unit, it could happen that an eight-member family would provide three or four units while another eight-member family might have five to six units in its labor force. Tasan counted each male adult above 20 years of age and below 60 years as one unit and, in the case of women, each female adult above 20 years and below 50 years as one unit.[26] Tasan regarded an eight-member family whose labor force amounted to five to six units, as the standard. He wrote:

> An eight-member farming family capable of providing three to four units of labor force cannot get much land.[27]
>
> An eight-member farming family capable of providing five to six units of labor force is entitled to 100 *myo* of land.[28]

According to Tasan, the acreage of one block of private land amounts to 100 *myo*, or one *kyŏng*. (One *kyŏng* is equivalent to 3,000 *p'yŏng*, that is about 9,900 m²) This corresponds to about 40 *turak* of seed rice. A farmer with an eight-member family or with a family of the standard size capable of providing five to six units of labor force is made "proto peasant" and is entitled to a block of private land amounting to 100 *myo*.

The residual peasant, on the other hand, is a farmer with a family of two members, he himself and his wife. This can be considered as the smallest family unit. The quantity of his family labor force is regarded as one-fourth of that of the proto peasant and he is given 25 *myo* of land or one-fourth of the allotment to the proto peasant. Tasan explained this as follows:

> On second thoughts, the residual peasant is a farmer who is incapable of cultivating an acreage of land exceeding the ability of a couple. A peasant

with an eight-member family capable of providing five to six units of labor force is given 100 *myo* of land. A couple who are unable to cultivate 100 *myo* is given 25 *myo*. As a family of eight members cultivates 100 *myo*, a tract of land amounting to 25 *myo* is given to a family of two.[29]

Thus, Tasan established the proto peasant in one corner as a qualified owner of one block of private land and the residual peasant in the opposite corner as qualified owner of one-fourth of one block of private land. He then dealt with units of land distribution for peasants located in the middle sphere between the two extreme points.

It is possible that there are many family compositions between the proto peasant and the residual peasant. There are many family compositions, some families having seven members each, some six members each, and still others five members each, and the composition of their labor force may differ. How can we solve this problem? Tasan tried to solve it in accordance with the principle that "families that are strong can get better land and families that are weak worse land," namely, according to the degree of land fertility, though all are given one block (100 *myo*) of land each. He wrote:

I found out after pondering again that the population decreases or increases every month and changes every year and so we cannot predetermine it. A family with less than seven less than half of whom are adults is not entitled to land of the highest grade. A family with less than six members less than half of whom are adults is not entitled to land of the medium grade. A family with less than five members less than half of whom are adults is not entitled even to land of the lowest grade. Families that exceed these figures will not be restricted.[30]

The figures seven, six, and five mean that they do not go below seven, six, and five. A family above the seven-member level can cultivate land of the highest grade and a family below the five-member level is not entitled to land of the lowest grade.[31]

It is clear to us that "in consideration of the amount" indicates the amount of family labor force depending on the case whether it is proto peasants or residual peasants, and "in consideration of the strength" the number of workers in families with five to eight members. However, Tasan here dealt only with the scope of agricultural operation and did not refer to problems connected with land ownership. He did not aim at transforming tenant farmers into independent owner-farmers.

One thing we must take note of is that Tasan emphasized that a proto peasant must have three male adults in his family as a condition for obtaining land. He also asked that every two households have one draft animal. It was not prohibited that each household later have its own draft animal. If there is a household without draft animal, the government was asked to supply one, on the condition that it be repaid in the form of a tax.[32] In other words, Tasan made it a precondition for receiving 100 *myo* of land that a family has more than three male adults and one draft animal in joint ownership with a neighbor family. He considered animal power as a supplement to the family labor force. This also discloses that the primary aim of the *Chŏngjŏn* theory was to expand agricultural productivity, and that the standard for land distribution was the labor force (man power and animal power).

As the standard for land distribution among peasants was the family labor force, Tasan excluded sick and effete persons and aged people from it. He explained this point as follows:

I think that the preceding kings gave land to people in consideration of their strength just like the government bestows official positions on people in consideration of their ability. No matter how many children one must feed in addition to one's parents and wife, one is not entitled to a government position if one lacks the ability. No matter how many children one must feed in addition to one's parents and wife, one is omitted from land distribution unless one is truly strong enough. Even though a peasant has more than 10 family members, he is not entitled to land of the highest grade if some of them are aged and weak, some disabled, and others sick, unable to till the farm forcefully. Whether a peasant had many dependents to feed or not did not bother the preceding kings.[33]

What really matters here is the possibility of enforcing Tasan's *Chŏngjŏn* theory. The question here is how much land the government could freely dispose of in accordance with a reform policy.

3) Method of Purchasing Public Land

Questions arise here. One is how the government could secure "one block of public land" out of the eight blocks in the *Chŏngjŏn* theory. The other is how much the government could interfere freely in the "eight blocks of private land" and redistribute them in accordance with the principle advocated in the

Chŏngjŏn theory. They were grave problems that had to be examined in circumstances where all the land was being made private.

First of all Tasan recognized that the land was being transformed into private ownership and conceived the idea that the government would purchase "one block of public land" at its own expense. He explained this point as follows:

> I think that adjustment of farmland does not require much expense. The government is asked to purchase one block of public land at its own expense. One block of public land generally comprises 100 *myo*. The acreage of 10 *myo* of paddy corresponds to 4 *turak*. Therefore, 100 *myo* amounts to 40 *turak*. 1 *turak* costs 10 *nyang*. 100 *myo* costs 400 *nyang*. If the government buys 10 blocks, the cost will be 4,000 *nyang*. If it buys 100 blocks, the cost will be 40,000 *nyang*. If it buys 1,000 blocks, the cost will be 400,000 *nyang*. If it buys 10,000 blocks, the cost will be 4,000,000 *nyang*. Even though the government mobilizes all the national strength, it will face difficulty when it tries to buy blocks of public land in several counties. How staggering the cost would be if it buys all blocks of public land in one province. But there are eight provinces.[34]

Tasan tried to explore the three routes below as a means of supplying money for the project of purchasing the necessary number of blocks of public land.[35]

(1) All the money in reserve in central and local government offices.

(2) All the income of all military and civil officials in the central and local government offices, but two-tenths of it to be reserved.

(3) All gold and silver deposits will be explored under supervision of officials appointed for this specific purpose. Royal secret inspectors will be sent with the mission of imposing penalties on corrupt officials. All the profits accruing from mining will be spent for the purchase of public land.

Tasan proposed a special government office to manage the purchase fund and the public land.[36]

4) Problems Connected with Redistribution of Privately Cultivated Land

Concerning the eight blocks of private land, Tasan asked for redistribution of cultivation but did not go so far as to ask for redistribution of ownership, thereby postponing a solution to the problem. In other words, although he criticized the growing trend of private ownership of land by the landlord class, he was far from conceiving the idea of purchasing or confiscating private land and redistributing it. In short, he tried to change peasants who were to cultivate private land in accordance with the principle of land redistribution in his *Chŏngjŏn* theory while permitting landlordism tacitly.

In his *Chŏngjŏn* theory, as a consequence, landlordism remained and the transformation of tenant farmers into independent owner-farmers did not take place. He conceived the idea that, if all of the eight blocks of private land belonged to the same landlord, the landlord was advised to select eight among his tenants for land redistribution. He also mentioned the case that two peasants divided one block of private land evenly. He advised that, if either of the two could not buy up the other half, they would cultivate it jointly. He explained this point as follows:

> Today there is no land in the country that is not privately owned. What shall we do in the future? We should not bother ourselves with minute matters if we are to achieve a great result. All farms, whether they are good or bad in quality, that can be divided in the form of 井, must be divided in the form of 井. The government is asked to spend money to buy up private land at generous price for public land. If all eight blocks belong to one owner, they should be let stay as they are, eight suitable tenants should be named to cultivate each of them. One peasant should be prohibited from cultivating two blocks. If half of one block belongs to Peasant A and the other half to Peasant B, and if either A or B is unable to buy the two halves, they should be asked to cultivate the block jointly.[37]

What becomes clear here is that Tasan's *Chŏngjŏn* theory did not contain any measure against the existing system of private land ownership and he himself did not discuss methods of solution to the landlord-tenant system. What attracted his concern most, what he discussed most zealously, what he tried to reform first of all was redistribution of land on the basis of the family labor force of peasants as a measure to expand agricultural productivity and increase social wealth. In his *Chŏngjŏn* theory, as a consequence, a proto peasant who cultivated "one block of private land" could be an owner-farmer or a tenant farmer. The social position of peasants would not change but the acreage of their land under crops and the system of taxes and other public dues would be reformed fundamentally.

In consideration of the practice of exploiting peasants that was rampant among local petty officials, Tasan's *Chŏngjŏn* theory should be evaluated as a reform plan with the aim to improve the welfare of peasants. If the peasants of the eight private blocks were united firmly, it would be easy for them to reject means of intermediary exploitation wrought by local petty officials.[38] Tasan emphasized this point. He wrote as follows:

> The most urgent task for us today is to increase the agricultural population. If there are many peasants, they can work out means of rejecting inroads by corrupt and crafty petty officials. If they are to reject the inroads, they must be united under the *Chŏngjŏn* system. Even if such sage kings as Yao (堯) and Shun (舜) are born here again, they would surely adopt this method.[39]

It is clear that Tasan's *Chŏngjŏn* theory was not a vague land reform ideal desiring to return to ancient institutions but a very realistic measure that tried to reform the land system based on reality, a measure the possibility of whose realization was high. Even though his theory did not intend to abolish landlordism, it tried to remove intermediary exploitation by petty officials, expand the state revenue, and provide jobs for roaming people in a systematic manner.

6. Problems Concerning Literati, Artisans, and Merchants in the *Chŏngjŏn* Theory

In the *Chŏngjŏn* theory of Tasan, literati were denied in distribution of land, This was in contrast to the ancient *Chŏngjŏn* system which called for a generous distribution of land among literati or to the *Kyunjŏn* theory of Yu Hyŏng-wŏn which demanded a share of two to four *kyŏng* of land for a literati while setting aside only one *kyŏng* for a peasant. The exclusion of literati from land distribution was Tasan's unique idea.

IIis exclusion of literati from land distribution was motivated basically by two reasons.

First, as the normal occupation of literati was to serve the government, they should be given salaries and not "land." According to Tasan, land in the capital area was divided and given to officials as "fiefs" in ancient times so that they could collect taxes from their land. This being the beginning, the salaries of their descendants all sprang from land. In later years, however, all crops in the country were transported to the capital and issued to officials as salaries. It would be proper in legislating the system of salary in his time merely to define salary as "a certain amount of millet and rice" without specifying the origin of the crops.[40] He pointed out that to give land to literati who received salaries was too excessive. He explained:

> All land is cultivated by peasants. What would happen if family members of literati and officials are given land? If public land is given to their descendants for tenant farming by peasants, this means that they would gain land in addition to their salaries. It is excessive to give land to descendants when their fathers are able to feed their families with their salaries.[41]

Tasan also emphasized that, when land was given to bureaucrats in ancient times, the government bestowed not the land itself but the right to collect taxes:[42]

> If land were distributed among literati in a situation in which the private landlord system was established firmly, those who were not engaged in farming could garner five-tenths of the harvest while sitting idle and those who were directly engaged in farming would be obligated to pay six-tenths of the harvest in tax. Was this the law of the preceding kings?[43]

He lamented that the so-called literati did not serve the government, did nor engage in farming, did not study, did not respond to labor conscription, and did not pay the cloth military-tax by using false title, while collecting taxes from peasants and exploiting them.[44]

Tasan lamented that petty officials exploited peasants and asserted that these problems should be solved by establishing a proper salary system.[45]

He wrote that, whereas a peasant could receive 100 *myo* of land only when the number of man power in his family reached seven, a literati enjoyed generous salary.[46] He stressed the need to establish a sound salary system. He also urged that a system be established under which a literati could get salary only after he obtained a government position. Tasan clearly rejected their access to land.

Quite contrary to the convention of the time, Tasan asserted that land be distributed among illegitimate sons. This was because, while legitimate descendants of literati with hereditary salary were not asked to engage in farming, descendants of illegitimate sons were, after all, destined to be farmers. Tasan, therefore, thought it proper to give a share of 100 *myo* to each of them like peasants.[47] This shows that Tasan criticized the system of his time discriminating against illegitimate sons in favor of legitimate sons and conceived a measure intended to help illegitimate sons settle as peasants and producers. We find here again that his *Chŏngjŏn* theory was not aimed at returning to ancient institutions but was a creative land reform measure designed to solve all existing problems at the time.

The second reason Tasan excluded literati from land distribution can be found in the fact that his *Chŏngjŏn* theory did not reject landlordism. At that time most literati already had settled themselves as landlords possessing huge tracts of land. Unless their land was subjected to redistribution, it was not necessary at all to discuss allotment of land to them.

What was a proper measure for those literati who did not serve the government or failed to become landlords? Tasan did not make separate mention of this question in the *Chŏngjŏn* theory. However, in view of the fact that he advocated "jobs for all" as one of the major objectives of the *Chŏngjŏn* theory, we may find the suggestion that these idling literati should find proper jobs in agriculture, handicrafts, or commerce and, if they wanted farming as an occupation, land should be allotted to them as in the case of peasants.

Tasan's exclusion of artisans and merchants from land distribution was based on two reasons. First, he advocated that handicrafts and commerce be kept separate from agriculture. He criticized some scholars who interpreted the *Chŏngjŏn* theories in such a way as to assert that land be given to merchants. He wrote: "Merchants, while sitting in the market with their commodities, can earn enough to feed eight dependents and so it is not proper to give land to their families."[48] He also wrote: "With goods artisans and merchants trade with peasants and earn their bread, and so land distribution among them is certainly contrary to reason."[49]

Tasan divided social occupations after the land reform into agriculture, handicrafts, commerce, and service to the government. He then divided agriculture into six divisions; 1. crop farming, 2. fruit farming, 3. vegetable farming, 4. yarn and weaving, 5. forestry, and 6. livestock farming.[50] From this point of view it was very natural that handicrafts and commerce should develop as separate social specializations.

Second, handicrafts and commerce had already achieved a considerable degree of development and income from them surpassed that from agriculture. Taking note of this trend, Tasan asserted that artisans and merchants be excluded from land distribution.

Tasan said, "Handicrafts and commerce bring about a rich profit. If persons who are engaged in these occupations are given land, this means that the wealthy will become wealthier. This certainly runs counter to reason."[51] As handicrafts and commerce promised a greater profit than agriculture, Tasan believed that people pursuing these occupations could enjoy a richer life than peasants even without land distribution.

7. Questions about Tasan's *Chŏngjŏn* Theory

As we saw, Tasan tried in his *Chŏngjŏn* theory to ① increase agricultural productivity, ② eradicate exploitation of peasants by petty officials, ③ restore state finances on a sound basis by doing away with embezzlement by petty officials, ④ provide jobs for roaming people, and ⑤ eliminate the evil from government lands. In this way he hoped the welfare of peasants would be improved. However, his *Chŏngjŏn* theory poses several questions.

First, his *Chŏngjŏn* theory failed to present a countermeasure for landlordism, one of the most serious land problems of his time. He proposed that, if the eight blocks of private land all belonged to one private landlord, he should select eight peasants to farm the eight blocks as tenants. This shows that Tasan dodged a solution to problems arising from the landlord system. Although he sought a measure to transform tenants into independent owner-farmers, this was not realized. The primary objective sought in his *Chŏngjŏn* theory was to increase agricultural productivity and this does not impair its value greatly. However, the landlord system was let unchanged, the landlord taking possession of half the harvest, and as long as landlordism existed, the landlord could take almost all of the net profit from increased land productivity, leaving almost nothing for tenants. A good result could have been achieved from efforts to increase agricultural productivity only if landlordism was abolished. Thus, it can be said that Tasan's *Chŏngjŏn* theory offered no solution to one of the most serious land problems of the time.

Second, Tasan did not work out a measure to impose limits on land ownership. Even though he permitted landlordism for the time being, he should have presented certain restrictive measures against land encroachment which was growing at an astonishing speed at the time. Emphasizing land distribution in proportion to family labor force, Tasan sought measures to expand the total social productivity through equalization of farms per labor unit. This means that he delayed confronting a trend of aggravating land relations as seen in land encroachment.

Third, although Tasan mentioned the cost of purchasing "one block of public land," he did not calculate the expenses needed for establishing the *Chŏngjŏn* system. He believed that dry fields on mountainous terrain and paddies could be embraced in the *Chŏngjŏn* system by measuring their acreage without being sectioned into squares. However, farms in the plains could be sectioned into squares and Tasan himself conceived this idea. Readjusting farms into squares in all parts of the country would cost a staggering amount and the expected result could hardly be achieved without considering how to raise the necessary funds.

Fourth, Tasan did not fully examine how to transform men of the ruling *yangban* class into producers. Literati who held government positions received salaries under the salary system and literati who became landlords could collect farm-rent from their tenants under the landlord system. However, how about those literati who did not serve the government or failed to become landlords? The *Chŏngjŏn* theory did not show concrete institutional measures to help these literati take productive jobs in agriculture, handicrafts, or commerce.

8. Conclusion

Despite containing several questionable points, *Chŏngjŏn* theory can be considered an epochal measure to realize the objectives Tasan sought.

The most questionable points in Tasan's theory were that he admitted the "continued existence of landlordism," and failed to establish full measures against land encroachment by *yangban* landlords.

Despite that he was a thinker of the Practical Learning School who knew the harm of landlordism more keenly than anybody else and criticized it sharply, Tasan did not assert its abolishment in his *Chŏngjŏn* theory but admitted its existence. It is interpreted that he wanted to make his *Chŏngjŏn* theory acceptable by the king and the *yangban* landlord class for relatively easier realization.

One of the greatest merits of the *Chŏngjŏn* theory was that it was very realistic and its enforcement was highly practicable. He distinguished labor from the labor force. On the basis of this view, he tried to realize "equalization of acreage under cultivation for each labor force unit" as a means of eliminating idleness in the labor force and maximizing total social productivity.

There is one thing we must take note of. Tasan's *Chŏngjŏn* theory cannot be utilized for "enterprising agriculture." This is disclosed by the fact that Tasan fixed the ceiling of land ownership for each household at 100 *myo* and he considered only the family labor force and neglected a hired labor force.

It is necessary for us, therefore, to recognize that his *Chŏngjŏn* theory belongs not to the category of modern land reform thought but to that of feudal land reform thought. He aimed at increasing agricultural productivity by alleviating structural contradictions of the land system within the framework of feudal institutions. An embryo of modern institutions would come after agricultural productivity was elevated. This was another question for Tasan.

Tasan's land reform thought was one of the epochal assertions of the time despite containing several questionable points. It was also a creative idea designed to solve land and agricultural problems. Tasan's land reform thought remains immortal in the history of Korean social thought as a highly creative and important legacy.

FOOTNOTES (Part I - 4)

1. In "Chŏnlon" (田論), *Yŏyudangjip* (與猶堂集) (Kyujanggak Tosŏ no. 11894), Book 28, Tasan said that he wrote this work at the age of 38 and he included this book in this collection although it was a little different from the *Chŏngjŏn* system.

2. According to *Saam Sŏnsaeng Yŏnbo* (Chŏng Kyu-yŏng (ed.), Kyujanggak Tosŏ no. Ancient 4650-167), Tasan wrote unfinished *Kyŏngse Yup'yo* (Design for Good Government) at the age of 56.

3. Pak Chong-gŭn, "Chŏng Yak-yong no Tochi Taikaku Shiso no Kosatsu‾ Noryoku ni ojita Tochibunpai o Chushin toshite (An Inquiry into Chŏng Yak-yong's Land Reform Thought‾ Centering on Land Distribution According to Ability)," *Chosen Gakkuho*, Vol. 28, 1964. Kim Yong-sŏp, "The Real Situation Facing Agriculture in the 18th and 19th Century and New Agricultural Operation Theories," *Han'guk Kŭndae Nong'ŏpsa Yŏn'gu*, 1975.

4. Shin Yong-ha, "Landlordism and the Tenant Class in the Last Part of the Chosŏn Period," *Ch'oe Mun-hwan Paksa Kinyŏm Nonmunjip*, 1977.

5. *Chŏng Tasan Chŏnsŏ* (丁茶山全書), Chŏngbŏpchip (正法集). *Kyŏngse Yup'yo*, Chigwansuje (地官修制).

6. *Kyŏngse Yup'yo*, Chigwansuje (地官修制), Chŏnje (田制) 4.

7. *Kyŏngse Yup'yo*, Chigwansuje, Chŏnje 10.

8. *Kyŏngse Yup'yo*, Chigwansuje, Chŏnje 8.

9. *Kyŏngse Yup'yo*, Chigwanhojo (地官戶曹) 2.

10. *Kyŏngse Yup'yo*, Chigwansuje, Chŏnje 7.

11. *Kyŏngse Yup'yo*, Chigwansuje, Chŏnje 8.

12. In *Chŏnlon* in which Tasan conceived a land reform on the basis of the *yŏjŏn* theory, he said that it was impossible to enforce the *Chŏngjŏn* system siding with the opinion of senior scholars such as Yu Hyŏng-wŏn, Yi Ik, and Pak Chi-wŏn. His criticism here of the opinion of his senior scholars that the *Chŏngjŏn* system was impossible can be regarded as criticism of his own former view.

13. *Kyŏngse Yup'yo*, Ch'ŏn'gwanijo (天官吏曹) 1.

14. *Kyŏngse Yup'yo*, Chigwansuje, Chŏnje 1 (Chŏngjŏnnon 1).

15. *Kyŏngse Yup'yo*, Chigwansuje, Chŏnje 1 (Chŏngjŏnnon 3).

16. *Kyŏngse Yup'yo*, Chigwansuje, Chŏnje 4.

17. *Ibid.*

18. *Ibid.*

19. *Chŏng Tasan Chŏnsŏ, Simunjip* (詩文集), Chŏnlon (田論) 2.

20. *Chŏllon 2.*

21. *Ibid.*

22. *Kyŏngse Yup'yo*, Chigwansuje, Chŏnje 5 and Chŏnlon 5.

23. Pak Chong-gŭn, op.cit.

24. *Kyŏngse Yup'yo*, Chigwansuje, Chŏnje 4.

25. *Ibid.*

26. *Kyŏngse Yup'yo*, Chigwansuje, Chŏnje 11 (Chŏngjŏnnon 3).

27. *Kyŏngse Yup'yo*, Chigwansuje, Chŏnje 4.

28. *Kyŏngse Yup'yo*, Chigwansuje, Chŏnje 1 (Chŏngjŏnnon 1).

29. *Kyŏngse Yup'yo*, Chigwansuje, Chŏnje 1 (Chŏngjŏnnon 3).

30. *Kyŏngse Yup'yo*, Chigwansuje, Chŏnje 4.

31. *Ibid.*

32. *Kyŏngse Yup'yo*, Chigwansuje, Chŏnje 4.

33. *Ibid.*

34. *Kyŏngse Yup'yo*, Chigwansuje, Chŏnje 9 (Chŏngjŏnnon 1).

35. *Ibid.*

36. *Ibid.*

37. *Ibid.*

38. It is necessary to take note of the possibility that this method would automatically abolish the government and palace farms.

39. *Kyŏngse Yup'yo*, Chigwansuje, Chŏnje 8.

40. *Kyŏngse Yup'yo*, Chigwansuje, Chŏnje 1 (Chŏngjŏnnon 1).

41. *Ibid.*

42. *Kyŏngse Yup'yo*, Chigwansuje, Chŏnje 4.

43. *Kyŏngse Yup'yo*, Chigwansuje, Chŏnje 4.

44. *Chŏng Tasan Chŏnsŏ*, Simunjip (詩文集), Nongch'aek (農策) and Nongjŏngso (農政疏).

45. *Chŏng Tasan Chŏnsŏ*, Chŏngbŏpchip, *Mongmin Shimsŏ*. Ijŏn Yukcho (吏典六條), Songni Yukchŏn (束吏六典) Chapter 1.

46. *Kyŏngse Yup'yo*, Chigwansuje, Chŏnje 4.

47. *Kyŏngse Yup'yo*, Chigwansuje, Chŏnje 1 (Chŏngjŏnnon 1).

48. *Kyŏngse Yup'yo*, Chigwansuje, Chŏnje 1 (Chŏngjŏnnon 1).

49. *Kyŏngse Yup'yo*, Chigwansuje, Chŏnje 4.

50. *Mongmin Shimsŏ*, Hojŏn Yukcho (戶典六條), Chapter 6, Kwŏnnong (勸農).

51. *Kyŏngse Yup'yo*, Chigwansuje, Chŏnje 1 (Chŏngjŏnnon 1).

5. Land Tenure System in Korea, 1910-1945

1. The Basic Structure of Land Tenure System

The land tenure system of Korea in the Japanese occupation period was one of its major social and economic institutions just as it was in the Chosŏn dynasty.

For instance, in 1920, 82.6 per cent of the total Korean household population was engaged in agriculture. Of that, 77.2 per cent were tenant and owner-tenant farmers, while the proportion of landlords was only 3.3 per cent of all agricultural households. That is, the 3.3 per cent landlords owned 64.3 per cent of all paddy-fields, 43.3 per cent of the dry-field acreage, and controlled 77.2 per cent of total farm population in 1920.[1] In 1930, 75.1 per cent of the Korean household population was farm household, and of that the 3.6 per cent were landlords who owned 66.6 per cent of all paddy-fields, 49.1 per cent of the dry-field acreage, and controlled tenant and owner-tenant farmers who constituted 77.5 per cent of the total agricultural household population.[2]

Therefore, in order to understand the structure of Korean village life and its changes in this period, it is absolutely necessary to know about the land tenure system and its related economic and social institutions.

If a simplified description is allowed, the structure of the land tenure system can be summarized in the following way.

The landlords had private ownership of vast acreage of cultivated land and made tenure leases with landless farmers and collected tenant rent from them.

There was two kinds of landlords in this period. First, there were absentee-landlords who never undertook cultivation at all but simply leased out all their lands to landless farmers. They were the biggest landlords and usually lived in Seoul or other large cities and towns. The second type was the so-called farmer landlords who leased out the larger part of their land to tenants but also undertook the cultivation of small holdings of their own, usually with the help of hired laborers called Mŏsŭm (머슴). These were rather small-scale landlords even though their total numbers were not insignificant.

The land possessed by landlords was sometimes a single large estate, but more frequently it consisted of small holdings scattered rather widely throughout various districts.

The absentee-landlords employed bailiffs called *Marŭm* (마름) *Saŭm* (舍音) or *Nonggam* (農監) as their proxies and required them to live near the leased lands. The major role of the bailiffs was as follows.

(1) Collection of rent

(2) Holding of rent

(3) Supervision of leased land

(4) Management of land leases

(5) Payment of land tax for the landlord

One big absentee-landlord usually employed several bailiffs. In this case the number of bailiffs employed was decided by two conditions: how much leased land the landlord possessed, and how widely his land was scattered.

The tenant rent was collected in three ways: *Chŏngjo* (定租), *T'ajo* (打租), and *Chipjo* (執租).

Under the *Chŏngjo* method, the amount of tenant rent was fixed by tenure lease between landlord and tenant farmer, and this fixed tenant rent was collected without consideration of the size of the harvest.

Under the *T'ajo* method what was fixed was not the amount but the rate or fraction of yield. Therefore, the amount of tenant rent fluctuated depending on the year's good or bad harvest.

Under the *Chipjo* method, the amount of tenant rent was not fixed. Every year the landlord (or bailiff) and the tenant jointly estimated the year's yield before the harvest and decided the year's amount of tenant rent based on the estimated figures and on the agreed terms of rate or fraction.

The ratio of the application of these three methods for the collection of tenant rent in 1920 and in 1930 are shown in the following simplified figures[3] as Table 1.

(Table 1) Ratio of Application of Three Rent Collection Methods

Year		*Chŏngjo*	*T'ajo*	*Chipjo*
1920	Paddy-field	24.2%	50.8%	25.0%
	dry-field	50.9%	46.4%	2.7%
1930	Paddy-field	32.0%	52.0%	16.4%
	dry-field	60.6%	38.0%	1.4%

As we can see it in the table, *T'ajo* was used in more than half of all cases in paddy-field and *Chŏngjo* was more than half of all cases in dryfield in both 1920 and 1930. In a dynamic fashion, *Chipjo* tended to become *Chŏngjo* in paddy-fields, whereas *T'ajo* tended to turn into *Chŏngjo* in dry-fields, throughout the colonial period.

The rate of tenant rent differed slightly according to the methods of rent collection.

The average rate of tenant rent in 1920 and 1930 are estimated as the following abridged Table 2.[4]

(Table 2) Average Rate of Tenant Rent

Year	*Chŏngjo*	*T'ajo*	*Chipcho*
1920	40-50%	50%	39-50%
1930	50-60%	50-55%	50-55%

As the above table indicates, the average proportion of tenant rent in paddy-field and dry-field to crop yield was 50-60 per cent under *Chŏngjo* method, 50-55 per cent under *T'ajo* method and also 50-55 per cent under the *Chipjo* method in 1930.[5]

Generally speaking, we can safely say that the rate of tenant rent in the colonial period was between 55-60 per cent of the gross product.

Tenant rent was collected in two ways: rent in kind and rent in money. In 1920, 94.6 per cent of the tenant rent for paddy-fields was collected in kind and the remaining 5.4 per cent in money. In dry-field, the proportion of the rent in kind was also 94.6 per cent against money-rent of only 5.4 per cent.[6] In 1930, in paddy-fields, 93.9 per cent of the year's tenant rent was collected in kind and 6.1 per cent in money. In dry-fields, the proportion of the rent in kind was 92.1 per cent to money-rent and 3.9 per cent substitute money-rent in 1930, while in dry-fields the money-rent of 7.9 per cent.[7]

However, this money-rent included so-called "substitute money-rent (代金納)." Here, "substitute money-rent" means that the amount of the tenant rent was expressed in terms of payment in kind such as rice, barley, etc., and the given amount was paid in money at current market prices. Therefore, in the paddy-fields the money-rent of 6.2 per cent was divided into 2.3 per cent real money-rent and 3.9 per cent substitute money-rent in 1930, while in dry-fields the money-rent of 7.9 per cent was actually 3.9 per cent real money-rent and 4.0 per cent substitute money-rent.[8]

2. Some Changes in Land Tenancy and Rural Stratification

The structure of both the land tenure system and the rural class system of Korea changed significantly during this period. We can point out the main aspects of change in the following ways.

First, the rate of the tenant rent had considerably increased in the colonial period compared with that in the Chosŏn dynasty period.

The comparison of the average rate of tenant rent of Chosŏn dynasty[9] and that of the colonial period[10] can be shown in the following simplified Table 3.

(Table 3) Comparison of Average Rate of Tenant Rent

Periods	Chŏngjo	T'ajo	Chipjo
Chosŏn dynasty period (early 19C)	33-50%	50%	33-50%
Colonial period (1930)	50-60%	50-55%	50-55%

As the table indicates, the rate of tenant rent had been considerably increased in all the three methods of rent collection. The increase in *Chŏngjo* is especially note-worthy.[11]

The strange fact is that, in spite of the development of modern economic organization in urban areas and its impact on rural agricultural sectors, the rate of tenant rent had risen significantly in the colonial period in comparison with that of the traditional economic organization of Chosŏn dynasty Korea. Generally speaking, the rate of tenant rent had risen from below 50 per cent to 55-60 per cent of gross products.

This surprising fact has caused serious controversies among social historians and economists in Japan and Korea. Anyone concerned with the study of this period or modern Korean society cannot avoid looking into these controversies especially regarding the fields of social history and economic history.

Secondly, in the colonial period, the structure of socio-economic classes had been remarkably changed.

(1) In the Chosŏn dynasty period, a considerable portion of independent owner-farmers had existed in rural areas as the middle class of the village community, even though a slow decline in their numbers had begun in the later Chosŏn dynasty period. In the colonial period, however, the fall or downward mobility of the owner-farmers to tenant farmers had become a nation-wide tendency as the encroachment and buying of land ownership had been accelerated by Japanese landlords. The major trends of the changes in rural socio-economic classes in this period are shown in Table 4.[12]

(Table 4) Trends of Changes of Rural Economic Classes

Year	Landlords	Owner-Farmers	Owner-Tenant	Tenants	Agricultural Laborers	Fire-field Tillers
1913	3.1%	22.8%	32.4%	41.7%		
1914	1.8	22.0	35.1	14.1		
1915	1.5	21.7	40.8	36.0		
1916	2.5	20.1	40.6	36.8		
1917	2.8	19.6	40.2	37.4		
1918	3.1	19.7	39.2	37.6		
1919	3.4	19.7	39.2	37.6		
1920	3.3	19.5	37.4	39.8		
1921	3.6	19.6	36.6	40.2		
1922	3.7	19.7	35.8	40.8		
1923	3.7	19.5	35.2	41.6		
1924	3.8	19.4	34.6	42.2		
1925	3.8	19.9	33.2	43.2		
1926	3.8	19.1	32.5	43.3		1.3%
1927	3.8	18.7	32.7	43.8		1.0
1928	3.7	18.3	32.0	44.9		1.2
1929	3.7	18.0	31.5	45.6		1.2
1930	3.6	17.6	31.0	46.5		1.3
1931	3.6	17.0	29.6	47.4		1.4
1932	3.6	16.3	25.3	52.8		2.1
1932		18.4	24.9	51.8	2.9%	2.0
1933		18.1	24.1	51.9	3.1	2.8
1934		18.0	24.0	51.9	3.4	2.7
1935		17.9	24.1	51.9	3.6	2.5
1936		17.9	24.1	51.8	3.8	2.4
1937		18.0	25.1	51.7	3.8	2.4
1938		18.1	23.9	51.9	3.8	2.3
1939		17.9	23.7	52.4	3.7	2.3
1940		18.0	23.3	53.0	3.3	2.2
1941		17.9	23.5	53.7	3.0	1.9
1942		17.4	23.9	53.8	3.1	1.8

As we can see in Table 4, the proportion of the owner-farmers had fallen from 22.8 per cent in 1913, to 19.7 per cent in 1918, to 19.5 per cent in 1923, to 18.3 per cent in 1928, and to 16.3 per cent in 1932. From 1932 on, the Government-General of Korea had changed the form of statistics to cover up the rapid decline in the number of owner-farmers. Absentee-landlords were omitted altogether from agricultural population statistics; farmer-landlords were combined with owner-farmers; and a new category of agricultural laborer was introduced, these being distinguished from tenants of the smallest land-holdings.

Even with the new categorization, the rapid decline of the owner-farmers continued with a drop from 18.4 per cent in 1932 to 17.4 per cent in 1942.[13]

(2) The decline from owner-tenants to pure tenants is also noteworthy. From 1915 on, the proportion of owner-tenant farmers had continuously declined from 40.8 per cent in 1915, to 37.4 per cent in 1920, to 34.6 per cent in 1925, to 31.0 per cent in 1930, to 24.1 per cent in 1935, and to 23.3 per cent in 1942.

(3) On the other hand, the proportion of landlords had slightly increased from 1914 on. Yet this slight increase is very meaningful because in any society the number of the richest people is rather small in proportion to the whole population. Therefore, this slight increase in the percentage of landlords indicates a somewhat significant increase in the number of landlords and also indicates the great concentration of land and wealth by them.

This increase in proportion and in number of landlords came mainly through the large scale land-lordization of wealthier Japanese immigrants. But accurate figures have not yet been calculated.[14]

(4) The most striking fact of this period is the increase in the proportion of pure tenant farmers. From 1915 on, the proportion of the tenant farmers had surprisingly increased from 36.0 per cent in 1915, to 39.8 per cent in 1920, to 43.2 per cent in 1925, to 46.5 per cent in 1930, to 51.9 per cent in 1935, to 53.0 per cent in 1940, and to 53.8 per cent in 1942.

If we combine this tenant farmer group with the owner-tenant farmers, 77.7 per cent of agricultural household population was involved in tenure relations with landlords in 1942.

This sort of tendency has been confirmed by another calculation of Professor T. Suzuki (see Table 5).[15] The only unsatisfactory point in this estimation is that we can not compare the mobility of various farmer groups with that of landlords.

From the above statements and statistical data presented, we can recognize a high mobility among various rural socio-economic classes, an undeniably strong tendency toward decline on the part of the independent owner-farmers and a polarization of various socio-economic classes into two major groups: the landlords and the tenant farmers.

This tendency towards mobility among various rural socio-economic classes occurred more drastically in the fertile paddy-field regions such as southern Korea. Table 6 shows the structure and proportion of rural socio-economic classes in 1937 according to agricultural regions.[16]

(Table 5) Trends of Decline of Owner-Farmers to Tenants

unit of number : thousand

Year	Owner-farmers		Owner-tenants		Tenants		Total	
	Number of households	%	Number of households	%	Number of households	%	Number of households	%
1913-1917	555	21.8	991	38.8	1,008	39.4	2,554	100
1918-1922	529	20.4	1,015	39.0	1,098	40.6	2,602	100
1923-1927	529	20.2	920	35.1	1,172	44.7	2,621	100
1928-1932	497	18.4	853	31.4	1,362	50.2	2,712	100
1933-1937	547	19.2	732	25.6	1,577	55.2	2,856	100
1939	539	19.0	719	25.3	1,583	55.7	2,841	100

(Table 6) Regional Differences of Structure of Rural Economic Class

	Paddy-field region	Mixed region	Dry-field region
Owner-farmers	13.7%	16.5%	31.3%
Owner-tenants	25.2	23.9	21.8
Tenants	55.8	52.6	40.7
Agricultural laborers	5.0	3.0	1.1
Fire-field tillers	0.3	4.0	5.1

Here, (a) paddy-field region means where paddy-fields took up from 50 to 100 per cent of the whole cultivated land; (b) mixed region means where paddy-fields occupied from 20 to 50 per cent of cultivated land; (c) and dry-field region means where the proportion of paddy-fields is less than 20 per cent.

As Table 6 indicates, the proportion of owner-farmers (including farmer landlords) in the paddy-field region is only 13.7 per cent,[17] while that of the tenant farmers is 55.8 per cent. If we combine these tenant farmers with the group of owner-tenants, 81 per cent of all agricultural households were involved in tenure relations, not to mention another 5 per cent who were agricultural laborers.

This tendency of downward mobility in the rural socio-economic classes is even stronger when it comes to the fertile Chŏlla plain area. For instance, in North Chŏlla Province, the proportion of owner-farmers was only 5.6 per cent, while that of pure tenants was 69.4 per cent and that of owner-tenants was 25.0 per cent of the total agricultural household population in 1926.[18]

Again, Professor Kenichi Hisama's field survey on Okku county, one of the most fertile paddy-field regions of North Chŏlla Province, proved that the proportion of landlords was only 0.6 per cent and that of the owner-farmers was only 2.9 per cent, while that of pure tenant was 73.4 per cent and that of owner-tenants was 23.1 per cent.[19] If we combine the two groups, tenants and owner-tenants together, surprisingly enough 96.5 per cent of the total agricultural households had entered into the tenure relation while only 0.6 per cent were landlords in this fertile paddy-field region.

In the early 19th century, Chŏng Yak-yong once estimated the proportion of various rural socio-economic classes of the fertile Chŏlla province paddy-field region and urged land reform. According to him, the proportion of landlords was 5 per cent, that of owner-farmers was 25 per cent and that of the tenure related peasants (pure tenants and owner-tenants) was 70 per cent in the fertile Chŏlla Province.[20]

We can compare Chŏng Yak-yong's estimation from the Chosŏn dynasty period with estimations in the colonial period in fertile Chŏlla region as in the following Table 7.[21]

(Table 7) Comparison of Composition of Rural Classes between the Chosŏn Dynasty and the Japanese Occupation Period

Periods	Landlord	Owner-farmer	Owner-tenant (A)	Tenant (B)	(A)+ (B)
Chosŏn dynasty period (early 19C)	5.0%	25.0%	70.0%	70.0%	70.0%
Colonial period (1926) N. Chŏlla		5.6	25.0	69.4	95.4
Colonial period (1930) Okku C.N.Chŏlla	0.6	2.9	23.1	73.4	96.5

From the above table, we can imagine how drastic was the mobility of the rural socio-economic classes, especially the fall of the rural middle class and the polarization of classes into landlords and tenants in the plain areas during the colonial period.

As with the increase in the proportion of the tenant-farmers, the proportion of tenured acreage of cultivated land also increased slightly during the colonial period as the following abridged Table 8 shows.[22]

(Table 8) Proportion and Acreage of Tenured Land

	Paddy-field		Dry-field		Total	
	%	*Chŏngbo*	%	*Chŏngbo*	%	*Chŏngbo*
1915	65.4	770,152	44.7	891,197	52.4	1,661,349
1920	64.3	992,849	43.3	1,202,297	50.8	2,195,045
1925	64.9	1,015,528	42.5	1,183,201	50.6	2,198,729
1930	66.6	1,093,920	49.1	1,386,606	55.5	2,480,526
1935	67.9	1,155,730	50.6	1,414,618	57.1	2,570,348
1940	67.7	1,197,726	51.6	1,409,438	57.8	2,607,164

To put it briefly, the proportion of tenured land had increased from 65.4 per cent in 1915 to 67.7 per cent in 1940 in paddy-field acreage, from 44.7 per cent in 1915 to 51.6 per cent in dry-field acreage, and for the total cultivated land increased from 52.4 per cent in 1915 to 57.8 per cent in 1940.

Unfortunately, the Government-General of Korea did not publish the statistics of acreage owned by various socio-economic classes or groups, such as absentee-landlord, farmer-landlord, owner-farmer, and owner-tenant. The-refore, we cannot calculate how much cultivated land each socio-economic classes owned in that period.

The only thing we can speak of precisely is the acreage owned by all landlords up to 1932. For instance, the landlords who made up only 1.5 per cent of the agricultural household population owned 65.4 per cent of the total paddy-field acreage, 40.8 per cent of the total dry-field, and controlled 76.8 per cent of the total agricultural household population in 1915. In 1920, the landlords, 3.3 per cent of the total agricultural household population, possessed 64.3 per cent of paddy-field and 43.3 per cent of dry-field acreage and controlled 77.2 per cent of the total agricultural household population. In 1925, the landlords constituted only 3.8 per cent of the population but owned 66.6 per cent of the paddy-fields, 57.5 per cent of the dry-fields and controlled 76.4 per cent of the agricultural household population. In 1932, 3.6 per cent of the landlords possessed 67.4 per cent of the paddy-field land, 50.2 per cent of dry-field acreage, and controlled 78.1 per cent of the agricultural household population.

Thus in the colonial period, there were five major socio-economic classes in rural society.

1) Landlord

This landlord class can be divided into two groups: the pure absentee-landlords and "farmer landlords," as we have already seen. The farmer landlords were engaged in the cultivation of a certain portion of their possessed land and leased out a larger part of it to tenants. These farmer landlords usually lived in villages or small towns. However, even though they undertook the cultivation of small holdings, they usually employed several *mŏsŭm* (traditional farm laborers) or else agricultural laborers and did not do the manual work themselves. And, even though they frequently lived in villages, they might also be absentee-landlords to tenant-farmers of other village areas since their lands were usually scattered over various districts. In that sense, I think both of these groups of landlords shared the common characteristics of being absentee-landlords. The proportion and number of these two groups of landlords is shown in the following Table 9.[23]

As Table 9 shows, up to 1930 the proportion of absentee-landlords had increased very slightly, but after 1930 it increased rather rapidly. The reason is that until the world economic depression the proportion and number of Korean absentee-landlords was rather constant, while that of Japanese absentee-landlords had increased continuously up to 1930.[24] After the world economic depression around 1930, Korean landlords had significantly decreased while Japanese landlords rapidly increased.[25] However, we can see some significant increase in the proportion and number of Korean farmer landlords up to 1929. That is, there was some upward mobility of wealthier Korean owner-farmers to farmer landlords up to 1929.[26] Of course there also was a more rapid increase in the number and portion of the Japanese small farmer landlords in this period.[27]

(Table 9) Proportion and Numbers of Landlords

	Proportion		Number	
	Absentee-landlord	Farmer landlord	Absentee-landlord	Farmer landlord
1916	0.6%	19.0%	16,079	50,312
1918	0.6	2.5	15,731	65,810
1920	0.6	2.7	15,565	75,365
1922	0.7	3.0	17,157	81,916
1924	0.7	3.1	18,663	85,520
1926	0.7	3.1	20,571	84,043
1928	0.7	3.0	20,777	83,824
1930	0.7	2.9	21,400	82,604
1932	1.1	2.5	32,890	71,933

However, during the period of world economic panic around 1930, the number of Korean and Japanese small farmer landlords and owner-farmers had drastically fallen mainly because of the sudden fall of rice price and the subsequent fall of land price.[28] Taking advantage of this opportunity, some wealthier Japanese immigrants and capitalists bought much acreage of land and became absentee-landlords from 1932 on.[29] We cannot trace this process further because the Government-General of Korea did not publish the statistics of landlords after 1932.

Generally speaking, as far as Korean landlords are concerned, the number and proportion of big absentee-landlords was rather constant and rigid, although later it began to decline slightly. Social and economic mobility was the matter of the lower classes from farmer landlord and below.

2) Owner-farmers

The owner-farmers owned their own land and cultivated it themselves. They usually had their own house and agricultural implements. They were quite independent freemen and formed the middle class of rural society.

During the colonial period, as we already have seen, a few of the wealthier owner-farmers could make upward mobility to become farmer landlords, but the majority of owner-farmers had fallen into the class of tenant-farmers. That is, the owner-farmers making up 22.8 per cent of the total agricultural household population of 1913 had declined to 16.3 per cent in 1932. And if we remove the farmer landlords from the mixed statistical categorization of owner-farmer, it is quite certain that the percentage of owner-farmers in total agricultural household population is below 15 per cent in 1942.[30]

(Table 10) Balance of Farm-Family Budget (1931)

unit: yen

	Total farm family income	Total farm expenditure	Balance
Owner-farmer	1,120	1,463	-393
Owner-tenant	874	976	-102
Tenant	757	832	-78

The major factor in the fall of the owner-farmer is the deficit of farm family budget which resulted from the lower farm family income, higher agricultural operation expenditures, and the final result, the accumulation of debts.

Many field surveys proved this face. For instance, the results of a survey of South Kyŏngsang Province in 1931 are seen in the previous Table.[31]

As the above table indicates, owner-tenants were in the position of having a chronic deficit balance of the farm family budget, a deficit balance that was far higher than those of owner tenants and tenant-farmers since the former were independent free owner-farmers and should buy new expensive production factors such as chemical fertilizers, new seed, new agricultural implements, and pesticides; and they also could operate their own land on their own independent budgets. After several years of accumulation of deficit balance, they became helpless debtor-farmers, and there was no other way to pay off debts unless they sold their land and finally fell the state of tenant-farmers.

The extreme weakness of the rural middle class farmer caused serious social and economic problems during the colonial period as well as after 1945.

3) Owner-tenant

This class had their own small land holdings, but because it was insufficient in comparison with their family manpower, they had to make land leases from landlords. That is, they were semi-owner and semi-tenant.

The direction of the mobility of this class must have been a crucial factor changing the class structure in rural society. If they could have made some upward mobility, there would have appeared a strong and stable middle class of free farmers in the rural areas. But, as we have seen, they mostly experienced downward mobility to tenant-farmers.

4) Tenant

The tenant class comprises the farmers who had no land of their own and leased all the land that they cultivated from landlords. They were the majority of Korean farmers during the colonial period.

They were also the poorest farmers as well as debtor-farmers, as we have already seen in Table 10. According to Professor Hisama's calculation in 1930, 68.1 per cent of tenant-farmers lived in an extreme state of near starvation without having any grain for the spring season, while 37.5 per cent of owner-tenants starved as the following Table 11 shows.[32]

(Table 11) Number and Proportion of Starved Tenants

	Number of households	Percentage
Owner-farmer	92,304	18.4
Owner-tenant	323,470	37.5
Tenant	875,111	68.1
Total	1,253,285	48.3

The proportion is to the total households of each group

5) Agricultural laborer

The agricultural laborer class can be divided into two groups. One is the traditional agricultural laborer called *mŏsŭm*, his group served to supplement the shortage of family labor force and had existed from the Chosŏn dynasty to the colonial period. The other one is the modern type agricultural laborer who was a wage earner, usually employed in rather large estate operations in the fertile plain area.

In this period, some former tenants who had lost their land lease or who had left their miniature plot of tenured land wandered around the plains area to be employed in plowing, transplanting, harvesting, and other agricultural works and finally became agricultural laborers. This type of modern agricultural laborer was a new class in the colonial period. In 1937, the proportion of agricultural laborers was 3.7 per cent of the total agricultural household population throughout the country, and it was 5.0 per cent of the total agricultural household population in the paddy-fields of south Korea.[33]

6) Fire-field tillers

Besides the above five socio-economic classes, there were "fire-field tillers" or "*Hwajŏnmin* (火田民)." These were the people who lost their land and went up in mountain areas instead of seeking employment in rural or urban areas. They then set fire to grasses and bushes in the mountain forests, planted cereals or potatoes for a few seasons and then left to seek still other mountain forests.

However, I do not classify these people as a normal socio-economic class in rural society but count them as a specific "tiller's group" in the specific area because we could hardly find it in the typical rural community.[34]

In the colonial period, the correlation between the traditional social estates and the new socio-economic classes was not close.

Already in the later Chosŏn dynasty period, this kind of disintegration phenomenon had appeared. Many bankrupted *yangban* became very poor and were economically compelled to undertake the cultivation of land while some industrious wealthier commoners had become wealthier than some *yangban* and became small landlords.[35] After the abolition of the traditional social estates system in 1894 and throughout the colonial period, this kind of two way mobility was further widened and deepened.

Because of the lack of accurate statistical data and sufficient case studies, we cannot precisely estimate this trend of mobility statistically. The only thing I can do is simply describe the general tendency.

(1) The major absentee-landlords were still composed mainly of descendants of the top class of the Chosŏn dynasty, the *yangban* estates, though later many wealthy Japanese immigrants and merchants joined the

group. Therefore, as far as the Korean major absentee-landlords were concerned, we cannot see any significant social mobility but rather it would be proper to say that this top class of *yangban* absentee-landlords stayed rather constant and rigid.

On the other hand, the small farmer landlord class was not only composed of former *yangban* but also of many former commoners and even merchants. Of course, many wealthy Japanese immigrants and merchants also joined this group. We can see some difference between the former social estates and the new socio-economic classes and can see some upward mobility from the owner-farmer to the farmer landlord and other still lower classes.

(2) The owner-farmer class was a mixed group of former commoners and former *yangban*. Many successful lower class people and many Japanese immigrants joined this group. In this period, the bankrupt *yangban* was rather eager to become an owner-farmer, and it was absolutely no shame at all for a *yangban* to undertake cultivation and do manual work in the field, rather it was considered to be proper and natural.

(3) The most drastic change had occurred in the make up of the owner tenant and tenant classes. In this period the tenant farmers were composed not only of former lower or slave classes but also of a much larger portion of commoners and helpless poor former *yangban* inevitably trapped by tenure leases. In other words, all the components of the traditional social estates of the Chosŏn dynasty period had become components of the owner-tenant and tenant farmers in this period.

(4) The agricultural laborer class is supposed to be composed of former slaves and commoners. Conservative former *yangban* were so insistent on living in their home districts that they willingly chose to be poor tenant farmers rather than to become wandering agricultural laborers.

Thus, while a small number of top class *yangban* remained consistently the biggest absentee-landlords, the majority of poor *yangban* had to take a downward move economically as well as socially. And, relatively many commoners had improved their social prestige, even though in many cases they had fallen to tenant-farmer status. Especially the former slave-tenants and lower classes had gotten rid of the bonds of the traditional social estate system and had gotten much more freedom and could become "freemen" from 1894 to the end of this period.

However, because I cannot present accurate statistical data to prove the above description, there is much room for controversy concerning my point of view, especially my view on former slave-tenants and tenants as "freemen."[36]

3. Controversies on the Character of Land Tenure and Rural Class Structure

How can we explain, all the changes in the structures of land tenure and rural classes, especially the strange fact of the rise of tenant rent and the tendency of the polarization of various rural classes into two groups of landlords and tenants in this period?

From the 1930s to the present, there have been elaborate controversies among social historians and economists who produced tremendous amount of literature on this subject in Korea, China, and especially in Japan. At first these controversies appeared among one of the ideologically oriented schools and became well-known as a "controversy of Japanese capitalism,"[37] but later the many modern positivistic historians and socio-economic historians who have been concerned with the study of this period also got unavoidably involved in the controversies. In reviewing all the existing research papers on this subject, one cannot avoid examining and commenting on the tremendous number of controversial articles, documents and many books, especially those published in Japan.

In Korea's case, I have reviewed this literature and re-examined the subject from the strictly positivistic, empirical standpoint and have derived my own interpretation, quite different from any of those schools.

The main points of the existing controversial views are as follows. One group of social historians and economists especially noticed the phenomena of the rise of tenant rent, its collection in kind rather than in money rent, and the unchanged character of the absentee-landlord. Then they considered the Korean landlordism or land tenure system of the colonial period as an equivalent of the "feudal" or "semi-feudal" landlordism which characterized the landlord system of the Chosŏn dynasty period. After examination of the rising rate of tenant rent and collection of various gifts, they concluded that the landlords of the colonial period were equivalent to the Chosŏn dynasty feudal landlords, the tenant farmers to serfs or semi-serfs, tenant rent to feudal rent, and the rise in the rate of tenant rent to the increase in feudal rent as a kind of feudal reaction in response to the impact of modern capitalism.

They theorized that the capitalist economy was dominant in the urban industrial sector; but in the rural agricultural sector, especially in agricultural production, the feudal system was still persistent and, in a sense, reinforced- far from being on the decline.[38]

Another group gave a quite opposite interpretation. This group maintained that the landlords of the colonial period were similar to the modern landlords or agricultural capitalists, the tenant rent had common characteristics with profit and the tenant farmers were just the same as agricultural laborers. According to this view, the Korean landlord system of this period is quite different from that of the Chosŏn dynasty period, that is to say, the one is a modern system while the other is a feudal one.

As a result, capitalism prevailed not only in urban-industrial sectors but in rural agricultural sectors too. They noticed the tendency of the polarization of various rural classes of landlord and tenant and explained it as the same phenomenon as the decline of small-scale industrialists and the polarization into two groups of industrialist and industrial laborer in the urban-industrial sector.[39]

These two opposite points of view have produced different interpretations in studying other specific minor phenomena which are not mentioned in this paper. But the most serious controversies have been concentrated on the strange phenomenon of the rise of the rate of tenant rent or the extremely high rate of tenant rent even after a money economy had developed even in rural areas, and the profit rate had gradually fallen in manufacturing sectors of the urban area.

I do not think either of those two views explain the facts as they are nor can they reach any convincing conclusions in spite of the long and elaborate controversies because they have been too speculative and ideologically oriented, lacking empirical positivistic basis.

I have found the field survey reports and primary sources do not accord with those interpretations. I have re-examined the strange phenomenon of the rise of the rate of tenant rent empirically, independent of any speculative views, using available survey reports and primary source materials published by the late Chosŏn dynasty Government and Japanese Government-General of Korea and some others.[40]

4. Rent and Land Tenure in Transition

At first, I felt I should re-examine the composition of tenant rent itself and analyze the components of tenant rent case by case. Formerly all the social historians and economists on this subject had treated tenant rent as a single unit, as a self-evident fact. I noticed, however, that there might be some other additional components or some change in the composition of tenant rent, especially in the case of the rise of rent rate. I was then able to isolate the fact that the tenant rent in the Korean land tenure system in the colonial period was composed not only of original rent but also of some additional components, mainly interests of various production factor costs.

During the Chosŏn dynasty period, tenant rent was nothing but the original rent itself. In the colonial period, however, the interest on the costs of agricultural production factors was included in the tenant rent because the Government-General of Korea drafted the Rice Production Increment Program and forced the landlords to invest in irrigation and land improvement projects to increase food production and its transmission to Japan. The program of the Government-General of Korea also introduced new production factors into agricultural operations, such as new seed, chemical fertilizers, new agricultural implements, pesticides, etc.

Under the pressure of the Government-General of Korea, the landlords were supposed to invest in agricultural production. But for, the most part, the landlords invested in irrigation and land-improvement projects not directly but indirectly through the programs of the Government-General of Korea.

The Government-General itself usually directed the irrigation and land-improvement projects and charged the expenses to the landlords who passed it on to the tenant and collected the interest on the costs together with the rent.

This also happened in the case of the supply of new production factors, such as new seed, new agricultural implements, chemical fertilizers, pesticides, and circulating capital.

The landlords lent these new production factors to their tenants in advance and charged them interest on the costs as well as the principal after harvest. In the most cases, the principal was collected separately, and the interest of various costs were added to tenant rent.

Thus, we can put the composition of the tenant rent of this period in five patterns:

   (1) Pattern I

      Tenant rent = original rent

   (2) Pattern II

      Tenant rent = original rent + the interest of irrigation and land improvement costs.

   (3) Pattern III

      Tenant rent = original rent + the interest of new production factor costs.

   (4) Pattern IV

      Tenant rent = original rent + the interest of irrigation and land improvement costs + the Interest Lof new production factor costs.

   (5) Pattern V

      Tenant rent = original rent + the interest of irrigation and land-improvement costs + the interest of new production factor costs+land tax.

If we use TR to stand for tenant rent, R to stand for original rent, I_1 for the interest for irrigation and land improvement costs, $I_{2,3}$–n for the interest of the new production factor costs, and T for land-tax, the five patterns listed above can be expressed in the following ways:

(1) Pattern I   TR=R

(2) Pattern II   TR=R+I_1

(3) Pattern III   TR=R+$I_{2,3}$–n

(4) Pattern IV   TR=R+I_1+$I_{2,3}$–n = R+Ii

(5) Pattern V   TR=R+Ii+T

In Pattern I, the rate of tenant-rent was 50 per cent of the gross product, and the landlord did not conduct any lending or investment. But in the case of Pattern II which includes the interest of irrigation and land improvement cost, the rate of tenant rent rose to 55-60 per cent of the gross product. And as is shown in Pattern III, IV and V, if the interest of new production factor costs and other components were added, the rate of tenant rent kept increasing, in some cases, even up to a ceiling of 90 per cent.

Therefore, it is clear that the tenant rent of this period is composed of not only the original rent "R" but both original rent and interest of various production factor costs, "R+Ii" basically.

According to survey data of that period, the rate of original rent in tenant rent has proved to be about 50 per cent of the gross product during this period. This is almost the same as in the Chosŏn dynasty period. With the interest of production factor costs "Ii," added to this original rent, however, the overall tenant rent rate had risen with the degree of rise as a whole being decided by the amount of production factors the landlords had lent to tenant farmers. This analysis is concerned with the condition of the landlords as the land suppliers.

On the part of the tenant farmers as the land demanders, what made possible the increase in the rate of tenant rent was the keen competition among them to get land leases under the pressure of surplus population in the rural areas.

Therefore, in my opinion, the view that the rise of the rate of the tenant rent is a reflection or a result of the reinforcement of feudal rent and of feudal landlordism deeply rooted in the field of agricultural production must have been influenced by superficial observation and led to the conclusion that the tenant rent was simply equivalent to the original rent.

I suppose that this is because they could not find the new additional element, "Ii," that is the interest of various production factor costs, and thus could not explain the strange facts of the rising tenant rent in spite of the development of capitalism in the urban-industrial sector. Therefore, they interpreted it as a feudal reaction responding to the impact of modern capitalism upon traditional agriculture.

The other view, the one which said the rise of the rate of tenant rent could be interpreted as an increase in profit rate, fell into the fanciful speculation that the tenant rent equals profit. To transform the rent to profit, the landlords had to turn into agricultural capitalists and managers, and the tenant farmers into agricultural laborers. However, as we have already seen, the Korean landlords of the colonial period were not agricultural capitalists but absentee-landlords. They might have supplied some capital and equipment besides the land, but that was simply lent to tenant farmers. On the other hand, the tenant farmers were farm operators and responsible producers as well as actual agricultural cultivators. The tenant farmers, therefore, were not agricultural laborers but the actual farmers though they could not possess land of their own.

Moreover, there is a strong tendency for the profit rate to be equalized among various industries. However, it is quite clear that the rate of tenant rent of 55-60 per cent is far beyond the average profit rate.

I also do not agree with the view that the fall of owner-farmers and its polarization into two major classes of landlords and tenants is the same as the fall of small-scale industrialists and its polarization into the big industrialist and the industrial laborer.

The fall of small or medium scale industrialists happens when the profit rate falls to near zero, or just below the zero mark in the process of the industrial competition at which moment they stop operating their plants, while the fall of the owner-farmers never occurs when the profit rate falls to zero or to below zero but happens when their farm family earnings usually a complex of various family incomes cannot meet their family expenditures, and when several years of accumulation of deficits make them debtor-farmers, and then they cannot help but to sell their land and thus fall to the state of tenant farmer. That is to say, the former is a phenomenon that is the result of modern industrial competition, while the latter is a phenomenon that is the result of poverty in a subsistence economy that is basically a part of the traditional economic sector.

Therefore, I think it is clear that the structure and process of the fall of owner-farmers in the colonial period is not the same as the fall of middle class industrialists in the modern industrial sector. I strongly feel that the fall of owner-farmers and small industrialists in the two sectors should be strictly distinguished from one another.

In conclusion, from my point of view, the tenant rent in the Korean landlord system in the colonial period is neither feudal rent nor capitalist profit in the process of the change in land system and rural society in Korea as the Marxian school and some modern economists have analyzed.

From the positivistic point of view, I conclude that the tenant rent of the colonial period was compound rent in the category semi-feudal rent, composed mainly of the original rent and additional interest of various production factor costs, that is, TR=R+Ii, in the age of transition.[41] And I also think the fall of owner-farmers to tenant farmers was also a phenomenon of the pre-modern peasant economy and society in the age of transition under the impact of the modern industrial system. At that time the Chosŏn dynasty traditional social estate system had legally been abolished and only the vestiges of it still remained. The land tenure system was conducted not according to the traditional social estate system but basically by economic contract. Chosŏn dynasty socio-economic organization was already in the course of disintegration though not completely finished, while a modern industrial system had not yet appeared. I think it is basically a transition period of colonial semi-feudal and colonial merchant capitalist system, and the compound tenant rent (TR=R+Ii) is a specific pattern of rent in this transition period marking the disintegration of Chosŏn dynasty socio-economic organization under the impact of the modern industrial system.

A similar tenant rent had appeared in China and Japan during the same period although it might be different to some degree. If the same pattern of compound tenant rent is found in the land tenure system of China and Japan in this period, there is a high possibility to generalize a specific "East Asian tenant rent" of the transition period in the course of the disorganization of traditional land tenure system and peasant economy and society under the impact of modern capitalism.

FOOTNOTES (Part I - 5)

1. Calculated from Chosen Sotokufu (Government-General of Korea): *Chosen Sotokufu Tokei Nempo* (Statistical Year Book of Government-General of Korea) of 1920, Seoul, 1922, and from Government-General of Korea; *Chosen no Nogyo* (Korean Agriculture) of 1920, Seoul, 1922.

2. Calculated from Government-General of Korea: *Chosen Sotokufu Tokei Nempo* (Statistical Year Book of Government-General of Korea) of 1930, Seoul, 1932; and from Government-General of Korea: *Chosen no Nogyo* (Korean Agriculture) of 1930, Seoul, 1932.

3. Calculated from survey report of Chosen Nokai (Korean Agricultural Association); *Chosen no Kosaku Kanko, Chidai to Kanko* (The Practices of Land Tenure of Korea, its Trends and Practices), 1930, Seoul and from Government-General of Korea: *Chosen no Kosaku Kanko* (Land Tenure practices of Korea), Vol. 1, Seoul, 1932.

4. Calculated on the rate of tenant rent of 1920, from Korean Agricultural Association: *Chosen no Kosaku Kanko, Chidai to Kanko* (The Practices of Land Tenure of Korea, its Trends and Practices), Seoul, 1930, and on the rate of tenant-rent of 1930, calculated from Chosen Sotokufu Chusuin (The privy Council of Government-General of Korea): *Kosaku ni kansuru kanshu chosasho* (Survey Report on the Customs of Land Tenure), 1930, Seoul, and Government-General of Korea: *Chosen no Kosaku Kanko* (The Land Tenure Practices of Korea), Vol. 1, 1932, Seoul; Government-General of Korea, *Chosen ni okeru Kosaku ni Kansuru Sankojiko Tekiyo* (The Essential References on Land Tenure in Korea), Seoul, 1934.

5. The calculation of the rate of the tenant rent of the Chŏngjo method must be varied whether we calculate it in the agreed terms of rent before harvest or calculate it in the actually practiced rent rate after harvest because the Chŏngjo method of rent-collection fixes a constant amount of tenant rent without consideration of good or bad harvest. Government-General of Korea estimated it before harvest as 45-51 per cent of gross products in *Chosen no Kosaku Kanko* (The Land Tenure Practices of Korea), Vol. 1. But the present author calculated it on the actually practiced rate of tenant rent after harvest.

6. Calculated from the survey report of Korean Agricultural Association: *op.cit.*, 1930, Seoul.

7. Calculated from Government-General of Korea: *Chosen no Kosaku Kanko* (The Land Tenure Practices of Korea), Vol. 1, 1932, Seoul.

8. Calculated from Government-General of Korea: *ibid.*, 1932, Seoul.

9. Calculated from Chŏng Yak-yong: *Mokminsimsŏ* (True Guide Book for Catering People), Vol. 5 in *Chŏng Tasan Chŏnsŏ* (Complete Works of Chŏng Tasan), Vol. 3. reprinted in 1961, Seoul; and from Takjibu (Ministry of Finance of the Great Han Empire Government), *T'oji Chosa Ch'amgosŏ* (The References for Land Survey), Vol. 1, 2, & 3. Seoul. 1905-1910.

10. Calculated from the same materials as Table 2. See note 5.

11. The higher increase in the rate of the tenant rent under Chŏngjo method is partly due to the fact that this method was mainly practiced in the fertile plains area.

12. Calculated from Government-General of Korea: *Chosen Sotokufu Tokei Nempo* (Statistical Year Book of Government-General of Korea), 1913-1941, Seoul, from Government-General of Korea: *Chosen Nogyo Tokeihyo* (Statistics of Korean Agriculture), Seoul, 1934-1941 and from Government-General of Korea: *Chosen no Nogyo* (Korean Agriculture), 1931-1942, Seoul.

13. If we accept the assumption that the proportion of the farmer-landlord was constant as 2.5 percent of total agricultural household population (in fact it might have increased a little during this period), the real proportion of the owner-farmers must be 14.9 percent of the total agricultural household population in 1942.

14. The Government-General of Korea did not publish the number of Korean and Japanese landlords separately. Therefore, we cannot calculate direct statistics of the increase of Japanese landlords and the upward mobility of Korean wealthier owner-farmer to farmer landlords, but still we can estimate it indirectly through the statistics of land tax payers. For instance, for the very biggest landlords (above 200 chŏngbo), the number of Japanese landlords was 169 households in 1921, 170 households in 1925, 187 households in 1930 and 195 households in 1932, while that of the very biggest Korean landlords was 66 households in 1921, 45 households in 1925, 50 households in 1930, and 46 households in 1932. For the small landlord of 10-20 chŏngbo, the number of Japanese landlords was 1,544 households in 1921, 2,389 households in 1925, 2,797 households in 1930, and 3,295 households in 1932, while that of Korean small landlords was 29,646 households in 1921, 32,747 households in 1925, 31,939 households in 1930, and 30,567 households in 1932. The number of Korean big landlords was rather constant but later had a little decrease while the Japanese big landlords increased very rapidly. For the small landlords, the number of Korean small landlords had slowly increased up to 1929, but later began to decrease, while that of Japanese small landlords had increased more rapidly. Source: Government-General of Korea, *Chosen Sotokufu Chosashiryo* (Survey Data of Government-General of Korea), *Series No. 26, Chosen no Kosaku Kanshu* (The Customs of Korean Land Tenure), 1929, Seoul and Government-General of Korea: *Chisei Tokei* (Statistics of Land-tax), 1928-1936, Seoul.

15. Calculated by Takeo Suzuki from *Chosen Sotokufu Nempo* (Statistical Year Book of

Government-General of Korea); T.Suzuki, *Chosen no Keizai* (Korean Economy), Tokyo, 1942, p. 246.

16. Calculated by Chogi Hashimoto from *Chosen Sotokufu Nempo* (Statistical Year Book of Government-General of Korea) of 1937; C. Hashimoto: *Chosen Bei no Kenkyu* (A Study of Korean Rice), 1938, Tokyo, p. 91. Rearranged by Andrew J. Grajdanzev; Also see A.J. Grajdanzev: *Modern Korea*, 1944, New York, p. 111.

17. The owner-farmer of 13.7 percent includes the farmer landlords in this statistic. If we take an assumption that the proportion of farmer landlords of 2.5 percent in 1932 was constant, then the real percentage of owner-farmers of the south Korea paddy-field region would be below 11.2 per cent.

18. Calculated by Kenichi Hisama from Zenrahokudo Nokai (Agricultural Association of North Chŏlla Province); *Zenrahokudo no Nogyojijo* (The Situation of Agriculture in North Chŏlla Province). See, K. Hisama: *Chosen Nogyo no Kendaiteki Yoso* (The Modern Phases of Korean Agriculture), 1935, Tokyo, p. 287.

19. Calculated by Kenich Hisama from his own field survey of Okku County: *ibid.*, pp. 159-210.

20. Calculated by Chŏng Yak-yong: *Simunjip* (Collections of Literature), Vol. 9 in *Chŏng Tasan Chŏnsŏ* (The Complete Works of Chŏng Tasan), Vol. 1, reprinted in 1961, Seoul, p. 198.

21. This cross table might not be fully accurate, but it clearly shows the tendency statistically.

22. Calculated from *Chosen Sotokufu Tokei Nempo* (Statistical Year Book of Government-General of Korea), 1915-1941, Seoul, and from Government-General of Korea: *Chosen Nogyo Tokeihyo* (Statistics of Korean Agriculture), 1941, Seoul.

23. Calculated from *Chosen Sotokufu Tokie Nempo* (Statistical Year Book of Government-General of Korea), 1916-1934, Seoul and from Government-General of Korea: *Chosen Nogyo Tokeyhyo* (Statistics of Korean Agriculture), 1934, Seoul.

24. No accurate statistics had been published, but still we can estimate it indirectly using the statistics of land tax payers. That is, the number of Korean bigger landlords above 100 *Chŏngbo* was 426 households in 1921, 388 households in 1925, and 357 households in 1930, while that of Japanese bigger landlords above 100 *Chŏngbo* was 414 households in 1921, 430 households in 1925, and 538 households in 1930. Source: *Chosen Sotokufu Chosashiryo* (Survey data of Government-General of Korea), *Series No-25, Chosen no Kosaku Kanshu* (The Customs of Korean Land Tenure), 1929, Seoul. and Government-General of Korea: *Chisei Tokei* (Statistics of Land-Tax), 1936, Seoul.

25. The statistics of land tax payers shows that the number of Korean bigger landlords above 100 chŏngbo had decreased from 388 households in 1925 to 351 households in 1933 after the world economic depression, while that of Japanese bigger landlords above 100 Chŏngbo had increased from 530 households in 1925 to 598 households in

1933. Source: *ibid.*, 1929 and 1936, Seoul,

26. The statistics for the land tax payers also show that the number of the Korean small landlords of 10-20 chŏngbo had slightly increased from 29,646 households in 1921 to 32,557 households in 1929. Source: *ibid.*, Seoul, 1929 and 1936.

27. The same statistics for the land tax payers also show that the number of the Japanese small landlord of 10-20 chŏngbo had rapidly increased from 1,544 households of 1921 to 2,677 households of 1929. Source: *ibid.*, 1929 and 1936, Seoul.

28. The statistics for land tax payers show that the Korean small landlords had been severely affected by the world economic depression. That is, the number of Korean small landlords of 10-20 chŏngbo had decreased from 32,557 households in 1929 to 29,993 households in 1934 after the depression. Source: *ibid.*, 1929 and 1936, Seoul.

29. The statistics for land tax payers show that the Korean bigger landlords had been severely affected also by the world economic depression. That is, the number of Korean bigger landlords above 100 chŏngbo had decreased from 380 households in 1929 to 351 households in 1933 after the depression, while that of Japanese bigger landlord had still increased from 534 households in 1929 to 598 households in 1933. Source: *ibid.*, 1929 and 1936, Seoul.

30. If we assume that the farmer landlord percentage of 2.5 percent in 1932 is constant, the percentage of owner-farmers would be below 14.9 percent of the total agricultural households. *cf.* note 292.

31. Calculated by Kamekichi Takahashi from Korean Agricultural Association: *noka Keizai Chosa* (Survey Reports on Economy of Farm-Households), K. Takahashi: *Chosen Kendai Keizairon* (An Essay on Modern Economy of Korea), 1935, Tokyo, p. 228.

32. Calculated by Kenichi Hisama from the Government-General of Korea: *Kosaku ni kansuru Sankojiko* (The Essential References on Land Tenure). K. Hisama: *Chosen nosei no Kadai* (The problems of Korean Agricultureal Policy), Tokyo, 1943, p. 45.

33. This figure for the whole country is calculated from *Chosen Sotokufu Tokei Nempo* (Statistical Year Book of Government-General of Korea) of 1937, 1939, Seoul. The figure for the paddy-field region was calculated by C. Hishimoto and A.J. Grajdanzev. *cf.* note 395.

34. This specific tillers group mainly appeared in the Northeastern mountain areas such as Kangwŏn Province, North and South Hamgyŏng Provinces. They were such very specific groups that one could not find them in ordinary rural society. However, the number of their households was not insignificant. That is, it was about 34 thousand households (1.3 percent of the total agricultural households) in 1926, about 38 thousand households (1.3 percent) in 1930, about 76 thousand households (2.4 percent) in 1935, and about 66 thousand (2.2 percent of total agricultural hoseholds population) in 1940. Source: *Chosen Sotokufu Tokei Nempo* (Statistical Year Book of Government-General of Korea), 1926-1941, Seoul.

35. No accurate direct statistical data is available on this, but still we can see this trend through the statistics of land-tax payers. *Cf.* note 393.

36. I have found many cases of this kind in field survey reports of the Government-General of Korea. However, no accurate statistical data can be presented to prove this description now. Actually, I have met strong opposition from a Korean socio-economic historian on my view that the tenant class realized relatively significant upward mobility in the sociological sense and became freemen, and I was offered case materials for the counterevidence.

37. This controversy originally arose among Japanese Marxist economists and historians and was known as the "Nihon Shihonshugi Ronso" (Controversy on Japanese Capitalism). The group which took the Japanese landlord and tenant rent system as feudal or semi-feudal consisted of Moritaro Yamada who wrote *Nihon Shihonshugino Bunseki* (An Analysis of Japanese Capitalism), 1934, Tokyo and his many followers; the other group which has taken the Japanese landlord and tenant rent system as a modern capitalistic one was formed by Itsuro Mukouzuka who wrote *Nihon Shihonshugi no Shomondai* (The Problems of Japanese Capitalism), 1937, Tokyo and his many followers. This controversy has been going on in Japan for about thirty-five years. Later non-Marxian modern economists and positivistic historians have inevitably gotten involved in this controversy in interpreting the phenomenon of this period, and a tremendous number of papers and books have been published especially in Japan. This paper includes some criticism on that speculative controversy and its theories from a positivistic point of view.

38. In Korea's case, the following are the major works that have taken the land tenure system and tenant rent of the colonial period as feudal or semi-feudal. (a) In Chŏng-sik: *Chosen no Nogyokiko no Bunseki* (An Analysis of Korean Agricultural Organization), Tokyo 1937; (b) Seichi Tobada and Kazushi Okawa: *Chosen Beikoku Keizarion* (An Essay on Korean Rice Economy), 1939, Tokyo; (c) Pak Tong-myo: *Han'guk Nong'ŏp Kyŏngje* (Korean Agricultural Economy), 1961, Seoul; (d) *Pak Kun-chang: Nong'ŏp Kyŏngjehak* (Agricultural Economics), 1962, Seoul; Ch'oe Ho-jin: *Han'guk Kyŏngesa* (An Economic History of Korea), 1962, Seoul.

39. In Korea's case, the following works are the major literature which have taken the land tenure system and tenant rent of the colonial period as a modern capitalistic one. (a) Pak Mun-byŏng: "Sezenkeizai (Natural Economy)," 1935, Seoul; (b) Kuranojo Tsumagari: "Chosen ni okeru Kosakumondai no Hattenkadei (The Development of Land Tenure Problem in Korea)" in Keijo Imperial University: *Chosen Keizai no Kenkyu* (Studies of Korean Economy), Tokyo, 1929; (c) Kenichi Hisama: *Chosen Nogyo no Kindaiteki Yoso* (The Modern Phases of Korean Agriculture), 1935, Tokyo; (d) Kim Jun-bo "Kumyung Chabon Haui Yŏngsenong ui Songgyoik-Ilche Haui Yŏngsesojakje rul Chungsimuro (The Caracteristics of Small Peasant under the

Financial Cpital– especially in reference to the land-tenure system under Japanese Colonial Rule)" in Seoul National University: *Seoul University Journal, Humanities and Social Sciences*, Vol. 5, Seoul, 1957; (e) Kim Jun-bo: *Nong'ŏp Kyŏngjehak Sosŏl* (Agricultural Economics), Seoul, 1967.

40. The major survey reports and primary source material used in this research are as follows: (a) Chŏng Yak-yong: *Mokminsimsŏ* (The True Guide Book for Catering People) in *Chŏng Tasan Chŏnsŏ* (The Complete Works of Chŏng Tasan), Vol. 3, reprinted in 1961, Seoul; (b) Chŏng Yak-yong: *Simunjip* (The Collections of Literature) in *Chŏng Tasan Chŏnsŏ* (The Complete Works of Chŏng Tasan), Vol. 1, reprinted in 1961, Seoul; (c) Takjibu (The Ministry of Finance of the Great Han Empire Government): *T'ojijosa Ch'amgosŏ* (The References on Land Survey), Vol. 1, 2 & 3, 1905-1910, Seoul; (d) Tokanfu (Residence-General of Korea): *Kankoku Tochinosan Chosahokoku* (Reports on Korea's Land and Agricultural Products), 1905-1910, Tokyo; (e) Chosen Sotokufu (Government-General of Korea): *Chosen no Kanshu Chosa Hokokusho* (Survey Reports on Korean Customs), 1912, Seoul; (f) Chosen Sotokufu Rinji Tochichosakyoku (Special Bureau of Land Survey of Government-General of Korea): *Chosen Tochichosajihyo Hokokusho* (Reports of Land Survey Work in Korea), 1918, Seoul; (g) Chosen Sotokufu Rinji Tochosakyoku: *Chosen Tochichosajihyo Hokokusho Tsuiroku* (A Supplement to the Reports of Land Survey Work in Korea), 1919, Seoul; (h) Chosen Sotokufu Chosashiryo (Survey Data of Government-General of Korea), Series No. 26, *Chosen no Kosaku Kanshu* (The Customs of Land Tenure of Korea), 1929, Seoul; (i) Chosen Sotokufu Chusuin (The Privy Council of Government-General of Korea): *Kosaku ni Kansuru Kanshu Chosasho* (The Survey Report on the Customs of Land Tenure), 1930, Seoul; (j) Chosen Nokai (Korean Agricultural Association): *Chosen no Kosaku Kanko-Chidai to Kanko* (The Practices of Land Tenure of Korea, its Trends and Practices), 1930, Seoul; (k) Government-General of Korea: *Chosen no Kosaku Kanko* (The Practices of Land Tenure of Korea), Vol. 1 and 2, 1932, Seoul; (l) Government-General of Korea; *Chosen ni okeru Kosaku ni Kansuru Sankojikyo Tekiyo* (The Essential References on Land Tenure in Korea), 1934, Seoul; (m) Government-General of Korea: *Chisei Tokei* (Statistics of Land Tax), 1928-1936, Seoul; (n) Government-General of Korea: *Chosen Nogyo Tokeihyo* (Statistics of Korean Agriculture), 1934-1941, Seoul; (o) Government-General of Korea: *Chosen Sotokufu Tokei Nempo* (Statistical Year Book of Government-General of Korea), 1913-1941, Seoul; (p) Government-General of Korea: *Chosen no Nogyo* (Korean Agriculture), 1931-1942, Seoul.

41. My theory of "compound rent" of Korea in the transition period will be reinforced if we can find out similar evidence in other countries' histories. Fortunately, we can find such one in "metayer-rent" of eighteenth and early nineteenth century French agriculture. However, French metayer-rent of the transition period developed in the

form of "rent + profit," while Korean tenant rent of the transition period developed in the form of "rent + interest." Anyway, it is an encouraging fact that we can find "compound rent" in the transition period even in European social and economic history.

6. Land Reform in Korea, 1950

1. Introduction

In all agricultural societies status-role designations are closely related to variations in the rights to use and control land. Various social ranks existed in the traditional Korean society were closely associated with the land tenure system of those days. Thus, the change in land tenure in contemporary Korea is of particular interest to social historians and social scientists. This paper examines the background, process, and results of a land reform which was tardily carried out in the liberated Korea after World War II.

It has been generally recognized that one of the pressing national tasks in Korea after World War II was a land reform, since the land tenure system had been the major obstacle to any social and economic development until Korea's liberation from Japan. In the pre-reform land tenure system the landlords had private ownership of vast acreage of cultivated lands, let their lands to landless farmers, and collected a high rate of rent from them. In fact, the landlords constituted a small minority of people but they owned the major part of arable land and could control a majority of farmers. In 1930, for instance, 77.5 per cent of the total households in Korea were tenant-farmers or part tenants (owner-tenant), only 3.6 per cent were landlords, and the rest included owner-farmers and a small percentage of "fire-field tillers." (See Table 2) In that year the landlords actually owned two-thirds of the total paddy-fields and nearly one-half of the total dry-fields.

There were two kinds of landlords: the absentee-landlord and farmer-landlord. However, it should be noted that most of the Korean landlords were parasitic absentee-landlords who never undertook operation of farm at all but simply leased out all of their lands to landless farmers and collected a high rate of rent from them. The average rate of tenant rent was between 55-60 per cent of the gross products and its form of payment was mostly share-cropping. A strange fact was that, in spite of the development of modern capitalistic economic organization in urban area and its impact on rural agricultural sectors, the rate of rent had been gradually increasing during the colonial period, comparing with that of the Chosŏn dynasty land tenancy, as shown in Table 1.

(Table 1)   Increase in Rate of Tenant Rent

Periods	*Chongjo* *	*Tajo* **	*Chipjo* ***
Chosŏn dynasty period (early 19C)	33-50%	50%	33-50%
1920	40-50%	50%	39-50%
1930	50-60%	50-55%	50-55%

Source : Yong-Ha Shin, Land Tenure System in Korea, 1910-1945
Social Science Journal, 1973. UNESCO/Korea
 * *Fixed amount of rent was collected regardless of yearly harvest.*
 ** *Share-cropping at a fixed rate, hence the amount fluctuated depending on yearly harvest*
*** *The rent was negotiated yearly.*

The rent was collected in two ways : rent in kind and rent in money. In 1930, for example, 93.9 per cent of tenant rent for paddy fields were collected in kind and only 6.1 per cent in money. For dry fields, the proportion of produce-rent in kind was 92.1 per cent against money-rent of only 7.9 per cent.

Korean tenant-farmers were burdened not only with tenant rent, but also with land-tax and various kinds of public and landlord's private imposts. In 1930, for example 48 per cent of the total tenant-farmers were charged with land-tax which was supposed to be charged to landlords.

This kind of land tenure system had greatly hindered the increase in agricultural production and productivity, since the increased share of production was returned only to the absentee-landlords and there never existed any incentives for tenant-farmers to increase their investment in work and input supply. The land tenure system in this period contributed only to Japanese imperialists who faithfully delivered agriculture products from Korea to Japan to support her industrialization. For such tenancy of high rate of rent functioned as the most efficient and convenient apparatus to collect surplus food (rice and other grains) through landlords, suppressing the food consumption of Korean farmers to a very low subsistence level.

Moreover, the land tenure system had intensified the chronic poverty of Korean peasants. Tenant-farmers and owner-tenants were always deprived and poverty-stricken. Even owner-farmers were not in a better condition. Most owner-farmers were also very poor, since they were small indepen-dent farmers who could not afford expensive new farming practices which were forced to be adopted under the Japanese colonial agricultural policy. Many small independent farmers were actually compelled to sell their lands to pay off their debts and finally fell into the position of tenant-farmers.

All the burdens levied on peasants by land tenancy had made Korean farmers extremely poor. According to the statistics of Government-General of Korea, 68.1 per cent of tenants were indigent farmers who usually suffered from hunger in the spring season in 1930. Similarly, 37.5 per cent of owner-tenants and 18.4 per cent of owner-farmers were also indigent.

(Table 2) Percentage Distribution of Farm Households by Types of Land Tenure

(1913-1942)

Year	Landlords	Owner-Farmers	Owner-Tenant	Tenants	Agricultural Laborers	Fire-field Tillers
1913	3.1%	22.8%	32.4%	41.7%	-	-
1914	1.8	22.0	35.1	41.1	-	-
1915	1.5	21.7	40.8	36.0	-	-
1916	2.5	20.1	40.6	36.8	-	-
1917	2.8	19.6	40.2	37.4	-	-
1918	3.1	19.7	39.2	37.6	-	-
1919	3.4	19.7	39.2	37.6	-	-
1920	3.3	19.5	37.4	39.8	-	-
1921	3.6	19.6	36.6	40.2	-	-
1922	3.7	19.7	35.8	40.8	-	-
1923	3.7	19.5	36.2	41.6	-	-
1924	3.8	19.4	34.6	42.2	-	-
1925	3.8	19.9	33.2	43.2	-	-
1926	3.8	19.1	32.5	43.3	-	1.3
1927	3.8	18.7	32.7	43.8	-	1.0
1928	3.7	18.3	32.0	44.9	-	1.2
1929	3.7	18.0	31.5	45.6	-	1.2
1930	3.6	17.6	31.0	46.5	-	1.3
1931	3.6	17.0	29.6	47.4	-	1.4
1932	3.6	16.3	25.3	52.8	-	2.1
1932	-	18.4	24.9	51.8	2.9	2.0
1933	-	18.1	24.1	51.9	3.1	2.8
1934	-	18.0	24.0	51.9	3.4	2.7
1935	-	17.9	24.1	51.9	3.6	2.5
1936	-	17.9	24.1	51.8	3.8	2.4
1937	-	18.0	25.1	51.7	3.8	2.4
1938	-	18.1	23.9	51.9	3.8	2.3
1939	-	17.9	23.7	52.4	3.7	2.3
1940	-	18.0	23.3	53.0	3.3	2.2
1941	-	17.9	23.5	53.7	3.0	1.9
1942	-	17.4	23.9	53.8	3.1	1.8

* *The statistical reporting system was changed in 1932.*

Calculated from Government-General of Korea: Chosen Sotokufu Tokei Nempo (Statistical Year Book of Government-General of Korea), Seoul, 1923-1941, from

Government-General of Korea: Chosen Nohyo Tokeihyo (Statistics of Korean Agriculture), Seoul, 1934-1941, and from Government-General of Korea: Chosen no Nogyo (Korean Agriculture), Seoul, 1931-1942.

During the Japanese occupation period, the proportion of independent farmers declined considerably and the rate of tenancy gradually increased. At the end of Chosŏn dynasty period, a sizable number of independent owner-farmers had existed as a middle class in rural communities although a slow decline had begun in the later Chosŏn dynasty period. In the colonial period, however, the fall of owner-farmers to tenant-farmers had become a nation-wide tendency as the encroachment and buying of land had been accelerated by Japanese and Korean landlords. As shown in Table 2, the proportion of owner-farmers had fallen from 22.8 per cent in 1913 to 16.3 per cent in 1932. Since 1932 the Government-General of Korea had changed the form of statistics to cover up the rapid decline of owner-farmers. Absentee-landlords were omitted altogether from agricultural population statistics; farmer-landlords were combined with owner-farmers; and a new category of agricultural laborers was introduced. Even with the modified categorization, the rapid decline of the owner-farmers had continued with a drop from 18.4 per cent in 1932 to 17.4 per cent in 1942. The proportion of owner-tenants had also declined from 40.8 per cent in 1915 to 23.3 per cent in 1942. On the other hand, the proportion of pure tenant-farmers had markedly increased from 36.0 per cent in 1925 to 53.8 per cent in 1942. If we combine these tenant-farmers with owner-tenants, more than three-fourths (77.7%) of agricultural households were involved in tenure relations with absentee-landlords in 1942.

The land tenure system under the Japanese colonial rule was so cruel that Korean tenant-farmers offered stubborn resistance against the land tenure system and the Japanese colonial rule over Korea. For instance, the number of cases of tenancy group-dispute had strikingly increased from 15 cases in 1920 to 31,799 cases in 1937. Most of the tenancy disputes, however, were not settled on the basis of reasonable bargain of both parties involved, but they were one-sidedly oppressed by the authorities of the Japanese Government-General of Korea who had always supported landlords. Japanese were so busy to facilitate the delivery of Korean foods to Japan, exploiting the efficient collection mechanism of agricultural products through the land tenancy. Therefore, in spite of the great discontent of Korean tenant-farmers and most of Korean people, the land tenure system could survive until the end of World War II with the strong support of Japanese colonial authorities. Under such circumstances, a land reform was urgently called for as soon as the Japanese colonial rule was collapsed.

2. Preparation of Land Reform

1) Attempt of First Land Reform

When Korea was liberated from the Japanese occupation in 1945, the demand of tenant-farmers for a land reform could not be overlooked, otherwise a violent revolt was imminent. And, it was quite certain that universal suffrage was to be given to the farmers for the first time in Korean history. Thus, a land reform was imperative to attain national unity by abolishing such an anachronistic semi-feudal land tenure system which had been serving to create a wide gap between the wealthy and the poor. It was also so urgent to attain overall national socio-economic development by increasing agricultural production and productivity. So, it was quite natural for all the political parties and social organizations at that time to advocate a land reform.

Although a land reform was the most imperative task of the nation after the liberation from Japan, different opinions prevailed as to the method of implementation among different social groups, and various proposals were presented by political parties and social organizations. Under strong political and social pressures from Korean people, the first attempt of land reform was undertaken by the American Military Government which came into being on September 8, 1945.

At first, the American Military Government promulgated Ordinance No. 9, "On the Determination of the Ceiling of Rent Rate," on October 5, 1945. The ordinance was intended to slash the high rate of rent, regulating the ceiling of rent rate at one-third of annual yields. By this measure, tenant rent should never exceed 33 per cent of gross products for a given year. The reduction of tenant rent was favorably received by Korean farmers, but they were not completely satisfied. In Spring of 1946, farmers strongly demanded the early implementation of land reform and some tenant-farmers even started radical movements.

In Spring of 1947, through the consultative body of Korean agricultural expertises, the Legislature Assembly (立法議院) and the American Military Government jointly drafted the South Korea Land Reform Law and referred it to the provisional legislation. The essence of this provisional law was to let the to-be-established Korean Government purchase tenanted lands from landlords and sell them to tenant-farmers at the same prices, with the ceiling of 2 *chŏngbo* (one *chŏngbo* is equivalent to 2.45 acres) per farm household. The price of the land to be sold was 300 per cent of the average annual yields of past five years, and should be paid in equal annual installments over a 15 year period. That is, the yearly payment was set at 20 per cent of average annual yields in kind.

This provisional South Korea Land Reform Law was generally viewed as for landlords' interests. However, some assembly men who seemingly represented landlords still opposed these measures, and finally the Legislature Assembly shelved the provisional law on the assertion that such a law should be enacted after the establishment of Korean Government.

American Military Government discontented with the evasion of Legislature Assembly and decided to take an initiative for the execution of land reform in Korea. It seemed to be intended to satisfy the aspiration of tenant-farmers for landownership, to prepare for the establishment of western form of democracy, and to avert the pressure of a radical revolutionary movement. On March 22, 1948, the Military Government promulgated Ordinance No. 173 to start the distribution of the government-vested lands owned by New Korea Company (新韓公社) among tenant-farmers. New Korea Company had been organized by the American Military Government to administer formerly Japanese-owned farm lands including those owned by the Japanese Oriental Development Company. New Korea Company owned a total of 282,480 *chŏngbo* of farm land which represented 13.1 per cent of the total farm land in South Korea. This included mostly fertile paddy-fields in plain regions. More specifically, the Company owned 205,988 *chŏngbo* of paddy-fields which actually represented 16.6 per cent of the total acreage of paddy-fields in South Korea.

As shown in Table 3, the American Military Government actually distributed 189,518 *chŏngbo* of paddy-fields and 56,036 *chŏngbo* of dry-fields to 554,067 tenant-farmers. The distributed paddy-fields represented 92 per cent of the total paddy-fields acreage owned by the New Korea Company and 87 per cent of the total dry-fields owned by the New Korea Company. The distributed lands by the American Military Government constituted 29.6 per cent of the total tenanted lands in South Korea at the time. More than one-third (35.1%) of the total tenanted paddy-fields were so distributed.

The first attempt of land reform by the American Military Government greatly influenced the later land reform of Korea in 1950. When the subsequent Land Reform was carried out by the Government of the Republic of Korea, the distributed lands by the American Military Government was recognized and confirmed as an established fact after reducing the price of the lands according to newly legislated Land Reform Act, within the limits of 3 *chŏngbo* per farm household. Since the first attempt of land reform by the

American Military Government had regulated the ceiling of the distribution at 2 *chŏngbo*, the results of the first attempt of land reform could be subsumed and recognized as established facts in the Land Reform by the newly-born Government of the Republic of Korea.

(Table 3) Distributed Land by American Military Government

unit : *chŏngbo*

Area	Administered Land		Distributed Land	
	Paddy-field	Dry-field	Paddy-field	Dry-field
Seoul	24,453	10,713	22,243	10,168
Taejŏon	28,962	11,024	24,648	10,216
Taegu	13,499	6,503	13,065	5,761
Pusan	26,084	7,327	22,946	5,161
Iri	47,905	8,496	56,828	8,610
Mokpo	55,085	18,568	49,788	16,120
Total	205,988	62,631	189,518	56,036

Source : Ministry of Agriculture and Forestry

2) Legislation

When the Government of the Republic of Korea was established on August 15, 1948, the land reform again became the most urgent task of the newly-born Republic. Several organizations and authorities proposed their own outlines of the land reform. Out of these, two major drafts emerged and they were presented by the Ministry of Agriculture and Forestry and by the Industry Committee of National Assembly.

In November of 1948, the Ministry of Agriculture of Forestry presented a draft of land reform which was prepared by agricultural specialists. This draft proposed that the state purchase the lands of absentee-landlords and excess farm lands of large farmers who owned excess of 2 *chŏngbo*. The price was set at 150 per cent of average annual yields, and landlords were to be compensated in equal annual installments over a 10 year period. And, the Government was to sell the lands to tenant-farmers with the price of 120 per cent of average annual yields in equal annual installments over a 6 year period. The difference between the prices of purchasing and selling of lands was to be appropriated from the payments of tenant-farmers for the government-vested lands and government finance. The draft also set the ceiling of distribution and possession of lands at 2 *chŏngbo* per farm household.

In March of 1949, on the other hand, the Industry Committee of National Assembly presented another proposal of land reform after careful study of the Ministry's draft. The draft of the Committee was designed to purchase by the Government the lands of absentee-landlords and the land of large farmers, which exceeded 3 *chŏngbo* per farm household, with the provision of issuing Land-value Bills to compensate landowners. The price of purchasing of these lands was to be determined on the basis of 300 per cent of average annual yields. The draft provided that these lands should be distributed by the Government among tenant-farmers and owner-farmers of submarginal scale of operation, with the repayments to be made in equal annual installments over a 10 year period at the same price of purchase.

On April 27, 1949, the National Assembly amended its Committee proposal and finally passed the Korean Land Reform Bill. In this Bill the price of compensation for landlords was cut down to 150 per cent of average annual yields, and the rate of repayment by farmers to 125 per cent. The difference was to be appropriated by Government finance. The term of repayments was also shortened to 5 years. On May 2, 1949, the Bill was transferred from the National Assembly to the Executive Branch of the Government to be promulgated and enacted.

However, the Bill was sent back to the National Assembly, calling for a revision of rates of compensations for landlords and repayments by tenant-farmers to be equally coordinated at the same price, since the Government had no enough finance to pay off the difference between 150 per cent compensation rate and 125 per cent repayment rate of average annual yields.

In January of 1950, the Industry Committee which conspicuously declined to be conservative, reproposed a revised land reform bill to the National Assembly, calling for a revision of compensation and repayment rates up to 240 per cent of average annual yields over a 8 year period, with the yearly payment set at 30 per cent. The proposed Bill was turned down by a general meeting of the National Assembly and it was finally agreed to fix the price of lands for purchase and sale by the government at the same rates of 150 per cent of average annual yields over a 5 year period. It was the final setting of the legislation of the Land Reform Act of Korea. On March 10, 1950, at last the Government promulgated the Land Reform Act as Law No. 108 and undertook the execution of the Land Reform starting April 10, 1950.

3. Execution of Land Reform

1) Land Purchased

The Land Reform Act of 1950 designated two types of farm lands to be redistributed: the government-purchased lands and government-vested lands. Government-purchased lands included the farmlands listed below:

(1) Farmlands owned by absentee-landlords.

(2) Farmlands owned by non-self-cultivators.

(3) Farmlands which exceeded 3 *chŏngbo* per farm household.

On the other hand, the government-vested lands comprised of the following farmlands:

(1) Farmlands owned by the Government.

(2) Farmlands confiscated by the Government (formerly Japanese-owned lands).

(3) Ownerless Farmlands.

The Land Reform Act, however, exempted many farmlands from the reform. The most distinguished exemptions were as follows:

(1) Farmland which was less than 500 *pyŏng* (about 0.17 *chŏngbo*) per household, owned by non-farmers as vegetable gardens.

(2) Orchards, nursery gardens, mulberry fields, and other farmlands cultivated with perennial plants.

(3) Farmland which was planned to be used for purposes other than farming by the Government, public institutions, and educational institutions as public ground, school sites, school experimental stations, military park, municipal planning lands, road and highway sites, waterway sites, reservoir sites, power plant, and dam sites, etc.

(4) Farmland cultivated by all types of schools, religious institutions and public welfare institutions.

(5) Farmland which was used for some special purposes such as academic researches and experiments.

(6) Farmland which was set aside for the care of ancestral tombs designated as *Wito* (位土), with a ceiling of 0.2 *chŏngbo* per tomb.

(7) Reclaimed lands unfinished.

(8) Reclaimed lands finished after the Enactment of the Land Reform Act.

The above exceptions allowed the landlords and large-scale farmers to evade the land reform. Of course, the Land Committees at the various administrative level were organized to administer and supervise the purchase and sale of lands. However, the Land Committees were usually composed of influential local magnates. With the approval of the Committee, mayors or provincial governors could defer certain purchases or sales. Even those landowners who had abandoned farming were allowed to defer their sale of lands to the government if they could convince the Committee that they were returning to farming. Actually a vast acreage of farmlands owned by various types of landlords could be left untouched by the reform. The Government actually could purchase only 331,766 *chŏngbo* of farmlands (226,465 *chŏngbo* of paddy fields and 105,301 *chŏngbo* of dry-fields) which represented 63.4 per cent of the total lands expected to be purchased.

2) Compensation for Landlords

The Government purchased the lands of absentee-landlords and large farmers with Land-value Bills called *Chika Chŭngkwŏn* (地價證券) which were issued in advance by the Government for the land value compensation expressed in the amount of produce such as rice and barley on the basis of 150 per cent of average annual yields over the past five year period. For the paddy fields, the Government chose the standard rice-fields with average fertility and calculated 150 per cent of average annual rice production of past 5 years. For the dryfields, the Government calculated the average annual yields of the highest priced crop of past 5 years. However, the actual calculation of compensation for landlords was carried out on the basis of sliding scale according to the acreage of the landownership of each landlord, as shown in Table 4.

(Table 4) Sliding Scale of Compensation for Landlords

Size of Compensation	Sliding Scale of diminution
Less than 75 *sŏk*	Non applied
75-100	3% of Excess of 75 *sŏk*
100-130	5% of Excess of 100 *sŏk*
130-200	8% of Excess of 130 *sŏk*
200-400	12% of Excess of 200 *sŏk*
400-1,000	17% of Excess of 400 *sŏk*
1,000-2,000	23% of Excess of 1,000 *sŏk*
2,000-5,000	30% of Excess of 2,000 *sŏk*
5,000-10,000	38% of Excess of 5,000 *sŏk*
more than 10,000 *sŏk*	47% of Excess of 10,000 *sŏk*

Source: Ministry of Agriculture and Forestry

The Government was to pay the compensation in cash to landlords according to the Land-value Bill in five annual payments, by calculating the legal cash price of the noted amount of crops of a given year. However, in the event that the amount of compensation was relatively small or the landlords were public institutions authorized by the Government, the payment was to be stretched.

The Land Reform Act originally intended to help landlords to transform themselves into industrial capitalists or entrepreneurs. When a landlord wanted to use his Land-value Bills as industrial capital or he applied for a loan from public financial institutions, the Minister of Finance had obligation to guarantee a low-interest loan. And, when a landlord wanted to buy government facilities at disposal such as factories, mines, ships, fishing grounds, breweries, printing facilities, cleaning mills, orchards, nursery gardens, mulberry fields, cocooneries, forests, reclaimed lands, etc., the Government had the obligation to give preference to the Land-value Bill holders. A small number of large-scale landlords were successful to establish themselves as industrial capitalists, taking advantage of the Land Reform Act.

3) Distribution of Lands to Farmers

Lands so purchased by the government and government-vested lands were to be sold to such farm operators as those who could be expected to devote themselves to farming according to the following priority:

(1) Tenant-farmers who had been actually cultivating the tenant lands at the time of the enactment of the Land Reform Act.

(2) Tenant-farmers or owner-farmer who were cultivating relatively small holdings comparing with his family labor force.

(3) Bereaved families of patriots who had experiences of agricultural operation.

(4) Agricultural laborers who had family labor for independent agricultural operation

(5) Returned countrymen from abroad whose original occupation was farming.

The Government adopted a scoring system to gauge the capacity of farm operation for the purpose of distributing the purchased lands. This scoring scheme is shown in Table 5.

(Table 5) Score for Family Capacity of Farming

Type of Resource	Score
1. Number of Family Members	30
2. Family Labor Force	60
3. Agricultural Implement	10
Total	100

Source: Ministry of Agriculture and Forestry

However, the Government decided not to apply the scoring system in case of ① tenant-farmers who were actually cultivating the tenant land at the time of the enactment of the Land Reform Act, and ② tenant-farmers or owner-farmers who were cultivating less than 3 chŏngbo. Therefore, the scoring system was only applied to ① tenant-farmers who were operating relatively very small holdings comparing with his family labor force, ② bereaved families of patriots, ③ agricultural laborers and ④ the returned countrymen from abroad. In practice, since average scale of operation of tenant-farmers was very small, the ownership right was transferred, in most cases, to the tenant-farmer who was actually cultivating the land. In general, the land reform merely transferred ownership to cultivators, leaving the size of farm almost unchanged. It was especially disadvantageous to small scale tenant-farmers and owner-farmers.

As mentioned earlier, the Land Committees at various administrative levels made decisions and supervised the redistribution of lands. First, the local government authorities drew up the lists of redistributable lands for every eligible farm household. The Land Committee reviewed and finalized the lists of redistributable lands. Then local governmental authorities opened the lists to the public and asked farmers to take their objections, if any, to the Land Committee within 10 days.

Finally it should be noted that the Land Reform Act exempted tenant-farmers from various taxes associated with landownership rights such as land-registration tax and immovable-acquisition tax.

4) Conservation of Distributed Lands

The Land Reform Act of 1950 provided for the transfer of ownership of the distributed lands to the cultivators as soon as the distribution was carried out. However, the Land Reform Act provisionally prohibited any sale, donation and mortgage of the distributed lands until the distributed land was completely paid off. When payments for the distributed land were delinquent without any acceptable reasons, the Government had the right to institute a suit to the court for the return of the distributed land to the Government. If any lands were returned to the government for such reasons, the Government was to pay the farmer over 75 per cent of the already paid amount by farmers plus the costs of land improvement. The Government had the same obligations when a farmer chose to quit farming or changed his occupation and decided to move to cities before he completed the repayment.

According to the Land Reform Act, the Government and local Land Committee had the right to consolidate, exchange, divide and improve the distributable lands, and also to change the use of the lands in order to enhance the agricultural productivity. In reality, however, little land consolidation works were carried out during the land reform. The Act also prohibited strictly any kind of new tenancy, lease or trusteeship of land operation, not only in the distributed farmlands but also in the original owner-farmers' lands. By this measure, the Land Reform Act of 1950 permanently abolished any forms of land tenancy in Korea. However, since the redistribution of lands was not effectively completed, some land tenancy was left illegally even though it was not significant.

4. Immediate Achievements of Land Reform

1) Effects of Distribution of Lands

We have two different sets of statistics about the immediate achievements of the land reform. The first one was compiled by the Ministry of Agriculture and Forestry immediately after the execution of the land reform. Another was prepared by the Korean National Agricultural Cooperative Federation more than 10 years after the land reform. Since the second source excluded the lost acreage of the distributed lands during the Korean War, the figures in the second source slightly underestimate the results of actual land reform.

(Table 6) Results of the Distribution of Lands

	Paddy field (in *chŏngbo*)	Dry field (in *chŏngbo*)	Total	No. of Household
Government-purchased Land	226,465	105,301	331,766	918,548
Government-vested Land	189,518	56,036	235,554	727,632
Total	415,983	161,337	557,320	1,646,180

Source : Ministry of Agriculture and Forestry

According to the first source, a total of 331,766 *chŏngbo* of government-purchased land was distributed to 918,548 farm households and 235,554 *chŏngbo* of government-vested land to 727,632 farm households. As shown in Table 6, 415,983 *chŏngbo* of paddy field and 161,337 *chŏngbo* of dry field were redistributed by the reform. According to the second statistics, on the other hand, a total of 470,022 *chŏngbo* of lands including 352,410 *chŏngbo* of paddy field and 117,612 *chŏngbo* of dry field, was distributed by the reform.

When we compare the first set of statistics with the tenant lands at the end of 1945, only 39.3 per cent of the tenanted acreage was redistributed by the land reform: 47.6 per cent of the tenanted paddy field and 27.8 per cent of dry field. When the same comparison is made with the tenanted acreage of June of 1949 which was one year before the execution of the land reform, only 69.4 per cent of the tenanted acreage was redistributed: 77.0 per cent of the tenanted paddy field and 51.3 per cent of the tenanted dry field. (see Table 7)

(Table 7) Comparison of Distributed Lands with Tenanted Lands (A)

Type of land	Tenanted Lands (in 1,000 *chŏngbo*)		Distributed Lands (C)	Percentage	
	Dec. 1945 (A)	June 1949 (B)		(C/A)%	(C/B)%
Paddy field	890	540	416	46.7%	77.0%
Dry field	580	291	161	27.8	51.3
Total field	1,470	831	577	39.3	69.4

Source: Ministry of Agriculture and Forestry

(Table 8) Comparison of Distributed Lands with Tenanted Lands (B)

Type of land	Tenanted Lands (in *chŏngbo*)		Distributed Lands (C)	Percentage	
	Dec. 1945 (A)	June 1949 (B)		(C/A)%	(C/B)%
Paddy field	895,313	560,196	352,410	39.36%	62.91%
Dry field	552,046	280,067	117,612	21.30	51.57
Total field	1,447,359	840,263	470,022	32.47	55.94

Source: National Agricultural Cooperative Federation

On the other hand, when we compare the second set of statistics with the tenanted lands at the end of 1945, only 32.5 per cent was redistributed by the reform: 39.36 per cent of the tenanted paddy field and 21.30 per cent of the tenanted dry field. Similarly, only 55.9 per cent of the tenanted acreage as of June, 1949 was redistributed by the reform: 62.9 per cent of the tenanted paddy field and 51.6 per cent of the tenanted dry field. (see Table 8)

Again, when we compare the first set of statistics with the actual goal of the reform of estimated in 1949, only 69.2 per cent of the goal was reached by the reform: 76.1 per cent of the estimated goal of distributable paddy field and 55.2 per cent of the estimated goal of distributable dry field. When the second set of statistics was compared with the goal of the reform estimated in 1949, only 56.4 per cent of the goal was reached: 64.5 per cent of the estimated goal of distributable dry field. (see Table 9)

It is clear that the immediate achievement of the land reform was far behind the estimated goal. The following reasons may be responsible for this account.

(Table 9) Comparison of Distributed Lands with Goal of Distribution

unit: *chungbo*

Type of land	(C) Goal of Distribution	(A) Distributed Lands*	(B) Distributed Lands**	(A/C)%	(B/C)%
Paddy field	546,410	415,983	352,410	76.1%	64.5%
Dry field	292,472	161,337	117,612	55.2	40.2
Total lands	833,882	557,320	470,022	69.2	56.4

*Source : * Ministry of Agriculture and Forestry*
*** National Agricultural Cooperative Federation*

First, it took too long to deliberate the legislation of the Land Reform. By the time the Act was put into effect, vast acreage of lands in the possession of landlords had been turned over to tenant-farmers either through 'black market' sales or credit sale at a higher rate than the price regulated by the Land Reform Act. Owing to social instability and uneasiness after World War II, landlords were already disposing their lands at their convenience. This can be evidenced by the fact that the lands transferred to tenant-farmers under the Land Reform Act of 1950 did not exceed 40 per cent of the total tenanted lands at the end of World War II.

Secondly, since the Land Reform Act allowed so many exceptions, surveillance over the execution of the land reform was very difficult and many landlords could manage to evade the reform. Even those landlords who had abandoned farming were allowed to defer sales of their lands if they were considered by the Government or the Land Committee as returning to farming. Actually the Land Committees were composed of influential local magnates. Moreover, landlords were given the right to entrust the operation of their lands to caretakers of their ancestral grave with the limit of 2 *tanbo* per tomb. Also, those farmlands owned by authorized schools, social welfare institutions and public organizations were excluded from the reform. Thus, vast acreage of lands earmarked for sale escaped the redistribution. While tenant-farmers were destitute of influential political power of their own, the power of local magnates was so strong that they could easily incorporate their lands as properties of school foundations or as lands set aside for disguised graveyards. Because of such irregularities, the land reform was carried out far less effectively than originally expected. This can be evidenced by the fact that the lands transferred to tenant farmers by the land reform did not exceed 70 per cent of the originally expected acreage.

2) Repayments of Farmers

The results of the repayment by farmers were far less than satisfactory. By the year of 1954 which was legal termination year of repayment, 43 per cent of required amount of repayment were still unpaid. (see Table 10)

(Table 10) Repayment of Farmers for Distributed Lands by 1954

unit : *sŏk*

	Required Amount of Repayment (A)	Repaid Amount	Unpaid Amount (B)	(B/A)%
Government-purchased Land	5,814,665	3,600,626	2,214,029	38%
Government-vested Land	4,398,375	2,201,790	2,196,585	50
Total	10,213,030	5,802,416	4,410,614	43

*Source : * Ministry of Agriculture and Forestry*
*** National Agricultural Cooperative Federation*

Following reasons can be considered for this unsatisfactory result: First, it was actually too heavy burden for former tenant-farmers to pay for the distributed lands at the rate of 30 per cent of average annual yield over a 5 year period. Farmers had already been suffered from the chronic poverty and yet they had to make the required payments even when they had bad harvests. This was already too heavy a burden for farmers to bear.

Secondly, farmers were required to pay land income tax at the rate between 5 per cent and 25 per cent of their yearly harvests according to the sliding scale on the basis of the farm size. For instance, a farmer who owned 1 *chŏngbo* was required to pay 23 per cent of his annual harvest as the land income tax. Such a high rate of land income tax was also a heavy burden for that farmer, considering that he was formerly a poor tenant farmer.

Thirdly, farmers had to bear a heavy burden of public imposts during the Korean War. The local governments imposed various kinds of taxes and imposts on farmers because farmers were usually stable sources of public finance at the time of a war. Actually it was recorded that more then 50 different taxes and imposts were levied on the poor shoulders of farmers during the Korean War. In other words, with all payments combined the charges imposed upon farmers for over the 5 year period were heavier than the tenant rents imposed on them before the land reform. For instance, a farmer with 1 *chŏngbo* was required to pay ① 30 per cent of annual yield as repayment for his distributed land, ② 23 per cent of annual yield as land income tax and ③ about 10 per cent of annual yield as his public imposts. Actually, that farmer was required to pay a sum total of 63 per cent of average annual yield for over a 5 year period. This was really heavy a burden for indigent Korean farmers. This conclusion can be reinforced by the fact that legally appointed completion year of repayment, about 99 per cent of repayments for the distributed lands were paid 9 years after the legal termination of repayment.

3) Compensations for Landlords

The compensation for landlords for their lands sold was unexpectedly far behind the schedule. Only 28 per cent of the required amount of the compensation had been paid by the legally appointed year of 1954. The Government could pay the estimated amounts of compensation for landlords only in two years of 1950 and 1951, and after that the Government was unable to pay according to the schedule. This means that the Land-value Bill which was given to the landlords for their lands sold was not exchanged in currency by the Government as designated in the Land Reform Act of 1950. By 1963, nine years after the appointed completion year of compensation, 97.2 per cent of the compensation-value was paid for landlords, with devaluated price since the fixed legal price was applied by the Government. (see Table 11)

(Table 11) Compensation for Landlords for Purchased-land by 1954

unit : Thousand *won*

Year	Required Amount of Compensation (A)	Compensated Amount (B)	Uncompensated Amount	(B/A) %
1950	318,805	302,115	16,690	95
1951	1,265,984	1,242,290	23,695	98
1952	3,885,537	2,620,123	1,265,414	67
1953	3,885,537	91,079	3,794,458	0.2
1954	5,971,625	-	5,971,624	-
Total	15,327,448	4,255,607	11,071,881	28

Source : Ministry of Agriculture and Forestry

As mentioned earlier, the Land Reform Act originally intended to transform the landlords into entrepreneurs or industrial capitalists. The Act stipulated that the Land-value Bill could be used prior to the currency in buying the industrial plants and facilities owned by the Government at its disposal. It was really a great favor for the landlords. However, this measure generally failed to produce new entrepreneurs except the case of a few large landlords. The following seem to be the two salient reasons for this failure.

First, the Korean War broke out shortly after the enactment of the Land Reform Act caused the economic and social collapse of most of the landlords. In fact, 82 per cent of 169,803 landlords were small scale landlords with less than 50 *sŏk* (1 *sŏk* is equal to 5.9568 bushels) of compensation. They actually consumed their indemnities to pay their living costs, since they used to live on tenant rents. Moreover, those landlords with more than 50 *sŏk* of indemnities also failed to invest the Land-value Bills in industrial projects. Instead of investing their Land-value Bills in the purchasing of the government-owned industrial plants and establishments, they sold them to the security brokers at a devaluated rate between 30 per cent and 60 per cent of the actual value, because the Government could not exchange and compensate the Land-value Bills in currency as scheduled. Most landlords only contributed toward the accumulation of capital for the newly-rising speculative capitalists.

Secondly, most landlords had long been accustomed to unproductive, parasitic, consuming, and pleasure-loving way of life. Therefore, they actually had no substantive ability to adjust actively to the changing situation resulted from the land reform and could not transform and establish themselves as entrepreneurs or industrial capitalists. They frequently considered their Land-value Bills as another form of the unearned income.

On the whole, the land reform of Korea and the followed Korean War actually stroke a fatal blow on the landlords. They could not help but selling their Land-value Bills at the devaluated rate of 30-60 per cent of actual value in advance to the speculative capitalists through security brokers. Only some capitalists who were in collusion with political power bought the government-owned plants and industrial facilities at low prices by using the actual value of the Land-value Bills. In addition, taking advantages of inflation, foreign aids and privileged public loans, new industrial capitalists emerged after the land reform, with strong ties with the political power, apart from farmers and landlords.

Under such circumstances, only a few large landlords could be exceptionally successful in transforming themselves into industrial capitalists. This group includes the following:

(1) A few very large landlords who had previously invested in the manufacturing sector could use the privilege given to the Land-value Bill and participated in buying the government-owned plants and industrial facilities as its disposal along with the newly-rising capitalists.

(2) A few large landlords who had previously invested or entrusted their lands in the school foundations and educational institutions could evade the influence of the land reform. Actually they could serve as directors or trustees of school foundations and as capitalists in various enterprises

(3) The landlords who had invested in their children's higher education could maintain their socio-economic status through their university-educated children who actively participated in the newly-rising business enterprise. They actually could turn into industrial capitalists through their descendents.

However, the landlords who could transform themselves into industrial capitalists through the land reform were extremely small in number. Most of the landlords eventually went bankrupt under the influences of the land reform and the Korean War.

5. Conclusion

Land reform has been generally viewed as having dual purposes of serving as both a redistributive instrument primarily for the achievement of greater social equality and a vehicle for achieving increased agricultural productivity.

The land reform of Korea did attain the former purpose to a large extent. The reform essentially abolished the transitional and semi-feudalistic land tenure system and the class of parasitic landlords. It was principally successful to transform the tenant-farmers to free owner-farmers and to establish social equality and social justice to a large extent in rural Korea. Thus, the reform dissolved basically the age-long structural conflict and antagonism between tenant-farmers, owner-farmers and absentee-landlords and helped to achieve the social stability to a great extent in rural communities. Abolishing the high rate of rent, it also created new incentives for increased agricultural productivity for the former tenant-farmers. It is believed that all of these changes resulted from the land reform provided a favorable setting for the modernization of agriculture and the advancement of democracy in Korea.

It is further believed that these achievements were dearly bought at the sacrifice of farmers, since the land reform was carried out rather ineffectively in some respects and the resulting changes from the reform have meant the following new challenges and problems:

First, the price of redistributed land at 30 per cent of average annual yield over a five year period was a too heavy burden to farmers, considering chronic poverty of tenant-farmers. To make matter worse, very heavy land income tax and various public imposts were levied on the newly-established owner-farmers. These heavy burdens of payments accelerated rural poverty. Thus, the newly-created owner-farmers were inevitably bound to the fetters of usury and became hopeless debtors.

Secondly, the land reform failed to take more effective provisions to mitigate the uneven distribution of tenanted lands among tenant-farmers. The provision that land should also be bought from tenant-farmers and owner-farmers who cultivated more than 3 *chŏngbo*-ceiling, had little effects upon the equalization, since the number of such a big holding which exceeded the ceiling was very small. The tenant-farmers with big holdings benefited automatically more than those with small holdings and the reform had little effects on economic equality among the cultivators who had less than 3 *chŏngbo* of land.

(Table 12) Farm-households by Size of Holding, 1947 and 1953

Size of land holding	1947		1953	
	No. of Households	%	No. of Households	%
Less than 0.5 *chŏngbo*	894,775	41.2	1,011,932	44.9
0.5-1.0	724,167	33.3	768,600	34.2
1.0-2.0	409,204	18.8	370,848	16.5
2.0-3.0	113,194	5.3	95,722	4.3
More than 3.0 *chŏngbo*	31,095	1.4	2,930	0.1
Total	2,172,435	100.0	2,249,132	100.0

Source : The Korean Reconstruction Bank

Thirdly, the land reform did not dissolve the system of submarginal farming operation. On the contrary, submarginal farming was slightly intensified as a result of the land reform. When we compare the size of farm in 1953 with that of 1947 which was directly before the reform, the proportion of farm-households with less than 0.5 *chŏngbo* increased from 41.2 per cent in 1947 to 44.9 per cent in 1953, and those with 0.5-1.0 *chŏngbo* increased from 33.3 per cent to 34.2 per cent. On the other hand, the proportion of the farm household with more than 1.0 *chŏngbo* decreased from 25.5 per cent in 1947 to 20.9 per cent in 1953. (see Table 12) Thus, those farm household engaged in less than 1 *chŏngbo* holding accounted for 79.1 per cent of total farm household in 1953 comparing with 74.5 per cent in 1947.

Fourthly, the land reform did not result in immediate increase in agricultural productivity even though it created new incentives for farmers. The land reform failed to provide the supporting services such as land improvement programs, land consolidation, two-crop farming, agricultural credit, research and extension, etc. Thus, agricultural productivity had not increased immediately after the land reform until 1958.

Nevertheless, the effects of the land reform of 1950 should not be underestimated. Because it fundamentally changed the whole structure of Korean rural community and hence the Korean Society. Although farmers paid so high costs and the reform itself was carried out unsatisfactory, it actually abolished the age-long land tenure system and parasitic absentee-landlords. Although some vestiges of tenancy were left illegally, the parasitic absentee-landlordism as a social and economic institution was clearly abolished.

The land reform improved the prospects for raising production and productivity since new incentives for increased work and investment were created as a result of abolishing tenancy and accomplishing more equitable redistribution of lands. It may be safe to say that the land reform of 1950 made a turning point for the modernization of agriculture and of rural community in Korea.

Modern Transformation of

Korean Society

7. The Establishment of *Tonghak* and Ch'oe Che-u

1. Introduction

In the mid-nineteenth century when the Western imperial powers were threatening Korea, the Korean people generated new ideologies to meet the challenge of national crisis. Of the various currents of thoughts which emerged at the time, *Tonghak* (Eastern Learning), *Kaehwa* (Enlightenment), and *Wijŏng Ch'ŏksa* (Protect Orthodoxy and Reject Heterodoxy) formed main currents of the modern Korean thought.

All these nationalist thought of the times are created out of the exigencies of coping with the rising Western pressure. But *Tonghak* is particularly significant because of its outstanding originality and creativity. This alone deserves *Tonghak* an important place in the history of modern Korean thought.

In addition, *Tonghak* followers started and spearheaded the *Kabo Peasant Revolutionary movement* in 1894. *Tonghak* thought informed and interpenetrated this revolutionary movement which in turn led to the introduction of the *Kabo Reforms*. Importance of *Tonghak* movement can be gauged by yet another fact.

Both Ching China and Japan seized the movement as an excuse to send their troops to the Korean peninsula which ultimately led to the outbreak of the Sino-Japanese War. Neddless to say, *Tonghak* is a topic of tremendous significance not only in the modern history of Korea but also of East Asia. The paper proposes to describe the process of the establishment of *Tonghak* and furthermore, it seeks to discuss ideological significance of the movement.

2. Backgrounds of the Establishment of *Tonghak*

Tonghak arose from the following historical background : first, deep inroad of Western powers and Western Learning (Catholicism) into China and Korea, and second, powerful undercurrents of domestic social unrest.

With the onset of the 19th century Western steamships (dubbed then in Korea as 'strange-shaped vessel') became a common sight on the Korean shores. The first Western ship to intrude into the Korean waters was the British ship Lord Amherst. It visited the coast of Hwang-hae and Ch'ung-chŏng provinces for a period of twenty days in June 1832 and demanded conclusion of trade pact. Afterwards, navigation of Western ships into the Korean waters became threateningly persistent. If we look at 1850's, the period when Ch'oe Che-u was engaged in the study of new thought, the following picture emerges. A Western steamship of unknown nationality visited Uljin in Kyŏngsang province in February 1850. The sailors got off the ship, and indulged in wanton shooting which caused the deaths of five civilians. In 1851 a French ship visited the coasts of Cheju island on a surveying mission. In 1852 an American whaling vessel appeared off the Tongnae coast in Kyŏngsang province. In 1853 a Russian warship commanded by Captain E.V. Poutiatin conducted reconnaissance off the east coast of Korea and clashed with the local residents. In 1854 another Russian warship named Vostok reached Korea on a surveying mission. In 1855 the British warship Hornet and Sylvia conducted reconnaissance of the part of the east coast as well as of Pusan harbor. A French warship Virginee reached Korea on a similar mission. So, year after year Western vessels made expeditions into the Korean waters causing immense alarm to the Korean people and forcing the Korean intelligentsia to look for ways and means to encounter the crisis.

Another related development which proved to be a source of immense uneasiness to the Korean people was active propagation of Western Learning (Catholicism) in Korea. Korea was detached from the jurisdiction of the Bishop of Peking and was made an independence diocese in 1831. A bishop of Korea was appointed but he died before he could set foot on the Korean soil. The second bishop Joseph Imbert entered Korea in utter secrecy in 1838 and supervised an organized and systematic propagation of the faith. Catholicism began to make rapid strides thereafter, so much so that in early 1839 the church membership reached the figure of nine thousand. The Korean court viewed the incursion of Catholicism and rapid rise of its forces with gravity and resorted to several measures to suppress the fledgling faith. Notwithstanding, the common populace and womenfolks who were discriminated and tyrannized by the *yangban* bureaucracy continued to embrace Catholicism even at the cost of their lives, because no other faith in the contemporary society of Chosŏn dynasty Korea held for them any spiritual appeal. At any rate, official persecution and proscription failed to curb the growing influence of Catholicism.

In addition, news of the circumstances in China engendered a deep sense of responsibility amongst the Korean intelligentsia for the protection of the country and its people. Several events transformed the alarm of the Korean intellectuals into a panic, such as the defeat of China in the Opum War and the subsequent conclusion of the humiliating and unequal Nanking treaty (1840-1842). The outbreak of the Taiping rebellion led by Hung Hsiu-Chuan in 1850. Arrow incident of 1856, joint Anglo-French occupation of Canton and invasion of Tientsin and the humiliating Tientsin Treaty of 1858 which was concluded to defuse the crisis. When China procrastinated in ratifying and implementing the terms of Tientsin Treaty, the joint Anglo-French troops mounted once again an armed assault on China, and occupied Tientsin in July 1860. Peking the capital of China fell to the Anglo-French forces in August 1860 and so formidable was the threat that the Chinese emperor had to flee to Jehol. A month later China completely recapitulated to the armed invasion of Western powers and signed Peking Treaty. The Korean court and literati was immeasurably shocked to hear these reports. Peking Treaty gave sweeping new privileges such as payment of indemnities of 16,000,000 dollars, concession of Kowloon island and opening of Tientsin port. The other privileges the Western powers secured through the treaty were rights of Catholic missions to hold land in China, build churches and propagate their faith, and rights of Westerners to employ Chinese coolies and send them overseas. Thus the Peking Treaty laid bare the nexus between propagation of Christianity and the use of armed force.

The complete surrender of China, so far regarded as the most powerful country of the East, to the invasion of the West sent serious shockwaves to the Korean officials and literati and made them explore possible strategy to curb the approaching threat. Ch'oe Che-u himself acknowledged that he was inspired to establish *Tonghak* in 1860 and propagate his doctrines a year later as a result of the shock that the complete collapse of the Chinese resistance to the Western invasion induced. He wrote :

> It was rumored in 1860 that Westerners were making inroads into other nations not for riches or power but for building churches and propagating their faith. They claim that such an act is in accord with the divine will. I felt highly skeptical of their motives and said, 'how can it be true.'[1]

The point which we need to underscore here is that the establishment of *Tonghak* by Ch'oe Che-u is directly linked with the terms of Peking Treaty which gave Westerners full freedom to propagate their faith in China.[2] We need to remember that Peking Treaty was imposed on China after the imperial capital of Peking was pillaged by the joint Anglo-French forces. China's complete capitulation to the forces of the Western powers made Ch'oe Che-u firm in his conviction that the clouds of Western military threat were bound to lower soon on the Korean horizon. He wrote as follows:

> The West made war and won, attacked and seized what they wanted. With China gone, we will feel cold like teeth without lips. And I pondered ways to protect the country and comfort the people.[3]

Ch'oe Che-u used the oriental adage "if lips are gone, teeth feel cold" to describe Korea's intimate and dependent relationship with China. He meant that since the protecting shield (lip) China was destroyed, Korea (teeth) was exposed to the menace of Western aggression. A vision of this reality inspired him to devise a plan of protecting the country and comforting the people. In other words, *Tonghak* was conceived and created as a stratagem to preserve the country from the invasion of Western powers and Christianity.

As already noted, domestic social unrest formed another component of the background of the establishment of *Tonghak*. Commoners suffered unbearable exploitation and injustice at the hands of the ruling *yangban* officials during the Chosŏn dynasty. Small-scale popular uprisings broke out frequently in the Chosŏn dynasty history. They weakened the foundation of the regime and signs of imminent collapse of the dynasty were evident everywhere.

With the onset of the nineteenth century the rebellion of commoners against excessive taxation and exaction and brutality of officials became a common phenomenon. Hong Kyŏng-rae rebellion of 1811 proved to be a turning point in the history of the Chosŏn dynasty, for in its wake popular uprisings broke out without interruption and crippled the administration in the northwestern region of the peninsula. Small-scale uprisings broke out ceaselessly even in the central and southern provinces. In the year 1862 when Ch'oe Che-u started propagating his doctrines, popular uprisings broke out in thirty counties. Chinju uprising was one of them. In fact it won't be an exaggeration to describe the 19th century Korea as the 'century of peasant uprisings.' Though these uprisings were suppressed, the hold of officials on the areas where peasants rose up in revolt remained tenuous. The administration of Chosŏn was shaken from its roots.

Collapse of the medieval, feudal administrative structure was accompanied by the process of rapid disintegration of social estate system, the cornerstone of the traditional society of Chosŏn dynasty. The microscopic minority of top-ranking *yangban* who monopolized government positions and wealth sought to consolidate the *yangban* dominated estate system and indulged in brazen and unbridled exploitation of the common people. However, new social phenomena seriously compromised the power and prestige of the *yangban* class. Instances of the sale of *yangban* status by déclassé *yangban* took place. Moreover, choice of *yangban* as the prime target of attack in peasant revolts contributed to the erosion of prestige of the *yangban* class. Commoners and lowborns demanded elimination of *yangban* system and establishment of an egalitarian social order. They avidly looked forward to the emergence of an ideology which echoed their sentiment and represented their views.

Under these social circumstances the moral precepts and ethical codes of Confucianism which was instrumental in the rule of the *yangban* class lost their relevance not only for the commoners but also for the ruling elite. Corruption was rampant. The extant religions had run their course, dried up their elan and energy and were too effete to hold an appeal as spiritual anchor of the common people.[4] Ch'oe Che-u knew that the powerful undercurrent of social crisis was about to swell and prove fatal for the Chosŏn dynasty. He was also aware of the fact that common people were waiting for a gleam of hope and strength in the age which was marked by abysmal gloom of spiritual bankruptcy. He wrote :

> Four hundred years have passed since the dynasty was established and set up its capital at Hanyang (Seoul) at the foot of Samgak mountain. But what has been its achievements it can leave to the posterity? None at all.[5]
>
> Alas! The whole world, the whole mankind is wallowing in the quagmire.[6]
>
> How ridiculous! People claim to be superior on the basis of their birth. People consider themselves qualified to discourse on morality on the basis of their knowledge of classics.[7]
>
> The whole world is doing as they please without following the heavenly principle and without obeying the heavenly mandate.[8]
>
> Alas, the world has run its course. Neither the Golden Age nor the virtues of Confucius will suffice.[9]

These sentiments demonstrate that the contemporary Chosŏn dynasty society, especially the commoners class was seized with a kind of spiritual crisis. Christianity could find a firm foothold on the soil because the existing faiths were incapable of addressing the needs of the people. Ch'oe Che-u, however, realized that Christianity was not only inadequate to meet the spiritual needs of the Korean people, but what was worse still, incompatible with the national interest. He regarded Christianity as dangerous because it was the wellspring of the strength of the Western powers, and the vanguard of the Western aggression. He felt that Western invasion of Korea would follow close on the heels of Christianity.[10]

This is the context in which Ch'oe Che-u felt the necessity to found a new thought and religion which would protect the country and comfort the countrymen, aiming furthermost, at the salvation of the whole mankind. Founding *Tonghak* became the sole mission of his life.

3. The Incentive and Process of the Establishment of *Tonghak*

The founder of *Tonghak* Ch'oe Che-u was born on October 28, 1824 in Kajŏng village, Kyŏn-gok township, Wolsŏng county which is now a part of Kyŏngsangbuk-do.

Ch'oe Ok, Ch'oe Che-u's father was endowed with enormous intellect. He was well-versed in both literature and philosophy and was an avid student of the philosophy of Yi ŏn-jŏk (1491-1553) and Yi Hwang (T'oegye, 1501-1570).[11] He repeatedly failed, however, in the civil service examination because merit was immaterial in the corrupt practices of Chosŏn dynasty. He married a woman of Chŏng family. She bore him a son but soon both she and the newly-born son died of disease. He was remarried to a woman of Sŏ family. She bore him two daughters but no son. He craved for a son, so at the age if sixty-three he took a young widow Madam Han, as a concubine. Ch'oe Che-u was born of this union.[12]

In Chosŏn society, Ch'oe Che-u was regarded as illegitimate. A son of Ch'oe Ok's second wife Lady Sŏ would have been eligible to inherit his father's social status, but unfortunately she bore only two daughters. Meanwhile, Ch'oe Ok adopted his nephew Ch'oe Che-hwan to continue the family line. Craving for a son induced him to take a concubine, but this union was without social legitimacy according to the current practice because it was consummated while his second wife was alive. Thus Lady Han was entitled only to the status of a concubine. Chosŏn dynasty law disqualified concubine-born sons of *yangban* to appear at the civil service examination. So intense was the discrimination and social prejudice against concubine-borns in the contemporary society of Chosŏn dynasty that they were not allowed even to call their father 'father.' To make the matter worse, Ch'oe was a son of a widow who remarried as a third wife. Therefore, Ch'oe Che-u was burdened with the stigma of an infcrior social class from his very birth.

Ch'oe was bereaved of his mother at the age of six and grew under the tutelage of his father. His father started giving him conventional education in the Chinese classics when he was eight. He possessed uncommon intellect and very retentive memory.[13] When he was ten, however, he realized that his low status and standing in the contemporary society disqualified him from seeking office through examination system, no matter how great his learning were. The sense of hopelessness and depression which afflicted Ch'oe Che-u in the early years of his life is not difficult to guess.

The aging father thought that he should get his unfortunate son married before breathing his last. So, Ch'oe Che-u got married at the age of thirteen to a girl of Pak clan. Four years later when he was eighteen he lost his father. Now left an orphan, bereaved of the only person of social status who loved him, he keened almost as if to spit blood.[14]

After three years of mourning he asked his wife to go to her parents' house and set off in quest of means of livelihood and spiritual enlightenment. He was 20 (1843) when he started wandering across the country, and he was 31 (1854) when he returned to his wife. For eleven years, he learned various trades, earning his bread at the same time.[15] During the period he learnt military arts, including horse-riding and archery with a view to taking the military service examination which was open even to concubine-borns.[16] Then he tried his hand on several trades in the market such as running linen shops.[17] He also tried his hands on such miscellaneous arts as medicine, acupuncture, and fortune-telling.

In addition, he is said to have studied various religious texts during his years of wandering. He learnt texts of Taoism from the famous Taoists of the country. He visited famous Buddhist temples of the country and learnt tenets of Buddhist philosophy from learned monks. Hearing that Catholicism possessed profound philosophy, he even studied it too.[18] But none quenched his spiritual thirst. He returned home in despair at the age of 31, without any solution.

Though the eleven long years of wandering did not satisfy his quest for spiritual enlightenment, they did not go in vain either. The travel broadened his outlook and gave him an insight into the reality of his country. He realized that the forces of Western nations and Catholicism to which China capitulated were making inroads into Korea as well. He also observed that common people were reeling under the abuses and exploitation of the officials and collapse of Chosŏn dynasty was imminent. Awakened to the reality of the deep crises which had engulfed his country, he was convinced that he was not alone in the search. And as a result he felt inspired to found religion and system of thought which reflected the aspirations of his countrymen, especially the common people, which echoed their mute sentiments and gave them strength to overcome the deepening national crisis.[19]

During the next five years after returning home Ch'oe Che-u engaged himself wholeheartedly in deep study meditation and prayer sustaining himself only with water. Thus he bent his whole spiritual energy on discovering the new thought and religion which could defend the interests of the nation and secure the livelihood of its people.

Especially the news of the Western invasion and depredation surrounding such incidents as the Tientsin Treaty of 1858 and the joint Anglo-French occupation of Peking in 1860 filled Ch'oe's heart with deep shock and anguish. Thus he experienced all on a sudden a revelation on May 25th of 1860 and heard the word of God. Ch'oe Che-u wrote about the incident as follows:

> Meanwhile in April 1860 the world was in state of chaos and confusion and people were bewildered. Strange news spread everywhere. "The Westerners established a doctrine which was unrivalled in its strength and through whose efficacy they could work wonders. None could match them in war." China lay in shambles and I thought "Won't we perish as well? If the lip is gone, the teeth will surely feel cold."
>
> The reason why Westerners are invincible is that their way is called the Western Way, their learning is called Western Learning or the Teaching of the Lord of Heaven. It was also rumored that they knew the heavenly order and received the Heavenly mandate.
>
> These are only a few samples. And I also felt remorse at being born late. Then I experienced trembling of my body, and I felt the Spirit and heard the word of God. I saw and couldn't see. I heard and couldn't hear.[20]

Thus Ch'oe Che-u explained that he was chosen by God to receive his doctrines. But if we scrutinize these doctrines minutely, it becomes obvious that what Ch'oe termed as revelation was an outcome of his own rigorous intellectual exercises. Ch'oe spent years of restless days and sleepless nights in order to create a way which could preserve the country from foreign forays and relieve the poor and helpless people from the quagmire of miseries. And as noted above, all the while he was engrossed in deep thought, sincere prayers, meditation and contemplation. All of a sudden he had an inspiration which led him to discover the new way. Sincc he was weakened in body, is it not likely the voice of God which he heard was the voice of his own soul, his internal voice?

After receiving the Way Ch'oe Che-u spent one year giving his new doctrine a theoretical framework, composing incantations made of 21 words and establishing prescriptions and rules for following the Way. He started propagating his faith in 1861,[21] and so successful was his evangelical work that he won about 3,000 converts only in six months time.[22]

4. Concept and Intellectual Resources Ch'oe Che-u's *Tonghak* Thought

It is clear from the extracts of Ch'oe Che-u's works which we cited above that it was primarily with a view to countering the menace of *Sŏhak* (Catholicism) that *Tonghak* was founded. Ch'oe Che-u saw that Western powers at whose hands China suffered crushing defeat were now forcing Korea to open its door. And he knew that as China which traditionally served as a shield of protection against any foreign attack on Korea lay in shambles. Western invasion of Korea was no longer a remote possibility. He founded *Tonghak* as a stratagem to protect the country and comfort the people.

Ch'oe Che-u analyzed the forces of Western powers as the Way (the Western Way) including the Western Learning or Catholicism, the doctrine of the Holy Bible as well as the arms and ammunitions which made them so successful in wars. In Ch'oe's view the former, i.e. the Western Learning was more formidable in its strength and more concrete in its manifestation and impact than military force. That is why he regretted the fact that he was born later than the founder of Christianity and founded *Tonghak* with an essential objective of curbing its challenge. The fact that *Tonghak* was founded as an antithesis to Sŏhak is further illustrated by the statement of Ch'oe which he gave to his followers. To quote :

Q. If so, what do you call your Way?

A. Ch'ŏndo, The way of Heaven.

Q. How is it different from Catholicism?

A. Though Catholicism seems analogous to Tonghak, it is different. Catholicism also has prayers but their prayers lack in substance. The Way of the Catholic faith is identical to that of ours, but our principles are different.

Q. If the Way of Catholicism is the same as that of yours, as you say, why don't you call your way also Catholicism?

A. I was born in the East and received my Way in the East, so even if my

Way is Heavenly Way, my learning is Eastern Learning (*Tonghak*). Moreover, as the world is divided into East and West, how can we call the West East or vice-versa. Confucius was born in the state of Lu and disseminated his doctrines in the state of Chou. So he imbibed and transmitted the culture of Lu and Chou states. Similarly, I received my Way and then spread it in this Eastern country. Therefore how can you call it Western Learning (or confuse it with Catholicism).[23]

What is remarkable in the above statement is the distinct national identity of *Tonghak* which Ch'oe seeks to assert and emphasize. He argues that *Tonghak* and Catholicism of the West have the Heavenly Way in common and even share the same destiny, but since their teachings and doctrines are different, *Tonghak* and Catholicism are basically two different religions and ideological entities.

In other words, Ch'oe Che-u stressed the fact that since different regions and cultures had cradled *Tonghak* and Catholicism, they were radically different in their essence and elements.

According to him, the Heavenly Way may be the same, but since the world is divided into East and West, *Tonghak* and Catholicism cannot but be different. It is to be remembered that Ch'oe uses the word '*Tong*' in his statements to convey two different shades of meaning depending on the context. For example, when Ch'oe talks about division of the world into East (*Tong*) and West (*Sŏ*), he means Eastern hemisphere of the globe. But when he says that he received the Way in the East and therefore, called his doctrine *Tonghak* (Eastern Learning) the word East refers to Eastern country (*Tong' guk*), the traditional name of Korea. Most of the Korean intelligentsia called their country 'Eastern country' rather than Chosŏn. Ch'oe's likening of the indigenous roots of his ideology to the Lu-Chou roots of Confucianism seeks to emphasize the same meaning. He wished to underscore the point that *Tong* in *Tonghak* stood for Eastern country, i.e. Chosŏn.

It is clear from the above analysis that Ch'oe envisioned a combination of two contents and contexts when employed the word *Tong* in *Tonghak*—first the East or the Orient and second the Eastern country (Chosŏn). Additionally we also notice that Ch'oe Che-u's *Tonghak* inheres two meanings at the same time—Heavenly Way of the East and Heavenly Way of the Eastern Country (Chosŏn).

If we scrutinize Ch'oe's views on the Western powers and Catholicism, we notice that unlike the exponents of '*Wijŏng Ch'ŏksa* (Protect Orthodoxy and

Reject Heterodoxy) school,' he did not denigrate Western powers as beasts not did he denounce science and technology as wicked skills and queer tricks. He held the Western powers as representatives of mighty forces, morally upright, successful in all the affairs and invincible in all the wars.[24] It demonstrates that Ch'oe's perception of the West and Catholicism was objective and realistic.

Ch'oe identified *Tonghak* with Catholicism in the way and its destiny, but differed them in their teachings and principles. He accepted the fact that both were flourishing and promising faiths and possessed the same Heavenly Way. Thus we see that unlike many religions which are sectarian and subjective in their character and profess and propagate that God belongs only to their religion, Ch'oe Che-u had a more universalistic and objective concept of God. He placed Eastern and Western civilizations on equal footing and his view was not colored by subjective pride or prejudices. Such a view stands in sharp contrast with the contemporaneous *Wijŏng Ch'ŏksa* school which despised the West as bestial and vicious, since Western culture and customs were incompatible with Confucian precepts and principles enunciated in the Three Fundamental Principles and Five Moral Rules in human relations which it held as sacrosanct and infallible.

As noted earlier, Ch'oe Che-u was well acquainted with the ideological systems and scriptures of Confucianism, Buddhism and Taoism. These three major religions of the East became basic sources of *Tonghak* thought. He believed that the three traditional religions had run their course and dried their vitality, and therefore, were unable to protect the country and provide for the people. *Tonghak* brought to a happy fusion the composite religious wisdom of the country. Moreover, *Tonghak* did not fail to realize the relevance of the new thought and religion of the West. Ch'oe Che-u told his disciple and successor Ch'oe Si-hyŏng :

> In reality our religion is neither Confucian nor Buddhist. It is nor even Taoist. But it is a systhesis of Confucianism, Buddhism and Taoism. In other words, though our religion is neither Confucianism nor Buddhism nor Taoism, these three religious streams constitute a part of Heavenly Way.[25]

In addition, diverse streams of knowledge — the doctrines of Wang Yang-ming,[26] theory of Yin-Yang and five elements,[27] thoughts of Ching (Philosophy of Change),[28] geomantic theories,[29] spirit-worship,[30] thoughts of *Chŏnggam-nok* — exercised a profound influence on *Tonghak* thought, some of whose ideas are reflected in *Tonghak* teachings[31]. Ch'oe acquainted himself with all the intellectual forces at work in the Orient. He opened his mind to all the confluence of Eastern thoughts and integrated them critically and creatively into the structure of *Tonghak* thought. Ch'oe Che-u did not stop here, but made use of the Western thoughts. He accepted the challenge of a new age and showed readiness to accept new ideas from the West. As a devil's advocate he wove them into the texture of *Tonghak*.[32]

5. Ideological Significance of *Tonghak*

Tonghak which underwent the above mentioned process of establishment has the following salient features.

1) Thought of Unitarian Ultimate Vital Force

Ch'oe Che-u believed that the whole universe was composed of ultimate vital force (*Chigi*). The point to note here is that Ch'oe Che-u differentiated between vital force (*ki*) and ultimate vital force (*Chigi*) and emphatically argued that the universe was not made of vital forces but of ultimate vital force. He believed that ultimate vital force does not have form nor can it be seen. It is the force which produces and dominates all objects of the world.[33] Ultimate vital force of Ch'oe may be understood to mean '*energy*' in the modern concept. Ch'oe advocated that 'Heaven' and 'Man' are the most divine, the loftiest of all the objects created of ultimate vital force. Since 'Heaven' and 'Man' are the most godlike, they can correspond and united into one force.

2) Thought of Unity of Heaven and Man

Ch'oe Che-u believed that God and Man are spiritual and divine in their essential character. Both influence each other and unite with each other through the medium of divine ultimate vital force. Thus, if one cultivates one's heart and rectifies one's ultimate vital force, one can achieve sagehood.[34]

Even before the establishment of *Tonghak* there existed some philosophical systems which professed the unity of heaven and man, but they were heaven-centered. God occupied pivotal and preponderant position and humans were subservient to the divine will. Uniqueness of Ch'oe's philosophy lies in the fact that he tilted the fulcrum in favor of man. He established a human-centered religious belief. *Tonghak*'s thought of unity of heaven and man can be called a Copernican break from the traditional Oriental belief.

3) Thought of Attending God in Humanity

Ch'oe Che-u preached the idea that god dwell in the body and mind of human beings[35] and established the principle of 'Attending God in Humanity.' In other wards Ch'oe put forward the epochal notion that the body and mind of every human being is the abode of God. Thought of attending God in humanity is the nucleus of *Tonghak* thought and essence of its moral precepts.

Ch'oe Si-hyŏng disciple of Ch'oe Che-u carried forward the tradition of his master. He said that human heart should be regarded as palace of God. He further warned against doubting the existence of God because in his view it amounted to doubting the existence of oneself.[36] Thought of attending God in humanity occupies a central place in the prayers and incantations composed by Ch'oe Che-u.

4) Thought of Calm Mind and Correct Vital Force (*Susim Chŏng-gi*)

Grounded on this philosophical thoughts, Ch'oe Che-u established thought of calm mind and correct vital force as the substance of discipline. It enunciates the idea that internally one should act according to one's awakened conscience and thus have clear and calm mind and externally one should have correct vital force reflected on one's face or in one's actions. Ch'oe said that Confucius taught four cardinal virtues, benevolence, righteousness, decorum and knowledge and he was adding another one, the virtue of calm mind and correct vital force.[37] He further explained;

> I put forward a fresh idea of calm mind and correct vital force. The gentleman's vital force is orthodox and his mind is stable so that he is united with the virtue of the Universe (heaven and earth). The amoral man's vital force is not orthodox and his mind is unstable. So it contradicts the will of the Universe. Is this not the principle of rise and fall?[38]

5) Thought of 'Man is God'

Consistent with the thought of unity of God and man and that of 'attending God in humanity,' Ch'oe put forward the thought of 'man is God.'[39] He said that since human heart is the abode of God, human beings are God. Ch'oe Si-hyŏng, the second patriarch of the *Tonghak* order preached that human beings are God and asked *Tonghak* followers to 'serve human beings as gods.'[40]

Tonghak's philosophy that human being are God revolutionized the thinking of the times by refuting the postulation of other faiths which believed that God is an absolute and separate entity and human beings are under God's overarching control. *Tonghak*'s thought of leveling God with human beings represents the loftiest and the noblest ideal of humanism. This concept of humanism infused hope and confidence in the hearts of the common people and lowborns who suffered inhuman abuses and exploitation at the hands of the *yangban* officials. That is why they greeted it with such enthusiasm.

6) Thought of Equality

Tonghak's equation of Man with Heaven, the thought of serving Man as God provided for a unique system of thought on equality. It was essentially aimed at dismantling social discrimination and inhered the idea of respect for all human beings irrespective of their social standing and status. Since God dwells in the heart of all human beings, discriminations and differences between one's wives and concubines, masters and slaves, men and women, old and young, rich and poor are arbitrary and untenable. All are basically equal and any form of discrimination and division including that between high and low is in contravention of God's will. For example, a *yangban* cherishes a god in his heart, and a commoner has the same god in his heart, who dwells in the heart of a lowborn too. Since all share the same god, they should be equal.

Thus Ch'oe Che-u repudiated the discriminatory *yangban*-based social estate system.[41] He also prophesized that the spirit of equality will be the hallmark of the coming age. The poor and low of today, he said, will be the rich and powerful of tomorrow.[42]

Tonghak also raised a strong voice of protest against low social status and standing of women. He argued that women's heart is also an abode of God and moreover, women beget God in the form of children.[43] So he espoused equality of sexes and besides, exhorted *Tonghak* followers to cherish and respect women as an invaluable component of human society.

Tonghak discerned spark of divinity even in children and forbade its followers to strike children because it was tantamount to striking God.[44]

7) Thought of the Evolution of New Age

Ch'oe Che-u divided the history of mankind broadly in two stages. Former Heaven and Latter Heaven, and contended that both these stages marked the evolution of a new age. He said that the Former Heaven spanned about fifty thousand years and could be divided into three periods. Civilization had not yet dawned during into the first periods. The second period started with the birth of Confucius and propagation of his teachings. The third period represented the most mature phase. It was in this period that Ch'oe Che-u was born and spread his doctrines.[45] He prophesized that at the end of the third period, the Former Heaven would be torn asunder by chaos, moral degeneration will reach climactic height and the Latter Heaven will make its advent.

Ch'oe further said that the coming age would be that of *Tonghak*. He contended that he was chosen by God to create a thought which was capable of protecting the country, comforting the people and salvaging the whole mankind.[46] It is obvious that Ch'oe negated the extant thought, wisdom and religion which dominated the Eastern mind since the dawn of the civilization and thus emphasized the revolutionary character of his religion and freshness of his thought.

8) Thought of Heaven on Earth

Ch'oe Che-u opposed the Catholic paradise and argued that paradise should be built on earth. He offered a vision and promise of heaven on earth by contending that all the commoners would become superior men if converted to *Tonghak* faith. Moreover, he said that if they lived unitedly, their dwelling place, the earth would change into paradise.[47] He further asserted that even Western invaders would be repelled, if the commoners embraced *Tonghak* faith.

Thought of paradise on earth was a utopian concept which Ch'oe conceived and constructed as a fitting response to the Catholic paradise.

6. Conclusion

Tonghak won large following and dug deep roots amongst commoners and lowborns ever since its inception in 1861.[48] *Chŏpju* (Overseer) system was organized in 1862 in the fourteen counties of Kyŏngsang province with a view to systematically administering *Tonghak* followers.[49] Rapidly growing popularity of *Tonghak* thought and the attendant expansion of the ranks of *Tonghak* followers caused immense alarm to the court and literati of Chosŏn dynasty. As a result Ch'oe Che-u was arrested in December 1863, incarcerated in Taegu prison and beheaded to death on March 10, 1864. Ch'oe mounted the scaffold with dignity and poise and told the magistrate as follows;

> *Tonghak* is not an outcome of my subjective wish but owes to heavenly command. Therefore, let it be known to you that even though you are putting me to death, generations to come will embrace my teachings.[50]

After marrydom of Ch'oe Che-u, Ch'oe Si-hyŏng (1827-1898) inherited the leadership of *Tonghak* order. Despite the fact that *Tonghak* thought was branded as heretical and subversive, that Ch'oe Che-u was killed and *Tonghak* order was prescribed, common people continued to join the ranks of *Tonghak*. They braved untold hardships to embrace its God. The fact that commoners of the times risked their lives to joint *Tonghak* demonstrates the extent of appeal *Tonghak* ideology held in the contemporary society. One drawback of *Tonghak* which needs to be pointed out is that it put undue emphasis on the religious dimension of Western powers; It did so, however, because it was created with an objective of encountering Catholicism, the ideological weapon of the West.

It ought to have paid due attention to science and technology, military force and political, economic and social system of the West. It may be considered as *Tonghak*'s weakness. nonetheless, *Tonghak* gave to the Korean people a strong ideology of nationalism by raising the slogan of 'protect the country from foreign invasion and comfort the countrymen.' It put forward the loftiest ideal of humanism by advocating 'man is God.' An attendant injunction was that man is not servant of God but at par with God. Its emphasis on equality gave considerable hope and confidence to the down−trodden and deprived populace of the nation who were victims of the rapacious avarice and exploitation of *yangban* officials. Its teaching that mankind, being from God, was essentially equal in its origin which everyman bears and serves deep within oneself proved to be an inexhaustible source of spiritual strength to the common people of Chosŏn dynasty living in an era of spiritual bankruptcy. Thus in 1894, that is, a generation after Ch'oe Che-u was put to death, peasants in south, central and partially in the northern regions of Korea rose up in revolt and started what is known in history as the *Kabo Peasant Revolution* of 1894. *Tonghak* provided ideology and organization to the peasants and became driving force of the *Kabo Peasant Revolution* of 1894.

FOOTNOTES (Part II - 7)

1. Ch'oe Che-u, "P'odŏngmun" (On Propagating Virtue) in *Tonggyŏng taejŏn* (Tonghak scriptures).
2. Ch'oe Che-u, "Nonhangmun" (A Discussion on Learning) in *Tonggyŏng taejŏn.*
3. "P'odŏngmun," *op.cit.*
4. Ch'oe Che-u, "Kyohun'ga" (Song of Instruction) in *Yongdam yusa* (Legacy of Yongdam).
5. Ch'oe Che-u, "Mongjung noso mundapka" (Talk with Young and Old While Dreaming) in *Yongdam yusa.*
6. Ch'oe Che-u, "Kwŏnhakka" (Song of Encouragement of Learning) in *Yongdam yusa.*
7. Ch'oe Che-u, "Todŏkka" (Song of Virtue) in *Yongdam yusa.*
8. "P'odŏngmun" (On Propagating Virtue).
9. "Mongjun noso mundapka" (Talk with Young and Old While Dreaming).
10. "Nonhangmun" (A Discussion on Learning).
11. Ch'oe Ok's extant work entitled *Kŭnamchip* bears testimony to the fact that he was an accomplished traditional scholar.
12. *Kyŏngju Ch'oessi Taedongbo* (Geneaological Record of Kyŏngju Ch'oe Clan), Vol. 1. Also see Yi Ton-hwa, *Ch'ŏndogyo Ch'ang'gŏnsa* (A History of the Founding of Ch'ŏndogyo), Ch'ŏndogyo Central Headquarters, 1933.
13. "Mongjung noso mundapka" (Talk with Young and Old While Dreaming).
14. Ch'oe Che-u, "Sudŏngmun" (On Cultivation of Virtue) in *Tonggyŏng taejon.*
15. "Kyohun'ga" (Song of Instruction).
16. Yi Ton-hwa, *Ch'ŏndogyo Ch'ang'gŏnsa* (A History of the Founding of Ch'ŏndogyo), Vol. 1, p. 4.
17. O Chi-yŏng, *Tonghaksa* (A history of *Tonghak*), 1944. p. 1.
18. *Ibid*, p. 2.
19. "Kyohun'ga" (Song of Instruction) and "Kwŏnhakka" (Song of Encouragement of Learning).
20. "Nonhangmun" (A Discussion on Learning).
21. Ch'oe Che-u, "Ansimga" (Song of Comfort) in *Yongdam yusa.* Also see "Nonhangmun" (A discussion on Learning).
22. "Sudŏngmun" (On cultivation of Virtue).
23. "Nonhangmun" (A Discussion on Learning).
24. "P'odŏngmun" (On Propagating Virtue).

25. Yi Ton-hwa, *Ch'ŏndogyo Ch'ang'gŏnsa*, Vol. 1. p. 47. Also see *Ch'ŏndogyo-sŏ* (Book of *Ch'ŏndogyo*), in *Asea Yŏn'gu*. Vol. 3, No. 1, p. 216.

26. "Kyohun'ga" (Song of Instruction).

27. "Nonhangmun" (A Discussion on Learning).

28. "Sudŏngmun" (On cultivation of Virtue).

29. "Yongdamga" (Song of Yŏngdam).

30. *Yongdam yusa* (Legacy of Yŏngdam).

31. "Mongjun noso mundapka" (Talk with Young and Old While Dreaming), *op.cit.*

32. *Tonghaksa* (History of Tonghak), p. 2, *op.cit.*

33. "Nonhangmun" (A Discussion on Learning). Also see *Tonghaksa* (History of Tonghak), p. 7.

34. "Nonhangmun" (A Discussion on Learning).

35. "Kyohun'ga" (Song of Instruction).

36. *Tonghaksa* (History of Tonghak), pp. 68-69.

37. "Sudongmun" (On cultivation of Virtue).

38. "Nonhangmun" (A Discussion on Learning).

39. "Nonhangmun" (A Discussion on Learning), *Tonghaksa* (History of Tonghak).

40. *Ch'ŏndogyo Ch'ang'gŏnsa* (A History of the Founding of *Ch'ŏndogyo*), Vol. 2, pp. 37-38.

41. "Todŏkka" (Song of Virtue).

42. "Kyohun'ga" (Song of instruction).

43. *Ch'ŏndogyo Ch'ang'gŏnsa* (A History of the Founding of *Ch'ŏndogyo*), Vol. 2. pp. 36-37.

44. *Tonghaksa* (History of Tonghak), p. 64.

45. "Podŏngmun" (On Propagating Virtue).

46. "Mongjung noso mundapka" (Talk with Young and Old While Dreaming).

47. "Kyohun'ga" (Song of instruction).

48. "Sudŏngmun" (On Cultivation of Virtue).

49. *Ch'ŏndogyo Ch'ang'gŏnsa* (A History of the Founding of *Ch'ŏndogyo*), Vol. 1, p. 42.

50. *Tonghaksa* (History of Tonghak), p. 18.

8. The Opening of Korea and Changes in Social Thought

1. *Tonghak* (Estern Learning) Thought

Faced with a national crisis created by the advent of the Western powers in the mid-19th century, Koreans evolved new social thought devoted to promoting the nation's independence and development in response to the challenge. Three representative schools of thought were: 1. *Tonghak* (東學; Eastern Learning) 2. The *Kaehwa* (開化; Modernization or Enlightenment) doctrine 3. The *Wijŏng ch'ŏksa* (衛正斥邪; Protect Orthodoxy and Reject Heterodoxy: Confucian scholars in the late Chosŏn dynasty asserted that the monarchy should follow the principles of new-Confucianism in ruling the country while rejecting the influence of Western culture which was, they believed, evil) doctrine and 4. The doctrine of *Tongdosŏgi* (東道西器; Eastern Culture with Western Technology).

All of this new social thought came into being prior to Korea's opening to the outside world in 1876. With the opening as a turning point, social thought developed keeping pace with the fast changing society of Korea.

Tonghak thought came as a reaction to the advance of the Western powers which were threatening China in the 1850s. *Tonghak* was started by Ch'oe Che-u who gave the name to his religion in 1860, 16 years before the opening of the country. It was the year when the Anglo-French allied fleet raided Peking and forced the Peking Treaty upon China.

In Ch'oe's view, the crisis facing Korea stemmed not only from the penetration of the Western powers but also from the dire distress in which the common people had to live at that time. Therefore, he insisted that the solution must be found in simultaneously coping with the external and internal challenges. China, he said, bowed to the Western powers not only because of their military supremacy but also because of the strength of Catholicism in the background.

The only way to save the people from distress at home and counter Catholicism from without would be, he claimed, to originate a new religion. According to him, the old Confucianism, Buddhism and Taoism had lost the dynamism required to fulfill the task. Therefore, he sought to amalgamate these three major religions of the East, plus his own philosophy, into a new religion called *Tonghak*. *Tonghak* thought is characterized by the following aspects.

First, it shifted emphasis from *ch'ŏn* (heaven) to *in* (man) in the traditional concept of *ch'ŏninhabil* (unity of heaven and man). Thus he presented the doctrine of *sich'ŏnju*, that every man esteems heaven at heart. Accordingly, all men are most worthy beings for they all respect the most worthy God.

Second, all men are not only worthy but are equally worthy, hence they are equal. Ch'oe explained that there should be no discrimination in terms of social status or sex. Such a concept of equality embodied the demands of the farm population and the common people for the abolition of *yangban* (nobility) and increased civil rights for all. It represented a most thorough equalitarianism and humanism in that it found god in every one's mind.

Third, he preached that one can attain enlightenment and become a "true gentleman" or a "divine being" even without profound learning if one serves God with sincerity, respect and trust. It was contrary to the thinking of neo-Confucianism which held that much learning and high official position attained through the civil service examination were essential for one to become a "true gentleman." It thus appealed to the common people who lacked intellectual training and an economic base.

Fourth, *Tonghak* claimed that all men converted to *Tonghak* can attain enlightenment and earthly divinity and that an earthly kingdom of heaven may come if all men have attained such divinity. The nation armed with *Tonghak* could resist *Sŏhak* (西學; Western Learning meaning Catholicism) and would turn into an earthly heaven. Thus Korea with its strong national power would be able to overcome the menace of the West, maintain security and widely benefit the people.

In short, *Tonghak* thought was motivated by a desire to tide over the national crisis by achieving an equalitarian society based on a peasant-centered democracy. The most outstanding feature of *Tonghak* is its too acute sense of antagonism toward Catholicism. *Tonghak* developed a pattern of responses to challenges from the West from a religious and spiritual standpoint, but failed to formulated new concepts in science and technology. The difficulties faced by the country were not to be overcome without understanding of Western science and technology, but *Tonghak* lacked that vital understanding. In spite of this weakness, *Tonghak* thought rapidly spread among the peasantry on the strength of its equalitarian stand. Alarmed by the propagation of this thought opposed to the *yangban* system, the aristocrats and bureaucrats went all out to suppress the religion. Ch'oe Che-u was arrested and executed in 1864, and *Tonghak* was outlawed.

But the death of Ch'oe did not put an end to the fast-spreading religion which was popular among the rural people because of its demands for the emancipation of the underprivileged class and the abolition of the *yangban* system. Ch'oe Si-hyŏng succeeded Ch'oe Che-u as leader and tried to revive the outlawed *Tonghak*. The *Tonghak* following snowballed by 1894 prior to the *Tonghak* peasant revolutionary movement. The followers of *Tonghak* were heavily concentrated in Ch'ungch'ŏng, Chŏlla, Kyŏngsang, Kyŏnggi, Kangwŏn and Hwanghae provinces.

2. *Kaehwa* (Enlightenment) Thought

Next to *Tonghak* thought, Koreans also evolved *Kaehwa* thought. It was formulated by a handful of intellectuals during 1853-1860s, before the opening of Korea. Pak Kyu-su and O Kyŏng-sŏk, who acted respectively as ambssador and interpreter for Korean missions frequently dispatched to China, had seen that China was subdued by the overwhelming military might and technological prowess of the Western powers, and concluded that a similar fate would befall Korea. With a view to preparing for this eventuality, they brought back many new books from China introducing Western civilization. One of O's friends Yu Tae-ch'i read the books and agreed on the need to provide for a crisis to come. These men of foresight felt that they should infuse a new thought in the young generation to take the helm of state in the future and instruct them in things Western. They opened a class for reading *Silhak* (Practical Learning) classics of the late Chosŏn dynasty and books on Western civilization. They enrolled talented youths from *yangban* families.

Among them were Kim Yun-sik, Kim Hong-jip, Ŏ Yun-jung, Pak Yŏng-hyo, Kim Ok-kyun, Pak Yŏng-kyo, Hong Yŏng-sik, Sŏ Kwang-bŏm and Yu KIl-jun. Through reading new books and examining internal and external conditions, they developed a new thought which was called *Kaehwa* thought. They found the challenge from the Western powers in a new social system founded on advanced technology and advocated a new way of response different from new-Confucianism. *Kaehwa* thought had the following characteristics.

First, it called for the introduction and adoption of the advanced technology of the West. They well recognized the technological lag of Korea and the Orient and believed that learning and adopting Western technology was necessary to make the nation strong and prosperous.

Second, it ascribed the technological lag to the defects in social institutions and called for an overall reform and the introduction of a modern capitalistic social system free from such defects.

Third, it called for a political transition from the old authoritarian monarchy to a constitutional monarchy and establishment of a modern nation-state.

Fourth, it called for the growth of industry and commerce by putting Western technology to economic use. It called for efforts to enhance productivity and introduce capitalistic institutions.

Fifth, it sought to realize the freedom and equality of the people through the abolition of the obsolete *yangban* system. Its adherents believed that recruitment of men should be made on the merit of the person and the entire people should be effectively mobilized for the defense and development of the nation. They demanded that modern schools should be immediately established to give new education to youths.

Sixth, they urged that Korea should embrace many cultures of the West, other than the Chinese culture, and thus develop Korea's own unique cultur, language, arts and history.

Kaehwa thought held that the national crisis could be overcome if and when Korea adopts not only the technology but also the good social institutions of the West.

The *Kaehwa* faction worked for sweeping reforms as the country was opened to intercourse with the Western world. The reforms included: 1. administrative reorganization such as the creation of *T'ongrigimuamun*; 2. dispatch of students to China for technical training; 3. dispatch of an observer mission to Japan; 4. establishment of modernized schools; 5. publishing of a modern newspaper; 6. inauguration of a customs house; 7. establishment of an agricultural experimental station; 8. introduction of a modern postal system; 9. publishing of new books; 10. introduction of Western technology and promotion of industry.

The military riot (*Imogullan*) of 1882 brought Chinese troops to Korea under the command of Yüan Shih-k'ai who attempted extensive intervention in the internal affairs of Korea and also attempted to put down the modernization policies of the early *Kaehwa* faction and indeed rid the government of this faction.

At this juncture, radical members of the faction launched a Coup d'Etat in order to take over the government and introduce general reforms. But the Coup d'Etat lasted only three days, and only a small number of the extremists exiled themselves to foreign countries while the rest were captured and executed by the Chinese army and the conservative faction. Thus, the modernization bid was foiled.

Those moderate members of the *Kaehwa* faction who did not participate in the Coup d'Etat survived but they were excluded from the government.

3. *Wijŏng Chŏksa* (Protect Orthodoxy and Reject Hetrodoxy) Thought

The doctrine of upholding justice and rejecting vice which was another main current of Korean social thought of the time may be regarded as a practical version of orthodox neo-Confucianism intended to counter the challenge of the Western powers. The doctrine was latent in the Weltan-schauung of Confucian scholars since new-Confucianism was introduced to Korea. It came to the fore as a response to the Western challenge in the late 19th century.

The idea of *Wijŏng ch'ŏksa* supported firm resistance to the military pressure of foreign powers to open up trade relations at the time of the General Sherman Affair in 1866 and Roger's expedition in 1871. The doctrine was spearheaded by Yi Hang-no and Ki Chŏng-jin and it also provided the backbone for the campaign against the opening of Korea in 1876. At this time, Ch'oe Ik-hyŏn led the theoretical campaign. Characteristics of the doctrine may be summed up as follows.

First, it subscribed to the neo-Confucianist dichotomy of *hwa* and *i*—the division of the world into two, the civilized (*hwa*; 華) and the savage (*i*; 夷). Under the dichotomy, China was the big *hwa* and Korea the little *hwa*, while Japan and the West all belonged to *i*. According to the theory, the center and legitimacy of civilization rested with the *hwa*, and therefore, no matter how strong and prosperous the West might be, it still was part of the savage world, and as such it is inferior to the civilized East.

Second, it applied the similar neo-Confucian dichotomy of *li* (理, Principle) and *ch'i* (氣, material force) and contended that China and Korea represented *li*, while Japan and the West represented *ch'i*. By neo-Confucianist reasoning, it believed that as *li* always prevails over *ch'i*, so the East will prevail over the West. The challenge of the West may appear formidable on the surface, but in substance, the East remains superior.

Thirdly, it did not approve of the advanced level of Western science and technology, branding them as intriguing and strange techniques. Therefore, the doctrine insisted, the science and technology of the West are not to be overcome by learning and adopting them, but rather they should be prevailed over philosophically and ethically by following the "right path" suggested by neo-Confucianism.

Fourth, it claimed that the way to conquer the intriguing and strange techniques lay in blocking their entry into the country by closing the country to foreign intercourse. It also contended that introduction of things Western by means of trade would result in trading our yearly yield (farm produce) for daily yield (manufactured goods), thereby impoverishing this country, in addition to corrupting public morals.

Fifth, it advocated a negative response to challenges from without, accompanied by renovations in domestic affairs — a doctrine of setting the house in order and excluding things foreign. It was opposed to the stand of the early *Kaehwa* faction members who sought to open diplomatic relations with foreign countries, while at the same time carrying out domestic reforms.

Sixth, it considered "unity of mind" as the cardinal element in domestic reforms, and that the doctrine of *Wijŏng ch'ŏksa* provides the base for consensus among the people. Adherence to the doctrine will enable Korea to deal with the challenges from the West. The most fundamental aspect of the doctrine was that it established the Confucian value system of *Samgang'oryun* (three principles and five moral rules in human relations) as the criteria for distinguishing justice from vice. Since it based its value judgment on the ethics and norms of neo-Confucianist human relations, it grasped the nature of Western challenges in spiritual, moral and ethical terms; thus, it identified the West with ethical inferiority. Therefore, its response to the challenge was also spiritual and moral. It sought to find the answer to all problems in spiritual integrity under neo-Confucianism.

The doctrine based its value judgment on neo-Confucianist ethical principles with reference to subjective circular reasoning and dogmatism. It thus led to intense exclusivism and anti-foreignism, and was lacking in scientific rationalism.

After the opening of the country the doctrine emerged as the most powerful force opposed to the modernization policy of the early *Kaehwa* advocates. Youthful members of the *Kaehwa* faction vigorously pursued the modernization policy. In 1881 Confucian scholars subscribing to this doctrine presented a petition opposing the modernization policy and started a great debate with the *Kaehwa* faction (the so-called controversy of 1881). In 1882 the faction temporarily took over the government, taking advantage of the military riot: In 1884 a reform campaign attempted by extreme members of the *Kaehwa* faction failed, followed by the *Tonghak* rebellion of 1894.

4. *Tongdo sŏgi* (Eastern Culture with Western Technology)

The doctrine of *Tongdosŏgi* emerged as another main current of Korean social thought at the time of Korea's opening. Its influence was rather limited. Following the debate of 1881, some Confucian scholars came to approve *Kaehwa* thought. Representative of them were Kwak Ki-rak and Yun Sŏn-hak who set out on a petition campaign in 1882.

Advocates of this doctrine recognized the importance of Western technology and called for the combination of *do* (spirit, culture) and *gi* (technology) to cope with Western challenges. It had the following characteristics.

First, it held the view that *do* and *gi* could be separated and that the challenge of the West could be met by pitting Eastern *do* against Western *do* and Eastern *gi* against Western *gi*.

In the second place, it appreciated the superiority of Western *gi* (technology) and advocated the adoption of Western science and technology. Cannon, steamships, railroads and telegraph from the West were regarded as necessary vehicles of national development and prosperity; so they must be introduced into the country.

Third, the Eastern *do* originating from Confucian ethical norms was rated as superior to Western *do*, and therefore, we should stick to the Eastern *do*, for the Confucian ethics are in harmony with human nature. It criticized *Kaehwa* thought for being a radical doctrine opposed to both the Eastern *do* and Eastern *gi*, while the *Wijŏng ch'ŏksa* doctrine did not keep abreast of the times.

The *Tongdosŏgi* doctrine took a major step forward by putting things in a much more objective perspective and served a great deal toward finding practical answers to the problems of the day. However, it was problematical whether the science and technology of the West and the philosophy of the Orient based on Confucian ethics could be grafted together.

At the end of the 19th century the four main streams of social thought in Korea clashed with each other, giving rise to drastic changes. The *Kaehwa* faction suffered a major blow when the revolt in 1884 by its early members failed, and the doctrine of *Kaehwa* could no longer play a leading role. The conservative group which came to power through the help of Queen Min in 1885 and stayed in power until 1894 cracked down on the *Kaehwa* faction and stood by the doctrine of *Wijŏng ch'ŏksa* which opposed modernization. In the absence of a political power to counter the *Wijŏng ch'ŏksa* group which was firmly supported by Yüan Shih-k'ai, the conservative group became increasingly corrupt. It fattened on extortionary tax burdens on the people. Thus, the Korean people lost a valuable decade during which the nation could have nurtured its strength and capacity for achieving self-reliant modernization and coping with challenges from the West.

It was the *Tonghak* adherents who rose in violent protest against the prolonged exploitation of the faction subscribing the doctrine of *Wijŏng ch'ŏksa*. Joined by the farming populace, they staged a revolution in 1894 with a call for better preparedness against external challenges and for sweeping domestic reforms. The government dominated by Queen Min and her proteges failed to subdue the revolution and invited Chinese troops. Then, the Japanese who were looking for any opportunity to invade Korea sent army contingents, invoking the Tientsin Treaty. They clashed with the Chinese forces and touched off the Sino-Japanese war; the Japanese laid siege to the Korean court and had the *Kaehwa* faction take over the government from the conservative group led by Queen Min.

Tonghak ousted the Wijŏng ch'ŏksa faction but as a result it ushered in the moderate wing of the *Kaehwa* group. The moderate *Kaehwa* group instituted a major political reform in 1894. It succeeded in part of the reform attempt but it undermined the base for national independence and integrity by opening the door for Japanese intervention in the internal affairs of Korea. With the temporary transfer of King Kojong to the Russian legation in Seoul, the *Kaehwa* group went out of power in February of 1896.

In the wake of the incident, the *Kaehwa* group rallied again to form the Independence Club in 1896, and formulated a new social thought to inspire the nationalist movement. The ideology of the club represented a merger and evolution of *Kaehwa* and *Tongdosŏgi* doctrines. For three years after 1898 the Independence Club stimulated and developed the thought of modernization, modern nationalism and democracy. It was at this time that the people awakened to the idea of parliamentary democracy, republicanism and industrial revolution. The Independence Club was later suppressed by the conservative group and the Japanese.

The *Kaehwa* ideology permeated the ranks of the Korean people through the campaigns of the Independence Club and the People's Meetings. For this reason this ideology became the dominant social thought of Korea at the beginning of the 20th century. Under the influence of *Kaehwa* thought, the *Tonghak* also changed into the *Ch'ŏndogyo* religion. The doctrine of *Wijŏng ch'ŏksa* was also heavily influenced by *Kaehwa* thought and lost its influence. The doctrine of *Tongdosŏgi* also developed and was absorbed into *Kaehwa* thought. After 1905 *Kaehwa* thought prevailed throughout the country though in a form different from the immediate post-opening years. The later *Kaehwa* thought is often referred to as the doctrine of patriotic enlightenment directed towards loving and saving the nation.

9. The Thought of the Enlightenment Movement

1. Introduction

By *Kapshin Chŏngbyŏn*, or the Coup d'Etat of December 4, 1884, the Progressives, who demanded the nation's autonomy from China's suzerainty and commercial and trade relations with the outside world, took power from the Conservatives led by Queen Min. But they were driven out of power by the Chinese troops then stationed in Seoul.

However many historians attach importance to this coup and the ensuing short-lived Progressive government. This is because the thought underlying this coup and the policy the Progressives called for are considered to have had the epoch-making aim of building a modern nation-state in Korea.

But the historians do not necessarily agree on the historical significance of the Coup d'Etat of 1884. Rather they are more sharply split on the evaluation of this coup than on other issues of modern Korean history. In fact, the coup is the most controversial topic in modern Korean history among scholars of Korean history. At one extreme are those who see the coup simply as a power struggle between the pro-Chinese faction and the pro-Japanese faction that had nothing to do with the will to modernize the country. At the other extreme are those who praise the coup as the first modern civil revolution in Korean history.

One way to settle the disputes on the pros and cons of the Coup d'Etat of 1884 is to analyze and review the thought this coup pursued. The Progressives who launched the coup harbored the thought of enlightenment that the nation could become rich and strong only by opening the country to the outside world, and after having seized power in the coup they proclaimed progressive policy guidelines based on this enlightenment thought.

In this chapter, I will briefly discuss the course of development the enlightenment thought took in the late 19th century in order to bring to light the historical characteristics of the Coup d'Etat of 1884, and then deal in more detail with the platform the Progressives announced after the coup.

2. Development of Enlightenment Thought

In the middle of the 19th century Western powers made inroads into

Northeast Asia, and in the latter half of the 1860s the enlightenment thought arguing for opening the country to the outside world was developed chiefly by O Kyŏng-sŏk (1831-1879), Pak Kyu-su (1807-1876)and Yu Hong-gi (1831-?).

The enlightenment thought had two origins; one is *Shilhak* (Practical Learning) developed in the 18th century, and the other the Western thought introduced to the country by way of China in the 19th century.

Pak Kyu-su, took over both the academic traditions and ideas of the *Shilhak* titan Pak Chi-wŏn (pen name Yŏnam, 1737-1805) who was his grandfather. In 1860 when Pak Kyu-su was working in the government, an allied force of British and French troops occupied Peking, the capital of the Ch'ing dynasty China. This incident was a great shock to the Chosŏn dynasty government which believed that China was the most powerful country of the world. In January 1861 the Korean government sent a consolatory mission to Peking. Pak Kyu-su was deputy head of this mission, and he observed Peking exposed to danger under the influence of the Western powers. Anticipating Korea would also come under Western influence, he felt keenly the necessity of studying the Western world. He brought home many books on geography, history, politics, economy, culture and military affairs of the Western nations. China opened its ports to the West in 1842 and this prompted many Chinese scholars, especially those in Kuangtung, to publish books on the West. Pak Kyu-su developed the enlightenment thought on the basis of his grandfather's thought of *Shilhak* and his study of the books on the Western ideas and ways he brought from Peking.

In 1872 Pak Kyu-su made his second visit to Peking as chief of a royal mission and returned home with many books on Western ideas and ways again. He opened a class for young promising boys of *yangban* (aristocratic class) families at his home and taught them Western ideas and ways, while encouraging them to read the "new books" he brought from Peking and the *Shilhak books.*

Pak Yŏng-hyo, one of the leading figures of the Coup d'Etat of 1884, recalled how he learned the enlightenment thought from Pak Kyu-su as follows:

> The new thought came from the home of Pak Kyu-su, one of my relatives. I learned this thought with Kim Ok-kyun, Hong Yŏng-shik, Sŏ Kwang-bŏm and my eldest brother (Pak Yŏng-gyo).
>
> I learned the thought of equality from *Yŏnam-jip* (Collection of Yŏnam's Writings) as it contains essays attacking the aristocrat.[1)]

Shin Ch'ae-ho wrote How Kim Ok-kyun learned the enlightenment thought from Pak Kyu-su as follows:

When Kim Ok-kyun visited Right Prime Minister Pak Kyu-su at his home, Pak brought a globe from a wall closet and showed it to him. Pak told him that the globe had been brought from Peking by his grandfather, Yŏnam (Pak Chi-wŏn). Turning the globe once, Pak told Kim with a smile, "Where is the Middle Kingdom today? When you turn the globe that way the United States will be the Middle Kingdom, and when you turn it this way Korea can be the Middle Kingdom. Thus any country can be the Middle Kingdom, depending on which way you turn this globe. There is no absolute Middle Kingdom, is there?"

Kim Ok-kyun thus began to argue for trade relations with other countries on the basis of his study of the "new books" Pak brought from Peking. Kim woke up from the traditional thought of hundreds of years that China is the Middle Kingdom of the world and the nations surrounding it are barbarians. Kim came to know that so long as this thought of looking up to China as the Middle Kingdom of the world prevailed, Korea could not become independent of Chian. Later Kim Ok-kyun led the Coup d'Etat of 1884.[2]

O Kyŏng-sŏk, a Chinese translator-interpreter of the *chungin* (middle people) class, visited Peking 1853-1854 and returned home also with many books on the Western world. Naturally he studied these books and began to embrace the enlightenment thought. In 1872 he again visited China as interpreter for Pak Kyu-su who was chief of a royal mission. Observing the developments in Peking, he felt that Korea was also in danger of heavy Western influence, and that he had his friend, Yu Tae-ch'i (Yu Honggi), read the books he brought from Peking. They discussed these books, worrying about the future of Korea. Later, O Se-ch'ang wrote about his father as follows:

My father, O Kyŏng-sŏk, had frequently visited China as interpreter for the annual Winter Solstice Emissary and other envoys of the Korean government sent to Peking. While in Peking he witnessed the Chinese capital turning into an arena of power struggle among the Western powers and worried about the possibility that Korea might become such an arena. Later he studied the histories of Western powers. especially their rise and fall, and was aware that

Korea was far behind these Western countries. He also deplored the corruption that prevailed in the government and warned that Korea would face a big tragedy should the corrupt, conservative government continue to remain, in power, … My father had a friend named Yu Hong-gi, alias Taech'i. Taech'i was a man of both letters and character. My father gave him the "new books" he brought from Peking and encouraged him to study them. Later their friendship was solidified as they came to hold the same opinion that the only way to save the country from the brink of the danger of fall to the Western power is to launch a great reform movement. One day Yu Tae-ch'i asked my father how the reform movement should be launched, and my father said that they should first make friends with young people of the *yangban* families in Pukch'on (North Village) of Seoul and then infuse them with the reformist thought.[3]

Yu Hong-gi was born of an interpreter's family of the *chungin* class, but he studied herb medicine and practiced it near Kwanggyo in Seoul. After reading the books O Kyŏng-sŏk brought from China, he came to embrace the enlightenment thought. A devoted Buddhist, he tried to fuse the enlightenment thought into Buddhism.[4]

The enlightenment thought was thus developed by the above-mentioned three pioneers during 1853-1860s at the latest. The gist of the enlightenment thought developed by these three reformists can be summarized as follows:

First, a crisis is being brewed in the Asia because of the Western powers' encroachment, and Korea is also facing such a crisis.

Second, to overcome this crisis, Korea must be transformed from a pre-modern society to a modern society in a great reform movement.

Third, Ch'ing China has already succumbed to the Western powers, and Korea cannot be saved from such a crisis by relying on China.

Fourth, there is no absolute Middle Kingdom, and any country can be a Middle Kingdom. Korea should strengthen its independence from China and decide its national fate on its own, while striving to build a rich and powerful country of high civilization.

Fifth, Western science and technology are further advanced than Oriental science and technology, and Korea should import and apply Western science and technology to building a rich and powerful country.

Sixth, Korea should initiate commercial and trade relations with Western countries on an equal and reciprocal basis, and accept Western ideas and ways on a selective basis in building a rich and powerful country.

Seventh, the *yangban* estate system must be abolished because ruling class privilege based on this system has done the cost serious injury to the nation, and equal rights must be established for all in order to recruit competent and talented people for government positions.

Eighth, the government must be reformed and reorganized because it, being corrupt and pre-modern, has no capability of saving the country from the encroachment of the Western powers.

Ninth, the Western powers have a powerful force of artillery and warships, and Korea should establish a modern army equipped with new weapons so as to strengthen the defense system.

Tenth, a new political force should be established. But since to this end there is not enough time, promising young people of the ruling class should be first educated in the new thought and new knowledge, all based on Western ideas and ways.

It was in 1870 when Kim Ok-kyun was around twenty that Kim, who was to become the leader of the Coup d'Etat of 1884, first learned the enlightenment thought from Yu Tae-ch'i. O Se-ch'ang wrote about their meeting as follows:

> Kim Ok-kyun made the acquaintance of Yu Tae-ch'i when Kim was 20 years old. Kim learned the new thought from Yu and made friends with the young men who had interest in this thought. Kim passed *kwagŏ* (the civil service examination) to serve in the government, where he devoted himself to gathering the young enlightened people.[5]

The enlightenment thought was developed in the latter half of the 1860s, and from 1870, when Kim Ok-kyun was 20, young people of the ruling class began to study seriously this thought. O se-ch'ang said that Kim Ok-kyun learned the enlightenment thought around 1870 and gathered young enlightened people when he passed the civil service examination to serve in the government. It was in 1872 when he was 22 that Kim passed the examination and two years later he was appointed a member of *Hongmun-gwan* (office of Special Advisors). According to O Se-ch'ang, it was therefore in 1874 that Kim Ok-kyun started to gather young enlightened people of the ruling class.

At the same time, Kim Ok-kyun said that it was in 1874 that the *Kaehwa-dang* (Progressive Party) was formed. This is in agreement with the above-mentioned records of O Se-ch'ang. In his Kapshin Illok (Journal of 1884) Kim wrote as follows:

There is a court lady (Yi U-sŏk ?) who is 42 years old. She is so strong that she is a match for five or six ordinary men in strength. So we call her *Kodaesu* (an Amazon) and she, in addition to being strong, is one of the favorites of the queen. She has worked for our party as a court agent for 10 years.[6]

In 1884 Kim wrote that there had been a secret court informer of our party from 10 years before, and this, together with O Se-ch'ang's records, leads to the conclusion that the Progressive Party was organized in 1874.

The enlightenment thought was developed by Pak Kyu-su, O Kyŏng-sŏk and Yu Tae-ch'i, and it was developed into the Progressive Party as a political force by Kim Ok-kyun and his friends. Under the guidance of Pak Kyun-su, O Kyŏng-sŏk and Yu Tae-ch'i, Kim Ok-kyun infused his friends with the new thought. Kim sought and gathered friends widely from among the military *yangban* class, the *chungin* class, merchants and even commoners. He also won court ladies and eunuchs over to his side.

But when Korea opened its doors to Japan under the Treaty of Kanghwa-do concluded in 1876, the power of the Progressive Party was so weak that it could do almost nothing. Under the treaty, Pusan was opened in 1876., Wŏnsan in 1880 and Inch'ŏn in 1883, and this necessitated the Chosŏn dynasty government to employ young people who had knowledge of the outside world. As a result, many Progressives found their way to important government positions to propagate the enlightenment thought among government officials, thereby contributing to the propagation of the enlightenment thought. But in 1881 the conservative Confucian *literati*, who called for defending orthodoxy and rejecting heterodoxy, sent a letter to the king attacking the enlightenment policy based on foreign ideas. This letter was occasioned by Huang Tsun-hsien's *Chaohsien Ts'elüeh* (A Strategy for Chosŏn) which Kim Hong-jip brought from Japan in 1880. In reaction to this letter, young Progressives also sent letters to the king, explaining the need for an enlightenment policy. For instance, in September 1882 Ko Yŏng-mun wrote a letter to the king, recommending:[7]

(1) Introduction of Western Technology — A mission should be sent to Western countries to observe their culture and institutions and establish friendly relations with them. Western engineers should be invited to the country for technical training of young people.

(2) Establishment of a Public Council — A public council should be formed as a non-government organization, and this council should draw on those who

are well versed in specific problems in formulating its policy recommendations to the government.

(3) Development of the Mining Industry and the Monetary System—A law should be enacted to promote the mining industry, and precious metal money should be issued for permanent circulation so as to make nobody live in idleness.

(4) Establishment of a Police System—A police district should be established for every 50 households, and each district should have four policemen, in addition to the district chief, for control of theft, fire, flood and overdrinking in the district.

(5) Establishment of National Bank and Chamber of Commerce—A national bank and a chamber of commerce should be set up in Seoul for the development of commerce and industry.

(6) Establishment of a Navy — A navy should be established, with its base in Inch'ŏn, for the defense of the sea route and the capital from sea invasion.

(7) Tax Reform– Unnecessary posts in the government should be abolished, and a modern tax system should be established for a reasonable tax burden on the people. Under this system, public servants will get subsistent wages and the opportunity for competent people to enter public service will be broadened.

The Progressives, who found their way to important government positions after the opening of the country to Japan and Western countries, had such influence on the king that their enlightenment policy was pursued. Between 1880 and 1884 when the *Kapshin Chŏngbyŏn* broke out, the Progressives implemented the following enlightenment programs, among other things: [8]

(1) Establishment of a modern government office called *T'ongni Kimu Amun* (office for Extraordinary State Affairs) in 1880.

(2) Dispatch of *Yŏngsŏn-sa* (Mission of Ordnance and Technology) to foreign countries in 1881.

(3) Dispatch of an observation mission to Japan in 1881.

(4) Establishment of a modern army, called *Pyŏlgigun*, in 1881.

(5) Establishment of *Kimu-ch'ŏ* (Deliberative Council of Important State Affairs) in 1882.

(6) Establishment of *Kamsaeng-ch'ŏng* (Office of Budget Austerity) in 1882.

(7) Execution of balance of power policy to foreign countries in 1882.

(8) Announcement of sea defense policy in 1882.

(9) Establishment of *Hae-gwan* (Customs Office) in 1882.

(10) Establishment of a modern school, *Wŏnsan Haksa*, in 1883.

(11) Establishment of an English school, *Tongmunhak*, in 1883.

(12) Publication of a modern newspaper, *Hansŏng Sunbo*, in 1883.

(13) Establishment of modern post system in 1883.

(14) Establishment of *Ch'ido-guk* (Office of Road Improvement) and widening of streets in Seoul in 1883.

(15) Establishment of a modern police system in Seoul in 1883.

(16) Reform of custom system (introduction of Western custom) in 1883.

(17) Dispatch of students to foreign countries in 1881-1884.

(18) Establishment of agricultural and livestock-farming experiment stations in 1884.

(19) Establishment of 26 modern commercial and industrial companies in 1881-1884.

These modernization programs of the Progressives were designed to build a modern nation-state in Korea. Had the progressives been able to continue their modernization programs without facing any hindrance, Chosŏn dynasty would have become a modern nation strong enough to maintain its independence. But the situation began to deteriorate, with the Military Mutiny of 1882 serving as a turning point.

The military mutiny forced the Conservative Party led by Queen Min out of power and Taewŏn'gun took over the reins of government. The Conservatives asked for Ch'ing China's help, and Li Hung-chang, China's North Sea Minister, decided to sent troops to Korea to consolidate China's suzerainty over Korea. As a result, a force of 3,000 troops was sent to Seoul and Taewŏn'gun, the king's father, was invited to a Chinese warship off Inch'ŏn and taken to China aboard the ship. He was put under confinement at Paotingfu in China.

China put the Conservatives again in power on the strength of its troops stationed in Seoul and claimed its suzerainty over Korea with positive interference in Korea's domestic and foreign affairs, thus greatly infringing upon Korea's sovereignty. Wu Ch'ang-ch'ing and Yüan Shih-k'ai, commanders of the Chinese troops in Korea, took the reins of Korea's military affairs, and Ch'en Shu-t'ang, financial advisor to the Korean government, had financial control in hand. Paul Georg von Mölendorff, whom Li Hung-chang sent to Seoul as customs advisor, intervened not only in customs affairs but in foreign affairs.

Moreover, China, considering the Progressive Party's enlightenment movement under Kim Ok-kyun's leadership as having the aim of Korea's independence from Chinese suzerainty, employed all means to oppress the Progressives and hinder their movement. The modernization programs after the Military Mutiny of 1882 were carried out under Chinese oppression and persecution, and they were thus not satisfactory to the Progressives.

The Conservative party led by Queen Min was subservient to China's suzerain policy in return for Chinese assistance in their rise again to power which they lost after the Military Mutiny of 1882. The Conservatives were bent on pursuing self-interest, paying no heed to the infringement upon sovereignty and the hindrance to modernization programs due to Chinese suzerainty. Furthermore, they, in collaboration with China, oppressed the Progressives to eliminate them from the political world.

In 1884 when the Sino-French relation became tense over Annan, China moved 1,500 troops of its 3,000-man force in Seoul to Annan in May, leaving only 1,500 troops in Korea. In August of that year, war broke out between China and France in Annan. Taking advantage of the situation, the Progressive Party launched a coup d'Etat on December 4, 1884, employing 1,000 Korean troops and 150 Japanese troops stationed in the Japanese legation in Seoul.

In the coup, the Progressives executed Conservative ministers on the first day and established a new government on the following day. On the third day of the coup, they even announced a reform platform. But on the evening of the day their government collapsed under the attack of Chinese troops. The Progressive Party's social thoughts underlying the Coup d'Etat of 1884 is reflected in the reform platform they announced in the coup, and in the following I will introduce this platform of the Progressive Party as it is known today in an attempt to shed light on the nature of the coup.

3. Platform of the Progressive Party

Some thoughts of the Progressive Party which launched the Coup d'Etat of 1884 are directly reflected in the party's reform platform. Of course, the platform does not represent the whole of the party's social thoughts because it contains only those which can be put into practice immediately after the coup. But it still presents well the basic reform direction in which the Progressive Party wanted to lead the country in those days.

On the evening of December 4, 1884, the Progressive Party launched the coup, making opportune use of a banquet hosted by Hong Yŏng-shik, director of the Postal Administration, to celebrate the opening of the new building of the agency. The following day the Progressives took over the reins of government and immediately started formulating a reform program. On the evening of December 5, they met in Ch'angdŏk-gung palace to discuss the platform, without eating supper. Participating in the meeting were Hong

Yŏng-shik, Pak Yŏng-hyo, Kim Ok-kyun, Sŏ Kwang-bŏm, Pak Yŏng-gyo, Yi Chae-wŏn, Yi Chae-wan and Sin Ki-sŏn. They had an all-night meeting to finish the platform. Kim Ok-kyun presided over the meeting.[9]

Around nine on the morning of December 6, they announced this program of political reform in the form of a royal circular and pasted up it on the walls at major places of the capital, even before the king approved it.[10] The Progressive government occasionally announced major policy measures immediately after a cabinet meeting and sought the king's approval later in view of the urgent need of the situation. The fact that the Progressive government announced the reform platform to the public prior to the king's approval shows that these Progressives did not adhere to an absolute monarchy.

Two points deserve attention here. One is that the program of political reform was formulated as a collective thought after long hours of discussion at a meeting. The other is that government policy was announced to the public beforehand in the form of a political platform, which had never before occurred in Korean history. All the previous governments, including the one ruled by the Conservative party led by Queen Min, had never announced their policy to the people. According to Confucian political morality, people as the ruled need not and should not know government policy. Thus the Progressive government's policy announcement to the public was an unprecedented and epoch-making event at the time.

On December 6 Right Prime Minister Hong Yŏng-shik of the State Council submitted the reform platform to King Kojong for his approval, and at three in the afternoon the king issued an edict proclaiming that the country would be run on the basis of the reform platform.[11]

Today, all the Progressive Party's program of political reform is not known, because Queen Min's Conservative Party, which took over power again after the collapse of the Progressive Party, collected documents containing the platform and destroyed them. A Japanese who was in Seoul during the Progressive Party's coup said that the platform contained 80 planks, but this is not reliable because he failed to put down those planks. The authentic record of the platform remaining today is found in Kim Ok-kyun's *Kapshin Illok* (Journal of 1884) which he later wrote in exile. This journal contains 14 planks, and these are only part of the platform because Kim said, "the platform can be summarized as follows." The 14 planks Kim Ok-kyun put in his journal are the following:[12]

(1) Seek the immediate return of Taewŏn'gun and an end to the empty

formalities of tributary relationship with China.

(2) Abolish ruling class privilege and establish equal rights for all; stop making appointments on the basis of finding suitable office for privileged seekers of position and instead seek out men whose talents suit them for official appointment.

(3) Revise the land tax laws for every region of the country and root out the extortionate practices of the petty officials who administer them, thus alleviating the distress of the people and at the same time ensuring receipt of sufficient revenue to meet government expenditures.

(4) Abolish the Office of Eunuch Attendants (*Naeshi-bu*), but employ those eunuchs who are men of superior talent.

(5) Punish the most notorious officials whose evil and venal acts past and present have brought the nation to its present state of infirmity.

(6) Cancel all outstanding grain loan debts owed to the government.

(7) Abolish *Kyujang-gak* (privileged Palace Library).

(8) Quickly establish police patrols to prevent thievery.

(9) Abolish the Office for the Benefit of Peddler-Trade (*Hyesang Kong-guk*)

(10) Review the cases of those who have been banished or barred from office and, as warranted, revoke their sentences.

(11) Merge the Four Barracks Commands into a single unit, then select able soldiers among them and immediately form a Royal Guards Division under the command of the Crown Prince.

(12) Put all internal fiscal administration under the jurisdiction of the Ministry of Finance, abolishing all other fiscal agencies.

(13) Have the ministers and councilors convene on a regular schedule at the State Council chamber in the palace to discuss policy, submit proposals to the king, made his decisions known, and then transmit them for implementation.

(14) Abolish all superfluous government agencies, with the ministers and councilors to study the matter and submit proposals to the throne.

Inoue Kakugoro, a Japanese translator of the *Hansŏng Sunbo*, thrice-monthly gazette, published by the Office of Culture and Information (Pang-mun-guk), the Office for Extraordinary State Affairs, recalled the reform actions of the Progressive Party as follows (he witnessed the coup in Seoul):[13]

(1) Abolish tributary relation with China; immediately send an envoy to

China to declare Korea's complete independence from China and seek Taewŏn'gun's return.

(2) Elevate the status of the king to that of emperor so as to be equal to the Chinese emperor, and address him *P'yeha* (Your or His Majesty), and call his order edict. The emperor should address himself *Chim* (Imperial We) so as to establish the proper etiquette as an independent nation's sovereign.

(3) Control arbitrariness of the *yangban* class and promote civil rights of the commoner.

(4) Abolish the eunuch system, but employ those eunuchs who are talented.

(5) Severely punish all corrupt officials.

(6) Establish the Ministry of Imperial Household Affairs so as to separate court affairs from state affairs.

(7) Reform the government system and establish a cabinet consisting of eight ministries.

(8) Abolish the civil service examination (*kwagŏ*) system.

(9) Select young men of talent and send them abroad for study.

(10) Issue public bonds to raise funds for the promotion of industry, transportation, education and defense.

The historical characteristics of the Coup d'Etat of 1884 are well represented in the Progressive Party's reform platform, and the platform as it is known today is so briefly summarized that it requires annotations and explanations. In the following, I will review and explain the Progressive Party's reform platform on the basis of the 14 planks found in Kim Ok-kyun's *Journal of 1884* and other historical documents.

4. Analysis of Reform Platform

A. Declaration of Complete Independence

The first plank, to press for the immediate return of Taewŏn'gun from China and an end to the tributary relationship with China, was a declaration that Korea and the new Progressive government was completely independent form China.

With the Military Mutiny of 1882 serving as a turning-point, Ch'ing China intensified its suzerainty over Korea in its policy to put the country under its control, thereby greatly damaging the sovereignty of Chosŏn. The reform platform of the Progressive government was a flat rejection of the suzerain policy of China toward Korea and a declaration of Korea's complete independence from Chinese control. Before the Coup d'Etat of 1884 Kim Ok-kyun wrote his idea of national independence as follows:

> It is shameful that China has traditionally considered Korea its subject state, and it is partly because of this tributary relationship with China that we have no hope for development as an independent nation. So the first task facing us is to expunge the Chinese sway and establish a completely independent nation. To be an independent nation, we should build up our political and diplomatic power.[14]

Sŏ Chae-p'il recalled Kim's independence thought as follows:

> He (Kim Ok-kyun) had a strong humiliating sense of Chinese sway over Korea, and was absorbed in the thought of relieving the people of this humiliation by making Korea a free country equal to other countries of the world.[15]

> The ideal and goal Kim Ok-kyun sought at the time was to eliminate Chinese influence and take an independent government could be established.

> Kim Ok-kyun was indignant about China's abduction of Taewŏn'gun because he considered it an unbearable shame to Korea. So he started organizing a force to eliminate the pro-Chinese aristocrats.[16]

So the reform platform of the Progressive Party rejected in its first plank the suzerain policy China began to intensify in Korea after 1882 and abolished the empty formalities of tributary relationship with China which had existed before 1882. It was thus a declaration of Korea's complete independence from China. In other words, it was a declaration that Korea, being an independent nation, could now take rank with other nations of the world.

The reform platform of the Progressive Party marked a very important milestone in modern Korean history in that it not only flatly rejected China's suzerain policy in Korea after the Military Mutiny of 1882 but also pressed for bringing to an end the empty formalities of the tributary relationship with China for the first time in nearly 500 years since the founding of the Chosŏn dynasty, thus declaring before the world that Korea is an completely independent nation.

B. Abolition of Yangban System and Nepotism for Appointments of Talented People

The second plank of the reform platform called for the abolition of ruling class privileges and the establishment of equal rights for all so that men of talent could be appointed to official positions, instead of making appointments on the basis of finding suitable offices for privileged seekers of positions. This was the pronouncement of equal rights for all by eliminating social estate differences and the rejection of nepotism and by guaranteeing appointments on the basis of men's talent.

At the time the most evil system that checked development of the country was the *yangban* system. Kim Ok-kyun wrote in a letter to the emperor about the evils of the *yangban* system as follows:

> Your Majesty must still remember what I have told about the need to chop down the *yangban* system on the basis of my study for a long time. In ancient times when the nation was prosperous Korea was better than the two Oriental countries (China and Japan) in technology and industry, but today such prosperity has all gone with no trace remaining. This is because of the arbitrariness of *yangban.*
>
> When people manufacture articles *yangban* officials take them, and when people make a fortune with hard work *yangban* officials carry it away. People complain that when they support themselves by hard work *yangban* officials not only usurp the result of such hard work but even threaten to kill those who refuse to give up their property. As a result, many people have given up agriculture, commerce and industry, and the number of idle and wandering people is on the increase only to bring the nation to its present state of infirmity.[17]

Kim Ok-kyun wrote this letter requesting the elimination of the *yangban* system in 1886, and as he said in the letter that "… what I have told … on the basis of my study for a long time, "he had already called for the elimination of the *yangban* system before the coup of 1884. He used the phrase "to chop down" in requesting the elimination of the *yangban* system, and by this he must have meant that the *yangban* system should be chopped down as we chop down weeds with a sickle. So the phrase had a stronger meaning than the words, abolition and elimination. In other words, Kim Ok-kyun demanded that the *yangban* system be done away with once and for all.

Noteworthy in Kim Ok-kyun's demand for the abolition of the *yangban* system is that he was quite capitalistic and modern in his way of thinking. He attributed the declining industry of the nation in his days, though it was more prosperous in Korea than in China and Japan in the ancient times, to the *yangban* system and pointed out: ① *Yangban* officials took from people whatever goods they made; ② *Yangban* officials usurped a small capitals people accumulate; ③ As a result, people could not engage in productive activities and capital formation by people was impossible; ④ *Yangban* officials exploited people when they supported themselves with hard work; ⑤ When people refused to give what they made to *yangban* officials, these threatened to murder them; and ⑥ consequently, people gave up agriculture, commerce and industry bringing the nation to an infirm state. He considered the *yangban* system as a big barrier against industrial development and capital formation and called for the "chopping down" of this system for good and all. His reform idea can thus be called capitalistic.

Sŏ Chae-p'il said that Kim Ok-kyun's idea was the realization of Koras's complete independence and the destruction of the aristocratic (*yangban*) system.[18] A Japanese who witnessed the coup of 1884 said that the Progressive Party launched it to abolish ruling class privileges and promote civil rights.[19] Kim Ok-kyun warned that, in the age of commerce and industry in which nations of the world compete with each other in industry, Korea would fall should it fail to eliminate the *yangban* system which is the source of all social and political evils of the country.

> "Today nations of the world are competing for bigger production on the basis of commerce. In such a time of world history, should we fail to chop down the *yangban* system which is the root of all social and political evils of the country, we can only expect the fall of the country."[20]

The reform program of the Coup d'Etat of 1884 was based on such ideas of Kim Ok-kyun, and it called for immediate elimination of the *yangban* system and establishment of equal rights for all.

The abolition of nepotism was closely related to the elimination of the *yangban* system. At the time, the nation was in a crisis and there was the pressing need to seek men of talent and knowledge from among all walks of social life for appointment to government positions so as to save the country from the approaching encroachment of foreign powers. In spite of this situation, selected *yangban* families formed a power clique, and only those who belonged to this clique were appointed to government positions and others were rejected, no mater what talent and knowledge they had. In other words, only the clique members, however corrupt and talentless, could be appointed to important positions of the government. Immediately before the coup of 1884, those of the Min family and a few others held nearly all of the important government positions.

Before the coup Kim Ok-kyun had strongly argued that to save the country "men of talent must be appointed" to government positions.[21] He told in a letter to the emperor about the need to abolish nepotism and appoint men of talent to government positions as follows:

> I sincerely request that Your Majesty pay attention to this situation and dismiss conservative and narrow-minded ministers and other talentless ranking officials and dismantle the nepotist family power clique. I also request Your Majesty to seek men of talent for a solid centralized government based on the people's trust.[22]

Based on the thought of Kim Ok-kyun the reform platform of the coup of 1884 was a declaration against nepotism for appointment of men of talent, along with the elimination of the *yangban* system for establishing equal rights for all.

In view of the second plank of the platform, had the coup of 1884 succeeded, Korea would have seen the abolition of the *yangban* system and the nepotist family power clique 10 years before the *Kabo Kyŏng-jang* (Reform of 1894) and appointments of many men of talent from all social classes to government positions on the basis of equal rights for all. This would have saved the nation from Japanese aggression and led to the development of the nation as a modern nation-state.

All in all, the second plank of the Progressive Party's reform platform in the coup of 1884 marked an epoch-making milestone in the history of Korean politics in that it was the first government declaration of the abolition of the *yangban* system and the family power clique to establish equal rights for all the people.

C. Reform of Government Organization and Establishment of Cabinet System.

The reform platform of the coup of 1884 was also designed to reorganize the government system by establishing a cabinet. This was clearly expressed in the 13th plank which provided for a regular meeting of ministers and councilors at the State Council in the palace to make proposals to the king, to announce decisions to the public and then to transmit them for implementation, the 14th plank which called for the abolition of all superfluous government agencies, except for the six ministries, with the ministers and councilors to study the matter and submit proposals to the throne, and the fourth plank which also pressed for the abolition of the Office of Eunuch Attendants but the employment of those eunuchs who were men of talent.

The aims of the Progressive Party in these measures were: ① institution of a daily meeting of ministers and councilors at the State Council without the presence of the king, instead of the imperial meeting under absolute monarchy; ② discussion and decision of policy matters at this meeting to submit them to the throne; ③ abolition of all government agencies submitting proposals to the king, except for the six ministries, so that only the meeting of the ministers and councilors of the six ministries can discuss and decide on all policy matters for implementation; ④ implementation as decrees (laws) of the decisions made at the meeting of ministers and councilors.

Under these measures, all legislative and administrative decisions were to be made at the meeting of the ministers and councilors of the six ministries (cabinet meeting) and the power of the throne would be limited to the right to approve or refuse the meeting a decision. And the king would hardly refuse such decision except for a special case because the decision was to be made only at a meeting of ministers and councilors. This was designed to bring an end to the arbitrary exercise of power by the king for the institution of a cabinet having both legislative and administrative powers, the early form of constitutional monarchy.

The institution of such a cabinet system envisioned under the Progressive Party's reform platform can be said to be the expression of the coup leaders' plan to transform the absolute monarchy into a constitutional one.[23]

The establishment of a cabinet system behooved the coup leaders to reorganize the government system, and the above-mentioned three planks of their platform called for ① reorganization of the government on the basis of six ministries, ② abolition of all agencies except for the six ministries, ③ separation of court affairs from state affairs, ④ abolition of all pre-modern agencies, such as the Office of Eunuch Attendants. These reform measures were thus considered revolutionary at the time because they aimed at an end to the centuries-old absolute monarchy.

D. Economic and Financial Reforms

The reform platform of the Progressive government included the measures for economic and financial reforms. The 12th plank called for placing all internal fiscal administration under the jurisdiction of the Ministry of Finance, abolishing all other fiscal agencies, and the third plank provided for revision of land tax laws and elimination of the extortionate practices of the petty officials who administered them, thus alleviating the distress of the people and at the same time encouraging receipt of sufficient revenue to meet government expenditures. In addition, the Progressives wanted to cancel all outstanding grain loan debts owed to the government under the sixth plank and abolish the Office for the Benefit of Peddler-Trade under the ninth plank. These measures were efforts to bring about unified and centralized fiscal administration, reform taxes including land taxes, root out the extortionate practices of covetous officials, cancel grain loan debts owed to the government and bring an end to the commercial privileges enjoyed by packmen for encouraging the development of free trade.

The government finances at the time were under a pre-modern system, and every government agency had its own revenue sources for its expenditures. In addition, there was no government budget system, thus causing financial waste and confusion. Even before the coup of 1884 the Progressives deplored such financial confusion of the country and strongly argued that a modern government budget system should be established to put all financial administration under the jurisdiction of the Ministry of Finance.[24]

In the coup of 1884 the Progressive Party set the goals of their financial reform measures as follows: ① unified fiscal administration under the control of the Ministry of Finance; ② abolition of all fiscal agencies except for the Ministry of Finance; ③ establishment of a government budget system; ④ tax reforms; and ⑤ integration of revenue and expenditure system; ⑥ issuance of public bonds to raise financial funds. To achieve these goals, the Progressives put stress on placing all internal fiscal administration under the control of the Ministry of Finance.

Taking over power in the coup, the Progressives intended a great reform from above, and to carry out this plan they needed funds. As a result, they wanted to bring all fiscal administration under the Ministry of Finance's control and appointed Kim Ok-kyun vice-minister of Ministry of Finance without appointment of the minister in order to control financial administration.

The revision of the land tax laws was an effort to reform the land tax system and the defense tax system, two cases out of the most corrupt three of the time. The Progressive Party's tax reform plan was designed to lower tax rates and root out the extortionate practices of corrupt officials for the alleviation of people's tax burden. They hoped that such tax reform would encourage people to increase production and ensure sufficient revenues to meet government expenditures.

The cancellation of all outstanding grain loan debts owed to the government was designed to bring an end to the grain loan system which was also in disorder at the time, along with the land taxes and the defense taxes. The grain loan system was originally designed to provide food for farmers in time of emergency and bad harvest, but in the latter Chosŏn period it became an official usury system for covetous officials to exploit farmers and amass a fortune. As a result, farmers' grievance against the grain loan system was so great that in 1862 farmers in Chinju rose against it. But the Conservative government under the sway of Queen Min was not able to abolish the system because the high interest they collected from farmers on grain loans was a major source of government revenues and thier private income.

In the reform platform of the coup of 1884, however, the Progressive Party accepted the people's demand for abolishing the grain loan system and even announced the cancellation of all the outstanding grain loan debts owed to the government. This was a significant policy in that it aimed at alleviating the people's distress due to grain loans.

The abolition of the Office for the Benefit of Peddler-Trade was an effort to bring an end to the commercial privileges of packmen. In August 1883 the Conservative government established the office and appointed Min T'ae-ho its director to intensify the commercial privileges of packmen and organize them as a political force for the Conservatives. This was against the capitalistic trend of the time toward free trade.

On the other hand, the Progressive Party encouraged the development of modern industries, such as manufacturing, railroad and shipping, as well as agricultural development.[25] Kim Ok-kyun also stressed the need to develop modern industries[26] and argued that the country should develop mining, transportation and communication industries, among others.[27] Thanks to such encouragement of the Progressive Party, a total of 26 modern companies of commerce and industry were established in the country between 1883 and November 1884, just before the Progressive Party's coup.[28]

The reform platform of the Coup d'Etat of 1884 calls for the abolition of the Office for the Benefit of Peddler-Trade to eliminate the feudalist commercial system based on packmen in an attempt to keep packmen from being a political force for the Conservative Party, and at the same time to lay a foundation for the development of capitalist free trade. This means that in the coup of 1884 the Progressives wanted to do away with the pre-modern economic system once and for all in order to construct a capitalist system of economy and industry.

E. Reform of the Defense System

The 11th plank of the reform platform, to press for merger of the Four Barracks Commands into a single unit and selection of the most able soldiers among them to form a Royal Guards Division under the command of the Crown Prince, was aimed at a reform of the defense system.

The Four Barracks Commands at the time were under the command of Conservative officers, and had the mission of guarding the court, rather than that of defending the country. Of the four commands, two were organized and trained in the style of a Western army, and the other two, activated by Yüan Shih-k'ai, were trained in the Chinese army style. As a result, the four commands were divided into two groups differently organized and trained, and these two were antagonistic to each other.[29]

Under the circumstances, the Progressive Party argued before the coup of 1884 that the four commands should be merged into a single unit organized and trained in a uniform style.[30] In the face of the Western powers' aggressive policy, Kim Ok-kyun and his Progressive Party members stressed the need to have an army strong enough to defend the country from the Western powers' aggression. They proposed that young able men be sent to foreign military academies for study. Returning home after study, they should be appointed instructors of a new military academy to be established for the education of modern army officers. On the basis of these newly-trained officers, a modern army should be organized. On this point Sŏ Chae-p'il recalled:

> One day he (Kim Ok-kyun) told me that to defend the country we must have a strong army, adding that nothing is more urgent than organizing a modern army. He then suggested that I go to Japan to study military art. I immediately accepted his suggestion and soon left for Japan with 15 other students.[31]

In June 1884 when the students they had sent to Japan returned home, Kim Ok-kyun and his Progressive Party demanded the establishment of a modern military academy with the students returned from Japan as its instructors.[32]

The Progressives had a plan to organize a modern army and a modern navy with imported warships. In other words, they wanted to adopt the Western military system, and to achieve this goal they carried in almost every issue of the *Hansŏng Sunbo*, the Progressive newspaper, and article introducing the strength of Western armies and navies, as well as the military situation of the Western nations. This attests to the fact that the Progressives had a great interest in developing a self-reliant defense posture in the face of the Western powers' encroachment policy.

The merger of the four commands into a single unit and the forming of a Royal Guards Division to separate the mission of national defense from that of court guard, as included in the reform platform, were but the initial step of the Progressive Party's defense reform program. Placing the Royal Guards Division under the Crown Prince's command was to follow the general practice of a monarchy of the time.

F. Abolition of *Kyujang-gak* and Development of Modern Culture

The abolition of *Kyujang-gak* (Palace Library) under the seventh plank of the reform platform was the expression of the Progressive Party's plan to eliminate the aristocratic system of culture represented by *Kyujang-gak* and develop modern culture on the basis of "new" education of the people.

It may be that the abolition of *Kyujang-gak* can hardly be understood by superficial minds, but it must be noted that the Progressives, weighing the two characteristics of the Palace Library, that is, the archives of traditional culture and the representative of the aristocratic system of culture, decided to abolish the latter characteristic of the library to lay a foundation for the development of modern culture based on the people. In this regard, Sŏ Chae-p'il recalled:

> Kim Ok-kyun attributed the infirm state of the nation to the lack of technical training of the people and the ignorance of the ruling class about the development of other countries. He used to say, "The only way to save the country is to educate the people." Because old people could hardly be educated in modern knowledge, he pinned hope on the education of young people.[33]

What is noteworthy here is that Kim OK-kyun thought that the pre-modern knowledge of the ruling class was useless and even harmful, considering that the only way to save the nation is to give "new" education to the people. Kim Ok-kyun argued that the people should be educated in "new" civilization[34] by establishing many schools of "new" education.[35] He also called for the publication of government policies in Korean letters, instead of in Chinese characters, so that the people can understand them.[36]

All in all, this thought of the Progressive Party was expressed in its reform platform of the coup of 1884 in the form of a demand for abolition of *Kyujang -gak*, the library for the ruling class, and establishment of modern schools of education of the people in "new" civilization to lay a foundation for the development of modern culture.

G. Establishment of Modern Police and Judicial System.

Under the eighth plank of the reform platform the leaders of the coup of 1884 demanded the establishment of police patrols to prevent thievery, and under the 10th plank they called for a review of the cases of those who had been banished or barred form office and, as warranted, the revocation of their sentences. These measures were designed to establish a modern police system based on police patrols and a modern system of judicial affairs by releasing unjustly exiled or imprisoned people under the inhumane, feudalist judicial system so as to win the heart of the people.

Even before the coup of 1884 Kim Ok-kyun strongly argued for the establishment of a modern police system.[37] And when Pak Yŏng-hyo was serving as mayor of Seoul, he partially introduced a modern police system to the capital city. Kim Ok-kyun criticized the harsh judicial system of the time as follows:

> Examining the present judicial system, I find that the criminal codes are so outdated that their enforcement is in confusion and the abuse of the codes, such as threats against the life of a person and the usurpation of property, all over the country, but no action has been taken against such evils. The stealing of a nail or a drill and the name-calling of a government official banish one to a remote place, and such belittling of people's lives only damages the peace of society.[38]

Kim Ok-kyun demanded the making of new laws because he believed that only under the new laws all social injustice and irregularities could be corrected. He called for a reform of judicial affairs by enacting new laws and abolition of heavy punishments, including banishment, in favor of light punishments, such as labor or fines for minor criminals.[39]

All in all, the reform platform of the coup of 1884 pressed for the immediate establishment of police patrols in an attempt to establish a modern police system. It also provided for the release of the people unjustly imprisoned or banished under the harsh feudalist judicial system so as to show the progressive government's generosity in an attempt to win the heart of the people, and at the same time to abolish the feudalist judicial system.

H. Punishment of Officials Harmful to the Nation

The Progressive Party demanded under the fifth plank of its reform platform that the crimes of those most notorious officials whose evil and venal acts have brought the nation to its present state of infirmity be punished. This was aimed at a purge of the corrupt officials who amassed a fortune in the Conservative government and the punishment of such officials depending on the degree of harm they did to the national interest.

The purge of the corrupt officials who did great harm to the national interest under the old regime can be considered a natural course of action to be taken by the Progressive Party after it took over power in the coup of 1884.

As discussed above, the reform platform of the Coup d'Etat of 1884 was a list of actions the Progressive Party was to take in order to reform the whole spectrum of state affairs.

5. Historical Characteristics of the Reform Platform

The reformation thought of the Coup d'Etat of 1884, as expressed in the reform platform, was the pursuit of reform measures for construction of a modern nation-state. Sŏ Chae-p'il, who took part in the coup, recalled Kim Ok-kyun's ideal as construction of "a strong modern nation":

> Although he did not receive modern education, Kim Ok-kyun had a keen insight into the historical trend of the time and devoted himself to building a strong modern nation in Korea. He strongly felt the need to reform the government and society by introducing new knowledge and new technology to the country.[40]

In training members of the Progressive Party as its leader, Kim Ok-kyun said, "Japan is endeavoring to be the England of the Orient, and we must make Korea the France of the Orient." Sŏ Chae-p'il also recalled him as follows:

Kim Ok-kyun treated us as his brothers and told us everything in his mind. He was frank and honest with us. He told about our mission and responsibility in the reform program and expected and believed that we would make a great contribution to the development of Korea. He often told us that while Japan is endeavoring to be the England of the Orient, we must make Korea the France of Asia. This was his dream and ambition. We believed him and made up our mind to fulfill our responsibility, no matter what may happen to us.[41]

The strong modern nation Kim Ok-kyun and his Progressive party members wanted to build was the France of Asia. Seeing that Japan was becoming a strong nation and trying to encroach upon other countries, as England was doing, they thought that by making Korea the France of Asia Korea could be a strong modern nation to check the aggressive policy of Japan and other countries toward Korea.[42] In other words, the Progressive Party pursued the construction of a self-reliant, powerful nation in Korea.

To achieve this goal as soon as possible, they launched the coup of 1884 to seize power first and then carry out their reform program from above on the basis of power. To them the coup was necessary because the Conservative government led by Queen Min hindered such reforms in collaboration with Ch'ing China. Japan, which had once planned to invade Korea, was rapidly developing as a modern nation strong enough to encroach on Korea. Under the circumstances, the Progressives could no longer put off their program to construct a modern, self-reliant, strong nation because without this program Korea would soon be in the danger of fall to Japan. They planned to oust the Conservatives from power by force and form a new government capable of carrying out their reform program. The first guidelines of this reform program were the planks of the reform platform they announced after the coup of 1884.

The reform program of the Progressive Party covered the whole spectrum of state affairs, because it was designed to transform the country from a pre-modern society into modern one.

In the political and diplomatic area, it rejected China's suzerainty over Korea and declared Korea's complete independence from China. It aimed at transforming the feudalistic absolute monarchy into a modern constitutional monarchy and reforming the government organization on the basis of a cabinet system in order to make Korea powerful enough to be equal to other countries of the world and free from any foreign intervention.

In the social system, the reform platform pressed for an end to social estate distinction and the nepotist family power clique, and establishment of equal rights for all the people. In other words, it purported a transformation of society from the *yangban*-ruled pre-modern society into a modern free society in which all members of society are equal. The Progressive Party wanted to recruit men of talent from all walks of social life for employment in the building of a modern nation.

In the economic and financial area, the platform called for a drastic tax reform to bring to an end all corruption and irregularities involving the old feudalist tax system. it also provided for a modern capitalistic economic reform to abolish the medieval commercial privileges of packmen. Free enterprise of modern capitalism was encouraged in manufacturing, mining, commerce, agriculture, transportation and communication. The Progressives wanted to put all internal fiscal administration under the jurisdiction of the Ministry of Finance in order to control the treasury for the carrying out of their reform program.

In the cultural area, it pressed for an end to the *yangban*-oriented aristocratic cultural system for the establishment of modern culture based on popular education. To this end, it demanded the building of "new" schools across the country for education of the people in "new " knowledge.

In the defense system, the platform included measures to transform the medieval military system into a modern defense system and establish a military academy to train leaders of a modern army. Warships should be imported to build a modern navy and a Royal Guards Division should be activated. These measures were designed to establish a strong, self-reliant defense posture.

In the administration of justice, it sought to bring to an end the pre-modern police and judicial systems and establish new laws to pave the way for modern police and judicial systems.

All in all, the reform of the new government born of the coup of 1884 can be considered a declaration of the measures for transforming Korea from a pre-modern society into modern one. It was the first modern government's public announcement of a reform program to establish a modern society in Korean history, and this may be said to be the historical characteristic of the platform.

6. Conclusion

As seen in the above discussion, the Progressive Party's thought which gave rise to the coup of 1884 was a reform idea of building a strong, self-reliant nation in Korea in order to cope with the national crisis which hit the country in the latter half of the 19th century. But this idea was not materialized because of the failure of the coup. As a result, the Korean people lost the opportunity of building a self-reliant, strong nation to join the ranks of world powers through a great reform program at an opportune time in world history.

Although the coup of 1884 failed, the Progressive Party's reform thought remained providing for modernization movements in later days. *Kabo Kyŏngjang* (Reform of 1894) was a program that realized the Progressive Party's reform thought of the coup of 1884 under different circumstances. And the Independence Club and the *Manmin Kongdonghoe* (People's Assembly) movements in the 1896-1898 period and the patriotic enlightenment movement in the 1904-1910 period were the development of the reform thought of the coup of 1884.

Furthermore, the reform idea of the coup of 1884 was the spiritual source of all the independence movements against foreign aggression and oppression in the early 20th century. In this connection, the reform thought of the coup of 1884 can be considered the origin of modern Korea's nationalism. It may be thus said that the reform platform of the Coup d'Etat of 1884 marked an epoch-making milestone in the modern history of Korea.

FOOTNOTES (Part II – 9)

1. Lee Kwang-su, "My Meeting with Mr. Pak Yŏng-hyo," *Tanggwang*, March 1931.

2. *A Collection of Tanje Shin Ch'ae-ho's Works*, revised edition, Vol. 2, 1977, p. 384.

3. Kogyun Memorial Society (ed.), *A Biography of Kim Ok-kyun*, Vol. 1, 1944, pp. 48-49.

4. Lee Kwang-rin, *A Study of the Progressive Party*, 1973, pp. 67-92.

5. Kogyun Memorial Society (ed.), *op.cit.*, p. 50.

6. Kim Ok-kyun, *Kapshin Illok* (Journal of 1884), Dec. 1, 1884. *Collected Works of Kim Ok-kyun*, 1979, Asea Munhwa-sa, p. 73.

7. *Ilsŏngnŏk* (Records of Kings' Sayings and Doings), Vol. 264, Sept. 22, 1882.

8. Shin Young-ha, *Modern Korean History and Social Change*, 1980, pp. 24-27.

9. *Choein Sin Ki-sŏn Kugan* (Criminal Shin Ki-son's Letter to the King), Kyujang-gak.; *Ch'uan-kup Kugan* (Proposals and Letters to the King), Vol. 30, 1978, Asea Mungwa-sa, pp. 786-792.

10. *Ibid.*, p. 787.

11. Ito Hirobumi (comp.), "Accounts of Keijo Incident," *Hishoruisan, Chosen Kosho Shiryo* (Data on Korea Negotiation), Vol. 1, 1934, p. 298.

12. Kim Ok-kyun's *Kapshin Illok*, Dec. 5, 1884, in *Collected Works of Kim Ok-kyun*, Asea Mungwa-sa, 1979, pp. 95-96.

13. Inoue Kakugoro, Memories of Seoul, in *A Collection of Folk Paintings*, Vol. 7, No. 84, Extra, 1895, pp. 12-13. Yamabe Kentaro, "A Study of Kapshin Illok," *Journal of Korean Studies*, No. 17, 1960.

14. "On Korean Reformation," *Collected Works of Kim Ok -kyun*, pp. 110-111.

15. Sŏ Chae-p'il, "Recollection of 1884 Revolution," in Min T'ae-wan, *Kapshin Chŏngbyŏn and Kim Ok-kyun*," 1947, p. 82.

16. Kim To-t'ae (ed.), *An Autobiography of Dr. Sŏ Chae-p'il*, 1948. PP. 86-87.

17. "A Letter to King Kojong" (A Letter Criticizing the Chi Un-yŏng Incident), *Collected Works of Kim Ok-kyun* pp. 146-147.

18. Kim To-t'ae (ed.), *op.cit.*, p. 86.

19. Inoue Kakugoro, *op.cit.*, p. 12.

20. "A Letter to king Kojong," *Collected Works of Kim Ok-kyun*. p. 147.

21. "Ch'ido Ynagnon" A Discourse on (the Improvement of Roads), *Collected Works of Kim Ok-kyun*, p. 3.

22. "A Letter to King Kojong," *Collected Works of Kim Ok-kyun*, p. 147.

23. "Constitutional Monarchy in Europe and America," *Hansŏng Sunbo*, No. 10, Jan. 3,

1884.

24. *Yun Ch'i-ho's Diary*, Oct. 2, 1884 (lunar calendar; the rest same).

25. "On Modern Business Company," *Hansŏng Sunbo*, No. 3, Oct. 2, 1883.

26. "Ch'ido Yangnon," *Collected Works of Kim Ok-kyun*, p. 13.

27. *Ibid,*. p. 4.

28. Shin Yong-ha, "Early Progressive Policy," *Korean History*, Vol. 16, 1975, Korean History Compilation Committee (Comp.) , pp. 383-392.

29. *Yun Ch'i-ho's Diary*, Dec. 4, 1883.

30. *Ibid.*, Dec. 21, 1883.

31. Sŏ Chae-p'il, *op.cit.*, p. 84.

32. Yun Ch'i-ho's Diary, June 19, 1884.

33. Sŏ Chae-p'il, *op.cit.*, p. 83.

34. "A Letter to King Kojong," *Collected Works of Kim Ok-kyun*, p. 146.

35. *Ibid.*, p. 147.

36. "Ch'ido Yangnon," *ibid.*, pp. 16-17.

37. *Ibid.*, pp. 15-16.

38. *Ibid.*, pp. 14-15.

39. *Ibid.*, pp. 14-16.

40. Sŏ Chae-p'il, *op.cit.*, p. 82.

41. *Ibid.*, pp. 84-85.

42. "A Letter to King Kojong,"*Collected Works of Kim Ok-kyun*, p. 146.

10. The Coup d'Etat of 1884 and the Pukchŏng Army of the Progressive Party

1. Introduction

The prescribed version of the Coup d'Etat of 1884 which we are all familiar with is that the Progressive Party, led by Kim Ok-kyun, staged a short-lived coup in the winter of 1884, the goal of which was to institute a progressive modernization policy. Kim and his cohorts intended to fashion Korea into a modern nation, built on a civil society and a capitalist economic system. Actual political ramifications notwithstanding, the principle objective of the Coup d'Etat of 1884 (also known as the *Kapsin Chŏngbyŏn*) was the re-formation of the antiquated system of government unchallenged for centuries.[1] It was the first earnest reform movement of its kind in Korean history dedicated to rebuilding Korea into a more powerful and modernized nation through the vigorous importation of advanced culture and technology from the West. Even those scholars who are overtly sensitive about the way the Coup d'Etat and the reform movement were ultimately carried out recognize the significance of the 1884 coup in the formulation of modern Korean history.[2]

Previous research and interpretations dealing with the coup have propagated the view that in staging the coup, the Progressives relied heavily on the assistance of 150 Japanese troops stationed in Seoul to guard the Japanese legation. Scholarly papers in the past have completely overlooked the fact that at the time of the coup, Pak Yŏng-hyo, a leading figure in the Progressive Party, had already trained a modern army of 500 men in Kwangju, Kyŏnggi-do. To illustrate this oversight, I provide two examples. The first study was written in Korean and the second in English.

[Example One] In 1884, the Progressive Party launched their coup on the day of the grand gala held in celebration of the opening of the Postal Administration, at which Hong Yŏng-shik, a member of the Progressive Party, was serving as director. Conspirators of the coup marched into the palace and promptly relocated the King and Queen and assigned 50 of its military academy cadets and 200 Japanese soldiers to guard the Korean sovereign. Ranking members of the Min clan faction and commanders of army garrisons in the capital were promptly disposed of as soon as they unsuspectingly strolled into the palace grounds following a personal summons by the king. Upon seizing power, the Progressive Party set up a new government and notified the foreign legations of this fact. Later, they accompanied the king back to Ch'angdŏkkung palace, and it was there that they formulated the 14 Point Reform Program... This reformation program never got off the ground because the coup fell apart when Ch'ing troops stationed in Seoul intervened. Chinese troops numbering some 1,500, commanded by General Yuan Shikai, assaulted Ch'angdŏkkung palace. Quick to understand the hopelessness of their predicament, the Japanese soldiers guarding the king withdrew and the members of the Progressive Party suffered a defeat. In the aftermath, Kim Ok-kyun and Pak Yŏng-hyo went to Japan in exile, accompanying the Japanese minister. Such was the fate of the calamitous coup, which lasted but three days.[3]

[Example Two] In the meantime, however, Japan's attitude toward the Progressives had changed, and the Japanese minister, Takezoe Shinichiro, promised that in the event of the coup, the Japanese legation guards in Seoul would render assistance. The Progressives' plans were now complete. It was a serious miscalculation, however, to allow the fate of the enterprise to hinge on the support of less than 200 Japanese troops when, even after the withdrawal of some contingents, there were at least 1,500 Chinese soldiers stationed in Seoul.[4]

These two exemplify the way in which history books, especially school textbooks on Korean history, have rendered this significant episode in Korean modern history. Of course, there is no reason to assume that the authors of the two prominent studies have deliberately promulgated the inaccurate view that those who staged the Coup of 1884 did so because they unwisely placed too much value on the support from the 200-man Japanese troops in Seoul. It would be a fairer assessment to say that these authors are merely reiterating the popular view largely unchallenged through the years.

The point that this study attempts to bring to light is that actual historical facts do not support this popular view. It is a documented fact that the Progressive Party, in anticipation of the coup, not only raised a modern army of 500 in Kwangju but also another 500 in Pukch'ŏng, Hamgyŏngnam-do. Studies in the past have merely acknowledged the existence of the Progressive Army at Kwangju; however, practically nothing has been said about the Progressive Army at Pukch'ŏng. This paper will provide an overview of the Kwangju Army and then deal with the Pukch'ŏng Army in greater detail, tracing it from its beginnings to its commitment to the coup in Seoul. Furthermore, it will resolve the question precisely of what role these military forces played in the Coup d'Etat of 1884.

2. The Kwangju Army of the Progressive Party

This first thing that we must deliberate upon is the condition of the Progressive Party in April of 1883. It is widely speculated that it was around this time that the Progressives first formulated the ambitious plans for the coup. At the time, the Progressives had earned the favor of King Kojong, a fact well corroborated by several noted appointments to key administerial posts. In April 22, 1883, for instance, Kim Ok-kyun, the head of the Progressive Party, was designated the Head Supervisor of Development of the South-Eastern Islands and Whaling,[5] and on the very next day, Pak Yŏng-hyo was appointed Mayor of Kwangju and Yun Ung-yŏl, Commander of Military Forces (*pyŏngma chŏldosa*) in Hamgyŏngnam-do.[6]

Not long after his new appointment, Kim Ok-kyun was sent to Japan on his third official visit, in order to procure a loan agreement with the foreign diplomats in Tokyo, Japan. Forest lands of Ullŭngdo island were to be offered as collateral. The loan agreement fell through, but Kim returned to Korea having purchased a large amount of gun powder, which could only indicate that Kim and his followers had by this time moved into the preparatory phase of the coup.

For his part, Pak Yŏng-hyo began to organize a modern army unit as soon as he was appointed Mayor of Kwangju. At the time, Korea was sectioned into 8 provinces and 4 main cities. Of the 4 cities, Kwangju was strategically the most important to the defense of the capital, and thus one of the responsibilities entailed in the office of the mayor was to organize a military unit for defense. Likewise, raising and maintaining a military force was also well within the purview of the responsibility of the Commander of Military Forces in Hamgyŏngnam-do, which had its headquarters in Pukch'ŏng.

Other studies have stated that the appointments of Kim Ok-kyun and Pak Yŏng-hyo were in truth a demotion craftily orchestrated by the Min faction, but this point perits a more thorough re-examination. It seems more plausible to suggest that the Progressives understood precisely how significant these particular posts were to the success of their coup and, therefore, deliberately lobbied King Kojong to procure these appointments. This assertion becomes somewhat clearer when we exam the role of Pak Yŏng-hyo during his tenure as the mayor of Kwangju.

As mentioned earlier, Pak immediately recruited 500 young males and began the process of shaping a modern army unit. Pak appointed Sin Pok-mo the officer in charge of training, and this turned out to be a wise choice. Shin, in a matter of months, molded the crude country recruits into a formidable fighting force. Pretense aside, there is little doubt that this modern army was organized primarily as the fighting arm of the Progressive Party.

Before long, the Min faction got wise to the fact that a modern army of 500 under the command of Pak Yŏng-hyo, a member of the Progressive Party, was not only an embarrassment but a legitimate threat to them. In October 31, 1883, the Min clique successfully persuaded the king to transfer the command of the army to the Royal Guards Command (Ŏyŏngch'ŏng), at the time a military garrison responsible for the protection of the royal palace.[7] The irony of all this was that because of the interference of the Min faction, Pak's privately trained soldiers once incorporated into the Royal Guards Command, were now responsible for the guarding of the palace as well as the royal family.[8]

In November 6, 1883, Pak Yŏng-hyo was dismissed from his post at Kwangju, and in November 22, a training unit (now composed of the Kwangju unit) of the Royal Guards Command became the Front Garrison of the Capital Guards Command (Ch'in'gunyŏng Chŏnyŏng), which was placed directly under the commander of the Royal Guards Command, Han Kyu-jik.[9] Since Han was one of the central figures in the Min faction, it looked as if the Progressives had completely lost control over the Kwangju unit to their adversaries. In reality, Kim Ok-kyun and Pak Yŏng-hyo had in due course recruited a large portion of the officers of the Front Garrison into the Ch'ungŭigye, the secret shock organization of the Progressive Party, while the enlisted element had been carefully screened and trained by the Progressives. In time, the Front Garrison itself became a formidable unit dedicated to the Progressive cause.

On December 28, 1883 (Nov. 29 on the lunar calendar), King Kojong personally inspected the training exercise of the Front Garrison at the Ch'anggyŏnggung palace grounds.[10] The following is an article in the *Hansŏng sunbo* detailing the momentous occasion:

On the 29th (on the lunar calendar, ed. note) His Royal Highness was present at the Ch'undangdae to witness the training of the Front Garrison of the Capital Guards Command. On that day Han Kyu-jik, commander of the Front Garrison, led the 500 man Kwangju contingent, trained in the Japanese-style as a modern army unit, and His Royal Highness personally reviewed the troops. The 500 men were all trimmed with a yellow-colored leather backpack and held modern rifles in hand, and they seemed to move as one to their leader's very command. So skillful were these soldiers in their exercises that they left little to be desired even when compared to the Japanese army. The lesson that one readily derives from this spectacle is that a strong army can only become a reality through emphasis on training. In light of the fact that these able troops have only been training for a few months, one cannot help but laud their commander's diligence in supervising their training.[11]

This Front Garrison (largely composed of the original Kwangju Army) was trained and controlled by the Progressives, and as the military arm of the Progressive Party, it played an active and vital role in the Coup d'Etat of 1884.

3. The Progressive Party's Army in Pukch'ŏng

In April 23, 1883, the Progressive Party leader, Kim Ok-kyun, was instrumental in placing Yun Ung-yŏl in the post of Commander of Military Forces in Hamgyŏngnam-do.[12] Furthermore, in the *Yun Ch'i-ho ilgi* (Private Journal of Yun Ch'i-ho), Yun Ch'i-ho writes that Kim Ok-kyun was personally involved in the raising of the modern army at Pukch'ŏng.[13] In praising the fighting effectiveness of the Pukch'ŏng Army, Yun Ung-yŏl dubbed it "an important organization dedicated to modernization and progress."[14] In sum, Yun Ung-yŏl's appointment to the post of Commander of Military Forces in Hamgyŏngnam-do and his subsequent raising of the Pukch'ŏng Army were an integral part of elaborate plans laid out by the Progressives in preparations for the coup.

On May 23, 1883, Yun Ung-yŏl left Seoul after an audience with the king. On June 28, soon after his arrival at Pukch'ŏng in Hamgyŏngnam-do, Yun recruited 250 young men and started to drill them in Western military training (then referred to as "the Japanese style of training").[15] In December of the same year, Yun recruited another 250 men. Some documents quote s smaller figure of 200, but a report by Ŏ Yun-jung, Officer of Trading and Administration to the North-Western Region, in the *Nambyŏngyŏng kyerok* (Collection of Reports of Southern Barracks Command) clearly stipulates that the correct number is

250.[16]

Yun's 500 recruits proved to be avid pupils of modern military drills. In evaluating the skills of his men, Yun reported, "their training in military techniques improves from one day to the next, and watching them in formation is truly a delight."[17]

As the 500-men army in Pukch'ŏng was gradually being molded into a formidable fighting force, it inevitably attracted the attention of the Min faction who now considered the army as potentially threatening. Their campaign to eradicate that threat began in the spring of 1884. To begin with, Im Han-su, the governor (*kamsa*) assigned to Hamgyŏng-do, wrote in a report to the king that Yun Ung-yŏl had lost the support of the people by extorting heavy taxes and deliberately damaging the *hyanghŏnbi* (the monument which had inscribed on its surface the local codes and rules). Im concluded his report with recommendations that Yun be stripped of his post.[18] To punctuate their point, the Min faction had the State Council (Ŭijŏngbu) submit a separate report which also recommended that Yun be immediately dismissed and that criminal charges be leveled against him.[19] According to the *Yun Ch'i-ho ilgi*, the governor's condemning report on Yun was orchestrated by none other than Min T'ae-ho, a noted figure in the Min faction.[20]

This episode ignited a heated confrontation between the Progressives who wanted to protect Yun Ung-yŏl, and thus the Pukch'ŏng Army, and the Min faction, who obviously wanted to eliminate the problem before it became a real threat. As a representative of the Progressive Party, Pak Yŏng-hyo personally travelled to Pukch'ŏng to get a firsthand assessment of the conditions of the Pukch'ŏng Army.[21]

Not to be outdone, the Min faction incited the local Confucian scholars, still sore over Yun Ung-yŏl's desecration of their treasured *hyanghŏnbi*, to lodge a formal protest against Yun. This protest was received by Han P'il-ŭn, an official in the Office of the Inspector-General (*Sahŏnbu*), who wasted no time in recommending Yun's immediate removal and punishment on the grounds that he knowingly damaged the *hyanghŏnbi*, and that in raising a costly modern army, he needlessly depleted the local coffer.[22] Suffice it to say that Han's tireless effort to remove Yun from office was in accordance with specific instructions handed down from the Min faction leaders like Yun T'ae-jun.[23]

The leaders of the Progressive Party did their best to contain the damage. Yun Ch'i-ho, whose father was Yun Ung-yŏl, used his influence with the king to plead his father's case. Yun Ch'i-ho vigorously attacked Han P'il-ŭn's report concerning his father as groundless accusations and submitted his own appeal in defense of his father's character.[24] Pak Yŏng-hyo made several more trips to Pukch'ŏng to devise ways to counter the Min faction's attack from the end.[25]

In the end, King Kojong decided agianst the plea by the Min faction to dismiss Yun Ung-yŏl from his post.[26] However, the Min faction leaders were not about to give up the fight because they deemed that the fate of the Pukch'ŏng Army was closely tied to the fate of its leader, Yun Ung-yŏl. Within the central government, Kim Myŏng-gi submitted a petition to the king requesting Yun's dismissal.[27] In like fashion, local Confucian scholars such as Ch'oe Sŭng-ak,[28] Yi Ki-jong,[29] and Kim Sŭng-jun[30] submitted petitions of their own. These two occurrences were meticulously planned and executed by the Min faction leaders in Seoul.

However, the efforts by the Min faction were to no avail because Yun Ch'i-ho, who had spent endless hours lobbying within the royal circle, had already earned the confidence and favor of the king. Every measure that the Min faction devised was adroitly countered by Yun Ch'i-ho and other Progressive leaders, until the king simply refused to hear any more accusations against Yun Ung-yŏl. The Progressives now boasted a decisive victory over the Min faction.

Meanwhile, on May 17, 1883, when it appeared that it would soon go the war with France over the issue of Annam, Ch'ing China withdrew 1,500 of its troops stationed in Seoul to fortify the Annam front, which left some 1,500 Chinese troops still in the Korean capital.[31] The Sino-French War erupted in July of 1884, culminating in the mortifying defeat of the Chinese Fujian Fleet by the French Asian Fleet in September.

Kim Ok-kyun and his consorts felt that Korea's liberation from foreign powers was finally close at hand[32] and determined that in order to maximize the probability of success the coup had to be launched no later than September of 1884.[33]

4. The Relocation of the Pukch'ŏng Army to Seoul

Now that the continued existence of the Pukch'ŏng Army was secured for the time being, the Progressives focused their efforts on moving the Pukch'ŏng Army to Seoul, where they would do the most good during the impending coup.

On July 29, 1884, the Progressive Party hastily recalled to Korea the 14 military cadets, including Sŏ Chae-p'il, that had been sent to absorb the latest military tactics in Japan. On August 9, Yun Ch'i-ho, immediately following private deliberations with Kim Ok-kyun, proceeded to the palace to seek the king's audience. Yun relayed a request, on behalf of his father, that 100 crack Pukch'ŏng troops be allowed to be dispatched to the capital as part of their training, and that they later return to Pukch'ŏng or be permanently reassigned to Seoul as circumstances warranted.[34] The king endorsed the plan. It is also on this occasion that Yun recommended the establishment of a military academy in Seoul to accomodate the cadets recently back from their training in the Japanese military academy. King Kojong's favoable reception of a plan to dispatch a detachment of the Pukch'ŏng Army to the capital was promptly relayed to Yun Ung-yŏl in Hamgyŏngnam-do by private carrier.[35]

On the evening of September 12, Yun Ch'i-ho was reassured by the king that a special decree to bring the Pukch'ŏng Army to Seoul was being drafted, and that Yun Ung-yŏl would be allowed to personally lead his troops into the capital.[36] The next day Yun sent a second letter to his father detailing the latest development, and then called on Kim Ok-kyun to give his report.[37] True to his word, on September 16, King Kojong appointed Yun Ung-yŏl one of the top officers of the Ch'ongyung Chunggun under the title *ch'in'gun chŏnyŏng chŏngyŏnggwan*[38] and ordered him to personally bring the Pukch'ŏng Army to Seoul.[39] In short, the king had unknowingly legitimatized the Pukch'ŏng Army's presence in the capital.[40] Yun Ch'i-ho was in the palace on a courtesy call when he learned of the king's orders, and he rushed to Kim Ok-kyun's house with the good news.[41]

On October 23, Yun Ung-yŏl made his grand entry into Seoul at the head of his 470-man Pukch'ŏng Army, and in accordance with the king's orders, Yun set up his new command at the Front Garrison of the Capital Guards Command.[42] Everything seemed to be going as planned. Yet Kim Ok-kyun, cautious as always, urged that from this juncture Yun Ch'i-ho leave the lobby work at the palace to more experienced hands. Kim instructed Yun Ch'i-ho that it was imperative that any future contact with the king concerning Yun Ung-yŏl and his unit be handled with the utmost caution.[43]

On October 28, King Kojong reviewed the Pukch'ŏng troops, and was reportedly impressed by what he saw. Yun Ung-yŏl was complimented at length for this efforts.[44] Up to this point, the Progressives seemed to be on a winning streak against the Min clan factions.

To the Min faction this was a serious crisis which called for desperate actions. First of all, the Min managed to secure the help of Yu Chae-hyŏn, a court eunuch widely known for his influence with the king. Yu was at one time not only a ranking member of the Progressive Party but also a close associate of Kim Ok-kyun and Yun Ch'i-ho.[45] However, for reasons unclear, Yu Chae-hyŏn went over to the other side to become the Min faction's most zealous spokesperson at the court. In accordance with instructions given to him by the Min faction leader, Han Kyu-jik, Yu Chae-hyŏn made the following defamatory remarks about Yun Ung-yŏl before the king:

> It is difficult to comprehend what is in the minds of these soldiers from the northern regions. It is rumored that Yun Ung-yŏl has his troops in full readiness for battle, and I shutter to think of what dire consequence may arise if individuals like Yun Ch'i-ho sought to take advantage of the situation. It woud have been better not to have trained an army in the northern regions in the first place.[46]

It is recorded in the *Yun Ch'i-ho ilgi* that this particular slur campaign was concocted by Han Kyu-jik (Commander of the Front Garrison), Yi Cho-yŏn (Commander of the Left Garrison), Yun T'ae-jun (Commander of the Rear Garrison), and Min Yŏng-ik (Commander of the Right Garrison). All four commanders belonged to the Min faction and were determined to frustrate any and all endeavors by the Progressives and by Yun Ung-yŏl. Yu Chae-hyŏn proved to be the Progressive's worst enemy because he had not only betrayed his party but served as the principal instrument of its destruction.

At first, the king turned a deaf ear to the accusations submitted by Yu Chae-hyŏn and other leaders of the Min faction. As a gesture of his confidence towards Yun and his Pukch'ŏng Army, King Kojong had 70 of the best men selected and bestowed special awards and privileges upon them.[47] Eventually, however, the persistent and relentless lobbying by the Min faction and Yu Chae-hyŏn began to bear fruit. On November 2, the king decreed, "It is inappropriate that the whole of the Pukch'ŏng Army continue to be stationed in Seoul. Therefore, I order that they should be sent home on a rotational basis."[48] Simply put, this royal decree mandated that a portion of the original 470 men be left in Seoul, and the rest return to Pukch'ŏng. This was undoubtedly a serious blow to the Progressives.

Curiously enough, on November 4 Yun Ung-yŏl sent no less than 400 men back to Pukch'ŏng,[49] when he could have easily justified sending back only 250, approximately half of the orginal number of men brought to Seoul. It is highly likely that the 70 men left behind in Seoul were the same 70 men whose skills were honored by the king weeks earlier. Nevertheless, the 70-man force that stayed on was a far cry from the 250-plus men that might have remained had Yun Ung-yŏl chosen to interpret the king's order to his advantage.

One explanation for Yun's curious action is that he realized that contrary to what he had been told by the Progressive leaders, the king's sudden order to divide up the Pukch'ŏng Army meant that the king did not fully support the coup, or worse yet that the king had no inkling at all of the upcoming coup. Yun might have seen the writing on the wall and was now cautiously distancing himself from the coup that he judged was doomed to failure from the start.

In fact, a day before Yun Ung-yŏl sent 400 of his troops back to Pukch'ŏng, he and his son, Yun Ch'i-ho, concluded through hours of private discussions that conditions warranted that the coup planned by the Progressive Party be put off for the time being or cancelled indefinitely.[50] Furthermore, a week before the coup, Yun Ung-yŏl abruptly submitted his resignation to Han Kyu-jik, Commander of the Front Garrison and one of the leaders of the Min faction.[51] Yun eventually, completely, dissociated himself from the Progressive Party and the coup.

To Kim Ok-kyun and other leaders of the Progressive Party, Yun Ung-yŏl's actions were tantamount to treason; however, in their eyes, the betrayal of Yu Chae-hyŏn, an ardent Progressive at one time, was the most reproachable, for it was mainly through Yu's maneuvers at court that the king decided to send a large portion of Yun Ung-yŏl's troops back to Pukch'ŏng. Yu Chae-hyŏn was later apprehended and executed as a traitor during the initial hours of the coup. Had circumstances dictated otherwise, Yun Ung-yŏl might have suffered a similar fate during the coup. Following the coup's failure, King Kojong explained to Yun Ch'i-ho that Kim and Pak, of course, wanted to dispose of Yun Ung-yŏl, but thought better of it because his son, Yun Ch'i-ho, was working at the American legation.[52]

It is unclear exactly where the remaining 70 men of the Pukch'ŏng Army were restationed, yet there are enough clues to make an educated guess. On September 11, 1884, the king ordered the Rear Garrison of Capital Guards Command to be reorganized.[53] In the midst of the coup, the troops of the Rear Garrison were detailed to support the coup by guarding the perimeter of the palace.[54] As soon as the coup got underway, Pak Yŏng-hyo, who had been instrumental in defending the Pukch'ŏng Army during the dark days of the opposition's slur campaign and again in bringing the Pukch'ŏng Army to the capital, was appointed commander of both the Front and the Rear Garrisons.[55] It is not difficult to conjecture that the 70 men must have been reassigned to the Rear Garrison. Pak Yŏng-hyo later recalled in his memorials that the total number of troops the Progressive Party had at its disposal in the coup was about 1,000 men, the combined forces of the Rear and Front Garrisons.[56] To be more specific, each Garrison was comprised of 500 men, and the Progressive

Party was able to make use of 500 men of the Front Garrison (namely the Kwangju Army) and the 500 men of the Rear Garrison (which included 70 crack soldiers of the Pukch'ŏng Army).

5. The Structure of the Military Force Involved in the Coup

On October 30, 1884, Takezoe Shinichiro, the Japanese minister to Korea, returned to his post after an extended respite in Japan. The past relationship between Minister Takezoe and the Korean Progressive Party was, to put it mildly, somewhat less than amicable. In the past, Takezoe had been one of the loudest critics of the Progressives while expressing his endorsement of the Min faction. When Kim Ok-kyun, armed with King Kojong's personal letter, went to Tokyo to procure a loan agreement with the foreign diplomats, it was Takezoe who spread the rumor that Kim's letter was a clever forgery. That accusation all but killed Kim's credibility and effectiveness at the bargainning table.

However, Minister Takezoe seemed to have experienced a miraculous change of heart following his leave of absence in Japan, at which time Takozoe must have had consultations with his superiors. Takezoe approached Kim Ok-kyun and the other Progressives with a proposal that if the Progressives meant to proceed with the coup, then he was authorized to put at their disposal 150 Japanese troops stationed in Seoul for the protection of the Japanese legation. Kim and his cohorts accepted Takezoe's proposal.

Prior to the coup, the Progressives had succeeding in amassing a sizable armed force of about 1,200 men: 500 men of the Front Garrison (the Kwangju Army); 500 men of the Rear Garrison (which included 70 crack soldiers of the Pukch'ŏng Army); 14 cadets under Sŏ Chae-p'il; 40 men of the *Ch'ungŭigye* (a covert Progressive organization); and now 150 Japanese troops. One of the main reasons that the Progressives were quick to accept Japan's assistance was that although they were confident that they had a sufficient number of men to forcibly subdue the Min faction, they were worried about the 1,500 Ch'ing China soldier still stationed in Seoul. In numbers alone, the Progressives were still at a disadvantage, yet they were confident that once they had control of the palace and the king, they would be in an advantageous position to carry out the coup without too much opposition.

On December 4, 1884, Kim Ok-kyun launched his coup backed by a military force of 1,200. Kim seized power and established a new government, and promulgated sweeping reform programs. This was, of course, what we know as *Kapshin Chŏngbyŏn* (the Coup d'Etat of 1884).

During the coup, an elaborate defensive system was devised to maximize the force's ability to protect the king and to repel possible attacks by the Min faction forces and the Chinese army: the 1,000 men of the Front and Rear Garrisons of Capital Guards Command assumed the defense of the outermost perimeter; the 150 men Japanese force, the center perimeter; and finally, the 50 men composed of cadets and member of the *Chu'ungqŭigye*, the innermost perimeter.[57]

Nonetheless, the Chinese forces penetrated the defense lines at 2 p.m. on December 6, and launched a frontal attack on the Progressive army and the Japanese forces in the palace grounds. The fighting was fierce with heavy losses on both sides, but in the end, the defenders succumbed to the superior Chinese forces. This closed the book on the ill-fated Coup d'Etat, which lasted but three days. What should be remembered here is that the Korean forces made up the bulk of the men who fought on the side of the Progressives during the three-day escapade, and that the 150 men that were composed of the Japanese legation guards, which rank so prominently in most historical studies on the coup, made up only 12.5 per cent of the total force.

6. Conclusion

The one fact that has been made evident by this study is that the Coup d'Etat of 1884 was not, as is commonly postulated, a reckless gamble, the success of which hinged upon the support of a Japanese force of less than 200 men in strength.

The Progressive Party had, up to a year and a half prior to the coup, raised an effective modern army in Kwangju and in Pukch'ŏng. The categorization of the forces that fought on the side of the Progressives during the coup clearly indicates that the Japanese troops (numbering some 150) constituted only a fraction of the total number, and that they primarily played an auxiliary role.

The fact that the Progressives raised a modern army of some 1,000 men with the explicit intention of employing them in the coup manifests their conviction to carry out the coup fundamentally on the basis of their self-reliant strength. Therefore, I believe that in light of the new documents that seem to grant a more accurate picture of the Coup d'Etat of 1884, it is time we amend the outmoded interpretation that the Progressives unwisely placed too much reliance on Japanese troops.

FOOTNOTES (Part II - 10)

1. Lee Kwang-rin, "Kapshin Chŏngbyŏn-e taehan ilgoch'al," In *Kaehwadang yŏngu* (A Study of the Progressive Party), 1973, Ilchokak Publishers, Seoul.

2. Shin Yong-Ha, "Kapshin Chŏngbyŏn-ŭi kaehyŏk sasang," *Hankuk hakpo* (The Journal of Korean History), No. 36, 1984.

3. Pyŏn T'ae-sŏp, *Kaejŏngp'an Han'guksa t'ongnon* (Revised History of Korea), 1989, Seoul, Samyŏngsa Publishers, pp. 420-421.

4. Carter J. Eckert et al., *Korea Old and New: A History*, Seoul: Ilchokak Publishers; Cambridge, Mass; Harverd University Press, 1990, p. 210.

5. *Kojong sillok* (Annals of King Kojong). Consult entry for the lunar date March 16, 1883 (the 20th year of the reign of King Kojong).

6. *Kojong sillok*, lunar date March 17, 1883.

7. *Kojong sillok*, Oct. 1, 1883.

8. *Hansŏng sunbo*. See the article entitled "Kwangyu changgye" in No. 3 (dated Oct. 21, 1883 of the lunar calendar).

9. *Kojong sillok*, Oct. 23, 1883.

10. *Kojong sillok*, Nov. 29, 1883.

11. *Hansŏng sunbo*, Consult the article entitled "Yuji kongnok" in No. 7 (dated Dec. 1, 1883 of the lunar calendar).

12. *Nambyŏngyŏng kyerok*. Consult entry for the lunar date March 2, 1883.

13. *Yun Ch'i-ho ilgi*, Oct. 5, 1883 (Nov. 4 on the solar calendar).

14. *Yun Ch'i-ho ilgi*, April 21, 1883 (June 6 on the solar calendar).

15. *Nambyŏngyŏng kyerok*, Consult entry for the lunar date Dec. 29, 1883.

16. *Yun Ch'i-ho ilgi*, Nov. 25, 1883.

17. *Yun Ch'i-ho ilgi*, Dec. 29, 1883.

18. *Kojong sillok*, May 14, 1884.

19. *Yun Ch'i-ho ilgi*, May 21, 1884.

20. *Yun Ch'i-ho ilgi*, May 11, 1884 (June 4 on the solar calendar).

21. *Yun Ch'i-ho ilgi*, May 19, 1884 (June 12 on the solar calendar).

22. *Kojong sillok*, May 28, 1884.

23. *Yun Ch'i-ho ilgi*, May 24, 1884 (June 17 on the solar calendar).

24. *Kojong sillok*, Consult entry for the lunar date, intercalary month, May 5, 1884.

25. *Yun Ch'i-ho ilgi*, intercalary month, May 15, 1884 (July 7 on the solar calendar).

26. *Yun Ch'I-ho ilgi*, intercalary month, May 2, 1884 (June 24 on the solar calendar).

27. *Kojong sillok*, intercalary month, May 10, 1884.
28. *Ibid.*
29. *Ibid.*
30. *Kojong Sillok*, June 6, 1884.
31. *Yun Ch'i-ho ilgi*, April 23, 1884 (May 17 on the solar calendar).
32. *Yun Ch'i-ho ilgi*, Aug. 3, 1884 (Sept. 21 on the solar calendar).
33. *Kapshin illok* (Journal of 1884), Nov. 1 and Nov. 25, 1984 (both solar dates).
34. *Yun Ch'i-ho ilgi*, June 19, 1884 (Aug. 9 on the solar calendar).
35. *Yun Ch'i-ho ilgi*, June 21, 1884 (Aug. 11 on the solar calendar).
36. *Yun Ch'i-ho ilgi*, July 23, 1884 (Sept. 12 on the solar calendar).
37. *Yun Ch'i-ho ilgi*, July 24, 1884 (Sept. 13 on the solar calendar).
38. *Sŭngjŏngwŏn ilgi* (Journal of the Royal Secretariat), Consult entry for the lunar date July 27, 1884.
39. *Hansŏng sunbo*, Consult the article entitled "Yuji kongnok" in No. 34 (dated Aug. 1, 1884 of the lunar calendar).
40. *Sŭngjŏngwŏn ilgi*, Consult entry for the lunar date July 27, 1884.
41. *Yun Ch'i-ho ilgi*, July 27, 1884 (Sept. 16 on the solar calendar).
42. *Yun Ch'i-ho ilgi*, Sept. 5, 1884 (Oct. 23 on the solar calendar).
43. *Yun Ch'i-ho ilgi*, Sept. 9, 1884 (Oct. 27 on the solar calendar).
44. *Yun Ch'i-ho ilgi*, Sept. 10, 1884 (Oct. 28 on the solar calendar).
45. *Yun Ch'i-ho ilgi*, July. 28, 1884 (Sept. 17 on the solar calendar).
46. *Yun Ch'i-ho ilgi*, Sept. 11, 1884 (Oct. 29 on the solar calendar).
47. *Yun Ch'i-ho ilgi*, Sept. 14, 1884 (Nov. 1 on the solar calendar).
48. *Kojong sillok*, Sept. 15, 1884.
49. *Yun Ch'i-ho ilgi*, Sept. 17, 1884 (Nov. 4 on the solar calendar).
50. *Yun Ch'i-ho ilgi*, Sept. 16, 1884 (Nov.3 on the solar calendar).
51. *Yun Ch'i-ho ilgi*, Oct. 10, 1884 (Nov. 27 on the solar calendar).
52. *Yun Ch'i-ho ilgi*, Oct. 21, 1884 (Dec. 8 on the solar calendar).
53. *Kojong sillok*, Consult entry for the lunar date July 22, 1884; *Hansŏng sunbo*. Consult the article entitled "Yuji kongnok" in No. 34 (dated Aug. 1, 1884 on the lunar calendar).
54. *Yun Ch'i-ho ilgi*, Oct. 17, 1884 (Dec. 4 on the solar calendar).
55. *Kapshin illok*, Dec. 4, 1884 (solar date).
56. Park Yŏng-hyo, "Hanmal chŏnggaek-ŭi hoegorok," *The Dong-A Ilbo*, 5 Jan. 1930; "Hanmal chŏnggye-wa Pak Yŏng-hyo," *Chogwang*, Vol. 5, No. 11 (Nov., 1939).
57. *Kapshin illok*, Consult entry for Dec. 5, 1884 (solar date).

11. Conjunction of *Tonghak* and the Peasant Revolutionary Movement

1. Introduction

Tonghak, established in 1860 by Ch'oe Che-u, was a religious thought founded and propagated to "sustain the nation and provide for the people (*poguk anmin*)" and "save the oppressed people (*kwangje ch'angsaeng*)" by achieving a simultaneous breakthrough in the national and the feudal crises which the Korean people faced in the mid-19th century. Compared to previous religions, the *Tonghak* ideology was peculiar in its content and organization. On the other hand, the Peasant Revolutionary Movement, initiated by the *Tonghak* followers as well as the peasants in 1894, was a movement that concluded the numerous popular uprisings that had erupted, demanding the fundamental end to the old system of *yangban*-class society as well as the establishment of a new system clear of peasant extortions at the end of the 19th century.

What, then, is the relationship between *Tonghak* and the Peasant Revolutionary Movement of 1894? Hitherto, the following have been the main opinions on the linkage and relationship between *Tonghak* and the Peasant Revolutionary Movement:

1) The *Tonghak* Revolution Theory which views the Peasant Revolutionary Movement as a *Tonghak* Revolution, proposing that the *Tonghak* ideology is revolutionary and that the Peasant Revolutionary Movement arose based on this revolutionary thought.

2) The *Tonghak* Outer Cover Theory which argues that *Tonghak* did not have the power to contribute to the waging of the Peasant Revolutionary Movement and that it was merely the outer "cover" and outer "clothing" of the Revolutionary Movement.

3) The *Tonghak* and the Peasant Revolutionary Movement Conjunction Theory which holds that *Tonghak* provided the ideology and organization for the popular uprisings and thereby made it possible for the Peasant Revolutionary Movement to be held on a national scale.

The theoretical foundation of this paper will be based on the third, that is, The *Tonghak* and the Peasant Revolutionary Movement Conjunction Theory.[1]

The organizational and ideological elements are seen to have acted as the intermediary aspects of the conjunction proposed by the *Tonghak* and the Peasant Revolutionary Movement Conjunction Theory. In this paper, I will attempt to explain the *Tonghak* and the Peasant Revolutionary Movement Conjunction Theory by investigating in detail which of the *Tonghak* ideological elements appealed to the peasant army and how the *Tonghak* organization developed alongside the Peasant Revolutionary Movement.

2. Ch'oe Che-u and the Establishment of *Tonghak*

Ch'oe Che-u was born on December 18, 1824 (October 28 by the lunar calendar), the 24th year of the reign of King Sunjo, at Kajŏng-ri, Kyŏn'gok-myŏn, Wŏlsŏng-gun, Kyŏngsangbuk-do province,[2]

He belonged to the Ch'oe clan of Kyŏngju. His birth name was Pok-sul and his adult name Che-sŏn. To fully understand the background to Ch'oe Che-u's founding of *Tonghak*, it is necessary to understand the peculiar circumstances of his birth and origin. Ch'oe Ok (1762-1840), the father of Ch'oe Che-u, was a descendent of a fallen *yangban* family who was unsuccessful in his five or six attempts at the civil service examinations.

Another significant agony for Ch'oe Ok was that he had no son to continue the family line, which was very important for the continuation of the lineage. His first wife, Lady Chŏng, bore him a son but he lost both his son and wife due to an illness. He remarried Lady Sŏ with whom he had two daughters but no son. Ch'oe Che-u was born to Ch'oe Ok whose desire for a son led him to take a widow from his neighborhood, Lady Han, as his concubine at over 60 years of age.[3] Ch'oe Che-u, born of this relationship, was considered illegitimate. In the Chosŏn society, illegitimate sons were forbidden to take the civil service examinations.

Illegitimate sons of the time, no matter how competent and gifted, were not allowed to even enter the site where state examinations were administered. Not only that, but because of the strict discriminatory system against illegitimate sons, they could not even call their fathers "father."[4] The social practices of the times despised illegitimate children even more than the commoners (*yangin*) origin. That is, in the Chosŏn dynasty society, an illegitimate child was an outcast from birth, and Ch'oe Che-u was born such an outcast in 1824, toward the end of the Chosŏn dynasty.

Such were the odds against Ch'oe Che-u, who he possessed a brilliant mind.

He was loved by his father and received from him an education in Chinese characters and the Confucian classics.[5] As soon as he turned ten, he began to realize that he was illegitimate, of a low-class status as well as the contradictions of the social system. From this time on he began to resent that, no matter how hard he studied, he would never be employed or treated accordingly in Chosŏn society.

Ch'oe Che-u married a woman of the Pak clan of Ulsan at the age of 13, following his father's order. The early marriage was probably due to the wishes of his father who, at 75 years of age, wished to see his unfortunate son married befor he died. Ch'oe Che-u was bereaved of his mother at the age of 6 and 10 years later his father passed away at the age of 79.

As soon as the three years of mourning were over, Ch'oe Che-u, by then 20 years old, told his wife to return temporarily to her family. He then started wandering around the country to seek a means of livelihood. After he set off from his home, he partook in various studies and jobs and also sought spiritual enlightenment.

At first, Ch'oe Che-u learnt military arts including archery and horse riding intending to take the military service examination which was sometimes open even to the sons of concubines. When he realized that even this opportunity would be very difficult to come by, he engaged in commercial activities such as running a linen shop. He also tried his hand at medicine, hoping to become a doctor of Korean traditional medicine, as well as studying the science of divination.

In addition, he studied various Chinese scriptures to seek spiritual salvation and he visited the famous Taoists throughout the country to study Taoism in order to arrive at spiritual enlightenment. Thinking that profound truth may lie in Buddhism, he went about the famous Buddhist temples and grottos throughout the country meeting learned monks to receive Buddhist teachings. He even studied Catholicism upon hearing that profound philosophy lay in Western Learning.[6]

However, Ch'oe Che-u was unable to achive any of his goals. None of the religions, Confucianism, Buddhism, Taoism or Catholicism could quench his thirst for the truth. In despair, he returned to his family in 1854 at the age of 31, 11 years after he had left home. However, his 11 years of wandering throughout the country was not entirely in vain. Although he had yet to arrive at spiritual enlightenment, he was able to correctly see and understand the realities of his contemporary society, nation and the people as a result of his wandering across the country.

He confirmed through his wanderings that the means of livelihood and the

Way which he sought did not exist in this world. He became determined to create a new religion and system of thought in order to save the people, himself, society and the country.

Ch'oe Che-u, after all attempts to establish a new religion and system of thought had failed, left Ulsan in despair in October of 1859 at 36 years of age to return with his family to his hometown in Kyŏngju. He resolved to not return to the world if he failed to found a new religion and belief system which would save the world. Through arduous studies and meditation he finally arrived at spiritual enlightenment on May 25, 1860 (April 5 by the lunar calendar), his body in an extremely frail state.[7]

The crises facing the country which he had observed and experienced during his 11 years of wandering were the decisive factors and social background for his being able to attain spiritual enlightenment. Ch'oe Che-u observed that the Western powers' invasion, which led to the breakdown of China, while encouraging the people to seek spiritual salvation in Western Learning, meant that an identical national crisis was also imminent in Chosŏn (Eastern Country), which was in a "lip and teeth" relationship with China. The founding of *Tonghak* by Ch'oe Che-u was directly related to the occupation of Guangdong, Tianjin and Beijing (Peking) by the great powers of the West through military might and the propagation of Western Learning (Catholicism) which was allowed freely.

Ch'oe Che-u pointed out that the corruption and depravity of the Chosŏn dynasty had reached the extremes, with the evil persons enjoying riches and honor while the virtuous suffered poverty. Even those who had achieved virture were employed in consideration of the class and power of the family; the man of virtue and morality of which the *yangban* talked about were nothing more than meaningless words. The people were of disparate minds, not knowing where to go, having lost the way to spiritual salvation. He also pointed out that under such circumstances existing religions such as Confucianism and Buddhism were no longer effective, that they were without life or vitality. He despaired that the world had arrived at a state of extreme depravity which could not be saved, not even by the politics of Yao and Shun or the learnings and virtues of Confucius and Mencius.

During his years of wandering throughout the country, Ch'oe Che-u clearly observed that the people desperately wanted a new society, a new order, a new ideology, a new religion, a new morality and a new world and he too felt keenly his desire for the same. *Tonghak* was founded through the determination of Ch'oe Che u to respond to the people by founding a new Way. Like many other founders of new religions, Ch'oe Che-u explained that he had arrived at spiritual enlightenment through a conversation with God in which he received God's revelations.[8]

On May 25, 1860 (April 5 by the lunar calendar), Ch'oe Che-u began meditations after having washed himself. Soon thereafter, his body began to tremble and he felt a strange stirring in his heart. To overcome this, he composed his mind, and devoutly concentrated yet his body begans to tremble even more and his heart started to beat faster and his mind entered a state of ecstasy. At this moment, the heavens shook and he heard the words of God. The essence of God's words was; "I (God) have also so far not achived any merit. Therefore, I have let you (Ch'oe Che-u) be born into this world to teach the people the Way of Heaven (*Tonghak*), a new Way. Hence, teach well this Way to the people." According to Ch'oe Che-u, God's words were loud enough to shake the universe but neither his wife nor his son, who were next to him at the time, were able to hear any sound.[9]

In this author's opinion, from a scientific perspective, the creation of *Tonghak* can be viewed as an intellectual creation of Ch'oe Che-u himself through rigorous intellectual processes. To seek the Way, Ch'oe Che-u had wandered the country observing in detail and experiencing firsthand the situation around the country, and the problems of the society and the people while studying the various existing learings and religions. Upon returning home, he studied in earnest, depriving himself of sleep even, offering sincere prayers, meditating and contemplating for six years in order to found a new Way that would sustain the nation and provide for the people and save the oppressed people. Suddenly he was inspired, and discovered the principles of the new Way. Could not the words of God which were loud enough to shake the univers, yet heard only by Ch'oe Che-u, have been his inner voice in his weakened physical state, in his joy at the sudden inspiration and understanding of the principles of the new Way?

3. The Name *"Tonghak"* and the Beginnings of Propagation

Ch'oe Che-u named the new Way, system of thought and religion which he founded *"Tonghak"* or "Heavenly Way," emphasizing that it arose to confront Western Learning.[10]

It should be noted that in the term *"Tonghak,"* the dual concepts of *tong* exist: one is "Eastern Learning," and the other "Learning of the Eastern Country (Chosŏn)."

Ch'oe Che-u's *Tonghak* was a new Way, new religion and a new thought system created through a sublation of the principles of the then-existing

Confucianism, Buddhism and Taoism.[11] Confucianism to which Ch'oe Che-u refers here includes not only the classical Confucianism of Confucius and Mencius and the Neo-Confucianism of Zhu Xi, but the Learning of Lu Xiangshan and Wang Yangming as well.

Ch'oe Che-u did not stop at this and included some elements of Western Learning. He explained the relationship between *Tonghak* and Western Learning in the following manner: "Their Way and their destiny are the same but their principles are different."[12] He said that his *Tonghak* and Western Learning shared the same destiny because both were destined to flourish and that they follow the same Heavenly Way. This is understood as his acknowledgement that Western Learning was included in the founding of *Tonghak*.

Ch'oe Che-u recognized the mighty power of the West which was destroying China and he was afraid of it. He perceived the Western power on two levels: 1) Power of Western Learning including the Way (Western Way), learning (Western Learning), and religion (Catholicism); and 2) Military power of the West as demonstrated in weapons and warfare. Of the two, he regarded the power of Western Learning as the more fundamental. That is, Ch'oe Che-u saw Western Learning as the fundamental source of Western power and also believed that the military power of the West was ultimately based on this and guided by the same.

Ch'oe Che-u felt a serious crisis, thinking that the power of Western Learning, after destroying China through Western military force as an intermediary measure, would invade Chosŏn and destroy his motherland as well. He thus regretted that he was born after the founder of Christianity. He agonized, obsessed by this confrontational attitude against Western Learning, and criticized its problems. When he succeeded in founding *Tonghak* which he claimed to be a more superior Way compared to Western Learning, he was overjoyed.

Regarding his *Tonghak*, Ch'oe Che-u said "Our Way is something that no one has heard of either in the past or the present and a principle that is incomparable to any principle of the past or the present."[13] He confidently explained that it was the best Way of all ages and nations, and a "boundless great Way that was truly unique."[14]

For approximately one year after the founding of *Tonghak* Ch'oe Che-u concentrated on the theoretical framework for *Tonghak*. In 1861, he composed the "P'odŏngmun" (On Propagating *Tonghak*) and began the spread of *Tonghak*.

Initially, Ch'oe Che-u was successful in his propagations. People gathered from all corners of the country to study the new Way and in six months some 3,000 people came to see Ch'oe Che-u and to study *Tonghak* and became his disciples.

As Ch'oe Che-u began to succeed in the propagation of *Tonghak*, slander and defamations arose accordingly. Even many of his relatives defamed him, greatly shocking him. The most shocking of all was the allegation that Ch'oe Che-u was a believer in Western Learning (Catholicism) and that *Tonghak* was actually Western Learning. This rumour spread quickly among non-believers who did not know the meaning and content of *Tonghak*.

Despite persecution in the provinces, the success of *Tonghak* continued to grow. In particular, Kyŏngsang-do province had the largest number of followers and near the end of 1862 Ch'oe Che-u began to establish *chŏp* or *chŏpso* (local unit of *Tonghak*) in the provinces and appointed a head for each *chŏp* (*chŏpju*).

The central government of Chosŏn dynasty received a report of the rapid growth of the *Tonghak* force in Kyŏngsang-do province and felt so greatly threatened that in December 1863 a messenger and soldiers were sent to Kyŏngju and arrested Ch'oe Che-u, incarcerating him in a Taegu jail. The central government decided to execute him on February 29, 1864 and ordered it to be carried out in the Taegu jail. Accordingly, Ch'oe Che-u was executed on March 10, 1864. At the age of 40 he had become a *Tonghak* martyr.[15]

Following the martyrdom of Ch'oe Che-u, Ch'oe Si-hyŏng became the second leader. The central government of the Chosŏn dynasty, with the execution of Ch'oe Che-u, declared *Tonghak* an evil thought and made it illegal. In the provinces the persecution of *Tonghak* followers by local authorities was severe, and included the confiscating of property and the killing of the faithful.

Despite such cruel and severe persecution of *Tonghak* followers by the Chosŏn dynasty, *Tonghak* continued to spread among the peasants as an underground religion. This was because *Tonghak* appealed to the peasants who found in it some deep thought which they were willing to accept even if it meant their lives were on the line. What, then, was the ideological structure of *Tonghak* that so appealed to the peasants?

4. Socio-Ideological Chracteristics of *Tonghak*

This writer has mentioned the characteristics of *Tonghak* ideology, to borrow the terminology employed by *Tonghak*, as a thought in: 1) a unitarian ultimate vital force; 2) the unity of heaven and man; 3) attending God in humanity; 4) calm mind and correct vital force; 5) man is God; 6) equality; 7) the Later Creation; and 8) heaven on earth.[16]

Here, I attempt to observe the socio-ideological elements of *Tonghak* which captured the hearts of the peasants and which they warmly welcomed despite extreme persecution by the Chosŏn dynasty.

First, the nationalism and anti-foreign, anti-invasion thought of *Tonghak* seems to have captured the hears of the peasants. *Tonghak*, as afore-mentioned, was from the time of its founding a means to sustain the nation and provide for the people, a system of thought full of nationalism. The word *tong* of *Tonghak*, as mentioned before, referred to the East as well as the Eastern country (Chosŏn). The name *Tonghak* itself was a nationalistic name, established to counter Western Learning.

First of all, *Tonghak* saw the intrusion and invasion of Western powers and recognized Western Learning as spearheading the invasion of the East and Chosŏn and attempted to stop this. In this respect, it could be considered indentical to the movement of "defending orthodoxy and rejecting heterodoxy (*wijŏng ch'ŏksa*)." However *Tonghak* did not subjectively despise Western power nor did it look down upon it as a non-ethical and spiritually weak power. Rather, *Tonghak* viewed the West as powerful and fearful. *Tonghak* realistically and objectively observed the strength of Western power and tried to overcom it. This was very different from the subjective and unrealistic observation of Western power by the doctrine of "defending orthodoxy and rejecting heterodoxy."

Regarding Western Learning, *Tonghak* claimed "Their Way and their destiny are the same but their principles are different,"[17] well recognizing the thriving nature of Western Learning. In addition, the *Tonghak* see the *Tonghak* and Western Learning as following the same Heavenly Way thus demonstrating their universal view of God. This reveals that it was a far more universal and objective ideology compared to all the religions of the time which regarded God as their own. It was also a rational ideology which saw the cultures of East and West as being equal, not looking down on the Western culture from one's subjective perspective.

Also, *Tonghak*'s perception of China (Ch'ing) shows a very strong anti-Ch'ing sentiments as demonstrated in a hymn the verse of which reads "Let us take revenge on the Manchus,"[18] recalling the invasion by Ch'ing China and the humiliation of the surrender of King Injo of the Chosŏn dynasty to the Ch'ing emperor in 1636.

Tonghak's perception of Japan was even more hostile, showing a very strong bitterness toward the past Japanese invasions. The founder of *Tonghak* denounced the Japanese invaders as "Japanese dogs" and emphasized that since the Japanese Invasion of 1592 was unsuccessful they were waiting for another opportunity to invade, thus Chosŏn should be wary of them.[19] It should be noted that the founder of *Tonghak* was determined to destroy the Japanese should they invade the country again, even if in spirit after his death, and conveyed his determination to his followers.[20]

At a time when *Tonghak* was spreading in full force, another invasion by the Japanese was well under way after the opening of ports. It can easily be guessed how the strong nationalistic anti-Japanese sentiments and anti-invasion ideology of *Tonghak* captured the hearts of the peasants and were welcomed among them.

Secondly, the egalitarian ideology of *Tonghak*'s particular ideological structure can be seen to have captured the hearts of the peasants who occupied the lower strata of society.

According to *Tonghak*, each man had God in his heart and this God was the same regardless of social rank– legitimate or illegitimate, lord or servant– , sex, age or wealth. As each person had the same God, all men were equal. For example, the theory of equality of social rank explained that the *yangban* had God in his heart and the common people and the lower class all each had the same God therefore *yangban*, commoners and the lower classes were all completely equal. The founder of *Tonghak*, as an illegitimate son of a fallen *yangban* family, identified with the poor and low-class group saying that "the wealthy are the officials and the poor are the people. As the poor and the lowly we grew up in the backwoods."[21] The founder of *Tonghak* composed the following verse saying that after the Later Creation the poor and the lowly (the people) will become the wealthy: "The wealthy and the honored people were in the past the poor and the lowly, the poor and the lowly will be the rich and the honored in the coming age."[22]

Ch'oe Si-hyŏng, the second Patriarch of *Tonghak*, emphasized even more strongly the egalitarian ideology stressing that *Tonghak* was the Way of the peasants: "Those who want to follow our Way should be from among those who hold a hoe and bear a carrying rack."[23]

Tonghak also opposed the inequality of the sexes which was extreme in Chosŏn society and argued for the equality of the sexes.[24] According to *Tonghak*, women as well as men had the same God in their hearts, and moreover, woment were high and noble as they give birth to God. *Tonghak* emphasized that husbands should respect their wives and that husbands and wives should live in harmony.

Ch'oe Si-hyŏng stressed that "children were also God" and preached against striking or discriminating against children. He composed the "*Naesudomun*," suggesting a code of conduct for wives of *Tonghak* faith regarding their children: "Since the children also are abodes of God, striking them is equal to striking God,"[25] He said "striking a child in a family following the Way is equal to striking the Lord of Heaven and hence should be restrained"[26] and stressed that children should be respected on equal footing with adults.

Such an egalitarian aspect of *Tonghak* was warmly welcomed among the peasants who eagerly desired equality as they suffered extreme oppression, discrimination and ill-treatment at the hands of the *yangban* bureaucrats.

Third, the belief that "Mans is God," a unique humanism which viewed man as equal to God, strongly appealed to the peasants. Ch'oe Che-u, the founder of *Tonghak*, based on the idea of "Attending God in humanity," preached that "Man is God and God is man."[27] Ch'oe Si-hyŏng, the second Patriarch of *Tonghak*, taught that "Man is God. Therefore serve men as you would serve God."[28] He also taught that "In the family, if a man should come, say that the Heavenly Lord has descended from heaven."[29]

Tonghak emphasized the dignity of man, claiming that "man is Heaven." This thought appealed to the peasants even more than Western Learning. All the religions of the world at the time, including Western Learning, fixed God as a separate and absolute being that existed outside of man and preached that man should be ruled by God and should serve God as a servant of God. *Tonghak* viewed man, not as God's, but God himself, and put him on equal footing with God, establishing man as the most high and the most honored. This view seems to have contributed to the peasants' recognition of *Tonghak* as a more superior belief system and religion than Western Learning.

Fourth, the prophecy of the "Later Creation" strongly captured the hearts of the peasants. Ch'oe Che-u divided the history of mankind into two eras, that of the "Former Creation" and "Later Creation." Here the "Creation" meant the opening of a new period in which the universe and the world would change fundamentally. Accordingly, the Former Creation meant the changes had begun with the beginning of the society of mankind and would last approximately 50,000 years.

How, then, would the Later Creation begin? According to Ch'oe Che-u, as the end of the 50,000 years approached, God selected Ch'oe Che-u, spoke to him and taught him the Way of God so that he might propagate it, thus marking the beginning of the Later Creation. In other words, Ch'oe Che-u arrived at spiritual enlightenment through God's teachings, and *Tonghak* was founded, and this founding of *Tonghak* and its propagation are the beginning of the Later Creation, which would last yet another 50,000 years.[30]

Amidst the corruption present at the end of the Chosŏn dynasty the peasants could not find spiritual support in the existing morals and religions of Confucianism, Buddhism and Taoism. They must have whole heartedly welcomed the Later Creation of *Tonghak* which prophecized that *Tonghak* would usher in a new age in which the nation will be peaceful and people prosperous.

5. The *Tonghak* Organization

The organization of *Tonghak* was based on the *chŏpju* (head of a *chŏp*) system which was created by Ch'oe Che-u in 1862. As Ch'oe Che-u's *Tonghak* became very successful in Kyŏngju, Ch'oe Si-hyŏng, in November 1862, suggested to Ch'oe Che-u the appointment of *chŏpju* in various localities to foster the growth of *Tonghak*. Ch'oe Che-u accepted this suggestion and established *chŏp* (also known as *chŏpso*) in various localities as an organization to supervise the followers and instituted *chŏpju* (head) and *chŏpsa* (clerk) in each of the *chŏp*.[31]

However, as Ch'oe Che-u was executed on March 10, 1864 in Taegu, and *Tonghak* was strictly forbidden by the Chosŏn dynasty, this system seemed to have collapsed. The organization of *Tonghak* was broken up and Ch'oe Si-hyŏng was hounded by the authorities and had to eventually hide in Mt. Taebaeksan to escape them. With Mt. Taebaeksan as his base, Ch'oe Si-hyŏng travelled in disguise and was barely able to keep *Tonghak* alive.

In 1880, Ch'oe Si-hyŏng established a publishing house for the holy scriptures in Inje, Kangwŏn-do province and published to *Tonggyŏng taejŏn* (Bible of *Tonghak* Doctrine).[32] In the following year, 1881, he opened another publishing house in Tanyang, Ch'ungch'ŏng-do province and published *Yongdam yusa* (Anthology of Ch'oe Che-u's Hymns) in the pure vernacular.[33]

In February 1883, Ch'oe Si-hyŏng established a publishing house of the holy scriptures in Mokch'ŏn, Ch'ungch'ŏng-do province and published 1,000 copies of *Tonggyŏng taejŏn*, distributing them to various localities.[34] This clearly demonstrates that at this time, *Tonghak* was spreading to Ch'ungch'ŏng-do and Kyŏnggi-do provinces, and welcomed by the peasants, began enjoying a growing power base.

As the number of followers began to grow rapidly, in December 1884 Ch'oe Si-hyŏng newly instituted the "six responsibilities (*yugim*)"[35] system — *kyojang*, *kyosu*, *tojip*, *chipkang*, *taejŏng*, and *chungjŏng* — under each *chŏpju*, dividing the *Tonghak* work.

Ch'oe Si-hyŏng established the Toso at Poŭn in 1887. During this period, *Tonghak* was well received even among the peasants so that its power expanded rapidly among the farming communities. Innumerable followers from all provinces came to Poŭn to meet Ch'oe Si-hyŏng and to hear hime lecture on

Tonghak. In response, Ch'oe Si-hyŏng established the office in charge of the six responsibilities and made the heads of the office attend his lecture once a month in turn, and did not allow the common men to meet with him, unless they were recommended to do so by the *yugim*. This greatly enhanced the position of the *yugim* within the organization.

6. Poŭn Assembly and the Development of the *Tonghak* Organization

In Juanuary 1892, Ch'ungch'ŏng-do province Governor Cho Pyŏng-shik secretly banned *Tonghak* and ordered the *Tonghak* followers to be kept under control. Hence, life became difficult for *Tonghak* followers of Ch'ungch'ŏng-do who had to endure oppression, searches, and arrests by the authorities. In July of the same year, Sŏ In-ju and others met Ch'oe Si-hyŏng and said the posthumous exoneration of the *Tonghak* founder and the legalization of *Tonghak* were urgent and essential in order to protect the lives and property of *Tonghak* believers. They requested that a movement to exonerate the *Tonghak* founder be launched. However, Ch'oe Si-hyŏng did not allow this, saying that it was not the right time. Sŏ In-ju and others felt that *Tonghak* followers throughout the country could no longer endure persecution by the authorities. In October 1892, without the permission of Ch'oe Si-hyŏng, they called on *Tonghak* followers to gather at Kongju. At the Kongju assembly, requests for the posthumous exoneration of the *Tonghak* founder and a ban on the repression of *Tonghak* believers were presented in a civil petition.[36]

When the movement to exonerate Ch'oe Che-u was launched, Ch'oe Si-hyŏng decided to develop the movement in full force. He then sent notice to the *chŏpju* of all the provinces calling for a meeting at Samnye on November 1, 1892 in order to present a petition to Chŏlla-do Governor Yi Kyŏng-jik. The so-called Samnye assembly was held as thousands of *Tonghak* followers gathered at Samnye, and a petition was presented to Chŏlla-do governor on behalf of Ch'oe Si-hyŏng. The major points of the petition were: 1) to exonerate Ch'oe Che-u and to recognize and legalize *Tonghak*, just as western religions had been and 2) to prohibit local authorities from conducting searches, making arrests and confiscating the property of *Tonghak* believers.[37]

The Kongju assembly of October 1892 and the Samnye assembly of the following month signaled the introduction of a new method in which *Tonghak* demands were accomplished: by convening a mass rally of *Tonghak* believers to demonstrate and present petitions. After several petitions and replies, the Chŏlla-do governor said that the issues of the exoneration of the *Tonghak* founder and freedom to propagate could only be decided by the central government and were not something which the local government official could decide. However, it promised to forbid the arrests of *Tonghak* believers and confiscation of their properties by the local authorities.[38]

Tonghak believers then went to Seoul and on February 11, 1893 held a memorial for the exoneration of Ch'oe Che-u in front of Kanghwamun for three days and three nights. As there was a large number of *Tonghak* followers who had come to Seoul in secret in addition to those who held the memorial, it caused a great shock to the government and the residents of Seoul. Finally, King Kojong sent a reply that their wishes would be carried out if they returned home and to their jobs.

Tonghak followers, believing the promise of the king, dispersed their group and returned to the provinces. Upon this, the king and the central government, rather than carrying out the promise of exonerating Ch'oe Che-u, fired Chŏlla-do Governor, Yi Kyŏng-jik for not preventing the *Tonghak* believers from going to Seoul. On the other hand, an order was given to the local government to strictly control the *Tonghak* follower so as to prevent further disturbances. Therefore, the watch over *Tonghak* believers and their persecution by local authorities became more severe.

As the appeal for the exoneration of the *Tonghak* founder failed, Ch'oe Si-hyŏng, on March 11, 1893, returned to Poŭn and established the *Taedoso* (Headquarters of the *Tonghak* organization). He also created the *p'o* (*Tonghak* Parish) to administer over the several existing *chŏp*. *Taejŏpju* was placed in each *p'o* under the new system.[39] At this time, 19 *taejŏpju* were appointed.

The institution of Taedoso and the *p'o* system were important in the organizational development of *Tonghak*. The *Tonghak* leadership system saw the establishment of the *p'o-chŏp* system with the *Taedoso* (Ch'oe Si-hyŏng) → *p'o* (*taejŏpju*) → *chŏp* (*chŏpju*).

Tonghak believers began to gather at Poŭn, even before the arrival of Ch'oe Si-hyŏng, and ultimately the number of those present reached 27,000. As Ch'oe Si-hyŏng himself appeared at the Poŭn assembly and led the *taejŏpcju*, the meeting was very orderly

It should be noted here that the posthumous exoneration of Ch'oe Che-u was not demanded at this Poŭn assembly but rather a call was made for a "crusade to expel the Japanese and Westerners." They set up barricades along the flat land bordering the stream and erected entrances, and set up a banner in the center reading a "crusade to expel the Japanese and Westerners." Surrounding this were medium-sized banners representing each *p'o* and five small colored banners representing the five directions. The *Tonghak* followers chanted *Tonghak* verses (including *Yongdam yusa*) and carried out an intense demonstration. When the county magistrate of Poŭn came to the meeting place to ask them to disperse, citing the order of the central government, they replied they absolutely could not disperse as their purpose lay only in expelling the Japanese and Westerners.[40]

The call for a crusade to expel the Japanese and Westerners rather than the exoneration of Ch'oe Che-u signified a major shift in the goal of the *Tonghak* movement. This can be viewed as an official demonstration by the *Tonghak* followers that their movement was not limited to a religious movement but that it was also a nationalist movement and a movement to save the nation.

The Poŭn assembly was very orderly but, in the eyes of the central government, it was a subversive mass rally. Hence, the government fired the governer of Ch'ungch'ŏng-do province and both repressive and moderate measures were adopted. As a soothing measure, Ŏ Yun-jung was appointed and sent to placate the *Tonghak* followers and to disperse the Poŭn assembly. While as a repressive measure, 600 government troops were sent in under the leadership of Hong Kye-hun to disperse the meeting by force.[41]

When Ŏ Yun-jung arrived at Poŭn, the *Tonghak* followers sent him a written statement emphasizing the purpose of their meeting. Ŏ Yun-jung accepted this and called the *Tonghak* assembly a "meeting of the people" and called the *Tonghak* believers the "People's Party," recognizing their patriotism and loyalty. He also promised to exonerate Ch'oe Che-u and to forbid the local officials from repressing the *Tonghak* followers. Upon this, the negotiations progressed rapidly so that an agreement to dissolve the Poŭn assembly was reached before the arrival of the 600 government troops under the command of Hong Kye-hun.

The Poŭn assembly was dissolved before there was any need for military repression by the government troops even though this was a large-scale *Tonghak* demonstration which was held for 20 days beginning March 11, 1893 and was participated in by some 27,000 people from across the country. It was also a meeting in which a assembly for the exoneration of Ch'oe Che-u changed into a movement to save the country. This assembly, in its nature, was, in fact, a preparatory meeting for a peasant uprising that was the prelude to the Peasant Revolutionary Movement of 1894.

7. Theory of the Conjunction of *Tonghak* and the Peasant Revolutionary Movement of 1894

What then was the relationship between *Tonghak*, which we have observed, and the Peasant Revolutionary Movement of 1894? Regarding this, as afore-mentioned, there are three major opinions: 1) *Tonghak* Revolution Theory which states that the Peasant Revolutionary Movement occurred based on the revolutionary thoughts of *Tonghak*; 2) *Tonghak* Outer Cover Theory which argues that *Tonghak* was merely the outer cover or outer clothing of the Peasant Revolutionary Movement; and, 3) The *Tonghak* and the Peasant Revolutionary Movement Conjunction Theory which this author has been proposing.

This author believes that *Tonghak*, by providing the organizational structure and ideology (the nationalism and egalitarian ideology in particular), served to heighten the previous popular uprisings to the level of Revolutionary Movement based on size and content, instigating the Peasant Revolutionary Movement.

First of all, attention should be paid to the fact that the outbreak of the Peasant Revolutionary Movement of 1894 lay in the continuum of numerous popular uprisings that had been occurring since the end of the 18th century. One of the characteristics of these popular uprisings was that they erupted at the administrative units level such as *pu, kun, hyŏn* against repressions of the magistrates (*pusa, kunsu, hyŏn'gam*). These magistrates controlled the local government and enjoyed some leeway in their rule and thus had plenty of opportunity to corrupt. In these instances popular uprisings broke out on the level of *pu, kun* and *hyŏn*. However, these small-scale popular uprisings, when the central army intervened, were all defeated and easily suppressed. It was in such a situation that the *Tonghak* provided the previous popular uprisings at the local level with a large nation-wide organization to integrate the popular uprisings into a large-scale peasant revolutionary movement.

Organizational Structure of *Tonghak*

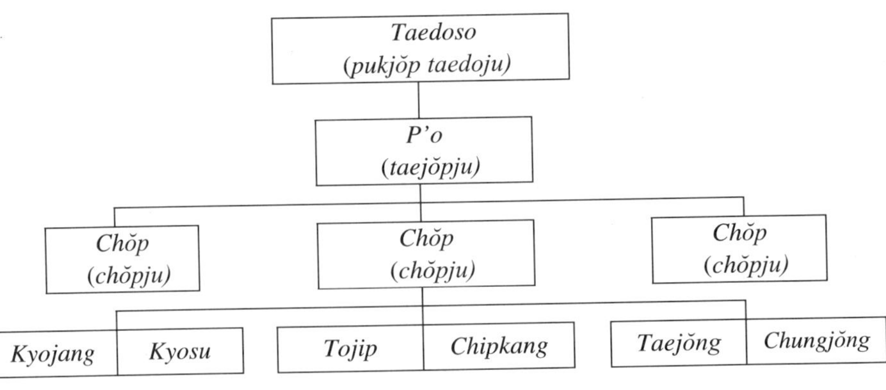

Ch'oe Che-u, as observed before, adopted the *chŏpju* system in 1862 as the organizational structure of *Tonghak* which continued to grow and in 1893, one year before the Peasant Revolutionary Movement of 1894, Ch'oe Si-hyŏng established a leadership structure of 1) taedoso (*pukjŏp taedoju*)→2) *p'o* (*taejŏpju*)→3) *chŏp* (*chŏpju*) and under each *chŏp* a "six responsibilities" system (*kyojang, kyosu, tojip, chipkang, taejŏng, chungjŏng*), and this system was also applied to *P'o* and *Taedoso*.

The most notable organizational unit in relation to the conjuction of *Tonghak* and the popular uprisings is the *P'o*. While *chŏp* covered (or were within) the range of *kun* and *hyŏn* as administrative units, *p'o* was inclusive of several *chŏp* under it so that it inevitably encompassed several *kun* and *hyŏn*. Therefore, the *p'o* (*taejŏpju*) organization, when it joined the popular uprisings, could provoke the large-scale peasant Revolutionary Movement in comparison with the local uprisings of the past.

In 1893, the *Tonghak* organizational structure had 19 *p'o* and *taejŏpju*. *P'o* was a powerful secret organizational unit: under each were *chŏpju* and believers of several *kun* and *hyŏn* units; above them was Ch'oe Si-hyŏng of the *Taedoso* (located at Poŭn). *Tonghak* believers referring to the peasant uprising as *kip'o* (which meant letting the underground *p'o* come up to the world to insurrect)[42] illustrates well the organizational peculiarities of *p'o*.

A nation-wide peasant Revolutionary Movement would have been inevitable if *Taedoso*, the Headquarters, had integrated with popular uprisings. However, even without the *Taedoso* moving into action, if a federation of several *p'o* had decided to integrate, revolt on the *kun* and *kyŏn* level could have escalted to large-scale provincial Peasant Revolutionary Movement.

Among these, an event of decisive importance was the Poŭn assembly of March 1893. At this meeting, *taejŏpju* and *chŏpju* in charge of *p'o* and *chŏp* across the country, together with *Tonghak* believers, under the leadership of Ch'oe Si-hyŏng, convened the largest ever meeting of some 27,000 peopel. Had the participants at the Poŭn assembly been given weapons, a large-scale peasant uprising would have broken out that very day. Therefore, no matter how often the importance of the Poŭn assembly is reiterated in relation to the start of the Peasant Revolutionary Movement on a national scale through the integration of *Tonghak* and popular uprisings, it would not be enough. This could be considered a prelude to the Peasant Revolutionary Movement which broke out the following year.

The Peasant Revolutionary Movement came on the heels of the Kobu Peasant Uprising of February 17, 1894 (January 11 by the lunar calendar) which caused the magistrate of a county to be changed and at the persuasion of the new magistrate Pak Wŏn-myŏng, dissolved itself. The Peasant Revolutionary Movement broke out at the provincial level when Chŏn Pong-jun who had travelled to Mujang in disguise, was able to persuade Son Hwa-jung of Mujang *p'o*, Kim Kae-nam of T'aein *p'o* and Kim Tŏk-myŏng of Kŭmgu *p'o* to combine the three *p'o* to establish Namjŏp Toso with Chŏn Pong-jun in charge.

Next in importance was the integration of *Tonghak* and the peasants. A strong nationalistic desire to defend the country from outside powers, solid democratism based on egalitarianism, high level of humanism based on believing "man is God" and expectations for an evolution of Later Creation captured the hearts of the peasants. The commoners and the peasants who had been discriminated against, oppressed and looked-down upon by the *yangban*-class bureaucrats did not have any spiritual support to depend on. It was at this point that *Tonghak*, which provided a strong nationalistic egalitarian and humanistic ideology, was eagerly welcomed by the peasants despite severe repression by the Chosŏn dynasty authorities, making possible for the *Tonghak* and peasants to join hands.

For example, the third Patriarch Son Pyŏng-hŭi admired the egalitarian ideology of *Tonghak* and became a follower as he had been discriminated against because he was the son of a concubine. Even Paekpŏm Kim Koo who participated in the Peasant Revolutionary Movement as a *chŏpju* of Hwanghae-do province became a follower of *Tonghak* at the age of 18 (1900) because of his admiration of the egalitarian and humanitarian ideology and recorded that it was mostly "low-class people" who became *Tonghak* followers because they admired the egalitarian ideology.[43]

In addition, *Tonghak*'s opposition to the Western powers and Japanese invasion was also enthusiastically welcomed by the peasants and became entrenched in their consciousness. For example, *Tonghak* founder Ch'oe Che-u in his writing *Anshimga* strongly criticized the Japanese invasion of 1592 and demonstrated his strong determination to destroy the Japanese should they invade again, even in spirit after death: "Also, even if I become an immortal, flying about the heavens, I will destroy the dog-like Japanese in one night, with God's agreement and make it omniscient and eternal."[44] This "*Anshimga*" became a part of the Holy Scripture which all *Tonghak* believers memorized and sang often at meetings. This determination to repel or destroy the Japanese had a profound influence on the ideology and consciousness of the *Tonghak* peasant army at both the Poŭn assembly and the Peasant Revolutionary Movement of 1894. One of the written records which this author relies on to argue the theory of the conjunction of *Tonghak* and the

Peasant Revolutionary Movement is the following statement made by Chŏn Pong-jun at his trial:

> Judge: At the time of the uprising, were there more *Tonghak* followers or more oppressed?
>
> Chŏn Pong-jun: At the time of the uprising, the oppressed and the *Tonghak* followers had conjuncted but the *Tonghak* followers were the minority and the peasants were the majority.[45]

At the same time *Maech'ŏn* Hwang hyŏn who had witnessed and experienced the Peasant Revolutionary Movement of 1894 at the time recorded the following, saying that from the time of the First Peasant Uprising by Chŏn Pong-jun and others, *Tonghak* followers and the insurgents had been conjuncted:

> "Rather, everyone said that while *Tonghak* promoted the interests of the nation and provided for the people according to the principles of heaven and beings, it did not promote killing or stealing but also did not forgive greed and the wrongdoings of the corrupt officials. The innocent people responded to this and 10 *ŭp* of the Chŏlla-do province rose up at once and within ten days reached several tens of thousands. This was the beginning of the conjunction of *Tonghak* and the peasants."[46]

"The conjunction of *Tonghak* and insurgents" mentioned by Chŏn Pong-jun and Hwang hyŏn refers directly to the "collaboration of *Tonghak* followers and insurgents" during the Peasant Revolutionary Movement of 1894. However, taken more abstractly and in retrospect, it may become the basis on which to make orthodox the conjunction of the *Tonghak* ideology, religion, and organization and the peasant army. This is because as *Tonghak* began to be propagated systematically, *Tonghak* began to integrate with the peasants, the popular uprisings and the Peasant Revolutionary Movement in turn.

8. Conclusion

As can be gathered from the above observations, the relationship between *Tonghak* and the Peasant Revolutionary Movement was not one in which the social-revolutionary ideology of *Tonghak* caused the Peasant Revolutionary Movement of 1894. It was also not one in which *Tonghak* was merely an outer cover or outer clothing for the Peasant Revolutionary Movement. At this point these two extreme explanations are not identical with the facts. *Tonghak* may be taken to have contributed the organizational structure and the ideology for the outbreak of previous popular uprisings and peasant uprisings so that the two could intergrate in solidarity and became the large-scale peasant Revolutionary Movement. At this juncture, I believe that the *Tonghak* and Peasant Revolutionary Movement Conjunction Theory on the relationship between *Tonghak* and Peasant Revolutionary Movement is the most rational explanation and one which is identical to the facts.

Among the *Tonghak* ideologies the most noticebale was the nationalistic ideology of strong anti-foreign power and anti-invasion.

In addition, the egalitarian ideology of *Tonghak* captured the hearts of the peasants, receiving enthusiastic welcome from the peasants and served as a major factor in integrating *Tonghak* and the Peasant Revolutionary Movement.

Another factor contributing to the conjuction was the belief that "Man is God. Therefore serve man as you would serve God" and this proved to be more appealing to the peasants than Western Learning. In addition, the thought of the evolution of the Later Creation made *Tonghak* very appealing to the peasant soldiers who were waiting for the coming of a new age.

However, the most important factor which *Tonghak* provided the Peasant Revolutionary Movement was the organizational structure of *Tonghak*. Prior to the organization and propagation of *Tonghak*, the peasants were without any systematic organization so that although popular uprisings spontaneously erupted at the *kun* and *hyŏn* levels, they were defeated and easily suppressed when the provincial and central governments intervened.

A monumental development in the *Tonghak* organizational structure was made during the Poŭn assembly in March 1893 during which the *p'o* system was newly established, *taejŏpju* system adopted and Taedoso instituted. *p'o* had several *chŏp* under it and the person in charge of *p'o*, *taejŏpju*, was in charge of a number of *chŏpju* who were responsible for *chŏp*.

P'o were the most important within the *Tonghak* organizational structure in the integration of *Tonghak* and the Peasant Revolutionary Movement. This is because while *chŏp* often paralleled administrative units of *kun* and *hyŏn*, *p'o* included several *chŏp* and hence included several *kun* and *hyŏn*. Therefore, when a single *chŏp* joined in a popular uprising generally one kun or hyŏn was shaken, but when one *p'o* joined in a popular uprising, unlike in the past, several *kun* and *hyŏn* were shaken and the government troops alone could not suppress the uprising.

The organizational structure of *p'o* had 19 *p'o* and *taejŏpju* by spring of 1893. The expression *kip'o* used by *Tonghak* followers to describe the rise up of the peasant Revolutionary Movement is an expression which well captured the characteristic of the *p'o* system.

The Poŭn assembly of March 1893 saw participation by all the *taejŏpju* of 19 *p'o* and many *chŏpju* and *Tonghak* believers under them. It was a *Tonghak* followers' meeting on a national scale. At this Poŭn assembly a call was made to "expel the Japanese and Westerners" rather than a demand to "exonerate Ch'oe Che-u." Thus, the Poŭn assembly becoming a prelude to the Peasant Revolutionary Movement of 1894. If weapons had been distributed at this meeting the Peasant Revolutionary Movement would have broken out on a national scale.

Although the enlightenment movement, *Tonghak* movement, movement of defending orthodoxy and rejecting heterodoxy and several other movements coexisted at the time to resolve the crises facing the Korean nation, *Tonghak* was selected by the peasants and integrated into the Peasant Revolutionary Movement. This could be interpreted as having occurred because of all the different movements, *Tonghak*, in its ideology and organizational features, had the most "elective affinity" to the peasants.

FOOTNOTES (Part II - 11)

1. Shin Yong-ha, "Tonghak-kwa kabo nongmin chŏnjaeng-ŭi minjok chuŭi (Nationalism of Tonghak and the Peasant War of 1894)," *Han'guk hakpo 47* (1987).

2. *Ch'oesŏnsaeng munjip towŏn kisŏ* (Record of the Origin of Tonghak Learning) (hereinafter: Towŏn kisŏ), in Tonghak *sasang charyojip* (Source Book on Tonghak Thought), Vol. 1, Asea Munhwasa, p. 159.

3. *Kyŏngju ch'oessi taedongbo*, Vol. 1 and Vol. 4; Yi Ton-hwa, ed., *Ch'ŏndogy'o ch'anggŏnsa* (A History of the Founding of Ch'ŏndogyo).

4. Yi Sang-baek, "Sŏŏl kŭmgo shimal (On Forbidding Illegitimate Sons to Take the Civil Service Examinations)," *Tongbang hakchi* 1, 1954.

5. *Yongdam yusa* (Anthologie of Ch'oe Che-u's Hymns).

6. *Tonghaksa* (The History of Tonghak), p. 2; *Ch'ŏndogyo ch'anggŏnsa*, chapter 1, pp. 3-4.

7. *Towŏn kisŏ*, p. 165.

8. "P'odŏngmun (On Propagating Tonghak)," in *Tonggyŏng taejŏn* (Bible of Tonghak Doctrine).

9. "Anshimga," *Yongdam yusa*.

10. *Towŏn kisŏ*, p. 171.

11. *Ch'ŏndogyo ch'anggŏnsa*, chapter 1, p. 47.

12. "Nonhangmun (A Discussion on Learning of Tonghak)," in *Tonggyŏng taejŏn*.

13. *Ibid.*

14. "Yongdamga," in *Yongdam yusa*.

15. *Towŏn kisŏ*, pp. 194-195.

16. Shin Yong-ha, "Tonghak-ŭi sahoe sasang (Social Thought of Tonghak)," in *Han'guk kŭndae sahoe sasangsa yŏn'gu* (Studies in Modern Korean Social Thought), 1987, Ilchisa, Seoul.

17. "Nonhangmun," in *Tonggyŏng taejŏn*.

18. "Anshimga," in *Yongdam yusa*.

19. *Ibid.*

20. *Ibid.*

21. *Ibid.*

22. "Kyohun'ga," in *Yongdam yusa*.

23. *Tonghaksa*, p. 42.

24. *Ch'ŏndogyo ch'anggŏnsa*, chapter 2, p. 36.

25. Ch'oe Shi-hyŏng, "Naesudomun," *Han'guk hakpo* 12, 1978.

26. *Tonghaksa*, p. 64.

27. *Ibid.*, p. 5.

28. *Ch'ŏndogyo ch'anggŏnsa*, chapter 2, pp. 37-38.

29. *Tonghaksa*, p. 64.

30. "Yongdamga," in *Yongdam yusa.*

31. *Tonghaksa*, p. 64.

32. *Towŏn kisŏ*, pp. 277-280.

33. *Ch'ŏndo kyohoesa ch'ogo* (Rough manuscript of the History of the Ch'ŏndogyo), in *Tonghak sasang charyojip*, Vol. 1, p. 428; *Ch'ŏndogyo ch'anggŏnsa*, chapter 2, p. 30.

34. *Ch'ŏndogyo ch'anggŏnsa*, chapter 2, p. 31.

35. *Ch'ŏndo kyohoesa ch'ogo*, p. 430.

36. *Tonghaksa*, pp. 70-71; *Ch'ŏndogyo ch'anggŏnsa*, chapter 2, pp. 45-46.

37. *Ch'ŏndogyo ch'anggŏnsa*, chapter 2, pp. 46-48; *Tonghaksa*, pp. 70-71.

38. *Tonghaksa*, p. 74.

39. *Ch'ŏndogyo ch'anggŏnsa*, chapter 2, p. 55; *Ch'ŏndo kyohoesa ch'ogo*, p. 54.

40. *Ch'wiŏ* (Collection of Manifestos and Slogans Related to the Tonghak Rebellion)," in *Tonghangnan kirok* (Records of the Tonghak Rebellion), tome 1, p. 111.

41. *Sokŭmch'ŏngsa* (Supplement to the Diary of Kim Yun-shik), Vol. 1, p. 262.

42. "Ch'och'o munmok (Record of the First Interrogation on Chŏn Pong-jun)," *Chŏn Pong-jun kongch'o* (Records of the Interrogations on Chŏn Pong-jun), in *Tonghangnan kirok*, tome 2, p. 525.

43. *Paekpŏm ilji* (Diary of Kim Koo), Paekpŏm Kim Koo Sŏnsaeng Kinyŏm Saŏp Hyŏphoe, pp. 27-29.

44. "Anshimga," in *Yongdam yusa.*

45. Chŏn Pong-jun kongch'o, in *Tonghangnan kirok*, tome 2, p. 525.

46. *Oha kimun*, Vol. 1, p. 25.

12. The Revolutionary Movement of the *Tonghak* Peasant Army of 1894:
Seen vis-a-vis the French Revolution

1. Sense of Problem

One of the most important research subject in the modern history of the nations of the world must be on how the medieval *ancien regime* was dismantled and how a new modern system was established in its place.

According to the orthodox interpretation of the French Revolution, the bourgeoisie of France brought down the *ancien regime* by revolutionary means and established a new modern system which opened the door to republicanism, civil society and capitalism. In other words, the French Revolution was a bourgeois revolution led by bourgeoisie (in alliance with other classes of farmers and laborers).[1]

My view of the modern history of Korea, however, is that Korea's medieval *ancien regime* was brought down by farmers through the revolutionary movement of the *Tonghak* peasant army in 1894 and, its wake, the Enlightenment faction (*kaehwap'a*) undertook the bourgois reforms. In other words, two forces played their own distinctive roles in bringing down the *ancien regime* in 1894 and establishing a new system. Farmers undertook the revolutionary movement in bringing down the medieval *ancien regime* and from there, the Enlightenment faction carried out the bourgeois reform of 1894 (*kabo kyŏngjang*). The collaboration of the two forces led the establishment of a new modern system in Korea.

I will attempt to construct "theory of the collaboration of the revolutionary movement of the peasant army and of the bourgeois reform" in relation to the issue of modernization in the modern history of Korea. We strongly advocate that even though the *Tonghak* peasant movement took the form of a peasant war in its outer appearance, it was a revolutionary movement of peasants in content and in its historical nature. I oppose the view which interprets the content and historical nature of the *Tonghak* peasant movement as a peasant war.

2. The Four Stages of the Peasant Revolutionary Movement

The revolutionary movement of the *Tonghak* peasant army in 1894 proceeded in four stages.

The first stage was the "peasant uprising at Kobu." About 1,000 peasants at Kobu, Chŏlla-do province, stromed the county office at Kobu under the leadership of Chŏn Pong-jun in protest against extortion and exaction by corrupt county officials. Meting out due punishment to the dishonest functionaries, they distributed to the original taxpayers the rice illegally collected by the county magistrate Cho Pyŏng-gap in the guise of an irrigation tax. In its consequence, the magistrate was replaced by Pak Wŏn-myŏng who as a new magistrate managed to persuade the peasants to disperse. This stage of unrest among the peasants was not yet in the nature of a peasant revolutionary movement; it was rather a prelude in a stage of a small-scale disturbance or uprising. The period from January 11 to March 3, 1894 according to the lunar calendar (February 17-April 8, solar calendar) corresponds to the first stage.

The second stage was the "first phase of the peasant revolutionary movement." In this stage, peasants from throughout the Chŏlla-do region set up a command post at Mujang under the leadership of Chŏn Pong-jun, Son Hwa-jung and Kim Kae-nam in preparation for a rebellion. Organizing a *Tonghak* peasant army of about 4,000 centering around the followers of *Tonghak* (Eastern Learning), they occupied several towns and counties starting from *Mujang* and entered the city of Chŏnju and defeated the government army. The peasant revolutionary movement started full scale in real earnest from this stage. The second stage can be dated on the lunar calendar from March 20 to May 7 (April 25-June 10 solar calendar) of the same year.

The third stage concerns the establishment of Local Directorates (*chipkangso*) for the *Tonghak* revolutionary movement. This occurred when a peace agreement was signed at Chŏnju between the *Tonghak* peasant army and the government army in order to expedite the withdrawal of the Chinese and Japanese armies which entered Korea to intervene in the *Tonghak* revolutionary movement. The *Tonghak* peasant army voluntarily disbanded *pro forma* in order to create a condition for the withdrawal of foreign armies. Local Directorates were established at 53 counties in Chŏlla-do province to conduct the rule by peasants. The period corresponds from May 8 to September 12 according to the lunar calendar (June 11-October 10, solar calendar).

The fourth stage concerns the "second phase in the peasant revolutionary movement." The Japanese army, far from moving out, provoked the Sino-

Japanese War in Korea. Japanese soldiers stormed the royal palace of Korea, disarmed the honor guards of the Korean Kingdom at will and interfered with the domestic affairs of Korea by manipulating the power relations in the royal court. This was when the *Tonghak* peasant army under the leadership of Chŏn Pong-jun arose again in bloody resistance to drive the Japanese army out the Korean peninsula. This period lasted from September 13 lunar calendar (October 11, solar) through the end of the year.

The signs of "revolutionary peasant movement" more became prominent in the second stage.

3. The Revolutionary Nature of Tonghak Peasant Movement

The Four Great Causes proclaimed at Paeksan on around March 25 in the "first phase" of the second stage contained as its third item, "Drive out the barbarous Japanese and clean up the ruling circles around the King." This was a proclamation for an anti-imperial struggle to drive out the Japanese imperial influences that had penetrated into Korea following the opening of the Korean ports. The fourth item read, "March into the capital with the army and crush all those in influence and nobility." This is interpreted as a proclamation for anti-feudal peasant revolution to bring down the Old Guard *ancien regime* centered around Queen Min and the *yangban* ("nobility") class on the top of society.

Again, the call to arms circulated in Chŏlla-do province and throughout the nation on around March 27 by the *Tonghak* peasant army manifested the anti-imperial and anti-feudal nature of its peasant revolutionary movement as follows.

We rise up in the cause of righteousness not for anything else but to save the multitudes from agony and to place the state on the firm rock-like foundation. Internally, we are to behead the corrupt and wicked officials and externally to drive out the arrogant hordes of our fearsome foes. People at large persecuted by the *yangban* and by the wealthy and rich, and petty government functionaries tramped down by magistrates and governors all share the same grievances as we do. They should not hesitate but rise up at this moment with us. If we should let this opportunity pass, it will be too late for us to regret... By the General for the Cause of Righteousness in Chŏlla-do Province at Paek-san.

The call to arms pinpoints the target of struggle as "*yangban* vs. people," thus manifesting itself as an anti-feudal struggle. In its reference to "driving out the arrogant hordes of our fearsome foes," the call also shows its anti-imperial nature, a national revolutionary movement by the peasants.

The *Tonghak* peasant army occupied more than 20 counties before it succeeded in entering the fortress of the city of Chŏnju. In the occupied areas, the administrative order of the *ancien regime* by the *yangban* bureaucrats was crushed to pieces and emergency measures for rehabilitation of the life of people were rapidly undertaken by the *Tonghak* peasant army.

Rule by peasants through Local Directorates in the third stage further clarifies the revolutionary nature of the *Tonghak* peasant army that put an end to the *ancien regime*. The essentials of the reform program proposed by the Loal Directorates were abolition of social estate system and enfranchisement of serfs in five areas; punishment of corrupt officials, the wealthy, the rich and pro-Japanese elements, annulment of high-interest loans and reform of the land-owning system each in one item. Basic practices actually implemented by the Local Directorates for a little over three months in the rule by peasants include ① stern punishment of the wealthy who owned their fortunes to high-handed extortionate practices, ② emancipation from the yoke of social estate system, ③ punishment and confiscation of wealth from venal and corrupt officials. ④ ban on collection of all arbitrary and irregular taxes, ⑤ cancellation of all outstanding debts, whether owed to government agencies or to private individuals, ⑥ annulment of high-interest loans, ⑦ ban on export of rice to Japan, ⑧ attempted annulment of landlord system, ⑨ disposition of complaints from people, ⑩ inspection and review of the official documents, ⑪ propagation of the *Tonghak* study and strengthening of the peasant army, ⑫ distribution of arms and horses among the peasant army and ⑬ stockpiling of money and rice for war preparation.

Of these, items ①, ②, ③, ④, ⑤, ⑥, ⑧, ⑨ and ⑩ mainly concern the anti-feudal struggle and items ⑦, ⑪, ⑫ and ⑬ the anti-imperial struggle. What is noteworthy here is that the peasant rule through Local Directorates was intent upon bringing down the conservative *ancien regime* of Queen Min, abolition of social estate system, emancipation of lower class people, abolition of the feudal landlord system and of the feudal taxation system, thus ranging over the entire compass of the *ancien regime*. In short, the peasant rule through Local Directorates actually implemented the revolutionary self-rule by peasant aiming to abolish the whole system of the feudalistic *ancien regime* and to establish a new regime of peasants aspired to by land-tilling farmers.

During the fourth stage of the "second phase of the peasant revolutionary movement," the movement spread out throughout the country spilling over from the Chŏlla-do region to Ch'ungch'ŏng-do, Kyŏngsang-do, Kyŏnggi-do, Kangwŏn-do and P'yŏngan-do provincial regions. The second phase ended in failure at the defeat inflicted upon the *Tonghak* peasant army by the Japanese army at the battle at Ugumch'i of Kongju. The original goal of the movement was to drive out the Japanese army from the Korean peninsula, to eradicate the *ancien regime* and to implement peasant rule through Local Directorates of the *Tonghak* movement. According to the estimate made by Pak Ŭn-sik, the casualties inflicted upon the peasants of the *Tonghak* movement in the series of two phases of the peasant revolutionary movement reached about 300,000 lives.

The revolutionary movement of the *Tonghak* peasant army of 1894 was a representative revolutionary movement in the modern chapter of Korean history. Though the anti-feudal and anti-imperial aspects were combined in the "first phase of the peasant revolutionary movement," the anti-feudal aspect was more conspicuous than the anti-imperial element. In the "second phase," both anti-feudal and anti-imperial elements were there but the anti-imperial character ws more markedly noted than the anti-feudal inclination.[2]

4. A Combination of Peasant Revolutionary Movement and Bourgeois Reform

On account of the weak sense of class consciousness among Korean peasants in the period of 1894, some views have been aired to underestimate the importance of the movement, claiming that the *Tonghak* revolutionary movement of 1894 can not be seen as a "peasant revolution" or "peasant revolutionary movement" and that at most the movement was in the nature of a "peasant war." Such arguments ignore the basic difference in the class structure of societies, namely, the class structure in Korea of the 19th century and the class structure in France prior to the outbreak of the French Revolution.

The class hierarchy of the West prior to the French Revolution was, in short, in the order of aristocrats, bourgeois and farmers (and laborers), or "nobility, tradesmen, artisans and peasants" in an Oriental paraphrasing. In the West, the bourgeois achieved a rapid growth right beneath the aristocrats while farmers were mostly in the state of serfdom in ignorance and illiteracy. To the contrary, the class hierarchy in Korea toward the end of the 19th century was in the order of "nobility, peasants, artisans and tradesmen" where peasants (or farmers) were situated right under the nobility; and artisans and tradesmen, which corresponded to the bourgeois of the West, were treated as belonging to despicable occupations with a social status much less respectable than the peasants and farmers.

Farmers in Korea in the 19th century were economically poor but in social status most of them were *yangin* (free-born). In the latter part of the Chosŏn dynasty, lecture halls spread out rapidly even in the countryside, markedly raising literacy among farmers, producing a sizable book-reading population in the farming communities with s subsequent rise in the level of their political consciousness. Therefore, the social status of Korean farmers was far better than for serfs in the medieval period of the West. Therefore, it is a mistake to apply the case of Europe to Korea and to claim that farmers were an underdeveloped class incapable of mounting a revolutionary movement and that only the bourgeois class could be the driving force of a revolutionary movement. Such a contention would commit an error of neglecting the paricular elements in the modern history of Korea.

In the modern history of Korea, the bourgeois was underdeveloped. Therefore, there is nothing strange in its historical development that the nobility class of *yangban* and aristocrats, the supporters of the *ancien regime*, became the target of attack in a revolutionary movement by the farming class which was relatively mature immediately beneath the aristocrats or *yangban*. Even though the *Tonghak* revolutionary movement could not afford to negate the monarchy itself in the light of the prevailing conditions of the time, the shifting trend from autocratic monarchy to constitutional monarchy was inevitable. A similar political stand was taken by the Enlightenment faction, the driving force for bourgeois reform. The latter, too, did not advocate republicanism in 1894 but was claiming for a constitutional monarchy.

Nevertheless, the revolutionary movement of the *Tonghak* peasant army managed to bring down the conservative Old Guard regime of Queen Min, the last stronghold of the *ancien regime*. It also achieved the emancipation of people from the yoke of social estate by completely abolishing the social estate system, the social backbone of the medieval *ancien regime*. It pursued a new modern system by resolutely negating the feudal landlord system and its exploitative system of extortion, the economic backbone of the medieval system. The *Tonghak* revolutionary movement of 1894 failed in establishing its regime in the capital. On this score, the event may be conceptualized as a "revolutionary movement" though it may fall short of being categorized as a "revolution." Though the *Tonghak* revolutionary movement of 1894 failed in establishing a new system, it succeeded in bringing down the medieval *ancien regime* in Korea through a revolutionary means.

The process of bringing down the *ancien regime* and establishing a new order in the modern chapter of Korean history shows that peasants of the *Tonghak* followers initiated a revolutionary peasant movement in March, 1894 bringing down the conservative Old Guard regime of Queen Min, the backbone of the *ancien regime*, the feudal landlord system and the feudal exploitative ecnomomic system in pursuit of a new system by the rule of peasants⁻ to be followed in three months by the Enlightenment faction which grabbed the power and began undertaking the bourgeois reform. But for the preceding revolutionary movement by the *Tonghak* peasant army, the weak power of the Enlightenment faction would have been incapable of grabbing the power in opposition to the *ancien regime*. But for the bringing down of the *ancien regime* from below through the revolutionary movement of the *Tonghak* peasant army and but for the subsequent undertaking of the radical change for reform implemented through Local Directorates of farmers, the legal reform undertaken by the Enlighenment faction in 1894 should merely have been "paper reform." In fact, the radical change for reform undertaken by the Enlightenment faction shortly following its grabbing of the power was patterned after the mode of the reform taken by peasants in the revolutionary movement of the *Tonghak* peasant army with some addition and revision suiting the style of the Enlightenment faction.

The reform undertaken in 1894 by the Enlightenment faction was basically a bourgeois reform in the eyes of the Westerners and most from the Enlightenment faction were from the *yangban* class. At the time, the Enlightenment faction had no potentiality or no aspiration to pursue "bourgeois revolution." What they pursued in actuality was not a bourgeois 'revolution' but a bourgeois 'reform.' The Enlightenment faction, which undertook the reform of 1894, proceeded resolutely with the bourgeois reform while the revolutionary movement of the *Tonghak* peasant army was in progress. Following the defeat of the *Tonghak* peasant army at the battle at Ugumch'i however, the speed of reform was notably slackened down.

In the light and methodology of history that merely records the chronicles of events, the *Tonghak* peasant movement may seem to be an event separate and independent from the bourgeois reform that was the reform of 1894 undertaken by the Enlightenment faction. However, in the light and methodology of history that focuses on structure, totality and depth in the study of social history, the *ancien regime* in the modern history of Korea in the 19th century was brought down in 1894 by the revolutionary movement of the *Tonghak* peasant army. The establishment of a new modern system based on that foundation was instituted by the bourgeois reform undertaken by the Enlightenment faction. Thus we can see that the modern social system of

Korea toward the end of the 19th century was established by a combination of the revolutionary movement of the *Tonghak* peasant army and of the bourgeois reform. These must be the characteristic elements in the modern history and the modernization process in Korea in contrast to the French Revolution.

FOOTNOTES (Part II – 12)

1. Shin Yong-Ha, "The Identity of the Driving Forces and Its Social Status in the Revolutionary Movement of the Tonghak Peasant Army (Kabo nongmin chŏnjaeng-ui chuch'eseryŏk-kwa sahoeshinbun)," *The Journal of Korean History* (Han'guksa yŏn'gu), Combined Issue of No. 50 and 51, December 1985; "Establishment of Farmers' Local Directorates in the Period of the Tonghak Revolutionary Movement (Kabo nongmin chŏnjaeng shigi-ŭi nongmin chipkangso-ŭi sŏlch'i)," *Journal of Korean Studies* (Han'guk hakpo), Vol.4, December 1985; "Activity of the Farmers' Local Directorates during the Tonghak Revolutionary Movement (Kabo nongmin chŏnjaeng shigi-ŭi nongmin chipkangso-ŭi hwaltong)," *Korean Culture* (Han'guk munhwa), Vol. 6, December 1985.

2. See Min Sŏk-hong ed., *Views on the History of the French Revolution* (P'ŭrangsŭ hyŏng-myŏngsaron), 1988, *Kkach'i* Publishing Co., related to the views of LeFebre, Soble and Prof. Min Sŏk-hong.

13. Social Thought of Korean Independence Club

1. Introduction

The social thought of *Tongnip Hyŏphoe* (The Independence Club) represents a system of social awareness created to preserve the independence of the nation through spontaneous strenghening of the power of the Korean people toward the end of 19th century when the great powers were out to colinize Korea in search of mining, railroad, forestry and fishery interests.

The prevailing concept of the social thought of the Independence Club seems in need of modification in some respects.

First, the philosophical lineage of the Independence Club can hardly be traced back to the heritage of Western bourgeois thought. Two streams of thought are noticeable; one stems from the influence of Western civil thought as introduced by Sŏ Chae-p'il and Yun Ch'i-ho; the other is the stream of indigenous thought of reform Confucianist tradition as represented by Namgung Ŏk, Chŏng Kyo, Chang Chi-yŏn and Pak Ŭn-sik. These two streams combine to form the social thought of the Independence Club. Yi Sang-jae played a most important role in amalgamating the two streams during the existence of the Independence Club and later came under the influence of Christianity in prison following the dissolution of the Independence Club.

The first stream was predominant on account of its sophisticated theory and the level perception of its advocates; mainly by means of the *Tongnip Sinmun* (The Independent) they criticized the premodern social institutions and awareness, and propagated nationalistic and civil ideas.

The second stream accounted for the majority opinion which was held by the middle stratum of the Independence Club membership. But the first stream was largely reinforced by the second stream. The second stream reflected the growth of national philosophy and helped in selective introduction of civil thought, thus constituting the backbone of the social thought of the Independence Club. The second stream began publishing *Hwangsŏng Sinmun* as its organ.

2. Social Background of the Independence Club

Those who regarded *The Independent* as the only organ of the Independence

Club failed to notice the second stream. Thus, the Independence Club had two more organs in the *Tongnip Sinmun* and *Hwangsŏng Sinmun* for the duration of its existence. Secondly, the social thought of the Independence Club mirrored the socio-economic state of Korea at the time, rather than the influence of foreign ideas. Characteristic of the socio-economic changes were:

1) Rise of bourgeoisie—Reorganization of market and the coming into being of various stores and modern joint-stock companies gave rise to a bourgeoisie.

2) Growth of farmer class— The Tonghak peasant revolutionary movement and its reform program evidenced the growth of the farming populace.

3) Emergence of miners and longshoremen— Mining industry and opening of ports for foreign trade created a class of wage earners.

4) Emancipation of outcasts— The Reform of 1894 recognized previous outcasts such as butchers and slaves.

5) Formation of a new intellectual class—Introduction and expansion of modern school system contributed to the rise and growth of a new educated class.

In the face of the mounting threat of aggression by big powers the emerging bourgeoisie, farming and wage earning classes and liberated outcasts were all gripped by crisis feelings and concerned about the future of the country.

The new intellectual class could be divided into several categories, of which the Independence Club members represented the most progressive wing, comprising the two streams as mentioned above.

The social thought of the Independence Club was the philosophy of this emerging social force, deriving its inspiration from the native *Silhak* (Practical Learning) school and the Western civil thought.

The social thought of the Independence Club has three aspects that should be looked into from three angles. They are the idea of independence, the idea of civil liberty, and the idea of self-help reforms. These components could be linkened to the three sides of a triangle. Formerly, the thought of the Independence Club was identified with the Western bourgeois thought of civil rights, but this was an overestimation of Western influence on the thought of the Independence Club. The social structure and the tasks of 19th century Korea were different from the nature and goal of 18th century Western civil society.

3. Idea of Independence

1) Concept of Sovereignty

The thought of the Independence Club is based on the theory of independence and sovereignty. The basic principles of the Independence Club were declared to be "the consolidation of the foundation of independence and strengthening of sovereignty." It was a reaction against a conservative segment of the bureaucracy which tended to rely upon a certain power for national survival.

The country was in a crisis, according to their belief. Since sovereignty is an essential quality of nation hood, their main interest was in maintaining the nation's sovereignty under the pressure of foreign powers.

By *Chajukwŏn* (sovereignty) they meant no dependence upon foreign powers, and the spontaneous spreading of justice throughout the country. This is to exercise sovereignty over the nation through independence.

In the midst of rivalries among imperialist powers, the country could not rely upon one big power to prevent the inroad of others. We could count on no one except our own countrymen, and the surest way to retain independence and sovereignty was not to depend upon any outside powers.

The Independence Club thought that upholding civil rights was necessary for independence. A nation is made up of individuals; therefore, an independent and strong nation must have independent and strong individuals whose rights should be respected and promoted. This is how the concept of independence espoused by the Independence Club led to the idea of civil liberties.

The conservative faction maintained that establishment of royal prerogatives should necessarily involve infringement upon civil rights; on the other hand, the Independence Club held that respect for civil rights was the basis of national strength and reinforced the power of the king.

On May 8, 1898, the Independence Club sought to persuade the conservative faction from the old line of thinking by organizing a public debate on the theme that higher status of the people results in stronger royalty and more prosperous nationhood. In a petition to Emperor Kojong on Oct. 25, 1898, the Independence Club made a strongly-worded and lucid criticism of the old-guard prejudice against civil rights.

All this implies that the old guard adhered to authoritarian monarchy, while the Independence Club came out in support of constitutional monarchy.

It was the conviction of the Independence Club that independence is hard to maintain under authoritarian monarchy, but that it could be better maintained under constitutional monarchy based on popular consensus born of respect for civil rights. The crowning of King Kojong as Emperor was merely a symbolic change meant for external independence.

Accordingly, the assertion that the Independence Club did not embrace the old-line group was not true. Rather, constitutional monarchy was thought to be the way to preserve independence, bringing the conservative faction into the same fold.

The Independence Club felt the need for greater sense of dignity and patriotism among the people for the sake of national independence. A prolonged period of suppression by the Chosŏn Dynasty Government misled the people to think that loss of independence was not so much loss of the nation as demise of the Chosŏn dynasty. Under the circumstances, the Independence Club emphasized the fact that the crisis involved not only a dynasty but the entire nation. This is why the Independence Club concentrated on advocating love of the nation.

The Independence Club contended that solid patriotism is generated by the participation of the people in government and enlarged civil rights. The ordinary people can love the nation only when they consider the country their own. This shows the democratic nature of the patriotism the Independence Club advocated. The Independence Club believed patriotism was inherent in man's nature and formed the primary spiritual defense of independence.

2) Protection of Econonomic Interests

Natural extension of the spirit of independence held up by the Independence Club was in opposition to the concession of economic interests to foreign powers. It insisted on recovering interests already yielded to foreigners.

Independence must be backed by economic independence, and could only be preserved by the development of one's own national resources and industries. The Independence Club likened government and finance to the body and blood vessels which have to be protected and nurtured for oneself.

Conceding resources, territory or other economic interests to foreign powers, therefore, is tantamount to yielding independence. The Independence Club would neither rely on foreign powers nor exclude them; friendly relations with them should be sought, but economic interests should not be given away.

If there was gold, silver and coal deposits within the country, we should explore them, not foreigners enrich themselves by exploiting these resources, thereby impoverishing the population. Conceding railroad, electric and mining rights to foreigners was like selling the country out to them, the Independence Club said. "The land of Korea is the great inheritance from our past kings and the abode of 12 million people; giving up an inch of it to foreigners is an act betraying the kings and millions of compatriots."

The Independence Club considered the already conceded interests as irecoverable by compulsion, but demanded that they be restored through diplomatic negotiation or purchase.

Opposition to foreign concessions was the main target of the Independence Club in 1898, and was instrumental in discouraging big powers from rending additional interests away from Korea.

3) Neutral Diplomacy

First, in order to gain time for achieving self-help after having checked the immediate exploitation of economic interests by foreigners, the Independence Club viewed maintenance of the then prevailing balance of power as necessary. It thought independence could be consolidated for the duration of such balance of power.

Secondly, the Independence Club called for fair and self-reliant diplomacy for the retention of the balance of power. The secret diplomacy of conceding interests to foreign powers that had been conducted by the conservative faction was denounced for its disservice to the nation, intensifying bickerings among big powers and foreign intervention in the internal affairs of Korea.

Thirdly, the Independence Club maintained that neutral diplomacy should be practiced, without favor or prejudice to any country. For this, two reasons were given. Independent and neutral diplomacy would keep foreign governments from attempting intervention and changes in the Korean government; moreover, partial diplomacy was likely to touch off a Russo-Japanese war, bringing hostilities and destruction to the Korean peninsula.

Fourth, the Independence Club was of the opinion that Korea's diplomacy, most befitting a weak country caught between big powers, should not embitter or provoke these powers. Unfavorable treaties ought not to be concluded, and the nation's economic and military prowess had to be strengthened to recover rights yielded through such treaties already entered into.

The Independence Club aimed at promoting independence and neutral diplomacy to maintain balance of power among big nations and to increase internal strength in the midst of intense conflicts, suspicious and aggressive designs. From this arises the idea of enlightened self-help.

4) Enlightened Self-help

The Independence Club thought independence at that time was only nominal, and we lacked the internal strength and foundation to sustain it.

"Independence in name will not be complete independence if it does not become independence in deed." Being based on the prevailing balance of power, independence might be lost whenever the balance tips. Therefore, the importance of self-reliance was brought to the fore, so that independence could be preserved even when the balance of power collapses.

The Independence Club contended that such self-help (or reliance) must be enlightened. In this respect the social thought of the Independence Club reached out in a different direction from the concept of *wijŏngchoksa* or *Tonghak* thought.

By enlightenment the Independence Club meant formation of a system by means of refining the ideas and customs to suit reason and the tide of the time, adopting the merits and discarding the demerits after comparing those of this country with others.

The principle of enlightened self-help encompasses a wide range of sweeping reforms in all aspects of national government. Such reforms and changes in laws were to be carried out on the strength of national consensus. This line of thinking was similar to the consensus theory of Knag Yu-wei of China, but anticipated the latter by one year.

The Independence Club claimed that enlightened self-help cannot be achieved without knowing two things– the "tide of the time and the world" and "one's self." The Independence Club thus endeavored to stimulate national consciousness and self-discovery, out of which its theory of national culture developed.

5) Theory of National Culture

The interest of the Independence Club in discovery of self evolved into a theory of national culture. It ascribed the spiritual weakness of the nation to preoccupation with Chinese history in ignorance of Korean history.

Coming from a background predominantly of reformed Confucianism, members of the Independence Club, including Chŏng Kyo, Namgung Ŏk, Ch'oe Kyŏng-hwan, Ch'oe Pyŏng-hŏn, hyŏn Chae, Chang Chi-yŏn, Pak Ŭn-sik, Sin Ch'ae-ho, Kwŏn Pyŏng-hun, Han Paeg-wŏn, Kim Yŏng-jin and Yu Ho-sik, tried to formulate Korean history from a nationalistic standpoint. The initial fruits of such effort appeared in *Taedong Yŏksa* (History of the Great East). The five-volume work was written by Ch'oe Kyŏng-hwan in 1896, but could not come off the press until after 1905 because of the official ban placed on its publication by Education Minister Sin Ki-sŏn for its allegedly excessive nationalism.

The book was a systematic reformulation of Korea's ancient history. It developed the theme of the orthodoxy of the Three Kingdoms, drawing upon

Sŏ Kŏ-jŏng's *Tongguk T'onggam* (Survey of the Eastern Country) and *Tongsagangmok* (Outline of Korean History). It thus clarified the fact that ancient Korea was a strong and civilized country equal to China. In the book, China is not called the Middle Kingdom; the author intended to replace the China-oriented historical interpretation by a nationalistic Korean viewpoint — a remarkable change at that time.

Taedong Yŏksa left a great impact on many Independence Club members and later historians, providing a point of departure for modern historical studies of Korea. Especially noticeable was the fact that the thought of *Silhak* embodied in An Chŏng-bok's *Tongsagangmok* had been carried over and further expanded by *Taedong Yŏksa*.

The Independence Club also insisted on using the national scripts, *Han'gŭl*; such Independence Club members as Chu Si-gyŏng (Chu Sang-ho), Chi Sŏg-yŏng, Ch'oe Kwang-ok and Sin Hae-yong took the lead in full-fledged and modern research on the Korean language, calling for the following programs:

(1) Formulation of unified Korean grammar;
(2) Adoption of spacing formula;
(3) Compilation of a Korean dictionary;
(4) Exclusive use of *Han'gŭl* (national scripts);
(5) Horizontal transcription in *Han'gŭl*.

All of these programs were considered revolutionary at the time and achieved considerable progress. These studies of the Korean language were all promoted as means of bringing about independence, civil rights and self-help.

The Independence Club adopted the first national anthem of Korea. In September 1896, it proposed a national anthem and in December proposed that it be sung at a gathering of the Independence Club; the ceremonial program of the Independence Festival of 1898 included the national anthem (Yun Ch'i-ho was the probable author of its lyrics, but data are insufficient to ascertain the fact). Moreover, the Independence Club organized nationwide campaigns to write patriotic lyrics for popular singing.

The Independence Club rediscovered the *Silhak* (Practical Learning) of the late Chosŏn dynasty period and introduced it to the poeple. At first, the Independence Club used the term *Silhak* to mean experimental social or natural sciences of the West, but later reformulated its concept as being unique to the Korean tradition of learning from practical things.

Usually, rediscovering and conceptualization of *Silhak* is attributed to the scholarly work of Ch'oe Nam-sŏn, Yi Nŭng-ha and Chŏng In-bo between 1916 and 1917, but actually it was done by members of the Independence Club toward the close of the 19th century, 20 years earlier than the afore-mentioned historians.

The results were first printed in the April 17, 1899 issue of the *Hwangsŏng Sinmun* under the title "Outlining the exposition of Korea's foremost economist, Chŏng Yak-yong." The August 3 and 4 editions of the same newspaper also carried articles on *Silhak* and its protagonist, Chŏng Yak-yong.

It is undeniable that these articles were the major intellectual sources of rediscovered *Silhak*. The national awareness of the Independence Club was advanced by its ideas about civil rights and self-help.

4. Concept of Civil Liberties

1) Rights to Popular Freedom

The Independence Club developed its concepts of rights to popular freedom in the belief that independence and prosperity of a nation are predicated on the civil rights and prosperity of its constituent individual members.

In the first place, the Independence Club insists on the right to life and property, by which the common people could be protected against premodern exploitation by the privileged and the bureaucracy.

Worthy of note was the fact that some of the Independence Club leaders espoused popular right to life and property prior to their exposure to Western civil thought. Inspired by *Silhak* thought, they developed their own conception of the people's rights to life and property for the protection of the farming and lowly populace from arbitrary exactions by the *yangban* and bureaucrats.

Treatment of criminals posed a serious problem. Opinions were still divided as to whether corporal punishment or forfeiture of property inflicted upon criminals should be regarded in the same light as the rights of ordinary people. Under the influence of Western civil thought, some thought that they should be treated on an equal footing.

Such ideas as "government must protect the life and property of the people," or "not a penny should be taken in tax except by law" had not been alien to Koreans. This line of thinking was long established; only the growth of the people was required to put the thinking into effect. Western civil thought exerted more influence upon technical and criminals.

The Independence Club also advanced the cause of freedom of the press and of assembly. This was intended not only to protect the people from exploitation by the *yangban* and bureaucratic class, but positively to nurture civil rights, thus enabling the common people to defend their own rights. Two trends are discernable in Independence Club's advocacy of the rights to freedom of the press and assembly. In Korea, freedom of the press on the part of the gentry was deeply rooted, and popular assemblies were rather prevalent, as was the case with the *Tonghak* groups. On this native base the Western civil ideas of freedom of the press and assembly were transplanted and amplified by the Independence Club. Available data indicate that the resolutions and procedures of the Independence Club and the *Manmin' gondonghoe* (Peaple's Assembly) combined the content and form of both East and West.

The concepts freedom of the press and assembly advocated by the Independence Club was a merger of the native stream and the current of Western civil thought, and was strengthened, instead of weakened, by the latter. The press and assembly of the *Manmin'gongdonghoe* since the spring of 1898 were led by the bourgeois class and its philosophy, but their persistent demand for freedom could not last long without the adamant tradition of the freedom of the gentry, press and the growth and vigor of the farming population.

The petition submitted by the Independence Club on October 23, 1898 stated that criticizing and denouncing cabinet ministers belong among the rights of the people, and a nation can hardly be sustained in the absence of a popular press, which absence erodes politics and law.

2) Right to Popular Equality

The Independence Club went beyond the advocacy of freedom and pressed for the right to equality. Stating that all men are born equal, it demanded the abolition of the social estate system, and the equality of the sexes.

Criticisms were made against the remnants of slavery; such criticisms had been anticipated by *Silhak* thinkers, and the institution was formally brought to an end with the emancipation of public slaves in 1801 and private slaves in 1894. Denunciation of the remnants of slavery was a typical example of the effective synthesis of Western civil thought and the indignenous *Silhak* tradition. Editorials in *The Independent* written by Sŏ Chae-p'il represent the same synthesis of the two currents.

The *Silhak* school of Chŏng Yak-yong was in favor of the complete elimination of the slaves, and out of it grew the idea of equality. *Silhak* scholars took issue with treating fellow men as property that could be bought and sold.

The concept of the equality of the sexes promoted by the Independence Club was most heavily influenced by Western civil ideology. Korea's reformed Confucianism had no established idea about feminine rights. Under heavy influence of Western philosophy, the Independence Club‒ especially

Sŏ Chae-p'il and Yun Ch'i-ho⁻ made many contributions to the enhancement of the rights of women.

3) Popular Sovereignty

The Independence Club advanced the theory of popular sovereignty that sovereignty rests with the people who are the masters of the nation; this is based on concepts of the rights to freedom and equality. Describing office holders as servants of the people as well as the king's subjects. The Independence Club criticized the fact that officials did not regard people as the masters of the nation.

Sŏ Chae-p'il said, "For centuries, the Korean people, believing that officials are all sages and respectable personalities, entrusted them with the life and property of themselves and their families; they paid taxes for the upkeep of these officials for them to take care of public affairs; the people delegated their role of master to those paid officials, but the servants soon turned out to be the masters, and the real master was reduced to servant, placing his life and property at the mercy of the former servant; for this the master has only himself to thank, because his inability causes such aberrance of the servant."

This version of popular sovereignty theory was explained along the line of traditional philosophy that the poeple are the foundation of the nation, and must be strong to make the country secure. The idea "for the people (*Wimin*)" and "of the people (*Minbon*)" was firmly rooted in reformed Confucianism, and merged with the impact of Western civil thought to constitute the popular sovereignty theory of the Independence Club.

The influence of Western socio-political thought becomes more manifest with the following ideas, beginning with universal franchise.

4) Popular Franchise

The development of Korea's native social thought that proceeded from the theory of popular sovereignty to universal franchise failed to institutionalize the participation of the citizenry and farmers in government.

The Independence Club leadership headed by Sŏ Chae-p'il and Yun Ch'i-ho broke through the failure to demand direct and institutionalized popular participation in government. In particular, Sŏ suggested that universal franchise be given the local people, so that they could elect local magistrates; this, he said, would be a solution to the problem of local maladministration and restive farm population.

When the local magistrate is chosen by popular vote, he argued:
1. The magistrate will be loved, not resented by the constituents.

2. Capable and conscientious persons will be elected.

3. They will be well informed of local conditions.

4. They will be more concerned about and interested in promoting the welfare of people who elected them.

5. Better administration to meet the popular trust is certain to improve the lot of the citizentry and people.

To have administrators elected by popular vote was a revolutionary idea at the time.

The concept of universal franchise was further broadened by the Independence Club to call for the inauguration of a legislature at the national level.

5) Formation of a Parliament

On April 3, 1898, the Independence Club called a forum on the political urgency of forming a parliament. Many Independence Club members and other participants attending the debate put forward a proposal for the establishment of a parliament.

Later, *The Independent* elaborated in its editorial on the advantages of inaugurating a parliament based on the principle of separation of powers. On July 3, a petition demanding the formation of a parliament was submitted to the Emperor.

The campaign of the Independence Club for a parliament actually meant the reorganization of Chungch'uwŏn (privy council), which was an advisory organ for administration and a depository of careerists, into a legislative body. It met with fierce opposition from conservative bureaucrats, but was supported by such reform-minded officials as Pak Chŏng-yang, Han Kyu-sŏl and Min Yŏng-hwan. After a series of revisions, agreement was reached between representatives of the government and the Independence Club to adopt a new privy council system. This marked the beginning of a parliament in this country.

(1) Under the new system the council had the power to:

    a) make laws,

    b) approve the decisions of cabinet,

    c) consent to cabinet recommendations, subject to royal sanction,

    d) advise on provisional recommendations of cabinet;

    e) decide on popular suggestions and petitions.

(2) The council chairman would be appointed by the Emperor and its vice chairman chosen by council members.

(3) The council consisted of 50 members, of which 25 were recommended by the government from among those who had rendered meritorious service to

the state, and the remaining 25 *chosen* from among the members of the *Inminhyŏphoe* (People's Association) above 27 years of age and well versed in politics and jurisprudence.

(4) The term of office of the council members was 12 months; new elections were to take place one month prior to the expiration of terms of the outgoing council.

(5) When the government and the council was in disagreement, a joint conference of the two was to be called to arriving at concurrence; the government could not act unilaterally.

(6) In the interim, the Independence Club would choose the 25 members who would be popularly elected.

These organizational rules were amended again by an intrigue of the old-guard faction to allow the participation of the *Hwangguk Hyŏphoe* (Imperial Association) in the new privy council. However, it represented the first institutional realization, albeit imperfect, of the concept of popular franchise presented by the Independence Club, and as such the first translation of the ideas of freedom and civil rights into parliamentary democracy.

It must be pointed out here that the Independence Club preoccupation with the formation of a parliament by reorganizing the privy council was motivated not only by respect for popular freedom and civil rights, but also by a far-reaching aspiration for the preservation of national independence. The Independence Club feared that the Emperor and the conservative factions might give away economic interests to foreign powers and this might pave the way for eventual surrender of the nation's independence under pressure. The Independence Club intended to install a parliament capable of preventing such irresponsible and weak-kneed decisions. The Independence Club sought to safeguard the national independence and integrity by means of a popularly-elected, responsive parliamentary body.

If the Independence Club and the embryonic parliament continued to exist for long, imposition of Japan's protectorate treaty upon Korea and the subsequent usurpation of the nations' sovereignty would not have been so easily attained. The combined forces of the Independence Club and the people could have frustrated the take over attempt.

5. Concept of Self-help and Reform

1) Constitutional Government

The Independence Club dwelt on specific self-help programs based on civil rights for the maintenance of independence.

First, authoritarian monarchy would be reformed and separation of powers introduced; the cabinet would be strengthened to enforce a policy of enlightenment and self-help. The Independence Club conceived of a cabinet that would include Pak Chŏng-yang, Han Kyu-sŏl, Min Yŏng-hwan and Yi Sang-jae.

Second, the parliament would be directly and popularly elected eventually, after a period of tutelage by the Independence Club. Yun Ch'i-ho would be named to lead the parliament.

Third, when the cabinet and the parliament became capable of executing self-help reforms, strict rule of law would be established in accordance with constitutional and other laws.

Fourth, upon the establishment of constitutional government. "nation-saving" self-help policies would be undertaken with the consent and support of the poeple. They reckoned five years would be required to achieve self-reliance and self-help sufficient to maintain independence in case international balance of power was affected.

2) Reform of Public Administration and Public Finance

The Independence Club asserted that overall modernization of the public administration and of the public finance system was necessary in preparation for self-help.

Important features of the reform plan were:

1. Overall modernization of the system of appointing central government officials.

2. Direct selection of local officials.

3. Increased professionalism and efficiency of administration.

4. Balanced development of regions.

5. Open management of administration and finance.

6. Unified control of finance by the Finance Ministry and budgeting in the black.

7. Repayment of Japanese loans.

8. Reform of taxation system and elimination of miscellaneous levies.

9. Conduct of agricultural survey and population census.

10. Taxation on foreign merchants.

The Independence Club planned to have the "budget in the black" spend one third in administrative expenditure and two-thirds on carrying out self-help programs. According to its blueprint, such programs would be pushed jointly by the government and the people, but financing was to be provided by the government.

3) New Educational System

The Independence Club gave priority in government spending to "new education, and manufacturing plants."

It considered the education of the rising generation and the masses as most essential to achieving national strength.

Establishment of schools devoted to new education was viewed as most urgent; plans were formulated to ring into being stage by stage, ① elementary schools, ② girls' schools ③ secondary schools or colleges, ④ vocational and professional schools; and private schools.

Especially elementary schools ought to be established for each community to expose all school-age children to new education. It was likened to sowing of seeds in spring.

The need for schools for girls where prospective wives and mothers could be taught and trained was pointed up with emphasis almost equal to that given to schools for men, on the grounds that women account for half of the entire population. The plan was presented in defiance of strong opposition from conservative groups.

It was also proposed that the duration of elementary, secondary and college education be equally three years. The proposal was conceived to suit the prevailing practice of starting elementary education at a late age.

The Independence Club proposed an overhaul of curriculum, putting greater stress on engineering, agronomy, medicine, military science, mathematics, chemistry, meteorology, astronomy, geography, physics, political science and economics, linguistics and athletics. Reformed Confucian schools included literature and Chinese classics as primary subjects.

This was a remarkable departure from the existing curriculum centered on Oriental classics and Chinese history. Members of the Independence Club also insisted that in all school education: 1. *Han'gŭl* be used as the primary national writing system; 2. Arabic, instead of Chinese, numerals, be introduced in teaching mathematics; 3. History of the West as well as of Korea be taught.

Fourth, the Independence Club requested and planned the publishing of textbooks for schools and books for the general public.

Fifth, for the sake of introducing natural science, technology and other new knowledge of the West, translation of foreign books, expansion of foreign-language institutes, and sending of students abroad were strongly urged.

4) Industrial Development

As part of self-help programs, the Independence Club emphasized industrial development next to education.

First, the Independence Club said that Korea should diversify from an agricultural economy in pursuit of commercial and industrial advancement. The modern economic structure it envisaged had the following breakdown in terms of population: 50% in agriculture, 30% in commerce and industry; 20% in public service and free professions.

Second, industrialization received top priority in the economic growth scheme of the Independence Club. Pointing out that Western powers had accomplished prosperity and military might through industrialization, it suggested that we must do likewise. The order of priority the Independence Club set was: ① spinning industry; ② iron mills; ③ timber industry; ④ paper making; ⑤ glass manufacture; ⑥ leather industry. The Independence Club showed most active interest in the spinning industry, for which it worked out a very concrete blueprint.

Third, the Independence Club proposed that industrial growth be attained by means of *Changguk* (manufacturing plants) equipped with steam engines and other machinery. Members of the Independence Club were well aware of the potential and effectiveness of steam engines and modern machinery, and they made many efforts toward enlightening the people on the scientific value and utility of the new energy and tools.

For the financing of these industrialization projects the Independence Club contemplated a combination of private capitalization through encouraging the formation of joint stock companies and financial investment by government. The government was advised to set up model plants where technical training could be given, while the creation of private industrial plants was liberally encouraged.

Fourth, introduction of modern technical knowhow from Great Britain was sought. The Independence Club was interested in bringing about an industrial revolution by building major industrial plants with steam-powered engines and mechanical equipment.

Fifth, the Independence Club emphasized the need for exploring such mineral resources as gold, silver, copper, iron and coal. It urged that development of mining be encouraged to serve the goal of national prosperity by producing raw materials and helping industrialization; it criticized mining concessions to foreign powers and the practice of dispatching official mining agents as reckless and damaging to the property rights of the people.

Sixth, the Independence Club made the following specific recommendations on agricultural, forestry and fishery development:

(1) Reclamation of uncultivated land and irrigation;

(2) Diversified farming and development of commercial agriculture;

(3) Introduction of new livestock breeds;

(4) Forestry development and timber export plan;

(5) Establishment of agricultural experimental stations, and develop-ment of new species and new farm implements;

(6) Development of coastal fishing and export of marine products.

Seventh, the Independence Club proposed the following reforms for the growth of commerce:

(1) Expropriation of commercial rights granted to foreigners and guarantee of complete freedom of commercial activity;

(2) Inauguration of modern banks;

(3) Uniform weights and measures, and intoduction of the metric system;

(4) Currency reform and double gold-silver standards;

(5) Improvement of international payments position.

Eighth, the Independence Club claimed that railroad construction was essential to industrial growth, and urged the return of the Seoul-Inch'ŏn, Seoul-Pusan and Seoul-Ŭiju lines from foreign management to Korean; it also planned the construction of a Seoul-Wŏnsan rail line. Purchase of engine-propelled coastal ferries and improvement of highways were also suggested.

5) Concept of Modern National Defense

Fearing a change in the balance of power in the Far East might bring military clashes between Japan and Russia on the Korean peninsula, the Independence Club advocated strong and self-reliant military preparedness to defend the nation against external invasion. It called for:

(1) Creation of a navy to support the army;

(2) Repair and expansion of arsenals;

(3) Intensive training by Continental drill techniques;

(4) Establishment of a military academy;

(5) Building up of military power strong enough to deter aggression by Japanese or Russians.

6) Reform of Social Customs

The Independence Club conceived of a sweeping reform of the nation's social customs. Important changes it proposed included;

(1) Elimination of early marriage;

(2) Liberation of women, and eradication of concubines and *kisaeng* entertainers;

(3) Introduction of scientific sanitation and hospitals, and ban on opium smuggling from China;

(4) Elimination of superstition and divination;
(5) End of geomancy;
(6) Elimination of nepotism and factionalism;
(7) Prohibition of gambling and speculative activities.

The Independence Club declared self-help reforms could only be carried out on the basis of articulate assertion of national independence and popular parti-cipation in government.

6. Conclusion

In retrospect, the balance of power around Korea existed for six years between 1898 and 1904. The Independence Club sought to take advantage of the period to insure independence on the strength of the combined energies of the people. Its social thought was embodied in the principles of spontaneity, civil rights, self-help and of freedom and independence-reform, which embraced the concepts of independence, civil rights, self-help, and reforms.

With the dissolution of the Independence Club, a major social thought and movement to save the nation from the danger of aggression by foreign powers came to an end. During the period 1881-1893, when Japan had the desire but not the capacity for aggression, Korea wasted valuable time under the pressure of Chinese intervention, failing to achieve national self-reliance. During the six years 1898-1904; when Japan had the capacity for aggression, but could not defy the prevailing international balance of power, the Independence Club was suppressed and could not prove effective in the face of the increasing collusion of the conservative ruling circles with the Japanese, depriving the nation of its second chance for survival.

However, the social thought of independence, civil rights and self-help advocated by the Independence Club continued to provide inspiration and momentum to the subsequent anti-Japanese independence movement. Inside the country, Yun Ch'i-ho organized the *Taehan Chaganghoe* (Korea Self-help Society) to undertake public enlightenment campaigns; it formed a base for the later 1919 independence uprising; outside the country, such leading members of the Independence Club as Yi Tong-nyŏng and Yi Sang-sŏl created the *Taehan Kungminhoe* and an independence army which was active in the Russian maritime provinces and neighboring Manchuria; Pak Yong-man and An Ch'ang-ho organized their independence movement in Hawaii and the mainland United States; and the former members of the Independence Club organized a provisional Korean government in Shanghai and published the newspaper *Tongnip Sinmun*. The social thought of the Independence Club marked a milestone in the evolution of modern social thought in Korea.

Independence Movement of

Korean People

14. *Sinminhoe*'s Independence Movement during the Late Years of Chosŏn Dynasty

1.Introduction

The year 1905 was a turning point in the history of modern Korea. In November of that year, Imperialist Japan had just won the Russo-Japanese war and forced the Korean Government to sign the five-article pact historically known as the *Ŭllsa Choyak*. The unsigned pact deprived Korea of its sovereignty and relegated it to the status of a Japanese protectorate. In February of the next year, the Japanese set up a Residency-General and, with the help of two Japanese army divisions stationed in Korea, began their semicolonial rule.

The Korean response was immediate and prompt: an independence movement was organized, including both "the righteous army" (*ŭibyŏng*) and a policy of "enlightenment education." The former consisted of Koreans who wished to defend national independence through armed resistance and were prepared to fight to the bitter end. The latter was based on the recognition that education alone was crucial in regaining national independence.

The prime movers of this educational movement were national leaders who had been devoted to the cause national modernization before 1905. Their strategy was to instill a patriotic spirit in young Koreans and teach them in such a way that they would become leading independence fighters. Their plan for the future was to setup military bases near the Manchurian border to develop a combat-ready independence army, and to await an opportunity to be provided by the inevitable clash of Japanese imperialistic expansionism with the interests of other great powers such as the United States and China. To carry out this vision, various movements were initiated such as "Save the Nation through Education" movement, the "Enlightenment Campaign" by the press, the campaign for the promotion of national industries, the campaign to repay the national loan, the new cultural movement, the movement for Korean Studies, the movement for a national religion, and the campaign for the establishment of independence army bases. These patriotic campaigns and movements received nationwide popular support and so achieved a great deal between 1905 and 1910. This period might well have been a period of despair, had it not been for the awakening patriotic spirit.

One secret organization operated on a national scale for the cause of independence during this period was the *Sinminhoe*. Being a secret association, the *Sinminhoe* was able to continue to operate undetected until the end of 1910. the *Sinminhoe* deserves our close attention for this reason and I attempt to examine it in as much detail as the scarcity of records and documents allows.

2. The Founding of the *Sinminhoe*

The *Sinminhoe* was founded in April 1907 under the leadership of Yang Ki-t'ak and An Ch'ang-ho. It came about through the combined efforts of five independence movement groups. The first constituent group was led by Yang Ki-t'ak. It founded a daily newspaper called the *Taehan Maeil Sinbo* (The Korea Daily News) in July 1904, through which it worked to regain national independence. First Pak Ŭn-sik and then Sin Ch'ae-ho served as editorial writers for this daily newspaper. They wrote inspiring lead articles in support of the movements for the righteous army and enlightenment education. Just before the founding of the *Sinminhoe*, the group had begun to concentrate on the campaign to redeem the national loan on January 29, 1907.

The second group was the Sangdong Church and its attached school, *Ch'ŏngnyŏn Hagwon*. Chŏn Tŏk-ki, Yi Tong-nyŏng, Yi Hoe-yŏng, Yi Chun, Kim Pyŏng-hŏn and Kim Koo were its leaders. Until 1905, the group had been rallying to oppose the *Ŭlsa Choyak*, but when this effort failed, the group switched to a long-term strategy of building schools and teaching young people, in the belief that education alone could lay a solid foundation for the restoration of independence.[1]

The third group consisted of former military officers, including Yi Tong-hwi, Yi Kap, Yu Tong-yŏl, No Paeng-nin, Cho Sŏng-hwan, and Kim Hŭi-sŏn. Seeing no point in fighting without being properly equipped, the group did not join the righteous army, although it supported the army wholeheartedly, and instead participated in the education campaign, waiting for a more opportune moment for military activity.

The fourth group was composed mainly of merchants and businessmen living in P'yŏngan Province. Yi Sŭng-hun and An T'ae-guk led the group. In March 1907, this group organized a traders' cooperative to effectively oppose Japanese authorities who had recently arrested An T'ae-guk, the president of *Hyŏptong Sa*. The group demanded the immediate release of An T'ae-guk and members closed their shops in the city of P'yŏngyang.[2]

The fifth group was the *Kongnip Hyŏphoe*, a cooperative society set up in the U.S. by An Ch'ang-ho. An went to the U.S. in 1902 to study, but when he saw the miserable state of Korean workers in San Francisco and Los Angeles, he gave up his study and began working for the betterment of their living conditions and for the protection of their interests. He formed a friendship society called *Hanin Ch'inmokhoe* in 1903. The organization continued to grow and was later renamed the *Kongnip Hyŏphoe*. The leader of this group included An Ch'ang-ho, Yi Kang, Chŏng Chae-kwan, Im Chun-gi, Kim Sŏng-mu, Song Sŏk-chun, and Yi Chae-su. They published an official organ called the *Kongnip Sinmun*.[3] When the news that Korea had been deprived of its independence by the *Ŭlsa Choyak* reached them, they became extremely bitter and indignant and decided to fight for Korean independence when the proper time came.

Most of the leaders of these five groups knew one another because they had belonged as young men to the *Tongnip Hyŏphoe* (The Independence Club). During the so-called Tongnip Hyŏphoe period (1986-1998) when the Club organized a movement for the self-government and self-strengthening of Korea, these men were too young to be its leaders, but they were in the vanguard of another organization, the *Manmin Kongdonghoe* (People's Assembly). By 1905 they were old enough to become leading figures in their own groups.

An Ch'ang-ho and his *Kongnip Hyŏphoe* initiated the founding of the *Sinminhoe* later in Seoul. An and his group members gathered at Riverside near Los Angeles during the New Year's holiday of 1907 and agreed to form the *Taehan Sinminhoe*. They drafted both its prospectus (*ch'wijisŏ*) and its general regulations (*t'ongyong changjŏng*).[4] They also agreed that, in order to make it more significant, they would form this society in alliance with leaders at home. The group chose An Ch'ang-ho for the mission of convincing leaders in Korea to join forces and it raised the money necessary for him to carry it out.[5] An left San Francisco on 20 January, 1907. He arrived in Tokyo in mid-February and stayed for several days to meet with Korean students. On 20 February, 1907, he arrived in Seoul.[6]

On 22 February An Ch'ang-ho paid a visit to Yang Ki-t'ak, the editor-in-chif of the *Taehan Maeil Sinbo*, and donated 35 *wŏn* for repayment of the national loan on behalf of the *Kongnip Kyŏphoe*.[7] An then informed Yang of the founding of the *Sinminhoe*. Subsequently, An was able to contact through Yang's connections a number of other leaders of the independence movement.

Yang Ki-t'ak, himself then an influential leader, had kept in touch with other patriotic leaders. In comparison, An Ch'ang-ho, though probably the abler of the two, was less influential in Korea because of his long absence. Realizing that he lacked Yang's background, An decided to support Yang, who was a comrade from the days of the *Manmin Kongdonghoe*, the head of the *Sinminhoe*. Yang was one of the key members of a secret association of reformists, *Kaehyŏktang* in 1902. These reformists, who were also members of the *Tongnip Hyŏphoe*, were pitted against the pro-Russian conservative political faction. Their secret association came to an end, however, when Yi Sang-jae was arrested and imprisoned. Another consideration was that since the conclusion of the *Ŭlsa Choyak*, Yang Ki-t'ak himself had apparently been thinking it necessary to form another secret association.[8]

An Ch'ang-ho's tremendous efforts came to fruition at last in April 1907 when representatives of the above-mentioned five groups—Yang Ki-t'ak, Yi Tong-hwi, Chŏn Tŏk-ki, Yi Tong-nyŏng, Yi Kap, Yu Tong-yŏl, and An Ch'ang-ho himself—gathered in great secrecy in Seoul, discussed the proposed secret society under the presidency of Yang Ki-t'ak, and founded the *Sinminhoe*.[9]

These seven men can thus be called the founding members. At the inaugural meeting, the prospectus and the general regulations, both of which had been drafted in America by An Ch'ang-ho and his group, were adopted almost in their entirety. The original idea of establishing headquarters in Riverside, California, was amended, however, and Seoul was chosen instead. It was also agreed that each province was to have one director and that An Ch'ang-ho was to be director for the American Continent.[10] The *Sinminhoe* was to be known in English as the "New People's Society."[11] In the initial organization, Yang Ki-t'ak was the director general, Yi Tong-nyŏng the general secretary, Chŏn Tŏk-ki the treasurer, and An Ch'ang-ho the executive officer. The rest of the founding members assumed provincial directors' posts. The duty of the executive officer was to deal with new membership.[12]

About four hundred new members were admitted to *Sinminhoe* immediately after the its inauguration, and membership increased to eight hundred by 1910.[13] Since nearly all the leaders of the patriotic enlightenment movement became its members, the newly formed *Sinminhoe* emerged as the most influential secret association, leading and guiding the independence movement.

The *Sinminhoe* would be thought of as a successor to the *Tongnip Hyŏphoe* and the *Manmin Kongdonghoe* in terms of leadership and to the *Kaehyŏktang* in terms of organization.

3. The Aims and Social Thought of the *Sinminhoe*

The ultimate aims of the *Sinminhoe* were, first, to regain national independence and build a free independence country, and second, to institute a republican form of government.[14] This was the first time in the history of Korea that a republic had been advocated instead of a monarchy. Even the

Tongnip Hyŏphoe had never thought of a republican form of government, although it was progressive enough to strive for a constitutional monarchy. Until then a republican form of government had been the ideal of only a few young members of the *Manmin Kongdonghoe*.

The members of the *Sinminhoe* realized that they lacked the strength needed to regain independence and that it was therefore imperative to gain strength. They maintained that Korean people must be "made new," that is, must become "a new people." These were the ideals of the *Sinminhoe*. The *Sinminhoe* was deeply committed to the concept of political democracy. It believed that the people are the master of the country and that national prosperity and power come from the prosperity and power of the people. According to the *Sinminhoe*, it was necessary for the people to renew themselves through their own efforts, without help from others.[15] Thus the *Sinminhoe* advocated new thoughts, education, morality, culture, industry, politics, and "earnestness" as prerequisites for creating a new nation and a new society.

In order to achieve its goals and realize its ideology, the *Sinminhoe* decided to carry out a variety of activities.[16] It published newspapers, magazines, and books to provide the people with the new knowledge. It attempted to instill the new national spirit in people. It built better schools with the idea of fostering talented boys, and directed the curriculum and teaching style of each school. It directed businessmen in the proper management of their businesses and set up a model business through partnership among *Sinminhoe* members. It established officers' training schools abroad in preparation for a war for independence and built military bases abroad as part of founding the independence army.[17]

4. The Organization of the *Sinminhoe*

As mentioned, the *Sinminhoe* was founded as a secret society. The reasons for secrecy were to minimize Japanese interference and oppression and maximize the effectiveness of the independence movement. Members also wished to avoid the dissolution of the society by any Japanese decree or suppressive measure and to secure a core organization to work for independence in the event that Japan gained complete control of Korea through coercion. They also wanted to strictly limit new membership so that Japanese secret agents could be prevented from penetrating the *Sinminhoe*. The central posts consisted of president, vice-president, direct general, councillors, treasurer, executive officer, and inspector. The first two posts, which were only created during the last years of the *Sinminhoe*, were honorary, and it was the direct general who had real control. Representatives of each province were chosen to fill councilor positions. The treasurer was responsible for financial affairs, and the executive officer examined the qualifications of prospective members and oversaw organizational matters. The inspector was in charge of disciplinary matters.

In addition, each province had a director, who was assisted by an advisory council. Similarly, each county had its own director and advisory council. The county members were divided into groups of five men called *pan*, each with one person in charge. Every twelve *pan* had one leader who oversaw the twelve group leaders, and every four *pan* were led by an associate leader. One striking feature of this organization of the *Sinminhoe* was that every level from the center down to the county level had its own legislative body.

During the last years of the *Sinminhoe* the holders of the key posts were as follows: Yun Ch'i-ho, president; Yu Tong-yŏl, vice-president; Yang Ki-t'ak, director general; Yi Tong-hwi, director of the Hamgyŏng provinces; Yi Sŭng-hun, director of North P'yŏngan Province; An T'ae-guk, director of South P'yŏngan Province; Kim Koo, director of Hwanghae Province; Yang Ki-t'ak, director of Kyŏnggi Province; and Chu Chin-su, director of Kangwŏn Province.[18] As for the director of other provinces, nothing is known about them since they were never arrested and consequently not exposed.

The *Sinminhoe* was so organized that no member was able to recognize more than two other memers, and no member was supposed to know even a single fellow member laterally. To qualify for membership, one had to be firm in one's patriotic thought and ready to sacrifice one's life to the cause of national independence. In addition, there was a period during which one had to meet the approval of the executive officer. A successful candidate finalized the procedure by declaring that he would offer both his life and propery according to the dictates of the *Sinminhoe*.[19]

By 1910, there were about eight hundred members, which means that almost all patriotic Korean leaders of the period belonged to the *Sinminhoe*. According to statistics revealed at the trial of 122 people in connection with the Case of One Hundred Five, the occupational distribution of *Sinminhoe* members was as follows: business, 37.71 per cent (merchants, 31.97% and other businessmen, 5.74%); education, 38.52 per cent (teachers, 22.95% and students, 15.57%); agriculture, 5.74 per cent; religion, 4.92 per cent; free labor, 4.92 per cent, manual labor, 1.64 per cent, and unidentifed, 6.55 per cent.[20]

This means that those in business and education together made up 76.23 per cent and thus were an integral part of the *Sinminhoe*. It is, therefore, fair to say that the *Sinminhoe*, though a nationwide society, was strongly dependent on middle-class citizens to carry out its various movements.

5. The "Save the Nation through Education" Movement of the *Sinminhoe*

Because it believed education to be the best and surest way to foster the national power necessary for the construction of a new nation, the *Sinminhoe* attached the highest priority to the movement for a new kind of education. The "Save the Nation through Education" Movement had been under way even before the founding of the *Sinminhoe*, but it was with the sponsorship of the *Sinminhoe* that the movement began to achieve notable results. After 1907, a number of inspired Korean patriots sold their lands and built new schools throughout the country.

The *Sinminhoe*'s education movement had three objectives: to make the people aware of the urgent need for the new education and to build schools for it; to direct the thrust of education in those newly built schools toward regaining of national independence; and to build *Sinminhoe*-sponsored model schools for educating young Koreans.

There were several reasons why the *Sinminhoe* itself had to build some schools in a number of important areas throughout the country. First, the *Sinminhoe* wished to provide a middle-school level of education to graduates of private schools established by local patriots, most of which were primary schools. Second, the *Sinminhoe* intended to establish schools which would be a model for others to follow in building middle schools. Third, it wished to offer teacher-training courses in order to have enough competent teachers for all the new schools. Such sponsorship of schools was considered the most important way for the *Sinminhoe* to achieve the goals of the "Save the Nation through Education" Movement.

With the aims in mind, the *Sinminhoe* sponsored the following schools: the Osan School in Chŏngju, Northe P'yŏngan Province; the Taesŏng School in P'yŏngyang, South P'yŏngan Province; the Poch'ang School in Kanghwa, Gyŏnggi Province; the Yangsil School in Uiji, North P'yŏngan Province; the Shinan School in Chŏngju, North P'yŏngan Province; the Kamyŏng School in Napch'ŏngjŏng, North P'yŏngan Province; the Hyŏpsŏng Anhŭng School in Anju, North P'yŏngan Province; the Sinhŭng School in Sŏnch'ŏn, North P'yŏngan Province; Hŭngyang School in Kwaksan, North P'yŏngan Province; the Myŏngnyun School in Yŏnghŭng, South Hamgyŏng Province; the Kyŏng-sŏng School in Kyŏngsong, North Hamgyŏng Province; the Yangsan School in Anak, Hwanghae Province: the Anak-kun Myŏnhakhoe Teacher Training Institute in Anak, Hwanghae Province; and the Sŏbuk Hyŏpsŏng School in Seoul.

A close examination of the Taesŏng School and the Poch'ang School will be sufficient to illustrate the characteristics of the *Sinminhoe*-sponsored schools. Since it was a school established in accordance with the purposes and values of the *Sinminhoe*, the Taesŏng School had the twin objectives of training leaders for the restoration of national sovereignty and of educating teachers to be employed in mass public education.[21] To achieve this goal, the school emphasized the acquisition of knowledge, the cultivation of patriotism, and the development of a sound character.

In order to instill the spirit of nationalism, the Taesŏng School made patriotism part of every course and lecture. It also made it a rule that students sing the national anthem and hear an admonitory speech on patriotism at every morning session.[22] A table printed in *Taehan Maeil Sinbo* gives the subjects and the textbooks used by Taesŏng School.[23]

As one can see from the table, the curriculum standard of Taesŏng School was rather high, indeed high enough to correspond to that of today's senior high schools or even junior college. Instead of the Chinese classics, the school used as its Chinese textbooks Liang Ch'i-ch'ao's collected works, *Yin-Ping-shih-wen-chi*, which are essays on how to save China from invading foreign powers. The idea was, or course, to teach schoolboys why and how national independence should be regained.

It is interesting to note the importance given to physical education, the instructor of which was a former Korean military officer. He gave lessons not only in physical education but also in military training and tactics. From time to time there were also emergency drills at night held for the sake of military training.[24] Military training was emphasized in order to terminate the traditional tendency to indulge in literary arts while neglecting military arts. It was also meant to keep the education offered in line with the *Sinminhoe*'s commitment to founding an independence army abroad. For the development of character, sincerity was emphasized as the basis. The school taught that sincerity consisted of righteousness, punctuality, keeping promises, and proper discharges of duty.[25]

The school encouraged students to govern themselves and so trained them in self-government. The student council consisted of five committees: lectures and discussion, music, sports, discipline, and social activities. The sports committee organized soccer and baseball matches between Seoul and P'yŏng-yang, and the lectures and discussion committee often held oratorical contests with patriotism as the topic. For the first time in the history of Korean schools, a military brass band was organized.[26] Because of these unique activities, graduates recalled the Taesŏng School as a kind of comprehensive institution that was a combination of middle school, school for political science, and military academy.[27]

With Yun Ch'i-ho as its honorary principal and An Ch'ang-ho as its acting principal, the Taesŏng School continued to function as a *Sinminhoe*-sponsored model school until 1911, when as a result of the Case of the One Hundred Five the Japanese authorities discovered the existence of the *Sinminhoe* and closed the school down. A number of other school were established throughout the country modeled after the Taesŏng School, and many of the Taesŏng graduates later became leaders of the independence movement.

The Poch'ang School was actually a chain of schools established mainly under the aegis of Yi Tong-hwi, The principal middle school located on Kwanghwa Island had branch schools at both the middle and primary school levels throughout the country. The main Poch'ang School was a three-year school, but it required a one year preliminary course.[28] The subjects and textbooks of this school were basically the same as those of the Taesŏng School.

In addition to the middle-school course, there were two other courses of study. One was a one-year intensive teacher-training course and the other was a night course. Boys between ages fifteen and twenty who already knew Chinese characters took the middle-school course, and men between ages twenty and forty who had already acquired considerable knowledge were placed in the teacher-training course to meet the ever-increasing demand for teachers as the "Save the Nation through Education" Movement continued to prosper. The night course was mainly for the working class and was designed to provide them with the new type of education. The Poch'ang School was so successful and flourishing that the number of students eventually amounted to 410.[29]

The principal middle school had twenty-one branch schools on Kanghwa Island alone. When these schools turned out to be extremely successful, Yi Tong-hwi formed a school board with the help of local leaders to enforce free and compulsory universal education for Kanghwa Island. The school board first added four schools — Chinmyŏng, Kyemyŏng, Ch'anghwa, and Konghwa— and later thirty-one more, thus increasing the total to fifty-six. It divided the existing sixteen *myŏn* and one hundred and fourteen *tong* of Knaghwa Island into fifty-six districts so that every district could have one school and so that school-age children could go to school in their own district.[30]

The Poch'ang branch schools located in areas other than Kanghwa Island were: Kaesŏng Poch'ang School in Kaesŏng, Kyŏnggi Province; Kŭmch'ŏn Poch'ang School in Kŭmch'ŏn-gun, Hwanghae Province; P'ungdŏk Poch'ang School in P'ungdŏk-kun, Hwanghae Province; Anak Poch'ang School in Anak-kun, Hwanghae Province; Hohŭng Poch'ang School in Hohŭng-myŏn, North Ch'ungch'ŏng Province; and Hamhŭng Poch'ang School in Hamhŭng-gun, South Hamgyŏng Province. There were more Poch'ang branch schools throughout the country, and according to Yi Kwang-su the schools established by Yi Tong-hwi during the *Sinminhoe* period numbered about one hundred.[31]

It appears that the Poch'ang School was even more independence-oriented and more militant than the Taesŏng School. In May 1908, some Poch'ang schoolboys held a meeting to discuss how to regain the country's independence, and seventeen of them cut their fingers to pledge their devotion to win back sovereignty, to work to save fellow countrymen, and their devotion glorify Korea's four-thousan-year history. The schoolboys also formed a "Finger-cutting Leagu" (*Tanji Tongmaeng*) and declared their determination to devote their lives to the cause of national independence.[32]

Other schools sponsored by the *Sinminhoe* were without exception imbued with essentially the same militant nationalistic thought. The *Sinminhoe*-inspired Korean leaders also turned to education and founded numerous private schools. The education movement was the most successful of all the activities carried out by the *Sinminhoe*. The simple fact that some three thousand schools were established subsequent to the founding of the *Sinminhoe* is evidence of this.[33] As of July 1, 1910, the number of private schools (whose establishment the Japanese were forced to endorse in spite of their oppressive anti-private-school decree) was 2,082.[34] The inspiration behind all these schools was the *Sinminhoe*. In short, the dream that the *Sinminhoe* would produce hundreds of national leaders through the "Save the Nation through Education" Movement came true.

6. Educational Association and Programs of "Enlightenment Lectures"

Both the *Sinminhoe*'s activities to promote educational association and their "enlightenment lectures" program were successful. One reason for the success of these activities was that they did not cost the impecunious *Sinminhoe*. The promotion of educational associations was carried out in two ways. First, the *Sinminhoe* itself moved around the country forming associations. Some of them were the *Anak-kun Myŏnghakhoe* (Anak-kun Educational Association) in Hwanghae Province, the *Haesŏ Kyoyuk Ch'onghoe* (Haesŏ Educational Association) in Hwanghae Province, the *Pyŏngyang Ch'ŏngnyŏn Kŭŏnjanghoe* (P'yŏngyang Youth Scholarship Foundation) in South Pyong'an Province, the *Yŏnhakhoe* (Research Society) in South Py'ŏng'an provinces, and the *Tongjehoe* (Tongje Society) in South Pyŏng'an Province.

Second, the *Sinminhoe* combined various existing educational associations. To cite one instance of this, the *Sŏu Hakhoe* (Sŏu Educational Association) and the *Hanpuk Hŭnghakhoe* (Hanbuk Educational Association) were integrated into the *Sŏbuk Hakhoe* (Northwest Educational Association) in January 1908 through the efforts of the *Sinminhoe*.[35] The *Sinminhoe* also attempted to merge the *Kiho Hŭnghakhoe* (Kyŏnggi-Ch'ungch'ŏng Educational Association) and the *Kwangdong Hakhoe* (Kangwon Educational Association) into a nationally united study society[36] based on the *Sinminhoe*'s principle of a unified alliance of a self-renewed people.[37]

As for the successful "enlightenment lectures" program, leading members of the *Sinminhoe* traveled around giving lectures and speeches whenever and wherever there were social gatherings. The *Sinminhoe* itself sometimes sponsored joint athletic meetings of private schools in order to take the opportunity to give "enlightenment" speeches.

The *Sinminhoe* used its "enlightenment" lectures as an opportunity to inculcate people with its patriotic ideas. Lectures presented the idea of regaining national rights and promoted recognition of popular rights. They pointed out the need for free and compulsory universal education and for the dissemination of new knowledge, and they advocated the establishment of schools and educational associations. They emphasized the importance of industry in saving the country. They urged the reform of old-fashioned practices and the cultivation of one's own potential resources.

Leading member of the *Sinminhoe* who took part in the lecture program included An Ch'ang-ho, Yi Tong-hwi, Chŏn Tŏk-ki, Kim Koo, Ch'oe Kwang-ok, Yun Ch'i-ho, Yi Sang-jae, Ch'oe Pyŏng-hŏn, Chang Ŭng-jin, Yŏ Chun, Yi Hak-p'il, An Pyŏng-ch'an, and Yun Ki-sŏp. All were noted for their eloquence. How devoted they were to this program is evidenced by the fact that Ch'oe Kwang-ok collapsed and died while giving a lecture.[38] Also noted for their persuasiveness were Yang Ki-t'ak, No Paeng-nin, Yi Hoe-yŏng, Yi Sŭng-hun, An T'ae-guk, Yu Tong-yŏl, Pak Ŭn-sik, Yi Kap, Yi Tong-nyong, Sin Ch'ae-ho, Chang Chi-yŏn, Cho Sŏng-hwan, Ch'oe Nam-sŏn, Nam Hyŏng-u, Kim To-hŭi, Chu Chin-su, Im Ch'i-jŏng, and Kang Yun-hŭi. But it was not these leading members alone who participated in the program; almost all the *Sinminhoe*'s members took part in one way or another. People were deeply moved by what the *Sinminhoe* had to say about the restoration of Korean independence.

7. The *Sinminhoe*'s Publications Activities

The *Sinminhoe* deemed it of great importance to enlighten the people through various publications and accomplished several noteworthy results in this area. First, the *Sinminhoe* took over the *Taehan Maeil Sinbo* as its organ.[39] It was easy for the society to secure the paper because the chief editor Yang Ki-t'ak and his staff were members. In addition, Yang carried out his duties as the director general of the *Sinminhoe* at his newspaper office, thus making the *Taehan Maeil Sinbo* the headquarters of the *Sinminhoe*. The *Taehan Maeil Sinbo* was a joint venture by Yang Ki-t'ak and the Englishman Ernest Thomas Bethel, who assumed the presidency. Because it had a foreigner as its head and part owner, the *Taehan Maeil Sinbo* was immune from Japanese censorship implemented under the Newspaper Decree. In this way the paper was able to be outspoken in what it said on behalf of the nationalistic cause of the *Sinminhoe*.

Second, the *Sinminhoe* published a monthly magazine called *Sonyŏn* (Boys).[40] Ch'oe Nam-sŏn was its head and he contributed to it regularly along with Hong Myŏng-hŭi, Yi Kwang-su, Sin Ch'ae-ho, and Pak ŭn-sik. This monthly not only inspired patriotic young boys but also promoted new culture and literature. It was discontinued when the Japanese found it to be one of the *Sinminhoe* organ in the trial resulting from the Case of the One Hundred Five.

Third, the *Sinminhoe* founded a publishing company called the *Chŏsun Kwangmunhoe*, which published a number of Korean classics. Pak ŭn-sik and Yu Kŭn were its directors and Ch'oe Nam-sŏn its executive.[41]

Fourth, the *Sinminhoe* established the *T'ae-guk Sŏgwan*, a chain bookshop, in cities like P'yŏngyang, Seoul, and Taegu with the financial support of Yi Sŭng-hun and An T'ae-guk. Its purpose was to promote national culture by publishing books and distributing them.[42] These bookshops also functioned as liaison organs for the *Sinminhoe*.

Fifth, the *Sinminhoe* established the *Myŏnhak Sŏp'o* in Anak; it was to function both as a publishing company and bookshop. It published Ch'oe Kwang-ok's *Taehan Munjŏn* (Korean Grammar) and *Kyoyukhak* (Pedagogics) and also distributed books in order to help the *Sinminhoe*'s campaign for enlightenment in Hwanghae Province.[43]

8. The *Sinminhoe*'s National Industry Movement

When the *Sinminhoe* carried out its national industry movement, its goals were to improve management among industrialists and to establish model industrial companies. The *Sinminhoe* considered Japan's economic invasion to be as serious and as dangerous as the military invasion. It believed that the promotion of national industry in addition to new education was the way to foster national strength.

The *Sinminhoe* set up model factories and companies that were jointly financed by its members and demonstrated to the general public and Industrialists alike how to run and manage them successfully. The ultimate goal was to facilitate the accumulation of national industrial capital.

The *Sinminhoe* established the P'yongyang Ceramic Joint-Stock Company (*P'yŏnyang Chagi Chejo Chusik Hoesa*) in Masan-dong, P'yŏngyang, in the belief that the production of Koryŏ celadons would help revive national industry, recapture the past glory of Koryŏ celadons, and fill the people with national pride.[44] It also established two trading and wholesale companies: the *Hyŏpsŏng Tongsa* in Napch'ŏnjŏng, North P'yŏngan Province,[45] and the *Sangmu Tongsa* in Sŏnch'ŏn and Yongch'ŏn, North Pyŏngan Province.[46]

In Pyŏngyang, the *Sinminhoe* raised stocks in order to establish a Korean industrial firm called the *Chosŏn Sirŏp Hoesa*.[47] It also established a small-scale model textile factory and a small-scale tobacco factory in Anak, Hwanghae Province.[48] Its plans to build a model farm village in Sariwŏn, Hwanghae Province, were aborted, however, when the Japanese authorities halted construction as soon as it was begun.[49]

The *Sinminhoe*'s national industry movement was not as successful as its educational movement. A possible reason for this is that patriotism and a small amount of capital were simply not enough to compete with Japanese monopolies backed by large amount of capital. It is significant, however, that despite difficulties the *Sinminhoe* put into practice almost all that it had planned for the promotion of national industry.

9. The *Sinminhoe*'s Youth Movement

The people were the main body of the independence movement but it was the younger generation, the future rulers of Korea, who were the main actors. That was why the *Sinminhoe* decided to inaugurate a separate youth movement.

The *Sinminhoe* founded a youth association called the *Ch'ŏngnyŏn Hagu-*

hoe in August 1909 to launch its youth movement. It was modeled after "Young Italy" and some other European youth associations. The founding members included Yun Ch'i-ho, Chang Ŭng-jin, Ch'oe Nam-sŏn, Ch'oe Kwang-ok, Ch'a I-sŏk, An T'ae-guk, Ch'ae P'il-gŭn, Yi Sŭng-hun, Yi Tong-nyŏng, Kim To-hŭi, Pak Chung-hwa, and Chŏn Tŏk-ki. The prospectus was wrtten by Sin Ch'ae-ho.[50] This association was recognized by the authorities as legitimate. It existed ostensibly to promote character cultivation, while in practice it pursued activities promoting national independence.[51]

In order to become a member, one had to be seventeen years old, with scholarly achievement and moral uprightness equivalent to those of middle-school graduates. A prospective member also was required to take a training course before becoming a regular member. The training aimed at engendering such cardinal virtues as sincerity, perseverance, self-reliance, faithfulness, diligence, sense of proportion, and courage. The training course consisted of three parts: moral, physical, and scientific education.[52]

The headquarters were located in Seoul, and any city, town, or district with more than fifty members could have its own branch association. As a result of this stipulation, the Hansŏng branch association came into existence in May 1910, followed by branch association in Ŭiju and Anju in June 1910. To these were added the Chŏngju, Kwaksan, Sŏnch'ŏn, Yongch'ŏn, and Samhwa (Chinnamp'o) branch associations.[53] Of all these branch associations Hansŏng was the best; it later moved to the western Kando (Chen-tao) in Manchuria where it established Sinhŭng Military Officers' School. Its leading members included Yi Tong-nyŏng, Yun Ki-sŏp, Kim Choa-jin, Yi Kyu-bong, Chang To-sun, and Yi Kyŏng-hŭi. The Hansŏng youth association continued to grow rapidly until it was disbanded by the Japanese in August 1910, only a year after its founding. It would have been more effective if it had been formed much earlier: as it was, the association did less than it could have done when Japan annexed Korea in August 1910.

10. Independence Army Bases and the "War of Independence"

The *Sinminhoe*'s purpose in founding military school and independence army bases abroad was to enable the independence army to initiate a war for independence. It was envisioned that the army would march into Korea and join with the people, who would rise in the cause of national independence. The *Sinminhoe* may have adopted the strategy of a war of independence because of An Chung-gŭn's influential lecture, "On Wars of Independence" ("*Tongnip chŏnjaeng non*"). An who first used the term "war of independence" was not satisfied with the "Save the Nation through Education" movement in Korea. An insisted on the need for an independence army to start the independence war from abroad, and he had a close relationship with the *Sinminhoe.*[54]

In August 1907, the *Sinminhoe* first began to examin the question of founding independence army bases and an independence army. In the wake of the forced disbanding of Korea's Imperial Armed Forces by the Japanese on 31 July 1907 (the formal ceremony took place the following day), many members of the military rose up in protest and subsequently joined the independence movement. Battles were conducted by the righteous armed corps with the full moral support of the *Sinminhoe.* From the *Sinminhoe*'s point of view, the problem was that the righteous army lacked the modern military training and arms necessary to fight the Japanese regular army. Under the circumstance it was impossible to expect victory. Thus the *Sinminhoe*'s need to modernize the righteous army was acute, but there was not much it could do, at least not until the end of 1908: At a time when it was expending most of its efforts and resources for the "enlightenment" movement, it was beyond the *Sinminhoe*'s power to do more than giving moral support and encouragement.

In the spring of 1909, when the righteous army movement had begun to decline, the *Sinminhoe* started to seriously consider founding military officers' schools and establishing independence army bases.[55] Finally at the director's meeting of the *Sinminhoe*, held at the house of Yang Ki-t'ak, it was decided that military bases and military schools should be established abroad in order to found an independence army strong enough to cope with modern warfare. The *Sinminhoe*'s most urgent priority, as it was felt, was to ensure a powerful independence army by means of systematic modern training and weaponry.[56]

Just before this decision of the *Sinminhoe* was to be put into practice. Ito Hirobumi was shot and killed by An Chung-gŭn on 26 October, 1909. The Japanese military police arrested key members of the *Sinminhoe*, including An Ch'ang-ho, Yi Tong-hwi, Yu Tong-yŏl, Yi Chong-ho, Kim Koo, and Kim Myŏng-jun, on suspicion of being connected with An Chung-gŭn.[57] Their periods of imprisonment lasted two to five months, and they were released one by one from the end of the following February.

The *Sinminhoe* held an emergency meeting in March 1910 and agreed that the "tactics of independence war" be adopted as the foremost strategy. It decided that the plan to establish independence army bases and military officers' schools should be put into effect immediately. The plan was for members who had been arrested to take refuge abroad in order to carry out this undertaking, and that those members remaining home would support the undertaking while continuing their activities in the "enlightenment" movement.[58]

The *Sinminhoe* planned to found independence army bases and deploy independence war tactics in the following:[59]

1) It was thought that Manchuria, especially the area near the Changbaek Mountain (Ch'ang-pai Shan), would be the most suitable area for the planned independence army bases, partly because it was outside Japanese rule and partly because it would facilitate the independence army's march into Korea.[60]

2) The selection of the most suitable site for a base would be followed by fund-raising and the purchases of the necessary land.

3) The land purchase would be followed by the recruitment of patriotic Korean emigrants both young and old.[61]

4) The recruited emigrants would settle on the purchased land and build a new Korean village. This new Korean village would form a powerful Korean emigrant association and construct a viable rural farming community. A school, a church, and other cultural facilities would also be built there.

5) A military officers' school would be established for the training of independence army officers.

6) With the graduates from the military school and other patriotic young Korean emigrants as its core members, an independence army would be founded. Officers and soldiers alike would be trained in modern military tactics and strategies so that they could be equipped with modern arms. Thus the independence army would be a select force which would be able to face the Japanese regular army.

7) To ensure the excellence of the independence army, a number of young Koreans would be sent to Chinese military officers' schools.[62]

8) When all preparation is completed, an independence war would be initiated at the earliest and most suitable opportunity. The "most suitable opportunity" would presumably arise, it was thought, when the Japanese imperialistic expansion policy would inevitably result in wars with China, Russia, or the United States.[63] While Japan was involved in such wars, the independence army would win its war and regain Korean independence with the help of other patriotic groups and association allied with the *Sinminhoe* at home.

11. High-ranking Members Found as Independence Army Base

After that, key members of the *Sinminhoe* (such as An Ch'ang-ho, Yi Kap,

Yu Tong-yŏl, Sin Ch'ae-ho, Kim Hŭi-sŏn, Yi Chong-ho, Yi Chong-man (the brother of Yi Chong-ho), Kim Chi-gan, and Chŏng Yŏng-do) left the country one by one for Peking. Later Yi Tong-nyŏng went to Manchuria and the Russian borderlands on a survey mission.

In April 1910, the political exiles held a meeting in Tsingtao, China, to discuss the details of the establishment of independence army bases. Those present were An Ch'ang-ho, Yi Kap, Sin Ch'ae-ho, Kim Hŭi-sŏn, Yi Chong-ho, Yi Chong-man, Yi Kang.[64] Yi Chong-ho took charge of fund-raising. He was the grandson of Yi Yong-ik, and it was believed that he had at his disposal thirty to fifty thousand *wŏn* which had been deposited by his grandfather in Te-hua Bank (Deutch-China Bank) in Shanghai.[65] At this meeting opinions were divided about how the money raised was to be used.[66] Yu Tong-yŏl ad Kim Hŭi-sŏn proposed that the money at the disposal of Yi Chong-ho be used for the publication of a newspaper and a magazine, and An Ch'ang-ho and Yi Kap wanted to adhere to the original plan to invest in the establishment of a new Korean village and a military officers' school. The dabate ended in favor of the new proposal, but their failure to obtain the endorsement of the German governor-general in charge of Tsingtao, which was a part of territory leased to Germany, forced them to resort to the original plan.

The exiles then purchased some 70 square li (11.2 sq. m. or 4.2 sq. mi.) of land owned by an American firm called T'ai-tung Industrial Company for the purpose of establishing an independence army base, a new Korean village, and a military officers' school. Yi Kap, Yu Tong-yŏl, and Kim Hŭi-sŏn, were to be the training instructors of the school, and Sin Ch'ae-ho was to teach Korean History and Chinese. Kim Chi-gan was to take charge of the farming activities of the village.[67]

In September 1910 they arrived in Vladivostok, where they heard for the first time the news that Korea had finally been annexed as a colony to Japan. Shocked, they began to formulate new ideas and plans. Yu Tong-yŏl and Kim Hŭi-sŏn argued that the long-term project of establishing an independence army base and military officers' school was quite inappropriate under the circumstances and that an independence army should be formed immediately using Korean residents in Manchuria and the Russian borderlands in order to march into the homeland. Again, An Ch'ang-ho and Yi Kap adhered to the original plan, but Yu and his supporters emerged victorious because Yi Chong-ho, who held the purse strings, took their side. Thus the founding of an independence army base ended in complete failure, and the task of forming an independence army was initiated instead.[68] However, even this project suffered a fatal setback when both Yu Tong-yŏl and Kim Hŭi-sŏn were arrested in Yen-t'ai while carrying out their mission there.[69]

12. The Founding of Independence Army Bases in Korea

When the *Taehan Maeil Sinbo* was taken over by the Japanese in May 1910 and Korea became fully colonized in August the same year, members of the *Sinminhoe* who remained at home found it almost impossible to continue the "enlightenment" movement. They decided that all those not engaged in teaching and publishing should emigrate collectively to the western Kando, Manchuria, in order to carry out the task of establishing independence army bases there. In September 1910, the director general, Yang Ki-t'ak assigned Yi Tong-nyŏng, Yi Hoe-yŏng, Chang Yu-sun, and Yi Kwan-jik with the mission. Disguised as paper dealers, they left Seoul for the southern part of Manchuria in order to look for suitable places for independence army bases.[70] This was not the first or the last mission of its kind: Ch'oe Myŏng-sik,[71] Chu Chin-su, Yi Chong-rok, and Kam Ing-nyong each carried out similar missions in October 1909, September 1910, November 1910, and December 1910, respectively. The destination was invariably the Western Kando area.[72] In addition, Yang Ki-t'ak sent Kim To-hŭi to Hwanghae Province to inform Kim Koo and other branch officers of the *Sinminhoe*'s plans for emigration and to have them prepare for it.[73]

Yi Tong-nyŏng and his group returned from their successful mission in November 1910 along with Chu Chin-su.[74] The land for a base had been secured in the western Kando, and now their plan for emigration made rapid progress. The *Sinminhoe* held the director's meeting four times within a month[75] — three times at the home of Im Ch'i-jŏng, and once at Yang Ki-t'ak's, Chu Chin-su, Yi Sŭng-hun, Kim Koo, Yi Tong-nyŏng, and Kim To-hŭi were among those who attended. They agreed on the following matters:[76]

1) Since the Japanese Government-General had begun to operate in Korea, in opposition to it, the *Sinminhoe* should establish a government called *Todokbu* in Seoul and *Ch'onggam* in the provinces, which would rule the country secretly.

2) The *Sinminhoe* should give the highest priority to the establishment of both independence army bases and military officers' schools in the western Kando by purchasing land there and making it a Korean "New Territory" with the ultimate purpose of regaining independence for the Korean peninsula.

3) The *Sinminhoe* should recruit as prospective Korean emigrants possessing at least one hundred *wŏn*.

4) The *Sinminhoe* should appoint provincial directors; Yang Ki-t'ak was selected·for Kyŏnggi Province and all the provinces south of the Kyŏnggi Province, Kim Koo for Hwanghae Province, An T'ae-guk for South P'yŏngan Province, Yi Sŭng-hun for North P'yŏngan Province, and Chu Chin-su for Kangwon Province.

5) The appointed provincial directors should recruit emigrants from their respective provinces and raise the necessary funds within fifteen days. The amount to be raised by Hwanghae Province, South P'yŏngan Province, and North P'yŏngan Province would be 150,000 *wŏn* each, that to be raised by Kangwon Province would be 100,000 *wŏn*, that to be raised by Kyŏnggi Province and the rest would be 200,000 *wŏn*.

The *Sinminhoe*'s recruitment of prospective emigrants to the western Kando made rapid progress. Hwanghae Province was the most successful in both recruting and raising funds.[77] The response from Seoul citizens was also great. Yi Sang-yŏng and Kim Tong-sam were among those who emigrated to the western Kando in response to the request from Yang Ki-t'ak, Yi Tong-nyŏng, and Chu Chin-su.[78] Chu himself sold all his property and prepared for emigration.[79] Yi Tong-nyŏng, Yi Hoe-yŏng and his four brothers, and Chu Chin-su and his family arrived in the western Kando between December 1910 and January 1911. In the wake of the "An Myŏnggŭn Incident" (*An Myŏnggŭn Sakkŏn*), the Japanese authorities began to arrest key *Sinminhoe* members both in Seoul and in Hwanghae Province in January 1911, and in September fabricated the "Case of the One Hundred Five" to make possible a full-scale roundup of the rest of the members, thus dealing the emigration plan a great setback.

13. *Sinhŭng* Military Officers' School

An advance party led by Yi Tong-nyŏng and Yi Hoe-yŏng settled in Tsou-chia-chien, San-yüan-pao, Liu-ho-hsien, Feng-t'ien-sheng, in January 1911. Together with their followers the advance party formed a new Korean village. In April 1911 they organized the *Kyŏnghaksa* for the purpose of achieving economic self-reliance through efficient farming and also set up an educational institute called the *Sinhŭng Kangsŭpso* to train army officers. This institute was later renamed Sinhŭng Military Officers' School (*Sinhŭng Mugwan Hakkyo*), and became the first independence army bases established by the *Sinminhoe*.

Yi Ch'ŏr-yŏng became the first president of the *Kyŏnghaksa*. Yi Hoe-yŏng and Chang Yu-sun were chosen to handle internal affairs and farming affairs, respectively. Yi Tong-nyŏng was elected treasurer and Yu In-sik secretary of education.[80] Yi Tong-nyŏng became the first principal of *Sinhŭng* Military Officers' School. Kim Tal was the head of teachers, both Kim Ch'ang-hwan and Yi Kwan-jik served as military instructors, and Yi Kap-su, Chang To-sun, and Yi Kyu-ryong were ordinary teachers.

Special attention should be paid to the literal meaning of the *sinhŭng*, "newly risen." The element *sin* (new) was derived from the name *Sinminhoe*, while *hŭng* (rising) was taken from the phrase *hŭngguk* (to make a nation "rise," that is, flourish). The reason the school was simply called an institute (*kangsŭpso*) was in order not to attract the attention of the native Chinese and to escape interference by the local Chinese warlords. The school offered two courses of study: one was the regular course and the other a special short course. The former aimed at providing a comprehensive middle and high school education, and the later at training military officers.[81]

The task of founding an independence army bases in San-yŭan-pao was a thorny one from the very beginning because of oppression by the native inhabitants and by the exclusive local Chinese warlords. The cold continental climate, and financial difficulties also caused problems. Nonetheless, the first year turned out to be a fairly successful one for the school, which graduated forty students, but the *Kyŏnghaksa* suffered complete failure when it had to be closed down due to a poor crop yield. The *Sinminhoe* members moved from San-yŭan-pao to Ha-ni-ho, T'ung-hua-hsien, some ninety *li* (10 *li* = 4km. or 2.5 mi.) southest of San-yŭan-pao. Ha-ni-ho thus became the second indepe-ndence army base. The members formed a Korean emigrants organization called the *Pumindan* with Hŏ Hyŏk as its first president. The second president was Yi Sang-yong. Sinhŭng Military Officers' School was also moved to Ha-ni-ho. The construction of the school was started early in the spring of 1913 and was finished in May 1913. The new class rooms were all spacious and every grade had its own building, with a big auditorium and office rooms for the teachers. There were also an editor's room, a night-duty room, a room for the school band, a dining room, a kitchen, and a supply room. In the corridors were rifle stands labeled with the students' names. A military drill ground of tens of thousand of *p'yŏng* (12.24 *p'yŏng* = 1 acre or 4,047 sq.m.) was leveled, and the interior work of several dozen class rooms was completed. This was accomplished almost entirely through the backbreaking labor of dedicated students.

The school offered a four-year regular course, a six-month course for army-officer candidates, and a three-month short course for noncommissioned officer candidates, thus accommodating the educational needs of a wide variety of young men and former righeous-army members who came to the school. It was compulsory for the graduates of this school to serve at least two years in whatever capacity ordered by school authorities.

The school curriculum also included a wide variety of modern subjects— infantry, cavalry, artillery, military engineering, surveying, the science of fortification, military law, disciplinary punishment, garrison duty, first-aid treatment, formation, drills, tactics, and strategies. Natural science and Korean history were also taught.

The military training included both individual drills and basic training. Simulated war games were repeatedly conducted against imaginary enemies on various nearby hills; both offensive and defensive strategies were practiced. Crossing the river at night in the dead of the winter, marching 70 *li*, skating, spring and autumn athletic meetings, fencing, judo, soccer, and horizontal bar exercises were all part of the physical education, the purpose of which was to cultivate strong bodies.[82]

On the whole, the education and training given at Sinhŭng Military Officers' School were extremely strict, and military discipline was so stern and rigid that during night emergency calls, there was an inspection to see whether even on button was undone. War-preparedness had to be so complete that a student could pick up his own rifle from the rifle stands without error even on a night as dark as pitch, having just been roused from sleep by the blare of trumphets.

The school had to struggle with financial difficulties, and part of its expenses were met by whatever the students could earn working during vacations. The staple food was millet, and a bean sauce made of picked beans was the only side dish. In spite of all these problems, the students were in high spirits, waiting for the day to come when they should serve their country and die for national independence. By the spring of 1917 the school had grown so much that a branch school called the Paeksŏ Farm Branch School (*Paeksŏ Nongjang Pun'gyo*) was established in Hsiaopeitai, T'ung-hua-hsien.[83]

After 1 March 1919, that is, after the March First Movement, patriotic young Koreans literally flooded the school for admission. When the school found itself too small to accommodate all the candidates, it moved to Ku-shan-tzu, Liu-ho-hsien. The original school continued to function as a branch school. More students meant that more teachers were needed, and Yi Ch'ŏng-ch'ŏn, Yi Pŏm-sŏk and other military instructors were added to the faculty.[84] The great success of Sinhŭng Military Officers' School was is indicated by the total number of graduates, which amounted to some 3,500 between the spring of 1911, when the school was founded, and August 1920, when it was closed by the Japanese.[85]

In 1919 a strong independence army was formed with Sinhŭng graduates as its core members. The army consisted of the *Sŏro Kunjŏngsŏ* (Military Administration for the Western Route) and the *Pungno Kunjŏngsŏ* (Military Administration for the Northern Route). When the latter established an Officer Training Center in Hsi-ta-p'o, Wang-ch'ing-hseien, in August 1919, Sinhŭng graduates alone were appointed to be drill master in accordance with a special request from the commander-in-chief of the *Pungno Kunjŏngsŏ*, Kim Choa-jin.[86]

This is only one example of how many of the Sinhŭng graduates fought for national independence in various capacities. It was also Sinhŭng graduates who masterminded the *Sŏro Kunjŭngsŏ* numerous raids and surprise attacks on the Japanese army and installation in Manchuria and North P'yŏngan Province in 1920. The Battle of Ch'ŏng-san-li independence war is yet another example of their activities. Indeed, the victory the independence army achieved at Ch'ŏng-san-li is the most striking example. When attacked by five Japanese regular army divisions, the *Pungno Kunjŏngsŏ* forces and allied independence armies with just twenty-eight hundred men, fought bravely, killing twelve hundred Japanese soldiers. Needless to say, the staff and other officers of the *Pungno Kunjŏngsŏ* were almost all Sinhŭng graduates.

14. *Tongrim* Military Officers' School

In addition to establishing *Sinhŭng* Military Officers' School, *Sinminhoe* members (including Yi Tong-hwi, Kim Lip, Yi Chong-ho, Chang Ki-yŏng, Kim Ha-sŏk, and O Yŏng-sŏn) founded another such school in Lo-tzu-kou, Wang-ch'ing-hsien, Manchuria, in 1913.[87] The Tongrim Military Officers' School (*Tongrim Mugwan Hakkyo*) eventually became another independence army base founded by the *Sinminhoe*, although the school closed a year later because of financial troubles and pressure from the local Chinese warlords. About forty students had gone to Russian areas to work for money to revive their school, which shows how great the financial pinch had been on the one hand and how much the school had instilled national spirit in its students on the other.[88]

Actually, the Tongrim Military Officers' School was reestablished inside Russian territory. According to the Japanese intelligence sources of 1916, there was a "Tongrim School" located in Chu-ch'uan-kou, Russian Maritime Territory (Yen-hai Chou), which was full of anti-Japanese sentiment. There were two teachers, Yi and Kim, and one hundred eighty students.[89] No further details are known about this school, but in all probability it must have been used as an independence army base by Yi Tong-hwi, Kim Ha-sŏk, Yu Tong-yŏl, Cho Sŏng-hwan, Pak Ŭn-sik, and Sin Ch'ae-ho when they organized an independence army. They planned to start an independence war by marching into Korea immediately after the March First Movement.[90]

15. *Milsan* Military Officers' School

The third officers' school established by *Sinminhoe* members was Milsan Military Officers' School in Feng-mi-shan-tzu, Mi-shan-hsien, Manchuria. According to a 1916 report by Japanese authorities, there was a military officers' school in Feng-mi-shan-tzu run by Yi Kap, who was the principal, and other Korean independence movement leaders.[91] Nothing more is known about it. Originally, some political exiles including An Ch'ang-ho and Yi Kap made a vain attempt to set up a military officers' school in Mi-shan in 1910; the 1916 report strongly suggests that comrades of Yi Kap and others did eventually succeeded in doing so.

From the evidence reviewed so far, it is clear that the *Sinminhoe* was only partially successful in its movement to found independence army bases. This was mainly because it needed a continual supply of funds and patriotic emigrants, and these were hampered by the wholesale arrest of *Sinminhoe* members in Korea in 1911.

Nonetheless, the *Sinminhoe*'s movement to found independence army bases achieved results in at least two respects. The first was that the *Sinminhoe* actually succeeded in establishing three military officers' schools (in western and northern Kando and in the Russian territory); these were used as bases for the independence army and independence movement. Further, these schools gave birth to a somewhat modernized independence army, small-scale though it might have been, that was basically different in both quality and quantity from the righteous-army corps and quite capable of competing with the Japanese regular army. Its rivalry with the Japanese army can be seen by its great victory achieved in the independence war of Ch'ŏng-san-li (*Ch'ŏng-shan-li Chŏnt'u*). The second was that the *Sinminhoe*'s movement to found independence army base and conduct a successful independence war brought together other national movements and provided a model for other political factions and associations to follow in their pursuit of national independence. During the period from 1910 to 1945, all political factions of the national independence movements, including the Provisional Government in Shanghai, nationalistic independence movement leaders, and communist independence movement leaders adopted the *Sinminhoe*'s strategy as their own.

16. The Dissolution of the *Sinminhoe*

In 1911 the Japanese fabricated incidents like the "Anak Incident" (*Anak Sakkŏn*), the "Yang Ki-t'ak et al. Violation of the Security Law" (*Yang Ki-t'ak Tŭng Poanbop wiban Sakkŏn*), and the "Case of the One Hundred Five" (*Paego In Sakkŏn*). This gave them an excuse to arrest and imprison the *Sinminhoe* leaders, thus disrupting its activities and fatally crippling the society. In December 1910, the Japanese military police arrested An Myŏng-gŭn, who had been raising funds for the recruitment of righteous-army volunteers in Manchuria. Although An was not a member of the *Sinminhoe*, the Japanese authorities took advantage of this opportunity and also arrested some 160 *Sinminhoe* members of Hwanghae Province.[92]

In January 1911, the Japanese military police arrested thirty-three Korean patriots beginning with Yang Ki-t'ak in Seoul. This incident was called the Case of Yang Ki-t'ak et al. Violation of the Security Law.[93] Then followed the arrest of six or seven hundred patriots of Southern and Northern P'yŏngan Provinces.[94] The Japanese military police fabricated the so called "Korean Conspiracy Case of an Assassination of Governor-General Terauchi" and applied it to the arrested Korean patriots.[95]

Conducting the investigation, the Japanese military police found out the existence of the secret association *Sinminhoe* and its organization. Of those seven or eight hundred people, 122 found the torture too much to bear, confessed their membership, and were brought to trial, and one hundred five received heavy prison sentences.[96]

Thus it was called the Case of the One Hundred Five. During the trial the defendants complained of the cruel torture they were subjected to and exposed the Japanese fabrication of the incident so logically that the Japanese authorities were put in extremely embarrassing position. Because a number of Christians were among the defendants, the American Presbyterian Foreign Mission, the Edinburgh Religious Council, and other foreign Christian bodies protested strongly against the false accusations of the Japanese, putting Japan into an even tighter corner.[97] As a result, only six of the defendants, Yun Ch'i-ho, Yang Ki-t'ak, Im Ch'i-jŏng, Yi Sŭng-hun. An T'ae-guk, and Ok Kwan-bin, received six-year prison sentences in July 1913, and the rest were released. The Japanese, nonetheless, had achieved their aims with this fabricated incident most of the indicted were disabled through torture and the *Sinminhoe* was virtually dissolved inside Korea by September 1911.

17. Conclusion

As demonstrated, the *Sinminhoe* was representative of the independence bodies and groups active during the critical years of 1907 through 1910 that preceded the complete colonization of Korea by Japan. The *Sinminhoe* was a secret society organized around a core of ordinary citizens, most of whom were intellectuals and members of a newly developing commercial class; it can be said to have changed the Chosŏn dynasty's last four years from a period of despair to a time of great awakening and building of national strength. The *Sinminhoe*'s "patriotic enlightenment" movement was so active that it became the driving force of the independence movement. It was through the efforts of the *Sinminhoe* that the "enlightenment" movement and the righteous-army movement were made complementary, in spite of their potential of mutual conflict. Consequently, both were fruitful.

Of the six great movements the *Sinminhoe* launched, the most epoch-making was the founding of the three independence army bases in Manchuria. The *Sinminhoe* alone was capable of such a grand enterprise. It made use of its accumulated experience in resisting invading foreign powers since the opening of Korean ports and combined that with the "enlightenment" movement and the righteous-army movement. Thus it formulated as its supreme strategy the concept of a "war of independence." To put this strategy into practice, the *Sinminhoe* overcame hardships and difficulties of all sorts to establish three military officers' schools in Manchuria and found a modern independence army, which moved the anti-Japanese independence movement into a significantly different stage.

Equally epoch-making was the *Sinminhoe*'s formal adoption of constitutional republicanism as the goal of its national movement. The adoption of this kind of goal was the first in the history of Korea.

The influence of the *Sinminhoe*'s activities over later independence movements was great. It was the national strength cultivated and fostered by the *Sinminhoe*, for instance, that became the main force of the March First Movement. It was again the *Sinminhoe*'s movement to found an independence army groups responsible for the various military independence campaigns carried out, the independence army groups formed, and the pitched battles and guerrila warfare conducted after the March First Movement. The great victory over the Japanese regular army in the Battle of Ch'ŏng-san-li was due largely to the *Sinminhoe*, for without the three independence-army bases the *Sinminhoe* had established, such a victory would not have been possible.

After the March First Movement, some former *Sinminhoe* members joined the communist-led independence movement. Yi Tong-hwi, the director of the Hangyŏng provinces, and the members of his branch are cases in point. Later, Pak Chung-hwa and some others from both Seoul and the provinces south of Seoul followed suit. As a result, the nationalistic independence movement subsequent to the March First Movement was led mainly by the former *Sinminhoe* members. For instance, all of the cabinet members of the Provisional Government of Korea established in Shanghai in 1919 except Syngman Rhee were the former *Sinminhoe* members.

In conclusion, because of human shortcomings and organizational limitations the *Sinminhoe* was not always successful in its undertakings, but no other society, faction, or group in the modern history of Korea achieved so much of importance or contributed so much to national independence in such a short period of time.

FOOTNOTES (Part III-14)

1. Kim Koo, *Paekpŏm Ilchi* (The diary of Paekpŏm Kim Koo), 1968, Paekpŏm Kim Koo Kinyŏm Sa'ŏphoe, Seoul, pp. 178-182.

2. *Taehan Maeil Sinbo* (Korea Daily News), 26 March and 27 March, 1907.

3. *Sokp'yŏn Tosan An Ch'ang-ho* (Supplementary Volume: Tosan An Ch'ang-ho), 1954, Tosan Kinyŏm Sa'ŏphoe, Seoul, pp. 117-133; Yi Kwang-su, *Tosan An Ch'ang-ho*, 1948, Seoul, pp. 8-13; Chu Yohan, ed., *An Tosan Chŏnjip* (The complete works of An Tosan), 1971, Seoul, pp. 40-54.

4. Kuksa P'yŏnch'an Wiwonhoe, ed., *Han'guk tongnip undong sa* (A history of the Korean independence movement), 5 Vols., Vol. 1, Kuksa P'yŏnch'an Wiwŏnhoe, 1965-1969, Seoul, p. 1028.

5. *Sokp'yŏn Tosan An Ch'ang-ho*, p. 135.

6. *Chŏsen no hogo oyobi heigŏ* (The protection and annexation of Korea), Vol. of Kim Chŏng-ju, ed. *Chŏsen tochi shiryo* (Historical records of the Japanese rule of Korea), 10 Vols., Vol. 3, 1970-1972, Kankoku Shiryŏ Kenkyŭjo, p. 73.

7. *Taehan Maeil Sinbo*, 24 February, 1907.

8. Yu Cha-hu, *Yi Chun Sŏnsaeng Chŏn* (A biography of Yi Chun), 1947, Tongbang Munhwa Sa, Seoul, pp, 59-68.

9. *Sokp'yŏn Tosan An Ch'ang-ho*, pp. 86-87.

10. *Han'guk tongnip undong sa*, Vol. 1, p. 1023.

11. *The Japan Chronicle*, 12 July, 1912.

12. *Sokp'yŏn Tosan An Ch'ang-ho*, pp. 86-87.

13. *Paekpŏm Ilchi*, p. 195; *Pak Ŭn-sik chŏnsŏ*, 3 Vols. (The complete works of Pak Ŭn-sik), Vol. 1, 1975, Tan'guk Taehak Pusŏk Tongyanghak Yŏn'guso, Seoul, p. 479.

14. *Han'guk tongnip undong sa*, Vol. 1, p. 1024.

15. *Ibid.*, p. 1026.

16. *Ibid.*, pp. 1028-1029; Yamagata Iso, ed., *Chŏsen inbŏ jiken* (The Korean Plot Incident), 1912, Seoul, pp. 26-153.

17. *Han'guk tongnip undong sa*, Vol. 1, p. 1024, p. 1027.

18. Yamagata, *Chŏsen inbŏ jiken*, pp. 2-177.

19. *Han'guk tongnip undong sa* (A history of the Korean independence movement), 1956, Aeguk Tongji Wonhohoe, Seoul, p. 91.

20. These statistics were from pp. 54-81 of Yamagata, *Chŏsen inbŏ jiken*.

21. Yi Kwang-su, *Tosan An Ch'ang-ho*, p. 25.

22.　*Ibid.*, p. 89.

23.　*Taehan Maeil Sinbo*, 6 October, 1908.

24.　Yi Kwang-su, *Tosan An Ch'ang-ho*, p. 240.

25.　Chu Yo-han, *An Tosan chŏnsŏ*, pp. 80-82.

26.　Yi Kwang-su, *Tosan An Ch'ang-ho*, p. 89.

27.　Chu Yo-han, *An Tosan chŏnsŏ*, p. 82.

28.　*Taehan Maeil Sinbo*, 25 April, 1909.

29.　*Ibid.*, 5 March, 1908.

30.　*Ibid.*, 18 March, 1908.

31.　Yi Kwang-su, *Tosan An Ch'ang-ho*, pp. 45-46.

32.　*Taehan Maeil Sinbo*, 16 May, 1908.

33.　*Hwangsŏng Sinmun*, 8 May, 1909.

34.　*Kwanbo* (The Government Gazette), No. 4756, 13 August, 1910, p. 64.

35.　*Sŏbuk Hakhoe Wŏlbo* (Monthly report of the Northwest Educational Association), 3.15 (February 1908), pp. 44-45.

36.　*Ibid.*, pp. 8-9.

37.　*Han'guk tongnip undong sa*, 1965, Vol. 1, p. 1024.

38.　*Paekpŏm ilchi*, p. 187.

39.　*Han'guk tongnip undong sa*, 1965, p. 91.

40.　Yamagata, *Chŏsen inbŏ jiken*, p. 27.

41.　*Sonyŏn* (Boys), 3.9:57.

42.　Yi Kwang-su, *Tosan An Ch'angho*, p. 33.

43.　Ch'oe Myŏng-sik, *Anak sakkŏn-kwa samil undong-kwa na* (The Anak Incident, the March Movement, and I), 1970, Kŭnghŏ Chŏn'gi Wiwŏnhoe, Chinhae, pp. 18-19.

44.　*Han'guk tongnip undong sa*, Vol. 1, 1965, p. 1024.

45.　Yamagata, *Chŏsen inbŏ jiken*, p. 27.

46.　*Ibid.*, p. 46.

47.　*Ibid.*, pp. 50, 96.

48.　Ch'oe Myŏn-sik, *Anak sakkŏn*, p. 23.

49.　*Ibid.*, pp. 25-26; Anak-kun Chi P'yŏnch'an Wiwonhoe, *Anak-kun chi* (Anak County Journal), 1976, Anak-kun Minhoe, Seoul, p. 109.

50.　*Taehan Maeil Sinbo*, 17 August, 1909.

51.　Koryŏ Taehak Asea Munje Yŏn'guso Yuktang Chŏnjip P'yŏncha'n Wiwonhoe, ed., *Yuktang Ch'oe Nam-sŏn's Chŏnjip*, 15 Vols.(the complete works of Yuktang Ch'oe Nam-sŏn) Vol. 10, 1973, Hyŏnam Sa, Seoul, p. 247.

52.　*Sonyŏn*, 2.8:15.

53.　*Ibid.*, 3.6:78.

54.　Sŏnu Hun, *Minjokŭi sunan: Paego in sakkŏn chinsang* (National sufferings: The truth of the "Case of the one hundred five"), 1954, Tongnip Ch'ŏngsin Pogŭphoe, Seoul, p. 33.

55. Won Ŭi-sang, "Sinhŭng Mugwan Hakkyo" (Sinhŏng Military Officers' School), in *Sindong'a*, May 1969, p. 236.

56. *Tongnip undong sa* (A history of the Korean independence movement), 10 Vols., Vol. 5, 1970-1978, Tongnip Undong Sa P'yŏnch'an Wiwŏnhoe, Seoul, p. 163.

57. Kim Yun-sik, *Sok ŭmch'ongsa* (Supplementary Volume: History of clouds and sunshine), 2 Vols., Vol. 2, Kuksa P'yŏnch'an Wiwonhoe, Seoul, 1960, See especially the item for 22 February, 1910.

58. *Sokp'yŏn Tosan An Ch'ang-ho*, pp. 134-145; Chu Yo-han, *An Tosan Chŏnsŏ*, p. 896.

59. *Sokp'yŏn Tosan An Ch'ang-ho*, pp. 26-154; Sae Charyo Anak Sakkŏn Kwa Sinmin-hoe sakkŏn (New discovered research materials: Trial documents of the "Anak Incident" and the "Sinminhoe Incident"), *Han'guk Hakpo* (Journal of Korean Studies), Vol. 8, Winter 1977, pp. 222-250.

60. *Ibid.*, p. 228.

61. It seems that the Sinminhoe's movement, the Ch'ŏngnyŏn Haguhoe, was related to the plan.

62. *Han'guk Hakpo*, No. 8, p. 233.

63. Yamagata, *Chŏsen inbŏ jiken*, p. 2, 26, and 83.

64. *Sokp'yŏn Tosan An Ch'ang-ho*, p. 144.

65. Chu Yo-han, *An Tosan Chŏnsŏ*, p. 896.

66. *Ibid.*

67. *Sokp'yŏn Tosan An Ch'ang-ho*, p. 144.

68. *Ibid.*, pp. 147-148.

69. Chu Yo-han, *An Tosan chŏnsŏ*, p. 897.

70. Yi ŭn-suk, *Minjok-undongga Anae-ŭi Sugi* (Memoirs of the wife of an independence movement leader), 1975, Seoul, p. 155.

71. Ch'oe Myŏng-sik, *Anak sakkŏn*, pp. 26-38.

72. *Han'guk Hakpo*, Vol. 8, pp. 233-237.

73. *Ibid.*, pp. 228-229.

74. Yi ŭn-suk, *Minjok undong.* pp. 15-16.

75. *Han'guk Hakpo*, Vol. 8, pp. 233-237.

76. *Paekpŏm Ilcki*, pp. 195-196; *Han'guk Hakpo*, Vol. 8, p. 234.

77. *Han'guk Hakpo*, Vol. 8, pp. 236-240.

78. Yi Sang-yong, *Sŏkchu yugo* (The posthumous works of Sŏkchu), 1973, Koryŏ Taehakkyo Ch'ulp'anbu, Seoul, p. 173.

79. *Han'guk Hakpo*, Vol. 8, p. 236.

80. Yi Ŭn-suk, *Minjok undong*, p. 160; *Sŏkchu yugo*, pp. 208-209.

81. Yi Ŭn-suk, *Minjok undong*, p. 160.

82. Won Ŭi-sang, "Sinhŭng Muhwan Hakkyo," p. 241.

83. *Ibid.*, p. 242.

84. *Ibid.*, pp. 242-243.

85. *Ibid.*, p. 243.

86. *Ibid.*, p. 243.

87. Kang Tŏk-sang, ed., *Hyŏndae sa charyo* (Records of modern history), Vol. 27, Seoul, 1970, p. 155.

88. *Tongnip Sinmun* (The Independent), 20 April, 1920.

89. Kang Tŏk-sang, *Hyŏndae sa charyo*, p. 167.

90. *Han'guk tongnip undong sa*, Vol. 5, 1973, p. 410.

91. Kang Tŏk-sang, *Hyŏndae sa charyo*, p. 157.

92. *Han'guk Hakpo*, Vol. 8, pp. 222-230.

93. *Ibid.*, p. 233.

94. Sŏnu Hun, *Minjok ŭi sunan*, p. 24; Yamagata, *Chŏsen inbŏ jiken*, p. 23.

95. Yamagata, *Chŏsen inbŏ jiken*, pp. 20-54.

96. *Ibid.*, pp. 54-177.

97. *Ibid.*, pp. 178-250.

15. The Life and Thought of Pak Ŭn-sik

1. His Life

Pak Ŭn-sik (1859-1926) was a remarkable patriotic enlightenment thinker, as well as a brilliant historian and independence fighter. He has become widely known in recent years for his achievements.

He was born into household of an indigent scholar in Hwangju, Hwanghae-do in 1859, the year in which Korea began to face a national crisis as the influence of the Western Powers swept the peninsula. As a young man he studied the orthodox school of Chu Hsi philosophy from Pak Mun-il and his brother Pak Mun-o, who had been disciples of Yi Hang-no (Hwasŏ). At 22, he visited Kwangju, Kyŏnggi-do, where he had a valuable opportunity to read the works of Chŏng Yak-yong (Tasan) through the courtesy of Sin Ki-yŏng and Chŏng Kwan-sŏp, and this provided him with a turning point in his thought. But actually, Tasan's works influenced him belatedly when he was nearly 40. Until then his learning centered on the orthodox Chu Hsi school.

He had thoroughly mastered Chu Hsi's doctrines already at the age of 30 and became the greatest Confucian scholar in the western province next to Sŏnu Hyŏp of the late 16th century. He revered Chu Hsi deeply. He once wrote: "As a child I studied the work of Chu Hsi and paid reverence to him every morning before his portrait in my study."[1]

Pak Ŭn-sik witnessed a sequence of shocking events, such as the opening of Korea in 1876, the Coup of 1884, the *Tonghak* Peasant Revolution in 1894, and the Kabo Reform.

Confronted with the turbulent situation of his day, Pak Ŭn-sik became skeptical as to whether the Chu Hsi school was ideologically capable of coping with such grave national crises.[2] "The Chu Hsi school was a learning intended for the unilateral benefit of the ruler, of his ministers and aristocratic bureaucrats, a learning that forced blind obedience on the part of the grass-roots," he thought in retrospect. "It neglected the introduction of sciences and technologies, new systems and new military science which were necessary for the survival of the Korean people. It was such an arbitrary learning that if one changed one word of Chu Hsi's Confucian interpretations, one was accused of being a rebel." Finally in 1898, when he was 40, Pak Ŭn-sik refused to be a legalist advocating *Wijŏng Ch'ŏksa* (衛正斥邪, Protect orthodoxy and reject heterodoxy). Instead, he turned to the camp of enlightenment and independence and accepted modern learning.

The following two facts can be seen as the factors responsible for the conversion of his thought.

In the first place, he inherited the tradition of Practical Learning by studying the work of Chŏng Yak-yong as a young man.[3] This seems to have functioned as an immanent factor in the conversion of his thought.

The second factor was the influence of a campaign launched by the People's Assembly (*Manmin Kongdonghoe*) in 1898, when the movement of the Independence Club was at its height. His contact with the ideas and movements of the Independence Club seems to have been an external factor for the conversion of his thought.

In the same year, Pak Ŭn-sik departed from the Chu Hsi school and accepted new Western learning in response to the Independence Club. In October of the same year, he voluntarily served as a leader of the *Manmin Kongdonghoe* affiliated with the Independence Club.[4]

But the conversion of his thought was accompanied by anguish, for the basis of his learning had been the Chu Hsi school and the rejection of this school meant a self-denial. He contemplated his departure from the Chu Hsi school and criticized himself, which was not an easy task for an ordinary scholar. It was hardly possible for a Confucian scholar to reject the system of his scholarship at the age of 40. It was possible only for a person who was in pursuit of the intrinsic value of learning disregarding his personal interest, a person who was devoted to his nation and society.

When the *Hwangsŏng Sinmun* was founded in September, 1898, the year in which Pak Ŭn-sik converted from the Chu Hsi school to the camp of enlightenment and independence, he worked as an editorial writer for the newspaper together with Namgung Ŏk, Na Sun-yŏn, Yu Kŭn and Chang Chi-yŏn, supporting the activities of the Independence Club and its *Manmin Kongdonghoe*.

After the dissolution of the Independence Club, he realized that the propagation of modern knowledge and information on changing world situations were imminent for the public and advocated the establishment of modern schools at the first opportunity. In 1900, he became a teacher of *Hansŏng* normal School and wrote *Hakkyo Sinnon* (New Theory of the School System). He also wrote many editorials on education including one entitled "The Theory for Promotion of Learning." Published in 1904, his book *Hakkyo Sinnon* contributed to the development of education and to the enlightenment of the public.

When Korea was forced by Japan to conclude the *Ŭlsa* Treaty (1905), the *Hwangsŏng Sinmun* carried an editorial by Chang Chi-yŏn, which was titled "Wailing Over the Sad Day" (*Siilya pangsŏng taegok*). The *Hwangsŏng Sinmun* was temporarily closed in the wake of this incident and Chang Chi-yŏn resigned from the newspaper. In 1906, Pak Ŭn-sik became editor-in-chief and acting publisher of the reinstated *Hwangsŏng Sinmun* and devoted himself to the newspaper energetically despite vicious Japanese oppression.

In 1906-1910, Pak Ŭn-sik wrote bold editorials in order to promote enlightenment and patriotism and to restore national sovereignty. Rebuking the Japanese invasion of Korea with a lethal pen, he encouraged a nationwide campaign to organize the Righteous Army and called on the public to nurture national strength for the restoration of sovereignty. To discourage his activities, the Japanese military police detained him, but he remained unshaken.

Pak Ŭn-sik participated in the activities of the *Taehan Chaganghoe* (The Korean Society for Self-Strengthening) founded in April, 1906 by Yun Ch'i-ho, Chang Chi-yŏn and Yun Hyojŏng, and contributed articles to the monthly journal published by the society.

In the same year, he founded Sŏu hakhoe (The Educational Association of Friends of the Western Provinces) and became editor of the *Sŏu*, a magazine published by the society. He inspired the public with patriotism and enlightenment with his articles carried in the magazine.

The Korean Society for self-strengthening was dissolved by the Japanese authorities in connection with the 1907 incident in which Korea dispatched an emissary to the international peace conference in the Hague. When the Japanese forced Emperor Kojong to abdicate, society opposed the Japanese decision and initiated a staunch demonstration. When *Sinminhoe* merged the *Hanpuk hŭnghakhoe* and *Sŏu hakhoe* into the *Sŏpuk hakhoe*, Pak Ŭn-sik became editor of the *monthly Sŏpuk hakhoe*. He clarified the activities of the society in a manifesto carried in the monthly and spearheaded the enlightenment movement by contributing a brilliant article to every issue of the magazine. The magazine also carried articles by other Korean enlightenment thinkers of the times.

When the *Sinminhoe*, a secret society aimed at restoring sovereignty, was organized by Yang Ki-t'ak and An Ch'ang-ho in April, 1907, Pak Ŭn-sik was active as a member in charge of education.

Written with his profound knowledge and ardent patriotism, Pak Ŭn-sik's articles played an important role in the awakening of the public and in the propagation of modern knowledge. In fact, intellectuals and young students of the times read his articles avidly and nourished their patriotism. Besides, innumerable conservative literati and Confucian scholars also realized the acute need of enlightenment and self-strengthening and turned to modern learning under the influence of Pak Ŭn-sik's articles. Pak Ŭn-sik was respected by the entire people as the most influential patriotic thinker toward the end of the Tae-Han Empire.

Korea was completely deprived of its sovereignty by the Japanese in August, 1910. Pak Ŭn-sik crossed the border and went to Huanjen district in west Chientao in April, 1911. He was 53. He chose Huanjen district for various reasons. There he wanted to meet his comrades and to investigate the territory of ancient Korea in preparation for a new book of ancient Korean history. He wrote in this place such works on ancient Korea as *Mongbae kŭm t'aejo* (I saw the Founder of Chin Dynasty) and *A Biography of Ch'ŏn'gae Somun*. The books revealed that ancient Korea was a powerful and prosperous nation in parallel with China, and that Palhae (Pohai in Chinese) and Kŭm (Chin in Chinese) were ancient Korean tribes. Thus the books exerted an influence on the study of Korean History and the development of the independence spirit for the restoration of Korean sovereignty.

In 1912, Pak Ŭn-sik went to Peking, Tienchin, Shanghai, Nanching and Hongkong where he conferred on methods for the independence movement with his comrades. Together with Sin Kyu-sik and Hong Myŏng-hŭi, he founded the *Tongje-sa*, a fraternity of Korean residents aspiring for Korean independence and became its chairman. In 1913, he founded the *Pakdal* School in the French settlement in Shanghai and devoted himself to the education of children of Korean residents in China.

In 1914, he became editor of *Kuo Shih Jihpao* at the request of K'ang Yu-wei, but the newspaper was closed after a short period. The elite of Chinese society, however, held him in respect for his scholarship and intelligence. He was especially intimate with such eminent Chinese leaders as K'ang Yu-wei, Liang Ch'i-ch'ao and T'ang Shao-yi.

He wrote the biography of An Chung-gŭn in 1914. He also authored *Han'guk T'ongsa* (The Painful History of Korea), for which he had prepared over a long time. Published in 1915, the *Han'guk T'ongsa* became an epoc-making classic in the history of modern Korea.

In the same year, he participated in the founding of the *Sinhan Hyŏkmyŏng-dan* (the New Korean Revolutionary Corps) and the *Taedong Poguk-dan* (the Corps of Great Union for the Nation) and became leader of both organizations.

Until 1918, he kept visiting Korean settlements in Manchuria and the coastal areas of Russia and China, founding patriotic organizations for Korean independence, teaching Korean history and inspiring the Koreans with the spirit of independence.

Meanwhile, the Independence Movement was successfully launched at home on March First, 1919, when Pak Ŭn-sik was 61. Pak Ŭn-sik was deeply touched by the spontaneous devotion of his compatriots.

He wrote many impassioned articles on the independence campaign, and in despite of his old age (61) he founded the *Taehan Noin Tongmaeng-dan* (the Corps of the Aged Koreans) and dispatched Kang U-gyu, Yi Pal and others to Seoul and had them attack the Japanese government offices and then the Japanese governor-general in Korea.

Learning of the March First Independence Movement launched at home, he was convinced that the day of independence was nearing. Participating in the founding of the provisional Korean government in Shanghai and becoming publisher of the *Tongnip Sinmun* (The Independent), he was active in formulating the ideological and theoretical background of the independence movement.

Encouraged by the independence movement, he began to write the *Han'guk Tongnip Undongji Hyŏlsa* (The Bloody History of the Korean Independence Movement). The book was published in 1920. Since it was wrtten while he was engaged in the compilation of materials on the independence movement in close collaboration with the Committe for the Compilation of Historical Materials for the Provisional government in Shanghai, the book was based on valid materials. In this work, he revealed his conviction that Korean could win national independence and liberation based on the March First Independence Movement. In this book, meanwhile, he examined and evaluated the history of the Korean independence movement. His *Hyŏlsa* (Bloody History) and *T'ong-sa* (Painful History) became two great classics in Korean modern history.

After the publication of *Hyŏlsa*, Pak Ŭn-sik wrote many articles on the Korean independence movement for the *Independence Press* in Shanghai. Among them was an editorial titled "To My Affectionate Young People."

In 1922, Pak Ŭn-sik was elected honorary chairman of the committe for the preparation of the Convention of National Representatives. When the provisional government in Shanghai became shaky following the resignation of Yi Sŭng-man (Syngman Rhee) as its President, he assumed the post of Prime Minister and functioned as acting President. He became President of the provisional government in March 1925. In order to assure the solidarity of Korean leaders, he revised the Constitution and by revising the Presidential system into the cabinet system, he rooted out internal conflicts within the provisional government. But reaching the age of 67, he conceded his

Presidency to Kim Koo and retired from active service. He became gradually infirm with age and illness and died on November 1, 1925, bequeathing his ideas for the independence movement.

Starting his career as an orthodox scholar of the Chu Hsi school, he devoted his whole life as a leader of the enlightenment and independence movement, as a great patriotic thinker, as a brilliant historian, and as an unflinching independence fighter. He was a giant symbolic of all the force and anguish underlying modern Korean history.

2. Patriotic Enlightenment Thought

Pak Ŭn-sik deplored that Korea had failed in strengthening herself for national sovereignty before she was to be put at the mercy of neighboring Japan. In preparation for the restoration of national sovereignty, however, he was active in implanting patriotism and enlightenment thought in the minds of Koreans from 1904 to 1910.

The following five points can be seen as constituting his patriotic enlightenment thought. The first is his theory of national salvation by education. The second is his theory of national salvation by industry, a theory advocating the development of modern industry using modern science and technology to secure an independent and prosperous life for Koreans. The third is his theory of national salvation by creating national culture embracing national history, national language and national religion. The fourth is his theory of reform in Confucian studies aimed at eradicating the ills of past bigotry and enhancing a revolutionary spirit of self-reliance. The fifth is his theory of independence struggle aimed at securing independence by force with the help of the Korean army trained in Manchuria.

1) Theory of National Salvation by Education

The core of Pak Ŭn-sik's patriotic enlightenment thought was his theory of national salvation by education.[5] Korea failed to propagate new knowledge through new education, and he saw this as the basic factor for the loss of her sovereignty. He advocated, therefore, that in order to restore sovereignty Koreans should be equipped with new knowledge and wisdom through modern education. The new knowledge advocated by him can be interpreted mainly as 1. science and technology, 2. social sciences, and 3. national culture.

He insisted that Western technology and social sciences are required for the self-strengthening of Koreans. Admitting that Oriental learning lagged behind in scientific fields, he bitterly criticized the legalists school and conservative

Confucian scholars who refused to accept Western science. But he did not mean to recommend Western learning unconditionally. He emphasized that Koreans should adopt Western learning by choice to suit their own environment.

Pak Ŭn-sik also emphasized the development of national culture by which he meant national history, national language, national script (syllabary) and national religion. Although they did not neglect their history, he pointed out, Koreans leaned on the study of Chinese history as a result of their blind respect for China. He deplored that this led them to belittle their national identity throughout 4,000 years of their history.[6] Criticizing the concept of Korea as "a Small Middle Kingdom (Small China)" held by corrupt Confucianists, he advocated the development of Korean history, language, syllabary and religion.

It seems that he emphasized the development of national culture because it would enable Koreans to nourish their "national soul" or "Taehan spirit." The "national soul" or "Taehan spirit" can be interpreted as "patriotism" or "self-reliant, independent thought," which he defined as "the morale that boosts independence." The study of national culture (Korean studies) was important because it would enhance "the Taehan spirit" which in turn would be conductive to "self-strengthening" for Koreans, according to him.[7] He thought it was important because even if Koreans could build large plants and produce warships and artillery by using modern technology and social sciences, they would be useless if they were not used for national salvation but for the interest of Japanese invaders.

He believed that modern technology and the new social sciences could be introduced from the West within a short period of time. But no one but Koreans could develop their own national culture (Korean studies), he thought, hence his emphsis on study and education in the field. He emphasized this at every available opportunity.

Considering modern education as essential for the entire people, he advocated the institution of compulsory education.[8] He further contended that the exclusive use of *Han'gŭl* is necessary for compulsory education.[9]

The exclusive use of *Han'gŭl* that he proposed in his attempt to develop the national salvation by education can be seen as a natural consequence. He studied the traditional Chu Hsi School and Chinese classics as a child and established himself as an eminent Confucian scholar at 30. But he boldly rejected the old framework of thought in response to the changing world and proposed the exclusive use of *Han'gŭl* before anyone else when he was 50. These facts are sufficient to illustrate his caliber as a great scholar and thinker.

We can easily imagine what a great impact his proposal gave to his society.

As a member of the National Language Research Society organized by Chu Si-gyŏng, he ws active in supporting researchers of Korean language and literature. He engaged himself also in the study of Korean language.

For the institution of compulsory education, he proposed urgent training of teachers and founding of schools for modern education. He also advocated night schools for adults who were unable to attend school in daytime. His proposal was widely accepted by the public and night schools became popular toward the end of the Tae-Han empire.[10]

Pak Ŭn-sik emphasized the importance of physical education as well. Pointing out that the traditional educational system neglected physical education and led to national ruin, he advocated training of sound and healthy Koreans through physical education.[11] He especially stressed physical education, for it was closely related to the founding of the Korean Independence Army Corps in Manchuria. He believed that training of a young generation in modern knowledge and martial arts was instrumental in winning independence at the first opportunity.

Pak Ŭn-sik took an active part in the movement of national salvation through education by founding the Sŏpuk Hyŏpsŏng School together with his friends and serving as principal of the school for some time. He also organized the *Kwangmunhoe* which was devoted to the publication of Korean classics.

2) His Theory of National Salvation by Industry

Pak Ŭn-sik emphasized the importance of the development of industry and business as well as education as part of his theory of naiotnal salvation through enlightenment.

His theory of national salvation by industry was established: 1. as a measure of self-strenthening required for the restoration of sovereignty, as a practical measure to be taken in the face of Japanese invasion; 2. as a means of self-development of the weak in defiance of the aggression of imperialism by deformation of the theory of social evolution encouraging the principle of the survival of the fittest. His theory shows that he was not a spiritualist nor an ideologist as errorneously interpreted by some scholars.[12]

He thoroughly understood the Industrial Revolution that took place in England and introduced its contents in detail to the public at the last stage of the Tae-Han Empire. He did not see the origin of the Industrial Revolution in association with the economic system of capitalist society but in association with the invention and innovation in science and technology.[13]

Observing the competition of nations as a competition of power, he decided that superiority and inferiority in terms of power, or victory and defeat, depends on the degree of industrial development. He further concluded that the development of industry depends on the development of productive capacity, and that the degree of the development of productive capacity depends on the standards of scientific technology achieved by a nation. The competition of nations will develop into the competition in productivity and a nation will win or lose in this competition depending on whether it is technologically advanced or backward, he observed.[14]

He emphasized scientific and technological reform and industrial development above all things as powerful factors for winning in the competition in productivity. Industrial plants of highly efficient productivity based on advanced technology will play a decisive role in the tough international industrial competition, he stressed. The self-reliance of a nation's economy will be achieved by this method alone, he believed. He stressed the importance of military buildup in the face of imperial invasion of big powers, but he also held a consistent view that a powerful military capability should be based on advanced industry and advanced scientific technology.

From these viewpoints, Pak Ŭn-sik proposed as methods of industrial development: ① development of up-to-date scientific technology, ② installation of plants equipped with modern machines, ③ installation of joint-stock firms, ④ training and employment of skilled technicians, ⑤ a reform in manufacture designed to win in international competition in quality production, ⑥ the development of export trade.

With regard to agricultural development which he stressed next to industrial development, he was bitterly critical of the Japanese colonial policy which resulted in the illegal occupation of Korean land. His ideas for the development of agriculture centered on diversified farming and technical reform. He proposed: ① a reform in agricultural technology, ② improvement of seeds, ③ development of sericulture, ④ development of cotton farming, ⑤ cattle raising, ⑥ promotion of forestation and ⑦ land reclamation. His ieas for agricultural development, however, lacked in a plan for land reform involving landowners and tenants.

In his theory of national salvation by industry we can detect the tendency to emphasize industrialism as well as science and technology. It can be appreciated from the fact that he used to neglect the commerce which other enlightenment leaders of his period ever laid stress. Seeing "industrial capitalism" as the source of Western power, he apparently sought the source of Korean power in industrialism.

We can assume that he formulated an "industrial philosophy" calling for industrious labor based on his industrialist ideas for national salvation by industry. His emphasis on "labor" was extremely basic and comprehensive and this distinguished his point of view from that of other leaders.[15]

3) Theory of Reform in Confucianism

A sailent feature of Pak Ŭn-sik's patriotic enlightenment thought is his theory of reform in Confucianism which is characteristically his own.[16] It is to be noted that emphasizing the importance of religion Pak Ŭn-sik did not abandon Confucianism which was criticized by his colleagues. He sought to reform and revitalize Confucian studies. Although his ideas contained some ideological elements, it would be a mistake to think that his entire enlightenment thought was dominated by the ideological elements. The fact that he was a realistic patriotic enlightenment leader can be detected in the following statement on science, philosophy and religion:

> "Spiritual Civilization is generally sought by science. Since this is an age in which all mankind seeks the benefit of material civilization in competition, scientific research is an imminent issue for our academic circles. However, it is essential to grasp the truth in philosophy in order to remedy the weakness of the human mind and thereby secure the noble domain of man's personality."[17]

It should not be overlooked that Pak Ŭn-sik's advocacy for a reform in Confucianism was derived not only from his personal interest but also from his far-sighted insight into the national goal of restoring sovereignty.

Confucianism was accepted nearly as a national religion. But Pak Ŭn-sik realized that a harmful influence of Confucianists of his period was serious enough to ruin the country. He sought, therefore, to uproot the impediment of Confucian circles by reforming Confucianism and attempted to utilize the Confucian tradition for the restoration of independence and social progress. While thus criticizing the impediment of the Chu Hsi school involving Korean Confucian circles, he strove to pursue a reform in Confucianism. He had a progressive attachment to Confucianism and he was a unique enlightenment thinker in that he tried to seek social progress in alliance with Confucian tradition.

Pak Ŭn-sik realized the need for the renewal of Confucianism at an early stage of his scholarship. But he contended that a reform in Confucianism is impossible through the Chu Hsi school. It, he insisted, is possible through the school of Wang Yang-ming, to whom "man manifests his spirit by acting in the concrete situation which confronts him." To Pak Ŭn-sik, Chu Hsi's notion of the knowledge of all the principles underlying the myriad phenomena is incoherent. But he judged that Wang Yang-ming's thought is simple and straight and is suitable in an age in which various intricate sciences are being developed. There is a deeper reason for his advocacy for the Wang Yang-ming school. In other words, he did not see "intricate explanations" and "principles" found in Chu Hsi's doctrines as essential in carrying out the national task of restoring independence from Japan. Believing that *liang chih* (man's latent intellect) emphasized by Wang Yang-ming could lead to self-awakening, he contended that what is imminent in the struggle for the restoration of sovereignty is the "unity of knowledge and action."

In order to achieve the ultimate national goal, Pak Ŭn-sik sought to use the Confucian tradition by developing the Wang Yang-ming school in lieu of the Chu Hsi school which lost vitality resulting from its accumulated harms. In coping with the issues of his period, he interpreted *liang chih* by classifying it into: ① a capacity for awakening, ② a capacity for immaculacy and inno-cence, ③ a capacity of craving for knowledge, ④ a capacity for wide response, ⑤ a capacity to disregard wiseness and dullness, ⑥ a capacity to know the union of Heaven and man. He emphasized more dynamic and democratic factors of man's latent intellect than the Wang Yang-ming School itself.[18] Thus he came to creatively interpret the Wang Yang-ming School as a learning that can effectively promote "social evolution," "public intellect," and "civil rights."

He also creatively interpreted the "chih" in "*chih liang chih*" (awakening to latent intellect) emphasized by Wang Yang-ming as a unity of "awakening-learning-action," or an action based on new knowledge that can satisfy the demand of a new age. His competency as a great thinker lies in the fact that he could interpret the Wang Yang-ming school in alliance with "new thought" to meet the demand of his times.

If Pak Ŭn-sik had considered Wang Yang-ming's doctrines as abstract ethical theories apart from the social conditions of his times, his ideas would have been more or less ideological rather than practical. But he did consider them in connection with the social conditions and established them as the theories of a new dimension.

He elicited the idea of "Great Union" from his creative interpretations of Wang Yang-ming's doctrines. The thought of "Great Union" held by Kang Yu-wei exerted a considerable influence on his thought of "Great Union." However, Kang Yu-wei's "Great Union" tended to be a "visionary" idealism in nature, whereas Pak Ŭn-sik's "Great Union" was from the beginning a "practical" idealism, and they seem to intrinsically differ from each other in this respect. Emphasizing "practice," Pak Ŭn-sik's idea of "Great Union" called for such things as: ① public virtue and public benefit, ② national salvation, ③ equal benevolence, ④ respect for the nation, ⑤ unity of knowledge and action in patriotism, ⑥ world peace.

Meanwhile, Pak Ŭn-sik's idea of "Great Union" was related to his critical absorption of the theory of social evolution which was the representative social thought of his times. Of the four elements of the theory of evolution— ① the principle of competition, ② the survival of the fittest, ③ individualism, and ④ the principle of evolution—he fully accepted only the principle of evolution. He was reluctant to adopt other elements which were largely utilized by big powers for their imperialistic aggression. In short, he thought, the principle of competition can be adopted among different nations. The principle of "Great Union" should be adopted within a nation instead of the principle of competition, he thought.

It is also to be noted that his idea for a reform in Confucianism developed into the thought of "Great Union," which in turn led to his idea for a new national religion called the religion of "Great Union." He made this move as a struggle against the Japanese political intrigue to make Korean Confucian circles pro-Japanese. As a move to make Korean religious circles pro-Japanese, the Japanese organized the so-called Taedong Hakhoe (the Great East Society) and attempted to make Korean Confucian circles pro-Japanese. Pak Ŭn-sik tried to found the Taedong-gyo (the Great Union religion) based on his thought of "Great Union" and through this religion he attempted to prevent the Japanese from such a political infiltration. He was fairly successful in leading the Confucian circles as a force to restore national sovereignty.

By means of a reform in Confucianism, Pak Ŭn-sik sought to creatively develop the Korean tradition in Confucianism which could meet the demands of the times in such a way that Korean intellectuals immersed in the ills of the Chu Hsi school could discard outdated concepts and respond to a new national demand.

Even if he advocated a reform in Confucianism, it did not contradict his progressive, patriotic enlightenment thought. It was rather an important and unique element of his patriotic enlightenment thought. Intrinsically, it was aimed at restoring sovereignty.

4) Theory of Winning Independence

Pak Ŭn-sik's theory of winning independence was not his own idea but a strategy adopted by the *Sinminhoe*, of which he was a member. The *Sinminhoe* was aimed at: ① training the public in patriotism and modern learning and training young people as new leaders in the campaign to restore national independence, ② establishing a military academy abroad and traning an independence army corps at an overseas outpost, ③ deploying the independence army corps into Korea and launching a war against Japan when Japan enters a hard-pressed war against China or the United States and consolidating the strength of the entire people at home and thereby driving imperialistic Japan out of Korea and winning national independence.[19] Pak Ŭn-sik developed his patriotic enlightenment thought with this idea of winning independence as a premise.

3. View of Modern History

Pak Ŭn-sik made a notable achievement especially in the study of modern history.[20] He seems to have organized his work on modern Korean history in three parts.

The first part was *Hangguk T'ongsa* (韓國痛史, Painful History of Korea) published in 1915. The *T'ongsa* vividly brought to light the Japanese invasion of Korea covering the period from the time of Taewŏn'gun's regency to the 1911 Incident of *Sinminhoe* (Case of 105 People). In this work, Pak distinguished national soul from national vigor, or national body-strength. His conception of national soul comprised national religion, national learning, national language, national script, and national history. And his conception of national vigor comprised money and grain, army, fortification of cities and moats, warships, and machinery.[21]

According to Pak Ŭn-sik, Korea was deprived of its national vigor by militant Japan in 1910. But he contended that although Korea was deprived of its national vigor, Japan could not deprive Korea of its national soul as long as Koreans willed to maintain it. With the national soul as a basis, Koreans could nurture its capabilities and could restore independence through an independence movement, he insisted.

Pak Ŭn-sik's conception of national soul and national vigor was derived from Confucian ontology. According to Confucian ontology, man's soul and vigor are in unity while he is alive, but when man dies, his soul ascends to Heaven while his vigor is reduced to ashes. Enhancing this philosophy into a national dimension, he held that even if national vigor is lost with the fall of sovereignty a national soul will survive. And organizing his conception of national soul into "national culture" and "independence spirit," he sought to reunite the national soul with the national vigor through an independence movement. In short, the reunion of national soul and national vigor was the means to pave the way for the restoration of national independence.

Exposing and accusing the history of Japanese invasion of Korea in his *T'ongsa*, he taught Koreans that Koreans could eventually restore their independence if they maintained their national soul even when they were deprived of their national vigor.

His *T'ongsa* was originally prepared in manuscript as *A Secret Memoire on the End of the Taehan Empire*. It was systematized as a book through deliberation over a long time. Being a book based on his vivid experiences, it reveals his deep insight into the intrinsic nature of the history of Japanese invasion. Every chapter of the book contains his commentaries revealing his own views and estimations of events and facts behind them. It is a classic containing his deep thought about the history of modern Korea.

Copies of the book were brought to Korea soon after its publication in China and were widely read by Koreans at home. In 1916, the Japanese Government-General in Korea organized the Society for the Compilation of the History of the Korean Peninsula in preparation for the publication of *History of the Korean Peninsula* which was later titled *Chosŏn-sa (The History of Chosŏn)*. The preface of the book stated that it was an attempt to "purge" Pak Ŭn-sik's *T'ongsa*. Pak's book was important to such an extent.

Pak Ŭn-sik's second work on history was *Han'guk Tongnip Undongji Hyŏlsa (The Bloody History of the Korean Independence Movement)* published in 1920. It deals with the Koreans' resistance movement against Japanese invasion covering the period from the Coup of 1884 to the time after the March First, 1919 Independence Movement.

In his *Hyŏlsa*, Pak Ŭn-sik analyzed and evaluated each incident in the history of the Korean independence movement. He presented especially in detail the contents of the March First Independence Movement. The addendum of the book contains foreign documents supporting Korean independence and materials related to the public opinion of the world.

Hyŏlsa was written with a more modern methodological approach than *T'ongsa*. He dealt with each incident and fact from strikingly modern and progressive viewpoints. The first chapter is devoted to the Coup of 1884, which is one of the focal points of debate among Korean historians today. He saw this move as "a revolution of the Independence Party" and attributed its failure to the group's attempt to rely on an outer force and its hasty move taken without the support of the populace. This is a bold and penetrating observation that even a most progressive historian can hardly follow today. Meanwhile, he saw the *Tonghak* Revolution as "a revolution of the common people." No residue of his Confucian prejudice can be detected in this book.

He wrote *Hyŏlsa* while serving for the Committee for the Compilation of Historical Meterials for the Korean Provisional Government in Shanghai. So it was based on valid materials made available for the committee. In this work, he manifestly defined the protagonist of historical development as the "nation" or the "populace" and interpreted the March First Independence Movement as "a non-violent revolutionary movement of the Korean populace." He further foresaw that we would regain our independence and liberation through the March First Independence Movement.

Thridly, Pak Ŭn-sik had intended to write *A History of the Founding of Korea* which he conceived was useful for Koreans of a younger generation in their founding of a new, independent nation. But he died leaving this work undone.

His *T'ongsa* and *Hyŏlsa* are the historical works systematized for the first time by a Korean with a sense of national identity. The books deserve our admiration, for they unveil not only the intrinsic nature and obscure fragments of historical events but also the author's creative and appropriated estimations. His conclusions are identical with those reached by today's investigations based on rich research materials. This seems to illustrate that he authored a live history with his keen insight into his actual experiences and with a modern historical viewpoint. His *T'ongsa* and *Hyŏlsa* are exemplified by everybody today as the two foremost classics in modern Korean history.

4. Conclusion

On his deathbed, Pak Ŭn-sik did not bequeath a will of a personal nature to his family but a will addressed to his compatriots in connection with the independence movement. In a memorandum dictated by An Kong-gŭn, he proposed three points for a successful independence movement:

First, he called on his people "to be firmly united without the slightest hint of sectionalism and to form a united front against the foe."

Secondly, he explicitly stated that "any extraordinary measure or tactics can be used in so far as it does not defame the Korean people or pose as an impediment to the future of Korea."[22] "Our most basic need is an independent nation upon which everything is reliant," he stated.

Thirdly, he stated: "Since our independence movement is the vital issue of the entire people, we should cope with personal emotional relationships among ourselves." He again called on his people to "take united action."

The life of Pak Ŭn-sik was spent to satisfy national demands. His life underwent changes in response to changes in modern Korean history. At first he was a traditional Confucian scholar of the Chu Hsi school. He was a member of the camp of enlightenment and independence, a patriotic enlightenment thinker, and an independence fighter as well. The social thoughts that he developed during his dramatic career exercised a profound influence upon the Korean people of his times. His brilliant achievements will remain in the minds of Koreans as part of tradition in modern Korean history.

FOOTNOTES (Part Ⅲ-15)

1. "Seek truth in learning in pursuit of doubt," *The Complete Work of Pak Ǔn-sik* (to be abbreviated as Chǒnsǒ), Vol. 3, 1975, p. 197.
2. "Ha Odongmun Chewu," *Chǒnsǒ*, Vol.3, pp.32-33 and "Seek truth in learning in pursuit of doubt," *ibid.*, p.197.
3. "A Brief Personal History of Paekam Pak Ǔn-sik," *ibid.*, p. 287.
4. *A Brief Record of Independence Society* and *Changjak Kwa Pip'yǒng*, the spring issue, 1970.
5. Shin Yong-ha, "On Pak Ǔn-sik's Idea of National Salvation by Education," *Han'guk Hakpo*, the first issue, 1975.
6. "Rubbing of Monument of King Yǒngnak of Koguryǒ," *Chǒnsǒ*, Vol. 3, p. 42.
7. "Questions and Answers on Capabilities of Self-Strengthening," *ibid.*, pp. 68-69.
8. "Theory of Promotion of Learning" in *Kyǒm-gok Mungo, ibid.*, Vol. 2, p. 412.
9. "Teaching of Korean Script" in *New Theory of the School System, ibid.*, pp. 17-18.
10. "Night School for Workers," *Chǒnsǒ*, Vol. 3, pp. 97-98, and "Regulations on Commendation and Punishment," in *New Theory of the School System, Chǒnsǒ*, Vol. 2, p. 23.
11. "Nonhak Yohwal-pǒb" in *New Theory of the School System, Chǒnsǒ*, pp. 9-12.
12. Shin Yong-ha, "Pak Ǔn-sik's Idea of National Salvation by Industry" in *A Collection of Monographs of the Academy of Sciences*, No. 18, 1979.
13. "Who can save our nation?..," *Chǒnsǒ*, Vol. 3, p. 36.
14. "Theory of Improvement of Goods," *ibid.*, pp. 37-39.
15. " People's self-reliance can lead to the nation's self-reliance," *ibid.*, pp. 21-22.
16. "Shin Yong-ha, Pak Ǔn-sik's Theory of Reform in Confucianism, His Theory of the Wang Yang-ming school, and His Theory of Great Union," *Journal of History* (Yǒksa Hakppo), the 73rd issue, 1977.
17. "Seek truth in learning in pursuit of doubt," *Chǒnsǒ*, Vol. 3, pp. 196-197.
18. "Account of Wang Yang-ming," *Chǒnsǒ*, Vol. 2, p. 48.
19. Sin Yong-ha, "Founding of Sinmin-hoe and National Campaign for Restoration of Independence," *Journal of Korean Studies* (Han'guk Hakppo), No. 7 and 8, 1977.
20. Sin Il-ch'ǒl, "Pak Ǔn-sik's Idea of National Soul as a Historical Conception," *Korean Thought* (Han'guk Sasang), No. 11, 1974, and Yi Man-yǒl, "Pak Ǔn-sik's. Theory of History," *Suktae Saron*, Vol. 9, 1976.
21. "*Han'guk T'ongsa*," *Chǒnsǒ*, Vol. 1, p. 376.
22. "Yuch'ok," *Chǒnsǒ*, Vol. 3, p. 203.

16. Pak Ŭn-sik's Idea of National Salvation by Industry

1. Introduction

I had published three manuscripts about the ideas of Pak Ŭn-sik (1859-1926)[1] one of the outstanding patriotic thinkers and prime movers of enlightenment in the last stage of the Korean empire and one of the representative leaders of her independence movement, but it appears that there are some misunderstandings about his thoughts. In particula, some students of history take a view of Pak as an ideologist and a thinker prone to spiritualism because of his over-emphasis on national spirit (Korean soul) in dealing with national history as one of the constitutents of national spirit only.

Nevertheless, by a closer view of the internal structure of Pak's ideas of patriotic enlightenment we can see that one of the important features of his thought was that he accentuated well-balanced development in each field of culture and society. Pak thought that all persons living in independence nations with good development had substantial identities which were in perfect union without separation of the national soul from the national body-strength.

In the conception which Pak called national soul at that time were included national religion, national learning, national language, national script, and national history; in the conception which he called national body-strength were included money and grain, army, fortification of cities and moats, warships, and machinery.[2] Even though Pak used two different words — *Kuk-hon* and *Kuk-paek* (national soul and national body), in his conception are shown two distinct meanings different from the definitions of these words. Thus he established a dual division method of analyzing culture which corresponds to the division of spiritual culture and meterial culture or the upper structure and the lower structure of the West.[3]

On thing worthy of note about the State of an advanced independence nation is its well-balanced development, the perfect harmony of national soul (national religion, ntional learning, national language, national script, and national history) and national body-strength (money and grain, army, fortifications of cities and moats, warships and machinery) in unity. According to Pak, national states in which only national spirit is developed with the national body inactive easily fall prey to foreign aggression; on the contrary, national states in which only the national body-strength is developed without related development of the national spirit may become powerful countries and swallow other countries for some time, but soon they fall into decay with national spirit withered to some limited sphere of inactivity.[4]

To Pak the development of an ideal national state is the well-balanced progress of the national soul and national body-strength mentioned above, and only by this method of two cultures can a nation become a self-governing country of power and wealth. Pak held the view in his patriotic enlightenment movement of 1904-1910 that even though Korea had lost her rights of diplomacy and defense through the forced protectorate treaty of 1905, her national state was not yet completely destroyed, so the nation was still living. For this reason he strongly emphasized the development of national body-strength as shown above along with a high national spirit.

Accordingly, until 1910 there was no clear appearance of any trend of conceptional spiritualism in his patriotic enlightenment idea.[5]

Pak's objective in emphasizing the patriotic enlightenment idea was the restoration of national rights which could be realized by organized, systematic methods. Pak declared the cultivation of real power[6] through strenuous efforts[7] to be the only means. To achieve this purpose he stressed education, industry, and reform of social customs (old habits).

Accordingly, the first constituent of Pak's patriotic enlightenment idea is national salvation by education and the second is national salvation by industry,[8] which was to be constituted with scientific methods formulated by cool-headed observation of the real condition at that time to build the foundation of the self-governing power of his own nation on a scientific basis.[9]

Pak distinguished national soul from national body-strength even after August 1910 (annexation of Korea by Japan), saying that the colonization of Korea did not necessarily mean the loss of the Korean soul, thereby clearly showing a trend of conceptional spiritualism after 1910.[10]

At that time Pak distinguished the things which the Japanese imperialists could and could not take by force of arms. He said that our national body-strength including money and grain, army, fortification of cities and moats, warships, and machinery had been taken away by the Japanese imperialists, but they were unable to take away our national soul which consisted of national religion, national learning, national language, national script (*Hangŭl*), and national history to destroy it, so we Korean people could preserve, strengthen, and develop them, because, if we did not lose our national soul we could cultivate our real power in this basis to develop our struggle for independence to regain our national body-strength, thereby reuniting it with the national soul for the restoration of our national independence.[11]

Because of his enthusiasm about national soul there have been some biased opinions of Pak's spiritualism and conceptionalism from a superficial viewpoint, but if we look more deeply we can see that in the status of a man without a country one of the motive powers of the independence movement comes from moral strength, for such things as national culture, language, letters, and traditional usages do not go to ruin overnight. Therefore, in view of the historical conditions at that time Pak's conceptionalism should be given deeper consideration at having particular significance. However, this is a great and controversial problem related to the views of culture and the independence movement, so for the time being we had better drop it from our main theme.

In the present treatise we shall only observe Pak's idea of national salvation by industry, which he stressed next to education in his patriotic enlightenment. Such an observation may help us understand Pak's scientific designs, which were neglected by leaders of the patriotic enlightenment movement in his time as well as give information on the special features of patriotic enlightenment which were the general tendency in the closing days of the old Korean empire when the country had not become a full colony of the Japanese.

2. Imperialistic Aggression and National Salvation by Industry

It may be viewed that in Pak's patriotic enlightenment idea industry occupied a central position next only to education because of his theoretical understanding of imperialistic aggression and his reflections on the causes of loss of national rights.

Pak viewed his time as an age of imperialism and he gave explanations of imperialism on the basis of social evolutionism. He said that after Darwin enunciated the power of authority, imperialism unfurled its banner of sole power all over the world, destroying nations and exterminating human races to make it an axiom of its own as a natural law, whose evils of competition increased tragedies to the extreme as the days went by.[12]

According to Pak, the two most important factors in determining the rise or fall of a nation and the existence or destruction of a race in the struggle for existence or all national states in the age of imperialism are the brightness or darkness of knowledge and the strength or weakness of power. Throughout all ages and climes history bears witness to the rise and fall of nations as well as the vicissitudes of races on the earth through bright or dark knowledge and strong or weak power.[13]

Pak says that which takes charge of enlightening knowledge is education and that which is imposed with the expansion of power is industry. In other words, in this age of imperialism in national competition which calls it the heaven-sent principle or the struggle for existence and the axiom of the survival of the fittest, the only was to emerge victorious is to develop intellectual faculties by education and promote power by industry.[14] For these reasons, in order to develop intelectual faculties national salvation by education had become the first objective of his patriotic enlightenment movement and in order to expand industries national salvation by industry came to the fore as the second objective.

Pak says only large nations with knowledge and power may become superior and strong, which govern themselves as powers with no reliance on other powerful nations.[15]

On the other hand, any race or nation with dark knowledge and weak, inferior power becomes weaker and is subject to decay and destruction by the aggression of larger nations.

> "In the present age the five oceans are open and the six continents are in touch with one another for traffic among the five races in mutual competition. The civilized ones with bright knowledge and expanded power call themselves the superior race and the uncivilized ones with dark knowledge and reduced power are called inferior races. The superior race treats the inferior race as savages, driving them out of their homes with plunder and killing at liberty without the least scruple like birds and beasts of prey, thus robbing the inferior race of their right to existence till they gradually decrease in numbers and fall to extinction. The African negroes and the American red Indians are living examples. Ah, miserable! Today inferior races are expelled by the superior races as birds and beasts were chased by man in ancient times, so they call the struggle for existence a heaven-sent principle and the survival of the fittest an axiom of natural law. Alas! Men are born equal as common human creatures, but some enjoy the blessings of comfortable life by occupying superior positions while others have to lead unedurably hard lives as slaves. Why is this so? The big gulf between the rich and the poor, safety and danger, the ups and the downs, glory and disgrace, joy and sorrow, pain

and pleasure are like the difference between heaven and earth. We must stande on our guard by taking them as a mirror for reflection on ourselvs."[16]

Of course Pak did not praise the logic of social evolution which advocates the aggression of imperialism. On the contrary, be criticized it, calling it immoral outlawry of the victors and the powerful which set out to destroy the weaker because the theory of competition of imperialistic aggression and social evolutionism raised endless wars in the world, calling the law of the jungle an axiom and a public example.

"Why is it that the more world civilization advances and the more human knowledge grows the more rises with warcry the crescendo of severe competition in killing called the competition of nations, competitive religions, competition of politics and competition of races so that there is no end of war on the earth? Rather the conflicts become more cruel and wider spread; thus the great wars fought a hundred years ago have become a history of children's play and the big theaters of bloodshed ten years ago are now scenes of comedy or tragedy, taking human lives in countless number with more elaborate and meticulous weapons such as Krupp guns, machine guns, ironclad warships and dirigible balloons, which swoop down over land and sea, shaking heaven and earth till human blood flows in streams and human bones heap up mountain high, yet they call it the axiom of the law of the jungle and a heaven-sent public performance, destroying nations and extinguishing their seeds to make it the best politics of statesmen in flagrant delicto- in this way the so-called Palace of Justice of World Peace and the parleys of international law have become nothing but official organizations of the victors and the superiors, yet the inferiors and the vanquished find no place to appeal for relief of their pains or to bring suit for redress of grievances. it is against the cosmopolitan love of God and the universal affection of the sages for the whole creation."[17]

Moreover, Pak prophesied by inferring from the principles of social evolutionism, the time was not far off when imperialism and militarism would disappear and the principles of equality come back and prevail. Thus he foresaw the interchange of militarism and equality.[18]

Nevertheless, Pak declared the aggression of imperialism and the law of the jungle to be a stern reality from an objective view. Then he continued, "the only way to confront this bloodthirsty reality calling the jungle law an axiom and a public law is to achieve the independence of our country with our own strength without borrowing the strength of others by cultivation of our self-governing qualities and building the foundation upon which we can stand on our own feet[19] with the growth of our strength of self-support and self-nourishment."[20] In this way, he emphasized self-help and integrity.

While criticizing the nature of militaristic social evolutionism, Pak affirmatively accepted the theories of evolution and progress. Based upon the theory of social evolution he pointed to his time calling it 'an age of seeking the new' which marched toward epoch-making progress in each field of society.

> "It is a natural trend that all people who can see and hear with their eyes and ears, move with their hands and feet, and feel with their hearts should follow the examples of evolution by watching the signs of the times. The signs of the present age — in the field of daily life agriculture changes to undustry and commerce, log cabins become brick and stone houses; in transportation and communications post-horse relays become telegrams and telephones; in vehicles sedan chairs become railroads; in the competition of weapons bows and arrows become guns; in navigation sailing boats become iron-clad steamships; in government absolute autocracy becomes equality; in thought respect for the old becomes new seeking. Without fitting oneself to the phenomena of universal change none could exist."[21]

Pak declared if we wish to confront imperialistic aggression in order to maintain our independence and existence we must adapt ourselves to the new mode of life fitting our new age. In other words, in industries we must develop industry and commerce; in transportation and communications we must develop telegraphs, telephones and railroads; in military and weapons we must develop guns and iron-clad warships; in government we must develop equality, and in thought we must adopt and develop methods fitting the seeking for the new.

According to Pak, therefore, education aimed at cultivating intellectual faculties must be new education; industry aimed at expanding power must be industry which utilized machinery.[22] Pak accentuated national salvation by industry to regain initiative strength in preparation for the restoration of national rights by confrontation with imperialistic aggression and he put it next to national salvation by education, because industry must be modern industry employing machinery which relies on scientific technology which depends on learning. Therefore, he found in learning and education the background resources for expansion of power brought back by the development of industry.

Pak tersely declared that superiority and inferiority in knowledge and power were the two determining factors which gave a sentence of life or death to each nation in the present age. Power comes from knowledge, and knowledge comes from learning, so a nation advanced in education may live and a nation wanting in education may die out. All who had ears could hear this truth.[23]

> "Because power is born of knowledge, and knowledge comes from learning, all civilized peoples of wealth and power in the present-day world are the fruits of advanced knowledge acquired through the encouragement of study in each country. Why should you seek it in another field?"[24]

One thing was clear to Pak, and that was that the idea of national salvation by industry comes next to the idea of national salvation by education.

When dwelling upon national salvation by industry for self-ruling power, Pak on many occasions referred to industrial schools, making a tie between industry and learning or education. For example, he proposed the theme, "who will deliver our country and who will give life to our people?" And he answered, "the industrial educationis is he." Thus he accentuated industrial education in the following words:

> "Today we Koreans under the present circumstances cry for a life-giver and seek a national leader, but where can we find them if it is not in the academic world? Even in the academic world whom should we call? Is it a political scientist, a doctor of laws, a doctor of science, a religous man, or an orator? These are all useful in the organization of government and society, but the most important man who can deliver our country from destruction and bring our people back from death is the industrial educationist."[25]

After stressing industrial education, Pak put emphasis on industrial establishments, saying that the establishment of industrial plants was the easiest way to build the foundation of national salvation by conquering poverty and winning wealth. He remarked as follows:

"The victory or defeat of a nation and the life or death of an individual depend on wealth and poverty, power and weakness. Nations and men are born equal, but some are rich and strong while the others are poor and weak. Why is that so? It is solely caused by full development or under-development of industry."[26]

Pak found industry to be the second method of national salvation which could help preserve the national strength and guarantee the existence of the weaker and smaller peoples through confrontation with the imperialistic aggression, as he declared that material civilization becomes the foundation of power and wealth.[27]

3. The Causes of Underdevelopment of Modern Industries

Pak first called the attention to his countrymen to six cardinal points which had become the fundamental causes of our underdevelopment of modern industries up to a standard of competition with foreign powers in his time.

1) Respect for empty literature without seeking practical utility.[28]

Pak sharply criticized the old learning in Korea centered on the study of Chinese philosophy, classics, decorum, poetry and odes which were useless in practical life. His statement was as follows:

"What is our learning? What are its arts and sciences? The philosophers sat erect on their bottoms with bent knees as they talked about the rule of heaven and human hearts and human nature or read Chinese classics and preached etiquette with which they spent their precious time, making it their · life task; the literati pirated some fine verses from archaic Chinese scriptures to construct line in flowery rimes for their imitation peoms and odes, thus dissipating their energies and idling away their golden hours,"[29]

He described the neglect of practical learning of natural science and technology in the old learning as the first cause of underdevelopment of modern industry.[30]

2) The plunder of people's property by the *yangban* mandarins and petty officials.

Pak severely criticized the corrupt officials of the *yangban* class for their theft and robbery of the accumulated wealth of the common people by unlawfully accusing them of all kinds of flase crimes and even by throwing them into dungeons, thus discouraging them from all thoughts of free trade to make their fortunes, because the accumulated wealth would often bring big misfortunes to their families. Pak stated as follows:

"The common people, having been oppressed and stripped by graft-happy officials, not only dared not run free business but the thrifty ones who enjoyed well-to-do lives with their honest products of labor were wrongfully arrested by government officials on false charges of various sorts such as unduti- fulness to parents and family discord, et cetera. They were flogged till they bled and their property confiscated and sometimes they died in prison. In this way their possessions of small farms and a few head of plowing cattle brought big missfortunes upon their families and their own bodies, ... They say robber, but the corrupt officials are the first-class robbers; they talk about traitor, but the official thieves are the worst traitors, aren't they."[31]

Pak also made a stern criticism of the gentlemen of noble birth as well as the petty *yamen* officials and clerks in the local governments for their plunder of the people's property.

"The so-called gentlemen of noble birth make it their family law to hang round the guest halls of powerful courtiers for office hunting and for stripping the country folks of everything valuable for their living while the country petty officials extort the people with the collection of heavy taxes which they put into their private purses and steal public and private property under the pretence of official power to fatten their black bellies."[32]

3) Pak pointed out the loafing country squires, local chieftains, prodigal bowmen (*hallyang*) geomancers and fortune-tellers— these free eaters of idle life were left to their easy going without any productive business to create more troublesome evils. He figured out the numbers of these kinds of parasites, free eaters hanging about their well-to-do friends and kinsmen instead of making their own living by honest labor, to be 3/4-4/5 of the total population of the country. An astounding fact, indeed! Pak deplored that the *laissez-aller, laissez-faire and laissez-passer* of these human locusts had becom the cause of the industrial backwardness of our fair land.

Pak made a comparison between Occdentals and the Orientals in the Land of the Eastern Sea (Korea), saying that the former of both sexes, young and old unless they were crippled went to work to earn their bread without hanging on other people, but on the contrary Koreans lived by mutual dependence, not only among family members of blood-relationship but among old acquaintances and distant kinsmen, expecting food and clothes with princely treatment for many days if not for life. That meant, even though there were twenty million people in the country only four or five million engaged in any productive business for livelihood, and the rest were parasites. Was there a hope to make them all happy with self-supply of comfortable life necessities?[33]

Pak says, still worse, the local chiftains and military playboys of free-eating clans roam about the country, bullying the peace-living and hard-working people, corrupting public morals, and damaging national life. His statement follows:

"The geomancers and divinators eat people's food and wear people's clothes for nothing while cheating the public with their weird soothsayings and the local chieftains and the military playboys run over the people to harass our brethren. These monsters are omnipresent throughout the country to corrupt public morals and hurt the national life beyond descrption."[34]

Pak pointed out the inability of twenty million people doing some productive job each by choosing some technical or vocational work without eating for nothing as a big problem and he always deplored it.[35]

4) Holding industry and commerce in contempt and maltreating artisans and merchants, a chief cause of hindrance to the progress and development of productive business.

Pak criticized the attitude of the educated toward industry and commerce, which they despised as the jobs of low-class people, looking down upon the artisans and merchants with the greatest scorn and contempt for their inferior skills. For this reason, far from making progress and development, handicrafts in domestic industry were degraded more and more till they dropped to the lowest point.[36]

5) Agriculture was regarded as of great importance,[37] but no serious attention was paid to the technical improvements of crop cultivation or the benefits of stock raising and seed breeding, a chief cause of hindrance to the development of agriculture.

Pak remarked; 'The farmers sing 'agriculture is on top; it is the fountain of life,' but their method of crop cultivation is primitive and they are wholly careless about the profits of stock raising and selection of new breeds ...[38]

6) Lack of international competition, a basic cause of underdevelopment of modern industry.

About this cause Pak showed a peculiar macroscopic insight into the matter. According to Pak, Western nations of similar magnitude rise vis-a-vis one another and develop various enterprises in competition. If a nation falls behind another nation it cannot exist by the law of survival of the fittest, so each nation compares strong points and weak points with one another, and when it finds a rival one step ahead in progress it makes strenuous efforts to march two steps forward. Thus new inventions and new manufactures appear endlessly to succeed in holding the power of civilization with national wealth. As a result, there arose in Europe world powers contesting for supremacy to becomes masters on land and mistresses at sea.

On the other hand, Pak continued, in the East, China, for instance, believing herself to be an unrivaled Celestial Empire with her vast territory, became haughty as Number One under heaven, looking down upon all other nations as barbarians and holding them in contempt. Due to this psychology of exaggerated vainglory which ruled the hearts of the Chinese the Celestial Empire dropped far behind the European nations in modern civilization for want of competitive spirit. Japan also had no power to compete with other nations but when she entered into treaty relations with Western powers she realized the world tendency and rose up to compete with other nations. As a result, she made swift progress in all fields of enterprise. As for Korea, even after the bitter experience of the Hideyoshi Invasion (1592-1598) and the Manchu barbarian conquest (1636) she had no heart to compete with other nations while her *yangban* sons were only busy in office hunting contests behind her closed doors. His statement is as follows:

"... But we the Oriental peoples are not so. China, which has a vast territory, regards herself as an unrivaled big power, assuming a big face and looking down upon other nations with scorn without a competitive spirit, so she drew back her head (like a turtle's head) and her national fortune gradually withered till she had fallen into decay in the present on earth today; Japan is a small country lying on the islands of the Eastern Sea. Until forty years ago her warlords contested with each other for political supremacy in endless armed conflicts to become shogun in the *Mikado* government minus competition with other nations, but since her entry into treaty relations with the Western powers she has awakened to the great tides of the world situation and she has made astonishing progress in leaps and bounds in all fields of enterprise.

As for Korea, she occupies a peninsula in the Eastern Sea with the least heart to compete against other nations to keep abreast of the times. Even though she experienced national disgrace in the Hideyoshi War of 1592 and in the Manchu barbarian conquest of 1636, still she placed sword below pen and her *yangban* were busy with factional strife and office hunting competition. How could she expect the development of enterprises or the expansion of national strength? Competitive heart! Is it not the decisive factor which determines the ups and downs of mankind?"[39]

Pak thought that it was a prerequisite to find the causes of under-development of modern industry in order to work out the ways and means of its progress. Thus in his patriotic enlightenment campaign, apart from relative success in national salvation by education, he pointed out the poor progress of the campaign for national salvation by industry, and urged industrialists to make strenuous efforts toward that goal of success.[40]

4. Reform of Scientific Technology and Industry.

In his idea of national salvation by industry Pak emphasized the reform of scientific technology most for its development. In his time, in view of the industrial conditions in the existing society and economy, not only the reform of scientific technology but the importance of the establishment of enterprising organizations by investments of capital was also keenly felt.

Pak of course urged capitalists and men of public spirit to collect shares to open businesses[41] and he also called upon them to establish stock corporations,[42] but the heaviest weight in his essays was on the development of technology in the natural sciences, which is the foundation of modern industry. He mentioned the scientific technology of the most advanced nations which developed after the Industrial Revolution. He accentuated the study of the same technology, and he drew the attention of the public to the importance of new inventions by men of science and new manufactures by captains of industry.[43]

It was Pak's thought that the evolution of civilization sprang from the evolution of scientific technology and also the law of the survival of the fittest as well as the principle of natural selection appeared in the evolution of technology.[44] Pak declared: "When telegraph and cable lines are laid out, post-horse stations and beacon fire towers must go out of existence; when steamships and railroad coaches offer services, sailboats and palanquins must be forsaken; when kerosene oil becomes the fuel of the lantern, sesame oil must to away; when matches makes ignition, flint must be of no use; when the demand for foreign paper increases, the production and sale of domestic paper must decrease; when spiral guns and repeating rifles become weapons, old-fashion cannons and fire-locks must fall into disuse. When and if cotton cloth as clothing material is imported in increasing quantities from foreign countries, the varieties of our native linen and cotton, silk and china grass must decrease. Pak repeatedly gave explanations of the following facts:

"When we observe the history of each nation on the earth, we find a definite truth. That is to say, when a civilized nation rose to power the barbarous race in the same land perished. As living evidence, we may mention the following facts: when telegraph and cable lines were laid out, post-horse stations and beacon-signal towers were done away with; when wheel-ships ploughed the sea and iron horses (trains) ran on the land, sailboats and sedan chairs were discarded; when petroleum oil came into use for fuel in lamps, sesame oil retreated; when matches made their debut as ignition tools, flints disappeared; when foreign paper satisfied its frequent demand local paper fell in supply; when spiral guns and repeating rifles appeared, old-fashioned cannons and matchlocks fell into disuse; when foreign cotton cloth and carpets overcrowded our markets, our native hemp cloth silk and china grass decreased in variety."

"Judging from the above facts, it is clear as daylight that the vicissitudes of human races are like this—when civilized nations dominate the world, barbarous nations must fall to extinction. In the face of an age of struggle for existence— our Han nation must stand on guard with awe and fear!"[45]

As an example, Pak mentioned the case of England, the wealthiest and most powerful nation in the world in his time. According to him, England was a small country in Europe, occupying land less than one-third of the area of Germany, with only a few million of population, but she developed civilization and expanded national strength to rise above all other nations, and within a few decades she acquired colonies (overseas possessions) far over the seven seas and increased her population to a hundred millions, because she was ahead of all other nations in the national scientific world and in material inventions, with the extraordinary development of industrial interests.[46]

In holding such a view Pak found the origin of British power and wealth in her Industrial Revolution, which had its origin in material inventions by improvements of scientific technology.[47] Moreover, Pak found the background of the successful overseas expansion of British imperialism in the advanced performance of the industrial Revolution.

As the most representative material inventions in the British Industrial Revolution Pak mentioned the following examples:[48]

1. James Watt, steam engine.
2. Richard Arkwright, hydraulic power weaving loom.
3. Pierre Martin, new blast furnace.
4. Samuel Crompton, new weaver.
5. William Murdock, gas lamp.

Pak said, "Besides, there are so many epoch-making new inventions related to the British Indutrial Revolution that I have no time to mention all of them. In brief, thanks to these material inventions of English brains the British empire has increased its national strength a hundredfold, unparalleled in world history, and the Union Jack has spread its influence of civilization all over the globe on which the sun never sets. Great is the power of material learning!"[49]

Pak mentioned steamships, railways and telegraph lines as exemplary inventions of the 19th century, then he described the following new inventions which appeared at the dawn of the 20th century to offer *de luxe* services for the convenience of mankind in modern living:[50]

1. The success in the Arctic and Antarctic Polar explorations and the support of scientific technology thereof.

2. The invention of an airship and its successful trial flight.

3. The American invention of a submarine which had a speed of more than 10 knots successfully.

4. The invention of a bicycle with which man made a round-the-world trip in 40 days at top speed.

5. Wireless receiving sets were operated over 3,000 miles on land and 6,000 miles at sea, and news was transmitted by wireless.

6. Wireless telephony was open as far as 550 miles.

7. Trains ran 99 miles and trams ran 92 miles an hour.

8. The *de luxe* (British) passenger boat Lusitania crossed the Atlantic in four days.

In comparing the above triumphs of scientific technology, Pak regretted deeply the backwardness of Korea at that time. He looked back on the great developments of scientific technology in ancient Korea when her manu- facturing industry was leading all other countries in the East. As genuine

evidence he mentioned the leather works of Koguryŏ; the ceramics, metal-
lurgy, saddlery, lacquerware and art decorations of Paekche; the iron-smithy,
lathe-works, embroidery, Buddhist image foundry, weaving work and ship-
building of Silla; and the cannon-making of Ch'oe Mu-sŏn of *Koryŏ*.[51]
Pak declared that the discontinuation of development of the ancient
scientific technology in Korea was due to her failure to continue study of
material civilization. His argument follows:

"Speaking of Korean civilization, she solely respected ethical culture
while despising material culture, resulting in the total lack of welfare
resources, the decline of industries and the corruption of national strength to
the extreme. Korea is endowed with natural products and human intelligence.
Had she studied her ancient culture of material civilization and continued it
she would not be lagging far behind other nations. When we look back on the
past, the Silla potters taught Japanese students, *Koryŏ* ceramics were prized as
world treasures, her movable type printing and her ironclad warships led all
other nations as the first inventions, and her proposal of coal mining
astonished the world, but alas! due to the absence of respect for material
civilization among our countrymen no one in the afterages was brave and
intelligent enough to promote the same arts and crafts with continued
study."[52]

Pak dilated upon the above subject, saying that in the Chosŏn period (Chosŏn dynasty) there appeared wonders like Yi Sun-sin's ironclad warships and
Hŏ Kwan's proposed use of coal for fuel, but the people failed to improve
ship-building technology or put in practice the use of coal, losing even the
original turtle boat and the empty essay on coal mining till they forgot to use
their own alphabet. Pak showed his regret as follows:

"Three hundred years ago Admiral Yi Sun-sin produced some iron-clad
warships called *Kŏbuk-sŏn* or Turtle boats which hand never been designed
by any Western Navy until that time (of the Japanese invasion under
Hideyoshi) and at that time a Korean called Hŏ Kwan expounded the benefits
of exploitation of coal mines, which was also unknown to the Europeans. Had
the Korean people continued the building of the Admiral's iron ships and
expanded naval strength and developed machine power by listening to Hŏ
Kwan's words to use coal, the Korean flag would have been flying in the

skies of Europe and America; but why did they look the other way and idle away the golden hours in noonday dreams and midnight revelries tell they fell into the present misery?"[53]

Pak's observation on the importance of reforms and new inventions of scientific technology was connected with the scientific insight of the future. When he heard the news of the new inventions of aircraft, airships, and flying pavilions and their flying tests he prophesied that in the near future there would be air living and world wars in the air. Then he gave a warning to his countrymen to awake to the fact that in an age of swift development of scientific technology a nation which boasted its archaic skills could handly compete with nations which performed such wonderful feats with advanced scientific technology. His statement follows:

"The occidentals make and break more records and fewer necks each day with their wonderful inventions of aircraft, airships, and flying pavilions which foretell their lives and wars in the skies. While the Western peoples are doing such wonders how can the Eastern peoples who sit and talk about the rule of sage kings under the trees of birds' nests in ancient caves make comfortable lives with competition? I wish to see the nose-diving birdmen make somersaults in the ninety-thousand *li* long skies!"[54]

Pak clearly saw the new scientific technology increase productivity a thousand-fold above human labor and increase national strength in the same ratio, and he summarized and effects in the following words:

"Their material research promotes the fruit of artificial labor by a thousand-fold, so their national power increases by a thousand-fold."[55]

Based upon these ideas, Pak put great emphasis on the reform of scientific technology as the foundation of industrial development, and this is a big feature of his idea of national salvation by industry.

For the intellectual background of his emphasis on the reform of scientific technology as the foundation of industrial development we may mention the following factors:

1. Pak found the strong points of the capitalistic structure of Western Europe in the capitalistic structure of industry. For this reason, he sought the special features of the capitalistic structure in the manufacture of goods in

industrial plants,[56] which view made him emphasize the reform of scientific technology as of decisive importance, and this view was different from that of some other thinkers on enlightenment who found the special features of capitalistic structure in commercial corporations.[57]

2. The backwardness of scientific technology in Korean society at that time made Pak emphasize the importance of the reform of that technology all the more.[58]

3. Pak's view of social evolution, which greatly influenced the intellectual structure of his patriotic enlightenment movement, made him emphasize the importance of the reform of scientific technology all the more[59] because the scholars who were greatly influenced by social evolution at that time and afterwards strongly felt that social evolution and technological evolution were cause and the effect.

4. When Pak pursued the substance of education as a means to cultivate self-governing real resources for the restoration of national rights he pursued the field of training scientific technicians for practical use as a matter of course — I mean industrial education and engineering education[60] together with military training in which he was deeply concerned in view of the general condition at that time. Resultantly, not only did he emphasize domestic education to acquire scientific knowledge, he urged the dispatch of young men abroad to study industrial sciences in wide fields in order to make his home country strong and his people happy.[61] The first importance of the reform of scientific technology appeared as one of the big features of his idea of national salvation by industry.

5. Industrial Development

Pak's idea of national salvation by industry conceived industrial development among all fields of productive industries as of the greatest importance. As we will see below, of course he also spoke about the importance of agricultural development, but he realized that in his age agriculture was changing to industry and commerce[62] and it was directly connected to the reform of scientific technology.

According to Pak, if one is to win in the struggle for existence one must win in the competition in production which must be done by manufacturing goods with renovations of producing methods considered to be the best and the fastest way. He explained it as follows:

Today if we are to escape failure and win victory in the struggle for existence we should emerge victorious from the competition in production of goods which are the elements of our living. If a country is rich with products its people will be well off in living; if the living is well off the people will be prosperous as a definite principle, because the products give us life. Then what is the plan to multiply products? It is the best way to make goods fast with improved processing methods.[63]

Pak said that the wealth and power of the European nations were the products of their development in industry and art manufacture (scientific technology) and the fall of Eastern country into decay was caused by the decline of industry and art manufactures. In connection with this view, he emphasized industry and scientific technology as the elements of all industries. He declared that even the military power of warships and guns would not be forthcoming without industry, goods transacted through commerce and trade would not be produced without industry, and agricultural implements, too, would not be furnished without industry, so the decline industry corrupted all industries. He described the reasons as follows:

"They respect industry to develop art manufactures, but we despised it, and this resulted in the decline of art manufactures. Engineering is the root of all sciences and the basic element of all business activities. A soldier or a sailor may have military science, but he cannot fight without warships and guns; a merchant may have commercial science, but he cannot do business unless he has the instruments which are the capital of his trade; a farmer may have agricultural science, but he cannot till the soil unless he is equipped with hoes, spades, and ploughs. Therefore, the decline of engineering means the decline of all sciences and the decay of art manufacture brings the decay of other manufactures. Therefore, the boom or slump of art manufactures is directly related to the rise or fall of a country."[64]

Pak declared that in our forthcoming commercial war, too, we could hope to emerge victorious only if we could produce goods of the best quality in the largest quantities. In this way he repeated his emphasis on the importance of the quickest industrial development.[65]

According to Pak, in ancient times Korea, too, made good development in industry to lead other countries in the East,[66] but for some centuries since the pre-modern days the philosophers, the poets, and the *yangban* officials had occupied the highest seats in the government to enjoy unlimited privileges, holding artisans in the greatest contempt and expelling them with their crooked arts and impure subtleties.[67] As a result, Korean industry had fallen into decay so that now Korea could not produce even her own clothes and her daily necessaries for home use, but had to rely on foreign imports, not to speak of the manufacture of steamships, trains, electric machines or ironclad warships. Pak said that if Korean people did not study scientific technology and did not develop industry Korea could never hope to enjoy happiness in this age of competition. Pak went on:

"The white-collar *yangban* despised industry and commerce and excluded artisans and merchants for shame as inferior people engaged in the lowest skills. Far from development, their standards dropped gradually to extremities thereby still our countrymen are unable to produce our clothing materials or daily goods for home use with our own handicrafts while relying on imported goods, much less the manufacture of steamships, trains, electric machines or ironclad battleships. Can these things fall from heaven or shoot from earth? While forsaking the study of industrial sciences can we hope to enjoy the blessings of existence in this age of competition?"[68]

Pak continued by criticizing the logic of the stubborn Confucian scholars for denial of modern industry in the following words:

"Some people with distorted views say — in the olden days our countrymen enjoyed happy living by using domestic products only. Even today if we wear linen, silk and China grass of our own country by boycotting foreign cotton or carpets they will have to produce or sell their goods to us no more; even though they lay out railroads, if we do not ride the trains they will have to remove the rails naturally for loss; if we use the sesame oil and flints only they will have to decrease imports of petroleum oil and matches— this is the best plan for our self-protection and self-integrity."[69]

But Pak made a rebuttal against the view of such Confucian scholars with his own argument declaring that view to be infeasible and impossible.
The following is Pak's argument:[70]
(1) In the living of mankind, it is natural that men seek profitable goods

instead of losing goods; demand quick services instead of slow services; take refined things instead of crude things.

(2) Comparing the products of our country with those of foreign countries, theirs are of superior quality and ours are of inferior quality; their goods are fine and our goods are crude. Who would buy expensive, crude, inferior quality goods instead of economic, fine, superior quality goods? Who would not seek profit and incur loss by saying categorically that the purchase of foreign goods means national loss?

(3) Now a man who wishes to travel between Seoul and Pusan (450.5 km) or between Seoul and Sinuiju (499.3 km) may reach his destinations in a day by rail whereas he has to consume a full ten days by palanquin. When he compared the time and speed required for his trip and calculated his travel expenses he would prefer the de luxe fast train to the palanquin or a native horse for hire unless he was a great fool. When a box of matches and a bag of flints are put in a room side by side before a man who wants a light, which would he prefer to take for use? About clothing materials, European cotton and velvet are superior in soft texture and long wear as against Korean linen, silk and China grass which are of inferior quality because of thinness and narrowness in size — which would you prefer to buy?

Pak says it is a rational mode of living to buy high quality goods economical in price and convenient for use which nobody can prevent. Likewise, in the love of one's country reasonable patriotism may be successful, but unreasonable patriotism may not be successful.

Pak declared the first road to Korean success in the solution of Korean national problems was to undertake industry at great speed, thereby to improve the process of mass production. Pak reiterated the above declaration as follows:

> "In this age of profit-making competition the Koreans, too, should undertake the production of native goods in large quantities by improved processes in order to preserve their national life."[71]

Then Pak said the fallen fortunes of Korean nation were caused by the decay of industry, and he urged the speedy development of industry in order to regain Korean national prosperity. His statement follows:

> "Since the fall of our country is in the fall of industry, on the day of the revival of Korean industry we can bring new life to it. Therefore, we the

whole people shall unite Korean hearts and souls to cooperate in industrial development to bring about good results."[72]

As the best method of the development of modern industry Pak emphasized the following points:

1) Study and extend the technology of the newest natural science.[73]

2) Finaciers and public-spirited men should collect capital stocks to invest in enterprises to establish factories with machine equipment.[74]

3) The people should invest their assets in the founding of stock corporations to operate joint businesses.[75]

4) Train and employ industrial technicians of superior ability.

5) Reform the process of mass production of domestic goods for competition with foreign imports.

6) Improve the quality of Korean goods for export to meet demand abroad.

Pak mentioned the cotton of Hwanghae-do and silk, silk gauze, and the fine-textured hemp cloth of Hamgyŏng-do in northern Korea which were highly reputed within the country, saying that due to the under-development of their reeling and weaving methods they looked too thin and inferior to foreign cotton and velvet for competition. He urged publicspirited financiers to establish textile companies with the installation of reeling and weaving machines, train and employ good workers, and to turn out high quality fabrics which could stand comparison with foreign-made goods.[76]

Pak also mentioned Korean native handicraft fabrics such as embroideries inter-woven with all kinds of designs—flowering vines, roses, maples, flowers and clouds, mountain chrysanthemums, and paulownia leaves, saying that these were finer than the Chinese products, and he praised the Royal Household Department for its planned production under a factory system by the establishment of a bureau of weaving.[77]

Pak mentioned the Ceramics Corporation in P'yŏngyang, the Integrated Iron & Steel Mill in Yŏngbyŏn, and the textile plant in Anju as the harbingers of representative factories in Korea.[78]

Not only the weaving mills mentioned above, Pak also cited the pig iron mill in Yŏngbyŏn and the sapphire mill in Tanch'ŏn which supplied the domestic needs of brass bowls and candlesticks inlaid with sapphire gems, urging further reform of its technology to produce export goods to satisfy demand abroad.[79] He declared that only by such production in modern factories to win in the international competition of specialites could Koreans hope to enjoy the blessings of life.

Emphasis on the reform of scientific technology together with industrial development forms one of the big features of his idea of national salvation by industry[80] and its intellectual background is social evolution.

6. Agricultural Development

Pak felt deep sympathy for farmers. He looked upon the agricultural community as the best society in the country, because the farmers' simplicity excluded sumptuous goods, their industry expelled idleness so as to dedicate their full measure of devotion to the country and to promote friendliness among the members of their community.

His statement follows: "Moreover, the agricultural community is the most ideal society under heaven, Farmers do not want luxuries, for they possess natural simplicity; they do not know idleness, for they are industrious. Being loyal and friendly, thy fair name is farmer!"[81]

Pak said that Korea was essentially an agricultural country, the overwhelming percentage of the entire population being engaged in agricultural pursuits of one kind or another, so she could expect wealth and power and civilization of her nation within a definite period if she could achieve agricultural development. He laid importance on industry as the element of all industries and he called agriculture the main body forming the fount of life.[82] Here we can see that he dealt with agriculture in a way somewhat different from industrial development. In other words, when he emphasized industrial development he proposed it with a methodological argument in principle for survival of the fittest of the times by emerging victorious in the struggle for existence externally. On the other hand when he emphasized agricultural development he urged the creation of a countermeasure for extrication from its traditional backwardness and against the Japanese policy of land exploitation internally.[83] Some special features of Pak's argument on agricultural development may be summarized as follows:

1) He had the deepest concern for the improvement of cultivation methods,[84] and among other things he emphasized new agricultural technology and the selection on new varieties of seeds.[85]

2) he emphasized sericulture (rearing of tussah-silkworms) in order to increase the incomes of farming families and to export raw silk for the reeling industry. Based upon the good results obtained from the collection of cocoons in Ch'ŏng-ju and Yŏ-ju by public-spirited capitalists of the Chŏndong tussah-silk company, Seoul, he mentioned the profit of sericulture as follows:[86]

(a) The climate and geological conditions of Korea are better fitted to silkworm raising than those of China and the planting of white-oak saplings occupies the greatest areas of forests throughout the country, making it most convenient for sericulture. That means all mountains and fields in the three-thousand-li-long peninsula are full of rich natural resources for that enterprise.[87]

(b) An official survey reports that if Korea fully developed her sericulture she could increase wealth up to 200,000,000 *hwan* (*won-yen*). equal to $100,000,000 annually.[88]

(c) The income is very high in comparison with the required investment of individual capital.[89]

(d) After short-course training from an instructor even women and children can engage in this vocation.

(e) In China exports of silk yarn increase yearly, occupying first place among her export items imported into Europe and America in recent years. Korea, being possessed of more favorable conditions than China, is more endowed with possible exports.

Pak said that unless we made strenuous efforts in sericulture now and did not put it off, the quick-witted Japanese would get the most profit. On this point he awoke the people to a desire for sericulture:

"My countrymen and lovers, look at the gardens, forests, and moun-tainsides in our fair land! You see everywhere the greatest natural resources that will bring you wealth as well as national power. Be diligent from today! If you don't and wait for tomorrow, someone with quick hands and swift feet will get it. A good opportunity once gone, may never come again. You cannot afford to be idle! Awake, brethren!"[90]

3) Pak emphasized the cultivation of cotton. He said that except for the mountainous districts in Kangwŏn and Hamgyŏng Provinces, the soil of the whole country was suitable for cotton cultivation, persisting that by supplying raw material to the cotton textile industry with the production of cotton bells Korea should prevent its importation and meet her own requirements for self-support. His argument is as follows:

"Except for two provinces — Kangwŏn and Hamgyŏng- the whole country, being favored with a mild climate and fertile soil, is suitable for cotton cultivation. Its rich soil is worth native gold as compared to that in Manchuria so the quality of Korean cotton boils is superior to that of India and it can contest for supremacy with the cotton bells of South America of high repute, as foreigners prove with praise. This inexhaustible rich natural resource appears before our naked eyes without waiting for foreign products— why do you sit idle without stretching your hands? Ah, miserable! I call upon domestic industrialists to pay attention to the fact that planting cotton seeds is encouraged even in Manchuria, unsuitable for cotton growth, and to engage in the cultivation of cotton plants."[91]

4) Pak encouraged the introduction of stock raising, too,[92] as he pointed out the drawbacks of the sole operation of the primitive agriculture of the plough, neglecting stock farming.

5) Pak also encouraged forestry development. As indirect effects brought about by the growth of trees in the forests he mentioned the following: (a) conservation of water sources, (b) prevention of sand-drifts, and (c) supply of pure and fresh air. Then as direct effects he mentioned building materials for houses, ships, and vehicles besides coffins, charcoal, and raw materials for tissues, and other forest products which forestry business could provide in more abundance.

As the chief causes of the under-development of forestry in Korea Pak mentioned the lack of guiding power of the government and the absence of an enterprising spirit among the people. As a special case, he cited a contemporary model gentlemen called Kim Ŭi-myŏng, who had planted Uch'i Hado-myŏn, Yangju-gun 10 years before to provide raw materials for sericulture, and cultivated weeping willows on Sŏk-to Isle in Miŭm-py'ŏng in Yangju-gun where 300,000 young willow trees of three to four years' growth stood and several millions of its saplings grew in perfect beauty. Pak praised this man as a national hero and exhorted his countrymen to model themselves on Kim Ŭi-myŏng and do their utmost in forestry enterprise.[93]

6) Pak also stressed the urgent need for reclamation of virgin soil and uncultivated land. He declared his age to be an age when the powers had adopted a colonial policy to transplant their own people to other countries to reclaim uncultivated land, so if Koreans do not exploit the virgin soil in her own land strong Japan will send out immigrants daily in growing numbers to occupy hers for good. Thus he rang an alarm bell to awake the senses of his people in the following words :

"Today the powers of the world make other countries colonies of their own by sending their immigrants to exploit waste land overseas under cover of big guns and super-dreadnoughts as vanguards and seize the possessions of the ignorant and inferior races. They cross over the wide oceans of tens of thousands of miles far away to execute their colonial policies by spending many millions of pounds and dollars. At this time if the power and intelligence of our race are inferior to those of other races our land, our houses, our products, and even our lives will not be our own. See the American red Indians. Formerly, there were several millions of them inhabiting the North American Continent, but now they have perished from the face of the earth leaving only ten thousand or so. In a few decades they will become an extinct race altogether. Heaven prefers the principle of the struggle for existence and the axiom of the survival of the fittest so exactly."

"At present, a strong race is squatting just across a narrow strip of water. Its colonists come over daily in growing numbers by boat and by rail to manage their colonization business in full swing to exploit our land and increase production here for their own benefit. How, can a poor race with an archaic mode of living in a dreamy land of Shan-gri-la without the knowledge of the times hope to exist?"[94]

By that time, in the wake of the "Protectorate Treaty" of 1905 the Japanese imperialists were preparing to begin occupation of uncultivated land in Korea,[95] so Pak gave an alarm to his countrymen to wake to danger and he urged a counter-measures to meet the emergency.

7) Pak urged tree planting.[96] In January 1908 the Japanese government promulgated a forestry law which aimed at the seizure of Korean forests. So he awoke his countrymen to prepare counter-measures to protect their private forest land. His warning is shown below:

"A law governing forestry and the regulations of its enforcement have been announced in the official Gazzette and the various newspapers by order of the government. Alas, our country! Do you know what a forestry law is? It is a law which fixes the areas of state and private forest land by the method of surveying to distinguish one from the other. Applications for certification of private forest land, duly measured by surveying methods, are required to be registered with the Department of Agriculture-Commerce-Industry. In default of this instrument (title deeds) all land is to be incorporated in state property; when private forest land becomes state property it might be occupied by a foreigner for exploitation. In that case the rightful owner may not be able to claim his ownership as private property. Then the large mountain estates together with hundreds of years' old pine trees which have been preserved by the owners for many generation as the sentinels of his forefathers' graves will be lost and the pallid bones underground will`find no repose. Even though he cries to heaven and stamps his feet on the earth all is unavailing."[97]

At that time the Japanese government (Resident General) promulgated a forestry law through the Korean government, announcing incorporation into state property of all forest land minus official registrations of title deeds.[98] Therefore, Pak gave the above warning in order put up direct resistance to the aggression of the Japanese imperialists, protect private forest land, and develop forestry undertaking with Korean land.

Pak's argument on agricultural development was concentrated on the reform of agricultural technology and on polygonous agricultural development aimed at a direct resistance to the Japanese policy of extortion of farmland, uncultivated land, and forest land in Korea in order to keep the landed property of Korean farmers and to develop Korean agriculture, it is thought, but regrettably, he did not present the requirements of land reform or proposals therefor. For these reasons, we need further observation in the future.

7. National Military Power and Industries

Pak developed his ideas in connection with his patriotic enlightenment campaign which he expanded in full swing in the period after military Japan robbed the Korean empire of her sovereign powers by coercing a protectorate treaty in the year 1905 under duress and at the point of the sword in the wake of her victory in the Russo-Japanese War; hence he had a strong concern for armed forces and military power.

Here, our attention is drawn to the fact that he believed the foundation of military power to be industry — in particular, an industry based on highly advanced scientific technology. For close inter-relations between military power and industry Pak mentions the following four points:

(1) Peter the Great of Russia arose in the vast wasteland of Northern Europe and annexed many neighboring countries and wielded his power all over the globe in confrontation with Western Europe as a result of his denial of the pleasures in his palaces and his pursuit of engineering in shipyards abroad as a plain workman.

(2) Had Germany had no Krupp guns or Thomas repeating rifles early produced in her arsenals she could hardly have emerged victorious in the

France-Russian War even with the political strategies of Bismarck and the military tactics of Moltke.

(3) Had America had no gigantic iron and steel mills or petroleum oil she could hardly have made the influences of the great merits of Geroge Washington and the great tasks of Abraham Lincoln widely felt all over the world.[99]

(4) There will be air battles due to the invention of aeroplanes, sky dreadnoughts, and flying pavilions in the future world.[100]

Based upon the above observations, Pak averred that the manufacturing industry was the first element of national power and wealth.[101]

Pak's modernistic view of military power on the foundation of industry appears in all his writings. In his *"Mongpae Kŭm T'aejo,"* too, he placed military training and industrial education side by side to show their essential mutual relations in national power and wealth.[102]

It is interesting to note that Pak had an early insight into the coming dogfights in the sky. It seems that he hit on this idea by making a connection between the development of aeroplanes and sky dreadnoughts and military power as soon as he had heard of their flying tests. Of course his opinion dawned upon him from a combination of foreign news and various reports received, but nobody at that time made a forecast of air battles after reading such reports, whereas Pak foresaw tragic scenes in the air with his keen observation and introduced the foreign news with his commentaries in his leading articles in the *"Hwangsŏng Sinmun"* telling of the arrival of an age of air battles,[103] then he rewrote his manuscript about the subject and had it inserted in *"the Sŏbuk Hakhoe Wolbo"* to enlighten the members of the same Hakhoe (educational association).[104]

To be sure, at that time foreign news agencies reported the following: ① Graf von Zeppelin of Germany floated his balloon (Luftschiff) which flew about two or three hours covering 300 miles between Lake Konstan and Bittelfield; ② the Zeppelin-type air boat made a successful trial flight with 36 passengers and various cargoes on board and obtained good results; ③ Regular airship services were begun for the convenience of traffic between Lake Lucerne in Switzerland and the Friedrich River in Germany: ④ A new-type military planc of England made a successful flight; ⑤ The Wright brothers of America made secret experiments with airships on return from their trip to Europe; ⑥ Claytole of the Bluebill Astronomical Observatory in America, charged with the duties of measuring wind power for sixteen years, announced his plan to fly across the Atlantic in a light balloon from Boston to England, saying that he could cover the distance of 3,000 miles in four days in a favorable wind; ⑦ A billionaire in England ordered from an airship building company attached to the Luinuxe Shipyard a flying pavilion, which was then in the making.[105]

While editorializing on such a topic for the introduction of new events based on reports an inference flashed into his inward eye, reasoning "Where do air life and air battles come from? Since the Occidentals invent aeroplanes, airships, and flying pavilions to bring good results in succession, why not air lives and air battles in the future world?"[106] Then he arrived at that conclusion with conviction,[107] and he forecast air battles by the invention of aeroplances to be a big revolution in war in the future world.[108]

After the reception of the above foreign reports with a combined analysis, Pak foresaw a big convulsion in the social life of mankind with air living and air fighting in future, because he knew that the changes in scientific technology would bring big changes in social life and big changes in the military power of the imperialistic age, thereby bringing big changes in the mode of war, it is thought.

Such an insight of Pak was inferred from his idea that manufacturing industry was the first element of a nation's power and wealth. Pak, who had personally experienced the aggression and military strength of the imperialistic powers, made his intellectual orientation emphasizing the development of business and manufacturing industry as the prerequisites for augmenting national military strength for confrontation with those aggressions. This idea of Pak was further developed in connection with his conclusion that manufacturing industry was the first element of a nation's power and wealth, it is interpreted.

8. National Wealth by Labor

At the root of Pak's idea of national salvation by industry lies a supporting reason; "Labor and service are the foundations of national wealth." He avers that labor is the chief factor in making wealth for national power and the personal independence of individuals. He says, "From labor comes freedom of the people and independence of the nation."[109] Then he says, "Labor is the root of life and the source of wealth."[110]

Pak pointed out the idle habits of the people without respect for labor as the root of the national poverty as he declared in the following words:

> "The agricultural yields from our fields, the aquatic goods in our seas, and the forest products in our mountains are out rich natural resources which heaven has given us as gifts, but why are we so poor and exhausted in life,

both public and private? This is because our brethren are in the habit of idleness and leisure, being ignorant of the dignity of labor. If we had kept ourselves busy in our daily trades like the people in the civilized countries we could have made our country rich and strong long ago with the development of our land and its products."[111]

"Today Korea is poor, weak, and exhausted in the extreme. Why is that so? Because, having enjoyed peace without war calamities for many hundred years the society in general has been accustomed to leisure and idleness to eat without going to work. Our misery today is the result of our hatred for work yesterday."[112]

Pak sharply criticized all kinds of unproductive modes of life including idle poets who only foster eating without work.[113] He said that if all people, every one of them, engaged in productive occupations to work hard each individual home and the state would become rich and independent — the harder they worked the more wealth they would acquire,[114] Then he concluded: "The self-supporting life of oneself comes from his labor. If one man's labor brings self-supporting independence to himself, his family will be independent with self-support; if one family is independent with self-support by labor the state will be independent through self-support."[115]

Pak's idea of labor and its basic importance has a deep root, for he thinks that man's body, mind, intelligence, productivity, business, and fortunes grow with labor and the energy of labor. He stated as follows: "Man's body becomes strong with labor; his mind is tempered with labor; his knowledge grows with labor; his production increases with labor; his business develops with labor; and his fortune prospers with labor. God loves a man of labor and gives him blessings, but a man without labor becomes weak and suffers illness; he becomes idle and low-spirited, ignorant, foolish, and must hunger, his business withers, his virtue is extinguished, his fortunes go away, and calamities arrive. The rise or fall of a nation depends on labor or laziness."[116]

From his view of labor the power of a nation is not found in the houses of wealth but in the sources of wealth — the inexhaustible labor power. He declares that the capital of our life is in our labor power and national power is also in our people's labor. Therefore in order to cultivate our national power we must increase our labor power. His argument went on:

"Those who talk about national power must not demand it from the houses of wealth but from the sources of wealth, for the houses of wealth may fall to poverty in due course, but the sources of wealth are inexhaustibly supplied from labor, ... " He continued:

> "Our living capital is in our individual labor; our national wealth is also in the sum total of labor of our people. Laborers foster the moral virtue of simplicity which extinguishes evil deeds of immoral outlaws, so the men who eats the fruits earned by the sweat of their brews never lust after unreasonableness. All public-spirited men who wish to cultivate the power of our nation and to purify the public morals should stand at the foremost front to increase the labor power of our countrymen."[117]

Pak's above view on labor came from his thorough-going observation of the evils of habitual idleness and his relentless criticism of the philosophical thought and mode of life of the *yangban* and Confucian scholars and after the orientation of his own thought on the foundation of modern science.

Pak's argument on national wealth by labor represents his idea of national salvation by industry and his idea of patriotic enlightenment, and it forms the intellectual background of his proposed reform of the existing social customs and bad habits.

9. Conclusion

From the above observations on Pak Ŭn-sik's idea of national salvation by industries we can understand that he was not a spiritualist or a conceptionalist, by which names he was known in the past.

Methodologically his idea of national salvation by industry was aimed at the orientation of Korea's self-strengthening efforts toward the restoration of national rights by practical resistance to the Japanese imperialistic aggression and her theft of Korea's national sovereignty, and theoretically it presented a change of phase in resistance to the aggression of imperialism from the standpoint of a weaker nation with the explanations of the social evolution of the jungle law.

The subjects which were dealt with in his idea of national salvation by industry were later represented in the phrase, "national body-strength" which included money, grain, army, fortified cities and moats, warships, and machines. In brief, national spirit is the basic problematic-consciousness in his idea of national salvation by industry.

As a self-strengthening method for restoration of national rights Pak mentioned industry next to education. This is a highly rational constituent for the solution of the national tasks enunciated in his patriotic enlightenment at that time.

Pak surprisingly grasped the contents of the Industrial Revolution begun in England, but he found its source in the reforms of inventive scientific technology rather than in the structures of the capitalistic social economy, as a special feature of his observations.

Pak observes national competition as power competition, so he looks upon the superiority and inferiority of power as reflections of the development and underdevelopment of industry, saying that the standards of industrial development are determined by the standards of development of their productivity which are determined by the standards of their scientific technology. Accordingly, he takes the view that national competition becomes competition in products of industries, whose superiority or inferiority are determined by the advanced or backward nature of their scientific technology.

From this point of view Pak's idea of national salvation by industry emphasizes most of all the reform of scientific technology and the development of industry as a method of cultivation of real power which could lead Korea to victory in the competition in products. For this reason, he mentioned factory industry of high productivity based upon the newest advanced scientific technology as the only factor which could decide the status of Korea whether it was victor or vanquished in the fierce competition in products with the powers, adding that this rule should apply to the economic independence of Korea. He laid stress on the importance of national military force in connection with the imperialistic aggressions of the powers at that time, but he kept his ground consistently that a strong military force could only be maintained on the basis of advanced industry and advanced scientific technology.

Based on this viewpoint, Pak proposed as the methods of industrial development the following requirements; ① Study and expansion of technology of natural science, ② Establishment of factories equipped with machines, ③ Establishment of stock corporations, ④ Training and employment of skilled technicians in industrial plants, ⑤ Reform of the manufacturing processes of our goods capable of competing with foreign goods, and ⑥ Methods of production of desirable exports.

Pak's emphasis on industrial development was related to the fact that he viewed the essence of the modern capitalistic structure as industrial capitalism and not as commercial capitalism.

In his argument on agricultural development, too, Pak laid stress on a resistance struggle against the Japanese colonial policy of land occupation on one hand and the reform of agricultural technology, improvement of varieties, sericulture, cotton growing, stock raising, forestry exploitation and land reclamation on the other, but he dropped his argument on land reform against the landlord-tenant system which had done much evil at that time.

Finally, we find in Pak Ŭn-sik's idea of national salvation by industry his stress on industrialism and scientific technology minus commerce, which had been emphasized by many other leaders in the campaign for patriotic enlightenment as he found the fountain of the power of Western Europe in his age in industrial capitalism and he tried to find the same power also in industrialism in Korea for his people to struggle against the inroads of alien imperialists.

In Pak's idea of national salvation by industry labor was stressed; thus he made an orientation of his industrial philosophy with good logic, which was represented by fundamental and comprehensible requirements in strong terms unlike other thinkers on patriotic enlightenment.

From the viewpoint of today Pak's idea of national salvation by industry reached many marginal points. Nevertheless, the writer thinks his idea to be an appropriately high standard intellectual system which approached a most scientific and reasonable realism to solve the knotty problems of national tasks in his age. Moreover, the scientific substance of this idea is good enough to disarm the mistaken criticisms which charge him with being prejudiced in favor of spiritualism and conceptionalism in his idea of patriotic enlighten-ment.

FOOTNOTES (Part III–16)

1. Shin Yong-ha (1) "About Pak Ŭn-sik's Idea of National Salvation by Education," *Hankuk Hakpo*, No. 1, 1975. (2) "Pak Ŭn-sik's the Theory of Seeking New in Confucianism, the Philosophy of Wang Yang-ming, the Ideology of Grand Union," *Yŏksa Hakpo*, No. 73, 1977 (3) "Pak Ŭn-sik's View of History," *Yŏksa Hakpo*, No. 90 and 91, 1981.

2. Pak Ŭn-sik, *Hankuk T'ongsa*, Section III, Chapter 61, Conclusion, 1915, Shanghai; *cf. Pak Ŭn-sik Chŏnsŏ*, Vol. 1, pp. 376-377.

3. Pak Ŭn-sik's Law of Bisection is similar to that of Western Europe, but the substance is somewhat different from the latter in which government and law are not included in the national spirit in express provision as institutional culture, so the sphere is not clear, but in Pak's case government and law are theoretically included in the national spirit even though there is no express provision of them. Then about the relationship of the two, Pak emphasized their union and balance in his conception from the beginning whereas in the conception of Western Europe there was a premise regarding the separation and unbalanced provision on one side in the beginning.

4. *Pak Ŭn-sik Chŏnsŏ* (hereafter Complete Works), Vol. I, p. 376. As examples of countries which had wielded power by conquering other countries when their national bodies were stronger than their national spirits, but even the capabilities of their national spirits shrank back when their military strengths became weak he mentioned Hsienpi, Khitan, and Mongolia; as an example which had suffered foreign aggressions for time when her national spirit was stronger than her national body, but soon she assimilated the aggressors upto the spheres of capabilities of their national spirit he mentioned China (Middle Kingdom); as an example which came back to new life when her national spirit became strong, he mentioned Turkey.

5. In Pak's thought alleging the theory of seeking new ideas in Confucianism on the basis of Wang Yang-mings study there were potential powers of conceptional prejudices in the theory itself, except for the trends of contemporary Confucian scholars who aligned themselves in the pro-Japanese camp and those who utilized Confucianism for practical purposes by its general mobilization in the campaign for recovery of the national rights.

6. "Korean Spirit, Written in Blood (series)," *Taehan Maeil Sinbo*, issue No. 623, dated September 26, First year of Yunghui (1907), *Complete Works*, Vol. 2, p. 73.

7. "Questions and Answers about Self-Strengthening Capabilities," *Taehan Cha'gang-*

hoe Wŏlpo, No. 4, *Complete Works*, Vol. 2, pp. 68-69.

8. "Happy New year!" *Sobuk Hakhoe Wolpo*, Vol. 1, No. 19, *Complete Works*, Vol. 2, p. 64. "Alas! We cannot censure the past, but we can pursue coming events... Develop education and promote industries with all capabilities available." This kind of argument appears everywhere in his articles on patriotic enlightenment.

9. "Thanks to our brethren in Hawaii," *Taehan Cha'ganghoe Wŏlpo*, No. 5, *Complete Works*, Vol. 2, p. 75.

10. In this case this trend of conceptional spiritualism was expressed after the loss to Japanese imperialism of national rights and all parts of the national body‒ money, grain, army, fortified cities, moats, warships, and machines, except national religion, national learning, national language, national script, and national history, corresponding to national spirit, together with national culture, which might be preserved, therefore, it is emphasized getting an understanding by connecting it to the peculiarities of the contemporary social conditions.

11. *cf.* Shin Yong-ha, "Pak Ŭn-sik's, View of History."

12. *Mong-pae-kŭm-T'aejo*, *Complete Works*, Vol. 2, p. 209.

13. "No education, No life," *Sŏu*, No. 1, *Complete Works*, Vol. 3, p. 86.

14. Korean Spirit, *Taehan Cha'ganghoe Wŏlpo*, Issue, No. 4, *Complete Works* Vol. 3, p. 67.

15. "Questions and Answers about Self-strengthening Capabilities," *Complete Works*, Vol. 3, pp. 68-69.

16. "No education, No life," *Complete Works*, Vol. 3, p. 87.

17. *Mong-pae-kŭm-t'aejo*, *Complete Works*, Vol. 2, pp. 213-215.

18. *Mong-pae-kŭm-t'aejo*, *Complete Works*, Vol. 2, p. 309.

19. "Questions and Answers about Self-strengthening Capabilities," *Complete Works*, Vol. 3, p. 69.

20. *Mong-pae-kŭm-t'aejo*, *Complete Works*, Vol. 2, p. 215.

21. *Mong-pae-kŭm-t'aejo*, *Complete Works*, Vol. 2, p. 217.

22. "No education, No life," *Complete Works*, Vol. 3, p. 87.

23. *Mong-pae-kŭm-t'aejo*, *Complete Works*, Vol. 2, p. 247.

24. "No education, No life," *Complete Works*, Vol. 3, p. 87.

25. "Who will save our country? Who will help our people? The industrial scientist is he." *Sŏbuk Hakhoe Wŏlpo*, Vol. 1, No. 7; *Complete Works*, Vol. 3, p. 35.

26. "Who will save our country? Who will help our people? The industrial scientist is he." *Complete Works*, Vol. 3, p. 36.

27. "Material civilization becomes foundation of power and wealth," *Hwangsŏng Sinmun*, September 27, 1908, Editorial.

28. Shin Yong-ha, "About Pak Ŭn-sik's idea of national salvation by education."

29. "Who will save our country? Who will help our people? The industrial scientist is he.," *Complete Works*, Vol. 3, p. 36.

30. *Mong-pae-kŭm-t'aejo, Complete Works*, Vol. 2, pp. 225-228.

31. "Congratulations with hundred bows on the founding of the Sukch'on-gun-Kalsan-dong Agricultural Cooperative," *Sŏbuk Hakhoe Wŏlpo*, Vol. I, No. 5; *Complete Works*, Vol. 3, p. 34.

32. "Who will save our country? Who will help our people? The industrial scientist is he." *Complete Works*, Vol. 3, p. 36.

33. "People's self-support in life brings national independence," *Sŏu*, No. 8; *Complete Works*, Vol. 3, p. 22.

34. "Who will save our country? Who will help our people? The industrial scientist is he." *Complete Works*, Vol. 3, pp. 36-37.

35. *Mong-pae-kŭm-t'aejo, Complete Works*, Vol. 2, pp. 242-244.

36. "Who will save our country? Who will help our people? The industrial scientist is he." *Complete Works*, Vol. 3, p. 37.

37. "Congratulations with hundred bows on the founding of the Sukch'on-gun-Kalsan-dong Agricultural Cooperative," *Complete Works*, Vol. 2, p. 246.

38. "Who will save our country? Who will help our people? The industrial scientist is he." *Complete Works*, Vol. 3, p. 37.

39. "Man's enterprises develop for themselves through competition," *Sŏbuk Hakhoe Wŏlpo*, Vol. 3, No. 16; *Complete Works*, Vol. 3, pp. 65-66.

40. "Happy New Year!" *Complete Works*, Vol. 3, pp. 64-65.

41. "Who will save our country? Who will help our people? The industrial scientist is he." *Complete Works*, Vol. 3, p. 37.

42. "Company Booms Bring Life's Bloom," *Hwangsŏng Sinmun*, December 29, 1905, Editorial,

43. "Man's enterprises develop for themselves through competition," *Complete Works* Vol. 3, p. 65.

44. "New Inventors of the Twentieth Century," *Hwangsŏng Sinmun*, November 13, 1909, Editorial.

45. "An Essay on the Improvement of Materials," *Sŏbuk Hakhoe Wŏlpo*, Vol. I, No. 8; *Complete Works*, Vol. 3, p. 38.

46. "Who will save our country? Who will help our people? The industrial scientist is he." *Complete Works*, Vol. 3, p. 36.

47. The opinion of seeking the ultimate source of the Industrial Revolution of England in the reforms of technology by inventions of scientific technology still prevailing as a powerful academic theory today.

48. "Who will save our country? Who will help our people? The industrial scientist is he." *Complete Works*, p. 36. In the background of such an opinion of Pak is the influence of K'ang Yu-wei's argument on national salvation by materials, it is presumed. *cf.* "Top Urgency of Study of Materials," *Hwangsŏng Sinmun*, November 13, 1908, Editorial.

49. "Who will save our country? Who will help our people? The industrial scientist is he."

Complete Works, Vol. 3, p. 36.

50. "New Inventors of the Twentieth Century," *Hwangsŏng Sinmun*, November 13, 1909, Editorial.

51. *Mong-pae-kŭm-t'aejo, Complete Works*, Vol. 2, p. 301.

52. "Material Civilization Becomes the Foundation of Power and Wealth," *Hwangsŏng Sinmun*, September 27, 1908, Editorial.

53. *Mong-pae-kŭm-t'aejo, Complete Works*, Vol. 2, pp. 218-219.

54. "Air Life and Air War in Future World.," *Sŏbuk Hakhoe Wŏlpo*, Vol. 1, No. 15, *Complete Works*, Vol. 3, pp. 55-56.

55. "Who will save our country? Who will help our people? The industrial scientist is he." *Complete Works*, Vol. 3, p. 36.

56. "An Essay on the Improvement of Materials," *Complete Works*, Vol. 3, p. 38.

57. For instance, Yu Kil-chun regarded the capitalisti structure as a commercial capitalistic system in essence.

58. "New Inventors of the Twentieth Century," *Hwangsŏng Sinmun*, Nov. 13, 1919, Editorial.

59. "New Features of our Weaving," *Hwangsŏng Sinmun*, Nov. 18, 1909, Editorial- 'Today man's vital energies and the production of goods have reached an age of intensive and extreme competition. It is as clear as daylight that we can never hope to enjoy happiness of existence without the progressive capabilities of our home-made manufactures.'

60. *Mong-pae-kŭm-t'aejo, Complete Works*, Vol. 2, p. 305.

61. "Who will save our country? Who will help our people? The industrial scientist is he." *Complete Works*, Vol. 3, p. 37.

62. *Mong-pae-kŭm-t'aejo, Complete Works*, Vol. 2, p. 217.

63. "An Essay on the Improvement of Materials." *Complete Works*, Vol. 3, p. 38.

64. "Chamber of Industry," *Hwangsŏng Sinmun*, September 11, 1909, Editorial.

65. "Look out for the preparations of a commercial war!" *Hwangsŏng Sinmun*, February 5, 1910, Editorial.

66. *Mong-pae-kŭm-t'aejo, Complete Works*, Vol. 2, p. 301.

67. "Chamber of Industry," *Hwangsŏng Sinmun*, September 11, 1919, Editorial.

68. "Who will save our country? Who will help our people? The industrial scientist is he." *Complete Works*, Vol. 3, p. 37.

69. Pak's proposition of this problem is against the xenophobies who cried out for prohibition of foreign commerce and a ban on alien goods.

70. "An Essay on the Improvements of Materials," *Complete Works*, Vol. 3, pp. 38-39.

71. *Complete Works*, Vol. 3, p. 37.

72. "Chamber of Industry," *Hwangsŏng Sinmun* , September 11, 1909, Editorial.

73. "New Inventors of the Twentieth Century," *ibid*, November 13, 1919, Editorial; "Chamber of Industry," *ibid*, September 11, 1909, Editorial.

74.   "Who will save our country? Who will help our people? The industrial scientist is he." *Complete Works*, Vol. 3, p. 37.

75.   "Company booms bring blooms to life," *Hwangsŏng Sinmun*, December 29, 1908, Editorial. − 'Facing tragedy to this extreme. This shall be our first aid− that industrialists quickly establish stock corporations with joint management of business. At present, the people in the civilized nations enjoy happiness in life by expansion of their industrial companies. If we should raise shares from the public and set up manufacturing factories and textile mills the capitalists will obtain profits by providing funds and the poor will find employment by offering labor, so all will enjoy the benefit with equal opportunity to make their living in the companies by hundreds and thousands. If such companies expand their business operations throughout the country there shall be no unemployed people. Thieves and burglars shall cease to exist and the wealth of the private persons and the public institutions shall increase daily.'

76.   "An Essay on the Improvement of materials," *Complete Works*, Vol. 3, p. 39.

77.   "New Features of Our Weaving,"*Hwangsŏng Sinmun*, Nov. 18, 1909, Editorial.

78.   "Harbingers in the Industrial World," *ibid.*, June 3, 1910, Editorial,

79.   "An Essay on the Improvement of Materials," *Complete Works*, Vol. 3, p. 39 − 'The cotton in Hwanghaedo, the silk and silk gauze in P'yŏngando, and the fine-textured hemp cloth in Hamgyŏng-do are the most illustrious products of our country, but the reeling and weaving methods are primitive without improvement− the textiles, being narrow in width and thin in quality, cannot stand competition with the broad cotton cloth and velvet of foreign exports.'

80.   Pak also laid importance on commerce, but he regarded it as in adjust to industry, for he always said, "Who will save our country? And who will help our people? The industrial scientist is he." *cf. Complete Works*, Vol. 3, pp. 35-37.

81.   "Congrarulations with hundred bows on the founding of the Sukch'ŏn-gun-Kalsan-dong Agricultural Cooperative," *Complete Works*, Vol. 3, p. 35.

82.   "A Complimentary address to the graduates of the Agricultural Vocational Training Institute," *Hwangsŏng Sinmun*, March 31, 1910, Editorial.

83.   Course of Survcying attached to the school, *Sŏu*, No. 17; *Complete Works*, Vol. 3, pp. 98-99.

84.   "Congratulations with hundred bows on the founding of the Sukch'ŏn-gun-Kalsan-dong Agricultural Cooperative," *Complete Works*, Vol 3, p. 35.

85.   "Who will save our country? Who will help our people? The industrial scientist is he," *Complete Works*, Vol. 3, p. 37.

86.   "An encouraging address to our country brethren on the occasion of opening business of Tussah-silk," *Sŏbuk Hakhoe Wŏlpo*, Vol. 1, No. 15; *Complete Works*, Vol. 3, pp. 52-53.

87.   *Ibid.*, p. 53 − 'The Tussah-silk business was commenced in Shantung, China, where the production of silk, yarn increased annually, leading all items of Chinese exports of

Enurope and America in recent years. The climate and geological condition in our country are more suitable to the rearing of tussa and the Tussal-oak saplings are most numerous of all trees in our woods, so this kind of sericulture is very convenient everywhere in Korea.'

88. "An encouraging address to our country brethren on the occasion of opening business of Tussah-silk," *Complete Works*, Vol. 3, p. 53⁻ 'More recently, the Japanese conducted an investigation of the tussah-silk belt throughout Korea and submitted a report in which it was estimated that if tussah-rearing was developed in full swing it would make increased production of silk valued at 200,000,000 hwan (yen at the rate of 2 yen to the dollar) by years. Formerly, our brethren had no information on its business, its way, and its profit, but now have seen and heard of its experimental results. Still don't you want to obtain a property of 200,000,000 won each year in this business!'

89. *Ibid.*, Vol. 3, p. 53 — 'The tussah-silkworm rearing business requires very little capital. If you invest a fund of 200-300 won in it you will get a profit of 2,000-3,000 won or at least 1,000 won. It means by cultivation of tussah-oak saplings on land of 50 hectares you will get a profit worth ten-fold the amount invested. It is worth trying by all ambitious farming families. Those who wish to get information on its rearing methods are required to obtain membership in the Chŏn-dong tussah company. Instructions and silkworm eggs will be provided on request. After a rearing experiment all women and children may learn the trade without difficulty...'

90. *Ibid.*

91. "Impressions of the theory of cultivation of cotton of the Manchurian species," *Hwangsŏng Sinmun*, September 14, 1909, Editorial.

92. "Who will save our country? Who will help our people? The industrial scientist is he." *Complete Works*, Vol. 3, p. 37 and *"Mong-pae-kŭm-t'aejo, Complete Works,"* Vol. 2, p. 246.

93. "Pioneer industrialists in Korean forestry World," *Hwangsŏng Sinmun*, September 15, 1909, Editorial.

94. "Course of surveying in the school," *Complete Works*, Vol. 3, pp. 98-99.

95. Shin Yong-ha, "Land Survey by the Japanese Government-General and the State Property, *Yŏktŏ Tuntŏ* (Postland and land for the border guards)," *Seoul National University Economic Review*, Vol. 17, No. 4, 1978.

96. "Gongratulations with hundred bows on the founding of the Sukch'ŏn-gun-Kalsan-dong Agricultural Cooperative." *Complete Works*, Vol. 3, p. 34.

97. "Course of Surveying in the school," *Complete Works*, Vol.3, p.99. Pak's establishment of a course of surveying attached to the Sŏbuk Hyŏpsŏng Hakkyo at that time is viewed as one of his efforts to protect the forest land and uncultivated land of the people from Japanese occupation.

98. Shin Yong-ha, "Land Survey by the Japanese Government-General and the State

Property, Yŏktŏ Tunto."

99. "Who will save our country? Who will help our people? The industrial scientist is he." *Complete Works*, Vol. 3, p. 36 —'Peter the Great of Russia arose in the vast wasteland of Northern Europe and annexed many neighboring countries and wielded his power all over the globe in confrontation with Western Europe as a result of his denial of the pleasures in his palaces and his pursuit of engineering in shipyands abroad as a plan workman, because he had a keen insight into the truth that the manufacturing industry is the first element of power and wealth of a large nation; Had Germany had no Krupp guns or Thomas repeating rifles early produced in her arsenalsshe could hardly have emerged victorious in the Franco-Prussian War even with political strategies of Bismarck and the military tactics of Moltke; Had America had no gigantic iron and steel mills or petroleum oil she could hardly have made the influences of the great merits of George Washington and the great tasks of Abraham Lincoln widely felt all over the world.'

100. "Air lives and air battles in the future world," *cf. Complete Works*, Vol. 3, pp. 55-56.

101. "Who will save our country? Who will help our people? The industrial scientist is he." *Complete Works*, Vol. 3, p. 36.

102. "*Mong-pae-kŭm-t'aejo*" *Complete Works*, Vol. 2, p. 305.

103. *cf.* "Portents of the War History of Flying Boats," *Hwangsŏng Sinmun*, Oct. 3, 1909, Editorial.

104. *cf. Sŏbuk Hakhoe Wŏlpo*, Vol. 2, No. 15, August 1, 1909 (the third year of Yunghui), pp. 23-25.

105. "Air lives and air battles in the future world," *Complete Works*, Vol. 3, pp. 55-56.

106. *Sŏbuk Hakhoe Wŏlpo*, Vol. 2, No. 15, p. 24.

107. "Air lives and air battles in the future world," *Complete Works*, Vol. 3, p. 56.

108. *cf.* "Portents of history of flying boats," *Hwangsŏng Sinmun*, Oct. 3, 1909, Editorial.

109. "Self-supporting life of each person brings the independence of the nation." *Complete Works*, Vol. 3, p. 21.

110. *cf.* "Labor is the capital of life," *Hwangsŏng Sinmun*, Nov. 4, 1909, Editorial.

111. "Self-supporting life of each person brings the independence of the nation." *Complete Works*, Vol. 3, p. 22.

112. *cf.* "Labor is the capital of life," *Hwangsŏng Sinmun*, Nov. 4, 1909, Editorial.

113. *Mong-pae-kŭm-t'aejo, Complete Works*, Vol. 2, pp. 242-244.

114. *cf.* "Labor is the capital of life,"*Hwangsŏng Sinmun* , Nov. 4, 1909, Editorial.

115. "Self-supporting life of each person brings the independence of the nation." *Complete Works*, Vol. 3, p. 22.

116. *Mong-pae-kŭm-t'aejo, Complete Works*, Vol. 3, pp. 235-236.

117. *cf.* "Labor is the capital of life," *Hwangsŏng Sinmun* , Nov. 4, 1909, Editorial.

17. Enlightenment Thought of Sin Ch'ae-ho

1. Sense of Problem

Sin Ch'ae-ho (pen name Tanjae) was a great patriotic enlightenment thinker, historian, and independence leader whose activity stretched from the latter half of the 19th century to the first half of the 20th century.

Sin's career and achievements can be reviewed by dividing them into five stages. The first stage was a period of growth from his birth to the time when he embarked on social activity. Sin Ch'ae-ho was born a son of Sin Kwang-sik, a poor family in Sannaeri, Taedok County, South Ch'ungch'ong Province in November 1880. His family originally came from the ruling *yangban* class, a descendant of Sin Suk-chu. Sin Ch'ae-ho's grandfather was a *yangban* who, having passed the civil service examination, served in a post of the senior sixth rank at the court. The fortunes of his family, however, went to ruin at the time when his father was married. Consequently his father had to move his family to Ch'ae-ho's grandmother's home in order to seek a livelihood. The new place was located in a different *ri* of the same county. When Tanjae was born, his family plunged into a state of greater impoverishment so much so that they had to live on soybean gruel. Making matters worse, his father died when Ch'ae-ho turned eight years of age.

After his family lost its head in extreme poverty, it moved to join Ch'ae-ho's grandfather at his home at the Sin family's original home in Kwirae-ri, Nangsŏng-myŏn, Ch'ŏng-wŏn County, North Ch'ungch'ŏng Province, because it could find no other recourse. These vicissitudes finally made Ch'ae-ho grow up under the tutorage provided by his grandfather.

Sin Ch'ae-ho's grandfather was strongly imbued with the *yangban* consciousness as a descendant of Sin Suk-chu of the Sin of Koryŏng; and it seems that he was considerably rigid and strict in personality. When Sin Ch'ae-ho failed to grasp or recite immediately what was taught by his grandfather, he used to whip his little grandson severely. Under such feudalistic education provided by his grandfather, Sin Ch'ae-ho received lessons on Chu Hsi's Neo-confucianism early in his life, finishing reading *Chach'itonggam* (資治通鑑) by the age of nine and the Four Books and Three Classics (of Confucianism) by the age of 13. At a tender age he already displayed his genius, showing the talent of keeping in memory whatever he had read once. In other words, Sin Ch'ae-ho received education in orthodox Neo-Confucianism in a thorough manner under tutorage of his grandfather.

On the other hand, it seems, Sin Ch'ae-ho was indifferent to or lagged behind other boys in matters other than study. He looked ignorant of the world dull and indistinct, indifferent to food and clothing, and unable to express his feelings adequately. Consequently his friends and villagers used to criticize Sin Ch'ae-ho as being ignorant of affairs of the world, dull, and foolish except that he was excellent in study.

At the age of 18 years, Sin Ch'ae-ho obtained an opportunity to use a private collection of books housed at the paternal home of Sin Ki-sŏn, an intimate friend of his grandfather's, in Mokch'on. Sin Ki-sŏn was a cabinet minister from the conservative clique and exerted great influence in political circles. Struck with admiration by the boy's astounding talent, Sin Ki-sŏn sent him to Seoul for admission to *Sŏnggyun'gwan* (National Academy). Presumably Sin Ki-sŏn's intention was to bring up Sin Ch'ae-ho, a talented young man who had been educated in orthodox Neo-Confucianism, into an important scholar-bureaucrat for the conservative faction by providing him with an opportunity for advanced study at the nation's highest institute for Confucian learning in Seoul.

In 1898 when he came up to the capital and was enrolled at *Sŏnggyun'gwan*, however, Sin Ch'ae-ho witnessed the rise of an independence, civil rights, and self-help movement winning enthusiastic support from all the citizens until December that year under the leadership of the *Tongniphyŏphoe* (Independence Club) and the *Manmin Kongdonghoe* (People's Assembly). Seeing the movement, Sin Ch'ae-ho was initiated for the first time into the thought of civil rights and could avail himself of an opportunity to learn modern knowledge. He realized that Chu Hsi's Neo-Confucianism was already an old learning for his times and that it was unable to help people solve the problems of the new age. At last Sin Ch'ae-ho took part voluntarily in the civil rights movement organized by the *Manmin Kongdonghoe* in autumn 1898. He was elected to a post as a member of the youth cadre at the Department of Documentation. We find him in the list of more than 430 members who were arrested up to December 25, 1898, when the two organizations were disbanded forcibly. His participation in the movement marked a start in his official social activities with the aim of creating a new chapter in the nation's modern history. His participation and activities in the independence, civil rights, and self-help movement led by the *Manmin Kongdonghoe* marked a decisive moment for the conversion of his thought.

After his participation in the *Manmin Kongdonghoe* activities, Sin Ch'ae-ho was no longer a conservative scholar-bureaucrat but began to convert into a modern youth who shared the same ideal with the enlightenment and independence faction. One example was that, in 1901 after the disbandment of the *Tongniphyophoe* and the *Manmin Kongdonghoe* Sin Ch'ae-ho returned to *Mundong hakwon*, an institute established in Inch'a-ri near his native village, where he emphasized a change in the trend of the times and asserted the uselessness of the Chinese classics while teaching at the school to be finally rejected by rural scholars.

The assertion of the uselessness of the Chinese classics was a very radical view by the standard of his times; and this was clear evidence that Sin Ch'ae-ho had already converted himself into a young scholar of the enlightenment party.

The second phase of Sin Ch'ae-ho's career began in 1905 when he devoted himself literally with a self-sacrificing spirit to a patriotic enlightenment movement with the aim of restoring the national sovereignty after the so-called *Ŭlsa* Treaty under which Korea was forced by imperialist Japan to degrade herself in to becoming the latter's protectorate and ended in April 1910 when he exiled himself abroad.

In 1905 Sin was employed by the *Hwangsŏng sinmun* as an editorial writer of the recommendation of Chang Chi-yŏn (pen name Wiam). After an editorial by Chang, entitled "We Wail Aloud This Day," in which he exposed the true intention of and bitterly criticized the so-called Ulsa Treaty, incited the Japanese authorities to take the measure of suspending the publication of the newspaper, Sin Ch'ae-ho moved to the *Taehan maeil sinbo* as an editorial writer on the recommendation of Yang Ki-t'ak (pen name Un'gang) in 1906. With the foundation of the *Sinminhoe* (新民會) as a secret organization by patriotic enlightenment leaders in April 1907 on the initiative of Yang Ki-t'ak and An Ch'ang-ho, Sin became its leading member. It was during this period that the name Sin Ch'ae-ho came to the fore to remain immortal in the history of Korea and his patriotic enlightenment thought and his launching in earnest of a patriotic enlightenment movement exerted profound influence on the public.

Sin wrote a very large number of commentaries in the *Taehan maeil sinbo* with a view to awakening the people, while contributing editorials to the *Taehanhyophoe wolbo* and *Kiho hunghakhoe wolbo*, both monthlies. On the other hand, he edited the *Kajong chapchi* (1908), a home magazine written purely in, for the purpose of enlightenment the womenfolk. His patriotic zeal, new thought, magnificent style, and sharp criticism which were contained in his editorials and commentaries impressed and awakened all readers and the people of his times, including young men and women.

His writings elucidated well the thought to which the *Sinminhoe* dedicated itself; and Sin was an outstanding theoretician and spokesman for the organization even though he was not named so officially.

Sin was also deeply absorbed in historical study at that time. In 1908 he authored *Toksasillon* (讀史新論), a serial essay on Korean history, which is rated as an immortal achivement since it founded the science of history for Korea's modern age on the basis of nationalism. In 1907 he translated into Korean *The Biographies of the Three Greatest Heroes at the Time of founding Italy* written originally by Liang Chi-chao of China. Afterward he authored biographies of three Korean heroes who are eminent historical figures: *The Biography of Yi Sun-sin, the Greatest naval Hero* (1908), *The Biography of Ulchi Mun-dok* (1909), and *The Biography of Ch'oe To-t'ong, the Giant in the Eastern Country* (1909). With these works he tried to stimulate patriotism among young students and the public.

Seen from the socio-historical point of view, it was during this period that Sin Ch'ae-ho exerted the greatest influence on the Korean people and society and made the greatest contribution to study on Korean history.

After An Chung-gŭn shot Ito Hirobumi to death (in October 1909) and the Japanese military police arrested leaders of the *Sinminhoe* and released them on an individual basis in February in the following year, Sin Ch'ae-ho, in accordance with a decision reached at a conference of *Sinminhoe* leaders, exiled himself abroad in April 1910 as a member of a group of the leaders who decided to do so.

The third phase of Sin's career covered the period from 1910 to 1925 when he engaged in the independence movements as a popular nationalist leader and in historical study.

In accordance with a decision reached at a conference of exiled *Sinminhoe* leaders in Chingtao, Sin went to Vladivostok during this period for the purpose of founding a military academy and establishing a base for the independence army outside Korea. Hearing the news of the annexation of Korea by Japan in August 1910, the leaders, as indignant as they were, decided to form an independence army with Korean youths abroad and make an attack on the Japanese occupation army in Korea immediately instead of embarking on the long-range plan of founding the military academy and establishing a base for the independence army. However, the plan of organizing an independence army immediately failed on account of the shortage of funds and the arrest of some of the leaders. Afterward Sin Ch'ae-ho was invited to the *Kwŏnŏp sinmun*, an organization newspaper of Korean residents in Vladivostok, as its editor-in-chief.

At the invitation of Sin Kyu-sik (pen name Yegwan) Sin Ch'ae -ho went to Shanghai in 1913. Until the outbreak of the Independence Movement on March First, 1919, Sin spent his days without relation to any organizations in order to explore remains from ancient history scatted in many places of Manchuria including the monument in the tomb of the Koguryŏ King Kwanggaet'o, to visit his colleague who were scattered in many places throughout China for discussions to formulate an independence movement strategy, to study Korean history, and to contribute articles to Chinese newspapers. At one time during this period he formed connections with Taejonggyo (大倧敎).

With the establishment of the Korean provisional government in shanghai after the outbreak of the March First Independence Movement at home, Sin joined, becoming a member of the legislature at first and elected chairman of the Whole-House Committee at the fifth conference of the legislators in July that year. As the provisional government named Syngman Rhee (Yi Sŭng-man) as its temporary president and Rhee's request for trusteeship over Korea came to his knowledge, Sin voiced his object to the plan and withdrew from the provisional government. In October 1919 Sin was named editor-in-chief of the *Sin taehan*, a weekly newspaper which was opposed to the provisional government. Sin criticized the provisional government and fought the *Tongnip Sinmun*, its organ, in a battle of words. In January 1921 Sin inaugurated the, *Ch'ŏn'go* (天鼓), a magazine, criticizing the direction the previsional government was taking for independence. When the provisional government broke up into two factions - the Reconstruction group and the Creation group - and a conference of national representatives was held at around that time, Sin sided with the Creation group.

In compliance with a request by the Ŭiyŏltan (義烈團), Sin drafted "the Declaration of Korean Revolution" in 1923. He also promoted his historical studies energetically, making public a series of dissertations such as "An Inquiry into the Former and Latter Three Han States (1924)," "Changes in Korea's Ancient Literature and Poetry (1924)," "On the Method of Interpreting Nouns Described by the Idu System (1924)," "Research on the East and the West Referred to in *Samguksagi* (1925)," "Corrections on Some Descriptions in Biographical Notes on the Eastern (Korean) Nation in San-Kuo-Chi (1925)," "An Inquiry into the River P'aesu in P'yongyang (1925)," and "The Greatest Incident in 1,000 Years of Korean History (1925)." (These dissertations were published at home in 1930 in a book entitled *Excerpts from*

My Study of Korean History.) He contributed *Ancient History of Korea* to the Chosŏn *Ilbo* in 1931 to be published serially. He contributed another work, *Ancient Cultural History of Korea* to the same newspaper, which carried it in serial form from 1931 to 1932. It seems that the two works were written during the 1921-1924 period.

The fourth phase of Sin Ch'ae-ho's career covered the period from 1926 to 1928 when he was arrested by the Japanese after activities as an anarchist.

There were three courses taken for national independence after the March First Independence Movement. They were the nationalist independence movement, the communist independence movement, and the anarchist independence movement. While the first two courses were overwhelmingly strong, the last course was insignificant in terms of influence.

Having expressed dissatisfaction at the civic nationalist trend which emerged after the March First Independence Movement, Sin began to incline to anarchism with his drafting of "the Declaration of Korean Revolution" in 1923 as a turning point, writing *New Years Free Notes by a Wanderer* (1925) in which he expressed his anarchist thought and affiliated himself with the Anarchist Eastern League in 1926, through which he launched anarchist activities. Sin engaged in positive organized activities at around that time while contributing articles to *T'alhwan* (Recapture) and *Tongbang* (The East), propaganda magazines for anarchism.

In cooperation with his Taiwanese comrade named Lin Ping-wen, Sin Ch'ae-ho played the leading role in holding a conference of the Anarchist Eastern League at Peking in April 1928. He drafted a declaration at the Peking conference; and he and his comrades agreed to publish a magazine or a newspaper as a propaganda organ for the Korean independence movement and establish a bomb manufacturing plant with the purpose of blasting Japanese offices.

In order to raise money needed to put the decision into practice, Sin and Lim who worked at the Postal Affairs Management Bureau in Peking decided to forge foreign drafts. They printed 200 forged foreign drafts amounting in value to 64,000 yüan; and Lim succeeded in drawing out 4,000 yüan in Tairen in April 1928 but was arrested by the Japanese police while he was making an abortive attempt to exchange another 2,000 yüan at Kobe, Japan. Under an assumed name, Yu Pyŏng-t'aek, Sin Ch'ae-ho arrived at Keelung, Taiwan, by way of Kobe in May 1928 in order to obtain 12,000 yüan, an amount he was held reponsible for raising; but he was arrested by the Japanese maritime police shortly before landing and escorted to Tairen.

Although Sin's activities in earnest as an anarchist continued only for a relatively short period of three years, this period witnessed a surprising change take place in the process of his independence movement. In "The War of the Dragons"which Sin wrote in 1928, he expressed his anarchist thought in a frank manner.

The fifth phase of Sin Ch'ae-ho's career covered the eight years from 1928 when he was arrested by the Japanese police, sentenced to ten-year imprisonment, and began to serve his term at the Lushun prison in isolation from any organization and society to February 21, 1936, when he died of cerebral haemorrhage as a martyr for the nation ending his eventful career.

Any long-term imprisonment of an independence leader seems to require special research. If Sin Ch'ae-ho had not died in prison but had written a note on his life in prison after release from captivity, the public could have known something of the changes in his mental state. However, he did not leave behind anything like that; and consequently it would be difficult to judge his mental state while in prison. Nevertheless, we know something: While serving his prison term, Sin asked mainly for books of history and historical materials to be sent to his cell and told a newspaper reporter who interviewed him that he alone could write "The History of the Chosŏn dynasty's Four-Party Wrangling" and "The History of the Six Kaya States"in a proper manner. In a letter sent to Hong Myŏng-hŭi (Pyŏkch'o), he wrote to the effect that he was worried about the possibility that his manuscripts for "An Inquiry into Vicissitudes in the Great Kaya State"and "A Brief Biography of Chŏng In-hong" would be buried with his death. It can be presumed that while in prison he was more interested in Korean history than in anarchism and had plans for various writings.

Below we will review characterisitics of Sin Ch'ae-ho's patriotic enlightenment thought during the second phase of his career (1904-1910) when he exerted the greatest influence on the people and society and he played the greatest role in the historical perspective among his many achievements during his checkered career.

2. Imperialism and Nationalism

First of all Sin Ch'ae-ho observed that his time was "an age of imperialism and nationalism." According to Sin, imperialism was a gift given by Europe. Needless to say, it was a practice even in the primitive age that the stronger devours the weaker and the bigger annexes the smaller. However, Sin pointed out, it was due to European civilization that the time-honored practice was institutionalized, spreading all over the world in the form of aggression and territorial partition, he went on to say:

> "The world is now an imperialist one. The pratice already existed in the primitive age that the stronger devours the weaker and more vehement in the modern age, with the result that the great drama played by imperialism sways over the world. Strong European nations, armed with their powerful weapons, are overrunning to the east, occupying Africa to the south after dividing the continent, and taking possession of Oceania to the southeast. Wherever their feet touch, mountains and rivers quake, and wherever their banners flutter, heaven and earth change."[1]

He deplored the fact that "The so-called six world powers or eight world powers in the six continents in the East and in the West worship imperialism with all their might and all their efforts. While they competed with each other, all peoples in the world submit themselves to the imperialist thought and policies they pursue. The whole world has now become and arena for action dramas presented by imperialist powers."[2]

Sin interpreted imperialism on the basis of "socal Darwinism" which was prevalent at the time. For him imperialism was based on the principle that the weak fall prey to the strong, with strong nations occupying weak nations by employing their superior weapons, military might, and economic power. In short, imperialism was understood by him as aggression in all parts of the world in his times (around 1908) as follows:

First of all, England occupied all of southern Africa, constructing a railroad across it. On the other hand, England also occupied many places in south Asia, having already taking possession of Australia.

France robbed lands in and around the Sahara Desert, annexing Madagascar, conquering Indochina, watching for an opportunity to advance to southern China.

Czarist Russia invaded Eat Asia, constructing the Siberian railway as far as to the Pacific coast. To the right Russia subdued Afghanistan and to the left it invaded Mongolia and Manchuria.

Such other European countries as Germany, Portugal, Spain, and the Netherlands are competing with each other in exploring colonies in Africa, Latin America, the Pacific, and in all parts of the world.

The United States of America, having discarded the Monroe doctrine in the last years of the 19th century, adopted imperialism, provoked the Spanish War, and annexed the Hawaii Islands and the Philippines.

Even Japan, having established a modern state through reformation, though belatedly, came to be greedy for the vanity of imperialism in imitation of the European powers after winning the Russo-Japanses War. She devised a strategy to colonize Korea with the aim of establishing a base in Manchuria.[3]

According to Sin, any country which became a protectorate as a victim of imperialist aggression must do its best to restore its lost national sovereignty and any country which has already become a colony must launch an independence movement and recapture its independence. Also the most effective means of opposing imperialist aggression is to promote nationalism. However, Sin observed, nationalism can be divided into two patterns when seen in a broad perspective. One is expansionist nationalism which aims at expanding abroad. Sin saw that imperialism was too one form of expansionist nationalism like the one pursued by the European power and Japan. The other was nationalism with which the weaker nations tried to resist imperialist aggression. This form of nationalism was aimed not at expansion abroad but at resisting espansionism and protecting the nation. Therefore, according to Sin, nationalism has two sides. Namely, "imperialist nationalism" and "nationalism resisting imperialism." The form of nationalism which Sin ch'ae-ho stressed was the latter, namely, "nationalism resisting imperialism." Sin emphasized that the only way to repulse imperialist aggression and protect the nation was to encourage nationalism. He said:

"What, then, is the method of resisting imperialism? This is to encourage nationalism (the ism of rejecting intervention by other nations). This form of nationalism is truly the only method of protecting the nation. When this form of nationalism becomes strong and formidable, any hero, however great he may be, has to lose his men just like Napoleon who had to throw his soldiers into the flames of the capital of Czarist Russia. When their nationalism grew weaker, even the eminent fighters of Arabia had to weep at the loss of their national sovereignty. Alas! Any nation which wants to protect itself has on other recourse than to stick to nationalism. If, consequently, nationalism displays its masculine fortitude, it can protect the nation from an aggression attempted by any expansionist form of nationalism, that is, imperialism, no matter how atrocious and sinister it may be. In short, imperialism can find its way into a country whose nationalism is enfeebled.

Why has the Korean peninsula, as beautiful as silk and flowers, been degraded into a dark den? It was because the Korean people failed to develop their nationalism strong enough.

It is sincerely hoped the my dear compatriots will promote their nationalism greatly, believing that we are the masters of our nation and we must make all decisions for ourselves in our endeavor to insure our national survival."[4]

Sin emphasized that, if nationalism is to grow into "one that can effectively resist imperialism" and if nationalism is to prevent itself from being degraded into imperialist nationalism, it must by all means combine itself with "liberalism."

According to Sin Ch'ae-ho, a country can realize "reform, revolution, independence, self-strengthening, self-reliance, unification, national welfare, and national autonomy" for itself only when it succeeds in combining nationalism with liberalism. Sin presented examples which he found in Occidental history. When nationalism was combined with liberalism, Sin observed, "the first English revolution could sing a triumphal song, the second French revolution could spread its great waves, the United States could obtain independence, Germany could strengthen herself, Belgium could become self-reliant, Italy could achieve national unification, the European powers could broaden the scope of their national welfare, and South American countries could win independence."[5]

One thing we must pay attention to here is that the form of nationalism which Sin asserted and emphasized was one that was based on liberalism, namely, "liberal nationalism" in order to repulse Japan's imperialist aggression and achieve national reform, revolution, independence, selfstrengthening, self-reliance, unification, welfare, and autonomy.

3. Restoration of National Sovereignty and Patriotism

First of all, Sin Ch'ae-ho asked the Korean people to look squarely at the fact that their country was deprived of parts of its national rights, such as diplomatic, military, financial, and other rights, by Japan's imperialist aggression under the *Ŭlsa* treaty of 1905 and the *Chŏngmi* seven-article treaty of 1907. He explained to his 20 million compatriots that the deprivation of their national rights under the name of "protectorate" meant their being placed on thorny mats and their "enslavement" in a colony which was as bad as hell.

According to him, the first thing the Korean people were asked to do was to recognize correctly "the objective point toward which they should advance their country." Sin explained that some people stressed the promotion of education as the most urgent task for the Korean people, some the development of business, some the reform of social customs, some the establishment of new morals, etc., but these might become methods to reach the objective point but could not be recognized as the object itself. Sin Ch'ae-ho clearly defined that "the objective point for the Korean people to strive to reach at that time was to restore their national sovereignty, independence, and freedom."[6]

Sin emphasized that, once the "object for the people" was fixed to be "restoration of national rights," the Koreans were called upon to make all-out efforts to realize that purpose.

Nevertheless, the Korean people lacked the power to restore their lost national rights at the moment. According to Sin, it was apt that the Korean people would fall into despair when they saw the enormous "disparity" between the ability of the imperialist aggressor and that of the Koreans who had been deprived of their national rights. Sin flatly rejected such "despair" which arose from comparison between imperialist Japan and Korea as they were at that time. If one was gripped by despair, all would end in vain.

Sin encouraged his compatriots that, even though their ability to oppose imperialist aggression was actually very weak, their future would be bright because their "national hope" for restoring their national rights and establishing a strong and wealthy, self-reliant, independence, free, and civilized country was very deep-rooted.[7]

According to Sin, the Korean people could first undertake the task of building up their ability by displaying patriotism while recognizing their fragile reality but never losing hope for the future even though their ability to oppose imperialist aggression was actually very insufficient at the moment.

According to him, if the whole people were filled with patriotism, they would be able to restore their national rights in the not distant future of the basis of their patriotism as generation power. Sin saw that patriotism is the mother who gives birth to the power to oppose imperialist aggression when a nation lacks it. He said: "The rise or fall of a country depends on whether its people have patriotism or not."[8] With this saying Sin stressed the importance of patriotism under the circumstances in which the Taehan Empire was situated at that time.

Sin saw that patriotism was the ultimate generating power with which to build up the ability to restore the lost national rights when a nation was short of or lacked the power to resist imperialist aggression. For this reason he emphasized "patriotism as the base for restoration of national rights" above anything else.

4. Discourse on New Nation

Never giving himself up to despair upon seeing the miserable reality facing the nation, Sin Ch'ae-ho devised various plans to nurture the ability to restore national rights and establish a new nationalist independence state with patriotism as generating power and presented them to the people.

Sin clearly declared that the political system of the new state to be constructed after restoring national rights should be a constitutional government. He divided the process of development in the state life of mankind into ① the age of tribal chieftains, ② the age of aristocrats, ③ the age of autocracy, and ④ the consitutional age, explaining that his time corresponded to the constitutional age.[9]

Sin asserted that a constitutional state could be regarded as a "national state" and, citing European examples, positively praised the constitutional republican system by saying that "the gospel of constitutional republics is spreading far and wide, the stage becoming a paradise for the people, and the people becoming the master of the state."[10] His praise of the constitutional republican system seems to be related to the fact that the *Sinminhoe* for which Sin had once acted as spokesman decided the policy to a new state to be established to be a republican system.[11]

According to Sin, the motive power for the competition among national states which was taking place in the 20th century rested not with one or two leaders but with the people as a whole and a victory in the competition was owing not to one or two leaders but to the people as a whole. Politicians competed in politics, religious leaders in religion, businessmen in business, some with military might, and some in science; and those who proved themselves to be superior won and those who proved themselves to be inferior were defeated. Their competition could be considered to be a "competition among the people as a whole," he said.

Consequently, according to sin, the "whole Korean people" should become a "new people" if they were to restore their lost national rights from Japanese imperialism, establish an independent "constitutional republic," and guarantee the nation's development and happiness. In other words, the whole Korean people should be made new and become a "new people" in the political, economic, educational, scientific, social, cultural, moral, military, and all other fields in order to enable them not only to build up their modern-age ability and restore their national sovereignty but to establish a new constitutional republic and insure their own happiness.

Explaining that the cause of Korea's defeat by Japan was that the Korean people were not a new nation, Sin made various proposals aimed at making the Koreans a "new nation" in all fields, as we will see in the following chapter.

Sin also asserted that, when the new nation was educated, its organization had to be created at the same time for the restoration of national rights. This was because the new national strength to be displayed by the new nation could be exercised effectively only through organization.[12)]

5. Discourse on New National Salvation Education

As a means of bring up the people into a "new nation" and establishing a "new country," Sin Ch'ae-ho asserted "new education" and "national salvation education."

Characteristics of his discourse on new national salvation education were as follows: First, he asserted "patriotic education." According to him, education and patriotism are in mutually inseparable relations. He explained that education without patriotism is incomplete and patriotism without being accompanied by education is liable to become blind and to be unable to attain purposes. Good education is essential for filling the mind of people with patriotism and patriotism can arise from good education. The effect of good education, according to him, will result in giving birth to national unity and strength able to restore national rights.

Second, Sin divided education into three categories: home education, school education, and social education. At that time most patriotic enlightenment leaders stressed only school education. However, Sin emphasized home education and social education as much as school education, accentuating adult education at home and in society with a view to helping them acquire new knowledge and promoting patriotism in their minds.

Third, Sin, concerning school education, proposed "early-age commencement of education" in view of the tense situation of his time. Details of his proposal were as follows: At the age of four years children are admitted to kindergartens in order to make them observe what classroom lessons are like. At the age of seven children are enrolled at primary schools to attend elementary courses. At the age of 10 they advance to middle schools for higher courses. At the age of 13 they are enrolled at colleges to be trained in specialized courses for graduation at the age of 15.

Answering the question if his proposal for a system of early-age commencement of education was too excessive, Sin explained as follows: There are four-year-old children who are already well versed in the Book of One Thousand

Letters, beginning to learn *Tongmongsŏnsup* (童蒙先習, a reader for beginners). In the old days in Korea we found 10-year-old children who were well versed in the Confucian classics, also proficient in versification. This means that such children surpass the academic background which is required to attend today's middle school courses providing the new learning. In view of this fact, there seems no reason why a child who displayed such ability in the old learning cannot display the same in acquiring the new learning.

Furthermore, Sin sought the necessity of early-age schooling in the requirements of the situation. In an emergency, a boy who has turned 15 years of age can be regarded as a fully grown man. He must make a firm decision and sharpen his spirit, assuming the duty of joining talented young men of the whole country in the movement to restore national sovereignty with courage and vigor. In order to make this possible, boys must be helped to be graduated from college at the age of 15 years, so that they will be able to pour their youthful vigor into the drive to restore lost national rights. In short, Sin asserted early training of useful men for the restoration of national sovereignty.

Fourth Sin emphasized the importance of physical education very much.[13]

Accepting the theory of dividing pedagogics into education for knowledge, education for virtue, and physical education. Sin said that the most ideal form was balanced development of the three. In the Taehan Empire, according to Sin, the importance of education for knowledge and education for virtue was well recognized but the importance of physical education was rather neglected. He observed that "physical education can make the body vigorous, elate the spirit, cultivate skills, and train students in the martial arts." As the reason he thought physical education was most urgent, Sin explained that, unless one's body is healthy, one cannot acquire knowledge and cultivate virtue because an unhealthy body destroys the sources of both knowledge and virtue. For this reason he emphasized that bodily health should be placed above all.

It seems that the background of Sin's emphasis on physical education went beyond this. He stressed physical education because he attached importance to "education holding the martial spirit in esteem." Sin believed that, without "education holding the martial spirit in esteem," it would be impossible to display and maintain the national spirit, nationalism, and a civilization-centered attidude in the age of militarism and imperialism, with the world powers fighting each other, and without it, it would also be impossible to restore national sovereignty. His emphasis on physical education and military education must have been one salient characteristic of his discourse on the new national salvation education.

Fifth, Sin also emphasized "emotional education" very much in the belief that it could stir up patriotism which he stressed as a means of restoring national sovereignty.

"As love is emotion," Sin said, "there would be no love without emotion and there would be no emotion without love; and, therefore, the people must cultivate love for the country if they are to get patriots."[14] If patriotism was to spread all over country, the Korean people would have to pay attention to emotional education.

In connection with emotional education, he also emphasized the "beauty of the country" and the "beauty of the national culture." According to him, beauty is a vessel in which love is contained. The reason why one wants to stay on a beautiful mountain or near a clear brook and hates to leave it is that one loves the splendid scenery. There are the "beauty of the country" and the "beauty of the national culture" in any state or nation. Beauty comprises various merits unique to a nation such as its customs, language, history, religion, politics, natural features. climate, etc. To say that one loves one's country without knowing the "beauty of the country" and the "beauty of the national culture" is tantamount to patriotism without contents. Emotional education should be designed to cultivate patriotism firmly by teaching the "beauty of the country" and the " beauty of the national culture."

Sixth, Sin attached great importance to book publication in connection with the new education for the people. He emphasized greatly the publication of both classical and new books. The new books he stressed should be those which could impress the minds of the Korean people and promote their knowledge by stating the position of their country after it was examined by Korean authors with Korea's unique thought instead of merely translation foreign books or introducing foreign theories.[15]

6. Discourse on Reform of Social Customs

Sin Ch'ae-ho also asserted reform of the old social customs in order to transform the Koreans into a "new people" and establish a "new country." Characteristics of the social reform he asserted were as follows:

First, he emphatically stressed the destruction of familism. He pointed out that it was a medieval custom that the Korean people were still strongly imbued with familism while their ideas of the state and nation were relatively weak in the emergency situation when they were asked to achieve the national task of restoring the nation's sovereignty. From this standpoint he strongly emphasized that familism be destroyed.[16]

Second, he asserted the destruction of cliquism among Confucians. He deplored that the vestiges of the four-party strife still remained in Confucian circles attaching greater importance to private cliques while slighting the people and the state.

Third, he asserted that the social estate system be destroyed and the egalitarian principle be promoted.

He saw that all men are equal and the "principle of inequality" is a devil which is the cause of destroying all– politics, religion, economy, law, science, military affairs, etc. He stressed that all countries which believe in the principle of equality would certainly become prosperous and all those which were swayed by the principle of inequality were destined to go to ruin.

He pointed out, even though the Korean people were awakened and were striving toward prosperity after the Kabo Reform abolished most elements of the unequal system of the country, there still remained its vestiges, such as the discriminations and illegitimate sons among clans, between the government and the people, between a legitimate sons and illegitimate sons, among the classes of scholars, farmers, artisans, and merchants, and between the male and the female.[17]

Fourth, he asserted that liberal thought and a liberal pattern of life be put into practice. He termed "freedom" to be our second life, saying that the death of our bodies is a visible death while the death of freedom is an invisible death. As all people are endowed with personality, those who have lost freedom have also lost their personality, being no better than beasts or trees. Those who failed to restore their freedom were destined to go to ruin even if they could manage to maintain their shameful life. This was because the death of freedom is just like the death of the body.

According to Sin, Korea was a society where the notion of freedom was not developed to the fullest extent, and, therefore, it was urgently required to develop liberal thought and the custom of leading a liberal pattern of life.

Fifth, he asserted that selfishness be destroyed and righteousness be defended. Pointing out that the growing attitude of seeking personal gains had been a great evil practice which prevailed in the Korean people's life custom, he criticized bitterly that selfishness prevented a considerable number of people from joining in the struggle for the restoration of their national rights and the defense of righteousness at this moment of emergency.

Sixth, he pointed out that superstition was another evil of the Korean people and must be uprooted.

Sin classified superstition into the following three types: Misbelief in wicked magic such as exorcism, necromancy on the basis of topographic features, sun-divination, and other conjuring tricks. These are groundless evils imperiling the people: Misbelief in destiny. Without making due efforts, people tend to impute their failure to destiny. This habit does great harm to building up the national strength: Misbelief in natural phenomena. This prevents progress in science, causing disaster for the nation.

Seventh, he emphasized the cultivation of the virtue of bravery. According to him, the Koreans were greatly insufficient in terms of bravery because of their custom of respecting letters and oppressing the martial art. Any thought can be put into practice only with bravery and any plan for statecraft can succeed only with bravery. He emphasized that it was very important to cultivate bravery for the restoration of national rights.

Eighth, he asserted that public morality and public spirit be nurtured.

Sin observed that among Korean people of his time there were still many who failed to discard the thought of bygone days and were weak in public morality and public spirit but strong in selfishness and exclusivism. A considerable number of Koreans knew that only individuals and families existed, paying no heed to the existence of society and the state. Therefore, he asserted, it was necessary to provide education which could nurture public morality and public spirit for the transformation of the Koreans into a "new people" and the establishment of a "new country."

Ninth, he asserted that, when they were about to undertake an enterprise, the Koreans should choose a right one and specialize themselves in it for proper development.

Tenth, he emphasized that the Koreans should be diligent in all undertakings and cultivate the will and habit of formulation a long-term plan and achieve the desired aim with a long perspective.[18]

7. Discourse on the New National Economy

Sin Ch'ae-ho pointed out that the competition in imperialist trade among the world powers was becoming as vehement as their struggle in military policies. He observed that a country, when confronting another, first provoked an economic war and a stronger country, when dealing with a weaker one, aimed at seizing and aggressing its economy at first. Under these circumstances, he asserted, Korea had to prepare herself for a war supremacy in economy.

He proposed a new national economy for the competition. Characteristics of his theory of the new national economy can be found in proposals for construction of various modern factories, foundation of large-scale vocational schools, sending of students to overseas, provision of vocational and technical education for the people, and advancement in world trade and strengthening of the nation's international competitiveness.

Sin's assertion as explained above was aimed at constructing a self-reliant modern industrial system on the basis of new scientific technology and at laying the economic foundation for a new country with the ultimate aim of stemming the tide of Japan's imperialist economic aggression.

8. Preservation and Development of National Culture

One most notable characteristic of Sin Ch'ae-ho's patriotic enlightenment thought was that he asserted the preservation and development of the "essence of the national culture." This he terms as "kuksu" (essence of national culture), which, being entirely different from fascism, meant "merits unique to Korea in customs, language, history, religion, politics, natural features, climate, and all other matters."

He said that, when seeing conservatives touring the Western world with their long bamboo pipes in their mouths, boasting of their books of family genealogy, and debating about the four-party strife, any patriot naturally inclined to the mood of destroying everything with an axe. In this case, however, he should distinguish "what is beautiful in the national culture" from "what is ugly," preserving the former and destroying only the latter. If we should fail to distinguish beautiful aspects of the national culture from the ugly aspects and destroy all, we would ruin the base or ground on which patriotism could be promoted.[19]

Sin asserted that the national culture inherited from the old should rediscovered and its merits preserved and further developed. Even in the case of importing foreign culture, he asserted, only its merits should be accepted so that the national culture could play the leading role continuously. On the other hand, Sin vehemently assailed the worship of Chinese culture. He also bitterly criticized the attitude of following Western culture without preserving the "essence of the national culture."[20]

From this standpoint Sin advocated the preservation and development of the national culture. As a concrete means, he asserted collection of "old books" and their republication.[21]

His deep interest in the national culture reflected itself well in his theory of *Han'gŭl*. He pointed out that the evil influence of Chinese characters could be found more in nourishing a slavery disposition than in the fact that they were difficult to learn.[22] He asserted that in order to promote the independent spirit, books of korean history and geography had to be written in *Han'gŭl* and they had to be used in teaching at school. He pointed out that *Han'gŭl* could not be developed because it was used by the womenfolk and ordinary people while persons in the ruling class used the Chinese characters exclusively abandoning the Korean writing system which was devised with so great talent by a wise monarch. Sin believed that the exclusive use of Korean letters was right in principle at a time when it was urgently necessary to enlighten all the people. It was impossible to abolish Chinese characters at one time because they had been used from generation to generation for hundreds of years and they had nurtured the national culture for so long. For this reason Sin thought it would be wise to use both the Korean and Chinese letters in mixture for some time before shifting to the exclusive use of Korean letters. He proposed that a certain rule be fixed for the mixed use of Korean and Chinese letter.[23]

Concerning literature, Sin attached greater importance to its value as a tool of enlightenment than to its artistic value. His view of literature was consistently that of "patriotic enlightenment literature." Among many genres of literature, he valued novels, especially "novels written in Korean," most. He likened novels to a "compass" for the people. According to Sin, novels are greatly liked by the people, and so novels have great influence on them. Novels, like history, can play a great role in making ordinary people "patriots" and a "new nation." Criticizing bitterly that many new novels published at his time were ribald, Sin emphasized that novels should play the role of enlightenment.[24]

9. Creation of New History and a Modern Nationalist Science of History

Sin Ch'ae-ho's assertion for the preservation and development of the national culture was closely connected with his advocacy of the importance of history. He stressed that history was the best means of promoting patriotism which was essential for restoring national sovereignty. This was in contrast to Chu Si-gyong's assertion that the Korean language and letters were the key leading to patriotism. If we can term Chu's enlightenment thought to be "nationalism based on language and letters," one characteristic of Sin's patriotic enlightenment thought can be termed "nationalism based on history." Sin consistently treated history not as a science but as an instrument with which to promote patriotism among the people for the purpose of restoring national rights. For this reason his historical science can be called the "science of history of patriotic enlightenment."

History which Sin emphasized for promoting patriotism saw, of course, "Korean history" and "political history" occupied the central position in it.

The national history should be taught to the people as the best method of promoting their patriotism: but he made the following proposals; They are encouraged to read books on Korean history from childhood. Not only boys but girls should read Korean history. They should be taught to read Korean history until they get old. Persons not only in the ruling class but in the lowest class, namely, all people should read Korean history.[25]

However, Sin deplored the fact that there were not many books of Korean history which were good enough to be recommended to the whole people. He pointed out: Most old books of Korean history fell victim to the notion of revering Chinese culture and flunkeyism, treating China as the host and Korea as the guest. A distorted view of Korean history by Japanese historians was prevalent. Even textbooks on Korean history written by Koreans themselves were influenced by the above view.[26]

Viewed from Sin's nationalism based on history and his historical science aimed at patriotic enlightenment, these unpatriotic views and inferior books should be expelled. Once this was achieved, patriotism devoted to the restoration of national sovereignty would spring forth spontaneously. Sin recognized that to write new history clarifying the origin of the Korean nation and the process of its evolution was the most urgent and important task for the restoration of national rights and the formulation of a long-range plan for future national development. He recognized that to achieve this task was his mission. The book Sin wrote with this problem consciousness was *Toksa sinnon* (讀史新論) published in 1908.

Toksa sinnon dealt a great shock not only to the circles of historians but on the cultural circles during the enlightenment period (1904-1910). This was a "revolutionary" new book of history when compared with the former and existing textbooks of Korean history. The book can be considered to be a work which established the modern nationalist science of history of Korea.[27]

He encouraged the whole people and especially young men to learn his patriotic enlightenment thought and become "new heroes," without merely waiting for an opportunity for the restoration of national sovereignty but making it with a positive attitude and fighting for the supreme aim.[28] With his patriotic enlightenment thought, Sin succeeded in overcoming the medieval thought and the medieval culture with harsh and thorough criticism and in founding the liberal modern nationalist thought. Seen objectively, his patriotic enlightenment thought made a very significant contribution to the movement aimed at restoring national rights and to the development of Korea's social thought.

FOOTNOTES (Part III-17)

1. "The Twentieth Century New Nation," *Complete Works of Sin Ch'ae-ho (Tanjae) A Separate Collection*, 1977, Seoul, p. 212.
2. "Imperialism and Nationalism," *Complete Works*, Vol. 2, p. 108.
3. "I Tell Supporters of Korea-Japan Annexation," *Complete Works, A Separate Collection*, p. 207.
4. "Imperialism and Nationalism," *Complete Works*, Vol. 2, pp. 108-109.
5. "The Twentieth Century New Nation," *Complete Works, A Separate Collection*, p. 213.
6. "The Objective Point for Today's Korean people," *A Separate Collection of Complet Works*, pp. 175.
7. "Hope of Korea," *Complete Works*, Vol. 2, pp. 64-68.
8. "Soho dialogue," *Complete Works, A Separate Collection*, p. 141.
9. "Evolution and Retrogression," *Complete works, A Separate Collection*, pp. 208-209.
10. "The Twentieth Century New Nation," *Complete works, A Separate Collection*, p. 213.
11. Shin Yong-ha, "Establishment of Sinminhoe and Its National Sovereignty Restoration Movement," *Han'guk hakpo*, Vols. 8 and 9, 1977.
12. "Sŏho Dialogue," *Complete Works, A Separate Collection*, p. 142.
13. "Physical Education is Most Urgent Among Education for Virtue, Knowledge, and Physique," *Complete Works, A Separate Collection*, pp. 129-130.
14. "New Education (Emotional Education) and Patriotism," *Complete Works*, Vol. 2, p. 132.
15. "On the Necessity of Collecting Old Books," *Complete Works*, Vol. 2, pp. 99-100.
16. "Destruction of the Familism Idea," *Complete Works, A Separate Collection*, pp. 164-165.
17. "The Twentieth Century New Nation," *Complete Works, A Separate Collection*, pp. 215-216.
18. "It is Right to Fix the Purpose of Life," *Complete Works, A Separate Collection*, pp. 192-195.
19. "A Discourse on the Preservation of National Characteristics," *Complete Works, A Separate Collection*, pp. 116-118.
20. "On the Necessity of Collecting of Old Books," *Complete Works, A Separate Collection*, pp. 169-170.
21. "On Publication of Old Books," *Complete Works*, Vol. 2, pp. 99-104.
22. "Comparison of Korean and Chinese Letters," *Complete Works, A Separate*

Collection, pp. 73-76.

23. "On unification of Grammar," *Complete Works*, Vol. 2, pp. 95-96.
24. "The Trend of Novelists," *Complete Works*, *A Separate Collection*, p. 81. "The Recent Attention of the Authors of Novels Written in Korean Letters," *Complete Works*, Vol. 2, pp. 17-18.
25. "The Relations Between History and Patriotism," *Complete Works*, Vol. 2, pp. 72-79.
26. "Toksa sinnon." *Complete Works*, Vol. 1, pp. 495-496.
27. Shin Yong-ha, "Comparative Analysis of Sin Ch'ae-ho's Toksa sinnon-Rise of the Civic Modern Nationalist Science of History in 1908–," *A collection of Dissertations in Commemoration of the 100th Anniversary of the birth of Sin Ch'ae-ho (Tanjae)*, 1980.
28. "New Korean Heroes in the Twentieth Century," *Complete works*, Vol. 2, pp. 112-116.

18. Re-evaluation of the March First Independence Movement

1. March First Movement and Self-Determination

Many papers and books have been published on the March First Movement, an popular uprising against Japanese rule on March 1, 1919. In this paper, I will comment on some of the points of this independence movement which have been, in my opinion, misunderstood or misinterpreted.

One of the important misinterpretations of this anti-Japanese movement which I would like to point to is that the movement was launched under the influence of U.S. President Woodrow Wilson's self-determination doctrine. But this point of view is far from the historical facts, thereby requiring modification. To understand correctly the cause of the movement, we must review the nationalism and "the Taking-chance Strategy" that prevailed in Korea during the declining days of the Taehan Empire.

Nationalism was very strong in those days when the dynastic rule of the country was about to fall. Demanding absolute independence of the country, nationalists called for constructing a modern strong nation state. After 1905, this nationalism was so strong among young people that they organized even guerilla war against the Japanese forces stationed in the country. Between 1904 and 1910, nationalists launched a movement to save the nation by education and enlightenment, and many youths were infused with the thought of absolute independence and patriotism. This patriotic enlightenment movement and the youths educated in this movement were to provide the driving force for the March First Movement in 1919.

In 1910, the Korean people underwent the most inhuman colonial rule of Japan in history, and came to feel how precious national independence was to their life. Under the circumstances, they craved more for the absolute independence of a sovereign state.

On the other hand, the Wilson doctrine of self-determination was for the colonies of the defeated powers of World War I (Germany, Austria, Turkey and Bulgaria), and it called for independence, autonomy and even mandatory rule of these colonies. So the doctrine was a weak concept of self-government intended to solve international problems after the war.

But the thought of national independence which provided the motive power for the March First Movement was based on a strong and developed doctrine of independence which was far more specific and appropriate to the situation of Korea at the time than the mandatory rule-included Wilson doctrine. Thus, the March First Movement had no ideological relation with the Wilson doctrine.

What relationship, then was between the March First Movement and the Wilson doctrine? In short, the answer to this question is that "the Taking-chance Strategy" in the nationalist movement at the turn of the century related the Wilson doctrine to their struggle for national independence in an attempt to make the most of change in the international situation of the time for this struggle.

These chance-seekers in the nationalist movement wanted to build a strong power first and then to launch an independence movement on the basis of this power when change in international situation provided an opportune time for such a movement. In other words, they hoped to make use of change in the international situation for their independence movement. (Chance and Power, *Taehan Maeil Sinbo*, Jan. 13, 1910). This "Chance-strategy" characterized the nationalist movement at the turn of the century and the independence movements thereafter.

Independence fighters though that the chance would come in the form of war. So when World War I broke out in 1914, they tried to make the most of this change in the international situation for their movement against Japanese rule. This was before the announcement of the Wilson doctrine. When Japan joined the Allied side, Koreans wished Germany to win the war, and when Germany turned the tide of war in her favor in the early part of the war, independence fighters prepared in 1917 an anti-Japanese movement plan similar in scale to the March First Movement. But the war ended in Germany's defeat and the victory of the Allied Powers, including Japan, and Korean independence fighters, greatly disappointed, decided to give up their 1917 independence movement plan.[1]

On January 8, 1918, president Wilson of the United States, the strongest of the Allied Powers, announced a 14-point peace plan, including the self-determination doctrine for the colonies of the defeated powers of the war, and in November of that year an armistice was signed with Germany accepting Wilson's 14-point peace plan. This encouraged Korean independence fighters, and they thought that the international situation was not necessarily in disfavor of their anti-Japanese movement, though Japan was a victorious power in the war. They considered the armistice as a chance for them to rise against Japan.

But the independence fighters were well aware of the fact that the Wilson doctrine of self-determination was applicable to the colonies of the defeated powers and not to those of Japan, like Korea, because Japan was a member of the victorious Allied Powers. This was proved by the Japanese investigation records on the March First Movement leaders. In spite of their knowledge of this, they wanted to make use of the Wilson doctrine and the New Korean Youth Party, located in Shanghai, dispatched its representative to the Paris peace conference and secretly informed the independence fighters at home of its plan to rise against Japan. In other words, this party in exile wanted to make the most of the Wilson doctrine, demanding that the Allied Powers apply the Wilson doctrine not only to the colonies of the defeated powers but also to the colonies of Japan. This was included in the independence declaration issued on February 8, 1919 in Tokyo.

> "Ⅲ. We demand that the Paris peace conference decide on application of the self-determination doctrine to Korea. We have already presented this demand to the legations stationed in Tokyo for delivery to their governments and dispatched three representatives to Paris. The representatives dispatched to Paris have joined other representatives of Korea who had earlier arrived in Paris for a united movement."

In the course of preparing the March First Movement, its leaders over-publicized the meaning of the Wilson doctrine, but they well knew in the early stage of the preparation that the doctrine was not applicable to Korea. They understood the doctrine as a means of settling the problems of the colonies of the defeated powers. But some independence fighters who were seeking the opportunity of an anti-Japanese movement considered that had the Paris peace conference decided on application of the Wilson doctrine to the colonies of the defeated powers, they could make use of such a decision in turning world opinion in favor of their demand for application of the doctrine to the colonies of the victorious powers, including the independence movement in Korea.[2] In view of "the Taking-chance Strategy" developed toward the end of the 19th century, this can be considered as an attempt to make a small chance a big chance for the independence movement.

Lying herein is the relationship between the March First Movement and the Wilson doctrine. The movement was not a under any ideological influence of the Wilson doctrine. Its leaders did not start it with the hope that the doctrine would bring about independence for Korea. They knew that the doctrine was for the colonies of the defeated powers, but they nevertheless tried to make use of it in their independence movement, hoping that world opinion would move toward the application of this doctrine to the colonies of the victorious powers. In other words, they wanted to make a positive use of change in the international situation for the independence of Korea.

To repeat, the March First Movement was not ideologically influenced by the Wilson doctrine of self-determination. It was a movement developed from the nationalistic power built through the nationalist and enlightenment movements, such as the 1884 coup d'Etat, the 1894 peasants revolution, the movements of the Independence Club and the People's Assembly 1896-1998, the patriotic enlightenment movements and guerilla wars of the righteous army 1904-1914 and various independence movements in and after 1910, making use of change in the international situation of the time.

In asserting this opinion, I do not mean that I disregard the international situation of the time, while considering the domestic situation only. If there had been a similar independence movement in Manchuria, China, Vietnam or in India in those days and if such a movement had had a spill-over effect on other countries, I would willingly stress the influence of the Wilson doctrine on the March First Movement in Korea.

But the Wilson doctrine of self-determination was not of such a nature; it was related to the policy of the Big Powers for redivision of colonies among themselves. In Korea "the Taking-chance Strategy" was developed as a strategy for national independence toward the end of the last century when the Chosŏn dynasty was on the decline, and under this strategy independence fighters wanted to make a small chance provided by the Wilson doctrine for their independence movement a big chance.

Nearly all the independence fighters of the time knew the nature and limits of the Wilson doctrine. Yet, they over-publicized it, making the small chance a big chance in an attempt to make the most of it for their anti-Japanese movement. Only a few people had an illusionary hope in this doctrine. What I want to stress here is that nearly all the two million people who took part in the March First Movement did not know anything about the Wilson doctrine. They voluntarily participated in the movement, considering it one of the many such movements being promoted in the country at the time. So I can conclude that the established theory that the March First Movement was under the influence of the Wilson doctrine must be fundamentally revised or thrown away.

2. Non-violence and Violence

Another established theory on the March First Movement that I must revise here is that the movement was more meaningful because it did not use no force. This theory is, I think, based on the observation of only the style or method of the movement. In other words, this theory fails to see the nature of the independence movement in those days.

The independence fighters of the time attached importance to both violence and non-violence. Violence and non-violence are but a style or method of such a popular struggle even today, and therefore with only the style or method of a popular struggle, we cannot correctly understand the nature of such a struggle. So the effectiveness and appropriateness of non-violence as a method of the March First Movement should be measured by both the objective and subjective conditions of the independence movement in those days. To understand this problem correctly, we must understand the independence war strategy which was adopted in the early 20th century when the Taehan Empire was falling to Japan and which afterwards supported the independence movement until 1945 when Korea was liberated from Japan at the end of World War II.

This strategy for independence was adopted by the New People's Society in 1909 when national representatives of the society held a meeting at the home of Yang Ki-tak, president of the society. The gist of the strategy follows:[3]

1. To organize and develop an army strong enough to defeat the Japanese in a modern war. The army should be based in areas not under Japanese control, such as Manchuria and the Maritime Provinces of Siberia.

2. To educate and train youths of the country to infuse them with a strong spirit of nationalism as a means of building the power for independence.

3. To make a war that Japan would wage against China, Russia or the United States under her expansionist policy a chance for an independence war against Japan.

4. To win independence in the war against Japan, the independence army based in Manchuria and Maritime Provinces will march into the country to form a united front with domestic independence fighters trained and organized by the New People's Society.

As seen in the above, under this independence war strategy violence was adopted as the main approach and non-violence as the secondary approach. And this strategy tells that the independence fighters of the time attached great importance to violence as an approach to independence.

But this approach was not considered appropriate at the time of the March

First Movement in 1919, and it had to be modified for this movement. As independence fighters expected, a war involving Japan (World War I) broke out in 1914, but Japan emerged victorious from the war in 1918, along with Great Britain, France and the United States,, contrary to their expectation. This forced them to revise the above strategy for the March First Movement.

To understand further the appropriateness of the non-violence approach adopted for the March First Movement, we must consider the objective (international and domestic) conditions and the subjective conditions of the time.

The domestic conditions were closely related to the Japanese policy for suppressing the independence movement in the country. Under this policy, Japan had one infantry division at Nanam to control the northern part of the country and another one at Yongsan to control the southern part. In addition, she had a naval base at Chinhae on the southern coast. Moreover, some 15,000 military policemen were stationed at 457 points across the country. And there was a tight administrative network of the Japanese colonial government, called the Government-General of Korea, to rule the Korean people by force. In Japan were many army divisions which were ready for movement to Korea, Manchuria and the Maritime provinces at any time.

As for the subjective conditions of the independence movement in the country in those days, the Japanese suppressive policy by force did not allow a Korean to have any weapon. Thus, Korean independence fighters in the country were not able to arm themselves. Furthermore, the Japanese did not approve of any association or assembly of Koreans, except schools and religious meetings, and even religious meetings were subject to prior approval of the Japanese authorities concerned.

Between 1911 and 1912, the Japanese colonial government fabricated the so-called assassination attempt at Governor-General Terauchi in an attempt to suppress all independence movement in the country. Some 800 members of the New People's Society were arrested and many underground cells of the society were raided. Of the 800 New People's Society members arrested, ... 105 were sentenced to prison terms. In addition, more than 90,000 people were in custody on the Japanese black list of possible insurgents for police sur-veillance.

Under the circumstances, most under ground organizations in the country were cracked down on by the Japanese police, and the independence movement in the country was greatly shrunk. Stricken by the fear of arrest, the independence fighters trained in the enlightenment movement of the late 19th century could not organize themselves into an effective group fighting the

Japanese, and some of them, such as Yi Sŭng-hun, Kwŏn Tong-jin and O Se-ch'ang, found a retreat in religions, including Christianity and Chondo-gyo, the Korean religion believing in the Heavenly Way. But they clandestinely inspired the young people coming to their churches with nationalism. However, the more suppressive the Japanese policy was, the stronger the aspiration of the masses for independence, though they could not launch an organized independence movement under the Japanese suppressive policy.

On the other hand, the movement for organizing the independence army abroad was not as smooth as expected in the early years. Leaders of the New People's Society who went into exile in Manchuria established three military schools in Manchuria, Sinhŭng, Tongrim and Milsan. Small in scale, these schools could not fully function as the trainer or independence army soldiers because of the financial problem and the suppression of the Chinese warlord in Manchuria.

Of the three schools, the largest, Sinhŭng Military School, established in 1911, turned out about 40 officers a year. But there were no enlisted men for these officers to lead and the army these officers organized was a small one with officers only. Then these officers became teachers of Korean children in southern Manchuria and inspired these children with patriotism. But because the children were mostly of poor tenant farmer families, they could not join the independence army. If they joined the army, their parents could not support their families because of labor shortage.

The Korean independence army in Manchuria before the March First Movement in 1919 was a very small one and therefore not capable of making a war against the Japanese in Korea even if the people at home rose for independence. In the face of this condition, which approach should the leaders of the March First Movement adopt, violence or non-violence?

I am of the opinion that the movement leaders had no choice but the non-violence approach. Among the leaders were some men who had knowledge and experience of the violence approach. For example, Son Pyŏng-hŭi was commander of the northen force in the 1894 Tonghak Peasant revolution and Yi Sŭng hun was head of the North Pyongan Province of the New People's Society who attended the meeting in which the society's strategy for independence war was adopted. So they well knew that they must have arms to use violence in the March First Movement. When the people were not allowed to have even a pistol how could the leaders tell the people to fight the fully-armed Japanese forces with had done so, would the people have risen against Japan?

In view of he above objective and subjective conditions of the time, it is unrealistic to criticize the March First Movement leaders for not using violence in the movement. Moreover, the view of attributing the failure of the movement to its non-violence approach is not based on the realities of the country in those days.

In view of the historical facts of the times, it may well be said that if the March First Movement had used violence, the movement would have become a small-scale riot which could early be controlled by a company of a battalion of Japanese troops, instead of a mass uprising which involved some two million of the 17 million people in the country at the time. When the masses know a big gap in arms with their enemy, they do not approve of the use of violence against the enemy. The people are basically empirical and see the fact of life as it is.

As for the objective international conditions of the time, the chance of a decisive independence movement which Koreans so longed for came not in a war that would defeat Japan but in the Paris Peace Conference in which Japan took part as a victorious power after the First World War. This war, which broke out in 1914, did not provide such a chance for the independence movement of Korea because Japan joined the war as an Allied Power. When the peace conference was held in Paris on January 18. 1919 in which the Wilson doctrine of settling the colonial problems of the defeated powers, including Germany, this peace conference was made use of a chance to advance the independence movement. Because of this chance provided by change in the international situation at the time, a non-violent demonstration could be an effective approach.

In short, the non-violent approach is considered an inevitable and wise choice for the March First Movement in 1919, in view of the objective and subjective condition of the time.

What First want to stress in particular here is that the demonstration march in the March First Movement was a unique non-violent effort in the independence movement in Korea. When the non-violence approach was introduced to India, the indians staged sit-in demonstrations. In Korea, the first non-violent demonstration march was organized by the People's Assembly for its anti-Imperialist movement in 1898, and this demonstration march had since been used as a non-violence approach to the independence movement until 1945.

In spite of this non-violent approach in the March First Movement in 1919, the Japanese killed 7,509 Koreans, wounded 15,961 others and destroyed 715 houses and 47 churches. Japanese soldiers and policemen mercilessly fired at the unarmed people marching in demonstration in the streets. While students, workers and city people were non-violent in the movement, many peasants used violence to lead the movement in a violent manner. Why the peasants used violence is a major subject of study of the March First Movement in the future.

Although the March First Movement started with a non-violent demonstration, it developed into a half-violent and half-peaceful movement. This can be said to be the natural and unavoidable course because the movement was basically a struggle for independence.

3. 33 Leaders and the Masses

The third wrong view of the March First Movement I want to point out in the paper is that the 33 national leaders who signed the Declaration of Independence should be separately treated from the masses who joined the movement. Some people see the movement as an exclusive one of the 33 national leaders only, while other people see it as movement of the masses, disregarding the role of the 33 leaders. These two opposite views have long been hotly discussed.

I think that the two opposite view are due to a failure to see the whole course of the movement. To understand the whole picture to the movement, we must divide it into two stages; the early organization stage and the later mass movement stage. It was in the organization stage that the 33 leaders played a major role, and the masses played the leading role in the later stage of mass movement.

What should be noted here is that the scope of organization made by the 33 leaders in the early stage was quite limited. In other word, it can be said that the organization by the 33 leaders was limited to the areas where copies of the Declaration of Independence were delivered. According to my study,[4] the areas which got copies of the Declaration of Independence were Seoul, Sŏnchŏn, Pyŏngyang, Wŏnsan, Yŏnghung, Pyŏnggang, Kŭmhwa, Haeju, Sariwŏn, Sŏhung, Suan, Koksan, Kaesŏng, Ch'ŏnju, Taegu, Masan, Tongnae, Kunsan, Chŏnju and Imsil. But the movement actually spread across the country, from the northernmost part of the country in North Hamgyong Province to the southernmost part of the country on Cheju Island. There was no city, country and town of the nation where the people did not rise against Japan in March 1919. In fact, in the later stage of the mass movement, the masses voluntarily organized and launched local independence movements.

So it should be made clear that the 33 leaders planned and organized the movement in the early stage. In other words, they were the igniter of the later stage of mass movement across the country. There is no doubt that they were all ready to down their lives of national independence when they signed the Declaration of Independence, though some of them turned round later. But their role in the later stage of mass movement was quite limited and indirect. In this stage, the masses voluntarily planned and organized local movements, without the central leadership, and developed them into a nation-wide movement against Japanese rule.

The masses were more active in the March First Movement and suffered more from the Japanese oppression during and after the movement than the 33 leaders. During the movement, 7,509 people were killed and 15,961 others were wounded by the Japanese soldiers and policemen. Included in the killed were the activists who were sentenced to death.

The Japanese authorities first planned to mete out capital punishment to the 33 leaders, but seeing the movement spreading to every corner and nook of the country, they mitigated this plan to deliver a maximum term of three years in prison to the 33 leaders. This appeasement policy was apparently due to the pressure of the masses who rose in nation-wide uprising.

The March First Movement in 1919 was launched in two stages, and it was basically of the nature of a mass movement. Without the early organization stage, it would have been different from what it really was in March 1919. Without the mass movement stage, it would not have become an event whose historical meaning we highly appreciate today.

Today, we highly appreciate the historical meaning of this movement because it developed into a mass movement in the later stage. If we overlook this and emphasize too much the role played by the 33 leaders, we would misunderstand the movement more than we would do by overlooking the 33 leaders' role and emphasizing too much the activities of the masses. The 33 leaders were the igniter and the masses were the bomb ignited by these leaders.

4. Evaluation of March First Movement

The last wrong view of the March First Movement I want to correct here is that the movement was a failure from the start.

But the movement achieved more than the objective of the 33 leaders who planned and organized it, unlike similar movements before and after it. But it failed to achieve the goal of immediate independence. So I propose that the historical evaluation of the movement be made by two criteria.

The first criterion is the object set by the 33 leaders in the early stage of organization. By this criterion, the movement was far more successful than any of the leaders expected in the organization stage. Thus the movement is not comparable to the 1894 peasant revolution which ended in failure.

None of the early organizers of the movement expected that the movement would immediately result in independence of the country. For example, the Japanese investigation report on Kwŏn Tong-jin, one of the 33 leaders, includes the following statement:

> "Question (Japanese prosecutor): Are you going to participate in the independence movement in the future?
>
> Answer (Kwŏn Tong-jin): Yes. I will continue this movement at any cost until we win independence. I know that we cannot win independence now, but I firmly believe that if we sow the seed with our present will to achieve independence we will certainly see the fruit." [5]

Thus Kwŏn saw the movement as a course of action to win independence and as sowing the seed of independence which would certainly grow to be a tree bearing the fruit of independence.

This opinion was also shared by O Se-chang, another of the 33 leaders.

> "Question (Japanese prosecutor): Do you know about U.S. President Wilson's doctrine of self-determination which has been reported in newspapers?
>
> Answer (O Se-chang):Yes, I do.
>
> Question: What do you think of this doctrine?
>
> Answer: I don't think that Korea can be independence because we have submitted a petition for independence on the basis of this doctrine.
>
> Question: Do you think that the doctrine is applicable to the annexed and defeated countries or all the countries which were directly involved in the war?
>
> Answer: I think that the doctrine is applicable to the countries involved in the war and not to the other countries.
>
> Question: Then why did you decide to issue the Declaration of Independence of the basis of this doctrine and start an independence movement in the meeting held at the home of Son Pyŏng-hŭi?
>
> Answer: In view of the rapid development of the world today, we felt the need to announce before the world that the Korean people have the will to determine their own fate and to record this will in history, though such an announcement will not bring about independence. We also thought this

better than doing nothing about our country which is being left behind, while other countries are rapidly developing.

Question: Then do you want the independence of Korea now?

Answer: Yes, I want Korea to be independence as soon as possible." [6]

As seen in the above, O Se-ch'ang knew that the Wilson doctrine of self-determination was not applicable to Korea, but he and 32 others signed the Declaration of Independence in order to tell the world that the Korean people had the will of self-determination, availing themselves of the Wilson doctrine, though they knew that such a declaration would not bring about the immediate independence of the country. Other national leaders also had such an opinion Son Pyŏng-hŭi said, just before the March First Movement, as follows:

"If we declare independence, the country will not be independence immediately. But we must declare independence in order to infuse the people with the spirit of independence." [7]

None of the 33 leaders expected and imagined, that the movement they planned and organized would develop into a nation-wide uprising against Japan. But it actually became a great mass movement in which some two million people actively took part. Such a successful development of the movement is attributed to the masses, especially to their voluntary participation, not to the 33 leaders. So to understand the successful aspect of the movement, we must analyze the cause for the voluntary participation of the masses, and this, I think, is an important subject in the future study of the Movement.

If we consider the independence movement as a prolonged war against Japan, the Movement in 1919 was certainly a successful campaign of this war. Although it took the lives of 7,509 people, along with 15,961 wounded and 46,948 arrested, its achievements can be said to be far greater than these sacrifices, as discussed later in this paper.

The second criterion is the goal of a immediate independence of the country. By this criterion, the Movement was a failure. Why Korea failed to win independence immediately after the movement is, I think, a subject that requires a scientific analysis and criticism in the future study of the movement.

First of all, it can be pointed out that the power of independence fighters was much weaker than the power of the Japanese militarist forces. In addition, there was a weak central leadership incapable of organizing the voluntary local movements across the country into a decisive one.

Japan annexed Korea in 1910, and I think that there should have been a government in exile in Shanghai, Manchuria or in the Maritime Province of Siberia to organize and lead centrally all the independence movements. If that had been the case, the March First Movement would have been led by such a government in exile, not by the 33 religious and intellectual leaders. But this is simply my wishful assumption, and this problem should be studied in depth by many scholars.

5. Historical Meaning of March First Movement

The March First Movement in 1919 was a very significant event not only of Korean history but also of world history. Its historical meaning to Korea can be summarized as follows:

First, the movement fundamentally defeated the Japanese colonial rule by military force and the eradication policy against Koreans as a people, which Japan imposed on Korea for 9 years between 1910 and 1919. While executing the iron-fist colonial policy to eradicate Koreans and exploit their economy internally, the Japanese externally made false propaganda that Koreans were happy under their rule. Because of the March First Movement, the militarist Japanese colonial rule in Korea was almost broken and their inhuman treatment of Koreans was brought to light before the world.

Second, the movement strenghtened the indestructible power of the Korean people to achieve independence, thus providing the driving force for the independence movement thereafter. Under the unprecedented oppressive policy of Japan, many independence movement organizations in the country were dissolved around 1917. But the March First Movement in 1919 encouraged such organizations to emerge again and saved the independence movement from extinction. This is attested to by the far more active independence movements after 1919 than before. The movement provided an opportunity for the Korean people to build the subjective power to win independence, while presenting the possibility of winning independence sooner or later.

Third, the movement resulted in the establishment of a provisional government of the Republic of Korea in Shanghai, thereby introducing a republic system to the country for the first time in its history. In its early days, the provisional government was represented by all independence movement organizations and all social and political groups of the country, and it led and controlled all independence movements in and out of the country. But in 1923, it was split and thus weakened as a government, which is not the subject to be dealt with in this paper.

Fourth, the movement also resulted in strengthened armed independence movements in Manchuria, and some Independence Army units crossed the border to operate in the country. It must be noted that the strengthened armed struggles of the Independence Army in Manchuria and the Maritime Province were entirely due to the March First Movement. Many youths who took part in the movement went to Manchuria and the Maritime Provinces to join the Independence Army units there, along with the Korean youths living in Manchuria. For instance, Sinhŭng Military School, which turned out only 40 officers a year before 1919, had to move to a larger building and even establish a branch school to accommodate the increasing applicants after the March First Movement. It turned out some 600 officers and enlisted men a year. In 1920, the Northern Independence Army killed and wounded 3,300 Japanese troops on the battleground in Chŏngsan-ri, and the officers of this army were mostly graduates of Sinhŭng Military School, while its enlisted men were Korean youths who were trained for six months in the same school. It is noteworthy that the March First Movement caused the Independence Army to grow strong enough to win battles with regular Japanese army divisions in Manchuria.

Fifth, as a result of the movement, the Japanese had to grant the limited freedom enabled the people to start cultural, agrarian and labor movements for the building of national power. The so-called 'cultural colonial policy' of Japan in Korea after the movement was aimed at appeasing Koreans, especially nationalists, so as to split the nationalist force of the country. But it must be noted that this shift in the Japanese colonial policy in Korea was entirely due to the March First Movement, and therefore it can be considered the achievement of the movement.

Sixth, because of the movement, the Korean people was internationally assured of the independence of their country in due course of time. Because they declared the independence of their country in this nationwide uprising against Japan, the world came to recognize their independence when Japan would be a defeated power in a world war, though in those days the world was not in a position to give such recognition to the Koreans because Japan was a victorious power of World War I. During World War II, the independence of Korea was treated as a foregone conclusion in various meetings of the Allied Powers even though Korea was not represented in such meetings, and this was basically due to the March First Movement in 1919.

In addition, the historical meaning of the March First Movement is not limited to Korea; it is also a historical event of the world. It provided an opportunity of independence movement for colonial peoples of the victorious powers of World War I. During and after the war, colonial peoples of Germany, Turkey, Italy and Austria launched active independence movements because they knew that these powers would lose the war. But colonial peoples of Great Britain, France, the United States and Japan could not consider their independence until the March First Movement of 1919 in Korea because these powers won the war. Under the circumstances, they were greatly encouraged and influenced by the independence movement of Korea in 1919.

First, the May Fourth Movement of China was inspired and influenced by the March First Movement of Korea. This Chinese movement which marked an epoch in modern history of China was externally influenced by the March First Movement of Korea. Chinese nationalists of the time greatly praised the Korean people for their March First Movement and called on the Chinese people to learn from Korea's March First Movement. Leaders of this Chinese Nationalist Movement left many records telling that the May fourth Movement was inspired and influenced by the March First Movement of Korea.

For example, Ch'en Tu-hsiu, who led the May foruth Movement as a liberal nationalist but later became a communist to organize the Chinese Communist Party, said in his article on the independence movement of Korea published in a weekly dated March 23, 1919, that the March First Movement of Korea marked an epoch in the world history of revolutions and added: "the recent independence movement of korea was based on a great, sincere, courageous, clear and just thought. It wrote a new chapter in the history of revolutions in the world because it was a revolution based on the people's will, without violence. (…) In the face of this glorious movement of the Korean people, the Chinese people should be ashamed for their inactivity."

Nationalist Pu Ssu-nien in an article, The Lesson from Korea's Independence Movements, published in the April 1919 issue of *Hsinchao* (New Tide) and Anarchist Chen Mei-chiu in his paper on the situation of Korea praised the March First Movement of Korea. In short, the March First Movement had great influence on the May Fourth Movement of China.

Second, in India, the independence movement of the National Congress Party rapidly grew under the influence of the March First Movement of Korea. Making use of the British indirect colonial rule, the Indian people introduced the non-violence approach of Korea's March First Movement and rapidly developed their independence movement to the extent that they won independence by themselves. The Gandhi-led independence movement in April 1919 was under the influence of March First Movement of Korea. Indian nationalists, including Nehru, highly appreciated the March First Movement.

In Glimpses of World History which Nehru wrote for his daughter Indira, he described Koreas Movement of 1919 on December 30, 1932 as follows:

"Korea was given its old name again Chosŏn, the land of the morning calm ... For many years the struggle for independence continued and there were many outbreaks, the most important one being in 1919. The people of Korea, and especially young men and women, struggled gallantly against tremendous odds. On one occasion, when a Korean organization fighting for freedom formally declared independence, and thus defied the Japanese, the story goes that they immediately telephoned to the police and informed them of what they had done! Thus deliberately they sacrificed themselves for their ideal. The suppression of the Koreans by the Japanese is a very sad and dark chapter in history. You will be interested to know that young Korean girls, many of them fresh from college, played a prominent part in the struggle."[8]

Third, the influence of the March First Movement in Korea was felt in Indochina, the Philippines and some Arab countries.

The world history of the 19th and early 20th centuries was written by the Big Powers, disregarding the peoples suffering from colonial or semi-colonial rule of these powers though they accounted for three fourths of the world population. Because the independence movements of the oppressed peoples of this period carry weight in the world history, the future world history must be written objectively by all the peoples of the world, including the peoples of minor countries. In that case, the March First Movement of Korea will be treated in a new chapter as the first signal light for the oppressed peoples to rise against the Big Powers emerged victorious from World War I to win independence.

6. Conclusion

When Nobel literature laureate Tagore, who was also a leader of the Indian independence movement, visited Tokyo in 1929, the 10th anniversary of the March First Movement of Korea, Korean students in the Japanese capital city visited him. He told them about his impression of the March First Movement and wrote an impromptu poem on Korea at the request of the Korean student. His poem follows:

In the golden age of Asia

Korea was one of its lamp bearers,
And that lamp is waiting to be lighted once again
For the illumination in the East.

This poem of Tagore gives a new impression of the March First Movement to us today just 80 years after the movement took places.

FOOTNOTES (Part Ⅲ-18)

1. Association of Patriotic Comrades (ed.), *History of Korean Independence Movement*, pp. 95-96.

2. Shin Yong-ha, "The Subjectivity and the National self-determinism in the Samil Independence Movement," *Hanguk-sasang*, Vol. 15.

3. Shin Yong-ha, "The Initial-founding of Shinmin-hyoe and her Retrieval Movement of Sovereignty," *Hanguk-hakpo*, Vols. 8-9, 1977.

4. Yun Pyong-sok, etc. (ed.), *Essays on Korean Modern History* Ⅱ, pp. 182.

5. Yi Pyŏng-hŏn (ed.), *History of the March First Movement*, pp. 182.

6. *Ibid.*, pp. 514-515.

7. *Biography of Sŏn pyŏnghui*, pp. 342.

8. Jawaharlal Nehru, *Glimps of World History*, Korea translation edition, 1939, pp. 272-273.

19. "Modernization" Theme during the Colonial Period: A Criticism of the Argument that Japanese Colonial Rule Modernized Korea

1. Sense of Problem

Did Japan's colonial rule over Korea from 1910 through 1945 begin the modernization of Korea? Recently, scholars in various parts of the world have begun reevaluating Japanese imperialism and its effect on those nations Japan colonized. The view that Japanese colonial policies promoted modernization and economic development has been gaining support.

Although those who hold this view recognize that Japan colonized Korea in order to exploit it for the benefit of Japan, they argue that it is unfair to dismiss Japanese colonial rule as merely exploitative, since Korea experienced the beginnings of economic development and modernization while under Japanese rule. Moreover, these scholars contend that we should view the history of Korea during the colonial period primarily in terms of the modernization and economic development which occurred. Their aim is to locate the origins of contemporary Korea's rapid economic growth in the colonial policies Japan adopted toward Korea. Though they claim this is a new interpretation of the impact of Japanese colonial rule, they are mistaken. Their argument that Japanese rule brought modernization to the Korean peninsula is the same argument the Japanese Governor-General and his colonial bureaucracy preached to the "Chosenjin" from 1910 until 1945.

Japanese imperialists claimed that Korea had never in its history been a truly independent nation and that instead the Korean race and society had been dominated by non-Korean rulers. The Japanese went on to denigrate the Koreans and their society as stagnant and charged that Koreans could never "progress" and achieve "modernization" and "economic development" on their own. However, once Japanese colonialism　embraced Korea, Korea was able to "modernize" and "develop" thanks to Japanese "assistance." Koreans, therefore, should be thankful for Japanese benevolence and forswear dreaming "nationalistic" dreams of "self-determination." Such was the argument of Japanese imperialists that Korea modernized because of Japanese colonial rule.

In the fifty years since liberation, Korean academia has consistently and vehemently criticized this justification for colonial rule put forward by Japanese imperialists. Korean scholars have successfully refuted the Japanese imperialist approach to Korean history by engaging in research on Korean history from a realistic perspective using scientific methodologies.

Moreover, in recent years whenever Japanese cabinet ministers suggested that Japanese colonial policies had "modernized" Korea or stimulated "economic development" on the peninsula, the Korean people and media denounced such statements as absurd. In fact, such statements have created such problems for Japanese-Korean relations that those cabinet ministers had have to either apologize or resign. This being the case, why then are a few scholars both within and without Korea trying to revive arguments originally formulated by the bureaucracy of the Japanese Government-General?

2. The Concept of "modernization" and the colonial policies of Japan

To determine scientifically whether or not Japan's colonial policies promoted "modernization," it is first necessary to establish the framework of the "modernization" concept using social science methods to establish a standard.[1]

Though it is difficult to agree on the details of what exactly the concept "modernization" means, there can be agreement on its fundamental components. Politically, modernization implies that a country which has become independent is transformed from an autocratic polity into a constitutional state, thus becoming a modern nation-state. Economically, a medieval economic structure and mode of production is transformed by commercial capitalism into an industrialized economy. Socially, a pre-modern estate-based social system is replaced by a modern civil society composed of citizens who hold civil rights. And culturally, modernization implies a revolutionary change from an elitism centered on an aristocracy to a modern national culture centered on the common man. We can weight the impact of Japanese colonial rule by evaluating the, "modernization" of Korea according to those four defining components of the concept of modernization.

Since the sovereignty of Korea, an independent country, to promulgate its own constitution was obliterated by Japan's imperialist seizure of Korea, there was no political "modernization" to speak of Political Modernization was partially achieved, and then only for a short while, with the establishment of the Korean Provisional Government in Shanghai, China, in 1919 by Korean nationalists. The Shanghai Korean Provisional Government drew up a constitution and created a national assembly, achieving political modernization through the establishment of the first Korean democratic republic in Korean history, though this did not take place within Korea. However, it is important to note that Japan did everything within its power to destroy the Korean Provisional Government, making the Korean Provincial Government the principal target of destruction of Japanese colonial policies. Rather than promoting the political modernization of Korea, Japanese colonial rule was based on a policy of destroying the one manifestation of that modernization, viewing it as a thorn in its side.

Economically, Japanese colonial policies failed to further the establishment of industrial capitalism on the peninsula. Moreover, under colonial rule, socio-economic exploitation intensified. Private ownership of land (a defining feature of a modern agrarian economy) was not introduced into Korea through the implementation of Japan's Land Survey Act. Private ownership of land had been recognized in Korea since the fifteenth century. By the end of the nineteenth century, the private purchase and sale of land was a common practice throughout the peninsula. Japan carried out its land survey in order to more efficiently exploit Korea's land. The Japanese Government-General seized 50.4% of the entire Korean peninsula and then wielded its land exploitation policies to terminate the rights of Korean farmers. Land survey under colonial rule was nothing more than a colonial socio-economic exploitation policy devoid of any elements of real reform. Up until the end of colonial rule on August 15, 1945, the Government-general continued to use its authority to actively promote the semi-feudal landlord system, relentlessly suppressing the movement by Korean tenant-farmers for the reform of the semi-feudal landlord system.

When conducting research on the economy during the Japanese colonial period, it is above all crucial to keep in mind that one must clearly distinguish along national (Korean and Japanese) lines. The only valid way to gauge the economic impact of Japanese colonial rule is to compare actual development during the colonial period to the development which would have occurred on the peninsula had there been no colonialization. Comparing the statistics of 1945 with those of 1910 is not a scientific way of examining the issue. Since the colonial economy of Japanese imperialism and the economy of the Korean nation were in actuality usually opposed to each other and in conflict, it is necessary to distinguish clearly between the two, more importantly, if such a distinction along national lines is not made, the achievements of Koreans while they were suffering under the Japanese will be mistakenly treated as the fruit of Japanese colonial policies.

Moreover, much of the so-called "industrialization" after 1930 was only a statistical increase in industrial productivity. For example, the industrial facilities Japan established in South Hamgyŏg province near Ch'angjin lake and Pujŏn lake should not be counted as contributing to the industrialization of Korea since they functioned as a military supply base supporting Japan's invasion of China. These military facilities in South Hamgyŏng province, which was the core area within the Korean peninsula for Japanese capital, was regarded as the spoils of war; it was disassembled and taken to the Soviet Union after World War II.

Of the industrial capital within Korea in 1941, approximately 94 per cent was Japanese capital. Korean capital amounted to a mere 6 per cent. Under the Japanese, not only did an industrialization of the Korean national economy not occur, the handful of industrial facilities which were erected were part of Japan's military industrial complex. The industrial sector of the Korean economy was so underdeveloped that Korea was far from having an industrial national economy, nor did industrial capitalism play a significant role in that economy. Furthermore, the semi-feudal landlord system which dominated the agricultural sector was supported by the Japanese. The Korean national economy under Japanese was scarcely a case of "modernization." Rather, so little industrialization occurred that it is clear that Japan retarded Korea's economic modernization.

Tracing the origins of Korea's rapid economic growth over the last four decades back to Japanese colonial economic policies is illogical and can not be substantiated. Under Japanese rule, most industrial facilities within the Korean peninsula were in northern Korea in order to better serve Japan's military needs. Those few factories which were erected in the southern half of the peninsula were completely destroyed between 1950 and 1953 when the Korean War raged across Korea. Look at the two thousand companies which contributed the most to the rapid growth of the Korean economy after 1960. Very few originated in the colonial period. Koreans started ninety-nine percent of the new companies which operated after liberation. Not even one percent can be linked to the Japanese. It is necessary to keep in mind that a discontinuity exists between the Japanese colonial period and the rapid economic growth in Korea after 1960.

Furthermore, Japan's colonial policies did not aim at the creation of a modern citizenry enjoying civil rights, nor did the Government-General promote the growth of a civil society. Instead, even the most fundamental human rights of Koreans were violated. Under Japanese colonial rule, Koreans were denied such fundamental human rights as the right to personal liberty and freedom, the right to vote, and the right to own property. They were not allowed to enjoy freedom of speech, freedom of assembly, freedom of association, freedom of the press, or freedom to protest. They were denied sovereignty in their own land, and were denied the rights enjoyed by their Japanese neighbors. Koreans who fought to gain such rights were treated as participants in the independence movement and were death with harshly.

At the time of the Kabo reform, in 1894, the traditional rigid estate hierarchy was abolished by the Korean government. Korean society was in the midst of changing into a civil society when the Japanese invasion and subsequent colonial policies arrested this social modernization. Not only was the expansion of civil rights halted, the Japanese even deprived Koreans of those few civil rights they had already begun to enjoy. Koreans fell to the status of slaves with no civil rights under Japanese rule. Japanese colonial policies clearly did not promote modernization. On the contrary, Japan actively obstructed the modernization of Korean society.

Culturally, Japan enforced policies designed to suppress the modernization of Korea's national culture. What little modernization of culture occurred under Japanese rule was achieved by the March First movement. This movement carved out a space in which Koreans could use their creativity in the field of literature to struggle against the Japanese while being subjected to Japanese censorship and suppression. The modernization of Korea during the colonial period was achieved in the Korean national sector by such resistance to Japanese oppression. Japan pursued a colonial cultural policy of resorting to all sort of censorship and oppressive measures in order to obstruct the modernization of Korean culture. Clear proof of this can been seen in the countless hank marks stamped by censors on material published under Japanese rule.[2]

Similarly, it would be inaccurate to claim the Japanese colonial authorities promoted Korean education. Modern Korean education took its first giant steps in the late Chosŏn period. By the time the dynasty fell, there were 3,000 private schools already in existence, and several professional schools. A new educational system was expanding rapidly with the support of the Korean government. However, shortly after they annexed Korea and turned it into their colony, in September, 1911, the Japanese proclaimed the "Chosen Education Ordinance." Seeing a link between the Korean enlightenment movement and private schools, the Japanese banned them. In accordance with the provisions of the Chosen Education Ordinance, no private elementary schools were recognized. Instead, all *sohakkyo* (equivalent to modern elementary schools) were declared to be Japanese government-run public schools. Private foundations were allowed to operate four-year higher schools as well as two to three-year vocational schools, as long as they taught their students to be loyal subjects of the Japanese emperor. The colonial Government-General refused to authorize the establishment of' universities for Koreans. Only vocational junior colleges were permitted. As far textbooks, the Government-General would not allow the use of any textbooks which were not produced or authorized by the Government-General.

With the Japanese assumption of control over the approximately 2,250 private schools which had been run by Koreans, along with the restrictions the colonial government placed on higher education for Koreans, Japanese colonial policies resulted in second-class education for Koreans.

After the March First movement, Koreans challenged "the Chosen Education Ordinance" by pushing for the establishment of a Private Korean university consisting of six colleges. Just before that Private Korean university was to open its doors, in 1924, Japan opened Keijo Imperial University in Seoul to provide higher education for the children of Japanese who had moved to Korea. In order to made its colonial policies more palatable to Koreans, Japan allowed a few Koreans to join the predominantly Japanese student body.

As part of an its overall goal of eradicating the Korean nation, the colonial government interfered in Korea's schools, placing strict controls on textbooks, the subjects to be taught, and the curriculum. Such an educational policy was designed to repress Korea's effort to establish a modern Korean educational system.

Japanese colonial policy obstructed rather than promoted Korean modernization. As some Japanese and Korean scholars of Korean history have pointed out, after 1930 Korea "industrialized" under colonial rule, yet per capita consumption of rice among Koreans declined sharply. Koreans were forced to seek nourishment from wild roots and tree bark when the Japanese plundered the grain Koreans had grown and harvested. Moreover, Korean wives and mothers lost husbands and sons to Japanese conscription, and parents saw their daughters taken away to serve as comfort women for Japanese troops. Koreans were powerless to resist such exploitation by the Japanese. They had no civil rights whatsoever. Can this be considered "modernization," "industrialization," or "economic development? The little modernization which did occur under the Japanese was achieved by Koreans who fought against Japanese attempts to obstruct Korean modernization and repress the Korean people.

3. The Goal of Japanese Colonial Rule: The Destruction of Korean Nation

What common elements do we see in the various policies Japan adopted toward its Korean colony? There are at least two: all those policies were designed to eliminate through assimilation any remnants of a distinctive Korean identity, and they were designed to further Japan's socio-economic exploitation of Korea.

The colonial policies of Japanese imperialism were essentially different from the colonial policies of Western imperialism in that, along with socio-economic exploitation, the Japanese also attempt to permanently obliterate the Korean nation and to create an entire slave class to run errands for the Japanese. Japan did not consult Koreans in drawing up policies for Korea, nor did the Japanese policy of assimilation assume that Koreans would become just another group of Japanese citizens, sharing equal rights with other Japanese. Instead, the goal of Japan's colonial policies was to erase Koreans from the face of the earth and to turn the few who survived into a subordinate slave class of "Chosenjin" who would be discriminated against and subservient to the Japanese empire and people.

Therefore, when Japan began implementing this policy of "national obliteration," discrimination against Koreans became public policy and was institutionalized in official laws and regulations. Koreans suffered from severe prejudice in all areas of public life simply because they were Koreans. This discrimination was social, political, and economic. For example, a Korean with the same job as a Japanese in the same company, working the same number of hours, and producing the same quantity and quality of goods, would, in accordance with government regulations, receive approximately half the wages a Japanese counterpart would receive.

The colonial policies of Japan were the worst among the various colonial policies adopted by imperialist powers in modern times because Japan implemented a policy of "national obliteration" toward Koreans, and because, when this policy of "national obliteration" was added to policies of socio-economic exploitation, the hardships suffered by Koreans were exacerbated.

A nation is a human community, embedded in history, which becomes firmly united through a common language, shared territory, kinship ties, a common culture, shared political experience and history, and economic interaction. For Koreans to develop a national consciousness and see themselves as a separate and distinct nation, a precondition for the development of a modern Korean nation-state, they needed to maintain their own distinctive language, territory, kinship ties, cultural heritage, historical memories, and modes of political and economic interaction.

As soon as Japan seized control of Korea through brute force in August 1910, it began implementing colonial policies designed to eradicate the Korean nation by eliminating those characteristics which bound Koreans to one another as members of the same national community.

Japan first stole Korean national territory away from the Korean people, ripping sovereignty over the peninsula from Korean hands, and then subjugate and exploited the Korean economy. If the remaining defining characteristics of a Korean national identity, such as the Korean language, Korean culture, shared visions of Korea's past, and Korean ethnic pride, had been eliminated as well, the Korean nation would have been annihilated, and the Korean people would have become nothing more than a kinship group. Though there still would have been families which could have been labeled "Korean," they would have been nothing more than slaves of Japan. Korean national identity would have been eradicated.

A. The Attempt to Eliminate the Korean Language and Script.

Japan's colonial Government-General implemented a policy designed to eliminate the Korean language and the Korean writing system in order to extirpate the Korean nation. Beginning in 1910, Japanese was declared the national language of Korea, and the Korean language was suppressed. By 1930, Korean schools were no longer allowed to teach the Korean language. Starting in 1937, all Koreans, including even peasants, were ordered to use Japanese instead of Korean as they went about their daily activities. Using the Korean language was strictly prohibited. If a peasant wished to mail a parcel or to submit a document to an administrative office in his local township, he had to speak in Japanese. Otherwise, he would be ignored, The Japanese also punished elementary school children who slipped up and blurted out Korean.

As soon as Japan annexed Korea in 1910, a ban was imposed on the publication of Korean-language newspapers and magazines. Shocked by the strength of nationalist movements Koreans displayed in the March First movement, Japan in the 1920s reluctantly allowed the publication of some newspapers and magazines in Korean. However, the lid was put back on in the 1930s. In 1936, *Sintonga* was shut down. Four years later, all Korean-language newspapers, including *Tonga ilbo* and *Chosŏn ilbo*, were banned. In 1941, *Munchang*, *Inmun p'ylngron* and other Korean-language periodicals suffered the same fate. The following year, the *Chosŏnŏ hakhve*, a scholarly organization engaged in research on *hangul* in order to preserve the Korean language, was disbanded by force, and many of its members were arrested and incarcerated.

B. Attempts to Eliminate Korea's National Culture

Japan also implemented policies designed to eradicate the traditional culture of the Korean people. Organs of the Japanese imperial government were mobilized to investigate Korea's unique national culture and its cultural products. These "investigations" led to the devastation of Korea's national cultural heritage, A large percentage of Korea's countless cultural treasures were either destroyed or pillaged and taken to Japan. Moreover, in the schools of colonial Korea, the Japanese taught the fallacy that indigenous Korean culture represented an inferior culture.

C. An Attempt to Eliminate Korean Names

As part of their scheme to eradicate the national culture of Korea, the Japanese even went so far as to order Koreans to change their names, both their personal names and their surnames, to Japanese names. This policy was designed to eliminate visible signs of the kinship ties which bound the Korean national community together and, therefore, erase any remaining consciousness of a distinctive Korean identity.

D. Attempts to Distort Korean History and Eradicate Korean Historical Memories.

Japan also distorted the history of the Korean nation, introducing falsehoods and fabrications in order to support the imposition of colonial rule on Korea. In 1916 the Japanese Government-General established the *Chosŏnsa p'yŏnsu-hoe* (Association for the Compilation of Korean History). That asso-ciation systematically distorted Korean history in order to eradicate any evidence of an autonomous history of the Korean people and nation. The Japanese inserted into their accounts of ancient Korean history a number of unsubstantiated claims. For example, they claimed that Korea had been subordinate to China and Japan since ancient times; that Silla and Paekche did not introduce advanced civilization to Japan but instead were both under Japanese rule; that over a thousand years ago Japan had established a military base in the Kimhae area and had colonized the region around that base; that Silla, Paekche, and Koguryŏ had paid tribute to Japan; and that the Koreans were the younger brothers of the Japanese, since the Japanese were the legitimate offspring of the goddess Amaterasu and the Koreans were illegitimate sons, etc. Since the Korean nation had created a brilliant and advanced civilization and culture as far back as the ancient state of Tan'gun Chosŏn, and had latter transmitted the products of that advanced civilization to an as-yet-uncivilized Japan, the

Japanese version of Korean history was clearly distorted and fabricated.

The Japanese economic historian Fukuda Tokuzo even went so far as to claim that, up until 1902, Korean economic development had not advanced beyond the level of a household economy, like that which prevailed elsewhere in ancient times. He claimed that put nineteenth century Korea at the same stage as Fujiwara Japan ten centuries earlier. He went on to argue that, thanks to the grace of Japanese colonialism, Koreans for the first time in their history were beginning to break out of that economic stagnation and embark on economic modernization.[3] Such an analysis of Korean economic history is utter nonsense and an outright distortion of history. However, since his views were systematically diffused through the colonial education system, their impact was immense.

E. Attempts to Eliminate Pride in Korean National Identity

Japan not only schemed to obliterate any outward evidence of Korean autonomous historical developement, it also schemed to erase completely from the minds and hearts of the Korean people any notions stimulating national pride. To accomplish this, Japan taught that Korean history was merely a branch of Japanese history, attempting in this way to eradicate Korean history.

F. Requiring Worship of Japanese Gods

To eradicate Korean national consciousness and replace it with a Japanese identity, the Japanese required every Korean to have in his home an altar enshrining Japanese deities before which he was to bow every morning in worship. Moreover, the Japanese Government-General erected Shinto shrines on hills throughout the peninsula and forced Koreans to worship there as well.

G. Attempts to Promote Belief in Japanese Superiority

Starting in 1937, Koreans were required to bow daily toward the east as a sign of respect for the emperor of Japanese. That same year Koreans, as subjects of the Japanese emperor and the Japanese empire, were ordered to recite aloud the "Oath of Imperial Subjects," vowing to render their devoted service to the emperor and the empire.

In conclusion, Japanese colonial rule over Korea did not industrialize the Korean economy, did not democratize Korean politics, and did not promote a pride in a distinctive Korean national community. Therefore, when the impact of Japanese colonial rule is evaluated in accordance with the standard definition of modernization, it is clear that Japanese colonial rule did not modernize Korea.

FOOTNOTES (Part Ⅲ-19)

1. Shin Yong-ha, "Criticism of Japanese Imperialism," *Studies of the History of the Korean Independence Movement*, Vol. 6, 1992; "The Obstruction of Korea's Modernization Under the Japanese," *Korea and Change in the World System*, 1994, Chimmundang.

2. At a debate entitled "Problems with Modernization under Japanese colonialism Theory," sponsored by the research Centre of Modern History, one participant proposed Yun Tongju's "The Sky, The Wing, The Stars and Poetry" as an example of modernity which supported the notion of modernization under colonialism. However, this modern poem is not evidence for any modernizing impact of Japanese colonial rule. On the contrary, Japanese colonial policies hindered and repressed modernization by incarcerating Yun Tongiu, who died from the effects of biological experiments in Japanese prison.

3. Tokuzo Fukuda, "Kankoku no Keizaisoshiki to Keizai Tani," *Naigai aonso*, 1904. Fukuda's essay began to be taken seriously and influence the thinking of others when it was revised and published in *Keizai gaku Kenkyu* in 1915.

20. A Historical Study of Korea's Title to Dokdo

1. First Written Record on Dokdo

The first written records on Dokdo are traced to *"Silla pon'gi* (Annals of the Kings of Silla)" and *"Yŏljŏn* (Biographies)" both in *Samguk sagi* (History of the Three Kingdoms). These entries state that Dokdo became a part of the Korean territory in 512 A.D. when Usan'guk was subjugated by Silla.[1]

Some Japanese scholars question whether Usan'guk comprised Dokdo as part of its territory in addition to Ullŭngdo when the country was brought under the dominion of Silla. To this query, *Man'gi yoram* (Handbook of State Affairs) of 1808 quotes *Yŏjiji* (Geographical Gazetteer) in its chapter on military administration: "Usando and Ullŭngdo all belonged to Usan'guk, and Usando is what Japanese call Matsushima."[2] The Japanese scholar accede to the fact that, up to 1900, Ullŭngdo had been called Takeshima and Dokdo, Matsushima, by Japanese. As for the Korean appellation, Dokdo was originally called Usando, implying its derivation from Usan'guk.

Around the end of *Koryŏ, waegu* (Japanese pirates) had become increasingly rampant, plundering coastal areas, and as Ullŭngdo had been subject to their frequent and severe pillage, King Taejong of the Chosŏn dynasty sought the safety of the islanders by evacuating them inland and took a vacant island policy toward Ullŭndo.

Some of them escaped to Ullŭndo for re-settlement, but were brought back inland again and again. In this process, Dokdo acquired the official designation of Usando.

Although the Chosŏn dynasty had, since King Taejong, continued the vacant island policy for Ullŭndo and Dokdo, the latter presenting no problem as the rock island were uninhabited, and this did not mean they were abandoned. The administrative policy was adopted out of necessity to ensure the safety and security of the inhabitants.

Following in the footsteps of King Taejong, King Sejong adhered to the vacant island policy, but confirmed Korea's title to these islands in the gazetteer in *Sejong sillok* (Annals of King Sejong) as follow: "Two islands of Usan and Mulŭng are not far off from each other, so one is visible from the other on a fine day. They were called Usan'guk during the period of Silla."[3]

Usan refers to Dokdo, and Mulŭng to Ullŭndo, and the hyŏn to Uljinhyŏn (country).

The Chosŏn dynasty government compiled and published *Ton'guk yŏji sŭngnam* (Augmented Survey of the Geogrpahy of Korea) in 1481 and *Sinjŭng tongguk yŏji sŭngnam* (Revised and Augmented Survey of the Geography of Korea)[4] in 1531 to define and demarcate authoritatively the territory of Korea. Of these, the former has not survived but its contents are incorporated into the latter.

The Revised and Augmented Survey of the Geography of Korea states that "Dokdo and Ullŭndo are under the jurisdiction of Uljinhyŏn of Kangwŏndo as an administrative unit." On the map attached to the book are shown two separate islands of Usado (Dokdo) and Ullŭndo in the middle of the Eastern Sea.[5]

The old maps published in Korea thereafter follow, the example set by this gazetteer and its attached map in recording the two separate islands. Slightly different location of the islands are seen on the maps, which are attributable to immature cartographical skills, but which do not affect the fundamental question of Korea's title to these islands. In particular, the three major maps, i.e., *Tongguk chido* (The Map of Korea) by Chŏng Sang-gi (1678-1752), *Haejwa chŏndo* of 1822, and *Chosŏn chŏndo* (a Complete Map of Korea) by Kim Tae-gŏn (1821-1846) show the exact location and name of Usando (Dokdo)on the right side of Ullŭndo.[6]

2. First Japanese Record on Dokdo

The Japanese government cites *Onshu shicho goki* (Records on Observations in Oki Province) edited by Saito Hosen in 1667 as the first record on Dokdo. Saito was a retainer of the daimyo of Izumo (sesshu) and at his lord's behest made an observation trip to Oki Island and submitted the report to his lord. In the report, Dokdo and Ullŭndo were both ascribed to *Koryŏ* (Korea), and Oki to Japan as its westernmost boundary on the following way:

Oki is the middle of the North Sea, so it is called Okinoshima. Going further from there for two days and one night in the direction of northwest, one reaches Matsushima. Also there is Takeshima at another day's travel distance. These two islands are uninhabited and getting a sight of *Koryŏ* from there is like viewing Oki from Onshu. And thus Oki marks the northwestern boundary of Japan.[7]

Here again, Matsushima refers to Dokdo and Takeshima to Ullŭndo. This first Japanese record on Dokdo as an official document clearly places Oki within Japan's territory, and Dokdo and Ullŭndo within that of *Koryŏ*.

3. Disputes over Ullŭndo and Dokdo at the End of the 17th Century

Around the end of the 17th century, Japan attempted to seize Ullŭndo and Dokdo but was frustrated by the activities of a Korean named An Yong-bok and the hardliners in the government who prevailed over the appeasers and took tough measures to defend them.

Although the Chosŏn dynasty government adhered to the vacant island policy, the Korean fishermen along the southern and eastern coasts could not resist the temptation to fish in the rich fishing grounds off these two islands. On the other hand, the Tokugawa shogunate, being aware of this Korean government policy, granted licenses to Otani Jinkichi and Murakawa Ichihei of Yonago to take passage to Ullŭngdo and Dokdo without the knowledge of the Korean government in 1618 and in 1661 respectively. This enabled the Otanis and Murakamis to cross secretly to Ullŭndo to fish and fell trees. This often gave rise to conflicts between the fishermen from Korea and Japan.

At last, in the spring of 1693, in the 19th year of King Suk-jong, about 40 Korean fishermen from Tongane and Ulsan clashed with the fishermen of the Otanis and the Murakamis. The Japanese proposed that the matter be settled peacefully and asked the Koreans to send their delegates. An Yong-bok and Pak Ŏ-dun went over to the Japanese side as Korean delegates, but were taken by force to Oki. There An Yong-bok squarely confronted the lord of Okinoshima and protested against his detention while he as a Korean entered the Korean land of Ullŭndo.[8]

The lord found the case beyond his control and sent An Yong-bok to his superior the magistrate of Hokishu (shimane-ken today).Interrogated by the magistrate, An explained in a dignified manner that Ullŭndo was Korea's territory and demanded that the magistrate keep the Japanese fishermen off the island. The magistrate of Hokishu was aware that Ullŭndo belonged to Korea and transferred An to the Kanpaku (Imperial Regent) of the Shogunate, who in turn confirmed Korea's title to Ullŭndo, ordered the magistrate of Hokishu to write a note that Ullŭndo was not Japan's land, and to sent An back to Korea. While en route to Korea, An was seized by the lord of Nagasaki, the note he was carrying with him was taken away and he was jailed on the grounds that he had trespassed on Japanese territory.

Availing himself of this event, the lord of Tsushima, So Yoshitsugu, attempted to annex Ullŭndo and Dokdo to Tsushima. He apprehended An as an intruder into the Japanese territory of Takeshima and turned him over to the magistrate of Tongnae. So Yoshitsugu sent an envoy named Tachibana Masashige to Tongnae with his letter to be transmitted to the Chosŏn dynasty government through the magistrate. In the letter, So pretended there existed a Takeshima that belonged to Japan and that was similar to but was different from Ullŭndo. He stated that he would not allow any Korean boat to go to Takeshima and demanded that the Korean government strictly keep the Korean fishermen from Takeshima.[9] The lord of Tsushima who knew that Takeshima was but another name for Ullŭndo might have tried to inveigle the Korean government into accepting the existence of a japanese-owned island of Takeshima in written form, to start a dispute over the possession of Takeshima alias Ullŭndo, and finally to absorb the island into his possession. This was a multi-stage stratagem.

The Chosŏn dynasty government leaders split over the issue between the hawks and the doves. First the moderate faction in power prevailed, cautioning against a head-on clash with the Japanese whose militancy and ferociousness were well proved during the Hideyoshi invasion of Korea (1592-1598). They feigned ignorance of the fact that Chukto (Takeshima) was another name for Ullŭndo and only made it clear that Ullŭndo was Korea's territory, recognized Takeshima as Japan's and promised to keep Koreans from fishing off the island. The response to the lord of Tsushima reads in part:

> Whereas our fishermen on the eastern coast are not allowed to go out to an ocean, and are even prohibited to travel at will to Ullŭndo that is our territory but is thought to be rather far off, how could they be authorized to go over to other places? Now that this boat had ventured into your territory of Takeshima and your side took the trouble of remanding them to us, and dispatching an official letter from afar, we should like to express our gratitude for your amities of good neighorliness.[10]

The moderate faction's equivocation over the designation of Ullŭndo that was also called Chukto (Takeshima) and its accedence to the Japanese claim to a Takeshima were typical of an easy-going expedient that might sow the seeds of a dispute over the title to Ullŭndo itself.

Tachibana Masashige, who was staying at the Japan House in Tongnae, thought he had half-accomplished his mission when he received Korea's reply stating "your territory of Takeshima..," but found objectionable the passage... "our territory Ullŭndo." He persistently requested for a fortnight that these words be deleted from the note, but to no avail.[11] The deletion of these words would place Ullŭndo at the disposal of Japan in the name of Takeshima.

At the news, the hardliners rose to action, censured the moderates, and drove them out of power. Now in power, Nam Ku-man, the leader of the hardliners, memorialized the King to punish the appeasers and recover the official letter they had given to the Japanese. This was granted royal sanction.

Nam Ku-man and his followers questioned An Yong-bok and others who had been kidnapped to Japan, and eventually became aware of the scheme concocted by the lords of Tsushima and Nagasaiki in disregard of the Kanpaku's directive to recognize Ullŭndo (Takeshima) as Korea's territory. Ignorant of this turn of events in the Korean government., So of Tsushima sent Tachibana to Tongnae again in August 1694, to repeat his request for expurgation of the words "Our territory Ullŭndo" from the letter.

The new Korean government turned this down out of hand, declared the first reply *null and void*, and sent a new, revised letter to the effect that Takeshima was another name for Ullŭndo which was Korea's territory. It reprehended the Japanese act of encroachment on the Korean territory and the kidnapping of An Yong-bok and others from the Korean territory. The letter strongly requested that the Shogunate in Edo be notified of this fact and that Japanese be barred from coming to Ullŭndo again. However, So Yoshitsugu of Tsushima took issue with this and confronted the Korean government without withdrawing his claim to Ullŭndo, calling it Takeshima. This led to tension between the Korean government and the shogunate in Edo.[12]

In the meantime, So Yoshitsugu died and was succeeded by So Yoshimichi who, on his inauguration, paid a courtesy call on the Kanpaku in January 1696. There in Edo, in the presence of the magistrates of Hoki and three other provinces, the Kanpaku raised some pointed questions to So Yoshimichi on the question of Takeshima. After a series of queries and answers and the ensuing discussions, a decision was reached to recognize Takeshima (Ullŭndo) and its adjacent island as Korea's territory.

The Kanpaku's instructions to So included the following: (1) Takeshima is about 160-*ri* (64 km) from Hoki while it is only about 40-*ri* (16 km) from Korea, and it can be considered to be a Korean territory as it is nearer to the country; (2) Japanese are to be forbidden henceforth to make passage to Takeshima; (3) the lord of Tsushima should communicate this to Korea; (4) he should also send the Osakabe Daisuke (judge) of Tsushima to Korea officially to notify the Korean government of this decision and report the result of his mission to the Kanpaku.[13]

This was an important decision by the Tokugawa shogunate as the central government of Japan to reconfirm Korea's title to Ullŭndo and its adjacent island,. Upon his return to Tsushima, So Yoshimichi sent a brief note to Korea through an official translator wherein he conveyed the decision of the Kanpaku,[14] but he resorted to a delaying tactic without sending the Osakabe Daisuke.

An Yong-bok, having realized So's stratagem to seize Ullŭndo and Dokdo eventually despite the Kanpaku's decision, decided to visit the magistrate of Hokishu again and negotiate the question personally.

According to the *Sukchong sillok* (Annals of King Sukchong), An Yong-bok enlisted 16 fishermen and went to Ullŭndo in 1696. There he found some Japanese fishing boats at anchor. An protested loudly against the Japanese for their transgression into the Korean territory of Ullŭndo and threatened to capture them. The Japanese said they were living in Matsushima (Dokdo) and strayed into the place while fishing and would return to where they came from. An Yong-bok retorted that Matsushima was also Korea's possession and demanded to know why they were living on a Korean island. Early the next morning, he and the Korean fishermen went to Usando (Dokdo) and there some Japanese were cooking fish in a cauldron. An and his company destroyed the cauldron and fulminated against them, and all the Japanese took flight to Japan.[15]

An and his company pursued the Japanese boats to Oki island. Asked by the lord of Oki what had brought him there, An explained that he had come to the island several years before, Japanese authorities had agreed to place the two islands of Ullŭndo and Usando within the boundary of Korea's territory, and he had been issued Kanpaku's official document to that effect. Then he pressed for the reason why the Japanese had invaded the Korean territory again, and the lord promised to transmit An's protest to his superior, the magistrate of Hokishu. However, no reply was forthcoming for a long period of time.[16]

An Yong-bok and his company decided to negotiate directly with the magistrate. Impersonating a Revenue Supervisor for the two islands of Ullŭndo and Usando, An met the magistrate and explained how the Kanpaku's letter issued to him, attesting to Korean sovereignty over the two islands, had been seized and doctored by the lord of Tsushima, who attempted to incorporate these islands into his possession by sending an emissary to the Korean government. An went on to say that he would lodge an appeal to the Kanpaku and debunk the whole frame-up.[17] The magistrate granted him permission and requested that Korea bring to his attention by means of an official note and a translator any future act of encroachment on Ullŭndo and Dokdo that were Korean possessions and any stretch of authority by the lord of Tsushima vis-a-vis the question of these islands and promised to mete out heavy punishment for any such act.[18]

The magistrate had been presented several months before when the Kanpaku decided to recognize Korea's claim to Ullŭndo and Dokdo and instructed the lord of Tsushima to send the Osakabe Daiske (judge) to Korea to notify the Korean government of his decision.

An Yong-bok's activity proved highly successful. Now, the lord of Tsushima sent Judge Tahirano Naritsune to Korea in January 1697, to notify the Korean government of the Kanpaku's decision. By 1699 the diplomatic notes had been exchanged and all the formalities had been cleared to recognize Korean title to Ullŭndo and Dokdo.[19]

After the Kanpaku reconfirmed Korea's title to Ullŭndo and Dokdo around the end of the 17th century with the An Yong-bok incident as the turning point, no documentary records of the period showed Japan's claim to these two islands. (This refers to the documents of the period released to date by the Japanese government.) Nor do any Japanese maps edited by the government or semi-governmental organizations since the end of the 17th century show these two islands as Japanese possessions.[20]

The *sangoku setsujozu* (A Map of Three Adjoining Countries), a map attached to the *sangoku tsuran zusetsu* (An Illustrated General Survey of Three Countries) by Hayashi Shihei (1738-1793), an eminent scholar of the day, published in 1785 shows international boundaries and foreign countries in different colors; Korea in yellow and Japan in green. On the map Ullŭndo and Dokdo are shown in their exact positions in yellow. Alongside the islands Hayashi writes, "Korea's possessions."

Hayashi also treats Korea and these two islands in the same way in color and explanatory note in the *Dainihonzu* (A Great Japan's Map), another map attached to *An Illustrated General Survey of Three Countries*. In the latter part of the 18th century, a Japanese geographer made a map called *Soezu* (A Complete Illustrated Map) which uses colors to distinguish national borders and territories: Korea in yellow and Japan in red. Ullŭndo and Dokdo are not identified by name but are shown in yellow in their accurate positions and described as "Korea's possessions."

These typical maps of the Tokugawa era are solid evidence that Ullŭndo and Dokdo are integral parts of Korea's territory, which the Japanese government cannot negate. The Tokugawa Shogunate and the Japanese people had since recognized and respected these two islands as Korea's until the Meiji Restoration of 1868.

4. Meiji Government's Reconfirmation of Korea's Title to Dokdo

When the Meiji government was established in 1868 in place of the Tokugawa regime overthrown by the samurai, the Japanese Foreign Ministry sent Sada Hakudo and Moriyama shigeru to Korea to study the Korean situation in December 1869. The list of items for investigation include the circumstances under which Takeshima (Ullŭndo) and Matsushima (Dokdo) had become Korea's possessions, and it was submitted to and approved by the Dajokan (the Council of State).[21]

This list is evidence that the Foreign Ministry and the Dajokan both recognized Korea's title to these two islands. The report of this study mission was included in the *Chosenkoku kosaishimatsu naitansho* (A Confidential Inquiry into the Particulars of Korea's Foreign Relations) and was incorporated in the *Nihon gaiko bunsho* (Japan's Diplomatic Documents).[22] This official document also substantiates the Japanese government's acknowledgment of these two islands as Korea's territory.

Among the official document released by the Japanese Ministry of Home Affairs are papers that attest to Korea's title to Ullŭndo and Dokdo. In 1876 the Ministry instructed all the prefectures to conduct a land survey in order to make a national cadaster and a map of the nation. At this time, Shimane prefecture inquired of the Ministry whether or not Takeshima (Ullŭndo) and Matsushima (Dokdo) were to be covered by this survey. The Ministry had examined for five months all the papers exchanged between Korea and Japan around the end of the 17th century and concluded that the question of the title to these two islands had already been resolved in 1699 (the 12th year of Genroku). The Ministry decided to exclude these islands from the survey.[23]

However, the Ministry considered it necessary to refer the matter to the Dajokan for its sanction. To this, Iwakura Tonomi, Minister of the Right, the third highest in the cabinet and the acting head of the Dajokan approved an instruction to be sent to the Ministry on March 20, 1877. It was on April 9, 1877, that the instruction was dispatched to Shimane prefecture. The directive made it clear that Japan had nothing to do with Takeshima (Ullŭndo) and Dokdo that were part of Korea's territory and that they should be excluded from the land survey.[24]

Not only the Ministries of Foreign Affairs and Home Affairs, and the

Dajokan, but also the Japanese Ministries of the Army and Navy, recognized Dokdo (Matsushima) as Korea's territory in the maps they edited and published.

Chosen jenzu (A Complete Map of Korea) published by the Staff Bureau of the Ministry of the Army in 1875 positions Dokdo in the territory of the Korea in the deliberately expanded righthand margin. The *Chosen tokai kaiganzu* (A Map of the Eastern Coast of Korea) by the Hydrographic Bureau of the Ministry of the Navy places the two islands inside the Korean territory.

The latter published in 1876 was based on the charts mapped by Russian and British warships and positions Dokdo in the Korean territory. It shows, in the lower righthand section, three accurate and vivid photograph-like drawings of Dokdo done by the Russians from three different distances.[25] The map was reprinted in 1887 and ran into many impressions until 1905.

The Ministry of the Navy also published *Chosen suiroshi* (The Korean Sealanes) wherein Dokdo appears in the Korean territory. *Kan'ei suiroshi* (The Sealanes of the World) by the Ministry of the Navy in 1886 first uses the name "Liancourt Rocks" for Dokdo in part 4, "Korea's Eastern Coast,"[26] in Vol. II (second edition). The publication of the chart was discontinued in 1889 when the sealanes of the world were treated separately by countries. The Japanese version does not include Dokdo.[27]

This practice by the Ministry of the Navy had continued until January 1905 when Japan incorporated Dokdo *sub rosa* into Shimane prefecture without the knowledge of Korea. This was immediately after the Japanese victory in the Russo-Japanese War when Korea was virtually under Japanese control. Then in 1907 Japan began to show Dokdo north of Okinoshima in the Vol. IV of the *Japanese Sealanes*.

5. Chosŏn dynasty's Re-development of Ullŭndo and Dokdo and Imperial Ordinance No. 41

While the Chosŏn dynasty government was taking the vacant island policy for Ullŭndo and Dokdo, foreign men-of-war began appearing in the Korean territorial seas from the close of the 18th century, and they gave Western names to these two islands.

In 1787, French Naval Captain Jean Francois Galaupe de Perouse took two warships, the *Bussole* and another, to the Korean seas off Chejudo and Ullŭndo and surveyed the coastal areas. Ullŭndo was named after Dagelet, an instructor at the French Naval Academy who had come with Captain de

Perouse. Then in 1849, anther French warship *Liancourt* surveyed Dokdo and christened it "Liancourt Rocks." After that "Dagelet Island" and "Liancourt Rocks" were used in the European maps and gazetteers.

Then Russians followed suit. In 1854, the Russian warship *palada* under the command of Putiatin made a survey of Dokdo and gave it the name of "Manalai and Olivutsa Rocks." Further in 1855, the British warship *Hornet* commanded by Cdr. Charles C. Forsyth gave the island another name, "Hornet Rocks." but Dokdo was popularly known "Liancourt Rocks" in Europe.

The Chosŏn dynasty government felt a tense atmosphere when Korea was forced by the Japanese to open its ports in 1876 and Japanese came in masse to Ullŭndo and indulged in felling trees and fishing. The Koreans from the mainland coast also began to settle down there.

The government sent Yi Kyu-wŏn as inspector to Ullŭndo to study the situation there in April 1882. He found 140 Koreans on the island; 115 of them (82%) were from Chŏllado; 14 (10%) from Kangwŏndo; and 10 (7%) from Kyŏngsangdo; and one from Kyŏnggido. The Japanese numbered 78.[28]

From June 1882, the Korean government began to file strong protests with the Japanese Foreign Ministry against the Japanese intrusion into and the felling of trees on the island and demanded that an immediate end be put to such illegal acts. In March 1883, the government appointed Kim Ok-kyun, a leader of the progressive group, Commissioner for the Development of the Southeastern Islands and Whaling, and set about developing and resettling Ullŭndo and Dokdo in earnest, thus abandoning the vacant island policy.[29] Apparent in the official title of Kim was the government intention to cover not only Ullŭndo but also Dokdo by "Southeastern Islands."

The government appointed a head for the island and encouraged resettlement. As a result the population of the island had increased to 1,134 (662 males and 472 females) dwelling in 397 houses in 12 villages as of March 1897. A total of 1,160 acres of land had come under cultivation. But fishing off the island and Dokdo was the most important industry to support the population.[30]

The Chosŏn dynasty was renamed Taehan Cheguk or the Empire of Korea in 1897 and as Japanese encroachment on Ullŭndo and logging had become a serious problem, the government sent an investigation team headed by U Yong-jŏng to Ullŭndo in October, 1899.[31] U found about 70 Japanese intruders there while the head of the island could do nothing without any troops to enforce the law. A dire need was felt for a counteraction.[32]

To cope with the situation, the government promulgated Imperial Ordinance No. 41 on October 25, 1900, which renamed Ullŭndo Uldo and upgraded the office of the head to *kunsu* (county magistrate). The new *kun* covered Ullŭndo and its adjoining islands which had been under the control of Uljinhyŏn in Kangwŏndo.[33]

Article Ⅱ of the ordinance designated Taehadong as *kun* office venue and defined the jurisdiction of the Uldo county magistrate as extending over the whole of Ullŭndo and Chukto, and Sŏkdo. Here Chukdo refers to Chuksŏdo, a rocky islet adjoining Ullŭndo that was confirmed by Yi Kyu-wŏn in his diary during his inspection trip there. Sŏkdo is Dokdo.

A majority of the people settled down on Ullŭndo had come from Chŏllado. In the dialect of that region, tol (돌 in the vulgate; 石 in Chinese character) become tok (독), thus dolsŏm (rocky island) becomes doksŏm. Having been reported this way, the government registered the island as Sŏkdo 石島 in the Chinese writing system, which was preferred by the literati-official (as was Latin under Roman occuption and French after the Norman conquest in Great Britain) even after the creation of the *han'gul*, an indigenous alphabet in 1447.

A plethora of similar cases is found in Korea, particularly in the southern region, not only in the names of islands, but also those of valleys and villages. In some cases doksŏm becomes Dokdo 石島: dok 獨 standing for the sound of dok (corruption of dol) and do 島, a Chinese character, meaning sŏm (island).

Although the government adopted the name of Sŏkdo for Dokdo when the ordinance came into effect, the residents of Ullŭndo called the island Sŏkdo or Dokdo interchangeably.

The Japanese first referred to this island as Dokdo in 1904 during the Russo-Japanese War when the Japanese warship *Niitakago* was sent to Ullŭndo to investigate the area in preparation for building a watchtower on Dokdo. An entry in the report dated September 25, 1904 reads: "The Liancourt Rocks are called Dokdo by the Koreans while it is referred to as Liancourt by the Japanese fishermen."[34] The important fact here is that the Korean government exercised its sovereignty over Dokdo (Sŏkdo) in 1900 by the promulgation of Imperial Ordinance No. 41 and by the appointment of the county magistrate.

6. Japan's Annexation of Dokdo

As the Russo-Japanese War broke out on February 8, 1904, the Japanese Navy built many watchtowers with wireless telegraphs on Korean coasts including two on Ullŭndo (in August 1904) to keep watch on the movements of the Russian Vladivostok fleet.[35] In order to construct another on Dokdo , the Navy sent the warship *Tsushima* to the area to prepare for the work in November 1904.[36]

At this time a Japanese fisherman living in Shimane prefecture by the name of Nakai Yozaburo intended to obtain a Korean government exclusive license for sea lion hunting and fishing off Dokdo. He applied to the Japanese Ministry of Agriculture and Commerce for negotiations with the Korean government on his behalf.[37] This information was passed to the Navy by the Director of the Fisheries Bureau of the Ministry. Adm. Kimotsuki Kenko, Director of Hydrographic Bureau of the Ministry of Navy, assumed Dokdo (Liancourt) to be a *terra nullius*, and told Nakai to apply to the Japanese government, not the Korean government, for "incorporation of Liancourt into Japanese territory and also for lease of the island."[38] Adm. Kimotsuki apparently tried to take advantage of the stationing of Japanese troops in Seoul and the prevailing Japanese influence over the Korean government for annexation of Dokdo and the establishment of a Japanese surveillance network there.

That Nakai was cognizant of the legal status of Korea's Dokdo is evident in "*Nakai Yozaburo rirekisho* (Nakai's peronal History),"[39] "*Nakai jigyo keiei gaiyo* (An Outline of Nakai's Business Operations),"[40] and *Shimane kenshi* (Annals of Shimane prefecture).[41] But he followed Adm. Kimotsuki's demand and filed the afore-said application to the Ministries of Home Affairs, Foreign Affairs, and Agriculture and Commerce on September 27, 1904.

At the Japanese cabinet meeting on January 28, 1905, Nakai's application was approved and it was decided "to incorporate into Japan's territory a *terra nullius* in lat. 39° 9.30″ N. and long. 131° 55″ E., 85 nautical miles off Okinoshima, there being no evidence of its being occupied by any country; to call it Takeshima, and to place it under the jurisdiction of the administrator of Okinoshima."

The Ministry of Home Affairs notified Shimane prefecture of this cabinet decision, and the prefecture, in turn, put the decision on public notice (Prefectural notice No. 40) repeating the information given in the parentheses above (on the bulletin of the prefecture and local newspapers) on February 22, 1905. Now, this Japanese action is to be examined in light of international law, precedents and practice.

First, Japan's claim to prior occupation of a *terra nullius*. As has been seen already, there are many documents attesting to Korea' title to Dokdo before January 1905, and the Japanese documents that ascertain Korea's possession of Dokdo before this period abound, too. There is also a Russian publication on the topography of Korea by the Ministry of the Treasury of the Russian government, edited in 1898 and published in 1900, which recognizes Dokdo as part of the Korean territory, and which shows the accurate location of the island, drawing on the survey conducted by the Russian warships.[42] These documents provide tangible evidence that Dokdo was not a *terra nullius* at the time of Japan's annexation of Dokdo .

Second, the mode of notification of the acquisition of the territory should be called into question. The acquisition of a new territory is to be notified to the countries involved if it is to satisfy the requirements of international law and practice. The Japanese government had neither contacted the Korean government for inquiry on the question beforehand no served any notification afterwards.

This contrasts sharply with the Japan's action when it acquired the Bonin (Ogasawara) Islands in the Pacific. Then Japan contacted Great Britain and the U.S. several times, which were only remotely involved in them; it notified 12 European countries of its establishment of control over the islands.

Considering that the Meiji government recognized Korea's title to Dokdo in 1870 through the Foreign Ministry and the Dajokan, in 1877 through the Ministry of Home affairs and the Dajokan, in 1875 through the Ministry of the Army, in 1876 and several times thereafter through the Ministry of the Navy, and in 1905 through the Ministry of Home Affairs when it opposed the plan to incorporate Dokdo, the question naturally follows why Japan did not contact the Korean government beforehand and did not notify it of the action afterwards.

The answer seems simple: the Japanese knew that the island had been under Korean sovereignty and the Korean government would have reacted immediately and strongly, had it known of Japan's intent or act of annexation. Another point for consideration is that foreign diplomatic missions posted in Seoul were still active then, and Japan may have concluded it inadvisable to incur their suspicion of its aggressive designs on Korea after the end of the Russo-Japanese war by making public announcement of the acquisition of Dokdo.

Accordingly, the Japanese government may have tried to veil the matter from public knowledge. This action was followed by the construction of a watchtower on Dokdo by the Japanese Navy in July 1905. It was eventually removed after the end of the war with Russia.[43]

7. Korcan Government's Reaction

The Korean government became aware of the matter on March 28, 1906, one year after the event took place, when the lord of Okinoshima of Shimane prefecture and party called on magistrate Sim Hŭng-t'aek of Ullŭndo during their inspection trip to Dokdo and told him that the island had become Japan's possession.

The date, March 28, 1906, is important. On September 5, 1905, the Portsmouth Treaty was signed ending the Russo-Japanese War, and on November 18, 1905, Japan used its troops in Seoul and forced a Protectorate Treaty it had drafted upon Korea. The whole proceeding was illegal without obtaining the Korean Emperor's sanction and seal and with the royal court under duress because it was surrounded by Japanese troops.

The two essential points of the treaty are the transfer of full authority over foreign affairs to Japan and the appointment of a Japanese Resident-General under the Korean Emperor to supervise all aspects of the Korean government operation. It thus reduced Korea to semi-colonial status.

The Korean Ministry of Foreign Affaires was dismantled on January 17, 1906; the Resident-General's office opened in Seoul in February 1 that year and took over the conduct of the foreign affairs of the Korean government. Then the lord of Okinoshima was sent to Ullŭndo to inform, as if casually, the Korean country magistrate of the incorporation of Dokdo. Under these circumstances, Korea could not take any measures against the Japanese action on Dokdo.

Startled at the news, magistrate Sim Hŭng-t'aek reported the following day (March 29, 1906) to the Ministry of Home Affairs through the Governor of Kwangwŏndo that he had been apprised of the incorporation into the Japanese territory of Dokdo that was under the jurisdiction of "this county."[44] By "this county," Dokdo was meant to be part of the Korean territory.

The Minister of Home Affairs, upon receipt of the report, renounced the Japanese claim, stating that "it is totally groundless for the Japanese to lay claim to Dokdo and I am shocked at the report."[45] Having thus been reported, the *Ch'amjŏng taeshin* of the Uijŏngbu (State Council)–the acting head of government then–issued Directive No. III on April 29, 1906, wherein he denounced the Japanese claim as groundless and ordered a full inquiry into the matter.[46]

Taehan maeil sinbo[47] and *Hwangsŏng sinmun*,[48] two major papers of the day, reported the Japanese action in full and protested vehemently against it. Also, Hwang Hyŏn (1855-1910), a known savant of the day, bitterly criticized and protested against the Japanese invasion of Dokdo in his writings: *Ohakimun* (A Miscellany)[49] and *Maech'ŏn yarok* (personal Accounts of maech'ŏn)[50]

The Japanese government today has often pointed out the non-action on the part of the Korean government when Dokdo was annexed and tended to take it as its acquiescence, but it fails to take into account the fact that the Japanese Resident-General in Korea conducted foreign affairs and the Korean government had no dipolmatic channel of its own to make representation against the Japanese claim. It was five years prior to the Japanese annexation of the Empire of Korea that Dokdo fell prey to the Japanese machinations.

8. SCAPIN No. 677 and Reversion of Dokdo

Following the surrender of Japan, SCAP GHQ was set up in Tokyo, which began implement the Cairo and Potsdam Declaration. As the intial step, a Memorandum for Government and Administrative Separation of Certain Outlying Areas from Japan was issued as SCAPIN (Supreme Command for Allied Powers Instruction) No. 677, on January 29, 1946.

This directive limited Japan's territory to the four main islands of Hokkaido, Houshu, and Shigoku, and about 1,000 smaller islands. Excluded from the definition in Clause 5 of Japan's territories were Ullŭndo, Dokdo and Chejudo.

Clause 5 of the instruction provides that "the definition of the Japan contained in the directive shall also apply to all future directives, memoranda and orders from the Headquarters unless otherwise specified therein."

Therefore, without another specific instruction by SCAP this definition could not be changed and would continue to be binding.

In accordance with this instruction, SCAP transferred the jurisdiction over Dokdo to the U.S. Military Government in Korea on January 29, 1946. When the Republic of Korea, was proclaimed on August 15, 1948, all territories of Korea, including Dokdo, automatically reverted to the Korean government.

On June 22, 1946, SCAPIN No. 1033 was issued, in which Clause 5 set up a fishing and whaling area permitted for Japanese fishermen and prohibited Japanese ships and crew from entering the 12-nautical mile seas off the Liancourt Rocks at lat. 37° 15″ E., and approaching the island. SCAP recogniged again Dokdo as Korea's territory.

9. A Need to Change Korean Policy toward Dokdo

From this brief study, it is clear that Dokdo has since 512 A.D. been an integral part of the Korean territory. It is an island appended to Ullŭndo.

There are not any ancient documents published by the Japanese government that claim Dokdo as a Japanese territory. Nevertheless, the Japanese government has been advocating the principle of "prior occupation of a *terra nullius*" and trying to justify the incorporation of Dokdo into its territory in February 1905. But as so many old documents prove, Dokdo had not been a *terra nullius* before February 1905, but had long been part of the Korean territory.

Now, the Japanese government is shifting its position to its "historical title." Here again the Japanese side has the burden of proof to substantiate its historical ownership of Dokdo. This assertion also contradicts the action Japan took in February 1905 under the pretext of acquiring a *terra nullius*. Why should Japan have had to acquire the island anew if it had been an inherent part of its territory?

Today the Japanese government is considering proclaiming a 200-mile exclusive economic zone and is asserting its ownership of Dokdo. The maps appended to the Japanese government-authorized geography textbooks for elementary and secondary schools show Dokdo as Japanese territory. This is not a salutary action since it is a continuation of an imperial expansionist policy of the past and is detrimental to the promotion of good neighborliness between the two countries.

To the Korean people, Dokdo is not simply the question of small rocks, but that of the emergence of neo-expansionism in Japan.

FOOTNOTES (Part Ⅲ-20)

1.　Kim Pu-sik, compl., *Samguk sagi* (History of the Three Kingdoms, 1146). Photographic reproduction in the Kyujang-gak Library, Seoul National University, Vol. IV: *Silla pon'gi* (Annals of the Kingdom of Silla); the entry on the Summer June, 13th Year in Part 4 (King Chijung) reads: In June in the 13th year, Usan'guk surrendered and has since paid a tribute of staple products each eyar. Usan'guk is an island in the middle of the sea due east of Myŏngju and is also called Ullŭngdo. The area is 100 *ri* (One *ri* is about 2.44 miles.). The people were fierce and did not surrender, so Ich'an (Ich'an is the second highest rank in the 17-grade hierarchy.) Isabu was appointed the lord of Asulnaju to subjugate them⋯the people of Usan'guk were horrified of him and soon surrendered, Vol. 44: "*Yŏljŏn* (Biographies)." the entry on Isabu in Part 4 reads: Isabu was a native of Silla with the surname of Kim and was a 4th generation descendant of King Naemul. During the reign of King Chijung (King Chidoryak) he became a border garrison commander and, applying an old ruse of an equestrian game first used by Gen. Isabu, took Kayaguk (also Kara). In the 13th year, he became the lord of Asulnaju and set out to annex Usan'guk. "They are benighted and fierce, and cannot be subjugated by forces along. Better use a ruse." said he. Then he had a large number of wooden lions made and carried them in the warships. Arriving on the shore, he commanded in a loud voice : "Surrender, or we will let loose all these ferocious beasts to trample you all to death." Much frightened, the people of Usan'guk yielded. According to another entry on Isabu in the *Yŏljŏn*, Gen. Isabu had trained his cavalry in the guise of an annual equestrian show seemingly for recreation in peace time, and used his cavaliers in a surprise attack on the foe in war.
2.　"Kunjŏng P'yŏn (Military Administration)" in *Man'gi yoram* (Handbook of State Affairs), edited by Sim Sang-gyu *et al.* in 1808. Photographic reproduction in the Kyujang-gak Library, Seoul National Univ. In classic Chinese.
3.　*Chiriji* (Gazetteer) in *Sejong sillok* (Annals of King Sejong), Vol. 153, Section on Uljinhyŏn, Kangwŏndo.
4.　*Tongguk yŏji sŭngnam* (Augmented Survey of the Geography of Korea) was compiled by No Sa-sin *et al.* by order of King Sŏngjong (9th King of the Chosŏn Dynasty) in 1481. It has not survived, but most of its contents are incorporated in the *Sinjŭng tongguk yŏji sŭngnam* (Revised and Augmented Survey of the Geography of Korea) edited by Yi Haeng during the reign of King Chungjong (11th King) in 1531. Typographical edition in classic Chinese, 55 Vols, 25 bks., in the Kyujang-gak Library,

Seoul National Univ.

5. Revised and Augmented Survey of the Geography of Korea, *ibid.*, Vol. 45, Section on Uljinhyŏn.

6. Yi Ch'an, "Chosŏn kojido esŏ bon tokdo (Dokdo as Seen in the Old Korean Maps)" in *Ullŭngdo Dokdo haksŭl chosa yŏn'gu* (Academic Survey and Research on Ullŭngdo and Dokdo), Seoul, Han'guk sahakhoe (Society of Korean History), 1978.

7. Saito Hosen, *Onshu shicho goki* (Records on Observations in Oki Province), Vol. I (Kokudaikibu) in Kawakami Kenzo, *Takeshima No rekishi chirigakuteki kenkyu* (A Historical and Geographical Study of Takeshima), 1966, Kokonshoten, Tokyo, p. 50.

8. *Sukchong sillok* (Annals of King Sukchong), Vol. 25, Feb. Sinmyo, 1694.

9. *Ibid.*, Vol. 26, section on February, Sinmyo, 1694.

10. *Ibid.*

11. *Ibid.*

12. *Ibid.*, Vol. 27, Ŭlyu, August, 1694.

13. Japan, Dajokan, ed., *Kobunrok, 1877: Naimusho No bu* (Official Documents 1877: The Ministry of Home Affairs, National Archives), Tokyo. See section on "Nihonkainai takeshima hoka itto chiseki hensankata ukagai (Inquiry about Cadastral Compilation on Takeshima and Another Island in the Japan See)," Annexed document No. 1 of the Genroku Period (1688-1704).

14. Kuksa P'yŏnch'an wiwŏnhoe (National History Compilation Committee: NHCC hereafter), *Pyŏnye chipyo* (Seoul: NHCC, 1967), Vol. 17, part 2, Feb. 1667 (Chong Ch'uk). This is a collection of case studies of all facets of diplomatic relations with Japan for two hundred years from the 15th King Sŏnjo (1567-1608) to the 23rd King Sunjo (1800-1834).

15. *Sukchong sillok* (Annals of King Sukchong), Vol. 30, Sept., Muin, 1696.

16. *Ibid.*

17. *Ibid.*

18. *Ibid.*

19. *Kobunrok, op.cit.*, Annexed Document No. 4 of the Genroku era (1688-1704).

20. *Sangoku setsujozu* (The Map of the Three Adjoining Countries) attached to *An Illustrated General Survey of Three Countries* and *Tainihon chizu* (The Map of Great Japan) are considered to be the same map originally, but were made into separate maps by later compilators.

21. Nihon gaimusho chosabu (Japanese Foreign Ministry Research Div.), ed., *Nihon gaiko bunsho* (Japanese Diplomatic Documents), Vol. II, Bk, 3, Document No. 574, dated Nov. 1, 1869: "An Inquiry from the Foreign Ministry to the Secretary of the Dajokan (Council of State)" and "An inquiry for instruction in items to be studied by the officials dispatched to Korea and the decision on this by the Dajokan."

22. *Japanese Diplomatic Documents*, Vol. III, Item 6, Document No. 87, dated Apr. 15, 1870: "Chosenkoku kosai shimatsu naitansho (Confidential Report on the Particulars

of Korea's Foreign Relations)" by Sada Hakubo and others of the Foreign Ministry, *Confidential Report on the Particulars of Korea's Foreign Relations,*" p. 137.

23. *Kobunrok, op.cit.,* dated Mar. 17, 1877.

24. *Ibid.,* Dajokan shirei bunsho (The Documents on the Dajokan's Instructions), dated Mar. 20, 1877; Hori Kazuo, 1905; *nen nihonno takeshima ryodo hennyu* (Japan's Incorporation of Takeshima into its Territory in 1905), *Chosenshi kenkyu ronbunshu* (Collection of Article on Korean History), No. 24, 1987; Shin Yong-ha, "A Study of Korea's Territorial Rights to Dokdo," *Journal of Korean Independence Movement Studies,* Vol. 3, 1989.

25. *Chosŏn ilbo,* Feb. 24, 1983. The report on the *Chosŏn tonghaean chido* (The Map of the Eastern Coast in Korea) in the Kyujan-gak Library, Seoul National University.

26. Hydrographic Department, Japanese Ministry of the Navy, *Kan'ei suiroshi* (The Sealanes of the World), 2nd ed., Vol. II (Tokyo:Ministry of the Navy, 1886), pp. 397-398.

27. *Chosen suiro shi* (The Korean Sealanes), 1886, Ministry of the Navy, Tokyo, pp. 255-256.

28. Yi Kyu-wŏn, *Ullŭngdo Kamch'al ilgi* (The Diary of Inspection in Ullŭngdo), supplement to Yi Sŏng-gŭn, "Kŭndae Ullŭngdo munjaewa kamch'alsa Yi Kyu-wŏn ŭi t'amhŏm sŏn'gwa (The Question of Ullŭngdo in Modern Times and Results of Inspector Yi Kyu-wŏn's Exploration)," *Taedong munhwa yon'gu* (Taedong Cultural Research), Vol. 1, 1963.

29. *Kojong sillok,* Mar. 16, 1883 (20th year of the King).

30. *Tongnip sinmun* (Independence News), Apr. 8, 1897.

31. U Yong-jŏng, *Ullŭngdogi* (A Record on Ullŭngdo), Manuscript in classic Chinese Manuscript in classic Chinese.

32. U Yong-jŏng, *Pogosŏ-Ullŭngdo sahaek* (A Report on Research on Ullŭngdo).

33. *Official Gazette,* No. 1716, Oct. 27, 1900.

34. *Gunkan niitakago kodo nisshi* (The Logbook on the Operation of the Warship Niitakago), Sept. 25, 1904. The logbooks are kept in the War History Department of Japanese Defense Agency.

35. Nihon kaigun gunreibu (Japan Naval General Staff), ed., *Gokuhi meiji 37-8 nen kaisenshi* (Top Secret History of Naval Battles of the Years 37-38 in the Meiji Era), Part IV., Vol. 4, pp. 48-56.

36. *Gunkan Tsushima senji nisshi* (Logbooks of the Warship Tsushima during the War), Nov. 13, 1904, in the History Department of Japanese Defense Agency.

37. Shimaneken kohobunshoka (Public Information and Document Section, Shimane prefecture), ed., *Takeshima kankei shiryo* (Materials on Takeshima), 1953.

38. *Ibid.*

39. *Ibid.*

40. *Ibid.*

41. Shimaneken kyoyukukai (Board of Education, Shimane prefecture), ed., *Shimane Kenshi* (Annals of Shimane prefecture), 1923. See the entry on Takeshima.

42. Ch'oe sŏn, Kim Pyŏng-in, tranl. *Kukyok han'gukchi* (Korean Translation of the Geography of Korea), Seoul, Han'guk chongsin munhwa yŏn'guwon (Academy of Korean Studies), p. 118, The book was originally published by the Ministry of the Treasury, Russia.

43. Japanese Naval General Staff, *op.cit.*, Part I, Vol. 4, p. 276.

44. *Kak Kwamch'aldoan*, bk. I, appendix to the report; Yang T'ae-jin, ed., *Han'guk kukkyŏng yongt'o kwan'gye munhŏnjŏn* (References on Korean Territory and Boundaries, 1979, Seoul. *Kak Kwamch'aldoan* is in the Kyujang-gak Library, Seoul National Univ. It is a collection of the reports provincial governors and Uijongbu (the State Council) exchanged between Jan. 17, 1906 and Mar. 5, 1910. The documents cover the Japanese invasion of Korea, the Korea-Japan Treaty of Protectorate in 1905, the disposition of Japanese troops in Korea, Korea's relations with China and Russia and Japanese claim to Dokdo. Edited by the Foreign Affairs Bureau of the State Council.

45. *Taehan maeil sinbo*, May 1, 1906.

46. *Kak Kwamch'aldoan*, *op.cit.*, Apr. 20, 1906, The instruction No. 3, appendix to the report.

47. *Taehan maeil sinbo*, May 1, 1906.

48. *Hwangsŏng Sinmun*, May 9, 1906.

49. Hwang Hyŏn, *Ohakimun*, 1906, A Miscellany. Copy of the manuscript in the classic Chinese in the NHCC Library. In an entry dated April 1906, the author says: "100 ri away from Ullŭngdo, there is its appendant island called Dokdo, and Japanese have reportedly inspected the island claiming that it has become their territory."

50. Hwang Hyŏn, *Maech'ŏn yarok* (Personal Accounts of Mach'ŏn, 1906), NHCC, 1971, Seoul, p. 375. Maech'ŏn is the pen name of Hwang Hyŏn.

GLOSSARY

A. Lists

Ai ture	아이두레	Ch'ŏndo	天道
An Myŏng-gŭn Sakkŏn	安明根 事件	Ch'ŏndogyo Ch'anggŏnsa	天道敎創建史
Anak-kun Myŏnhakhoe	安岳郡勉學會	Chŏng Kyo	鄭喬
Anak Sakkŏn	安岳事件	Ch'ŏngae Somun	泉蓋蘇文
Ansimga	安心歌	Ch'onggak taebang	總角大方
Apriang-wich'ŏn	壓良爲賤	Chŏnggamnok	鄭鑑錄
Chabi	잡이	Chŏngjŏn	井田
Chach'itonggam	資治通鑑	Chŏngjŏnje	井田制
Ch'ach'ŏp	差帖	Chŏngjŏnnon	井田論
Chagŭnbuk	작은북	Chŏngjŏnŭi	井田議
Chajinmori	자진몰이	Ch'ŏngnyŏn Haguhoe	靑年學友會
Chajukwŏn	自主權	Ch'ŏngnyŏn Hagwŏn	靑年學院
Ch'amjŏng taeshin	參政大臣	Ch'ŏngsu	靑水
Changbaek San	長白山	Chŏngtojo	定賭租
Ch'angbu	唱夫	Chŏngtopŏb	定賭法
Changdan	장단	Chŏngyŏnggwan	正領官
Changgo	장고	Ch'ŏnmin	賤民
Changp'ungjang	장풍장	Ch'ŏpju	接主
Chaohsien Ts'elüeh	朝鮮策略	Chŏnsikwa	田柴科
Chapsaek	雜色	Chŏp	接
Ch'ido-guk	治道局	Chŏpju	接主
Chigi	至氣	Chŏpsa	接司
Chih liang chih	致良知	Chŏpso	接所
Chijŏngp'yo	支定標	Chosa ch'onggak	調査總角
Chika Chŭngkwŏn	地價證劵	Chosen jenzu	朝鮮全圖
Chikjŏn-pŏb	職田法	Chosen suIroshi	朝鮮水路誌
Chinbŏpnori	陣法놀이	Chosen tokai kaiganz	朝鮮東海岸圖
Ching	징	Chosenkoku Kosaishimatsu Naitansho	
Ch'in'gunyŏng Chŏnyŏng	親軍營前營		朝鮮國交際始末內探書
Chinsŏ	進鋤	Chosŏn	朝鮮
Chipkang	執綱	Chosŏn chŏndo	朝鮮全圖
Chipsa	執事	Chosŏn Ilbo	朝鮮日報
Chipsupŏb	執穗法	Chosŏn Kwangmunhoe	朝鮮光文會
Chŏllon	田論	Chosŏn Sirŏp Hoesa	朝鮮實業會社
Chŏn	錢	Chosŏno Hakhoe	朝鮮語學會
Ch'ŏndo-gyo	天道敎	Chuksŏdo	竹嶼島
		Chukto	竹島

Ch'umjangdan	춤장단
Chun-t'ien	均田
Chung	중
Chungin	中人
Chungjŏng	中正
Chungmori	중몰이
Ch'ungŭigye	忠義契
Ch'usugi	秋收記
Chwajang	座長
Ch'wiji sŏ	趣旨書
Dainihonzu	大日本圖
Dajokan	太政官
Dokdo	獨島
Feng-mi-shan-tzu	蜂蜜山子
Feng-tien-sheng	奉天省
Fujian	福建
Ha-ni-ho	哈泥河
Hae-gwan	海關
Haejwa chŏndo	海左全圖
Haengsu	行首
Haesŏ Kyŏyuk Ch'onghoe	海西教育總會
Hakkyu Sinnon	學規新論
Han'guk hakpo	韓國學報
Han'guk munhwa	韓國文化
Han'guk Tongnip Undongji Hyŏlsa	韓國獨立運動之血史
Han'guk T'ongsa	韓國痛史
Han'guksa yŏn'gu	韓國史研究
Hangŭl	한글
Hanjŏn	限田
Hanmin Ch'inmokhoe	韓民親睦會
Hanpuk Hŭnghakhoe	韓北興學會
Hansŏng Sunbo	漢城旬報
Hanyang	漢陽
Hayashi Shihei	林子平
Homi-modum	호미모듬
Homi-ssishi	호미씻이
Hongmun-gwan	弘文館
Hsi-ta-p'o	西大坡
Hsiao-pei-tai	小北垈
Hsinchao	新潮
Hŭngguk	興國
Hwajŏnmin	火田民
Hwangsŏng Sinmun	皇城新聞
Hwimori	휘몰이
Hyanghŏnbi	鄕憲碑
Hyesang Kongguk	惠商公局
Hyŏpsŏng Tongsa	協成同事
Hyŏptong Sa	協同社
Inmun P'yŏngron	人文評論
Kabo Kyŏngjang	甲午更長
Kabo nongmin chŏnjaeng	갑오농민전쟁
Kabo Peasant War	甲午農民戰爭
Kabo Reform	甲午改革
Kaehwa	開化
Kaehwa-dang	開化黨
Kaehyŏktang	改革黨
Kakssi	각시
Kallimbŏpko	갈림법고
Kamsa	監司
Kamsaeng-ch'ŏng	減省廳
Kando (Chien-tao)	間島
Kan'ei suiroshi	寰瀛水路誌
Kangsŭpso	講習所
Kanpaku	關白
Kapshin Chŏngbyŏn	甲申政變
Kapshin Illok	甲申日錄
Kasaemallim	가새말림
Ki	氣
Kilgunak	길군악
Kimu-ch'ŏ	機務處
Kisaeng	妓生
Kkwaenggwari	꽹과리
Kŏbuk-sŏn	거북선
Koguryŏ	高句麗
Kojidae	雇只隊
Kokpunpŏb	穀分法
Kŏllipp'ae nongak	걸립패농악
Kongbae	公配
Konghaejŏnsi	公廨田柴
Kongjŏn-je	公田制
Kongnip Hyŏphoe	共立協會
Kongnip Sinmun	共立新聞
Kongumjŏnsi	功陰田柴
Kongwon	公員
Koryŏ	高麗
Kosari-kkŏkki	고사리 꺾기
Kuk-hon	國魂
Kuk-paek	國魄
Kŭnamjip	近庵集
K'ŭnbuk	큰북
Kunho	軍戶
Kunin-jŏn	軍人田
Kuo Shih Jipao	國是日報

Ku-shan-tzu	孤山子
Kut	굿
Kutkŏri	굿거리
Kwagŏ	科擧
Kwajŏn-pŏb	科田法
Kwandong Hakhoe	關東學會
Kwangje ch'angsaeng	廣濟蒼生
Kwŏnhakka	勸學歌
Kwŏnŏphoe	勸業會
Kyohun'ga	敎訓歌
Kyojang	敎長
Kyŏl	結
Kyŏnghaksa	耕學社
Kyŏngju Ch'oessi Taedongbo	慶州崔氏大同譜
Kyŏngseyup'yo	經世遺表
Kyosu	敎授
Kyŏttŭri	곁드리
Kyoyukhak	敎育學
Kyujang-gak	奎章閣
Kyunjŏn	均田
Liang chih	良知
Liu-ho-hsien	柳河縣
Lo-tzu-kou	羅子溝
Maech'ŏn Yarok	梅泉野錄
Makkŏlli	막걸리
Man'gi yoram	萬機要覽
Manjangdan	만장단
Manmin Kongtonghoe	萬民共同會
Marŭm	마름
Matsushima	松島
Mi-shan-hsien	密山縣
Minbon	民本
Mongjung noso mundapka	夢中老少問答歌
Mongpae Kŭm T'aejo	夢拜金太祖
Mŏngsŏkmari	멍석말이
Mŏsŭm	머슴
Mudong	舞童
Munjang	文章
Myo	畝
Myŏn	面
Naeshi-bu	內侍府
Naesudomun	內修道文
Nallari	날라리
Nambyŏngyŏng kyerok	南兵營啓錄
Namjŏp Toso	南接都所
Namsadangp'ae	남사당패
Nihon gaiko bunsho	日本外交文書
Nongak	農樂
Nonggam	農監
Nongge	農契
Nonggi	農旗
Nongmak chuin	農幕主人
Nongmin chipkangso	農民執綱所
Nongsa	農社
Nonhangmun	論學文
Ohakimun	梧下紀聞
Oki	玉岐
Onshu shicho goki	隱州視聽合記
Ŏrŭn ture	어른두레
Osakabe Daisuke	刑部大輔
Ŏyŏngch'ŏng	御營廳
Paegoin sakkŏn	百五人事件
P'aeji	牌旨
Paeksŏ Nongjang Pun'gyo	白西農場分校
Pakdal school	朴達學院
P'alchindobŏp	팔진도법
Pangmokkam	放牧監
Pansu	班首
P'o	包
P'odŏngmun	布德文
Pok-sul	福述
Pokuk anmin	保國安民
Pŏpko	법고
Pŏpkojabi	법고잡이
P'osu	砲手
Pubyŏng	府兵
Pujanggo	부장고
Pujing	부징
P'umasi	품앗이
Pumin dan	扶民團
Pusoe	부쇠
P'yeha	陛下
Pyŏlgigun	別技軍
Pyŏngjak	竝作
Pyŏngjakpŏb	竝作法
Pyŏngma chŏldosa	兵馬節度使
P'yŏngyang Chagi Chejo Chusik Hoesa	平壤磁器製造株式會社
P'yŏngyang Ch'ŏngnyŏn Kuŏnhakhoe	平壤靑年勸學會
Sahoeshinbun	社會身分
Sahŏnbu	司憲府

Samgak mountain	三角山
Samguk sagi	三國史記
Samsoe	삼쇠
San-yŭan-pao	三源堡
Sangbŏpko	상법고
Sangdong Church	尙洞教會
Sangjanggo	상장고
Sangmo	상모
Sangoku setsujozu	三國接壤圖
Sangoku zsuran zusetsu	三國通賢圖說
Sangsoe	상쇠
Sangsogo	상소고
Sap'ae	賜牌
Sasajŏn	寺社田
Sat'ongbaegi	사통배기
Saŭm	舍音
Sejong sillok	世宗實錄
Shilhak	實學
Shimane kenshi	島根縣誌
Shinimnye	新入禮
Siilya pangsŏng taegok	是日也放聲大哭
Silla pon'gi	新羅本紀
Silla	新羅
Sindong'a	新東亞
Sinhan Hyŏkmyŏngdan	新韓革命團
Sinhŭng Kangsŭpso	新興講習所
Sinhŭng Mugkwan Hakkyo	新興武官學校
Sinjŭng Tongguk Yŏji sŭngnam	
	新增東國輿地勝覽
Sinminhoe	新民會
Sŏ	西
Sŏbuk Hakhoe Wolpo	西北學會月報
Sŏbuk Hakhoe	西北學會
Soezu	總繪圖
Sogojabi	소고잡이
Sŏhak	西學
Sohakkyo	小學校
Soim	少任
Sŏk	石
Sŏkdo	石島
Sonyŏn	少年
Sŏpuk hakhoe	西北學會
Sŏpuk Hyŏpsŏng School	西北協成學校
Sŏu Hakhoe	西友學會
Ssirŭm	씨름
Such'onggak	首總角
Sudŏngmun	修德文

Sujagin	首作人
Sujing	수징
Sukchong sillok	肅宗實錄
Susim Chŏnggi	守心正氣
T'aedong (T'aitung) Shih-yeh Hui-she	
	泰東實業會社
T'al Kwangdae	탈광대
T'ongni Kimu Amun	統理機務衙門
T'ung-hua-hsien	通化縣
Tadŭraegi	다드래기
Tae-han Empire	大韓帝國
Taedong Hakhoe	大東學會
Taedong Pokukdan	大同輔國團
Taedong Yŏksa	大東歷史
Taedoso	大都所
Taegŭmnap	代金納
Taehan Chaganghoe	大韓自强會
Taehan Kungminhoe	大韓國民會
Taehan maeil Sinbo	大韓每日申報
Taehan Munjŏn	大韓文典
Taehan Noin Tongmaengdan	
	大韓老人同盟團
Taejŏng	大正
Taejŏpju	大接主
Taet'aegin	大宅人
T'ajakkwan	打作官
Takeshima	竹島
Tangsanbŏllim	당산벌림
Tanji Tongmaeng	斷指同盟
Te-hua Yin-hang	德華銀行
Terauchi ch'ongdok	寺內總督
Todŏkka	道德歌
Todokpu	都督府
Togam	都監
Tojak	賭作
Tojakpŏb	賭作法
Toji	賭地
Tojikwŏn	賭地權
Tojip	都執
Tojip'yo	賭支標
Tojopŏb	賭租法
Tok	독
Toksa sinnon	讀史新論
Tol	돌
Tong	東
Tong	洞
Tonga Ilbo	東亞日報

Tŏngdŏkkkungi	덩덕궁이	Usan'guk	于山國
Tongdosŏgi	東道西器	Usando	于山島
Tongguk	東國	Waegu	倭寇
Tongguk Chido	東國地圖	Wang-ch'ing-hsien	汪淸縣
Tongguk T'onggam	東國通鑑	Wijŏng ch'ŏksa	衛政斥邪
Tongguk yŏji sŭngnam	東國興地勝覽	Wimin	爲民
Tonggyŏng taejŏn	東經大全	Wŏnsan Haksa	元山學舍
Tonghak	東學	Yang Ki-t'ak tŭng Poanbŏp Uiban Sakkŏn	
Tonghaksa	東學史		梁起鐸 等 保安法 違反事件
Tongje-sa	同濟社	Yangban	兩班
Tongmunhak	同文學	Yangin	良人
Tongnip Chŏnjaeng Non	獨立戰爭論	Yebunpŏb	刈分法
Tongnip Hyŏphoe	獨立協會	Yen-hai Chou	沿海州
Tongnip Sinmun	獨立新聞	Yin-ping-shih-wen-chi	飮氷室文集
Tongrim Mugwan Hakkyo		Yŏjiji	興地志
	獨立武官學校	Yŏjŏn	閭田
Tongsagangmok	東史綱目	Yŏjŏnje	閭田制
Tongyong Changjŏng	通用章程	Yŏjŏnnon	閭田論
Tosaŭm	都舍音	Yŏljŏn	列傳
Tsou-chia-chieh	鄒家街	Yŏnamjip	燕巖集
Tu	斗	Yongdam yusa	龍潭遺詞
Turak	斗落	Yongdamga	龍潭歌
Ture	두레	Yŏnggi	令旗
Ture-nori	두레놀이	Yŏngjwa	領座
Turep'ul	두레풀	Yŏngse	永稅
Ŭibyŏng	義兵	Yŏngsŏnsa	領選使
Ŭijŏngbu	義政付	Yŏngsu	領首
Ŭiyŏltan	義烈團	Yugim	六任
Ullŭngdo	鬱陵島	Yun Ch'i-ho ilgi	尹致昊日記
Ŭlsa Choyak	乙巳條約	Yusa	有司

B. Lists of Names

An Ch'ang-ho	安昌浩	Chen Mei-chiu	景梅九
An Chung-gŭn	安重根	Ch'en Tu-hsiu	陳獨秀
An Kong-gun	安恭根	Cho Chun	趙浚
An Pyŏng-ch'an	安秉瓚	Cho Pyŏng-shik	趙秉式
An T'ae-guk	安泰國	Cho Sŏng-hwan	曺成煥
An Yong-bok	安龍福	Ch'oe Che-u	崔濟愚
Ch'a I-sŏk	車利錫	Ch'oe Kwang-ok	崔光玉
Ch'ae P'il-gŭn	蔡弼近	Ch'oe Kyŏng-hwan	崔景煥
Chang Chi-yŏn	張志淵	Ch'oe Mu-sŏn	崔茂宣
Chang Ki-yŏng	張基榮	Ch'oe Myŏng-sik	崔明植
Chang To-sun	張道淳	Ch'oe Nam-sŏn	崔南善
Chang Ŭng-jin	張膺震	Ch'oe Ok	崔鋈
Chang Y-sun	張裕淳	Ch'oe Pyŏng-hŏn	崔炳憲
		Ch'oe Shi-hyŏng	崔時亨

Ch'oe Sŭng-ak	崔昇岳	Kim Tŏk-myŏng	金德明
Chŏn Pong-jun	全琫準	Kim Tong-sam	金東三
Chŏn Tŏk-ki	全德基	Kimotsuki kenko	肝付兼行
Chŏng Chae-kwan	鄭在寬	Ko Yŏng-mun	高潁聞
Chŏng Sang-gi	鄭尙驥	Kojong	高宗
Chŏng To-jŏn	鄭道傳	Kwak Ki-rak	郭基洛
Chŏng Yak-yong	丁若鏞	Kwŏn Tong-jin	權東鎭
Chŏng Yŏng-do	鄭英道	Liang Ch'i-ch'ao	梁啓超
Chu Chin-su	朱鎭洙	Maech'ŏn	梅泉
Chu Hsi	朱熹	Min T'ae-ho	閔台鎬
Chu Sang-ho	周商鎬	Min Yŏng-ik	閔泳翊
Chu Sigyŏng	周時經	Min Yŏng Hwan	閔泳煥
Han Kyu-jik	韓圭稷	Mokjong	穆宗
Han Kyu-sŏl	韓圭卨	Moriyama Shigeru	森山茂
Han Pil-ŭn	韓必㱕	Murakawa Ichihei	村川市兵衛
Hŏ Hyŏk	許赫	Na Su-yŏn	羅壽淵
Hŏ Kwan	許灌	Nakai Yozaburo	中井養三郎
Hong Myŏng-hŭi	洪命憙	Nam Hyŏng-u	南亨祐
Hong Yŏng-shik	洪英植	Nam Ku-man	南九萬
Hwang Hyŏn	黃玹	Nam Kung-ŏk	南宮檍
Hwang Tsun-hsien	黃遵憲	No Paeng-nin	盧伯麟
Hwasŏ	華西	O Chi-yŏng	吳知泳
Hyŏn Chae	玄采	O Kyŏng-sŏk	吳慶錫
Im Ch'i-jŏng	林蚩正	O Se-ch'ang	吳世昌
Im Chun-ki	林俊基	O Yŏng-sŏn	吳永善
Im Han-su	林翰洙	Ŏ Yun-jung	漁允中
Ito Hirobumi	伊藤博文	Ok Kwan-bin	玉觀彬
Kam Ing-nyong	甘翊龍	Otani Jinkichi	大谷甚吉
K'ang Yu-wei	康有爲	Paek Pŏm	白凡
Kang Yun-hŭi	姜玧熙	Pak Chi-wŏn	朴趾源
Kim Ch'ang-hwan	金昌煥	Pak Chŏng-yang	朴定陽
Kim Chi-gan	金志侃	Pak Chung-hwa	朴重華
Kim Chwa-jin	金佐鎭	Pak Kyu-su	朴珪壽
Kim Hong-jip	金弘集	Pak Mun-il	朴文一
Kim Hŭi-sŏn	金義善	Pak O-dun	朴於屯
Kim Ip	金立	Pak Ŭn-sik	朴殷植
Kim Kae-nam	金開男	Pak Won-myŏng	朴原明
Kim Koo	金九	Pak Yŏng-gyo	朴泳敎
Kim Myŏng-gi	金命基	Pak Yŏng-hyo	朴泳孝
Kim Myŏng-jun	金明濬	Pak Yŏng-sun	朴永順
Kim Ok-kyun	金玉均	Pu Ssu-nien	傅斯年
Kim Pyŏng-hŏn	金炳憲	Queen min	閔妃
Kim Sŏng-mu	金成武	Sada Hakubo	佐田白茅
Kim Sŭng-jun	金昇濬	Saito Hosen	齊藤豊仙
Kim Tae-gŏn	金大建	Sejong	世宗
Kim Tal	金達	Sim Hŭng-t'aek	沈興澤
Kim To-hŭi	金道熙	Sin Ch'ae-ho	申采浩

Sin Hae-yŏng	申海永	Yi Haeng	李行
Sin Ki-sŏn	申其善	Yi Hak-p'il	李學必
Sin Kyu-sik	申圭植	Yi Hang-no	李恒老
Sin Pok-mo	申福模	Yi Hoe-yŏng	李會榮
Sin Tal-won	申達元	Yi Ik	李瀷
Sŏ Chae-p'il	徐載弼	Yi Kang	李剛
Sŏ In-ju	徐仁周	Yi Kap-su	李甲洙
Sŏ Kŏ-jŏng	徐居正	Yi Kap	李甲
Sŏ Kwang-bŏm	徐光範	Yi Ki-jong	李基鐘
So Yoshimichi	宗義方	Yi Kwan-jik	李觀稙
So Yoshitsugo	宗義倫	Yi Kyŏng-jik	李耕稙
Son pyŏng-hŭi	孫秉熙	Yi Kyu-bong	李圭鳳
Song Sŏk-chun	宋錫俊	Yi Kyu-ryong	李圭龍
Sŏngjong	成宗	Yi kyu-wŏn	李奎遠
Suk-chong	肅宗	Yi Pŏm-sŏk	李範奭
Tachibana Masashige	橘眞重	Yi Sang-jae	李商在
Taejo	太祖	Yi Sang-sŏl	李相卨
Taejong	太宗	Yi Sang-yong	李相龍
Taewŏn'gun	大院君	Yi Sŏng-gye	李成桂
Takezoe Shinichiro	竹添進一郎	Yi Sun-sin	李舜臣
T'ang Shao-yi	唐紹儀	Yi Sŭng-hun	李昇薰
Tasan	茶山	Yi Ton-hwa	李敦化
Wang Kŏn	王建	Yi Tong-hwi	李東輝
Wang Yang-ming	王陽明	Yi Tong-nyŏng	李東寧
Won ŭi-sang	元義常	Yi Yong-ik	李容翊
Yang Ki-t'ak	梁起鐸	Yŏ Chun	呂準
Yi Chae-su	李在洙	Yu Chae-hyŏn	柳在賢
Yi Chae-wŏn	李載元	Yu Hong-gi	劉鴻基
Yi Chae wan	李載完	Yu Hyŏng-wŏn	柳馨遠
Yi Cho-yŏn	李祖淵	Yu Kŭn	柳瑾
Yi Ch'ŏl-yŏng	李哲榮	Yu Tae-ch'i	劉大致
Yi Ch'ŏng-ch'ŏn	李青天	Yu Tong-yŏl	柳東說
Yi Chong-ho	李鍾浩	Yun Ch'i-ho	尹致昊
Yi Chong-man	李鍾萬	Yun Ki-sŏp	尹琦燮
Yi Chong-nok	李鍾祿	Yun Sŏn-hak	尹善學
Yi Chun	李儁	Yun T'ae-jun	尹泰駿
		Yun Ung-yŏl	尹雄

INDEX

Z